ANGLISTISCHE FORSCHUNGEN
Band 265

Begründet von Johannes Hoops

Intercultural Encounters – Studies in English Literatures

Essays Presented to
Rüdiger Ahrens
on the Occasion of
His Sixtieth Birthday

Edited by
HEINZ ANTOR
KEVIN L. COPE

Universitätsverlag C. Winter
Heidelberg

Gedruckt mit freundlicher Unterstützung der Ernst Klett-Stiftung, Stuttgart

Die Deutsche Bibliothek – CIP-Einheitsaufnahme

Intercultural encounters: studies in English literatures; essays presented to Rüdiger Ahrens on the occasion of his sixtieth birthday / ed. by Heinz Antor; Kevin L. Cope. – Heidelberg: Winter, 1999

(Anglistische Forschungen; Bd. 265)
ISBN 3-8253-0849-9

ISBN 3-8253-0849-9

Alle Rechte vorbehalten.
© 1999. Universitätsverlag C. Winter Heidelberg GmbH
Photomechanische Wiedergabe und die Einspeicherung und Verarbeitung
in elektronischen Systemen nur mit ausdrücklicher Genehmigung durch den Verlag
Imprimé en Allemagne. Printed in Germany
Druck: Strauss Offsetdruck GmbH, 69509 Mörlenbach

Acknowledgements

The editors of this volume would like to express their gratitude to Michael Klett, Ernst Klett-Stiftung, Stuttgart, without the generous financial support of whom the printing of this *Festschrift* would have been impossible. Our further thanks go to Eilert Erfling, Universitätsverlag C. Winter, Heidelberg, who also liberally supported our project. Special thanks are due to Katja Zerck, Düsseldorf, whose untiring efforts and competent help in the production of the manuscript enabled us to bring out the book in time for Rüdiger Ahrens's sixtieth birthday.

H.A.   K.L.C.

Table of Contents

HEINZ ANTOR (Düsseldorf) and KEVIN L. COPE (Baton Rouge):
Introduction: Rüdiger Ahrens and English Studies xi

WILLIAM J. JONES (London):
Spuma linguarum: On the Status of the English Language in German-Speaking Countries Before 1700 1

WERNER HÜLLEN (Essen):
The Germans on English: Towards a Historiographical Treatment of Language Evaluation, 17th to 19th Centuries 31

JOHN E. JOSEPH (Edinburgh):
Basic English and the 'Debabelization' of China 51

PETER MÜHLHÄUSLER (Adelaide):
Towards a Dictionary of South Australian Pidgin English (SAPE) 73

WOLF-DIETRICH BALD (Köln):
Which ONE: Linguistic Category and Context 83

VERNON GRAS (Washington, DC):
How Not to Get Lost in Literary Theory, Especially Cultural Studies 93

MURRAY KRIEGER (Irvine):
The Language of Poetry and the Untranslatability of Cultures 103

GEORGE ROUSSEAU (Aberdeen):
The Riddles of Interdisciplinarity: A Reply to Stanley Fish 111

LAURENZ VOLKMANN (Würzburg):
Universal Truths or Ethnic Peculiarities? On Tensions Inherent in the Reception of Post-Colonial and Minority Literature 131

KLAUS STIERSTORFER (Würzburg):
Intercultural Developments in German EFL Teaching 153

SHINSUKE ANDO (Tokyo):
Displaced Heroes in Medieval Literature 169

THEO STEMMLER (Mannheim):
A Portrait of the Artist as a Young Man: Henry VIII's Early Songs 175

ERWIN WOLF (Erlangen):
'and tyranny tremble at patience': Patience and Impatience in Shakespeare's Plays 187

HEINZ-JOACHIM MÜLLENBROCK (Göttingen):
Don Quixote and Eighteenth-Century English Literature 197

KENNETH GRAHAM (Guelph):
Intercultural Conflicts: Godwin and his Counter-Revolutionary Reviewers 211

YASMINE GOONERATNE (Sydney):
Making Sense: Jane Austen on the Screen 259

JACQUELINE GENET (Caen):
On the Origin of Images According to Yeats 267

MALCOLM BRADBURY (Norwich):
Modernism and the Magazines 287

LUCIEN LE BOUILLE (Caen):
Inter- and Intra-Cultural Antinomies in Aldous Huxley 315

NORBERT GREINER (Heidelberg):
Silence in Pinter: Regression from the Everyday to the Poetry of Memory 327

HUBERT ZAPF (Augsburg):
The Discourse of Radical Alterity: Reading Process and Cultural Meaning in William Faulkner's *The Sound and the Fury* 335

IAN ROSS (Vancouver):
Cultural Interchange in 'Siouxland': An Approach to Frederick Manfred's Buckskin Man and Woman Tales 351

LOTHAR BREDELLA (Giessen):
Decolonizing the Mind: Toni Morrison's *The Bluest Eye* and *Tar Baby* 363

KEVIN L. COPE (Baton Rouge):
The Colossus of New Roads, or, The Reconstruction of Gulliver: Mineral Drama and the Colloquial Supernatural from the Colonial Era to the Age of Encounters 385

ULRICH BROICH (München):
Memory and National Identity in Postcolonial Historical Fiction 421

SUSANA ONEGA (Zaragoza):
Postmodernist Re-Writings of the Puritan Commonwealth: Winterson,
Mukherjee, Ackroyd 439

FRITZ-WILHELM NEUMANN (Erfurt):
The Moor's Last Sigh: Salman Rushdie's Intercultural Family Saga 467

PAUL GOETSCH (Freiburg):
Passing in South African Literature 479

ANDREW PARKIN (Hong Kong):
Migrations: Reading Louise Ho and Interleaving the Chinese Diaspora 497

HEINZ ANTOR (Düsseldorf):
David Malouf's *Johnno* (1975): A Study of Post-Colonial Self-
Constitution in Modern Australia 509

HANS-ULRICH SEEBER (Stuttgart):
Cultural Differences and Problems of Understanding in the Short Fiction
of Margaret Atwood 533

ALBERT-REINER GLAAP (Düsseldorf):
Intercultural Encounters: Plays by New Zealand, Jamaican and
Canadian Authors 547

UWE BAUMANN (Düsseldorf):
Katherine Mansfield and Witi Ihimaera: A Typology of Reception 563

List of Publications by Publications by RÜDIGER AHRENS 591

Tabula gratulatoria 605

Introduction: Rüdiger Ahrens and English Studies

HEINZ ANTOR (Düsseldorf) and KEVIN L. COPE (Baton Rouge)

The British Prime Minister Benjamin Disraeli, in a speech held in the House of Commons on 11th March 1873, pointed out that "[a] University should be a place of light, of liberty, and of learning." Although this statement was made in the late nineteenth century, it is as accurate today, more than one hundred years later, as when it was first made. But a university can only be such a place if the people who work in it, and particularly the professors who teach and do their research in it, are infused with the spirit conjured up by Disraeli in the definition quoted here. Rüdiger Ahrens is such a professor, and this book takes the occasion of his sixtieth birthday to celebrate the achievement of a scholar and an academic teacher who is a truly enlightened man, a keen thinker, a learned critic and a benevolent teacher, but also a staunch supporter of freedom of thought as well as of the academic freedom that provides an indispensable basis for any university that deserves to be called by that name.

It is not possible to characterize Rüdiger Ahrens's academic interests in one single sentence, even less with a general label or a formula. This in itself is symptomatic of the kind of scholar we confront in him, for he is a man who displays the advantages of a liberal education in the best sense of the word. Ahrens is no mere specialist in one subject or another. A brief glance at the impressive list of his major publications at the end of this volume shows that his academic interests range from the sixteenth century to the present, from the theoretical metalevels of philosophy and literary theory to the practical applications of English studies in the foreign language classrooms of this world, from poetry to drama and to the novel and further on to the interrelationships between literary texts and their extra-literary contexts.

Rüdiger Ahrens's first book, *Die Essays von Francis Bacon. Literarische Form und moralistische Aussage* (*The Essays of Francis Bacon: Literary Form and Moralistic Functions*, 1974), already hinted at much of what would characterize his subsequent academic career, and it already displayed many of his major interests. It is no coincidence that in this first major study, Ahrens chose to deal with a writer and philosopher who arguably was the first great English thinker to use a modern spirit of enquiry in his critical approach to the world. Ahrens's analyses of the form of the Baconian essays are firmly based on empirical evidence, and concrete reference to the texts he wrote about has always been one of the qualities that make his books and articles so accessible to the reader.

But it would be wrong to classify Rüdiger Ahrens only as a brilliant observer of literary forms, for this constitutes just one important aspect of his work. Never content with a mere description of the forms of literary texts in English, Ahrens always went beyond the material he dealt with and sought to put it in a wider context and a more comprehensive frame of reference, thus establishing its cultural functions within the social, political, religious, philosophical etc. traditions and movements of the respective historical periods. Ahrens thus already practised what is now popularly referred to as "cultural studies" at a period when the term itself and the critical practice it implies were only pursued by a small circle of progressive scholars.

Rüdiger Ahrens's book on Francis Bacon is indicative not only of his critical method and of his general approach to literature, but it also is the first major product of Ahrens's life-long interest in the early modern period, an interest that by now has produced many valuable contributions to this academic field, notably to the area of Shakespeare studies, but also to research in such fields as the sociology of literary life under the Tudors, problems of cultural transformation in the translation of early modern English texts, Renaissance poetics and the systematics of literary genres, the history of reception of Shakespearean and other related texts in Germany, twentieth-century adaptations of early modern texts and their cultural functions in a new context, Sir Philip Sidney's poetics, and many others.

Ahrens's work on Shakespeare, Sidney, and Renaissance poetics is infused with a keen spirit of enquiry into the phenomenon of literature as such, i.e. into a human cultural product Ahrens wrote about in numerous concrete analyses of individual texts, but also reflected upon on a metalevel in an effort that has provided us with many interesting and important studies in literary theory over the years. Ahrens's writings in this field range from diachronic analyses covering theoretical aspects of literary patronage in the fifteenth and sixteenth centuries or the poetics of eighteenth century pamphleteering to more synchronic studies of modern discourse theory and systematic surveys of contemporary critical theory. Both aspects mentioned here come together in his critical edition of major theoretical essays and statements from the history of English literature (*Englische literaturtheoretische Essays – English Critical Essays on Literary Theory*, 1975), in a massive two-volume collection of critical studies of English and American literary theory (*Englische und Amerikanische Literaturtheorie: Studien zu ihrer historischen Entwicklung – English and American Literary Theory: Studies on their Historical Development*, 1978), and, most recently, in his programmatic *tour d'horizon* published under the telling title of *Why Literature Matters*.

The question inherent in this title is a central one to Ahrens, and it is important to emphasize here that neither in his critical analyses of literary texts nor in his more general writings about the phenomenon of literature has Rüdiger Ahrens ever been an ivory tower scholar. Right from the beginning of his academic career, he has always reflected upon the legitimations of his doings both as a critical reader of texts and as an academic teacher of literature. Questions of why human beings produce and read literature and of why literature should be taught both at school and at university as an integral part of the education we receive there have always been at the centre of Ahrens's thought. This made it a matter of course to him never to restrict his academic activities to the library and to his desk, but always to go beyond. Going one step beyond the established boundaries of established patterns, as a matter of fact, defines much of Ahrens's academic life. His scholarly activities in the library always made him reflect on their relevance to the classrooms at universities and schools as well as to the world outside. He has thus become a successful mediator of literature both to his students and to many pupils in schools as well as to a general reading public. To a man like Rüdiger Ahrens, who looks upon literature not as an isolated phenomenon, but as one that must constantly be seen as integrated into a functional frame of reference that includes social history, politics, philosophy and many other neighbouring fields, literature cannot be studied properly without an awareness of what reception theory and such recent approaches as the New Historicism or Cultural Materialism have to tell us. This, in turn, means that the reader, including the young learner of English as a foreign language confronted for the first time with the major works of literature in his target language, as well as the reader's extra-literary horizons of understanding and the concrete contexts of reception have to be taken into account in our dealings with literature. Ahrens's constant awareness of this is amply documented in his publications on the teaching of literature in many different contexts. His three-volume collection of critical essays on the teaching of Shakespeare (*William Shakespeare: Didaktisches Handbuch – William Shakespeare: A Handbook for Teaching Shakespeare*, 1982), although published seventeen years ago by now, still is *the* standard work in its field even today, as a short glance at more recent publications in the field, which all take Ahrens as their point of departure and as their loadstar, documents very impressively.

Rüdiger Ahrens's works on the paedagogy of teaching literature and on the culture of education in general cover the whole of the history of literatures in English, but they also deal with more general questions of the aims and purposes of education. They are the results of the experience of an inspired teacher who knows the classroom from inside and who, over the years, has taught and lectured not only at German schools and universities, but in classrooms in Britain as well as in the United States of America, in Taiwan and in the People's Republic of China as well as in Canada and in Australia and in many other countries of this world.

Rüdiger Ahrens, then, is a man of learning, as required in a university teacher in Benjamin Disraeli's definition of a place of higher learning in the quotation given above. But the scholar we honour with the articles collected between the covers of this volume also is a man of light and of liberty. His publications and his teaching are enlightened by a spirit of rationality and of understanding, and the scope of his learning and teaching is enlightened by the will to transgress the boundaries of the walls surrounding the university, but also schools, academic and intellectual conventions as well as established academic fields and subjects. Rüdiger Ahrens has always taken the liberty of committing such acts of transgression and of shedding the light of critical enquiry into hitherto dark and largely unexplored fields, and he did so in a particularly fruitful way. This is documented by a growing interdisciplinarity and an increasing internationalization both of his thought as a scholar and academic and as a teacher. The international dimensions of the English language as well as interesting developments in the New English Literatures have always been one of Ahrens's major fields of interest, and he has accompanied and influenced the coming of age of post-colonial studies in English in Germany and elsewhere. This is illustrated by a collection of essays on international problems of English he edited and published under the title of *Text – Culture – Reception: Cross-Cultural Aspects of English*

Studies (1992). His chairmanship of a panel on anglophone South-East Asia at the recent German *Anglistentag* in the autumn of 1998 also is a good example of the way in which Rüdiger Ahrens always tries to give a new impetus to the future development of the subject he has influenced so profoundly during the past three decades.

The international dimension of Ahrens's work does not only shed light on new texts in English from hitherto neglected regions of this world. It has not only contributed to the enlightening and widening of the purely Eurocentric view that has dominated English studies for such a long period, but is has also had much more concrete repercussions – for Rüdiger Ahrens also is an eminently practical man. Since he has always been aware of the embeddedness of English studies in a social and political context, he has also constantly sought to establish concrete links with other spheres beyond that of the institutions of higher learning he worked at. As a result, Ahrens is the father of many international university cooperations at various levels. It is due to his merits as an international communicator and partner that both students and academic teachers were able to profit from the contacts he established with universities all over the world. German students and scholars were able to teach and study in the United States, Canada, Great Britain, France, Spain, Italy, Greece, and other countries due to Ahrens's mediation, and he has brought dozens of foreign scholars to Germany, scholars who came from places as far apart as the United States of America, Great Britain or China to enrich academic life here with different viewpoints and fresh new alternative visions. Ahrens himself was a visiting professor in Tokyo, Japan, he lectured at the University of Beijing in China, and he is a Fellow of Robert Black College at the University of Hong Kong. As a Fulbright Scholar he worked and lectured at Harvard, Princeton, Yale, Stanford, UCLA and Riverside. His contacts with George Mason University in Fairfax, Virginia, resulted in a number of very fertile academic exchanges, and the cooperation between George Mason and Würzburg is still an active one today.

Since 1988, Rüdiger Ahrens has been active as a European ERASMUS coordinator of various programmes aiming at increasing student and academic teacher mobility within the European Union. The first of his projects in this context was a three-year project entitled "National Traditions of Literary Criticism in Europe: England, France, Germany," which brought together students and scholars at the universities of Caen, London, and Würzburg. By now, he has managed to establish a wide-ranging network of contacts with many European universities, which offers his students and colleagues great opportunities of studying and teaching abroad and of widening their horizons. Ahrens also established contacts between his home university and institutions of higher education abroad on other levels, as is illustrated by the student exchanges he organized between Würzburg and Caen with the help of *Deutsch-Französisches Jugendwerk*.

Rüdiger Ahrens, then, is a scholar who cherishes the dialogic exchange not only between individuals, but between whole cultures, and he is not only a theoretician in this field, but an active agent, a man who has become an integral part of the process of international understanding. His practical acumen in such matters has been illustrated by his authorship of a project the aim of which it is to establish a European

Cultural Academy, an international agency the task of which it will be to foster exchanges and cooperations between European institutions of higher education. Rüdiger Ahrens's efforts in the service of international communication and the peaceful cooperation of nations have been rewarded by an honorary doctorate conferred upon him by the University of Caen (France) and by an honorary professorship from the University of Nanchang (China). His achievements as both scholar and international university co-ordinator also made him a member of the Academia Scientiarum et Artium at Salzburg, i.e. the European Academy of Sciences and Arts.

Not only has Rüdiger Ahrens been a driving force in the development of international academic partnerships, but he has also taken an active part in the politics of higher education in both Germany and the English-speaking world. His activities in this field have always been based on the ideal of a university as laid down by Wilhelm von Humboldt, and he has served in many committees and organizations to forward these ideas. For example, he was a member of the national governing board of *Deutscher Hochschulverband*, the German Association of University Professors, from 1990-1994, and he even served as its Vice-President from 1992-1994. Rüdiger Ahrens exerted an important influence in this period on the way universities developed in Germany. This applies in particular to the very difficult phase of reorientation of old universities in the eastern parts of Germany after 1989 and to the foundation of new universities there, a process Rüdiger Ahrens supported energetically through his devoted work in those years.

The international contacts established by the scholar and friend honoured through the essays collected in this volume were the result of and did of course also have an effect on Rüdiger Ahrens's academic interests. His never was a horizon that allowed itself to be hemmed in by the narrow boundaries of traditional university subjects, which is why Ahrens also worked extensively on the New English Literatures. A *Festschrift* such as this one can therefore only do justice to the achievement of the scholar it celebrates by taking into account the international dimension of his work – hence the plural in the title of the present volume and its intercultural orientation. Although the scope and impact of Rüdiger Ahrens's research and teaching are too wide to be addressed comprehensively by the contributors to this book, they reflect his many diverse interests and the multifarious ways in which they link up with the most important aspects of English studies today, ranging from cultural theory to critical practice, from the linguistics of World Englishes via (inter-)cultural aspects of British and American studies to analyses of post-colonial literatures in English. The internal structure of this book consequently also reflects the development of Rüdiger Ahrens's academic work as well as that of the subject that was influenced by it in so many ways. The following pages are a tribute to an excellent friend, a profound global thinker, a great scholar and a wonderful teacher whom the authors of the following articles as well as all those listed in the *tabula gratulatoria* would like to honour for his exceptional spirit of light, of liberty and of learning.

Spuma Linguarum: On the Status of English in German-Speaking Countries Before 1700

WILLIAM JERVIS JONES (London)

It is perhaps unwise to dwell on the earliest antecedents of English studies in German-speaking countries. Surveying the field as a whole, Thomas Finkenstaedt devotes barely four pages to the period before 1700; Bernhard Fabian, whilst far from ignoring earlier contacts, refers advisedly to the 'discovery' of England as a *terra incognita* in the early decades of the eighteenth century; and Eva Maria Inbar ventures to observe that until about 1750 English was "in Deutschland eine weitgehend unbekannte Sprache."[1] By the late eighteenth century, in the words of the fourth Earl of Chesterfield (1694-1773), English may have been "kindly entertained as a relation in the most civilised parts of Germany,"[2] but it is also considered to have remained for German speakers a "mühsam erworbene reine Lese-Bildungssprache [...], die sich nicht zur praktischen Verständigung eignete."[3] Evidence for the earlier status of the English language among German-speakers has inevitably highlighted much that is negative: the inability of visiting English players to communicate in their own language otherwise than by mime and gesture, and their use of German from 1608; the belated appearance of English in university curricula;[4] a surprising dearth of English books, even in Frankfurt and Leipzig round 1700; the continuing reliance on Latin editions of English works, and on Latin grammars of English; and the practice of translating from French or Dutch versions of English works.

Yet, as Konrad Schröder and others have reminded us, to every history there is a prehistory.[5] In this essay we bring together some testimonies, both positive and nega-

---

[1] Thomas Finkenstaedt, *Kleine Geschichte der Anglistik in Deutschland: Eine Einführung* (Darmstadt: Wissenschaftliche Buchgesellschaft, 1983); Bernhard Fabian, "Englisch als neue Fremdsprache des 18. Jahrhunderts," in Dieter Kimpel, ed., *Mehrsprachigkeit in der deutschen Aufklärung* (Hamburg: Felix Meiner, 1985), 178-96; Bernhard Fabian, *The English Book in Eighteenth-Century Germany: The Panizzi Lectures 1991* (London: The British Library, 1992); Eva Maria Inbar, "Zum Englischstudium im Deutschland des XVIII. Jahrhunderts," *Arcadia* 15 (1980): 14-27.

[2] Richard Weld Bailey, *Images of English: A Cultural History of the Language* (Cambridge et al.: Cambridge University Press, 1992), 99.

[3] Peter von Polenz, *Deutsche Sprachgeschichte vom Spätmittelalter bis zur Gegenwart,* vol. 2: *17. und 18. Jahrhundert* (Berlin and New York: de Gruyter, 1994), 102.

[4] Finkenstaedt, *Geschichte*, 212; Renate Haas, "Die Geschichte der Anglistik und Amerikanistik an deutschen Universitäten," in Rüdiger Ahrens, Wolf-Dietrich Bald and Werner Hüllen, eds., *Handbuch Englisch als Fremdsprache (HEF)* (Berlin: Erich Schmidt, 1995), 481-6.

[5] Konrad Schröder, "The Pre-History of English Studies in Germany 1554 to 1813," in Thomas Finkenstaedt and G. Scholtes, eds., *Towards a History of English Studies in Europe:*

tive, concerning English as a language prior to 1700, as viewed by speakers of German. We focus on the external image of English as a language, and on evidence for its acquisition and use.[6]

The English Stereotype

Scattered across the literatures of Europe from the sixteenth century onwards is an assortment of national stereotypes, often linguistic in character, and sometimes including a mention of English. For some commentators, prejudice against the English language had the deepest of theological roots. Thus in 1674 the Jesuit grammarian Dominique Bouhours (1628-1702) asserted that, whilst in Paradise Adam employed the manly language French, and Eve spoke an appropriately feminine Italian, the Serpent communicated in English, a language notable for its hissing quality.[7] This supposed characteristic had already been the object of adverse comment in Martin Luther's *Tischreden* (1538):

> Anno xxxviij. den xix. Decemb. ward mancherley geredet von den lendern Deudscher Nation / welche allzumal einfeltiger weren / vnd warheit lieber hetten / denn Frantzosen / Italianer / Spanier / Engellender etc. Welchs auch die Sprache vnd ausreden gnugsam anzeigte / Das sie leppisch vnd zischende die wort pronunciren vnd reden [...].[8]

English remained abysmally low in the ranking order well into the seventeenth century, if indeed it rated a mention at all. A collection of essays made by the Tübingen scholar Thomas Lansius (1577-1657), offering arguments for and against various

---

Proceedings of the Wildsteig-Symposium, April 30 - May 3, 1982 (Augsburg: Universität, 1983), 49-65.

[6] Informative, despite the heavily judgmental approach, is Gilbert Waterhouse, *The Literary Relations of England and Germany in the Seventeenth Century* (Cambridge: Cambridge University Press, 1914). On travel to England, see William D. Robson-Scott, *German Travellers in England 1400-1800* (Oxford: Blackwell, 1953), 136-7; William Brenchley Rye, *England as Seen by Foreigners in the Days of Elizabeth and James the First. Comprising Translations of the Journals of the Two Dukes of Wirtemberg in 1592 and 1610; Both Illustrative of Shakespeare. With Extracts from the Travels of Foreign Princes and Others, Copious Notes, an Introduction, and Etchings* (London: John Russell Smith, 1865). German visitors to England are considered more cursorily in Karl Heinrich Schaible, *Geschichte der Deutschen in England von den ersten germanischen Ansiedlungen in Britannien bis zum Ende des XVIII. Jahrhunderts* (Straßburg: Trübner, 1885); C. R. Hennings, *Deutsche in England* (Stuttgart: Ausland und Heimat, 1923).

[7] Arno Borst, *Der Turmbau von Babel: Geschichte der Meinungen über Ursprung und Vielfalt der Sprachen und Völker* (Stuttgart: Hiersemann, 1957-63), 1287-8, 1383, 1485.

[8] Martin Luther, *Tischreden Oder Colloquia*, ed. Johann Aurifaber (Eisleben: Urban Gaubisch, 1566), 606^r; also Weimar-Ausgabe, *Tischreden*, IV, 78-9, Nr. 4018. See Ewald Flügel, „References to the English Language in the German Literature of the First Half of the Sixteenth Century," *Modern Philology* 1 (1903): 19-30, here 23.

European cultures, contains a disparaging comment on English letters: "Quis non statuat mecum Anglos adeoq[ue] Britannos universos, in re literaria à Germanis, Gallis, Italis, Polonis, infinitis parasangis superari?"[9] In his *Schutzschrift für die Teutsche Spracharbeit* (1644), Georg Philipp Harsdörffer catalogues the qualities of specific languages (Hebrew, Greek, Latin, Spanish, French and Italian), but makes no reference at this point to English.[10] Perhaps mercifully, English receives no mention in Hans Jakob Christoffel von Grimmelshausen's inglorious catalogue (1673): "auff Böhmisch zu stehlen; auff Cretisch zu lügen / auff Italianisch zu lefflen: auff Spanisch zu schmeichlen und zu betriegen: auff Russisch zu prallen / und auff gut Frantzösisch zu potzmartern [...]."[11] But English does figure in other, equally unflattering, examples. The barking Englishman (perhaps a soldier, seaman or merchant?) is recalled by the nymph Germania in Justus Georg Schottelius's lament of 1640:

> Was redet der Frantzos mit fliessendem Gemenge /
> Was pralt der Spanier mit trotzigem Gepränge;
>   Was bellt der Engelsmann; was sagt der Welscher her /
>   Das ist vermengtes Werck / sind Hurenkinder nur.[12]

"Was hat man doch vor Lust," enquires the Pegnitzschäfer Johann Klaj (1645), "an dem Gelispel der Italiäner / an dem Flik- und Stikwerk der Frantzosen / an dem Sprachenschaum der Engelländer?"[13] This 'Sprachenschaum,' like Schottelius's "vermengtes Werck," points to that most abiding characteristic of English, as identified in earlier German sources: its peculiar genetic composition.

English as a Mixed Language

"Die Englische ist sie nicht durch zusammensetzung der andern zu einer Sprache worden?" asks Enoch Hannmann (1645) in his commentary to a re-issue of Opitz's *Buch von der Deudschen Poeterey*.[14] German linguists of our period concur in judging

---

[9] Thomas Lansius, *F. A. D. W. Consultationis de principatu inter provincias Europæ editio secunda* (Tubingæ: Eberhard Wild, 1620), 524. On a similar work by James Howell, *A German Diet* (London: Printed for Humphrey Moseley, 1653), see Werner Hüllen, "Some Yardsticks of Language Evaluation 1600-1800 (English and German)," in Vivien Law and Werner Hüllen, eds., *Linguists and Their Diversions. A Festschrift for R. H. Robins on His 75th Birthday* (Münster: Nodus, 1996), 275-306, here 296.

[10] Georg Philipp Harsdörffer, *Frauenzimmer Gesprächspiele*, ed. Irmgard Böttcher (Tübingen: Niemeyer, 1968-69), I (2nd edition, 1644), 15. See also Hüllen, "Yardsticks," 282, 288.

[11] Hans Jakob Christoffel von Grimmelshausen, *Deß Weltberuffenen Simplicissimi Pralerey und Gepräng mit seinem Teutschen Michel* (Nürnberg: Felßecker, 1673), 19.

[12] Justus Georg Schottelius, *Lamentatio Germaniæ exspirantis, Der numehr hinsterbenden Nymphen Germaniæ elendeste Todesklage* (Braunschweig: Gruber, 1640), Dij^r.

[13] Johann Klaj, *Lobrede der Teutschen Poeterey* (Nürnberg: Endter, 1645), 23; Hüllen, "Yardsticks," 285-6.

[14] *Prosodia Germanica, Oder Buch von der Deudschen Poeterey [...] Verfertiget von Martin*

language mixture adversely, and English as the archetype of a mixed language. Sebastian Münster (1488-1552) observed in the 1545 edition of his *Cosmographia*: "Die Englische sprach ist ein gemischte sprach / von vilen sprachen / besunder von Teütsch vnd Frantzösisch z sammen getragen."[15] In the 1556 version he added: "Aber vor zeiten ist jr sprach gar Teütsch gewesen / wie ich das spüren mag auß Beda / der ein geborner Engellender gewesen ist / der schreibt in eim büchlin des tittel ist / von der zeit also."[16] Strong influence from French had already been noted in 1548 by the Zürich theologian Theodor Bibliander (1504/09-1564),[17] whilst Conrad Gesner (1516-1565) in the general introduction to his linguistic survey *Mithridates* (1555) offered more detail:

> Anglica omnium maximè mixta hodie corruptaq[ue] uidetur. Primùm enim uetus Britannica lingua imperio Saxonum partim abolita, partim corrupta est: deinde Gallica etiam uocabula plurima assumpsit, siue propter multitudinem mercatorum ex Gallia uicina, uel aliorum homin ex eadem profectorum ut inhabitarent [.] Lingu etiam quarum in foro & in templis usus est aut fuit, non parum mutationis attulisse uidentur (3ʳ).[18]

In the section 'De Anglica Lingva'(8ᵛ-9ᵛ), Gesner adds: "Anglica lingua, (inquit Seb. Munsterus) mixta est ex multis linguis, præsertim Germanica & Gallica. Olim uerò merè fuit Germanica"(9ʳ). Finally, in his preface to Josua Maaler's dictionary (1561), Gesner lists English with Italian, French and Spanish, 'quæ omnes partim ex Latinis corruptis, partim Gothicis aut Saxonicis & alijs quibusdam uocabulis mixtæ confusæq[ue] sunt.'[19] Thus to Gesner contemporary English, even in its public forms, appears highly mixed because of the earlier adoption of French brought across the Channel by merchants and others, together with a more recent influx of Latin and French words which has occurred during the last two hundred years, and even within living memory, affecting and ornamenting oral and written usage. He writes also that the language contains still many Germanic or Saxon words which have somehow become 'distorted or altered,' but that the new mixed usage is unintelligible to the common people unless interpreted for them. These opinions are reflected by later commentators, for example the traveller Thomas Platter the Younger: "Die englische

---

Opitzen. Jetzo aber von Enoch Hannman an unterschiedlichen Orten vermehret (Franckfurt am Mäyn: Klein, 1645), 120.

[15] Sebastian Münster, *Cosmographia: Beschreibung aller Lender* (Basel: Henricpetri, 1545), xli; Flügel, References, 24-6.

[16] Sebastian Münster, *Cosmographei oder beschreibung aller länder* (Basel: Henricpetri, 1556), lv.

[17] Theodor Bibliander, *De ratione communi omnium linguarum & literaru[m] commentarius* (Tiguri: Christoph Froschauer, 1548), 8.

[18] Conrad Gesner, *Mithridates: De differentiis lingvarum tvm vetervm tum quæ hodie apud diuersas nationes in toto orbe terrar in usu sunt, Conradi Gesneri Tigurini Obseruationes* (Tiguri: Froschoverus, 1555). See Flügel, References, 25-6; George J. Metcalf, Konrad Gesner's Views on the Germanic Languages, *Monatshefte für den deutschen Unterricht* 55 (1963): 149-56.

[19] Josua Maaler, *Die Teütsch spraach* (Tiguri: Christoph Froschauer, 1561), *3ʳ.

sprach ist ein gemischte sprach von vielen sprachen, besonder von sächsisch unndt frantzösisch zesamen getragen."[20] Similarly, the French lawyer Claude Duret states in his encyclopaedic survey of languages (1613) that English is "vne langue composée de la langue Alemande, & de la langue Françoise."[21]

As the century proceeds, more lurid detail is supplied. In a defence of German (1642), the Hamburg clergyman, writer and purist Johann Rist portrays the genesis of English, as a deterrent to those who would similarly adulterate the German tongue:

> Würde nicht unsere sonst so hochgerühmte / edle u herliche teutsche Sprache bey denen ausländeren viel schlechter / geringer und verachteter gehalten werden / als heut zu tage die Englische / von welcher man schertzweise pflegt zu sagen / daß sie / dieweil die Engelländer bey austheilunge der Sprachen etwas zu späte angelanget / hernach von allen Völckern und Zungen mit dem Klinge-Beütel zusammen sey gebettelt / und also ihr Volck und Königreich damit versehen worden.[22]

The *locus classicus* for the theme of language mixture is to be found a year earlier, in the first edition of Justus Georg Schottelius's *Teutsche Sprachkunst* (1641):

> was würde man von derselben anders / als das sagen / was man von der Englischen Sprache zu schertzen pflegt *quod sit spuma linguarum*. Denn als in einem Topffe / wie man sagt / alle Sprachen gekocht worden / were der Schaum davon die Englische Sprache geworden: weil dieselbe ein lauter Geflick und Gemeng / wiewol im Grunde Teutsch ist.[23]

The topos recurs in Johann Klaj's reference to the 'Sprachenschaum der Engelländer.'[24] It is noteworthy that Schottelius, elsewhere scrupulous to acknowledge his sources, is here content with a vague jocular reference. Either the source was not to hand, presumably, or he is reporting hearsay. The corresponding passage in his *Ausführliche Arbeit* is no more precise (Schottelius, *Ausführliche Arbeit*, 141).

In his major work on language theory, the *Rosen-mând* (1651), Filip von Zesen places the issue in a theological-mystical context: the desire for novelty (in seven-

---

20 Thomas Platter der Jüngere, *Beschreibung der Reisen durch Frankreich, Spanien, England und die Niderlande 1595-1600 [...]*, ed. Rut Keiser (Basel and Stuttgart: Schwabe, 1968), 822.

21 Claude Duret, Thresor de l'histoire des langues de cest vnivers (Cologny: Berjon, 1613), 873.

22 [Johann Rist:] *Baptistæ Armati, Vatis Thalosi. Rettung der Edlen Teütschen Hauptsprache* (Hamburg: Heinrich Werner, 1642), Fjv^r-v.

23 Justus Georg Schottelius, *Teutsche Sprachkunst* (Braunschweig: Gruber, 1641), 169. The passage is reprinted in Justus Georg Schottelius, *Ausführliche Arbeit Von der Teutschen HaubtSprache 1663*, ed. Wolfgang Hecht (Tübingen: Niemeyer, 1967), 141. As Werner Hüllen notes ("Yardsticks," 295), the passage leaves Schottelius's own opinion open.

24 Klaj, *Lobrede* (1645), 23. The image is applied to Dutch in Andreas Helvigius, *Etymologiæ, Sive origines dictionum germanicarum* (Francofurti: Typis Iohannis Wolphij, Sumptibus AntonI HummI, 1611), 28-9: "De *Belgica* Lingva noli quærere! Spuria hæc est, sev (ut mitiùs dicam) spuma nostræ Germanicæ [...]."

teenth-century usage 'Neugierigkeit') itself a manifestation of Original Sin and of precisely that pride which had called down the wrath of God at Babel has led to language corruption, and hence to subservience, across most of Europe. Zesen continues: "Ein zeichen solcher leibeigenschaft ist die Spanische / Wälsche / Frantzösische / und am allermeisten die Englische / mit vielen andern sprachen."[25] A generation later, the satirist Joachim Rachel (1677) traces a centuries-old process of adulteration, affecting Classical languages and their derivatives as well as English and, he fears, German also, if its users do not remain vigilant:

> Welch 'eine Sprache solt' in Teutschland endlich seyn?
> So hat die Barbarey das gut Latein zerstükket /
> Und Gotisch / Wendisch / Teutsch mit Macht hinein geflikket /
> Dadurch kam allererst der Mischmasch auf die Welt /
> Denn Frankreich / Welschland selbst und Spanjen noch behelt [.]
> Der *Gentelman* hat auch sein Theil darvon bekommen /
> Ein Wörtlein hie und da / von allem was genommen /
> Und eben dieses wehr den Teutschen auch geschehn /
> Wenn nicht mit allen Ernst da wehre zugesehn:
> Der Lapperey gewehrt / das reine Teutsch erzwungen /
> Das nichts erbettlen darf von frembder Sprach und Zungen.[26]

English is cast elsewhere too in the role of the gentleman-beggar. The Breslau school teacher Georg Wende (1635-1705) in a school drama of 1670, *Actus Von der Hochlöbl. Fruchtbringenden Gesellschaft*, places a fictitious speech in the mouth of the Society's co-founder, Kaspar von Teutleben:

> Wir lächeln, wenn uns gesagt wird, das die Engelländer, (umb das sie zu spät kom[m]en, als der Höchste die Sprachen ausgetheilet,) endlich die Freyheit erhalten, aus der Ebraischen, Grichischen, Lateinischen, Sächsischen, Frantzösischen und andern sprachen sich eine zu dencken. Wer wird uns mit unser teütschen verhöhnen? Gewiß der Jude mengt Ebraisch, der weltweise Lateinisch, der Arzt Grichisch, der Weltmann Französisch oder welsch, der betler Rothwelsch, andre anders mit ein. Und bedenckt keiner, das die französische und welsche Töchter der Lateinischen und Zeügen der Römischen Dinstbarkeit, die teütsche aber eine Jungfrau, und zeügin der goldnen und unbestürmten Freyheit sey.[27]

Though well acquainted with England, the academic Daniel Georg Morhof (1639-1691) views its language still in 1682 as "eine bastard-teutsche," which "durch die vermischung / und die Weibische *pronuntiation* gar verdorben / daß sie schier nichts männliches an sich hat / was aber gutes an ihr ist / eintzig und allein der Teutschen /

---

[25] Filip Zesen, *Rosen-mând* (Hamburg: Papen, 1651), 15.

[26] Joachimi Rachelii Londinensis, *Neu-Verbesserte Teutsche Satyrische Gedichte* (Oldenburg: Zimmer, 1677), 8. Satire ("Der Poet"), lines 332-42.

[27] Georg Wende, *Briefe der Fruchtbringenden Gesellschaft und Beilagen: Die Zeit Herzog Augusts von Sachsen-Weißenfels 1667-1680. Mit dem Breslauer Schuldrama »Actus Von der Hochlöbl. Fruchtbringenden Gesellschaft« (1670) und mit den Registern der Mitglieder*, ed. Martin Bircher, collab. Gabriele Henkel and Andreas Herz (Tübingen: Niemeyer, 1991), 20.

die ihre Mutter ist / zuschreiben muß."[28] More extravagant claims for the composition of English are found in a publication of 1724 by the eccentric traveller Adam Ebert (1653?-1735), Professor of Laws at Frankfurt an der Oder, who visited England in 1678:

> Die Englische Sprache bestehet aus der Teutschen Holländischen / doch mehr aus dieser als aus jener [...]. Es ist in der Englischen Sprache Teutsch / Frantzösisch / Dänisch / Schwedisch / auch etwas Spanisch [...]; und berichtete einer / so die Polnische verstand / daß auch viel Polnisch darinn; vielleicht weil Pohlen damahls unter den Sachsen versteckt.[29]

Outlandish bastardisation, effeminacy and subservience are the recurrent themes. Nowhere in German sources before 1700, whether with reference to English or German, do we find a comment comparable in its confident receptivity with that contained in William Camden's *Remaines* (1605):

> it [the English language] hath beene beautified and enriched out of other good tongues, partly by enfranchising and endenizing strange words, partly by refining and mollifying olde words, partly by implanting new wordes with artificiall composition [...].[30]

Far from regarding external influences as undesirable, Thomas Rymer (1641-1713), the English translator of a work by the Jesuit René Rapin (1621-1687), capitalises on the fact in the following comparison (1674): "The *German* still continues rude and unpolisht, not yet filed and civiliz'd by the commerce and intermixture with strangers to that smoothness and humanity which the *English* may boast of [...]."[31] Morhof's

---

[28] Daniel Georg Morhof, *Unterricht Von Der Teutschen Sprache und Poesie / deren Uhrsprung / Fortgang und Lehrsätzen* (Kiel: Reumann, 1682), 230.

[29] Adam Ebert, *Auli Apronii vermehrte Reise-Beschreibung* (Franco Porto, 1724), 100-101; *Allgemeine deutsche Biographie*. Hrsg. durch die Historische Commission bei der Königl. Akademie der Wissenschaften (München and Leipzig, 1875-1912), vol. 5, 585; Robson-Scott, *Travellers*, 102-105; Andreas Selling, *Deutsche Gelehrten-Reisen nach England 1660-1714* (Frankfurt am Main et al.: Lang, 1990), 355.

[30] William Camden, *Remaines of a greater worke: Concerning Britaine, the inhabitants thereof, their Languages, Names, Surnames, Empreses, Wise speeches, Poësies, and Epitaphes* (London: G. E. for Simon Waterson, 1605), 20. Gesner's opinion is here directly challenged: "Whereas our tongue is mixed, it is no disgrace, whenas all the tongues of *Europe* doe participate interchangeably the one of the other, and in the learned tongues, there hath been like borrowing one from another. Yet it is false which *Gesner* affirmeth, that our tongue is the most mixt and corrupt of all other"(21-2).

[31] René Rapin, *Reflexions on Aristotle's Treatise of Poesie* [translated by Thomas Rymer] (London: T.N. for H. Herringman, 1674), A5^v. Rymer comments on other languages: "The *Spanish* is big and fastuous, proper only for *Rodomontades*, and compar'd with other Languages, is like the Kettle-drum to Musick. The *Italian* is fittest for *Burlesque*, and better becomes the mouth of *Petrolin* and *Arloquin* in their *Farces*, than any *Heroick* character. The perpetual termination in vowels is childish, and themselves confess, rather sweet than grave. The *French* wants sinews for great and heroick Subjects, and even in Love-matters, by their

reaction to this arrogant passage is understandably dismissive: "Die Englische habe diese Glückseeligkeit vor allen daß sie zur *heroi*schen *Poësie* bequem sey. Ist gar ein Kindisch und närrisch Urtheil" (Morhof, *Unterricht*, 229-30). He concludes that the translator must be ignorant of the German language and cannot have read German poetry. He observes, moreover, with surprise that English speakers unashamedly draw from other languages: "Dann die Engelländer nehmen ungescheut aus andern Sprachen was sie wollen und ihne[n] dienet / und ist nach ihrem belieben alles gut Englisch" (Morhof, *Unterricht*, 228-9). This statement makes unduly light of language debates which had been active within the English tradition, but in general a contrasting perception of the foreign word will persist for many years as a fundamental difference between language evaluations in the two cultures. A more receptive approach is adumbrated in Germany with Gottfried Wilhelm Leibniz. Already in his *Ermahnung an die Teutsche* (ca. 1680), Leibniz reports, with some indulgence, on contemporaries who use mixed languages as their models:

> Sey nicht das französische selbst eine vermischung des lateinischen und teutschen, so anfangs sehr ungereumt gewesen, an iezo durch vielen gebrauch alle gleichsam abgeschliffene rauhigkeit verlohren; So mache sich ein Engländer und Hollander kein gewißen, fast in einer zeile spanisch, welsch und französisch zu reden, was wolten wir uns denn zeihen, die wir doch selbst ihre bücher als zierlich geschrieben so hoch rühmen?[32]

In his posthumously published *Unvorgreifliche Gedanken* Leibniz repeatedly uses English as an example.[33] He shows, as one might expect from a highly informed scholar who had been elected to membership of the Royal Society in 1673, a sharp awareness of English language history, remarking that as a result of admixture the German of his day will soon be lost as Anglo-Saxon was in England (§ 20, 266, see also Selling, *Gelehrten-Reisen*, 92-3, 269). But he can also be heard developing a more receptive approach to lexical importation, albeit with some language-specific variation:

> Was die Einbürgerung betrifft, ist solche bey guter Gelegenheit nicht auszuschlagen, und den Sprachen so nützlich als den Völckern. Rom ist durch Auffnehmung der Fremden gross und mächtig worden, Holland ist durch Zulauff der Leute, wie durch den Zufluss seiner Ströhme auffgeschwollen; die Englische Sprache hat alles angenommen, und wann jedermann das Seinige abfodern wolte, würde es den Engländern gehen, wie der Esopischen Krähe, da andere Vögel ihre Federn wieder gehohlet. Wir Teutschen haben es

---

own confession, is a very Infant; the *Italians* call it the *Kitchin*-language, it being so copious and flowing on those occasions"(A5ᵛ-A6ʳ).

[32] Gottfried Wilhelm Leibniz, *Ermahnung an die Teutsche, ihren verstand und sprache beßer zu üben, sammt beygefügten vorschlag einer Teutsch gesinten Gesellschaft* in Paul Pietsch, *Leibniz und die deutsche Sprache*, Wissenschaftliche Beihefte zur Zeitschrift des Allgemeinen Deutschen Sprachvereins, 4. Reihe, Heft 29 (1907), 306.

[33] *Illustris viri Godofr. Guilielmi Leibnitii Collectanea etymologica, illustrationi linguarum, veteris celticæ, germanicæ, gallicæ, aliarumque inservientia. Cum præfatione Jo. Georgii Eccardi* (Hanoveræ: Foerster, 1717).

weniger vonnöthen als andere, müssen uns aber dieses nützlichen Rechts nicht gäntzlich begeben.

These words form a bridge to a more enlightened view of lexical borrowing. Despite the massive losses and replacements which had occurred in its history, English offered lexical resources which Leibniz was himself keen to use in his search for "Reichtum, Reinigkeit und Glanz." Reassuringly, as Schottelius before him had realised, the English language was still 'im Grunde Teutsch' (*Ausführliche Arbeit*, 33).

English as a Germanic Language

Awareness of the Germanic origin and character of English can be detected among German writers from an early date, but the theme grows in strength and clarity during our period.[34] "Ich gleub Engelland sey ein stück Deudschslandes /" remarked Martin Luther, "Denn sie brauchen der Sechsischen Sprache / wie in Westphalen vnd Niderlande / wiewol sie sehr corrumpirt ist / Ich halte die Deudschen sind vor zeiten hinein transferirt vnd gesetzt [...] Denische vnd Englische Sprache ist Sechsisch / welche recht deudsch ist."[35] In a Cologne edition of Bede (1537), Johannes Noviomagus observed: "ex utroq[ue] idiomate [Gallicana et Germanica lingua] quidem nata est similima Germanicæ seu Batauicæ linguæ."[36] Konrad Gesner was clear as to the Germanic basis of English, commenting in 1561:

> Anglica lingua hodie, ut dixi, è Saxonica & Gallica uulgari ferè constat, quam qui teneret, plurimas Saxonicæ & Germanicæ ueteris linguæ dictiones perciperet: unde ad explicandas origines, significationes & orthographiam, plurimum momenti accederet.[37]

Likewise, the (admittedly distorted) Germanic affinity of both English and Scots was evident to Andreas Helvigius: "*Anglicam & Scoticam,* differentes saltem idiomate

---

[34] On affiliations within the Germanic group, see Peter Schaeffer, "Baroque Philology: The Position of German in the European Family of Languages," in Gerhart Hoffmeister, ed., *German Baroque Literature: The European Perspective* (New York: Ungar, 1983), 74-84; William Jervis Jones, "König Deutsch zu Abrahams Zeiten: Some Perceptions of the Place of German within the Family of Languages from Aventinus to Zedler," in John L. Flood et al., eds.,*'Das unsichtbare Band der Sprache:' Studies in German Language and Linguistic History in Memory of Leslie Seiffert* (Stuttgart: Heinz, 1993), 189-213; Andreas Gardt, *Sprachreflexion in Barock und Frühaufklärung. Entwürfe von Böhme bis Leibniz* (Berlin and New York: de Gruyter, 1994), 341-64.

[35] *Tischreden* (ed. Aurifaber, 1566), 605^r; also Weimar-Ausgabe, *Tischreden,* V, 511-12 (Nr. 6146). See also Flügel, References, 23-4.

[36] *Bedae presbyteri anglosaxonis, monachi Benedicti, viri literatissimi opuscula cumplura de temporum ratione [...] authore Iohanne Nouiomago* (Coloniæ: Johannes Prael for Peter Quentel, 1537), XLVIII. See also Flügel, References, 27.

[37] Gesner, preface to Maaler (1561), *7^r. See also Gesner, *Mithridates* (1555), 8^v-9^r; Flügel, References, 26-30.

(quemadmodum & *Danicam ac Svecicam*) ex nostrâ Germanicâ ortas sev detortas esse, nemo dubitabit, qvi paulò diligentiùs illarum voces consideraverit."[38] Enoch Hannmann reports in 1645 (*Prosodia,* 163) the view, already seen in Gesner, that books written two or three hundred years ago in England were all in the Saxon language, a sure sign that English "meistentheils auß dem Deutschen herkömmt."

For Schottelius too in his *Lamentatio* (1640) (Dij^r) the source of English, Danish and Swedish lay in the German language, though in its truest, original state rather than in present-day corruption: "Die teutsche Sprache ists / daher gelernet reden / Der Nord-vnd Engelsmann / der Däne vnd die Schweden / [...]." His *Teutsche Sprachkunst* (1641) elaborates the theme, gathering support from the Dutch philologist Adrianus Scrieckius Rodornus:

> Was aber ferner die itzige Englische / Schottische / Norrische / Dänische und Schwedische Sprach anlanget / ist es gar unnötig / etwas weitläufftiges davon anzuziehen / weil es Weltkündig und offenbar / daß alle diese Sprachen in grunde lauter Teutsch seyn / wie denn auch diese Völcker alle Teutsches Namens Ankunfft und Uhrsprungs seyn / wiewol sie die Wörter in jhrer jetzigen Sprache guten theils zerzogen / verdorben und verwirret haben. *Scrieckius* sagt hiervon also; *Japhetica seu Europœa dialectus, perpetua usq[ue] traditione ad nostra usq[ue] secula devoluta est, aliquâ, ut sit, variatione, sed fundo quoq[ue] manente, adeo ut etiam hodie Teutones, Belgœ, Britanni, Dani & Septemtriones eo ipso utantur* (Schottelius, *Sprachkunst,* 161).

In the *Ausführliche Arbeit,* Schottelius moderates his criticism of these languages, replacing the words "wiewol sie die Wörter in jhrer jetzigen Sprache guten theils zerzogen / verdorben und verwirret haben" with the following: "wiewol die Wörter in jhrer jetzigen Sprache mit denen in Hochteutscher Mundart bekantlichen Wörteren und Redarten in vielen frömd / unbekant und abstimmig scheinen" (Schottelius, *Ausführliche Arbeit,* 130-1). In his mature work, the earlier perception of distortion, confusion and corruption has given way to a more accommodating sense of strangeness and remoteness, relative to High German. Schottelius proceeds to classify English with other Germanic and Celtic languages as "remotiores" or "abstimmige Sprachen:"

> Abstimmige / darin zwar die Teutschen Geschlechtwörter / Hülfwörter / Stam[m]wörter und also die Teutsche Eigenschaft befindlich / dennoch aber wegen der Ausrede / Verstümlung und unkentlich Machung der Teutschen und Einmengung der frömden Wörter / fast abstimmig von jetziger Teutschen Sprache scheinen / wiewol doch Ankunft / Grund und Wesen Teutsch annoch ist und bleibet / als da sind die Isländische Norwegische Dänische Schwedische Englische Schottische Wallische Altgotische / so annoch in *Taurica Chersoneso* verhanden (Schottelius, *Ausführliche Arbeit,* 153-4).

For Schottelius, all these languages are derived, like High German and Low German, from "Die Celtische od[er] alte Teutsche Spra[che]." Referring specifically to Danish,

---

[38] Andreas Helvigius, *Etymologiœ, Sive origines dictionum germanicarum, ex tribus illis nobilibus antiquitatis eruditœ Linguis, Latina, Graeca, Hebraea, derivatarum: [...]* (Francofurti: Typis Ioannis Wolphij, Sumptibus AntonI HummI, 1611), 28.

Swedish, Scots and English, he is well aware of the affinities linking the Germanic languages, but also of their mutual unintelligibility (Schottelius, *Ausführliche Arbeit*, 33). The genetic relationship of English and German remained a matter for careful equivocation. Morhof notes in 1682 that, despite its mixed character, English is "den Wörtern und der *Construction* nach Teutsch." It can therefore share in the renown enjoyed by the latter language, but, he adds guardedly, "jedennoch daß sie sich nicht unternehme der Mutter vorzugreiffen. Denn es ist beyweiten die rennlichkeit nicht in der Engelschen Sprach die in der Teutschen / die auß sich selbst bestehet" (Morhof, *Unterricht*, 228).

Seventeenth-century German language patriots frequently enhance the status of their language by emphasising its role as a donor, and this line of thought could only work to the further disparagement of English, which is pressed into the role of universal recipient. Thus, according to the bold genetic construct of the grammarian Johann Bödiker (1690), German has acted repeatedly as co-parent. In his view, a mixture of Hebrew and German produced Greek; Greek and German together produced Latin; Latin and German in turn produced Italian and French (and, with the addition of Arabic, Spanish); and finally, at the lowest point in the pedigree, "aus der teutschen und Französischen halb lateinischen die englische." A change of paradigm is signalled when Bödiker's reviser, Johann Leonhard Frisch, comes to portray German and English in a more modern way as cognate descendants of the older Germanic language.[39]

This truer picture of the co-equal place of English and German within the Germanic family of languages came to establish itself gradually from the late seventeenth century onwards. The most advanced state of the question round 1700 can again be illustrated from Leibniz, who explores the varying degrees of affinity among the German languages. The English are "halb Teutsch" (Leibniz, *Unvorgreifliche Gedanken*, § 42, 278); English and the Norse languages are "etwas mehr von uns entfernet, als das Holländische, und mehr zur Untersuchung des Ursprungs, als zur Anreicherung der Sprache dienen" (Leibniz, *Unvorgreifliche Gedanken*, § 70, 294). Leibniz carefully grades the other Germanic dialects as valuable sources, albeit of varying importance, for the recovery of primeval Germanic lexis and for its future development:

> Auch nicht nur was in Teutschland in Ubung, sondern auch was von Teutscher Herkunfft in Holl-und Engelländischen: worzu auch fürnehmlich die Worte der Nord-Teutschen, das ist, der Dänen, Norwegen, Schweden und Issländer (bey welchen letztern sonderlich viel von unser uralten Sprach geblieben,) zu ziehen: [...] Denn anders zu den wahren Ursprüngen nicht zu gelangen, [...] (Leibniz, *Unvorgreifliche Gedanken*, § 32, 272-3).

To house these philological riches, Leibniz looks to models elsewhere, including England:
> Was auch ein wohl ausgearbeitetes Glossarium Etymologicum, oder Sprach-Quell, vor schöne Dinge in sich halten würde, wo nicht zum menschlichen Gebrauch, doch zur

---

[39] Johann Bödiker, *Grundsäze Der Teutschen Sprache Mit Dessen eigenen und Johann Leonhard Frischens vollständigen Anmerkungen: Durch neue Zusäze vermehret von Johann Jacob Wippel* (Berlin: Nicolai, 1746), 282.

Zierde und Ruhm unserer Nation und Erklärung des Alterthums und der Historien, ist nicht zu sagen; Wenn nemlich Leute, wie Schottel, Brasch [i.e. Prasch] oder Morhoff bey uns, oder wie Menage bey den Frantzosen; und eben dieser mit dem Ferrari bey den Welschen, Spelmann in England, Worm oder Verhel bey den Nordländern sich darüber machten (Leibniz, *Unvorgreifliche Gedanken*, § 41, 278).

Leibniz is referring here to the work of the historian and antiquary Sir Henry Spelman (1564?-1641), presumably his *Archaeologus* (London, 1626) or the posthumous editions of the *Glossarium archaeologicum* (London, 1664 and later).

Cultivation and Study of English

As we have seen, the theme of English as a mixed language is counterpointed with an ever clearer articulation of its profoundly Germanic character. As a third voice in this polyphony, we now trace an awareness in German-speaking countries that the English language was copious, expressive and elegant, the product of conscious cultivation, and that in consequence it could hold its own among the languages of Europe, modern or ancient.

Again the starting point is low, and early testimonies are meagre. We have no evidence whatever that contemporary speakers of German shared the sanguine view of English put forth by Thomas Heywood (ca. 1570-1641): "from the most rude and vnpolisht tongue, it is growne to a most perfect and composed language, and many excellent workes, and elaborate Poems writ in the same, that many Nations grow inamored of our tongue (before despised.)."[40] It would be hard to argue, for instance, that the English players contributed anything to the standing of the English language in Germany. Performing in English from 1592, they appear to have met with a cool reception, and from 1608 they went over to the use of German in their performances.[41] A truer picture of contemporary perceptions of English language and culture can be gained from the work of the Swiss pastor and historian Johann Jacob Grasser, who visited England between 1604 and 1608. His work deals over-whelmingly with Italy and France. The section on English geography and history, with passing reference to language, is a significant addition, but comprises only some 28 out of nearly 1,500 pages.[42]

By the 1640s, opinion had decisively shifted. The anonymous poem *Deutsche Satyra* (Breslau, ca. 1640) refers to certain unspecified attempts to cultivate or purify the

---

[40] Thomas Heywood, *An Apology for Actors (1612)* [...] With Introduction and Bibliographical Notes by Richard H. Perkinson (New York: Scholars' Facsimiles and Reprints, 1941), F3ʳ.

[41] Lawrence Marsden Price, *The Reception of English Literature in Germany* (Berkeley, CA: University of California Press, 1932), 9-26; Horst Oppel, *Englisch-deutsche Literaturbeziehungen*, vol. 1: *Von den Anfängen bis zum Ausgang des 18. Jahrhunderts* (Berlin: Erich Schmidt, 1971), 43.

[42] Johann Jacob Grasser, *Newe vnd volkom[m]ne Italianische / Frantzösische / vnd Englische Schatzkammer* (Basel: Genath, 1610), III, 235-63; Robson-Scott, *Travellers,* 79-80.

language in England:

> Waß sol ich weiter sagen
> Von dir Tyberius? Der du dich vor zu tragen
> Dem Rathe hast geschewt ein eintzig Grichisch wort.
> O daß man dieses noch bedecht an manchem Ort:
> Daß thut auch Engellandt / dem folget meine Sinnen; [...].[43]

Harsdörffer is more specific in his praise. In a set of epigrams (1643) he characterises in turn the Hebrew, German, Dutch, Greek, Latin, Italian, French, Spanish, English and Slavonic languages. The order is probably significant, reflecting Harsdörffer's conception of the relative decline of each language from the most perfect state. On English, he writes:

> Die Englische Sprache.
>
> Ich bin von Teutscher Art / und hab genommen zu /
> An Kunst und Zierlichkeit / nun mangelt mir die Ruh
> (Harsdörffer, *Gesprächspiele*, III (1643), 444).

Captured here in miniature is a perception of the Germanic character of English, its prospering fortunes in the recent past, and the political unrest which now troubles it at home.

Though it seems few Germans living before 1650 had direct access to the language, respect for English thought had been fostered, in part through the availability of works by English writers in Latin, or sometimes in French translation, or in Latin translations made specially for a Continental readership.[44] More specifically, new perceptions of a cultured and expressive English vernacular were supported, usually at second or third hand, by the example of Sir Philip Sidney's *Arcadia* (1590).[45] The English version of the *Arcadia* (1590) was acquired in 1653 for the library at Wolfenbüttel, but we look in vain for evidence that the work was read in the original by seven-

---

[43] *Deutsche Satyra Wieder alle Verterber der deutschen Sprache* (Breßlaw: Christoph Jonisch, no date), lines 101-105.

[44] Irene Wiem, *Das englische Schrifttum in Deutschland von 1518-1600* (Leipzig: Becker & Erler, 1940; reprinted New York: Johnson Reprint Corp., 1967); Wilhelm Graeber and Geneviève Roche, *Englische Literatur des 17. und 18. Jahrhunderts in französischer Übersetzung und deutscher Weiterübersetzung: Eine kommentierte Bibliographie*, ed. Jürgen von Stackelberg (Tübingen: Niemeyer, 1988).

[45] *ARCADIA Der Gräffin von Pembrock. [...] fleissig vnd trewlich übersetzt Durch VALENTINVM THEOCRITVM von Hirschberg* (Franckfurt am Mayn: bey Caspar Rötell / In Verlegung Matthäi Merian, 1629). See Waterhouse, *Relations*, 18-37; Oppel, *Literaturbeziehungen*, 53, 72; Graeber, Roche and Stackelberg, *Literatur*, 111-13; Joseph Leighton, "On the Reception of Sir Philip Sidney's Arcadia in Germany from Opitz to Anton Ulrich," in D.H. Green, L.P. Johnson and Dieter Wuttke, eds., *From Wolfram and Petrarch to Goethe and Grass: Studies in Literature in Honour of Leonard Forster,* (Baden-Baden: Koerner, 1982), 473-88.

teenth-century Germans. Most, if not all, were (to say the least) more comfortable with a French version, as Harsdörffer shows by considerately listing "Arcadie par Philippe Sidnei" (Paris, 1642) in the bibliography to his *Frauenzimmer Gesprächspiele*, II (1657), Gg3ʳ. Nevertheless, the figurehead of Sidney was instrumental in raising perceptions of English as a cultivated language. Writers seeking an exemplar of English, particularly as part of an international canon of writers, turned readily to the name, and he is often the only English author to be cited in this way. Thus Schill, *Ehrenkranz* (1644, 194): "Es preise Engelland seine *Sidneos*." Revealing too is a passage in the anonymous *Sprachverderber* (1643, 16), which comments adversely on the popularity of the "Arcadien" among young ladies. Johann Balthasar Schupp, *Orator ineptus* (1638), in *Schriften* (1663) is exceptional in referring disparagingly to the "pompous words from the *Amadis* or the *Arcadia*" (Waterhouse, *Relations,* 35); among other academics, opinion was generally favourable. As early as 1634, Johann Matthäus Meyfart lauded the 1629 version as "die treffliche Vbersetzung der Engellendischen Arcadien / deß Hochwolgebornen Herrn von Sidney," adding the comment: "daß mich bedüncket / es habe der Dolmetscher von dieser artigen vbersetzung nit weniger ruhms / als hochgedachter Autor von der sinnreichen erfindung vnd stattlichen Außzierung zugewarten."[46] August Buchner's poetic manual (in the posthumous edition of 1663, though interestingly not in the more highly regarded text of 1665) praises the stylistic distinction of Sidney's work, whilst deploring the lexical impurity of the German translation (presumably the 1629 version):

> Was werden dann für bessern Lohn bey dem verständigen die jenigen haben / welche unter das Teutsche ohne alle Noth so viel Lateinisches oder ander frembdes einbrocken / welches so es der Dolmetscher der *Arcadien,* so der Herr von *Sitnei* in Englischer Sprache geschrieben / in acht genommen hette / würde dasselbe schöne gedichte mit mehrer Anmuth in unser Sprach gelesen werden / daß alle die Lust / ob den artigen Erfindungen / und reichem Zufluß schöner Gedancken und Worten wir empfinden / die wird uns alsbald zunichte / und fast zu einem Verdrieß gemacht durch die vielfältig vermengte Reden / da bald ein Lateinisch / bald ein Frantzösisch / bald ein Italiänisch oder auch Spanisch Wort zum öfftern mit eingeschoben wird / daß fast kein *Bettlersmantel* von so vielfältigen Flecken als dieses Werck von unterschiedenen Sprachen zusammen geflicket ist / [...].[47]

Schottelius provides the fullest statement of Sidney's position as a linguistic landmark, though again, we may suspect, at some remove, since in the bibliography to his *Ausführliche Arbeit* (c2ʳ) he cites a German translation of the *Arcadia*. In the seventh of the eulogies which preface this work, he writes of poets who have made languages "beliebt" (Schottelius, *Ausführliche Arbeit*, 111). His prime example for English is Sidney (Schottelius, *Ausführliche Arbeit*, 115-16), who is thus placed alongside du Bartas, Petrarch and others as having risen "zu solcher wolbekandten Zier und an-

---

[46] Johann Matthäus Meyfart, *Teutsche Rhetorica* (Coburg: Johann Forckel in Verlegung Friderich Gruners, 1634), vᵛ.

[47] *August Buchners kurzer Weg-Weiser zur Deutschen Tichtkunst / Aus ezzlichen geschriebenen Exemplarien ergänzet [...] durch M. Georg Gözen / Kais. gekr. Poeten / der Philos. Fac. zu Jehn Adjunctum* (Jehna: Sengenwald, 1663), 56-7.

genehmer Hoheit." Early in the dialogue "Wie man recht verteutschen soll," Schottelius allows the speaker Siegeraht the following more extensive, indeed fulsome, account:

> Es ist die Englische Sprache / wie bekant / in sothanem Mispreise gehalten / daß sich niemand sonderlich / solche zuwissen / vor diesem bemühet / und wil für ein zusammengeflikke anderer Sprache geschetzt werden: Bekant ist aber / wie der so sinnreiche und gelahrte als tapfere *Philippus* Sidnei seine *Arcadiam* in Englischer Sprache mit so hohen Reden und Erfindungen beschrieben / daß dieselbe nicht allein in unterschiedliche Sprachen übergesetzet / von hohen und gelahrten Leuten lieb und werth gehalten / sonderen dieses Zeugniß ist jhr auch beygeleget / *quod Libro huic, quò ad verba, flores & elegantiæ totius antiquitatis Græcæ & Latinæ, quò ad res characterismi omnium virtutum & vitiorum insint: ut Authorem hunc viri & Authores nostri temporis celeberrimi jure vocarint incomparabilem, inimitabilem Sidneium.* Dieses hat jhm die Englische Sprache / der er mit Kunst und nach Grund mächtig gewesen / zuwege gebracht / und weil er so künstlich / so schön und wolanständlich die Englischen Worte hat zufügen / anzulegen / und gutem Verstande nach anzuordnen und beyeinzubringen vermocht / und seine vortrefliche Sprachbaukunst bey so bewanten und bekanten Stoffe dennoch aufs daurhafste und geschmükste erwiesen / als hat er auch einen ewig-daurenden schönen Nachruhm jhm erbauet / und seine Landsleute zu gleichmeßigem und noch höheren Nachtritte angewiesen und angelokket; Wie dan erfolgt und bekant ist / was für trefliche Bücher in geistlichen und weltlichen Sachen in Englischer Sprache verhanden (Schottelius, *Ausführliche Arbeit*, 1220).

In these words, a powerful voice is being prominently raised in defence of the English language. Implicit throughout is the argument that, if such glory is possible for English, it must, *a fortiori*, be possible for the purer and more ancient "Haubt-sprache," German.

The years before 1650 saw a further significant attempt to present the English language in a favourable light, again in the context of the "Fruchtbringende Gesellschaft." Celebrating the achievements of that Society in 1647, Karl Gustav von Hille (ca. 1590-1647) comments on historical changes in the German language, and adds:

> Vnd solches nicht allein in unsrer angebornen / sondern auch in andern unterschiedenen fremden Sprachen; insonderheit in der Englischen / einer alten Teutschen Mundart; welche sich dann von Jahren zu Jahren / dergestalt in der Rechtschreib- und Ausredung aufs zierlichste gebessert / daß derselben Sprachverständiger sich darüber verwundern muß.[48]

As proof, Hille cites an Old English version of the Lord's Prayer "wie es nach Christi Geburt im Jahr 430 gebetet / auch mir von einem vornehmen gelehrten Mann / als ein

---

[48] Karl Gustav von Hille, *Der Teutsche Palmbaum [...] durch den Vnverdrossenen* (Nürnberg: Wolfgang Endter, 1647), 121; Jill Bepler, "Karl Gustav von Hille (ca. 1590-1647): Zu seiner Biographie und zu seinen Beziehungen nach England," in August Buck and Martin Bircher, eds., *Respublica Guelpherbytana: Wolfenbütteler Beiträge zur Renaissance- und Barockforschung: Festschrift für Paul Raabe* (Amsterdam: Rodopi, 1987) (Chloe: Beihefte zu Daphnis, 6), 253-90; Waterhouse, *Relations*, 118-19; Hüllen, "Yardsticks," 294-5.

altes Gedächtniß mitgetheilet worden," with a contemporary English version in parallel. Hille continues:

> Ob nun wol die Englische / vor eine aus vielen zusammengesetzte und verstümpelte Sprache gehalten wird; so ist sie dannoch mit Warheit nicht eine so gar geringschätzig und schlechte / wie sich solches dieselb Vnverständige einbilden: Sondern sie bestehet in einer solchen * [marginal note: *Our Englisch: I, vvil not say as sacred as the Hebreu or as Learned as the Greke) but es as fluent as the Latine, and as coerteous as the, Spanisch, as court like as the French, and as amorous as the Italien. Besihe The Remaines of England.*] Lieblichkeit und hohen Sinnbegriff / daß auch die allerwürdigste Geist- und weltliche Bücher / nicht von ihnen in der Lateinischen; sondern viel ehe in ihren eigenen Muttersprache beschrieben / zu lesen seynd: dannenhero hertzlich zu wünschen / daß wir Teutsche ein mehrern Fleiß an solcher Sprache legten / ols leider nicht geschiehet, damit wir ihre übrige Geistliche Bücher / die sie artlich und wol gegeben / in unsere hochteutsche Sprache gleichfalls übersetzen könten: geschweige der unterschiedlichen herrlichen Schriften / insonderheit der Arcadien des Ritters *Sidney:* welcher wegen dessen hohen Würde und tiefen Verstands / über die 30. mal / von unterschiedenen fremden Völkern / in ihre angeborne Sprache / mit Fleiß zwar übersetzet aber dannoch die Vollkommenheit und innerlichen Verstand desselben / sowol und eigentlich nicht begreiffen / nach die Tieffsinnigkeit dessen vollständig ergründen und ausarbeiten können (Hille, *Palmbaum*, 123-4).[49]

This passage is significantly located in the argument. Hille has already dealt with the other "Haubtsprachen" and the minor languages of Europe. He has reserved until last the ancient German language, together with its venerable dialect, English, and the modern cultivation thereof by Sidney, before proceeding to a severe critique and parody of lexical mixture in contemporary German. At this date it is highly unusual to find in continental sources an author championing the English language and citing English vernacular works in the original. But Hille had excellent reason for so doing. As the son of James Hill, an English soldier formerly in the service of the King of Sweden, he had visited England on several occasions from 1628, speaking the language as well as his father according to the latter's testimony, and himself writing in English to Landgraf Moritz von Hessen (Bepler, "Hille," 261-6).

Throughout the century, informed scholars were aware that in its history the English language had been the object of official support and cultivation, enjoying the favour of its kings, just as German was known to have been promoted by the emperors Charlemagne, Rudolf I and Maximilian. Using Polydor Vergil and Camden, Grasser knew in 1610 that Edward III of England (1312-1377) had "ordnet daß die Rechtshändel in Englischer Sprach verrichtet / vnnd beschrieben wurden" (*Schatzkammer*, 244-5), and similarly Schottelius remarked in 1663 "wie er [Edward III] den Gebrauch und Werthaltung der Englischen Sprache durch sein gantzes Reich bestetigt habe" (*Ausführliche Arbeit*, b3ᵛ).

---

[49] The English quotation corresponds to Camden, *Remaines* (1605), 20, and to page 24 of the third impression (London: Nicholas Okes for Simon Waterson, 1623), of which Hille purchased a copy on his visit to London in 1629 (Bepler, "Hille," 271).

A new stage in knowledge and understanding of English is marked by the section of Morhof's *Unterricht von der Teutschen Sprache und Poesie* (1682) entitled "Von der Engelländer Poeterey" (225-53).[50] Despite some adverse comments on the mixed character of the language (quoted above), Morhof acknowledges certain landmarks in English literature: Chaucer, Spenser, Jonson, Bacon, Donne, Herbert, Milton and Dryden, also Shakespeare, Beaumont and Fletcher, though he admits that he has seen nothing of these last three. He cites passages of English at several points. The survey is in general positive, and an advance on most previous references, though Morhof is not uncritical. In his concluding paragraph, stung by the comments of Thomas Rymer (cited above), he finds among the English a lack of "Bescheidenheit von ihnen selbst und von andern Völckern zu urtheilen."

To royal patronage and literary achievement was added scholarly nurture. By the end of the seventeenth century, news had reached Germany of major lexicographical projects under way in England, which would set the seal on English as a major European language:

> Als mir nun auch vor einigen Jahren Nachricht geben worden, dass die Engländer ebenmässig mit einem grossen Werck umgiengen, so dem Frantzösischen damahls noch nicht erschienenen Wörter-Buch nichts weichen solte, habe ich so fort angehalten, dass sie auch auff Kunst-Worte dencken möchten, mit dem Bedeuten, was massen ich Nachricht erhalten hätte, dass die Frantzosen sich auch in diesem Stück eines bessern bedacht, vernehme auch nunmehr, dass die Engländer würcklich mit dergleichen anietzo begriffen (Leibniz, *Unvorgreifliche Gedanken,* § 38, 277).

Competence in English Language

These changing evaluations of the character of English are paralleled by advances in English language competence, which forms our fourth chronological theme. Early evidence is again sparse. Most German speakers, had they ever given thought to the matter, would probably have concurred with the view of Richard Mulcaster (1532?-1611) that "our English tung [...] is of small reatch, it stretcheth no further then this Ilad of ours, naie not there ouer all."[51] The Volksbuch *Fortunatus* (1509) provides us with a remarkably early fictive example of the use of English.[52] For the rest, most early German travellers are likely to have shared the pragmatic, utilitarian view expressed by Claude Duret in his survey of languages (1613):

> Ceste langue Angloise est si peu estimee des estrangers qui vont en Angleterre, qu'il y en

---

[50] Waterhouse, *Relations,* 119-22.
[51] Richard Mulcaster, *The First Part of the Elementary (1582)* (Menston: Scolar Press, 1970), 256.
[52] John L. Flood, "*Fortunatus* in London," in Dietrich Huschenbett and John Margetts, eds., *Reise und Welterfahrung in der deutschen Literatur des Mittelalters: Vorträge des XI. Anglodeutschen Colloquiums 11.-15. September 1989 Universität Liverpool* (Würzburg: Königshausen & Neumann, 1991), 240-63.

a peu qui veulent se pener de l'apprendre, & de la parler, si ce ne sont les seruiteurs ou facteurs pour l'vsage des choses vtiles & necessaires à la vie, lesquelles dependent du menu peuple qui ne sçait parler autre langue (Duret, *Thresor*, 876).

A few early instances of such contacts are recorded. German speakers were called upon to show some facility in the English language already before 1600, for purposes of Hanseatic trade. In 1554 an ordinance at the London Steelyard required incoming German youths to demonstrate to the satisfaction of their seniors that they had a year's acquaintance with the English language.[53]

Evidence for the use of Latin by German travellers to Britain is found from the fifteenth century onwards. In 1483, the Silesian nobleman Nikolaus von Popplau delivered an oration in Latin to King Richard III (Robson-Scott, *Travellers*, 14). Latin was naturally also the primary medium of the Swiss theological student and later lexicographer Josua Maaler (1529-1599), who came to Oxford in 1551.[54] Maaler took the opportunity to improve his French, but, as to English, "Ich wollt mich ye uff des Lands Sprach in keinem Wäg begäben, zum theil uß Kürze der Zyt, zum theil das sy ußert irem Land und Marchen nienen gebrucht wirt." He adds with disarming piety: "Die rächt waar englisch Spraach wöllend wir erst auch im waaren Engelland, in Gottes ewigem Himmelrych erlernen, und mit dißer by der Gmeinsame aller Säligen und Ußerwälten, Gott ewigklich loben und prysen" (Maaler, *Teütsch*) In German-English diplomacy, Latin, French and Italian were the languages of choice, as in the negotiations of Elizabeth I of England and the Earl of Leicester with Johann Casimir, Administrator of the Palatinate, in the late sixteenth century. "Fuit peritus linguarum, Gallica, Italica, Anglica præter Latina[m]," we read of the Strasbourg-born Palatine lawyer and poet Peter Denaisius (1560-1610), who visited England before 1590 and subsequently translated a pamphlet of King James I.[55] During a diplomatic mission in the 1590s, the Württemberger Hans Jakob Breuning von Buchenbach used Latin, Italian and French in meetings with Elizabeth, Essex and Cecil.[56] On the 'Badenfahrt' of 1592 (so called because of the rough Channel crossing), Friedrich von Württemberg used French in audience with Elizabeth.[57] According to Johann Wilhelm Neu-

---

[53] Konrad Schröder, "Kleine Chronik zur Frühzeit des Fremdsprachenlernens und des Fremdsprachenunterrichts im deutschsprachigen Raum, unter besonderer Berücksichtigung des 16. Jahrhunderts," *Die Neueren Sprachen* 79 (1980): 114-35, here 116, 118; Konrad Schröder, *Linguarum Recentium Annales: Der Unterricht in den modernen europäischen Sprachen im deutschsprachigen Raum* (Augsburg: Universität, 1980-85) (henceforth Schröder, *LRA*), nos. 002 and 011.

[54] Johann Georg Müller, ed., *Bekenntnisse merkwürdiger Männer von sich selbst* (Winterthur: Steiner, 1792-1822), VI, 187-464, here 225; also Robson-Scott, *Travellers*, 23-30; Flood, "Fortunatus," 240-63.

[55] Melchior Adam, *Vitæ Germanorum jureconsultorum et politicorum* (Haidelbergæ: Impensis heredum Jonæ Rosæ, Excudit Johannes Georgius Geyder, 1620), 444-7, here 445; *Allgemeine deutsche Biographie*, vol. 5, 49; Waterhouse, *Relations*, 91.

[56] Hans Jakob Breuning von Buchenbach, *Relation über seine Sendung nach England im Jahr 1595, mitgetheilt von A. Schlossberger* (Stuttgart: Literarischer Verein, 1865).

[57] Rye, *England*, 12; Robson-Scott, *Travellers*, 53-9.

mayr von Ramssla (1570-1644), James I conversed in Latin and French with Johann Ernst der Jüngere von Sachsen-Weimar (1594-1626) during his visit to London in 1613.[58] Entertaining Otto von Hessen two years previously, the King had commiserated with his guest on the bad Latin pronunciation which prevailed in England, a feature which continued to mystify travellers from Germany after the Restoration.[59]

There is varied evidence as to how other early visitors to Britain coped. Even if they were interested in acquiring a knowledge of the English language, short visits can have given but little opportunity. In 1585 Samuel Kiechel (1563-1619) was glad enough to find a pastry-cook who could converse in French; like many other visitors, he went to the theatre, but he remarks that foreigners found it annoying not to be able to understand the language (Robson-Scott, *Travellers*, 49-50). On his visit to London, Thomas Platter the Younger attended church services in French. Inspecting Hampton Court, he relied on an English-French interpreter, and on other occasions he used Latin, but at the Lord Mayor's banquet an interpreter was again required, "dann wier nichts verstunden, weder waß sie auf latein, frantzösisch oder spangisch mitt uns redeten."[60] Philip Julius, Duke of Pommern-Stettin, visited England with his entourage in 1602, a German tailor Leinvert acting as their guide for some of the time. The party saw plays in English, but it appears they lacked competence in the language, because on one occasion when an interpreter was not available they were relieved to find that they could make themselves understood in Latin.[61] The Thuringian Justus Zinzerling (Jodocus Sincerus) visited England about 1610, publishing his account (*Itinerarium Galliae*) in 1616 (with several later editions). By then, there are signs of regular traffic. The landlord of the Post Inn at Sittingbourne can understand Latin, Zinzerling assures us. He refers also to resident interpreters, some of them unreliable, who offer their services for the benefit of travelling Germans: he recommends one Frederick, an "excellent youth" and a native of Hesse-Kassel.[62]

In Germany, proficiency in English generally remained of little interest or value, particularly at the cultural and social level which is predominantly reflected in surviving testimonies. It is therefore not surprising when in a scholarly work Valentin Arithmaeus, Professor of Poetry at Frankfurt an der Oder, excuses himself from citing English-language inscriptions from Westminster Abbey and St Paul's with the comment "Anglicam enim paucissimi intelligunt."[63] Yet a knowledge of English was an

---

[58] Johann Wilhelm Neumayr von Ramssla, *Des Durchlauchtigen Hochgebornen Fürsten vnd Herrn / Herrn Johann Ernsten des Jüngern [...] Reise In Franckreich / Engelland vnd Niederland* (Leipzig: Henning Grosse d. J., printed by Justus Jansonius, 1620); Rye, *England*, 150; Robson-Scott, *Travellers*, 86-8.
[59] Rye, *England*, 144; Robson-Scott, *Travellers*, 85.
[60] Platter, *Beschreibung*, 778, 782, 784, 788, 831, 834, 866; Flood, *Fortunatus*, 257-8.
[61] Herman Hager, "Diary of the Journey of Philip Julius, Duke of Stettin-Pomerania, through England in the Year 1602," *Englische Studien* 18 (1893): 315-18; Robson-Scott, *Travellers*, 61-5.
[62] Rye, *England*, xxxvii, 131-3; Waterhouse, *Relations*, 3; Robson-Scott, *Travellers*, 80-2.
[63] Valentin Arithmaeus, *Mausoléa Regum* (Francof. Marchion., 1618), Praefatio of 1617, 6ᵛ; Robson-Scott, *Travellers*, 25.

accomplishment to which some Germans of note were willing to admit, even before 1650. Harsdörffer writes in 1644 of a hard-won oral and literary knowledge of English, alongside the Romance languages: "Mit was kostbarem Vngemach / mit was Leib-und vielmals auch Seelengefahr erwanderen wir der Welschen / Frantzösischen / Spanischen und Engeländischen Rede-und-Schriftenkundigung?" (Harsdörffer, *Gesprächspiele,* IV, 459). Philipp von Zesen claims in 1647 a linguist's passive knowledge of English, listing that language alongside Hebrew, Greek, Latin, French and Dutch as "alle sprachen / die ich zur noht / nuhr aus diesen uhrsachen habe verstehen lärnen," namely for purposes of comparison with High German.[64] And to acquire true proficiency in an obscure foreign language was always possible, given a favourable combination of circumstances and talent, as a few case histories show.

Georg Rudolf Weckherlin (1584-1653), having spent three years in England sometime between 1607 and 1615, was fully at home in the language by the latter date, thanks to his contacts with Elizabeth Raworth and her family in Dover.[65] Weckherlin writes in the preface to his highly accomplished translation *Triumphall Shews* (1616): "I was glad to find out all my best English, I had learned within three yeares, I lived in England."[66] Hieronymus Hainhofer (1611-1683), nephew of the art collector Philipp Hainhofer, visited England in 1634 and on at least four later occasions. In 1637 we find him corresponding fluently in English, and he subsequently translated texts from German into English. His contacts included the early German expatriates Weckherlin, Hartlib and Haak.[67] Samuel Hartlib (1600?-after 1662) was a native of Elbing and one of a family of merchants, his mother a daughter of John Langthon, "Vorsteher der englischen Kaufmannschaft in Elbing." He came to England in 1628, published many works in English from 1641 onwards, had close links with Hobbes, Evelyn, Pepys, Boyle and Wren, and was the dedicatee of Milton's treatise *On Education* (1644).[68] Heinrich (Henry) Oldenburg (1618-1677) from Bremen spent many years in England, becoming Secretary of the Royal Society from 1662 to his death; already in 1654 Milton felt moved to pay him the handsome compliment: "You have indeed learnt to speak our language more accurately and fluently than any other foreigner I have ever known" (Selling, *Gelehrten-Reisen,* 40, 234). Theodor(e) Haak

---

[64] Filip Zesen, „Sendschreiben an Adolf Rosel," in Johann Bellin, ed., *Etlicher der hoch-löblich Deutsch-gesinneten Genossenschaft Mitglieder* (Hamburg: Wärner, 1647), E^v.

[65] Leonard Wilson Forster, *Georg Rudolf Weckherlin: Zur Kenntnis seines Lebens in England* (Basel: Schwabe, 1944), 21.

[66] *Georg Rudolf Weckherlins Gedichte,* ed. Hermann Fischer (Tübingen: Literarischer Verein in Stuttgart, 1894-1907), I, 41; III, 37; Waterhouse, *Relations,* 11-17; Forster, *Weckherlin, 140;* Konrad Schröder, *LRA,* no. 133.

[67] Jill Bepler, "Augsburg England Wolfenbüttel: Die Karriere des Reisehofmeisters Hieronymus Hainhofer," in Jochen Brüning und Friedrich Niewöhner, eds., *Augsburg in der frühen Neuzeit: Beiträge zu einem Forschungsprogramm.* (Berlin: Akademie-Verlag, 1995), 119-39.

[68] *Dictionary of National Biography,* ed. Leslie Stephen et al. (London: Oxford University Press, 1885-1927), vol. 25, 72-3; *NDB,* VII, 721-2; F. Althaus, *Samuel Hartlib, ein deutschenglisches Charakterbild: Historisches Taschenbuch* (Leipzig: Brockhaus, 1884).

(1605-1690), co-founder of the Royal Society, was born at Neuhausen near Worms.[69] He settled in Oxford from the 1630s. To him we owe the first (fragmentary) German translation (ca. 1680) of Milton's *Paradise Lost*, which impressed the Heidelberg professor of Greek and history, Johann Seobald Fabricius, with its "gravitas stili, et copia lectissimorum verborum." Benthem mentions Haak posthumously as a helpful contact for visiting students.[70]

Evidence of this kind points to a growing and influential number of German emigrants to Britain, who absorbed both language and culture, and were instrumental in fostering further links, in some cases already by the middle of the century. Abundant documentation is also available for the intensity with which the English Civil War was followed by German speakers, though generally through the medium of other languages.[71] With the Restoration, interest in English language and culture entered a new, richer phase. Travel to Britain became more frequent. According to the "Heldengedicht" which the young Quirinus Kuhlmann (1651-1689) delivered at Breslau in 1670, the experience of visiting England was already putting its stamp on the faces, if not also the tongues, of contemporary travellers:

> Der voller Tugenden auß seinem Teutschland zog /
> Verwechselt' alte Lufft / wann er sich selbst verflog;
> Ward Franckreich kaum ersehn / so ward er zum Frantzosen /
> Genaß er Welsche Lufft / ward Welsch der Augen Losen /
> Satz' er den einen Fuß in Spanien erst ein /
> So muste bald sein Gang / sein Leben Spanisch seyn;
> War er in Engelland kaum eine Nacht gewesen;
> So ward auß dem Gesicht / was Englisch bald zulesen.[72]

"We find," writes Robson-Scott, "that for the first time it is possible to discover a certain unity of type among the heterogeneous variety of the travellers, and even to trace the emergence of a new conception of England and the English among Germans."[73] Interest in theology, philosophy, classical and oriental scholarship, and sci-

---

[69] *Dictionary of National Biography*, vol. 23, 412; Pamela R. Barnett, *Theodore Haak, F.R.S. (1605-1690): The First German Translator of 'Paradise Lost'* ('s-Gravenhage: Mouton, 1962); Waterhouse, *Relations*, 114-15, 136-40; Selling, *Gelehrten-Reisen*, 80-84.

[70] Henrich Ludolff Benthem, *Engeländischer Kirch- und Schulen-Staat* (Lüneburg: Lipper, 1694), 56-7.

[71] Günter Berghaus, *Die Aufnahme der englischen Revolution in Deutschland 1640-1669*, vol. 1 (Wiesbaden: Harrassowitz, 1989).

[72] A. Z. *Entsprossende Teutsche Palmen [...] Vorgetragen Von Qvirin Kuhlmann / Breßlauern. Oels, bey Johann Seyfferts nachgelassener Buchdrucker-Witwen Druckts Gottfried Güntzel / Factor. 1670.* Reprinted in *Briefe der Fruchtbringenden Gesellschaft und Beilagen: Die Zeit Herzog Augusts von Sachsen-Weißenfels 1667-1680. Mit dem Breslauer Schuldrama »Actus Von der Hochlöbl. Fruchtbringenden Gesellschaft« (1670) und mit den Registern der Mitglieder*. Martin Bircher, collab. Gabriele Henkel und Andreas Herz ed. (Tübingen: Niemeyer, 1991), Aiij^v.

[73] Robson-Scott, *Travellers*, 92; Waterhouse, *Relations*, 113-16.

entific discovery drew German visitors to Britain, and shaped the external image of its culture, society and language. Andreas Selling has examined in detail the contacts made by some 200 German scholars who visited Britain during this period. Typically, they were drawn by the resources of the Bodleian Library, and by the lustre of the Royal Society (founded 1660), which had well over twenty native German members by 1700, some permanently resident in Britain.[74]

As early as 1675, Franz Anton Freiherr von Landsberg (1656-1727) noted: "Die Teutschen reißen anietzo sehr viel in dieß Landt, undt es ist auch woll des Besehens wehrt" (Selling, *Gelehrten-Reisen,* VII). Visiting luminaries included Daniel Georg Morhof (1660, 1670-71), Christian Knorr von Rosenroth (1660s), Martin Kempe (1670-71), Gottfried Wilhelm Leibniz (1673, 1676), Christoph Fürer von Haimendorf (1683), Christian Heinrich Postel (1683), Christoph Wegleiter (1685-88), Heinrich Ludolf Benthe(i)m (1687-89), Johann Burkhard Mencke (1698-99), Johann Friedrich Riederer (1698), Christian Franz Paullini, August Adolf von Haugwitz, Hiob Ludolf, Paul Jakob von Marperger, Heinrich Offelen.[75] Two cases are worth exploring for their linguistic interest.

The Nürnberg Pegnitzschäfer Christian Arnold (1627-1685) visited England as part of his tour of Europe in 1651, followed by his son Andreas (1656-1694) in 1681-82.[76] Christian moved with ease in British scholarly circles, making contact with Franciscus Junius and others. He was familiar with English authors including William Camden (1551-1623), Richard Verstegen (1550?-1620), Sir Henry Spelman and William Lisle (L'Isle) (1569?-1637). He retained a good knowledge of English long after his visit, translating from the work of Sir Thomas Browne, and both father and son were avid collectors of English books. One in ten of the works in the important Bibliotheca Arnoldiana relates to England, including Francis Holyoke's Latin-English and English-Latin version of John Rider's *Dictionarie* (London, 1649) and Elisha Coles, *A Dictionary, English-Latin, and Latin-English* (London, second edition, 1679).

Another special case, researched by Jill Bepler, is the avid polyglot, traveller and collector Ferdinand Albrecht, Duke of Braunschweig-Lüneburg-Bevern ("Der Wunderliche" in the *Fruchtbringende Gesellschaft*), who spent ten months visiting England in 1664-65.[77] He arrived eager to attain, in particular, oral proficiency in English. His method, which he had already used in France, was to purchase a dictionary and some language handbooks, to converse with as many people as possible, and to secure the services of a language teacher (Bepler, *Ferdinand Albrecht*, 145-46). Ferdinand Albrecht was made Fellow of the Royal Society, where he declined the offer of an inter-

---

[74] Robson-Scott, *Travellers,* 92; Selling, *Gelehrten-Reisen,* 23, 52-88, 379.

[75] Selling, *Gelehrten-Reisen*; Waterhouse, *Relations,* 115-16.

[76] Frans Blom, *Christoph and Andreas Arnold and England: The Travels and Book-collections of Two Seventeenth-century Nurembergers* (Nürnberg: Schriftenreihe der Stadt, 1982), in particular 48, 53-4, 66, 69, 135ff.

[77] Jill Bepler, *Ferdinand Albrecht, Duke of Braunschweig-Lüneburg (1636-1687): A Traveller and his Travelogue* (Wiesbaden: Harrassowitz, 1988); Robson-Scott, *Travellers,* 97-101; Jill Kohl (Bepler), "The Curious Traveller: Literary and Non-Literary Documents of a Visit to Restoration England," *German Life and Letters* 36 (1983): 219-31.

preter: "His *Highness* told them, that it was not necessary, they should put themselves to that trouble: for he well understood our Language, having been drawn to the study of it, out of a desire of reading our *Philosophical Books.*"[78] His active competence in written English, however, does not appear to have been strong (Bepler, *Ferdinand Albrecht,* 154).

As well as providing awareness of the history and antiquity of English, these years brought with them a more detailed knowledge of contemporary English and a clearer sense of its internal variety. Commenting on the dialects of various European languages, Georg Neumark observed in 1668:

> In *Engeland* sind nicht weniger / der statlichsten Werke ausgangen / man sieht aber daß solche alle auf gut *Middelessexische* Sprachahrt / wie solche üm die Königliche *Thronstadt London* gebräuchlich / und nicht auf *Argylisch* / *Cumberländisch* / *Pembrokkisch* und dergleichen unförmlichere Außrede / gestellet sind (*Palmbaum,* 98).

Later in the century, scholars still came hoping to employ their Latin, but visitors continued to find the radical shifts in its Anglicised pronunciation, and evidently also the dwindling local competence, a serious barrier to comprehension.[79] Significantly, visitors also complain that they find the English reluctant to use French (Selling, *Gelehrten-Reisen,* 188-91, 207, 315).

Though in Germany the linguistic climate was now increasingly favourable to the learning of English, appearances can be deceptive. Andreas Gryphius is said to have known twelve or more languages. He used a few English-language sources for his *Carolus Stuardus* (1657), but most were in Latin, French and Italian.[80] It is also revealing that, even in the case of so linguistically gifted a figure, his translations of religious works by Sir Richard Baker (1568?-1645) were based, not directly on the original English, but on an intermediate Dutch version.[81] Similarly, the medic Johannes Lange (active 1670-96) reputedly translated over 30 works from English, including Bunyan, but his versions of *Pilgrim's Progress* and *The Holy War* (Hamburg, 1685 and 1693 respectively) were based on Dutch translations.[82] In all, we have as yet few signs of the vast activity which would generate over 8,000 translations of separate works from English into German during the years 1680-1800.[83]

---

[78] Bepler, *Ferdinand Albrecht,* 149; Selling, *Gelehrten-Reisen,* 91-2, 268-9.

[79] Ebert, *Reise-Beschreibung,* 101: "Die Lateinische Sprache wird in England so außgesprochen / daß die Außländer wenig aus dem *Discours* begreiffen können;" Robson-Scott, *Travellers,* 105.

[80] Andreas Gryphius, *Carolus Stuardus,* ed. Hugh Powell (Leicester: University College, 1955), cxxxv ff.; Günther Berghaus, *Die Quellen zu Andreas Gryphius' Trauerspiel "Carolus Stuardus"* (Tübingen: Niemeyer, 1984).

[81] Sir Richard Baker, "Udo Sträter, Sir Richard Baker und Andreas Gryphius, oder: Zweimal London-Breslau via Amsterdam," *Wolfenbütteler Barock-Nachrichten* 11 (1984): 87-9.

[82] Auguste Sann, *Bunyan in Deutschland: Studien zur literarischen Wechselbeziehung zwischen England und dem deutschen Pietismus* (Giessen: Schmitz, 1951), 13-15, 103-13.

[83] Marie-Luise Spieckermann, "Übersetzer und Übersetzertätigkeit im Bereich des Englischen in Deutschland im 18. Jahrhundert," in Konrad Schröder, ed., *Fremdsprachenunterricht*

To the Lutheran theologian Henrich Ludolff Benthem (1661-1723) we owe the first detailed guide book to England for German visitors, printed in 1694, and designed specifically for German students of theology.[84] Benthem is the first German traveller to advise visitors to acquire the language. He himself had visited England in 1686-87 during the reign of James II. He not only states the necessity of reading the language of the host country, because "dieselbe [die Engländer] schreiben fast alle ihre Bücher in der Muttersprache"(Benthem, *Kirch- und Schulen-Staat*, c6^v-c7^r), but also he stresses the long-term benefits of proficiency: "Es erfodert solches von ihm nicht nur die daselbst angeführte Nothwendigkeit; sondern damit er auch den Nutzen von Engeland noch behalten möge / wenn er diese Insul längst aus den Augen verlohren hat" (Benthem, *Kirch- und Schulenstaat*, d3^r). Noting the reluctance or inability of English scholars to use Latin, he reassures the would-be traveller that the task of learning English will be facilitated by the Germanic and Romance elements which it contains:

> Weil nun / wie ich kurtz vorher über die Frantzosen geklaget / auch in Engelland bey den meisten Gelehrten die Kranckheit gemein ist / daß sie die lateinische Sprache entweder aus Mangel der Ubunge und Fertigkeit nicht reden können / oder wegen allzuzarter Liebe und aus zu grossen *æstim* ihrer *national* Sprache nicht reden wollen / so muß einer / der sonst gedencket mit Nutze seiner *Studien* da zu leben / es sich lassen die allererste Sorge seyn / daß er die Engelländische Sprache wol fasse und rede. Es wird aber einem / welcher der lateinischen / frantzösischen und teutschen Sprache etwas erfahren ist / diese Arbeit nicht schwehr fallen / wie ich denn Teutsche / wie auch Schweden und Dähnen gekennt / welche durch Hülffe dieser dreyen und ihrer mütterlichen Sprache / die Engelländische in drey Monaten nicht alleine verstehen gelernet / sondern auch fliessend geredet haben; Denn diese Sprache ist / wie das Blut dieses Volckes / ein Mischmasch von alten Brittischen / Römischen / Sächsischen / Dähnischen und Normannischen oder Frantzösischen; [...] (Benthem, *Kirch- und Schulenstaat*, 9-10).

He warns, however, of basic phonetic difficulties:

> Wiewol sich keiner einbilden muß / daß er es darinn zu solcher Vollkommenheit bringen werde / daß man nicht noch allezeit solte hören können / er sey ein Ausländer; Denn daß ich anderer Schwierigkeiten jetzund nicht gedencke / so ist der eintzige *Articulus The* von solcher eigensinnigen Art / daß er deinen Fleiß eher ermüden wird / als du ihm den rechten Klang geben wirst; ob aber jemand könne diese Sprache in einem Tag lernen / wie sie der Herr Schurtzfleisch so leicht angesehen / zweiffele ich sehr [...] (Benthem, *Kirch- und Schulenstaat*, 11-12).

Benthem gives a few hints on linguistic preparation, privately at home, in the Academy in Hamburg, or in Holland, "wo die beste Gelegenheit" (Benthem, *Kirch- und Schulenstaat*, 12), a statement which brings home to us the pivotal (and under-researched) role of the Low Countries in English-German linguistic relations. Wallis's scholarly grammar in Latin will be of little use, Benthem feels, so instead he provides

---

1500-1800 (Wiesbaden: Harrassowitz, 1992), 191-203.

[84] Benthem, *Kirch- und Schulen-Staat*; Robson-Scott, *Travellers,* 92-7; Selling, *Gelehrten-Reisen,* 353.

his own sketch of English phonology and grammar (13-27). During his tour, he had himself found it helpful to read an English Bible aloud in the presence of a native speaker who would correct his pronunciation. For language as well as content, he claims to have benefited from Edward Chamberlayne (1616-1703), *Angliæ Notitia, or the Present State of England* (1669-71), and from attending Church services, armed with the *Book of Common Prayer* (26-27).

Learning and Teaching Aids

Interest in acquiring a working knowledge of English called forth, and was supported by, a range of other aids in the years before and after 1700.[85] Well before this, aspects of English grammar and vocabulary had become gradually accessible to some German speakers through the medium of Latin, French or Dutch. Grammars of English written in Latin are extant from 1593 and 1619. Later works include George Mason's *Grammaire Angloise* (London: Nat. Butter, 1622), Guy Miège's *Nouvelle methode pour apprendre l'Anglois* (Londres: Thomas Bassett, 1685), the *New double grammar French-English and English-French* of Claude Mauger and Paul Festeau (Leide: Peter Vander, 1690), and John Wallis's *Grammatica linguæ Anglicanæ* (Oxoniæ: Leonard Lichfield for Thomas Robinson, 1653).[86] During his London visit, Duke Ferdinand Albrecht is known to have purchased Wallis's work, together with a French grammar written in English, and a French-English-Latin conversation manual.[87] Grammatically, the two languages were drawn closer together with the *Double Grammar* (1687) of Heinrich (Henry) Offelen.[88] Several other grammatical works on English for German users appeared before the end of the century.[89]

---

[85] Approximately 2,400 titles (about 288 of them first published before 1800, and some ten before 1700) are listed in Konrad Schröder, *Lehrwerke für den Englischunterricht im deutschsprachigen Raum 1665-1900: Einführung und Versuch einer Bibliographie*, collab. Gerhard P. Drescher (Darmstadt: Wissenschaftliche Buchgesellschaft, 1975).

[86] Robin Carfrae Alston, *A Bibliography of the English Language from the Invention of Printing to the Year 1800* (Bradford, 1967), I, 14; II, 160, 181, 192.

[87] Bepler, *Ferdinand Albrecht*, 150; Selling, *Gelehrten-Reisen*, 269. In Latin, but with some sections translated into German, was S. Tellæus, *Grammatica Anglica* (Argentinae: Typis Carolinis, 1665) (Schröder, 1977a; Alston, II, 344), which offered guidance on pronunciation, grammar and syntax. Pronunciation and an outline of grammar were also provided in Johann Podensteiner, *Clavis linguæ Anglicanæ* ([Wittenberg?], 1670 and 1685) (Schröder, 1608; Alston, II, 345-6).

[88] Henry Offelen, *A Double GRAMMAR for GERMANS to learn ENGLISH; AND FOR ENGLISH-MEN To Learn the GERMAN-Tongue; [...] Composed, and set forth by Henry Offelen, Doctor in Laws and Professor of Seven Languages, (viz.) English, French, Spanish, Latine, and High- and Low-Dutch* (London, 1687). See Wilhelm Viëtor, "Die alteste deutsch-englische und englisch-deutsche Grammatik (1686-7)," *Englische Studien* 10 (1887): 361-6; Charles T. Carr, "Early German Grammars in England," *Journal of English and Germanic Philology* 36 (1937): 455-74; Schröder, 1503.

[89] J.N.S.: *Grammatica nova anglicana* (Jenæ: Ohrling, 1689) (Schröder 2353 with an attribu-

The lexicographical tradition reaches back much further, in that English is listed together with German and other languages in polyglot dictionaries from the 1530s.[90] A six-language edition of the *Dilucidissimus dictionarius*, with English words alongside Latin, French, Spanish, Italian and German, was printed in Augsburg circa 1530 (Claes, *Verzeichnis*, 317). English words are also listed in *Le dictionnaire des huict langaiges* (Paris, 1546) (Claes, *Verzeichnis*, 409), in Hadrianus Junius's topically-ordered *Nomenclator* (Antwerp, 1567), and in the perennially popular *Colloques ou Dialogues* first printed at Antwerp in 1576 (Claes, *Verzeichnis*, 586). In versions of Ambrosius Calepinus's multilingual dictionary, English first appears (alongside Polish and Hungarian) in the edition of Lyon, 1585.[91] Between 1600 and 1681, twelve or more editions of Calepinus appeared with English listings. Two new polyglot sources, several times reprinted, were Hieronymus Megiser, *Thesaurus polyglottus* (Frankfurt am Main, 1603) (Alston, II, 101) and John Minsheu, *Ηγεμον εις τα γλωσσας, id est ductor in linguas, the guide into tongues* (London, 1617) (Alston, II, 103). Available from 1629 was a six-language dictionary by Isaak Habrecht.[92] Alternatively, English vocabulary might be approached through a Latin-English or French-English dictionary. Coming to London in 1633, Hille purchased Randle Cotgrave's *Dictionarie Of the French and English Tongues* in an edition of the same year (Bepler, "Hille," 286). On his London visit in the 1660s Duke Ferdinand Albrecht von Braunschweig-Lüneburg used Christopher Wase's *Dictionarium Minus: a compendious dictionary English-Latin & Latin-English* (London, 1662) (Bepler, *Ferdinand Albrecht*, 150-53).

All these lexicographical aids were makeshifts, cumbersome in the extreme for the practical purposes of a German needing to make a way in England. As the first, modest example of English-German bilingual lexicography, we have the word list in Offelen's *Double Grammar* (1687) (Stein, "Lexicography," 147-8). Finally, in the early eighteenth century, the position of English-German bilingual lexicography was transformed with the appearance of Christian Ludwig, *A Dictionary English, German and French* (1706), and his *Teutsch-Englisches Lexicon* (1716).

Konrad Schröder has provided invaluable evidence of English tuition from the

---

tion to Johann Nicolay; Alston, II, 350) (also Gissæ, 1693 and Marburg, 1696, see Schröder 1469-70); the anonymous *Weg-Weisung / Die construction In der Englischen Sprache* ([Hamburg?], 1693) (Schröder 132a; Alston, II, 353); an anonymous four-language grammar, *The eloquent Master of Languages, [...] Der fertige Sprach-Meister* (Hamburg: Thomas von Wiering, 1693) (Alston, II, 147); and F. K.: *A little grammar, or Short guide to learn the Englisch Tongue* (Hamburg: Georg König, 1699) (Schröder 103a; Alston, II, 354).

[90] Franz Claes, *Bibliographisches Verzeichnis der deutschen Vokabulare und Wörterbücher, gedruckt bis 1600* (Hildesheim and New York: Olms, 1977); Gabriele Stein, "English-German / German-English Lexicography: Its Early Beginnings," *Lexicographica* 1 (1985): 134-64.

[91] Albert Labarre, *Bibliographie du Dictionarium d'Ambrogio Calepino (1502-1779)* (Baden-Baden: Koerner, 1975), no. 144. See also Claes no. 666; Alston, II, 81.

[92] Isaak Habrecht, *Ianua linguarum Silinguis, Latina, Germanica, Gallica, Italica, Hispanica, Anglica* (Argentinæ: Zetzner, 1629).

1650s.[93] From the 1680s onwards, English language tuition became available privately, and then officially, at the universities. At the University of Altdorf, formal tuition in English was available from 1685-86; English is further listed alongside French and Italian among the 'linguae exoticae' on offer there in the 1690s. In 1686, Johannes Sebastian Saltzmann ('linguae anglicae et gallicae peritus') was teaching the language at the University of Greifswald. A decree of the Landgraf von Hessen demanded the appointment of language teachers in French, Italian, Spanish and English at the University of Giessen in 1695. At Wittenberg, French and English were taught by Jakob Peter Stephani from 1696.[94]

Linguistic Effects

The changing status of the English language in German-speaking countries is reflected, not least, in the growing number of lexical transfers. Since the work of Peter Ganz, the 1640s have been recognised as the first true awakening of German interest in English culture and lexis.[95] The beginnings are modest: English was scarcely ever targeted in the intensely xenophobic German puristic activity of the 1640s, which focused on Latin, French, Italian and Spanish influences: we recall Johann Michael Moscherosch's comment that, if the heart of a "Newsuchtiger Teütschling" were to be opened, 5/8 would be found to be French, 1/8 Spanish, 1/8 Italian and 1/8 German.[96] By stages, however, the English language won itself a place in German hearts, and that former exemplar of a mixed, receptive language itself became a donor, in more recent periods on an unprecedented scale. Early Anglicisms surface in German newspapers of 1597, 1609 and 1667 (for example *alderman, mylord, lord major*).[97] Partly using French intermediaries, the traveller Thomas Platter the Younger refers to *the Water Worke, le millort maieur echevin, sterling* and *schilling* (Platter, *Beschreibung*, 781-3). In his description of England (1610), Grasser employs a few exotica (*alder-*

---

[93] Konrad Schröder, *Biographisches und bibliographisches Lexikon der Fremdsprachenlehrer des deutschsprachigen Raumes, Spätmittelalter bis 1800*, I, 2nd edition (Augsburg: Universität, 1991); Schröder, *LRA*, no. 272, 329, 436.

[94] Altdorf: Finkenstaedt, *Geschichte*, 212; Schröder, *LRA*, nos. 392 and 470; Selling, *Gelehrten-Reisen*, 129. Greifswald: Finkenstaedt, *Geschichte*, 16; Schröder, *LRA*, no. 426. Jena: Wolfgang H. Strauss, "Der Unterricht in den neueren Sprachen an der Universität Jena von den Anfängen bis 1800," in Konrad Schröder ed., *Fremdsprachenunterricht*, 205-15. Giessen: Schröder, *LRA*, no. 494. Wittenberg: Finkenstaedt, *Geschichte*, 16; Schröder, *LRA*, no. 499.

[95] Peter F. Ganz, *Der Einfluß des Englischen auf den deutschen Wortschatz 1640-1815* (Berlin: Erich Schmidt, 1957).

[96] Johann Michael Moscherosch, *Visiones de Don Quevedo: Wunderliche vnd Warhafftige Gesichte Philanders von Sittewalt* (Straßburg: Mülbe, 1642), I, 550.

[97] Thomas Gloning, "Bestandsaufnahme zum Untersuchungsbereich 'Wortschatz,'" in Gerd Fritz and Erich Straßner, eds., *Die Sprache der ersten deutschen Wochenzeitungen im 17. Jahrhundert* (Tübingen: Niemeyer, 1996), 141-93, here 174-6.

men, milord maier, schiriffs) (Grasser, *Schatzkammer,* 260). Some traces of the underlying cultural influences are also detectable. In an important testimony, the satirist and translator Johann Sommer of Zwickau (1545/59?-1622) alludes to a recently adopted fashion for the imitation of foreign customs ('Sitten / Religion / Kleidung / vnd gantzen Leben') and observes that, if the dead of twenty years past were now to rise from their graves, they would not recognise their fellow countrymen, "sondern meinen / daß es eitel Fratzösische / Spannische / Welsche / Englische / vnd andere Völcker weren."[98] That English fashions played some part in 'Alamode' is suggested by the remark of Schill (1644):

> Ich mag von den gemachten Haaren / die sie Bericken [see errata: Perruque] nennen nicht reden / ich geschweige andere Veränderungen in Hosen vnnd Wammes / vnd muß sich ein Kauffman darnach richten / daß er allerhand solcher alamodischer Gattung mit sich auß Franckreich / Engeland / Spanien bringe / will er anders auch Geld lösen / dann bey alten Wahren würd er frisch verderben (Schill, *Ehrenkranz,* 319-20).

Occasionally after 1650 specific lexical influences are commented on, as in the series of honorifics cited in the Low German *Scherzgedichte* of Johann Lauremberg of Rostock:

> Den *Monsör* up Frantzösisch is mit einem word
> Even so vel als up Engelsch ein Lord.
> Wen de Engelschen einen willen ehren / thor stund
> Nehmen se einen groten Lord in den Mund.
> *Lord Gentelmen, lord Biskop, lord Prelat,*
> *Lord Borgemester, lord Doctor, lord Advocat,*
> *Lord* hyr *lord* dar / *Monsör Monsör,*
> My deit de Bueck weh / wen ick idt hör.
> Laet de Frantzosen in ere Frantzösche Reden
> Beholden er *Monsör,* und syn darmit tho freden:
> Ein Engelsman mag *lord* in siner Spraeke bruken /
> Vnd einen groten dicken Denschen Lord upschluken.[99]

Peter Ganz recorded some 43 cases of English lexical influence which are first attested in German before 1700. His list includes *Adresse, Akte, Baronet, Bill, Bowling Green, Brownist, Debatte, dissolvieren, Gigue, Groom, Hackney Coach, Kaffeehaus, Kaliko, Kitz, Konvokation, nonkonformistisch, Paketboot, Presbyterianer, Pudding, Punsch, Quäker, quäkerisch, Rum.* Towards the end of the century, English words and phrases (sometimes in French guise) begin to be listed in German 'Fremdwörter-

---

[98] Johann Sommer, *Ethographia mundi* (n. p., 1607), Aij°. The remark may have been prompted by the splendid costumes of the English players, since Sommer (Olorinus) writes in the *Magdeburger Geldklage* (1614): "Da müssen die Kragen mit Perlen besetzet werden, und wird ein solcher Pracht gesehn, daß sie einhergehen, wie die Englischen Komödianten" (Price, *Reception,* 19).

[99] Johann Lauremberg, *Veer Schertz Gedichte [...] In Nedderdüdisch gerimet dörch Hans Willmsen L. Rost* ([Kopenhagen? Sorø?] 1652), poem no. 3, line 239.

bücher,' most typically in those reflecting journalistic usage. Johann David Scheibner's *Le Galant Interprete* (Helmstädt, 1695) has *Bil, Livre sterlin, Mylord, Ordre de la Jarretiere*. Kaspar Stieler, *Zeitungs- Lust und Nutz* (Hamburg, 1695) has *Exchester, Garde de Seaux, Jury, Lord Major, Messenger, Milord, Neugat, Quaker, Scherif, Sterling*.

Viewing the second half of the seventeenth century, we may concur with the verdict of Andreas Selling that Britain was then far from being a *terra incognita* in the German world-view. Admittedly, interest in its culture, and proficiency in its language, fell far short of the levels which were to characterise the mid and late eighteenth century. By then, the German-speaking community could no longer seriously doubt the historical antecedents and lexical composition of English, as set forth, for example, in a passage from the preface to Nathan Bailey's English-German dictionary, where language mixture, far from being a matter of shame and ridicule, calls forth a paean of lavish, not to say imperialistic, praise:

> Die *Englische Sprache* ist von solchem Reichthum, von solcher Weitläuftigkeit und Schwierigkeit, daß man diese Regel besonders darbey in acht zu nehmen hat. Denn sie ist aus dem alten *Britischen, (Welschen) Säxischen, Dänischen, Normannischen,* und dem neuern *Französischen, Lateinischen* und *Griechischen* zusammen gesetzt. Von den fünf ersten ist der conversable Theil, oder die in *Großbritannien* gebräuchliche lebendige Mundart, und von den zwey letztern sind die *Termini technici,* oder Kunstwörter, hauptsächlich hergeleitet. Obschon die *Britische* ursprünglich die Landes- oder Muttersprache ist, so machet sie nichts destoweniger den geringsten Theil davon aus. Denn da die *Briten* durch ihre Kriege mit den *Picten, Römern, Saxen* und *Dänen,* so über 1000 Jahre gewähret, nach und nach geschwächet worden, haben sie sich endlich genöthiget gesehen, sich über die Britischen Alpen zu begeben, da sie ihre Sprache mit in denjenigen Theil von *Britannien,* so *Wales* genennet wird, hinüber genommen, woselbst sie dieselbe bis auf diesen Tag unverfälscht erhalten haben. Mittlerweile haben ihre siegreichen Ueberwinder, nach Vertreibung der ersten Einwohner, nicht nur ihr Land eingenommen, sondern auch ihre eigenen Sprachen, darinnen ausgebreitet. Zwar haben die *Römischen Legionen,* ungeachtet sie etliche hundert Jahre in Britannien genistet, keine gar außerordentliche Veränderung in der *Britischen* Sprache gemachet: So steif und fest hielten die *Briten* damahls über ihrer Muttersprache! So haben auch die *Dänen,* wegen ihrer kurzen Regierung, so nicht über 27 Jahre gedauret, (etliche nördliche Länder, wo sie sich über 200 Jahre festgesetzt, ehe sie zur höchsten Gewalt gelanget, ausgenommen,) keine sonderliche Veränderung verursachet. Zumahl, da ihre Grausamkeit gegen die *Briten,* einen rechten Abscheu vor ihrem Regiment, ihren Personen, und ihrer Sprache bey diesen erwecket hatte. Die *Saxen* unterdruckten, durch einen längern Besitz, die *Britische* Sprache merklicher, und bemüheten sich, *ihre eigene* Sprache (mit einigem *Lateinischen* und *Dänischen* vermischt) durch das ganze Königreich einzuführen. Auf diese folgten die *Normannen,* welche großen Fleiß anwandten, die *Säxische* Sprache auszurotten, und die *Französische* an deren Statt fortzupflanzen. Aus dieser Ursache rühret die jetzige gemeine Sprache in *England,* größten Theils, von einem *Säxischen* und *Französischen* Ursprung her. Was aber die *Kunstwörter* anbelanget, sind solche nebst den Wissenschaften selbst, von den *Griechen* und *Lateinern* hergeholet. So sind auch durch die Handelschaft, und durch den Umgang (absonderlich zu Hof) sehr viel Worte von den *Franzosen, Dänen, Deutschen, Italiänern,* und andern Völkern, eingemischet worden. Durch diesen Zusammenfluß der Sprachen, und durch die tägliche Gewohnheit der Scribenten, ein jedes em-

phatisches und nachdrückliches Wort, das sie auf Reisen oder in fremden Sprachen anmerken, einzuführen, hat die *Englische* Sprache einen solchen Reichthum erlanget, daß sie die unerschöpflichste in *Europa,* ja, man mag wohl sagen, in der ganzen Welt.[100]

---

[100] Nathan Bailey, *A Compleat English Dictionary, oder vollständiges Englisch-Deutsches Wörterbuch. [...] Anfangs von Nathan Bailey in einem kurzen Compendio herausgegeben, bey dieser dritten Auflage aber um noch mehr als die Hälfte vermehret von Theodor Arnold* (Leipzig and Züllichau: Buchhandlung des Waysenhauses, Frommann, 1761), 2ᵛ - 3ᵛ.

The Germans on English: Towards a Historiographical Treatment of Language Evaluation, 17th to 19th Centuries

WERNER HÜLLEN (Essen)

1. Interest of Topic

The interest of the topic to be treated in this paper lies in the 20th century. It is a well-known fact that the fascist ideology between the ends of the first and the second World Wars asserted rights to all intellectual fields, consequently also to linguistics. Naturally, the topic of language evaluation lent itself quite readily to these activities. It is almost with incredulity that we read today what, besides serious academic work, was published at that time on *Herrensprache* and *Sklavensprache*, national characters expressed in languages of our friends and our enemies, etc. This incredulity even increases when we realise that such publications saw themselves (and indeed were located) in the tradition of a serious academic discipline, *Sprachwissenschaft*, in which Germany had gained world-wide fame during the 19th century. The general question of how such things can happen needs an answer. It does not suffice to show many publications for what they were, trivial and in many cases immoral. We must become aware of the history that lies behind them in order to understand better.[1]

So far, little historiographical research has been done on the history of language evaluation although, once you think about it, it discloses itself as a frequently occurring and almost popular topic. For centuries, linguists of (probably) all European languages have appreciated and scolded, praised and denounced "foreign" speakers, after the Greeks had called every language but their own 'barbaric.' General assumptions about languages and their relations to the members of speech communities were used as the underpinnings of these statements which, as a rule, appear as side-issues in works devoted to the explanation of language origins and language history, structural descriptions and language pedagogy. Most certainly, not all relevant sources have been found and interpreted so far. My own endeavours on the topic are bound not to be free from such gaps.[2]

---

[1] One of the outstanding examples where this is done is Ruth Römer, *Sprachwissenschaft und Rassentheorie in Deutschland* (München: Finck, 1989).

[2] Werner Hüllen, "On Calling Languages 'Foreign,'" in: John L. Flood et al., eds., *'Das unsichtbare Band der Sprache:' Studies in German Language and Linguistic History in Memory of Leslie Seiffert*. (Stuttgart: Akademischer Verlag Heinz, 1993), 393-410; "Good Language - Bad Language: Some Case-Studies on the Criteria of Linguistic Evaluation in Three Centuries," in Klaus D. Dutz and Kjell-Åke Forsgren, eds., *History and Rationality: The Skövde Papers in the Historiography of Linguistics*. (Münster: Nodus, 1995), 315-34; "Some Yardsticks of Language Evaluation 1600-1800 (English and German)," in Vivien Law and Werner Hüllen, eds., *Linguistis and Their Diversions: A Festschrift for R.H. Robins on His*

The following paper presents the topic of language evaluation with the focus on what the Germans thought about English as a national language, i.e. on one single case among many possible cases. The fact that 1900 is the limiting date entails that the result of my research is not visible yet. What I am going to present is the skeleton of a historiographical treatment rather than a treatment proper, and it should be read as such.

2. The Wide Horizon

As a rule, the comparison of languages with the aim of finding historical relationships and structural affinities between them is thought of as *the* central method of linguistic research in the 19th and the (beginning) 20th centuries. In fact, it had then already been a powerful tool of linguistic deliberations for more than 200 years. Even earlier, i.e. shortly after 1305, when Dante Aligheri (1265-1321) finished his *De vulgari eloquentia*, he derived the three Romance languages, Italian (in its various dialects), French, and Spanish, as daughter-languages from Latin. In *De causis linguae latinae libri XIII* (1557), the famous Humanist Julius Caesar Scaliger (1484-1558) described eleven language families which covered the European continent, four major and seven minor ones. The former correspond to what is today called the Romance, Greek, Germanic and Slavonic groups. He also did away with the theologically founded older concepts according to which all languages originated from Hebrew, and Latin was a direct successor of a Greek dialect. At the same time, an interest in empirical evidence arose. Samples from different languages were collected and juxtaposed. In his *Mithridates* (1555), Conrad Gessner (1516-1565), for example, presented the Lord's Prayer in twenty-two languages.

The experiential foundation of this linguistic work was people's growing awareness that many vernaculars were spoken (written and eventually printed) in Europe - a fact which had hitherto been hidden behind the all-powerful use of Latin. Together with the interest in genuine, not medieval, Latin, Greek and Hebrew, this awareness of the many European vernaculars was one of the outstanding features of the Renaisssance and Humanism. In many countries of Europe it led to what could be called a national linguistic consciousness.[3]

At that time, the most important languages on the Continent were French, Spanish, Italian, and German, each of which thrived for some time on a regionally influential cultural, political, or commercial superiority. For a long time, English, however, was not among them. It had some influence in the area around Antwerp and Bruges which was adjacent to the British Isles across the Channel, but otherwise it had the status of a

---

75th Birthday (Münster: Nodus, 1996), 275-306.

[3] For the linguists mentioned cf. the relevant entries in Harro Stammerjohann, ed., *Lexicon Grammaticorum: Who's Who in the History of World Linguistics*. (Tübingen: Niemeyer, 1996); for early comparative linguistics cf. R.H. Robins, *A Short History of Linguistics* (London: Longman, 1990), 114-15, 180-87. It goes without saying that 'national' has none of the semantic overtones which the word adopted in the 19th and 20th centuries.

language spoken on an island off Europe. This started to change in the first third of the 16th century. There was, for example, a German-Italian textbook, called *Introito e porta*, which appeared in Venice in 1477 and subsequently developed into a widely distributed multilingual textbook-family for all the important languages of the European continent. The author of the first edition was Adam of Rottweil. It was only in 1535 that English was added in a six-language edition. A similar textbook-family entitled *Colloquia et Dictionariolum*, whose first known Flemish-French edition appeared in Antwerp in 1530, had Noel de Berlaimont as its author. Again it was a six-language edition, this time of 1576, which contained English for the first time. The printing history of these two books, whose multilingual editions obviously dominated foreign language teaching in Europe outside the classically orientated monastic school-system for 200 years altogether, mirrors the regional influence at that time of (up to eleven) European languages, including the slow growth of people's interest in English, which was effectively supported by trade connections, but also by the Reformation.[4]

Under these conditions it is natural that English was not at the focus of early comparative linguistics, yet it was not totally absent from it, either. When looking today at the interest devoted to English by German scholars, we are guided by our historiographical hindsight and the knowledge that, for cultural and political reasons, English developed into a very important foreign language in Germany during the 18th century, that it gained more and more weight among the European languages, parallel to the extension of the British Empire in the world, and that finally it arrived at its position as the medium of world communication in which we know it today.[5]

3. From Schottelius to Jenisch (17th and 18th Centuries)

3.1 Schottelius and von Hille

Justus Georgius Schottelius (1612-1676) is the first scholar to be mentioned in the present context. Escaping from the evils of the Thirty Years' War with the help of his sponsor and friend, Duke Anton Ulrich of Braunschweig-Lüneburg in Wolfenbüttel, he devoted his scholarly life to demonstrating that German, at that time existent only in its various dialects, was, like the other European languages, of capital importance

---

[4] *Introito e porta* appeared first in 1477; the last edition of *Colloquia et dictionariolum* appeared 1671. See Werner Hüllen, *English Dictionaries 800-1700: The Topical Tradition* (Oxford: Clarendon Press, 1999).

[5] This long historical development is thoroughly analysed from the point of view of language learning and general reading culture by Friederike Klippel, *Englischlernen im 18. und 19. Jahrhundert: Die Geschichte der Lehrbücher und Unterrichtsmethoden* (Münster: Nodus, 1994); there are plenty of references for further reading in this book. The development is concisely analysed from the point of view of English as a world-language by Werner Hüllen, "ghoti – das Leittier der internationalen Kommunikation, oder: Das Englische als National- und als Weltsprache," in Ingrid Gogolin, Sabine Graap and Günther List, eds., *Über Mehrsprachigkeit* (Tübingen: Stauffenburg, forthcoming).

and prime standing and deserved more acknowledgment from and care by its speakers. In accordance with the programme of the *Deutsche Sprachgesellschaften* (*Frucht-bringende Gesellschaft* and *Pegnesischer Blumenorden*), whose member he was, he worked for the development of a national standard which would, first of all, end the intrusion into German of foreign elements, mainly French words and phrases. His main work is the *Ausführliche Arbeit Von der Teutschen HaubtSprache* (1663), in whose ten so-called eulogies (*Lobreden*) he laid the theoretical foundations of his grammar, in which he covered the lexicology, morphology, word-formation, and to a certain extent semantics and etymology of the language.[6] He does not deal with English in any detail, but mentions it in a significant context.

It is in the third eulogy that Schottelius explains an argument of great importance which was generally accepted at his time: There was perfect linguistic communication between God and Adam in Paradise and even later. After the flood, Noah's four sons migrated to the four points of the compass, i.e., according to the geography of time, to the various continents of the earth, but before doing so their language was confused in Babel. "Babylonicam confusionem nihil aliud fuisse, quam litterarum radicalium inversionem, tanspositionem, literaeve radicalis additionem aut ablationem, vocaliumque imutationem." Not new languages came into existence after Babel, but the old one became unintelligible. Consequently, that language of the post-Babylonian era is the most valuable which can claim to be nearest to the pre-Babylonian state. This claim is indeed made for the Germanic language. Its founder was supposed to be Ascenas, a direct descendant of Japhet, the son of Noah, who migrated towards the West, i.e. Europe. The claim could only be upheld because the Germanic peoples, who originally included the Celtic tribes, did not adopt any different language in the course of history or mix their own with others. "Ist also die uhralte Sprache bey den freyen Teutschen vornemlich nach dem Grunde geblieben / auch ihren Nahmen von den Teutschen / als dem vornehmsten Haubtgeschlechte der Celten / hernachmals behalten." All non-Germanic languages are said to have either become mixed with other ones or to have been lost altogether.[7]

English, however, although a Germanic language, has none of these merits. With reference to Valentin Ickelsamer (*c*.1500-*c*.1540),[8] but without giving the precise source, Schottelius criticises his German countrymen for their eagerness to find old

---

[6] For a concise introduction see the entry by Dieter Cherubim in Stammerjohann, *Lexicon Grammaticorum*, 838-41. There is a reprint (facsimile) of Schottelius' main work: Justus Georg Schottelius, *Ausführliche Arbeit Von der Teutschen HaubtSprache. 1663*, ed. Wolfgang Hecht. Two vols. (Tübingen: Niemeyer, 1967).

[7] Quotations: Schottelius, *Ausführliche Arbeit*, 33 and 35; cf. 29-49, 141-8 *passim*.

[8] First German grammarian, or rather phonetician, famous for his ideas about how to learn and to teach reading. He was a teacher in Rothenburg and in Augsburg. See Stammerjohann, *Lexicon Grammaticorum*, 457. Schottelius' quotation is neither in the issue of *Die rechte weis kürtzist lesen zu lernen* (1527) nor in that of *Ain Teütsche Grammatica* (1537) which I could get hold of (Reprint ed. by Karl Pohl, Stuttgart: Klett, 1971).

foreign elements in their own language and to introduce new ones into it. This, he says, makes the German *HaubtSprache*:

> [...] Was man von der Englischen Sprache zuschertzen pflegt / "quod sit spuma linguarum." Den[n] als in einem Topfe / wie man sagt / alle Sprachen gekocht worden / were der Schaum davon die Englische Sprache geworden: weil dieselbe ein lauter Geflikk und Gemeng / wiewohl im Grunde Teutsch ist. Und wegen solches vermengten Wesens / wird von der Englischen Sprache das jenige gehalten / was Duretus cap. 74,[9] in fin. davon sagt: "Ceste Langue Angloise est si peu estime des Estrangers, qui vont en Angleterre, qu'il y a si peu qui veulent se pener de l'apprendre, & de la parer, si ce ne sont les serviteurs ou facteurs pour l'usage des choses utile et necssaires à la vie."

Schottelius is obviously thinking of well-known facts in English language history: the clash of a West Germanic dialect with the indigenous Celtic idioms, the admixture of the resulting Anglo-Saxon with Scandinavian elements, the great blend of Anglo-Saxon and Anglo-French after 1066, and finally the acceptance of countless Latin and Greek words into Early Modern English.[10] He seems to be well-informed about these processes when speaking about the acceptance of structure-words, prepositions, prefixes and rules of word-composition from other languages, mainly from Greek and Latin.

Schottelius does not always follow the theories of other linguists without criticism. For example, he has his doubts whether Hebrew really is the original language of mankind. But in the case of English, he follows the mainstream: the admixture of linguistic elements alienates a language from its origins, and this is *per se* a bad thing. It is this kind of 'purity' which increases the value of German and decreases the value of English. In time-dependent garbs, this idea will be presented again and again in the course of evaluative linguistics. And so will the other idea which is quoted by Schottelius from Duretus, that an interest in English as a language is, if at all, grounded in the practicalities and necessities of everyday life which *serviteurs ou facteurs* have to deal with.

The ducal court at Wolfenbüttel, where Justus Georgius Schottelius had found a home and splendid conditions for his work, played an important role in the cultural exchange on a European scale at that time, i.e. under the reign of the Dukes August and Ferdinand Albrecht. Foreign languages were taught to the ducal children, foreign books were bought for the library. Karl Gustav von Hille (*c*.1590-*c*.1647), *Haushofmeister* to the Duke's mother Sophie Elisabeth, courtier and, like Schottelius, a member and follower of the ideas of the *Deutsche Sprachgesellschaften,* had an important

---

[9] Claude Duret (1565-1611) published his *Thresor de l'histoire des langues de cest univers [...]* in which European languages are classified according to seven matrices, following, among others, J.C. Scaliger (see above). Cf. the entry by Marie-Luc Demonet-Launay in Stammerjohann, *Lexicon Grammaticorum*, 162-3. Quotation: Schottelius, *Ausführliche Arbeit*, 141.

[10] Schottelius would argue that the early Latin loans in Anglo-Saxon were in fact older Germanic (Celtic) elements which wandered into Latin when it became an independent language.

share in these endeavours. He knew England from his travels and was well-read in contemporary English literature. In his *Teutscher Palmenbaum* (1647), i.e. even a few years before Schottelius' main work, he strikes a different note when characterising the English language:

> Ob nun wohl die Englische / vor eine aus vielen zusammengesetzte und verstümelte Sprache gehalten wird; so ist sie dannoch mit Wahrheit nicht eine so gar geringschätzig und schlechte / wie sich solches dieselbe Unverständige einbilden: Sondern sie bestehet in einer solche Lieblichkeit und hohe Sinnbegriff / dass auch die allerwürdigste Geist- und weltliche Bücher / nicht von ihnen in der Lateinischen; sondern viel ehe in ihren eigenen Muttersprache beschrieben / zu lesen seynd: [...].[11]

This means, von Hille does not query the common verdict of *spuma linguarum*,[12] but he counterbalances it with the simple statement that the English language has all the means to express 'the most dignified spiritual and secular thoughts' given in books. A secular, in fact a functional viewpoint is introduced instead of the theological one. Again, this argument will be met with in future centuries.

3.2 Zedler's Lexicon *and Jenisch*

So far, there is no historiographical treatment of the evaluation and characterisation of English as a national language by Germans in the period between von Hille or Schottelius and 1800. All we can say is that the convincing power of theological argumentation became weaker, which entailed that criteria like 'age' and 'purity' lost their hold on linguists. In the article *Sprache* of Zedler's *Universal-Lexicon* (1732-1750), the German counterpart to the French *Encyclopédie,* for example, the author Samuel von Pufendorf (1632-1694)[13] floated the idea that, contrary to the concept of a perfect *lingua adamica*, the oldest human language must have been quite imperfect and the idea of the 'holiness' of Hebrew was a myth.[14] This brought the notion of historical

---

[11] Karl Gustav von Hille, *Der Teutsche Palmbaum* (Nürnberg: Wolfgang Endter 1647). Reprint, ed. Martin Bircher (München: Kösel, 1970), 123-4. Cf. Jill Bepler, *Ferdinand Albrecht Duke of Braunschweig-Lüneburg (1636-1687): A Traveller and His Travelogue* (Wiesbaden: Harrassowitz, 1988), 96-7, and *passim*.

[12] The translation of *spuma linguarum* 'Sprachenschaum' appears in the works of other German writers, for example of Georg Philipp Harsdörffer (1607-1658). See Werner Hüllen, "Yardsticks," 286.

[13] Mainly known as a lawyer and historiographer of the Prince Elector Friedrich III of Brandenburg, the so-called *Grosser Kurfürst*. He also published on theology and philology. Zedler integrated an older paper of Pufendorf's, together with those of other authors, into the article on language (see note 14).

[14] Johann Heinrich Zedler, *Grosses vollständiges Universal-Lexicon Aller Wissenschafften und Künste, Welche bishero durch menschlichen Verstand und Witz erfunden und verbessert worden [...]*. Vol. 39. (Leipzig and Halle, 1744). Re. the article *Sprache* see Sigurd Wichter, "'Sprache, Rede, *Loquela*' in Zedlers Universal-Lexicon," in Hans Höfinghoff et al., eds.,

improvement into play, with new functional criteria of evaluation. They were quite international.[15] In the case of English this meant that the admixture of linguistic elements now appeared in a new light.

The (presumably numerous) sources of this development have still to be uncovered and analysed. But at the end of the 18th century we know of Daniel Jenisch (1762-1804), a *Hofmeister* preacher living first in Braunschweig and then in Berlin who worked as stylist, a historian and a translator of Greek, French, and Polish texts and published a considerable poetic oeuvre.[16] He brought the description and evaluation of English (and other languages) to a first scientific perfection. He did this in a *Preisschrift* advertised by the *Königlich Preußische Akademie der Wissenschaften* in 1794.[17]

Jenisch's merit is to have clearly defined the yardsticks which serve for the evaluation of languages. They are functional to the general task of all languages, *viz.* the communication of concepts (*Begriffe*) and emotions (*Empfindungen*). These yardsticks are: (i) 'copiousness' (*Reichtum*), i.e. the number of words for the denotation of objects (*sinnliche Gegenstände*) and abstractions (*Reflexionsbegriffe*), and also the potential of word-formation (*lexikalische Bildsamkeit*). This is a semantic criterion. (ii) 'effort' or 'energy' (*Nachdrücklichkeit, Energie*), i.e. the directness of expressions which is achieved by the fullness and range of concepts as well as by the intensity of emotions. This is a stylistic criterion operating on the lexical and the grammatical levels, where it shows in the brevity of expressions. (iii) 'clarity' (*Bestimmtheit*), i.e. the non-ambiguity of word-meanings and the nature of grammar. This is again a semantic, but most of all a syntactic criterion. And (iv) 'euphony' (*Wohlklang*), i.e. the interplay of vowels and consonants. This is an aesthetic criterion on the phonotactic level. These criteria give Daniel Jenisch the opportunity for almost excessive praise of the English language which turns old yardsticks into their opposite. Phenomena which caused the derisive description of a *spuma linguarum* now turn into linguistic merits.

Alles was Recht war: Rechtsliteratur und literarisches Recht: Festschrift für Ruth Schmidt-Wiegandt (Essen: Item, 1996).

[15] Cf. Brigitte Schlieben-Lange, "Reichtum, Energie, Klarheit und Harmonie: Die Bewertung der Sprachen in Begriffen der Rhetorik," in Susanne S. Anschütz, ed., *Texte, Sätze, Wörter und Moneme: Festschrift für Klaus Heger zum 65. Geburtstag* (Heidelberg: Orientverlag, 1992), 571-86. Moreover: Lieve Looken and Pierre Swiggers, "Enlightenment Reflections on the Nature of Languages: A Comparative Study of Frain du Tremblay (1703) and Thomas Stackhouse (1731)," Unpublished.

[16] See Herbert E. Brekle et al., eds., *Bio-bibliographisches Handbuch zur Sprachwissenschaft des 18. Jahrhunderts: Die Grammatiker, Lexikographen und Sprachtheoretiker des deutschsprachigen Raums mit Beschreibung ihrer Werke*. Bd. 5, J-L. (Tübingen: Niemeyer, 1997), 50-53.

[17] Daniel Jenisch, *Philosophisch-kritische Vergleichung und Würdigung von vierzehn ältern und neueren Sprachen Europens [...]* (Berlin: Friedrich Maurer, 1796). See Brigitte Schlieben-Lange and Harald Weydt, "Die Antwort Daniel Jenischs auf die Preisfrage der Berliner Akademie zur 'Vergleichung der Hauptsprachen Europas' von 1794," in Dieter Heckelmann ed., *Wissenschaft und Stadt. Publikationen der Freien Universität Berlin aus Anlaß der 750-Jahr-Feier Berlins* (Berlin: Colloquium Verlag, 1988), 1-26. Moreover: Werner Hüllen, "Yardsticks," 277-81, 296-300.

English is the most 'copious' language because of the happy mixture of its vocabulary and the generally favourable conditions for language development:

> Alles dies zusammengenommen, welches sich bei keiner Nation jemals vereinigt hat, noch jetzt vereiniget, [...] möchte ich fast behaupten, (so viel Anmaßung auch eine solche Behauptung vorauszusetzen scheint) daß die Englische Sprache unter allen Europäischen Sprachen, d.h. unter allen Sprachen der Welt, den größten extensiven Reichthum hat.

For Jenisch, this is also true for the potential of word-formation in English:

> Unter [den germanischen Sprachen] würde man der Englischen, auf den ersten Blick, den höhern Grad der Bildsamkeit zugestehen; indem sie, als eine Zwittergeburt der Lateinischen und Germanischen Sprache, die Bildsamkeit von beiden gewißermaßen in sich vereiniget.[18]

In semantic 'effort' or 'energy' Jenisch attributes a generally superior character to the Germanic languages over the Romance ones. But he highly praises the Latinate English vocabulary because the words have not only their special Germanic character but also the more general meanings of their Latin origins. He thinks that this is particularly propitious for poetry. His praise of the grammatical 'effort' of English is almost enthusiastic:

> Alle Sprachen Europens überraget durch die bewundernswürdige, und doch zugleich dem Ausdruck jeder Feinheit dieser Art vortheilhafte, Einfachheit ihres grammatikalischen Baues - die Englische [...]. Man könnte von der Englischen Sprache beinahe rühmen, daß sie von einer Gesellschaft von Philosophen erfunden worden, welche sich von alle dem entlediget, was Zufall und Eigensinn allen andern Sprachen anheftet [...].

Jenisch's arguments with reference to 'clarity' are similar to those with refrence to 'effort.' In grammatical easiness "steht der Britte, bei aller grammatikalischen Einfachheit seiner Sprache, oben an [...]. Die Ideen fließen ohne Zweifel leichter und gemächlicher in die Seele [...]" (Jenisch, *Vergleichung*, 331-2, 384, 390)

Only as regards 'euphony' is Jenisch's judgment full of reserve. Besides a happy mixture of consonants and vowels he, generally, expects a distinct pronunciation of all syllables, which however is lost in the English habit of truncating end-syllables and contracting two or more syllables into one.

4. The Narrow Horizon

The beginning of the new century saw the beginnings of new thoughts in linguistics and language philosophy during the Romantic era. They are usually said to cover two domains of the wide field, *firstly* historical linguistics pertaining to the Indo-European

---

[18] Jenisch, *Vergleichung*, 62 and 91. Note the considerable degree of eurocentrism in the assumption that European languages are anyway superior to other languages of the world.

group, and *secondly* ethnic linguistics.[19] The first group of linguists, embracing names like Rasmus Rask (1787-1832), Franz Bopp (1791-1867), and Jakob Grimm (1785-1863), were devoted to establishing genetic dependencies with the help of sound laws, syntactic affinities and etymology. Their work was carried on by Indo-European scholars like August Schleicher (1821-1868) and, in the last third of the century, by the so-called *Junggrammatiker*.[20] In the 20th century the neo-grammarian model developed as 'historical linguistics' and adapted itself to the changing methods of Saussurean, Bloomfieldean and transformational structuralism.[21]

The second group of linguists, embracing names like Johann Georg Hamann (1730-1788), Johann Gottfried Herder (1744-1803),[22] and most of all Wilhelm von Humboldt (1767-1835), were devoted to defining the interrelation between national cultures and languages. Their work was carried on as ethnic psychology (*Völkerpsychologie*) by Heymann (Hajim) Steinthal (1823-1899) and Wilhelm Wundt ((1832-1920) and experienced a so-called Neo-Humboldtian renaissance in the early 20th century with, among others, Jost Trier (1894-1970) and Leo Weisgerber (1899-1985), which ended in Germany only with the structuralist shift of paradigm around 1950.

Such grouping and periodisation always has its drawbacks. Even in what looks from the outside like a radical shift of paradigm at the beginning of the 19th century, the new generation of linguists stood on the shoulders of their ancestors. So each of the new topics and methods had already been prefigured earlier. Moreover, there were people who belonged to both groups such as, for example, Friedrich Schlegel (1772-1829) who in 1808 published *Ueber die Sprache und Weisheit der Indier: Ein Beitrag zur Begründung der Althertumskunde* by which he aroused the general German interest in Sanskrit, although this old language had been known much earlier to linguists in other European countries (see Gipper and Schmitter, "Sprachwissenschaft," 498-500). And there were people who do not fit into any of the two groups, although certain affinities cannot be denied. This is the case with the philosopher Johann Gottlieb Fichte (1762-1814) who, as is visible from his life-dates, preceded most of the representatives of Romantic linguistics and was not received by them with particular atten-

---

[19] Cf. Helmut Gipper and Peter Schmitter, "Sprachwissenschaft und Sprachphilosophie im Zeitalter der Romantik," in Thomas A. Sebeok, ed., *Historiography of Linguistics* (The Hague and Paris: Mouton, 1975), 481-606 (*Current Trends in Linguistics*, vol. 13). There is a separate edition of this essay with the same title, Tübingen: Narr, 1979 (second edition 1985).

[20] See Eveline Einhauser, *Die Junggrammatiker: Ein Problem für die Sprachwissenschaftsgeschichtsschreibung* (Trier: Wissenschaftlicher Verlag, 1989).

[21] See Theodora Bynon, *Historical Linguistics* (Cambridge: Cambridge University Press, 1977; many re-editions).

[22] As can be seen from the life dates, Hamann and Herder precede the linguists of the Romantic era with their works. This is particularly true for Herder's seminal *Preisschrift*: *Über den Ursprung der Sprache* (1771). A number of remarks made by Daniel Jenisch can be understood as being influenced by Herder, in particular his idea that, in their early stages, languages are more marked by 'poetic energy' than later when they show more intellectual 'clarity:'

tion either, but nevertheless developed ideas close to those of Herder and Humboldt and was, later, indeed understood in the contetxt of their deliberations. Among other reasons, this was the impact of Fichte's political commitment. Finally, both groups have at least one topic in common, and this is language typology. It was developed formally in genetic and in structural classifications, but it was also seen as the symptom of a cultural standard.[23]

There are two methodological features which the two groups of Romantic linguistics have in common. The *first* is its universalism. National languages are seen as tokens of higher ranking types, they are part of a system of historical development or typological classification. When Humboldt speaks of the national character of languages he is thinking of the conditions which must prevail for any of them to adopt this status and which must, consequently, be understood. The *second* feature is the comparative method. It is constitutive for the Indo-European group of linguists in any case. This is why they have been labelled 'comparative philologists.'[24] But the ethnolinguistic group was also devoted to comparing languages, if not for their own sake then for establishing the historical process by which national individuality in languages manifests itself as the linguistic form of *menschliche Geisteskraft,* which is the force that binds all linguistic development together. This entails finding differences before the background of a universal concept of human *Geist*. Humboldt explains the intention behind his introduction to the *Kawi-Werk* thus: "Die Betrachtung des Zusammenhanges der Sprachverschiedenheit und Völkervertheilung mit der Erzeugung der menschlichen Geisteskraft [...] ist dasjenige, was mich in dieser Schrift beschäftigen wird."[25]

From all this follows: Characterisations of the English language in the Romantic period are located in a complex situation of a linguistics with diverging tendencies. The universalism of the emerging discipline does not make such characterisations a favourite topic, but comparison as a general method leads the thoughts of linguists time and again in this direction. The historical linguists and neo-grammarians use English to support their ideas on language typology. The ethnolinguists use it to show their ideas on the national spirit of a language. Even where English is not explicitly mentioned, the linguistic deliberations of the Romantic period often served as a basis for language characterisations and evaluations in the following century.[26]

---

[23] See Anna Morpurgo Davies, "Language Classification in the Nineteenth Century," in Thomas A. Sebeok, *Historiography of Linguistics* (Hague and Paris: Mouton, 1975), 607-716.

[24] Note: "[...] and it is with Rask and Grimm that the comparative and historical study of the Indo-European family can be properly said to begin" (Robins, *History of Linguistics*, 188).

[25] Wilhelm von Humboldt: "Über die Verschiedenheit des menschlichen Sprachbaues und ihren Einfluß auf die geistige Entwicklung des Menschengeschlechts [1830-1835]," in: Albert Leitzmann ed., *Wilhelm von Humboldts Werke*. Vol. 7, first half. (Berlin: Behr, 1907); reprint (Berlin: de Gruyter, 1968), 15.

[26] This grouping is tentative, because there must be many more characterisations of English as a national language than I am aware of at the moment.

5. From Fichte to Delbrück

5.1 Schleicher, Misteli, Delbrück and Jakob Grimm

The various language typologies of the time were not only descriptive but also evaluative. August Schleicher, for example, differentiated between monosyllabic, agglutinative, and inflectional languages. For him the last ones represented the highest rank of linguistic and cultural development.

> Die flectirenden Sprachen stehen somit am höchsten auf der Skala der Sprachen: erst hier ist im Organismus des Wortes eine wahrhafte Gliederung entwickelt, das Wort ist die Einheit in der Mannigfaltigkeit der Glieder, entsprechend dem animalischen Organismus, von welchem dieselbe Bestimmung gilt.

This not only places the languages of the Indo-European group above all other languages of the world, it also places those highest among the Indo-European languages which have a rich inflectional morphology. Consequently, Schleicher's evaluation of English is negative:

> [...] die Sprache hat den angelsächs[ischen] Typus zwar bewahrt, ist aber eine der abgeschliffensten, an grammatischen Endungen ärmsten Sprachen unseres Sprach-stammes. Die meisten ursprüngl[ich] deutschen Wörter sind sogar zur Einsylbigkeit herabgesunken - wenigstens in der Aussprache, die hier allein massgebend ist.[27]

Franz Misteli developed a system of six language types, one of them being *flectirende Sprachen*. He is much more reluctant than other historical linguists and Neogrammarians in attributing a cultural value to a language type *per se*, and looks upon linguistic change as something occurring naturally in history rather than deterioration. Yet, his examples for this fact are stylistically telling:

> So sind von den modernen Vertretern des Indogermanismus die baltisch-slavischen Sprachen wohl die altertümlichsten, während die germanischen und romanischen sich weit vom Urtypus entfernten, besonders die englische Sprache, welche in rücksichtsloser Beschränkung der Formenmenge und in souvräner Behandlung der Syntax alle andern Glieder des Sprachstammes überholte.

Equal to English in this and some other respects is only modern Persian with which Misteli compares English in a detailed analysis.[28]

---

[27] August Schleicher, *Die Sprachen Europas in systematischer Übersicht: Linguistische Untersuchungen* (Bonn: König, 1850) with an introductory article by Konrad Koerner (Amsterdam, PA: Benjamins, 1983), 9 and 231. See also: Werner Hüllen, "Calling Languages," 404.

[28] Franz Misteli, *Charakteristik der hauptsächlichsten Typen des Sprachbaues: Neubearbeitung des Werkes von Prof. H. Steinthal (1861)* (Berlin: Dümmler, 1893), 489 and 597-601. Misteli starts the chapter on Indo-European (he says Indo-Germanic) languages with the sentence: "Unter den Völkern, welche die indogermanischen Sprachen reden, befinden sich unläugbar die begabtesten Völker der Erde: Inder, Griechen und Römer, Germanen. Aber nicht

The Neogrammarian Berthold Delbrück (1842-1922), finally, demonstrated that reckoning English among inflecting languages was problematical because we construct the morphology from history, although there is hardly any inflection left.[29] This is an interesting case of juxtaposing two principles of language description which were later, i.e. by Saussure, called 'diachronic' and 'synchronic.' For Delbrück, this observation served as a measure of general criticism *vis-à-vis* language classifications, as they had become popular.

The three applications of the Romantic language typology to English show various degrees of appreciation of inflecting languages. There can, however, be no doubt that the high degree of acknowledgment of inflecting languages with its preference for the Indo-European, the European, and finally the Germanic languages was widely accepted and even adhered to in the following century. It was not only the linguists of the first group who did this. Humboldt, for example, saw the *Geistesarbeit,* incorporated in languages, most clearly expressed in their grammatical systems. He maintains that there are more and less perfect languages in the world and that the inflecting ones, compared with the incorporating and agglutinative ones, belong to the most perfect. "Verglichen mit den einverleibenden und ohne wahre Worteinheit lose anfügenden Verfahren, erscheint die Flexionsmethode als ein geniales, aus der wahren Intuition der Sprache hervorgehendes Prinzip."[30] Most criticism of the grammatical structure is a direct corollary of this viewpoint and led to some unfavourable judgement concerning English.

However, the picture would not be complete if the ideas of Jakob Grimm (1785-1863) were left unmentioned. As is well known, he subsumed Anglo-Saxon, and consequently English, under *deutsch,* which made Rasmus Rask speak of "his [Grimm's] patriotism."[31] In spite of this, Grimm's high degree of evaluation of Anglo-Saxon and the later English is obvious in many comparisons when, for example, he says that the 'Low-German' dialects split up and their noblest part went away from the continent with the Anglos-Saxons: "aus dem schosz der anglesächsischen sprache aber erhob sich, mit starker einmischung des romanischen elements, verjüngt und mächtig die englische sprache."[32] Although the admixture of languages is even for him 'against nature,' he finds in the case of English that the inevitable loss of concrete (*sinnlich*) meanings under French influence is counterbalanced by a gain in abstract (*geistig*) ones. This means that, in order to understand the English language, the character of

---

alle Völker, welche indogermanische Sprachen reden, sind besonders begabt [...]" (Misteli, *Charakteristik,* 487).

[29] Berthold Delbrück, *Grundfragen der Sprachforschung: Mit Rücksicht auf W. Wundts Sprachpsychologie erörtert* (Strassburg: Trübner, 1901), 44-8.

[30] Humboldt, "Verschiedenheit," 163. The idea is mentioned time and again, so many quotations could be given.

[31] For the problem of this terminology see Stefan Sonderegger, "Jakob Grimms allgemeine Einstufung und Wertschätzung der englischen Sprache," in Andreas Fischer ed., *The History and the Dialects of English* (Heidelberg: Winter, 1989), 15-31.

[32] Jacob Grimm, *Geschichte der deutschen Sprache* (Leipzig: Hirzel, 1848; reprint: Hildesheim: Olms, 1970), 580.

the French and (Germanic) English languages must be seen as fully integrated. This is also true for understanding the English people.[33] The climax of all these thoughts is the well-known passage from Grimm's "Über den Ursprung der Sprache," in which he contradicted, for example, August Schleicher in literally every point. The passage is famous and deserves full quotation.

> keine unter allen neueren sprachen hat gerade durch das aufgeben und zerrütten alter lautgesetze, durch den wegfall beinahe sämtlicher flexionen eine gröszere kraft und stärke empfangen als die englische und von ihrer nicht einmal lehrbaren, nur lernbaren fülle freier mitteltöne ist eine wesentliche gewalt des ausdrucks abhängig geworden, wie sie vielleicht noch nie einer andern menschlichen zunge zu gebote stand. ihre ganz überaus geistige, wunderbar geglückte anlage und durchbildung war hervorgegangen aus einer überraschenden vermählung der beiden edelsten sprachen des späteren Europas, der germanischen und romanischen, und bekannt ist wie im englischen sich beide zueinander verhalten, indem jene bei weitem die sinnliche grundlage hergab, diese die geistigen begriffe zuführte.[34]

For Grimm, who cannot be reproached for a lack of German national feelings, these features gave the English language a chance to become *the* medium of world-wide communication. However, Grimm is not the only one to have this foresight.[35]

5.2 Fichte, Humboldt, Schopenhauer, and Abel

The difficult questions of how the ideas on the function of language in the process of 'humanisation'[36] as developed by Hamann, Herder, Fichte, and Humboldt influenced each other and in particular the latter's work are not in need of an answer in the present context. Their conceptual affinities are obvious. Moreover, Fichte and Humboldt share the concept of 'transcendentalism' in the way in which Immanuel Kant understood the term, i.e. they reflected on the conditions of the possibiliy ("die Bedingungen der Möglichkeit von [...]") of human existence, concentrating, contrary to Kant, on the role of language. The semiotic quality of (gestures and) sounds is the means by which the human individual as determined by *Geist* contacts other human individuals and establishes the web of actions which finally form human society. The most important feature of language in this function is grammar, a statement which shows the ideas of the two Romantic thinkers in their dependence on the idea of a universal human grammar in the preceding century.[37]

---

[33] See Sonderegger, "Einstufung." For Grimm's attitude towards indigenous and foreign words in a language see *Geschichte*, 5.
[34] Jakob Grimm, *Kleinere Schriften I* (Berlin 1879, reprint: Hildesheim: Olms, 1965), 293. The passage was translated into English in *Notes and Queries* 7 (1853): 294.
[35] See Sonderegger's, reference to K.M. Rapp ("Einstufung," 30).
[36] This is less a historical process in real time than a logical process in philosophical reflection.
[37] Cf. Kurt Müller-Vollmer, "Fichte und die romantische Sprachtheorie," in Klaus Hammacher ed., *Der transzendentale Gedanke: Die gegenwärtige Darstellung der Philosophie Fichtes*

Important in our context are only Fichte's *Reden an die deutsche Nation* which he held in 1807-1808 and which enjoyed great public acceptance. They exercised a strong influence, for good and for bad, in shaping the German national mentality until the middle of the 20th century. At a time when all of Europe was occupied by Napoleonic forces and when there was no German nation, he aimed at a pedagogical programme of national self-determinism. But again it is not this programme which is of interest here but only where it is concerned with the role of a national language in this process. This is explained in the fourth *Rede*.

According to Fichte, the origin of language is not only determined by man's free will to use sounds as the signs for something, but also by man's lack of free will in the choice of these signs. A language comes into being neither by the act of an individual nor by any convention established between several individuals but by a national principle which Fichte calls a *Grundgesetz* (basic law).

> So wie die Gegenstände sich in den Sinnenwerkzeugen des Einzelnen mit dieser bestimmten Figur, Farbe, u.s.w. abbilden, so bilden sie sich im Werkzeuge des gesellschaftlichen Menschen, in der Sprache, mit diesem bestimmten Laute ab. Nicht eigentlich redet der Mensch, sondern in ihm redet die menschliche Natur, und verkündigt sich andern seines Gleichen. Und so müßte man sagen: die Sprache ist eine einzige, und durchaus notwendige.

It is an idea which was later much more often attributed to Humboldt than to Fichte that language not as such ("nicht die Eine und reine Menschensprache") but as a national type ("eine Abweichung davon") appears in history. Of course, all languages change in the course of time, but they nevertheless remain identical with themselves when used by one indigenous linguistic community. "[...] die Sprache dieses Volkes ist notwendig wie sie ist, und nicht eigentlich dieses Volk spricht seine Erkenntnis aus, sondern seine Erkenntnis selbst spricht sich aus demselben." However, the condition for a speech community to enjoy this development is that its language is neither changed nor mixed with another one in the course of its history, which is regularly marked by migrations and settlements at various places. Fichte claims that the Germans are the only people in Europe to fulfill this condition. Without mentioning them, it is obvious that the verdict of having lost or polluted their own tongues is addressed to the speakers of the Neo-Latin languages and of English, whereas the speakers of the Scandinavian languages are subsumed under 'German' and the speakers of Slavonic languages are excluded from these deliberations. According to Fichte, it does not matter which language mixes with or replaces one's own; it is the incompatible foreignness of a different language (or of different languages) which does the damage.

The philosopher, who actually had little expertise in linguistics, pursued his ideas on another, more concrete level of deliberation. Denotation of what he calls "das Übersinnliche," i.e. abstract (mental, spiritual, moral, ideational) concepts is achieved

---

(Hamburg: Meiner, 1981), 442-61. Moreover, Jürgen Ziegler, "Warum die Sprache erfunden werden mußte: Fichtes Schrift 'Von der Sprachfähigkeit und vom Ursprunge der Sprache,'" *Beiträge zur Geschichte der Sprachwissenschaft* 7:1 (1997): 101-19.

by a metaphorical transposition of the denotation of concrete referents. His example is the Greek lexeme *idea* which can only be understood properly if the original meaning, i.e. 'vision,' 'dream,' is known. Without this background the word remains dead. In a language mixed with foreign elements (or in a foreign language altogether) people do not understand these transpositions intuitively but must learn them as something external to their genuine linguistic habitat. "So richtet alle Bezeichnung des Übersinnlichen sich nach dem Umfange und der Klarheit der sinnlichen Erkenntnis desjenigen, der da bezeichnet." The 'foreign' part of the language no longer follows its own *Grundgesetz*:

> Obwohl eine solche Sprache auf der Oberfläche durch den Wind des Lebens bewegt wird und so den Schein eines Lebens von sich geben mag, so hat sie doch tiefer einen toten Bestandteil, und ist, durch den Eintritt des neuen Anschauungskreises, und die Abbrechung des alten, abgeschnitten von der lebendigen Wurzel.

From this hypothesis, Fichte explains in words which have readily lent themselves to later political exploitation why Germans, if guided by their own language, are superior (in education, in culture, in morals) to everybody else in Europe.[38] He maintains that speakers of French, etc. do not understand their own languages because they cannot follow the genuinely Latin processes of denotation and the shifts of meaning. If at all, it is only the educated who are able to do this. But this has serious consequences, because it creates two kinds of nations:

> In einer Nation von der ersten Art ist das große Volk bildsam, und die Bildner einer solchen erproben ihre Entdeckungen an dem Volke, und wollen auf dieses einfließen; dagegen in einer Nation von der zweiten Art die gebildeten Stände vom Volke sich scheiden, und des letztern nicht weiter, denn als eines blinden Werkzeugs ihrer Pläne achten.

The first kind of nation is of course the *deutsche Nation* as Fichte wants to shape it by his public speeches, as the second kind he mentions the 'neo-Latin' nations France, Italy, and Spain. He never mentions English, but his ideas can be (and were) readily applied to the English language as a blend of Romance and Germanic elements and the estrangement between the educated and the non-educated members of the speech community that is said to follow from this.

It is not easy to explain in present-day linguistic terms what Fichte actually means. His idea seems to be that people (Germans), when using their language, should keep in mind the original denotations of words and follow the etymological shifts of meanings, in particular the metaphorical transpositions from the concrete to the abstract. Without explaining anything in the technical terms of linguistics, he agrees with the high estimation of etymology and the belief in the importance of the 'first' meaning of a lexeme. Both principles were generally accepted in the philology, most of all in the classical philology, of his time. Ultimately, they are part of the theological principle

---

[38] Werner Hüllen, "Good Language," 328-9. All quotations from: Johann Gottlieb Fichte, *Schriften zur angewandten Philosophie. Werke II* ed. Peter Lothar Oesterreich (Frankfurt: Deutscher Klassikerverlag, 1997), 595-612.

that the perfect language was always the language of the beginning, just as the perfect world was always the world of the beginning. As regards English, Fichte may mean a phenomenon as simple as 'unmotivated lexis' which has been described often in contemporary linguistics and also in its pedagogical consequences for the English speakers themselves.[39] Fichte himself regretted that he had to use the word 'philosophy' for his own thinking, although this is a perfect example of a word 'being cut off from its root.' He would have preferred *Lebensweisheit*. He denounces words like *Humanität*, *Popularität*, and *Liberalität*, which should be '*Menschlichkeit*,' '*Haschen nach Gunst*' and '*Entfernung vom Sklavensinn.*'[40] Such ideas have later served as authoritative arguments against the use of foreign words in German, in particular during the first half of the 20th century, when language purism was very much *en vogue*. They also supported a vague, in the bad sense: Romantic, understanding of *deutsche Bildung* as contrary to 'Western civilisation.' As mentioned, Fichte's hostility was mainly directed against France and French, but the adaptation of his ideas to Britain and English makes it necessary to see him in the ranks of those who determined the German evaluation of the English language in the later heyday of nationalism.

In spite of obvious affinities, Fichte's ideas differ from Humboldt in their rhetorical presentation, their aggressive patriotism and many statements on the relation between the individual and the speech community. His far-reaching influence in Germany on thinking about language in various disciplines circled around certain key words, like *ergon* and *energeia*, *Weltansicht*, *Nationalcharakter* of a language, *innere Form*, etc. with a distinct predilection for certain 'purple passages' which were quoted again and again. This is understandable *vis-à-vis* the fact that Humboldt's works are mostly unfinished, often contradictory, and difficult to understand. They almost begged for concretisation and exemplification.

One problem with Humboldt's deliberations is that they speak of historical processes which cannot be properly localised and which have no performing agent. Language is the cause as well as the effect of culture, and the individual speaker is an agent-member as well as a patient-member of a speech community. One way of coping with this difficulty was the psychological reading of Humboldtean ideas, as Heymann Steinthal and Wilhelm Wundt did. They paved the way for the idea that a worldview is the expression of a collective character and that the liberty of the individual is limited by it. The attempt to prove this by analysing one of the living languages in the context of its national history appears as a logical consequence from Humboldt's basic ideas. Steinthal and Wundt did not do this. *Völkerpsychologie,* in the way in which Wundt used the term, investigated the historical steps which mankind took in order to arrive at the present state. 'People' (*Volk*) here is any kind of society.[41] But the two

---

[39] For example, Victor Grove, *The Language Bar* (London: Routledge and Kegan Paul, 1949) and Ernst Leisi, *Das heutige Englisch* (Heidelberg: Winter, 1985), seventh edition.

[40] The comment on *Liberalität* '*Entfernung vom Sklavensinn*' gives Fichte a chance to prove his theory because the meaning of the Latin *liberalitas* (i.e. freedom from slavery) is indeed different from the meaning of the German *Liberalität*.

[41] Cf. the main chapters of Wilhelm Wundt, *Elemente der Völkerpsychologie* (Leipzig: Kröner, 1913): *1. Der primitive Mensch, 2. Das totemistische Zeitalter, 3. Das Zeitalter der Helden*

authors paved the way for a discussion which kept defining ethnic terms like 'nation' or 'people' and, most of all, 'race' in a historical perspective. All this happened more in the 20th than in the 19th century.

For linguists, interested in the languages of their own days, the question arose of how the Humboldtean individuality of a language could be proved, for example for English. Apart from analysing the grammatical structure and allocating a language its place in the current typologies, semantic investigations which included language comparisons obviously seemed appropriate. They provided an opportunity for pinning down the *Weltansicht* (or *Innere Form*) of a language in a concrete domain of its lexis. A generalisation might then be possible. Such investigations could theoretically be based on many of Humboldt's statements, for example on one like this:

> Denn der Zusammenhang aller Theile der Sprache unter einander, und der ganzen Sprache mit der Nation ist so enge, dass, wenn einmal diese Wechselwirkung eine bestimmte Richtung angiebt, daraus nothwendig durchgängige Eigenthümlichkeit hervorgehen muß. Weltansicht aber ist die Sprache nicht bloss, weil sie, da jeder Begriff soll durch sie erfasst werden können, dem Umfange der Welt gleichkommen muss, sondern auch deswegen, weil erst die Verwandlung, die sie mit den Gegenständen vornimmt, den Geist zur Einsicht des von dem Begriff der Welt unzertrennlichen Zusammenhanges fähig macht."[42]

In his essay "Über Sprache und Worte," Arthur Schopenhauer, for example, compared a series of related words in several languages, among them *ingénieux, sinnreich, clever, Geist, esprit, wit*; and *malice, Bosheit, wickedness* in order to show that they are not interlinguistic synonyms in the strict sense.[43] He symbolises their partial semantic identity with overlapping circles as they are familiar today from set theory. For foreign language learning this means:

> Daher also muß man, bei Erlernung einer fremden Sprache, mehrere ganz neue Sphären von Begriffen in seinem Geiste abstecken: mithin entstehn Begriffssphären wo noch keine waren. Man erlernt also nicht bloß Worte, sondern erwirbt Begriffe.[44]

---

und Götter, 4. Die Entwicklung zur Humanität.

[42] Wilhelm von Humboldt, "Grundzüge des allgemeinen Sprachtypus," in Albert Leitzmann ed., *Wilhelm von Humboldts Werke*. Vol. 5 (Berlin: Behr, 1907). Reprint (Berlin: de Gruyter, 1968), 387. There are also statements in which Humboldt warns people not to try and describe the individuality of a language because the task is too complex. Note, for example: "Die Untersuchung dieser Individualität, ja sogar ihre genauere Bestimmung in einem gegebenen Falle ist das schwierigste Geschäft der Sprachforschung. Es ist unleugbar, dass dieselbe, bis auf einen gewissen Grad, nur empfunden, nicht dargestellt werden kann, und fragt sich daher, ob nicht alle Betrachtung derselben von dem Kreise des wissenschaftlichen Sprachstudiums ausgeschlossen bleiben solle?" (Wilhelm von Humboldt, "Über den Nationalcharakter der Sprachen" in Albert Leitzmann, ed., *Wilhelm von Humboldts Werke*, vol. 4 (Berlin: Behr, 1907), reprint (Berlin: de Gruyter, 1968), 421.

[43] Cf. Werner Hüllen, "Calling Languages," *passim*. Schopenhauer also mentions *comfortable, disappointment, gentleman* as untranslatable.

[44] Arthur Schopenhauer, *Sämtliche Werke*, ed. Wolfgang Frhr. von Löhneysen (Darmstadt:

This sentence corresponds to Humboldt's statement:

> Die Erlernung einer fremden Sprache sollte daher die Gewinnung eines neuen Standpunkts in der bisherigen Weltansicht seyn und ist es in der That bis auf einen gewissen Grad, da jede Sprache das ganze Gewebe der Begriffe und der Vorstellungsweise eines Theils der Menschheit enthält.[45]

Schopenhauer goes on to explain that the sum total of all concepts expressed in the lexis of a language constitutes the spirit of the language to be learnt. A national language is related to this spirit of a nation in the same way in which a personal style is related to the spirit of an individual. We find a clear parallelisation here between the individual and the nation as a kind of super-individual. This idea will gain much ground in the following century, and there will also be much criticism levelled against it. Likewise, comparisons of related areas of lexis, of German and English *Wortfelder*, will then become very popular. Understandably, it is the theory of foreign language teaching which is highly interested in such concrete applications of abstract ideas.[46]

Another example of this method of language comparison is Carl Abel's juxtapostion of German and French words around the term *Freundschaft*, and of the German and English lexemes *fair* and *equitable* vs. *billig*, and *resolution* and *determination* vs. *Entschluß* and *Beschluß*. In the present-day era of corpus linguistics such intuitive analyses appear insufficient. Yet at their time they obviously aroused interest and stimulated imitators. In Carl Abel's essay "Über den Begriff der Liebe in einigen alten und neuen Sprachen" the same is done with reference to German, English, Hebrew, and Russian lexemes. Note the far-reaching generalisation that is attached to this comparative study:

Wissenschaftliche Buchgesellschaft Darmstadt, 1965). Vol. 5: "Parerga und Paralepomina. Kleine philosophische Schriften II," "Über Sprache und Worte," (Paragraph 298-303a), here 667.

[45] Wilhelm von Humboldt, "Über die Verschiedenheit des menschlichen Sprachbaus" in Albert Leitzmann, ed., *Wilhelm von Humboldts Werke*, vol. 7 (Berlin: Behr, 1907); reprint (Berlin: de Gruyter, 1968), 60.

[46] After all, Humboldt was *ex officio* the reformer of the *Preußisches Gymnasium*. Pedagogical reflections on how to apply the results of the new linguistics to foreign language teaching started quite early. Note, for example: David Asher, *On the Study of Modern Languages in General, and of the English Language in Particular: An Essay*. (Leipsic[!]: Charles Fr. Fleischer, 1859). In the same year: Bernhard Schmitz, *Encyclopädie des philologischen Studiums der neueren Sprachen* (Greifswald: C.A.Koch'sche Verlagsbuchhandlung, 1859). This book is very rich in reports on philological and pedagogical literature. It points out the importance of *Volkscharackter* for the teaching of foreign languages (mostly French), but the author also has its doubts concerning this vague term: "Es gibt immer noch Menschen genug, denen solches Gerede imponiert und Wunders tief klingt" (Schmitz, Encyclopädie, 28). The highly interesting topic must be left for a special investigation. See Karl-Heinz Flechsig, *Die Entwicklung des Verständnisses der neusprachlichen Bildung in Deutschland*. Diss. Göttingen 1952.

> Ein Volk, das viele Worte für irgend eine sinnliche oder geistige Vorstellung hat, muss sich viel mit derselben beschäftigt, muss sie nach mancherlei Seiten hin entwickelt und nüanciert haben; ein Volk, bei dem das Gegenteil der Fall ist, lässt uns den entgegengesetzten Schluss auf seine äussere und innere Geschichte machen. Das Wörterbuch, zumal wenn es die Bedeutung der Worte nicht nur oberflächlich angiebt, sondern aus ihrem Gebrauch heraus definirt, nimmt damit die Gestalt eines psychologischen Repertoriums an, und die Erkenntnis seines Inhalts wird zur scharf umrissenen Skizze einer nationalen Individualität.

This programme, i.e. interpreting the lexis of a language as it appears in a dictionary as a mental repertoire, would prove very productive in the future.[47]

6. Interest of Topic, Revisited

The foregoing historiographical overview leads to some noteworthy, if preliminary, results. Although the two periods under analysis are, of course, quite different in their basic assumptions, there is an astonishing parallelism. In the Romantic period the theological argument of Schottelius and others is repeated in a national variant. Whereas in the 17th century the originally divine quality of human language was the starting point of linguistic evaluation, this was in the 19th century its originally ethnic quality. Fichte's *Grundgesetz* takes the logical place of the *lingua adamica*. Consequently, the argument leads to similar results, viz. the critical rejection of English as a mixed language and a language with a poor inflectional system. The rational, in the historical sense of the word 'enlightened,' method of linguistic analysis by Daniel Jenisch got lost, at least in what would today be called the mainstream linguistics of the time. The way in which von Hille contradicted Schottelius in the earlier century is also repeated in Jakob Grimm's even more impressive praise of English in the later one. At the moment, the question must be left open as to whether there are more statements of this kind perhaps outside the mainstream, and whether this functional, non-ideological (i.e. neither theological nor ethnic) approach was stimulated by English authors. From the 17th century on and increasingly in the 18th and 19th centuries, English grammarians had already stressed the value of 'copiousness' against that of 'purity,' irrespective of where the 'copiousness' of words came from. Likewise, they had stressed the value of 'clarity,' i.e. a simple grammar, in the interest of learnability. This can be proved, for example, for the grammars of Guy Miège (1644), Robert Midgley (1692), Joseph Priestly (1761), and Robert Lowth (1763). The permanent historical pattern, as far as it is discernible now, is that an ideological (i.e. theological or ethnic) approach runs alongside a functional one, with the first much more in the foreground than the latter. It remains to be seen what happened to this competition during the 20th century. Here the ideological approach is certainly adopted by the followers of Neo-Humboldteanism, the functional approach, for example, by Otto

---

[47] Carl Abel, "Über den Begriff der Liebe in einigen alten und neuen Sprachen," *Sprachwissenschaftliche Abhandlungen* (Leipzig: Wilhelm Friedrich, 1885), 31-104, here 35.

Jespersen (1860-1943). The answer must remain open as to who eventually won (and when).

Seen in this perspective, the 'horizon' of the 19th century is indeed a narrow repetition of the wide horizon before. But there are, of course, also new problems. They were created by the massive intrusion of political and of economic thinking into the theoretical world of linguistics. The first sailed under the flag of 'nationalism' with its broad spectrum between patriotism and fascism, the second under the flag of 'world-traffic' (or something similar). It remains to be seen what effect this had and whether the dichotomy between the ideological and the functional approach to English as a national language repeated (and is repeating) itself once more. One of the most difficult questions in this context will be the role of ethnic terms like *people, nation, race, society,* etc. (*Volk, Nation, Rasse, Gesellschaft,* etc.). They were in extensive use during the Romantic period, but later on developed ethnic, psychological, anthropological, and political meanings besides their denotations in the linguistic context.

Whatever we will find can serve as a means of explanation for what some linguists published in the 20s and 30s of this century. It cannot take away these authors' responsibilities.

Basic English and the Debabelization of China

JOHN E. JOSEPH (Edinburgh)

1. The Riot at C. K. Ogden's Bookshop, 11 November 1918

History is shaped by small events. Who could have foreseen that the rampage at 18 King's Parade, Cambridge, while the ink was still wet on the Armistice, would turn out to be a pivotal event in the analysis and teaching of language in the 20th century? Here is an eyewitness's recollection:

> At noon on 11 November 1918, an excited Frenchman leapt off his cycle in King's Parade and cried: "They told me the war was over! But look!" Crashing out through the plate glass window of Ogden's Cambridge Magazine Book Shop and Art Gallery, No. 18, came canvas after canvas: Duncan Grant, Vanessa Bell, Roger Fry [...] Medical students, flown with the spirits of the occasion, were smashing the place up [...][1]

The rioters' choice of the shop belonging to Charles Kay Ogden (1889-1957) was not random, or so Ogden hinted in the *Cambridge Magazine* of 16 November:

> ARMISTICE DAY
>
> In this country at any rate, violence has not yet been recognised as the proper method of attaining communal ends, and the wrecking of the Cambridge Magazine premises within five minutes of the Armistice announcement was sufficiently lacking in spontaneity to rouse the suspicions even of non-legal observers [...]

Ogden was not being paranoid. His role in the anti-war movement had not only landed him in trouble with the government, but marked him as an enemy of Britain in the eyes of many.[2] Yet in his own mind he had done or said nothing unpatriotic. He had merely exercised, and helped others to exercise, the democratic values of freedom of thought and speech for which Britain had supposedly been fighting.

Late that night Ogden held his first serious discussion with Ivor Armstrong Richards (1893-1979), the eyewitness cited above. This was to be the start of an abiding collaboration, and Richards relates how it began in the aftermath of the noon-time event:

---

[1] I.A. Richards, "Co-Author of the 'Meaning of Meaning': Some Recollections of C. K. Ogden," in P. Sargant Florence and J. R. L. Anderson, eds., *C. K. Ogden: A Collective Memoir* (London: Elek Pemberton, 1977), 96-109, here 98.

[2] See further P. Sargant Florence, "Cambridge 1909-1919 and its Aftermaths," in Florence/Anderson, *C.K. Ogden*, 13-55.

> At that time I rented a room from him above one of his shops [...] and knew him only remotely as my landlord. About midnight, he came in to ask whether I could identify any of the rioters, if need be, to help him with his action for damages against the town [...]
>
> After collecting my useless impressions of the rioters, Ogden started off, steadily talking, for Top Hole, his fantastically cluttered attic above Mac-Fisheries in Petty Cury. Half-way down the tightly twisting stairs, under an aged, faintly whistling, Bat's Wing gas jet, he stopped to make some remark upon a recent controversy in *Mind*. An hour or two later when we went on downstairs, the main outline of *The Meaning of Meaning* was clear enough, and plans for a joint work to embody it were in being (Richards, "Co-Author," 98-9).

Ogden and Richards's *The Meaning of Meaning*, which appeared in serial form in *The Cambridge Magazine* before its publication as a book in 1923,[3] would prove enormously influential in the development of several strands of linguistic and philosophical study. It was no coincidence that this discussion followed the wrecking of Ogden's shop, any more than that the shop had been a chance target. "During a discussion with I. A. Richards on 11 November 1918 [actually the early hours of the 12th by Richards's account cited above] Ogden outlined a work to correlate his earlier linguistic studies with his wartime experience of 'the power of Word-Magic' and the part played by language in contemporary thought" (from Ogden's entry in the *Dictionary of National Biography 1951-1960*, 778). For amid the wreckage of the war, in the minds of Ogden and many others, were to be found the ruins of meaning itself. As will be discussed further in section 5 below, the Great War was portrayed both in Britain and abroad as largely a war of *propaganda*, in which the distortion of abstract words like 'freedom,' 'democracy' and even 'victory' was a key weapon. *The Meaning of Meaning* was motivated in part by a desire to understand how such distortion could happen, and could be prevented from happening.

Richards, recalling these events nearly 60 years later, has undoubtedly simplified them somewhat for narrative effect. As W. Terrence Gordon, our leading authority on Ogden, points out (letter to the author, 26 Jan. 1998), by 1918 Ogden had already spent a decade assembling a mass of quotations, jottings and references which would make up the bulk of *The Meaning of Meaning*, though this does not rule out the possibility that the book's overall framework might have been arrived at jointly by the two authors beginning with the discussion which Richards recounts.[4] Richards goes on to note that the chapter on Definition in *The Meaning of Meaning*

> [...] led us into long discussions of the number of radically different ways there may be of telling anyone what any word may mean. This inquiry was the germ of Basic English. Ogden had long been deep in the history and theory of universal languages, and it was no

---

[3] C.K. Ogden and I. A. Richards, *The Meaning of Meaning: A Study of the Influence of Language upon Thought and of the Science of Symbolism* (London: Kegan Paul, Trench, Trubner and Co.; New York: Harcourt, Brace and Co., 1923).

[4] See further W. Terrence Gordon, *C. K. Ogden: A Bio-Bibliographic Study* (Metuchen, N.J. and London: Scarecrow Press, 1990).

long step from our account of Definition to notions of a minimal English capable of serving all purposes [...] (Richards, "Co-Author," 108).

The development of Basic English will be sketched in section 3, where we shall look at the particular importance given to Asia, and China in particular, in its rationale. That importance was partly inherited from the tradition of 'the history and theory of universal languages' which, as Richards points out, was a long-standing interest of Ogden's.

2. China and the Western Dream of a Common Language

It was in the transition from late medieval to early modern thinking about language that the first widespread interest appeared in undoing the effects of God's punishment of humankind at Babel, where the original language was fragmented into mutually unintelligible tongues. The voyages of the 15th century and after had brought home an increasing sense of the world's linguistic diversity; and as the 16th century progressed, Europe itself found its own common language, Latin, losing ground against the rise of newly standardising national languages like Italian, Spanish, Portuguese, French, English, Dutch and German, to name just a few. The inability of nations to communicate had not been a major problem for medieval Europe, but was becoming an inescapable reality for the early modern Europe which emerged from the Renaissance.

Among the previously little known or unknown languages about which the voyagers of the Renaissance brought back information, one in particular fired the European imagination, because it seemed to point the way out from Babel.

> Intriguing details of China were beginning to percolate to Western Europe in the late 16th century from returning missionaries and travellers. According to these accounts, the Chinese language represented not sounds, but ideas [...][5]

By 'the Chinese language' is meant written Chinese; the reports which Large is describing regularly conflate the two. Some believed that Chinese characters consisted essentially of 'pictographs,' pictures of what they designate, while others insisted that the characters were essentially arbitrary and conventional, even if some characters like the numbers — 'one,' = 'two' and ☰ 'three,' and more obliquely 人 'man' or 馬 'horse' might indeed appear to depict what they mean. Either way, what mattered most was that this writing system was shared by large communities of speakers who could not understand one another when they spoke. This was sufficient proof that the existence of different languages need not in itself prevent the development of an *auxiliary* language making communication possible among people who did not share a mother tongue.

---

[5] Andrew Large, *The Artificial Language Movement* (Oxford: Basil Blackwell, in association with André Deutsch, 1985), 12.

One of the first Europeans to be taken with this idea was Sir Francis Bacon (1561-1626). "In his influential writing Bacon drew attention to the possibility of representing things instead of sounds by 'real characters' rather than letters, characters which could be understood regardless of language. His ideas had been triggered by Chinese which he thought offered a form of communication to solve the problem of language diversity" (Large, *Artificial Language Movement*, 4-5). Bacon's real characters were purely conventional symbols, as he conceived Chinese characters to be:

> [I]t is the use of China and the kingdoms of the high Levant to write in Characters Real, which express neither letters nor words in gross, but Things or Notions; insomuch as countries and provinces, which understand not one another's language, can nevertheless read one another's writings because the characters are accepted more generally than the languages do extend (Bacon cited by Large, *Artificial Language Movement*, 12).

This notion of creating a Universal Language became a dominant idea in British linguistic thought of the 17th century. The most influential of the systems of characters actually devised was that of Bishop John Wilkins (1614-1672), who like Bacon looked to Chinese,[6] but at least as much as a model of what to avoid as of what to imitate:

> As for the *China* Character and Language so much talked of in the world, if it be rightly represented by those that have lived in that Country, and pretend to understand the Language, there are many considerable faults in it, which make it come far short of the advantages which may be in such a Philosophical Language as is here designed. (Wilkins, *An Essay towards a Real Character and a Philosophical Language* (1668), cited by Large, *Artificial Language Movement*, 12-13)

Wilkins "emphasises the multitude of characters which must be learnt, the difficulty of pronunciation and the absence of analogy 'betwixt the shape of the Characters, and the things represented by them'" (Large, *Artificial Language Movement*, 13), and he set out to make his own system of real characters free from these faults. Numerous other cases of early universal language schemes in which Chinese played a direct or indirect part are cited by Large (*Artificial Language Movement*, 12, 17, 22).

When the movement for the creation of a spoken international language came to prominence in the late 19th century, Chinese was again very much in the picture, this time not because of the perceived nature of its writing system but by virtue of its being the mother tongue of more people than any other language. The international language Volapük (World Speech), invented by Johann Martin Schleyer (1831-1912) and published in 1880, had a number of Chinese-like features. "The fallacy which Schleyer committed," in the critical view of Jacob, "was to distort his vocabulary beyond hope of recognition in order to facilitate the pronunciation for every nationality. *R* was to be avoided as a concession to Chinese speakers, *fire* became *fil*, *red* became *led*, *world*

---

[6] A. P. R. Howatt, *A History of English Language Teaching*. (Oxford: Oxford University Press, 1984), 104.

became *vola*, and *speech* became *pük*".[7] Again echoing a process familiar in Chinese, "Schleyer preferred monosyllables; words not conforming to this principle were ruthlessly contracted" (Jacob, *On the Choice of a Common Language*, 8), so that for example *fermentation* became *fem*, and *chamber* became *cem*.

When in the 20th century linguists like Otto Jespersen (1860-1943) and Edward Sapir (1884-1939) became seriously involved in projects for the creation of an international auxiliary language, Chinese again came to the fore, this time for yet another reason: its 'isolating' or 'analytical' structure, foregoing all inflections and expressing grammatical relations purely through words and their order, was held up as the most economical form a language could take, and therefore the form which an invented international language would do best to imitate. Thus Sapir:

> [T]he ideal of effective simplicity is attained by a completely analytic language, one in which the whole machinery of formal grammar is reduced to carefully defined word order and to the optional use of 'empty' independent words (like 'several,' 'did,' 'of'). Inflection is reduced to zero. This is the ideal that English has been slowly evolving toward for centuries and that Chinese attained many centuries ago after passing through a more synthetic prehistoric phase.[8]

The last sentence brings in two ideas of particular significance. The first is the structural equation of Chinese with English, the language which by this time was reputed to be spoken by more people than any other tongue, though for most of them as a second language. Insofar as giving an auxiliary language the analytical structure of Chinese meant that it would also be quite like English greatly strengthened the argument that such a language would be accessible to the largest possible number of people. The second significant idea is that of evolution. For Wilhelm von Humboldt (1767-1835) writing in the first half of the 19th century,[9] the ideal linguistic structure was represented by the heavily inflecting Sanskrit. Humboldt believed that the conjoining of root and inflection as in Sanskrit, Greek, Latin and the Indo-European languages generally, directly reproduced the natural functioning of the human mind, endowing the nations which spoke these languages with the greatest intellectual power. The lack of inflection in Chinese was for him a defect, though one partly made up for by the language's

---

[7] H. Jacob, *On the Choice of a Common Language* (London: Sir Isaac Pitman & Sons, 1946), 8.

[8] Edward Sapir, "Memorandum on the Problem of an International Auxiliary Language" (1925), cited by Julia S. Falk, "Words without Grammar: Linguists and the International Auxiliary Language Movement in the United States," *Language and Communication* 15 (1995), 241-59, here 245.

[9] Wilhelm von Humboldt, *Über die Verschiedenheit des menschlichen Sprachbaues und ihren Einfluß auf die geistige Entwicklung des Menschengeschlechts* (Berlin: Königliche Akademie der Wissenschaften, 1836). English version: *On Language: The Diversity of Human Language Structure and its Influence on the Mental Development of Mankind*, trans. by Peter Heath (Cambridge: Cambridge University Press, 1989).

great consistency in applying the analytical principle.[10] The great changes that occurred between Humboldt and Sapir include Darwin, and a more general 'modernism' which takes the shedding of unnecessary features as providing evolutionary advantage.[11]

So it is that unlike their 19th-century predecessors such as Esperanto, which had inflectional systems as complex as those of the Romance languages, 20th-century invented languages like the Latine sine flexione (later renamed Interlingua) of the Italian mathematical logician Giuseppe Peano (1858-1932) (see Falk, "Words Without Grammar") and the Interglossa of the English biologist, mathematics *vulgarisateur* and linguist Lancelot Thomas Hogben (1895-1975) deliberately model their structure on that of Chinese. Hogben does so with a political motivation as well: Interglossa is presented as "a draft of an auxiliary for a democratic world order," and he hopes that making it as much like Asian languages as possible will help bring about the democratisation of China and Japan.

> *Interglossa* is a purely *isolating* language. It admits many compounds built from bricks which are independent elements, but it has no dead affixes prescribed in accordance with *a priori* considerations. In so far as it is a flexionless language, it resembles Chinese (or Peanese [i.e. Interlingua]), but it differs from P [i.e. Interlingua] because it has a large stock-in-trade of compounds sufficiently explicit in an appropriate context to anyone who knows or can recognize their parts [...]
>
> [...] Unlike its predecessors, designed exclusively, and admittedly, to meet the taste of *Western* Europe and the English-speaking peoples, *Interglossa* is for a world in which China, Japan, and eventually the peoples of Africa, will march in step with the U.S.S.R. and with western civilization.[12]

In Chinese fashion, the word for person (or man) is the truncated *pe*, which then becomes the second element in a large number of compounds: *agri-pe* 'farmer,' *amico-pe* 'friend,' *bibli-pe* 'publisher,' *pedio-pe* 'child' and so on. The fact that the word-stock of Interglossa is, like its name, Greco-Latin in origin, might be taken as a contradiction of Hogben's expressed aim of passing beyond 'the taste of Western Europe,' but his view is quite the opposite: "*Interglossa* has a vocabulary based on internationally current roots" (Hogben, *Interglossa*, 15).

Chinese, then, was kept at the centre of the movement for an international language by at least five reasons or beliefs:

---

[10] John E. Joseph, "A Matter of *Consequenz*: Humboldt on Chinese". Paper read at the annual meeting of the Henry Sweet Society for the History of Linguistic Ideas, The University of Luton, 12 Sept. 1997.

[11] On Sapir's Darwinian modernism vis-à-vis Humboldt see further John E. Joseph, "The Immediate Sources of the 'Sapir-Whorf Hypothesis'," *Historiographia Linguistica* 23 (1996): 365-404, esp. 369-70.

[12] Lancelot Hogben, *Interglossa: A Draft of an Auxiliary for a Democratic World Order, Being an Attempt to Apply Semantic Principles to Language Design* (Harmondsworth: Penguin, 1943), 14-15.

i.	Its writing system already furnished the basis for such a language, albeit with imperfections.
ii.	No other language had nearly so many native speakers.
iii.	Its simple analytical structure represented the evolutionary ideal of language.
iv.	Its analytical structure also brought it close to English, the world's most widespread second language.
v.	Making the international language resemble Chinese insofar as possible would help bring about political change on the world's most populous continent.

Rather than replacing them, the motives which came later simply added to the force of the earlier ones. Two other factors should also be borne in mind:

vi.	The sheer extent of the difference in structure between it and the Indo-European languages worked in favour of Chinese, especially for the modernist mind which sought to solve problems by breaking as completely as possible with Western tradition and not infrequently looked eastward for inspiration.
vii.	Because Chinese represented the ultimate in foreignness to the Western mind, recourse to it by a Westerner fashioning an international language could be fairly presented as complete lack of bias toward any of the more familiar languages or language families — virtually as objective a choice as Martian would be.

3. Basic English

The obvious alternative to an artificial international auxiliary language was for an existing 'natural' language to fill this role. Yet every such language faced huge political obstacles to acceptance as a universal second tongue. Moreover, 'natural' languages were inevitably more complex than an invented language needed to be, and therefore posed an obstacle to the kind of easy learning that would permit everyone on earth to acquire it.

In the July 1927 issue of his journal *Psyche*, Ogden began laying out his compromise solution for 'linguistic internationalization' or 'Debabelization,' which was fleshed out in subsequent issues through April 1930. Ogden believed that this end could best be achieved not by means of an artificial language, but by a 'simplified universal English' to be devised through vocabulary reduction.

> Conjugates [...] are words related to the same root [...] For example, in the case of 'House,' cottage, bungalow, hotel, sanatorium, palace, hut, hovel, home, city, room, chimney, etc [...]
>
> If the word we are studying proves to be part of our basic vocabulary, then its conjugates (*qua* single words) can usually be dispensed with. For a basic vocabulary on the

lines indicated in our January issue, any word which requires more than ten other words to knock it out would be retained.

Whether this would leave us with more than 500 essential terms is still doubtful; and these, together with a small number of simple devices for operating them, would enable everything that is at present said in the ordinary course of events to be dealt with, if not idiomatically, at least clearly and grammatically.

If a scientifically simplified language could thus place anyone, anywhere, in command of a medium of communication already used in one form or another by some 500,000,000 people, the problem of a universal language would have been virtually solved [...]

Meantime, of course, all research and experiment with artificial or synthetic languages will have both an educational and a psychological interest. Simplified universal English will differ sufficiently from literary English to be almost a new language[...].[13]

The January 1929 issue of *Psyche* opens with a full-page table headed "Panoptic English," giving the nouns, adjectives and "operators" which make up the vocabulary of this simplified system. The chart claims that the language has "no verbs," though the list of operators includes the items "come, get, give, go, keep, let, make, put, seem, take, be, do, have, may, will," and what is more the suffixes *-ing* and *-ed* can be added to 300 of the nouns. Thus Basic allows the forms *acted* and *acting* as derivates of the noun *act*, while claiming to have no verbs. The Editorial to this issue remarks:

So long as the essentially contractive nature of the verb was concealed by the existing grammatical definitions, there could be no reduction in the vocabulary sufficiently radical to affect the problem of a Universal Language, *nor is this now possible in any language other than English*; and it is the continuous approximation of East and West, as a result of the analytic character of Chinese and English (especially in its latest American developments), which makes this particular form of English *basic* for the whole world.

Many special captions or trade-marks for the system ahve been suggested, but BASIC = British American Scientific International Commercial (English) — is for the time being as good as any. The term *Panoptic* serves to emphasize that in its written or printed form it can [...], as it were, be seen at a glance.[14]

The fold-out vocabulary table in the January 1930 issue is headed "Basic English," and that term, or just "Basic," would henceforth be the name of Ogden's system. The following is an example of 'translation' from scientific English into Basic of a passage by the economist Sir Josiah Stamp:[15] (from Ogden 1944 [1930a]: 146):

Original: Narrow dispersions, skewed negatively, signify deliberate human restriction of output. Skewed positively, after the introduction of selection of em-

Basic: The tendency to a common level of output being more frequent, is a sign that output is being consciously kept inside a certain limit. When the lowest

---

[13] C.K. Ogden, "Editorial: Debabelization," *Psyche* 9:1 (1928), 1-3, here 2.

[14] C.K. Ogden, "Editorial: The Universal Language," *Psyche* 9:3 (1929), 1-9, here 4. Italics in original.

[15] From C.K. Ogden, *Basic English: A General Introduction with Rules and Grammar* (London: Kegan Paul, 1930. 8th ed., 1940; 9th ed., 1944).

> ployees by test or examination, a narrow dispersion indicates a successful system of selection.
>
> outputs are most frequent and the output of workers not widely different and generally high, after selection of workers by test has come into use, the tendency may be taken as a sign of the efficiency of the system of selection.

The adjective *narrow* is twice done away with in the translation even though it figures on the Basic Word List, because its metaphorical use in this passage is a specialised one, and one of the aims of Basic is to make specialised writing accessible to the common reader. *Output* does not appear on the list as a separate entry, but is a combination of two of the operators, *out* and *put*.

At first sight Ogden might not have seemed the likeliest inventor of a simplified English for use as an international auxiliary language, nor might one have expected the role of its chief advocate to fall to Richards, one of the most respected literary scholars of the 20th century. However this becomes less unlikely as one examines the intellectual climate of Cambridge University at the time they entered there.

Ogden arrived at Magdalene College on a classical scholarship in 1908, choosing as his specialisation the influence of the Greek language on Greek thought.[16] Among those with whom he became acquainted and associated in the following years were the two most important philosophers of language of the 20th century, Bertrand Russell (1872-1970) and Ludwig Wittgenstein (1889-1951), both fellows at Trinity College. Trinity had been the college of Francis Bacon, and from 1912 would be that of Lancelot Hogben, both of whose work on artificial languages was discussed in the preceding section. Ogden had a link as well to Peano through Russell, also a mathematical philosopher. Ogden, Russell and Wittgenstein came together most famously in the 1922 *Tractatus Logico-Philosophicus*, the only philosophical work Wittgenstein published in his lifetime, translated into English by Ogden and published by him in his Routledge and Kegan Paul series with an Introduction by Russell. Russell was convinced that our everyday language is the source of metaphysical traps which hinder clear thinking, and that reformulating philosophical language on a mathematical basis was the way to escape these traps. Wittgenstein began with similar assumptions, but finally came to believe that philosophical language posed even deeper problems of this nature than did ordinary language.

In 1923, a year after Wittgenstein's *Tractatus*, Ogden and Richards published *The Meaning of Meaning* in book form. Though claiming not to follow Russell, it took a partly Russellian view of the metaphysics of ordinary language (what Ogden termed 'word magic'). It was to prove highly influential, not least by provoking Edward Sapir and subsequently Benjamin Lee Whorf (1897-1941) to formulate what would become known as the 'Sapir-Whorf hypothesis' (see Joseph, "Immediate Sources"). Ogden would in retrospect locate in *The Meaning of Meaning* the germ of the principle of vocabulary elimination which would make Basic possible:

---

[16] Gordon, *C.K. Ogden*. See further John E. Joseph, "The Immediate Sources of the 'Sapir-Whorf Hypothesis'". *Historiographia Linguistica* 23 (1996), 365-404, esp. 380-381.

> The Panoptic Eliminator provides a very powerful and convenient instrument for grouping the whole material of lexicography.
> It is based in part on the theory of Definition set forth in *The Meaning of Meaning*. To find the referent of a given symbol from a starting point *x*, follow the route *y*. That is the formula of all definition, systematic or casuistic [...] The object both of description and of definition is to enable the reader to reach the referent (understand the meaning), and this can be achieved with varying degrees of conciseness and system.[17]

Ogden and Richards' theory of symbolisation is central to *The Meaning of Meaning*, and a full account of it can be found in Gordon.[18] In the present context, it is worth noting that it differs in a crucial way from the definition of the linguistic sign given by Ferdinand de Saussure (1857-1913).[19] For Saussure, the linguistic sign is the conjunction of a 'signifier' (sound-pattern) and a 'signified' (concept), and meaning derives from the value of these purely conceptual signifieds, not from their referents, the tangible things which they name. Ogden and Richards' model reincorporates the referent to form the third corner of a triangular conception of the sign — Term, Thought and Thing. In other words, against Saussure's notion of meaning as being generated by the language system and inseparable from the symbolisation process, Ogden and Richards cling to a more traditional view of meaning as standing apart from the language in which it is symbolised. Their famous triangle also probably shows the influence of the American pragmatist Charles Sanders Peirce (1839-1914), to whose work Ogden had been introduced some years earlier by Victoria Lady Welby (1837-1912), though Gordon (letter to the author, 26 Jan. 1998) speculates that by the time of *The Meaning of Meaning* it was Richards rather than Ogden who was pushing the Peircean triadic model.

What I wish to suggest is that in Saussure's model, the 'symbolisation' through which a thought (signified) is expressed as a term (signifier) is what makes meaning possible; meaning does not exist in any sense in advance of symbolisation. In Ogden and Richard's model, a crucial component of meaning *does* exist in advance of symbolisation: the referent, the Thing. In a sense, the referent is meaning itself, since as Ogden states in the quotation above, to *reach the referent* is to *understand the meaning*. Symbolisation, Thought expressed as Term, can be a direct path to the referent, but can just as easily be a misleading path filled with obstacles to the expression and comprehension of meaning. The purpose of Basic English was to clear the path of potential obstacles, so that symbolisation could be as direct as possible.

---

[17] C.K. Ogden, "Editorial: Penultimata; Scientific, Basic, Mnemonic; The Languages of Science; International Terms; Bilingualism in Bengal; Simplification and Irregularity; Methodological; Panoptic Conjugation; The Diagram of Operators; Opposition," *Psyche* 10:3 (1930), 1-28, here 9-10.

[18] W. Terrence Gordon, "Bridging Saussurean Structuralism and British Linguistic Thought," *Historiographia Linguistica* 21 (1994): 123-36.

[19] See Ferdinand de Saussure, *Cours de linguistique générale*, ed. by Charles Bally and Albert Sechehaye with the assistance of Albert Riedlinger. (Lausanne and Paris: Payot, ²1922, ¹1916.)

4. The Rise and Fall of Basic English in China

The importance of China within Ogden's programme has already been touched upon in the quotation from Ogden ("The Universal Language," 4) above, where in remarking on "the continuous approximation of East and West, as a result of the analytic character of Chinese and English" he echoes other modernist views seen in Section 2. A page later Ogden notes that in the course of testing Basic English,

> Its suitability for Oriental requirements was also verified, and the necessary contacts made to enable it in due course to secure a rapid diffusion in the chief educational centres of the East. Such a diffusion is now the next step; and during the coming months we shall be seeking the necessary financial support to initiate a programme of scientific Debabelization which it may take a hundred years to carry through (Ogden, "The Universal Language," 5-6).

Ogden financed the early activities of his Orthological Institute (founded in 1927) from his own pocket.[20] But the Debabelization of China looked like costing more than he was willing or able to fund. The preceding quotation was published in January of 1929, and the 'coming months' would bring the stock market crash and the Great Depression. Nevertheless, Ogden succeeded in getting major funding support from the Payne Fund of New York in 1932. The following year this was supplemented by the Rockefeller Foundation,[21] which also agreed to sponsor research programmes for Japan and China. This made it possible to establish a branch of the Orthological Institute in Beijing, its charge being to develop the teaching of Basic English in China, an enterprise which enjoyed the support of the Chinese government. Ogden would later write:

> [I]n 1933 a serious start was made in the Far East with a programme supported by the Rockefeller Foundation.
> [...] Special attention has been given to the needs of the education authorities in China, where the Orthographical Institute (Peking), under the direction of Professor R. D. Jameson of Tsing Hua University and Dr. I. A. Richards of Magdalene College, Cambridge, was working (till 1938) on the organization of material for the Middle Schools. They had the help of a Chinese Committee, and were profiting by the new developments in Radio, which is now coming to the front in all countries of the East. The parallel programme in Japan would have been complete in 1942, when the *Japanese-Basic Dictionary* [...] was ready to be printed for the use of teachers (Ogden, *Basic English*, 163-4).

The interruption in 1938 was of course caused by the Japanese invasion of China, and that in 1942 by the full-scale entry of Japan into world war the year before.

---

[20] Elsie Graham, "Basic English as an International Language," in Florence/Anderson, *C.K. Ogden*, 153-60, here 156.

[21] See further Raymond B. Fosdick, *The Story of the Rockefeller Foundation* (New York: Harper and Brothers, 1952), 250-251.

The Basic English project in East Asia would never entirely recover from these events, though Ogden and Richards worked hard to keep it going. Indeed, Richards returned to China as late as 1979 to continue the push for Basic, during which trip he fell fatally ill (see Richards' entry in the *Dictionary of National Biography 1971-1980*, 722). The following are excerpts from Richards' *Basic English and Its Uses*, published at the height of the war in 1943:

> No one who knows the Far East doubts that China and Japan must find linguistic access to the thought of the rest of the world if they are to join it in any real fashion (v).

> Neither those who learn English nor those who teach it as a foreign langauge have in general any feeling that they are submitting to or furthering a process of intellectual subjugation. On the contrary, they are more likely to feel that they are helping themselves or others to resist such influences. The Chinese, for example, are not in the least afraid of English. What they do often feel is that an excessive amount of time given up to learning English may be damaging to the study of their own language. And that, they rightly believe, would be disastrous (13-14).

> I am making no attempt to sketch the history of the spread of Basic through its first ten years. The war interrupted too many promising starts — in China, Japan, Czechoslovakia, Denmark, Greece, to mention only a few instances [...] (38).[22]

The key to Debabelization continued to be Asia, and particularly China, for reasons which will be explored in the following section.

But this battle was largely Richards' to fight, for Ogden was occupied on other fronts, including his 'counter-offensive' (the title of his 1935 book)[23] against the criticisms of Basic English being spread by a group led by Michael Philip West (1888-1973) (see further Howatt, *History*). West had been a supporter of Basic up until the year before the appearance of the 53-page 'critical examination' which he spearheaded,[24] and which appeared with the backing of another prominent and more senior applied linguist, Harold Edward Palmer (1877-1949), who also had previously expressed support for Basic to Ogden. (Ogden, *Counter-Offensive*, 176). Ogden suspected that they had perceived the potentially enormous market for Basic English and wanted a piece of it for their own texts and methods, which despite their criticisms of Ogden seemed to him to bear more than a passing resemblance to his ideas. The fact

---

[22] Other remarks concerning Chinese or China can be found at pp. 15, 21-22, 29, 37, 42, 44-6, 48.

[23] C.K. Ogden, *Counter-Offensive: An Exposure of Certain Misrepresentations of Basic English* (Cambridge and Peiping: The Orthological Institute, 1935. Repr. as vol. 4 of *C. K. Ogden and Linguistics*, ed. by W. Terrence Gordon, London: Routledge/Thoemmes, 5 vols., 1994), 176.

[24] M.P. West, E. Swenson, and Others [sic], *A Critical Examination of Basic English*. Bulletin No. 2 of the Department of Education Research, Ontario College of Education, University of Toronto (Toronto: University of Toronto Press, 1934).

that West et al.'s (1934) debunking of the Rockefeller-funded Basic project was supported by the Carnegie Corporation suggests that behind the 'Basic English wars' may also have been a certain amount of rivalry between American philanthropic bodies.

The high point of British public awareness of Basic came during the war, when Churchill and Roosevelt publically took interest in it. Within a few years however, Basic's newly heightened profile would lead to Ogden's giving up ownership of it:

> In 1943 (Sir) Winston Churchill set up a cabinet committee on Basic English [...] and made a statement to the House of Commons on its report on 9 March 1944. He outlined the steps which the Government would take to develop Basic English as an auxiliary international and administrative language through the British Council, the B.B.C., and other bodies[...] [Ogden] was requested to assign his copyright to the Crown which he did in June 1946 and was compensated by £23,000 [...] The Basic English Foundation was established with a grant from the Ministry of Education in 1947 (From Ogden's entry in the *Dictionary of National Biography 1951-1960*, 779).

The details of Ogden's compensation are uncertain; according to Lauwerys,[25] the £23,000 which the government paid to Ogden was actually in settlement of a claim he had submitted for £50,000 in damages and liabilities for delays in distribution which led to more than 100,000 volumes of Basic textbooks being destroyed by damp while in storage. "No payment was ever made by the Government for the copyright — only for material loss caused by delay and incompetence" (Lauwerys, "Basic English," 164). Lauwerys further notes that the £23,000 "is recorded in the Civil Appropriation Accounts as set off against the vote to the British Council, of which in that year £1,000,000 was shown as unexpended" (Lauwerys, "Basic English," 164).

Around this time a complex set of causes led Ogden to fall out with Richards. Matters were not helped by a book Richards co-authored with Christine Gibson, which has been described as

> [...] the one application of Basic that has survived in general use. It was originally called *A Pocket Book of Basic English* (1945) but is known to large numbers of people throughout the world as *English Through Pictures*, the first of a series of 'Through Pictures' spin-offs. Richards' decision to modify Basic for the book led to a split with Ogden, who disassociated himself from the publication (Howatt, *History*, 250-51).

The result of these events was that the future direction of Basic largely left Ogden's control. Over the next decade, the Basic English Foundation had to contend with lack of support and even outright hostility from the British Council, which had responsibility for the use of British government funds for the teaching of English worldwide. Sir Malcolm Robertson, Chairman of the Council when Ogden assigned his copyright to the government, "had never concealed his hostility to Basic," (Lauwerys, "Basic English," 164) and the British Council moved steadily toward a unified policy that

---

[25] J. A. Lauwerys, "Basic English — Its Position and Plans," in Florence/Anderson, *C.K. Ogden*, 161-8.

'natural' English was altogether preferable to Basic for teaching purposes (see Howatt, *History*, 254-5). By the time of Ogden's death in 1957, the Basic English project was but a shadow of what it had been in the 1930s and '40s.

5. *China as the Key to Debabelization*

It is not immediately obvious why China and the Chinese language occupy such a prominent place in the early literature of Basic English, more than any other of the thirty countries in which agencies for its propagation were established. At the end of Section 2 we resumed the various factors which account for the prominence of Chinese in the creation of artificial universal languages up through the first quarter of the 20th century, and we can begin by asking to what extent these carried over into the Basic project:

i. *The Chinese writing system already furnished the basis for a universal language.* This does not seem to play any part in the thinking about Basic English. On the contrary, Ogden (*Basic English*, 95) points out that "the time needed for the learning and writing of Chinese picture-words gives such a language very little chance of becoming more widely used". This is ironic, given the role played by 'Chinese picture-words' in inspiring Western universal language schemes for so many centuries.

ii. *No other language had nearly so many native speakers.* This was an important factor to which Ogden and others frequently alluded:

> It has taken 500 years for English to become the second language of the East, in addition to its development in the United States, Canada, and Australasia; and of the 30 languages now at the head of the list, English has the first place among the eight which are used by more than 50,000,000 persons. It is the natural language, or the language of government or trade, of some 650 millions. The seven others are:
>
> | | | | |
> |---|---|---|---|
> | Chinese | 450 | German | 95 |
> | Russian | 166 | Spanish | 85 |
> | French | 112 | Bengali | 60 |
> | Japanese | 100 | | |
>
> Though 'Chinese' is generally given as the mother tongue of 400 millions, it is not certain how far these are clear to one another in talking and writing. Some authorities put the number at 200 millions, others at 300, but the words have quite different senses at different voice levels [...] (Ogden, *Basic English*, 94-5).

(The figure for Japanese was up by two-thirds from the 8th edition of this book, published in 1940, which listed it as having 60 million speakers German, Spanish and Bengali were also up, though by much smaller amounts). It was unthinkable that the advances of Western science should be kept from so huge a proportion of the world's population.²⁶ In the last paragraph above Ogden introduces a novel rationale for an international language: the linguistic diversity of China, where the difference between northern dialects like Mandarin and southern ones like Cantonese is sometimes compared to that between English and Swedish. If it were not for such diversity among Chinese dialects, one would be hard put to defend the role of Basic English as universal auxiliary language rather than Basic Chinese. Richards directly entertains the latter possibility, though never with conviction:

> Which of the existing major languages can be made easiest for learners in general? [...] The two languages which lead in this respect are English and, much more doubtfully, Chinese.
> [...]
> On the most neutral grounds, the Chinese have a very strong claim to consideration by framers of a world language. There are so many of them, and the part they should play in the world should be second to none. A simplified English, if put forward as a planetary language, must be made as accessible as possible to peoples other than those of Indo-European tongues [...]²⁷

In fact the lack of a standard spoken Chinese would be a strong motivating force for the Chinese government to support the efforts to spread Basic English in China, so that it might serve as a shared language for Chinese from north and south as well as facilitating their contact and exchange with the rest of the world. It was only after the victory of the Communist forces led by Mao Zedong in 1949-50 that the project to spread Putonghua, a standardised form of Mandarin, as the common language of China got seriously under way, and indeed it was not until the Cultural Revolution of the 1960s and '70s that widespread use of Putonghua became a reality in China. Mao, who himself did not speak Putonghua, recognised that the power of English to open China to the rest of the world, and so placed strict limits on its teaching. As China has reopened its doors to the west since Mao's death, the teaching of English has increased accordingly. In 1994 English was made a compulsory subject in elementary schools throughout China.²⁸

iii. *Its simple analytical structure represented the evolutionary ideal of language.* Ogden's views on how "the analytic character of Chinese and English (especially in its latest American developments) [...] makes this particular form of English *basic* for the whole world" ("The Universal Language," 4) has already been cited twice above.

---

²⁶ See Charlotte Tylor, "The Teaching of English in China," *Psyche* 16 (1936), 178-187.
²⁷ I.A. Richards, *Basic English and Its Uses* (London: Kegan Paul, Trench, Trubner and Co., 1943), 15, 21-2.
²⁸ See further John E. Joseph, "English in Hong Kong: Emergence and Decline," in Sue Wright and Helen Kelly-Holmes, eds., *One Country, Two Systems, Three Languages: Changing Language Use in Hong Kong* (Clevedon: Multilingual Matters, 1997), 60-79 [= *Current Issues in Language and Society* 3 (1996), 166-85].

iv. *Its analytical structure also brought it close to English, the world's most widespread second language.* Same remark as the preceding.
v. *Making the international language resemble Chinese insofar as possible would help bring about political change on the world's most populous continent.* Although Ogden appears more reluctant than other proponents of Basic English to discuss its macro-level political ramifications, passages such as the following are occasionally found in his writings:

> More than ten years back Henry Ford gave the answer to this and other questions of the same sort when, in agreement with President Masaryk and H. G. Wells, he made English for Everyman his new peace-cry to take the place of war-cries of the past; but the different language groups got at one another's throats again, before the idea had time to take root. Now with the growth of that Everyman's English which is named Basic, the old arguments become ten times stronger. So, though the lights have gone out in country after country in Europe, there are hundreds of millions looking out from the dark into a future which is still bright with hope. (Ogden, *Basic English*, 176)

Ogden might have remarked, but did not, that the lights had gone out in China as well. There is no indication that China's politics are of particular concern to him in themselves, apart from their ramifications for the linguistic, educational and cultural development of the largest nation on earth. But it is crucial that the world's largest nation not be shut off from the modern international community. "Far more important, and overshadowing any other consideration" in the rationale for teaching Basic in China "is the need that educated China should be equipped to play its part in the modern world" (Tylor, "Teaching," 187).

vi. *The sheer difference in structure between Chinese and the Indo-European languages appealed to modernist mind as a complete break with Western tradition.* There is no direct evidence of Ogden having thought this; and it was, after all, English, an Indo-European language, which Ogden was trying to spread — albeit in a thoroughly 'modernised' form which a Humboldtian might see as removing it from its essential Indo-European nature and in the direction of an essential Chineseness. It is certainly the case that a strong motivation for Basic English was to help break with traditional ways of *thinking*, cluttered as they were with the effects of 'word magic.'
vii. *Fashioning an international language after Chinese meant no bias toward any of the more familiar languages.* Again, Ogden liked to stress that the Chinese-like features of Basic English and its supposed closeness to American English made it simultaneously Eastern and Western, Old World and New World. Of course no one could deny that the use of Basic gave certain benefits to English speakers, though the tight strictures on acceptable Basic vocabulary (and to a lesser extent, structure) meant that speaking in Basic English was no easy task for a native speaker of English to master.

It seems, then, that Ogden's interest in Chinese carried over some but by no means all of the factors which had impelled the inventors of artificial languages to look eastward, and added a new one: the fact that China itself lacked a common spoken language for all its people.

There is, however, at least one other potentially important factor for Ogden, which in some ways connects to the desire (weak in his case) to help democratise China (see (v) above), but has more to do with Ogden's and Richards' particular views about the nature of language and thought, alluded to in (vi). It does not find expression so much in Ogden's writings on Basic as in his theoretical work, but it can also be teased out of what others have to say about Basic, such as the views expressed in the second paragraph of this passage by Henry Jacob (b.1909):

> [I]t is possible and, indeed, probable that the 'English' of the future will be more like the language now spoken in the United States than like that spoken in Southern England or like that adopted by the British Broadcasting Corporation. How far this should be deplored is, of course, a matter of taste and *de gustibus non diputandum*. In any case, the change will be slow and not necessarily painful except to a few purists of old-fashioned outlook. The latter should be willing to pay this price for the unity of speech and outlook that the people of North American and of the British Empire would thereby preserve and enjoy.
>
> This anxiety of the purists has been expressed by Mr. Basil de Selincourt, who said that 'a [...] horror fills the mind of the humanist when it occurs to him that English may be destined to be the language of the human race. *What* English? he wonders. [...] In plain truth, it is already spoken too generally for its good, and [...] its expansion may yet prove its undoing.' While there is undoubtedly some truth in the assumption that English will be influenced by those national groups who will use it as a secondary auxiliary, we must leave it to the reader to judge how far fears like those of Mr. de Selincourt's are reasonable or justified (Jacob, *On the Choice of a Common Language*, 126).

The views of De Sélincourt (1875-1966) as laid out in his 1926 book *Pomona, or the Future of English* are more complex than this quotation out of context might lead one to believe. He is not so much a purist as a linguistic 'vitalist,' believing that languages are organisms in the truest sense and must evolve naturally, with the vitality of their evolution being directly connected to the spiritual vitality of their speakers. De Sélincourt believes that American English will be the salvation of the language, providing the necessary source of vitality to compensate for a spiritually exhausted England. He fears however that the still further spread of English will result in the meanings of words losing their vital connection to the Anglophone soul; for as he remarks about universal ancillary languages generally (but clearly with English foremost in his mind), "the adopted language would tend to be debased, since *men of different schemes of experience would use the same words in different senses*, so step by step obliterating their true sense and leaving them flavourless."[29] He is therefore concerned about *controlling* English at the level of meaning, an interest shared by the authors of

---

[29] Basil De Sélincourt, *Pomona, or the Future of English* (London: Kegan Paul, Trench, Trubner and Co.; New York: E. P. Dutton, 1926), 41, emphasis added.

The Meaning of Meaning. The difference is that De Sélincourt would achieve this control by containing the spread of the language to preserve its 'natural' development, whereas Ogden, who sees languages as functional tools rather than organic wholes, would intervene directly in the control of word meanings and put no limits on where the re-engineered language should be used.

It is hard to imagine anyone writing about language and meaning in the 1920s without the experiences of the Great War somewhere in their thoughts. The British war effort had included the creation of a massive propaganda machine, devoted to extolling the British over the German way of life, chronicling alleged German atrocities, and trying to persuade the United States to enter the War on the side of the Triple Entente. The propaganda was prepared by scholars like the historian Arnold Toynbee and the classicist Gilbert Murray, and was subtly distributed in conjunction with non-propagandistic writings by G. K. Chesterton, Arthur Conan Doyle, Joseph Conrad, H. G. Wells, George Bernard Shaw and Rudyard Kipling. It was sometimes critical of life in Britain but still portrayed British victory as more desirable than German victory.[30] This gave it the ring of objectivity. After the War it became received opinion in many quarters, including even Germany, that Britain's success owed more to propaganda than to military might:

> While many in Germany were over-lavish — for their own reasons — in praising the success of British propaganda during the First World War, the reaction to it in America was one of suspicion. This did not reveal itself fully until the outbreak of the Second World War, but then it came as somewhat of a shock in Britain. Many Americans felt — rightly or wrongly — that they had somehow been lured into the First World War, and certainly the many books and articles which those involved in Britain's efforts in courting the United States had written after the War, confirmed them in that impression (Roetter, *Psychological Warfare*, 89).

Ogden's particular concern with understanding the meaning of meaning seems to have been bound up with this fear that governments were now more capable than ever of manipulating language in such a way as to control the thoughts of the unwary citizenry. The same fear was exploited by Alfred Korzybski (1879-1950) in promoting his General Semantics movement.[31] Ogden saw Basic as a tool for protecting language, and through it, thought, from propagandistic manipulation, on the grounds that it is harder to dissemble and create bias using simple, concrete words than complex, abstract ones. Tyler, focusing on China, writes that

---

[30] Charles Roetter, *The Art of Psychological Warfare, 1914-1945* (New York: Stein and Day, 1974), 64-5.

[31] On the General Semantics movement see Christopher M. Hutton, "The Critique of Primitive Belief and Modern Linguistics," *Journal of Literary Semantics* 24 (1995): 81-103 and John E. Joseph, "General Semantics," in Gert Ueding, ed., *Historisches Wörterbuch der Rhetorik* (Tübingen: Max Niemeyer, 1996), Band 3, 721-23. On Korzybski's relations with Ogden see Joseph, "Immediate Sources," 389.

> Basic English [...] can be more of a factor in the training of acute critical intelligence, in China and in English-speaking countries, than the average unreflective thinker about the deeply rooted and far reaching problems of language realizes. The problem of the individual's control and understanding of his own and, when possible, others' thought-processes, through language, which is the major outward and visible sign of those processes, is obviously of the most fundamental importance in every effort to disentangle the larger world problems. (Tyler, "Teaching," 186)

Jacob, in the passage immediately following the one cited from him above, develops the notion that the limitations of Basic make it less culturally 'loaded:'

> Incidentally, it is well to note that Basic, being a much barer medium than Normal English, is not nearly so loaded with national and cultural implications and that its spread is therefore little likely to serve to extend mere Anglo-Saxon influence. It is entirely unsuited to be what some would call 'an instrument of Anglo-Saxon Imperialism!' (Jacob, *On the Choice of a Common Language*, 126-7).

This suggests that the spread of Basic English to China would have the effect not of Anglicising Asia, but of immunising it against mental takeover by any political party. Popular as well as psychological literature had for decades been filled with images of 'Asian hordes' acting as if with a single mass mind. If indeed the 'Chinese mind' could be overtaken with propaganda, the resulting stampede would be unstoppable.

Jacob's remark about 'Anglo-Saxon imperialism' has a more recent echo in Phillipson's[32] charge that the teaching of English as a second language is inextricably linked to a worldwide conspiracy of 'linguistic imperialism.' Phillipson believes that the spread of English is wiping out other cultural ways of thinking, in such a way as to serve the hegemonic purposes of the 'centre.' Jacob's point is precisely that Basic, being largely de-cultured, presents less of a threat than regular English does — a point which Phillipson and like-minded people might do well to consider, though one suspects that their distrust of English is so deep-rooted that even Basic would be unacceptable as an international auxiliary language.[33] In any case, Phillipson's view of language and hegemony is the polar opposite of Ogden's. Ogden believed that people left to their own language and culture would fall victim to tyrants from within controlling their minds through propaganda; Phillipson believes that, on the contrary, people left to their own language and culture will free themselves from externally-imposed hegemonic control. If Ogden was too pessimistic, Phillipson is optimistic beyond what any moderately realistic person who has lived through the last quarter-century could begin to swallow without choking.

Richards, writing at a time when Asia was in the grip of a fascist takeover, brings together the anti-propagandistic theme with the notion that English might be deformed in foreign mouths:

---

[32] Robert Phillipson, *Linguistic Imperialism*. (Oxford: Oxford University Press, 1992).

[33] Esperanto is their preferred choice for this function; on the relative merits of Basic and Esperanto see Ogden, *Basic English versus the Artificial Languages* (with contributions by Paul D. Hugon and L. W. Lockhart). London: Kegan Paul, Trench, Trubner and Co., 1935).

> Followers of Dr. Johnson at his most characteristic might be reluctant to give up words like abandon, abdicate, abjure, cede, desert, desist, forego, forsake [...] relinquish, renounce, resign, vacate, withdraw, and yield in place of give up — their homely Basic rendering — but a public unblessed by and unprotected by a sound training in philology escaped multiple dangers. So did the language itself. Every language is under constant attack by the tongues of its less expert users. One has only to watch — in a Chinese university, for example — the degradation of such learned words, when used without awareness of their implications, to see that they need protection. Basic English, by providing invulnerable but adequate substitutes for these more delicate instruments, can serve our language as a fender. It can guard full English from those who will blur all its lines and blunt all its edges if they try to write and talk it before they have learned to read it (Richards, *Basic English*, 29).

In effect, then, China was the key to Debabelization because unless China, with a quarter of the world's population, was inoculated against propagandistic control of language and thought, no other part of the world would ever be safe. As noted earlier, the politics of China do not appear to have particularly interested Ogden for their own sake; his concern was instead to keep China politically neutral at the level of linguistic manipulation. To this end, Basic English was not merely an international auxiliary language. It was the guarantor of freedom of thought, and ultimately of all liberty and civilisation.

6. Conclusion

As the 20th century draws to a close, Ogden's Basic English project is generally reckoned to have been a failure. A noble one perhaps, but a failure nonetheless. Yet it is remarkable how many aspects of Ogden's vision are coming to pass of their own accord. In recent decades the position of English as the world's most widely used second language has strengthened dramatically, largely as a result of technological progress. Since 1994 English has been a required subject in primary schools throughout China. Although the kind of mind control that Ogden foresaw has not really come to pass, people like Noam Chomsky believe very firmly that it has,[34] and that governments and big business conglomerates alike manipulate public thinking to a much greater degree than is apparent. In China, it is certainly true that the current totalitarian leadership manipulates language in order, for example, to describe themselves as democratic.

It would be naive to imagine that Ogden's solution might ultimately have kept these latter developments from happening. Or would it? Does my saying this reflect nothing so much as the total demise of the kind of utopian optimism which fueled all the projects for the creation and spread of an international language up through the middle of the 20th century? For a variety of reasons, such optimism has retreated in the face of a general 'naturalism' (not unrelated to the Romantic organicism of De Sélincourt,

---

[34] See for example Edward S. Herman and Noam Chomsky, *Manufacturing Consent: The Political Economy of the Mass Media* (New York: Pantheon, 1988).

discussed above) which takes human effort in the realm of language to be futile, since language finally will always follow its own course.

My wish for the new millennium is that it will see a better balance established between the natural and the cultural in the study of language, beginning with a recognition that in matters of language, as of everything else (even death and taxes), human beings are never entirely nature's lackeys. No one believed that more firmly than C. K. Ogden. In this context a reminiscence of him by Dora Russell (1894-1986), Bertrand's second wife, is particularly telling: "Ogden would often express contempt for the cult of fresh air and exercise, and assert that *everything artificial was preferable to the natural.*"[35] Not a balanced view, to be sure, indeed so extreme that one suspects it was exaggerated for shock effect. When the cult of the natural blinds us to the fact that human beings are ourselves part of nature, that our products are also, in a way, her products, it takes a strong voice speaking plain, basic English to provide the necessary shock back into reality.

Acknowledgments

This paper has benefitted from discussions about C. K. Ogden, Basic English and international auxiliary language schemes which I have had with J. C. Catford, who served as Ogden's assistant in the 1930s, Julia S. Falk, W. Terrence Gordon, A. P. R. Howatt and Vivian Salmon. In addition, Terry Gordon and Tony Howatt provided useful comments on an earlier draft. None of those named is responsible for any errors of fact or interpretation which may be contained herein. It was in Hong Kong, now China, that I first met Rüdiger Ahrens and came to admire his scholarship in and devotion to English language and literature, and to appreciate his personal warmth and kindness. It is an honour for me to take part in this salute to my friend on his sixtieth birthday.

---

[35] Dora Russell, "'My Friend Ogden'," in Florence/Anderson, *C.K. Ogden*, 82-95, here 86, emphasis added.

Towards a Dictionary of South Australian Pidgin English (SAPE)

PETER MÜHLHÄUSLER (Adelaide)

> [C]reole studies already form a complex and significant branch of university English research, particularly in view of the evergrowing worldwide importance of the English language.[1]

1. Introduction

I first met Rüdiger Ahrens on the occasion of the Anglistentag 1989 in Würzburg to which I had been invited to present a survey of creole theory to an audience of *Anglisten*. I have since written a contribution on South East Asian Englishes for the *Handbuch Englisch als Fremdsprache*[2] and I am very pleased to have been invited to contribute to Rüdiger´s *Festschrift* as, over the years, I have enjoyed greatly his contributions to scholarship. I particularly appreciate his catholic approach to what should be included under the heading of *Anglistik*. Having taught at the centre of the universe (Oxford) for many years and having missed out on describing the infamous St. Anthony College Pidgin (in use among overseas students) I have since moved to a more peripheral location (Adelaide in South Australia) where I have begun to document reduced and mixed varieties of English from the last century to the present. A first result is a joint article and several linguistic maps with Dinneen in Wurm, Mühlhäusler and Tryon[3], followed by a detailed analysis of the ubiquitous morphological suffix *-fela*[4] and remarks on the social functions of SAPE.[5] My paper today is about a joint project with Dr. Philip Clarke of the South Australian Museum on 19th century SAPE and 20th century Nunga (= South Australian Aboriginal people living in the Urban centres of the southern half of the state) English.

---

[1] Rüdiger Ahrens, "Preface," in Rüdiger Ahrens, ed., *Anglistentag 1989, Würzburg* (Tübingen: Niemeyer, 1990), vii.

[2] Peter Mühlhäusler, "Das Englische in Südostasien," in Rüdiger Ahrens, Wolf-Dietrich Bald and Werner Hüllen, eds., *Handbuch Englisch als Fremdsprache* (Berlin: Erich Schmidt, 1995), 49-50.

[3] Ann Dinneen and Peter Mühlhäusler, "Nineteenth Century Language Contact in South Australia," in Stephen A. Wurm, Peter Mühlhäusler and Darrell T. Tryon, eds., *Atlas of Languages for Intercultural Communication in the Pacific, Asia and the Americas* (Berlin: De Gruyter, 1996), 83-100.

[4] Mühlhäusler, Peter, "A Fellow´s Adventures in South Australia," in Philip Baker and Anand Syea, eds., *Changing Meanings, Changing Functions* (London: University of Westminster Press, 1996), 259-68.

[5] Robert Foster, Peter Mühlhäusler and Philip Clarke, "Give me Back my Name - the Classification of Aboriginal People in Colonial South Australia," in *Papers in Pidgin and Creole Linguistics* 5 (Canberra: Pacific Linguistics, 1998), A-91, 35-59.

2. Why a Dictionary for SAPE?

Dictionary makers, as Dr Johnson reminds us, can never hope to be praised. The best they hope for is to escape from blame, and even this is not granted to many. Dictionary makers' chances to get praised increase if the language they work on is at least a recognised language in the sense of having:

a) a bounded political unit within which it is spoken
b) prestige
c) a writing system

None of these enhancing properties are found with what I refer to as SAPE, a label that should not be taken to stand for a single self-contained language. The fact that it is not encountered in the literature should be taken as a warning. What I really mean is all sorts of informal Aboriginal varieties of English, some of which have names such as Cattle Station English, some of which have links with known varieties of Pidgin English elsewhere, and some of which are clearly not very felicitously labelled SAPE, as the political boundaries of South Australia have changed a few times since these varieties came into being. There are reasons, however, why a better knowledge of the lexical properties of the informal Englishes of South Australia is highly desirable:

i) A traditional reason linguistics/philology should be the handmaiden of other disciplines such as historical and literary studies. In order correctly to interpret older texts featuring Aboriginal speakers, it is a help to know that *killem* often meant "beat/hit," that *what name?* meant "who?," or *all the same* "like," *lanty* "a lot." It is also of use to know the number of terms borrowed from languages other than English such as *nanto, yaraman* "horse," *carpee* "water," *oo-ah* "yes" or *mukka* "no, not."

ii) The project further is meant to give temporal depth to the nearly finished *Nunga English Dictionary* (1995) compiled by Philip Clarke.[6] The present day speakers of Aboriginal English will thus be able to trace the roots of their language to the beginning of Aboriginal-European contacts.

iii) It raises the interesting question of the minimum size of a dictionary needed for efficient communication. Ogden and Richards' *Basic English* was meant to do with 800 words,[7] whilst my present draft contains no more than 600.

iv) It is most important for linguists that there is an urgent need to fill a gap in the documentation of Pidgin English in Australia and the Pacific, a gap which severely hampers comparative work, work on diffusion and work on general principles of lexical growth in pidgins and creoles.[8]

---

[6] A. Philip Clarke, The Historical Origin of Contemporary Aboriginal Language in Southern South Australia, MS, South Australian Museum, 1995.
[7] Ivor A. Richards, *Basic English and its Uses* (London: Kegan Paul, 1943).
[8] For the current state of the art see Stephen A. Wurm, Peter Mühlhäusler and Darrell T.

I shall briefly address these questions in the order I have raised them. Before doing this, however, I would like to outline what has been done thus far on this project.

3. The SAPE Dictionary Thus Far

The project arose out of my work for the *Atlas of Languages for Intercultural Communication in the Pacific, Asia and the Americas*,[9] for which a comprehensive corpus of pidgin/creole texts for the entire Pacific area has been compiled, and made into a computer databank which allows many applications in addition to that of mapping linguistic diffusion of informal English spoken in Australia. A number of researchers have compiled similarly brief vocabularies of varieties such as Kanaka English[10], New South Wales Pidgin English,[11] and more complex statements for Kriol,[12] and Torres Strait Broken.[13] For South Australia we are fortunate to have already mentioned Clarke 1995 MS on the lexicon of Nunga English, supplementing the rather meagre information contained in Knight and Ramson.[14] At the same time there has been a considerable amount of theoretical work on the growth and development of Pidgin English lexicons.[15] My own work on SAPE began in 1992 on taking up the position of Professor of Linguistics at Adelaide University. Thus far, the following results of fairly labour intensive archival work have been achieved:

1) A collection of records featuring SAPE have been made ranging from single sentences in large volumes to dozens of pages of connected court transcripts. A significant proportion of these has been entered on a databank for SAPE.
2) A preliminary list of lexical items in all texts has been compiled (a 543 page document), providing information about speaker, location, date and so on.

Tryon, eds., *Atlas of Languages for Intercultural Communication in the Pacific, Asia and the Americas* (Berlin: De Gruyter, 1996).

[9] Berlin: De Gruyter, forthcoming

[10] Tom E. Dutton, *Queensland Canefields English of the Late 19th Century* (Canberra: Pacific Linguistics, 1980), D-29.

[11] Jakelin Troy, *Melaleuka*, PhD thesis, Australian National University, 1994.

[12] T.R. Sandefur and T.L. Sandefur, *Beginnings of a Ngukurr-Bamyili: Creole Dictionary* (Darwin: SJC, 1979).

[13] Anna Shnukal, Broken: *An Introduction to the Creole Language of the Torres Strait* (Canberra: Pacific Linguistics, 1988), C-107.

[14] Anne Knight, "South Australian Aboriginal Words Surviving in South Australian English," in Tom L. Burton and Jill Burton, ed., *Lexicographical and Linguistic Studies: Essays in Honour of G.W. Turner* (Adelaide: P.S. Brewer, 1988), 151-62 and W.S. Ramson, "Some South Australian Words," in Tom L. Burton and Jill Burton, ed., *Lexicographical and Linguistic Studies* (Adelaide: P.S. Brewer, 1988), 145-49.

[15] Peter Mühlhäusler, *Growth and Structure of the Lexicon of New Guinea Pidgin* (Canberra: Pacific Linguistics, 1979), C-52 and Crowley, Terry, *Beach-la-Mar to Bislama* (Oxford: Oxford University Press, 1990).

3) From this unedited list a more structured edited list of about 200 pages is about to be finalised. The main job has been to decide on criteria as to sameness or difference (for example *fella, fellow, feller* or *kill, kill him, killem, killum*), word class membership and whether one is dealing with one or two words (*onefella* against *one fella* two words). The decisions were justified by my previous knowledge of Pidgin English in Western Australia, Victoria, New South Wales, Queensland and Northern Territory, and my having compiled a dictionary of Tok Pisin of Papua New Guinea. Still, it has not been an easy task to make decisions in all instances. Just as all grammars leak, all dictionaries also leak and the status of words can change over time (e.g. *fellow* was a separate word in the 1840s but became an affix in the 1860s).

4) The format that will be adopted for a final will follow the style guide for dictionaries prepared by Pacific Linguistics (Canberra) which has also been adopted for Clarke's Nunga English version (1995). It is intended that the two dictionaries will be published as companion volumes.

4. Applications

4.1 Accurate Information About Past Meanings

The language most commonly used in Aboriginal-European relations was SAPE. While some writers have normalised this pidgin to make it easily intelligible to Standard English speakers, others have not. Historians untrained in pidgin linguistics will experience difficulties with passages such as the following, culled from early manuscripts:

> No cut wood no get tea. Ooah, mucka wood, hungry plenty but not all finished up yet.
> "If you don't cut wood you won't get tea. Yes, no wood, then I'll be hungry but O am not finished yet."

> White woman no fire im little fella mucketty. Him afraid.
> "The white woman does not fire her pistol. She is afraid."

> Pickinniny tumble down, crack aback, and jump up white fellow.
> "The child died, was dead and came to life again as a white person."

> Lanty black fella come up here by n by.
> "Lots of Aborigines will arrive here."

> But plenty breakum coconut and no gammon.
> "He cracked his head very badly, it is true."

Words which will cause particular difficulty are:

tumble down	"to fall, to die"
crack a back	"to die"
lanty	"plenty"
mucka	"negator"

as well as words borrowed from local Aboriginal languages which are found in many pidgin passages, particularly those from the North of the state. The dictionary will provide both translations and information about the history of these words.

Pidgin languages tend to be semantically unstable and liable to rapid change over time. It is therefore important to provide dates as to when words were used in what meaning. Let me illustrate this with the example of the word *lubra* which in present day Australian English is perceived to be a racist term for an Aboriginal woman (as is another term, *gin* or *jin*).

Lubra, according to Troy, is documented first in the Bathurst district in the 1840s and is said to be "Kuntungera dialect for gin or woman" (Troy, *Melaleuka*, 598).

Jane Simpson believes *lubra* to be of Tasmanian origin and brought to the South Australian mainland via Kangaroo Island.[16] *Woman*, *gin* and *lubra* are all documented, with *lubra* by far the most common term. What is interesting is that it acquired its racial connotations only relatively late.

In Moorhouse's *South Australian Gazette*, the term *lubra* is encountered for the first time on 25th May 1844 in a report of a case:

> The native with one eye lifted the spear in an oblique direction close before her, and said 'lubra give me bread'.

The term *lubra* here refers to a European woman, and it is used in a quotation in Pidgin English. In the same year (South Australian Register, 31st July 1844), we find:

> Jimmy and Mary, a native man and his lubra, were charged with having struck and ill-treated John Garan, milkman.

Here *lubra* refers to a black woman and is used in English rather than in Pidgin.

Up to the mid 19th century, the meaning of *lubra* occasionally also was spouse. Among such examples of this meaning, the following one from Snell's diary (20th May 1850) illustrates this point: "They also told us that they had no 'Lubras,' i.e. husbands." Snell in a footnote observes: "'Lubra' was more commonly used at this time to refer to 'woman' or 'wife'."

However, the colour-neutral meaning of *lubra* persists. In the South Australian Register, 3rd May 1852, we found the following extra from a court hearing:

> She endeavoured to induce them to go away by saying that she had no flour to give them; to which one of several spokesmen replied "me no want plour, white lubra fery good."

---

[16] Simpson, Jane, "Early Language Contact Varieties in South Australia," *Australian Journal of Linguistics*, 16, 2 (1996): 169-207, here 177.

A similar use is documented in Hussey:

> Long after wood was carted to town for sale the natives proffered their services to cut it up for a small consideration; and to obtain this employment they presented themselves at the doors and windows of the early settlers with some such application as this: "Lubra, me cut wood; you give me black money picanninie bit of baccy"; again, "you bey good lubra, me bery hungry; you give me some bullocky and bread, me cut wood."[17]

Bolam in 1929 continues to use *lubra* to refer to both Aboriginal and white women: "I once said to a black whose lubra had died recently [...]" and " Toby, my white lubra lose 'em brooch."[18] The modifier "white" in the last sentence indicates that by the time the unmarked meaning of *lubra* was "black woman." That *lubra* had no racist overtones can be seen from the fact that Aboriginal self-reference employs the term *lubra* as for instance in the statements by various witnesses in the famous Willshire case (1891) in the early 1890s:

> Am donkey's lubra, me been sleep along camp, Chiuchewarra and all about lubra been sleep along a me [...]. Am Roger's lubra, native name Irra minta [...].[19]

From the 1920s onward, it is increasingly used with the connotations of racial inferiority, however. Historians will have to be sensitive to such changes when interpreting written documents. Similar problems will face those who carry out oral history, as many older Aboriginal people employ varieties of informal English that are difficult to follow for speakers of white Australian English. Consider the following extract in Cattle Station Pidgin English recorded in the north-west of South Australia in 1995:

> //ˆkunyu//ˆpalumpaˆColin Morton's son//ˆkunyu
> You know, his, Colin Morton's son, you know.
>
> //ˆI bin went back nganaku//ˆMimili//ˆbut that long time
> I returned to us, to Mimili, but that is a long time ago.
>
> //ˆI bin workin' cattle//Mimili//ˆthat's a long time
> I worked with cattle, at Mimili, a long time ago.
>
> //ˆbullocka we bin do cattle work
> With cattle, we do cattle work.

---

[17] Henry Hussey, *Colonial Life and Christian Experience* (Adelaide: Hussey & Gillingham, 1897), 29.

[18] A.G., Bolam, *The Trans-Australian Wonderland* (Perth: University of Western Australia Press, 1929, reprint), 122.

[19] W. Willshire, *Depositions in the Case of William Willshire* (Adelaide: State Records, 1891), GRG 52/90: 46-7.

//^fitj´im fence//^yard//^all these yard
Fix fences, do yard work, in many yards.

//^an we come back^Oodnadatta truck´em//^back
And we returned, took them by truck to Oodnadatta, returned.

Western Desert words such as in the above text are found over large areas of the Pidgin-using North of South Australia. That Pidgin English is still in use today is not widely known. Whilst Pidgin English in the nineteenth century was a fairly visible language, its visibility has diminished greatly since and it is regarded by its users as a language not to be used with white people, as a language to be ashamed of. During fieldwork I found the Cattle Station English to be widely used and known among teenagers in the Pitjantjatjara lands, particularly in informal contexts with members of the family. However, those who develop programs for teaching English to Pitjantjatjara speakers tend completely to ignore this knowledge and instead of using it as a transition to standard Australian English, they treat their learners as second language learners rather than learners speaking a related non-standard variety.

4.2 The Subsequent Fate of Nunga English

The variety referred to here as SAPE has changed greatly since the nineteenth century and like Cattle Station English it has changed from a language of Aboriginal-European inter-communication to a quasi esoteric Aboriginal language. There is ample evidence that all kinds of communication problems can arise if the separate nature of Nunga English is not given recognition in the courts, in the schools and in many other contexts. Having a dictionary and a historical account of the language will go a long way towards enhancing the status of the language and giving it the place promised to it by Australia´s national policy on language. In comparable instances, e.g. Torres Strait Broken, called informal English in 1960, the availability of a dictionary has made a great deal of difference to the status and to public awareness of the variety (see Shnukal, *Broken*, 1988).

Languages have traditionally been regarded as instruments of communication to which more recently has been added the idea that they also function as markers of identity. But neither characterization can be applied entirely felicitously to Nunga English. It is restricted in referential scope and in a diglossic relationship with English and at times it is used as a language of non-communication or deliberate miscommunication with outsiders. One of its main functions is to prevent whitefellows from participating in Aboriginal speech events. To call it a language of Aboriginal identity would be too simplistic, however. This became clear when I discussed the social role of Nunga English with some members of the Kaurna community. (The Kaurna are the traditional occupants of the Adelaide plains). Their language of identity is clearly Kaurna; this goes even for those who have only a very limited knowledge of this language. For them Nunga English fulfills the dual role of expressing regional identity (thus distinguishing South Australian Nungas from the Nyungars of Western Australia or the Koories of Victoria and New South Wales) and, at the same time, that of a buffer against non-Kaurna, particularly whites and more traditional desert dwelling Aboriginal people. Its metacommunicative roles thus mirror those of the traditional regional trade pidgins of North America such as Mobilian Jargon.[20]

4.3 Minimum Lexicon

The quest for the minimum number of words needed is one that has occupied a number of people. It is a practical question for designers of Basic English, World English, Maritime or Aviation Control English, and it is also a question about the nature of the early varieties of pidgin English both in Australia and the Pacific. SAPE in the nineteenth and early twentieth centuries had a total of 600 entries - at any one time probably not more than 400 - as there were many homonyms (*nanto, yarraman // datfella // I / me/ mine // mucka / no // palya / good // muckaty / gun // mia, miamia, worley, house // plenty, mob, too much//*). What is obvious is that the domains and functions of SAPE were fairly restricted, something which reflected social and communicative distance between the members of different races.

4.4 Linguistic Applications

One of the first things I hope to do with my data is to use the list of diagnostic pidgin words developed by Baker and myself for the Pacific area (see Wurm et al., *Asia* for relevant information). At a rather superficial level, SAPE shares only 50 of the list of 100 diagnostic Pacific English words. Absent are words such as *mary*, "woman," *sugar bag*, "honey," *capsize*, "to call," *savey*, "to know" and many more. Those items that are shared in virtually all instances postdate their use in New South Wales and/or Queensland, suggesting that while South Australia was a centre of some local innovation, none of those innovations travelled far beyond its state boundaries. A particularly interesting question is the role of Kangaroo Island which provides a link with the sealing industry of the Bass Straits. It seems likely that both the word "*lubra*," "woman" and "*krak-abakka, crackaback*" "to die" are of Tasma-nian origin. It may not be the case, as Earle opined in 1889: "It is doubtless the custom of keeping the body so long until it cracks or begins to fall away that the native terms now generally used to signify death, viz "tumble down" and "krack-a-back" originated". However, it is a widespread phenomenon in pidgin for words to be the result of cross linguistic encounters and consequently to have multiple etymologies[21] and both etymological accounts may be correct.

---

[20] Cf. Drechsel, Emanuel, *Mobilian Jargon: Linguistic and Social Historical Aspects of a Native American Pidgin* (Oxford: Clarendon Press, 1996).

[21] Peter Mühlhäusler, "Etymology and Pidgin and Creole Linguistics," *Transactions of the Philological Society* (1982): 99-118.

The question of inheritance from other pidgins or local developments is one that can only be decided with quite detailed studies. My first such study, the behaviour of *fellow* as an adjective marker (*good fellow*), number marker (*one fellow*) and demonstrative (*that fellow*), shows that SAPE behaves very differently from New South Wales and other Australian pidgins (Mühlhäusler, „A Fellow's Adventures"). Similarly, the SAPE solution for plural pronouns *me and all together, me all, me and you, you all together*, and so on, are not easily explained in terms of inheritance from other pidgins. This also goes for the incipient word formation one can observe, e.g. *white money*, "silver coins," or *paper yabba*, "letter," though lexical creativity of this type is very much reduced when compared, for instance, to Tok Pisin (Mühlhäusler, *Growth*, 1979).

5. Conclusion and Outlook

Whilst many of the major or central pidgins of the Australian and Pacific area have been well described in recent years there remains a great deal of documentation to be done for more peripheral varieties such as those of South Australia. There is of course a difference between varieties of informal English spoken within the present-day boundaries of South Australia (and they have changed several times in the course of history) and a claim that we are dealing with one (or several) languages bounded by state boundaries. The label SAPE is meaningful only in the former sense - it signals that we are dealing with varieties of informal English spoken in an area that other researchers on Australian pidgins, creoles and non-standard/informal varieties of English have not looked at: there are some quite comprehensive accounts of the pidgin/creole scene of N.S.W. and Queensland, for instance, but S.A. until recently has remained grossly under-researched.

The use of a dictionary of SAPE is primarily for historians and students of literature who wish to interpret texts featuring Aboriginal speakers of English. Linguists will find its most useful feature that the diffusion of individual words (e.g. *lubra, gin*) through Aboriginal Pidgin English can now be better documented. The fact that arbitrary geographical boundaries had to be chosen does not have to affect the usefulness of such an exercise, as Trudgill[22] has shown. To what extent the speech habits documented here can be related to other more focused pidgin and creole varieties remains to be seen.

Finally, the study of SAPE may help strengthen the link between philology/ linguistics, literary and historical studies. While the days are gone when philology was merely the handmaiden to the other two fields, being in the role of a beautiful handmaiden serving morsels of creolist wisdom to the members of older disciplines is not an altogether unpleasing image.

---

[22] Peter Trudgill, *On Dialect: Social and Geographical Perspectives* (Oxford: Blackwell, 1983)

Which ONE: Linguistic Category and Context

WOLF-DIETRICH BALD (Köln)

1. Numerous linguistic studies are available in which the indeterminacy of some linguistic item as regards its category membership has been analysed and has produced the well-known notions of *serial relationship*, of *category squish*, or categorial continuum, and other circumscriptions of the same phenomenon.[1] In such studies syntactic or lexical context has been taken into consideration as a rule, but it appears that phonological context may also play a role which is relevant to categorization. This situation seems to obtain in the uses of the element ONE, if the suprasegmental context is taken into account.

2. The word ONE has received a great deal of attention from historical linguists, traditional grammarians, and also from transformational theoreticians, but they all studied it for at least partially different reasons. To the historian of the language the development of ONE, linked with the indefinite article *a*, the disappearance of the Old English form *man*, and the rise of forms like *atone*, have presented a case study of some basic processes in language.[2] To the transformational grammarian, its pronominal behaviour has provided, among other points, support for the analysis of the noun phrase into determiner and „small" noun phrase (Det + N').[3]

In this study the form ONE will be investigated with its three basic functions of numeral, indefinite personal pronoun, and nominal pro-form. Special attention will be paid to the separation of these three functions, particularly when prosody is taken into consideration.

Method and material are closely interrelated. We shall draw on two kinds of material, authentic corpus data, and examples formulated by the author and checked with one or two native speakers of English. It is obvious that the weight of the evidence

---

[1] *Serial relationship* in Randolph Quirk, "Descriptive Statement and Social Relationship," *Language* 45 (1965): 205-17, *category squish* in J.R. Ross, "The Category Squish: Endstation Hauptwort," in P.M. Peranteau, et al., eds., *Papers from the Eighth Regional Meeting Chicago Linguistic Society* (Chicago: Chicago Linguistic Society, 1972), 316-28; cf. e.g. the study of -ing-forms in Randolph Quirk et al., *A Comprehensive Grammar of the English Language* (London: Longman, 1985), 1290 ff.), or the older study by Jan Svartvik, *On Voice in the English Verb* (The Hague, Paris: Mouton, 1966), on the past participles as adjectival or verbal (esp. 132 ff., 156 ff.), or the notion of conversion relating to the categorial status of items like *love-* verb or noun in Wolf-Dietrich Bald, "Zero Coming to Naught," in Edgar Schneider, ed., *Englishes Around the World: Studies in Honour of Manfred Görlach*, vol. I (Amsterdam, Philadelphia: Benjamins, 1997), 27-31.

[2] Cf. e.g. M. Rissanen, *The Uses of ONE in Old and Early Middle English* (Helsinki: Société Néophilologique, 1967)

[3] Cf. e.g. A. Radford, *Transformational Grammar: A First Course* (Cambridge: Cambridge University Press, 1988), 175.

and the value of generalisations or interpretations have to be related to the kind of data used. This correlation will be apparent in the subsequent sections and need not be detailed here.

With the exception of a few quotations from grammars or other written sources, all our corpus material has been derived from the *Survey of English Usage*.[4] The occurrences of ONE or ONES have been selected - in first stage analysis - from 160 texts, each of approximately 5,000 words in length, i.e. the texts amount to about 800,000 words. 102 texts (i.e., ca. 510,000 words) represent spoken English and 58 texts (i.e., ca. 290,000 words) written English; in this count of spoken and written English we have reclassified and thus changed the Survey classification of 13 texts of written English as spoken, because these texts were read aloud and were supplied with a prosodic transcription.

3. In present-day English an analysis of ONE will encounter a situation that might be called characteristic of this language, in which a single form (if the distinction between plural and singular is disregarded) is employed with different syntactic and semantic functions. It seems that three major types of use can easily be distinguished as is illustrated in the following examples:

(1) (a) numeral
He can already count from **one** to seven.
(b) (replacive) pro-form
They didn't have red apples, but only green **ones**.
(c) indefinite personal pronoun
One should be tolerant with children.

The distribution of the occurrences of ONE and ONES among the three fundamental functions is illustrated in *Table 1:*

Numeral	simple	1,277	1,836
	one of	531	
	one another	28	
Pro-form			852
Indefinite personal pronoun			482
Total			3,170

Table 1

---

[4] This collection of present-day English language data has been described, e.g. in Randolph Quirk "The Survey of English Usage," in Randolph Quirk, *Essays on the English Language Medieval and Modern* (London: Longman, 1968) and in Jan Svartvik and Randolph Quirk, *A Corpus of English Conversation* (Lund: Gleerup, 1980), 9ff. I am very grateful to Lord Randolph Quirk, who as former director of the *Survey of English Usage* gave me free access to the wealth of data collected at University College London.

However, comments in various grammars of English[5] indicate that the distinction between these functions is not always clear-cut if different contexts are taken into account so that a closer investigation is necessary to determine the factors that influence the interpretation of particular occurrences of ONE. Authentic data from educated British English have been gathered, as was pointed out above, from the *Survey of English Usage*.[6]

3.1   ONE as a numeral is illustrated in the following quotations:

(2) (a) |number N ′**one** # and|number ˋ**five** #   S.9.2.d.1
     (b)   as described in Part **One**   W.7.7.50
     (c) |forty 'nine ! ˋSkipton ′Place #|W ;ˋ**one** #   S.9.2.a.13
     (d)   My present employment requires me to give **one** month's
           notice.   W.7.8.57
     (e)   even|**one** old :tartar   :ˋdriver 'said # -   S.6.6.73
     (f)   the|news came !**one** ᵛevening #.|that...   S.6.6.57
     (g)   and we usually have **one** or two such students...   W.17.1.38
     (h)   This included two teaching practices, **one** at school and
           one at a College of Further Education,...   W.7.7.3
     (i)   so that the|peak of :ᵛ**one** 'wave #. coin|cides with the
           !trough of the : ᵛother # - -   S.10.9a.24
     (j)   for the|simple : ᵛreason # that|two 'inside 'servants and
           :**one** ᵛout'side #|full ᵛtime # - is e|quivalent to...   S.1.13.62
     (k) |even to :bandage " !ˋ**one** 'man # - |H ˋproperly #
           would|take at 'least five , ˋminutes #   S.6.6.37
     (l)   on|ˋ**one** occ ′asion # I|got "!so ˋangry #.   S.6.5.51

Examples (2a-c) contain undisputable citations of the numeral. In (2d-f) the element occupies the position of a determiner, shading into the meaning of 'a particular', 'a

---

[5] Cf. E. Kruisinga, *A Handbook of Present-Day English, Pt. II: English Accidence and Syntax* (Groningen: Noordhoff, ⁵1932), 2:283: "The many uses of *one* can best be arranged systematically and intelligibly if, starting from its meaning as a genuine numeral, we show the gradual disappearance of the numerical meaning, until the word ceases to have any meaning at all. We distinguish: (1) attributive *one*, (2) *one* denoting persons; (3) anaphoric *one*." Cf. also Otto Jespersen, *A Modern English Grammar on Historical Principles*, 7 vols. (Copenhagen, Heidelberg, London: Munksgaard, Winter, Allen & Unwin, 1909-49), II, 248 *et passim*, H. Poutsma, *A Grammar of Late Modern English*, 5 vols. (Groningen: Noordhoff, ²1914-28), pt II, sec. IB, 1171f. *et passim)*.

[6] The classification numbers at the end of the quotations give the location of the material in the *Survey*. The prosodic notation of examples of spoken English is that used in the *Survey*; cf. David Crystal and Randolph Quirk, *Systems of Prosodic and Paralinguistic Features in English* (London: Mouton, 1964); some of the spoken English texts have been published by Svartvik/Quirk, *Corpus*, reduced, however, to a few essential phonological features. The bold typing of the element *one* is mine unless otherwise stated.

certain' if it premodifies 'time-words' (*evening, day, year*), and even more clearly with proper nouns like *Peter, Mr. Brown*[7], etc but retaining "much of its original character of a numeral" (Poutsma 1914-29: ptII, sec. IB, 1172) in cases like (2d). The phrase *one month's notice* in (2d) could be replaced by *a month's notice* without a decisive change of meaning,[8] but clearly the numeral value is subdued. The wider context of (2e) also seems to allow the substitution of *a* or *some* for *one*, thus reducing the numerality of the expression:

(2e') I went|back to the ˅front # - and was re|΄ceived # - with|open((ed)) \arms # by|all the : personn΄el # I was "|H very 'very \glad # - even|**one** old :tartar :\driver said # - ...   S.6.6.73

i.e.: even an old tartar driver ... *or* some old tartar driver.

In examples (2 g-j), the occurrence of other numerals or the word *other* in the vicinity of ONE make its numeral character clear, even if, as in (2h), ONE appears on its own. The phrase *one or two* in (2g) may be treated as a fixed expression (cf. Poutsma 1914-29: pt II, sec IB, 1233; OED s.v. *one* 2c), which does not allow a substitution of *a* for *one*. The case is not quite as clear with respect to (2h); a sentence like

(2h') This included two teaching practices, a teaching practice at school and a teaching practice at a College of Further Education

is stylistically cumbersome but not unacceptable. (2h) could thus be grouped together with (2d,e).

In the previous examples the syntactic and the lexical contexts determined the function of ONE. But in the examples (2 i-l) the prosody plays a role in the interpretation as well. In (2 i,j) there is the lexical context of *other* and *two*, but also additional pro-

---

[7] It should be noted that the contextual semantic relationship between ONE and items like *evening, day, year*, etc., is not identical to ONE and proper names like *Peter, Mr. Brown*, etc. In sentences like *the news came one evening that..., We had a bad harvest one year which caused...*, ONE singles out a specific evening or year (of an infinite number of countable times), thus adding to it the meaning of singularity or particularity, while in expressions like *One Mr. Brown called this morning*, the referential uniqueness of the proper name *Mr. Brown* seems to be counteracted by ONE resulting in the meaning 'a certain Mr. Brown', 'some Mr. Brown'. One could perhaps say that the added singularity in the one case and the weakened uniqueness of the other come rather closely together semantically. Cf. Poutsma, *Grammar*, pt.II, sec. IB, 1171ff. It may also be noted that the two constructions admit different substitutes in determiner position: while *one Mr. Brown* and *a Mr. Brown* are semantically close variants (cf. Quirk et al., *Comprehensive Grammar*, 289), *one evening* in (1f) and similar colligations cannot be replaced by **an* evening*, **a year*, etc.

[8] Cf. also *a hundred* or *one hundred* in contexts like *They are a hundred / one hundred per cent certain*. Cf. Quirk et al., *Comprehensive Grammar*, 274.

sodic support for the interpretation of ONE as a numeral: the nucleus on ⱽ*one* (wave), and the prosodically parallel construction of |*two 'inside* and *:one* ⱽ*out'side* [9] emphasize the numeral. No substitution of *a* is possible. In (2k) the "oneness" is underlined by the nucleus on ONE, which forbids any other than a numeral meaning, although no other numerals provide support in the context. Clearly, neither *a* nor *some* can replace ONE here, i.e. the numerality is strong. Example (2l) is of a special nature and deserves a comment. The indistinct lexical content of *occasion* requires ONE as a numeral to make it more distinct, or some attribute has to provide the distinction.

*on one o | cc ′asion # I | got so ˋangry #
*on some o | cc ′asion # I | got so ˋangry #
*on an occasion I got so angry
on a particular occasion I got so angry
on an occasion which all will remember I got so angry

In other words, the prosodic emphasis on ONE is semantically obligatory in this construction with *occasion*.

In (2k), however, the prosodic emphasis may be reduced, which then would allow *a* or *some* as determiners (|*even to 'bandage a man* ˋ*properly #* or |*even to 'bandage some 'man* ˋ*properly #*). ONE in example (2e) on the other hand could receive prosodic emphasis, and would thus be turned into a strongly numeral element, although this would not suit the given context:" ˋone old tartar ′driver said # - but the other (or the others) differed ..."

The following structure should perhaps briefly be mentioned, in which the numeral character of ONE cannot be influenced by prosody:

(3) (a) He gives lectures in **one of** our main courses here..... W.17.2.76
 (b) I'll | just go and 'work in **'one of** the ! ˋstores # -   S.2.12.13
 (c) |and E I !think that E . :this is !**one of** the ! ˋproblems # -S.6.5.105
 (d) : but | ⱽ**one of** them # | has . E: a !little ′tab saying # |D 'K : ˋfiles #
                                         S.5.11.a.83

Whether the prominence of ONE in this construction is uncertain (3a), whether the form is not prominent (3b) or clearly prominent (3c,d), does not influence its numeral function. Prominence as in (3c,d) would be interpreted as contrastive emphasis, *only one of them, but not the other(s)* without affecting the numeral aspect.

The construction ONE OF needs to be neatly distinguished from the following type in which the context requires ONE as a proform:

---

[9] Note the oddity of: *|*two 'inside 'servants and :one outⱽside #* . In (1j) it would be possible to say: *and : one* ⱽ *outside 'one#*, which seems impossible with: **one outⱽside one#*.

(4) (a) | all but 'our /house # | which has !been . E : pre:ˇserved # as | **one** of archi:ˇtectual : \value and #   S.6.4b.32
(b) | so - the !argument has /been # | **one** of | of !words and ! \feelings #   S.5.7.13
(c) the po | litical :reasons in:ˇvolved # ((I mean the **ones** of)) | national pres:ˇtige # are en | tirely 'ones of : \timing #   S.2.8a.7

To summarize, one can state that the function of ONE as a numeral is usually determined by syntactic and lexical context, but may also be weakened or strengthened through prosodic emphasis.

3.2 Replacive ONE occurs in the following examples:

(5) (a) B | will you rem\ind me # to | ask your <u>N</u> \mother # if she's | got an !extra \button # for | that \cape # - -
A | \why # is [I] is ((there)) | **one** !ˇmissing #.
B I | <u>H</u> \lost '**one** # \yester'day # -   S.4.41
(b) NSB will you have a drink
C.. | <u>H</u> \yes # \love '**one** #   S.2.7.3
(c) the | order of /merit # . the com | panion of \honour # - down to the 'service medals # | cam'paign medals # - | ranging from 'one for some :"early 'skirmish in <u>N</u> \Cuba # - to the | Malam 'Kand 'field 'force 'medal and \clasp # -   S.10.5.25

In example (5a) ONE could each time be replaced by *a button*, and is thus the replacive ONE, corresponding to *an extra button* in the opening remark. The prosodic arrangement in (5b) is the same, but here it would be contextually possible to emphasize ONE prosodically :" \yes # | I'd love \one # but | then I need to \hurry #". Usually if people are invited to have a drink they are offered a second or even a third one, so a speaker could turn the replacive ONE prosodically into the numeral to make his or her position clear, which would change the whole syntactic relationship from a substitutive correspondence (*a drink - one*) to an elliptical construction (*a drink - one [drink]*). In example (5c) the prosodic as well as the lexical-syntactic context leave the interpretation of ONE vague, as replacive or numeral, although perhaps the relative prominence of stressed ONE in an unstressed immediate context suggests a numeral interpretation.

In example (5d) the list of three occurrences of ONE results in a more strongly numeral interpretation from the second occurrence:

(5d) B I'm not 'sure of the :two [i.e.wills] in 'fifty \nine #
A | <u>N</u> \I 'see # . | well # - ((let me)) | try and . 'help you a : \little about :<u>N</u> /this # she | <u>H</u> made **one** on the :twenty ! \fifth # of | ˇFebruary # | nineteen 'fifty \nine # | <u>LW</u> /didn't 'she # -
B | well # | that I 'couldn't be <u>N</u> ˇcertain of # | \no # - - -

A |one of the "!\thirtieth # of No| \vember 'nineteen 'fifty W̲ /nine # -

...

and |one - - 'on δi ! \sixteenth of /June # |nineteen 'sixty ! \one #

S.11.1.65

It would have been easy for the speaker to indicate from the first ONE onwards that the number of wills was recounted by saying for instance: "she |made \one on the 'twenty /fifth # ...", and so on.

There seem to be contexts in which not only the presence of a nuclear tone on ONE but the type of nuclear tone seems to be relevant to the interpretation:

(5e) B it's |a. !waste of : \time # |going to a :ˇregistry 'office # *((2 sylls))*
A * | \m #* -. I | don't think 'I've ever ˆ been #
B ((I've)) |been to ,one # it's a |N̲ /drag #   S.7.3f.55

The low level tone (low being indicated by the comma in the transcription), although it is the nucleus, makes a replacive interpretation most likely; a fall, however, would turn ONE into a numeral: "I've |been to \one #" (i.e. one registry office).

The discussion of examples has shown that there is some contextual vagueness even between the numeral and the replacive ONE, which can be disambiguated through prosody.

3.3. ONE as an indefinite personal pronoun is illustrated in the following quotations:[10]

(6) (a) |H̲ well one ! [H̲ \always] :\has /friends like 'this # |\doesn't one #

S.4.3.34

(b) |even 'if one .: walked to one's 'work in the N̲ ˆmorning #   S.6.4a.51

(c) but it |also - ":[H̲ \does sort of] 'make one slightly : \nervous #

S.6.4a.69

(d) but the problem ˇis # does one | have to 'cast 'out :all δi: diagnoses of the psy! \chiatrists #   S.6.5.106

(e) one's |ˇschool # [w E] was of |H̲ prime im: ˆportance to 'one # -

S.6.4a.19

(f) " | I think the :ˇsoft 'options # |make it \harder for 'one in the /end # -

W.5.2.76

---

[10] Only a few typical instances will be discussed here. Cf. the highly informative articles by K. Wales, "Further Notes on Personal Reference in Colloquial English," *University of East Anglia Papers in Linguistics* 7 (1978): 1-10 and "'Personal' and 'Indefinite' Reference: The Uses of the Pronoun ONE in Present-Day English," *Nottingham Linguistic Newsletter* 9 (1980), as well as K. Wales, *Personal Pronouns in Present-Day English* (Cambridge: Cambridge University Press, 1996) for a detailed analysis of the present-day English uses of ONE as a personal pronoun.

The indefinite personal pronoun is used as subject, object, prepositional complement, and attributive genitive. The most obvious characteristics of this item ONE are its structural and its prosodic patterning. It is always completely unmodified (and does not even admit constructions like *There is greedy him again*). Of the 482 instances found in the Survey material, spoken and written, there are 410 in which ONE functions as the subject of the clause; the attributive genitive ONE's appears 48 times, 16 times ONE is the object, and in 8 cases it is preceded by a preposition.[11] The prosodic analysis, taking into account nuclear tone, onset, stress, and boosters as possible markers of prominence, results in the following table:

Function / Prosody	Subject	Object	attributive Genetive	after Preposition	Total
Unstressed	205	8	29	4	246
Stressed	27	-	2	3	32
Onset	79	-	2	-	81
Booster	2	-	-	-	2
High booster	1	-	-	-	1
Nuclear tone	1	-	-	-	1
Total	315	8	33	7	363

Table 2

The large number of unstressed occurrences of the personal pronoun ONE confirms its indefiniteness. Also the frequent occurrence as subject seems to support the lack of prominence, because the subject as the theme of the sentence tends to be less prominent than the rheme part.

The relatively high number of onsets with ONE does not contradict this observation since the onset marks the beginning of the tone unit but is not especially prominent within it, unless it is additionally marked (e.g. with a high pitch, a booster, extra-strong stress, etc.).[12] The singular case of a nuclear tone on ONE deserves to be men-

---

[11] It may be interesting to note that the spoken and the written data show a similar distribution as regards the syntactic functions of ONE as indefinite personal pronoun:

	Spoken	Written	Total
Subject	315	95	410
Object	8	8	16
Attributive Genitive	33	15	48
After Preposition	7	1	8
Total	363	119	482

[12] Cf. Crystal's definition of onset in David Crystal, *Prosodic Systems and Intonation in English* (Cambridge: Cambridge University Press, 1969),143: "In defining *pitch-range* contrasts in both these cases [=direction and range of pitch], it seems best to isolate the range distinction by hypothesising a *pitch constant* [italics mine; WDB] for any speaker. This constant is

tioned especially: it is the level tone, which, because of its non-changing pitch, is not very prominent:

(7) |when **one** # is |looking at m. the :way in 'which 'one - δi |tech"!niques #. by |which one - !N ˇanalyses. | ʹmarkets # ...   S.6.1b.4

The passage is characterized by hesitation and pauses as well as a new start, and the level tone is not conspicuous in this context.[13]

The instances in which the indefinite personal pronoun ONE is stressed, has a booster or even a high booster are always cases in which the context is prosodically either more prominent than, or at least as prominent as, ONE producing the effect that ONE in fact is not prominent. Quotations (6e,f) provide illustrations of such situations: in (6e) ONE has only a post-nuclear stress, and in (6f) the stress is surrounded by two far more prominent dynamic tones. Thus with regard to the indefinite personal pronoun ONE it seems to be the case that the vagueness of meaning which could be observed in relation to numeral and replacive ONE does not seem to recur with the indefinite pronoun. If the function is ambiguous it would be a matter of insufficient context; compare the subsequent quotations:

(8) (a) and |if **one** ! keeps N ʹlow # and |((comes)) through a bit !
  ˇquickish #   S.2.76-32
 (b) al|though it's [the ball or shot] coming at a ! ˋmore even ʹheight #.
  δi the |odd one [:does ˋtend]. to keep: ˋlow #. and |if **one** !keeps N ʹlow # and|((comes)) through a bit !ˇquickish # if you're |on the back N ˋfoot # you've got to be |awful ˋquick #. to |come ! ˋdown on it #   S.2.76-32

In (8b) it becomes apparent that ONE is the pro-form and not the indefinite personal pronoun. The examples in the data do not permit the interpretation of an unclear function between personal pronoun and numeral or pro-form. If an indefinite personal pronoun needs to be prosodically emphasized, speakers can resort to *everyone* or *anyone*:

(9) (a) there's an|ˋother ʹinteresʹting # |ˇside to this # and |that N ˋis that #.
  |N ˋ**everyone** # is |very ˋbusy ʹnowaʹdays#. trans|ˇferring   S.2.4b.37
 (b) I |don't think there's : ˋanyone #   S.2.6.220[14]

---

taken to be the first prominent syllable (the 'onset') of any stretch of utterance definable as a tone-unit.... For any speaker, the first prominent syllable of a tone-unit is articulated at or around a *stable pitch-level* [italics mine; WDB] for the majority of his tone units.... Occasionally, a speaker begins a tone-unit at a distinctively higher or lower level than normal, for a particular contrastive effect... this is taken to be the 'marked' form of onset... "

[13] The level tone has a doubtful existence if considered on a par with the tones involving a pitch change. Cf. Crystal's discussion in *Prosodic Systems*, 215ff.; J.D. O'Connor and G.F. Arnold, *Intonation of Colloquial English: A Practical Handbook* (London: Longman, ²1973) introduced the level tone only in their second edition.

4. It appears that the numeral and the pro-form uses of ONE are still closely related in present-day English, whereas the indefinite personal pronoun is more sharply differentiated. The uses of the first two are not always clearly distinguished, and they can be changed with changing the prosody, while the latter remains separate because prosodically and contextually it cannot be influenced. It is common knowledge in the field of lexical phonology that sometimes stress patterns correlate with lexical classes, as in *abstràct* (verb) and *àbstract* (noun). A comparison of numeral and pro-form ONE shows that there are probably further category shifts which are linked to prosodic emphasis. One swallow does not make spring (or another type of category squish), but probably there are more such instances (*èveryone* vs. *every òne, èach one* vs. *each òne*), which, however, are still waiting to be analysed in their prosodic contexts.

---

[14] Quote from Svartvik/Quirk, *Corpus*, 522, Text 2.6., tone unit 220.

How Not to Get Lost in Literary Theory, Especially Cultural Studies

VERNON GRAS (Washington, DC)

My relationship with Professor Rüdiger Ahrens has been very student centered because in 1985 we initiated a student exchange program between the University of Wuerzburg and George Mason University in Fairfax, Virginia. Since then, we have had two to six students from each institution exchange their place of learning each year. It has been a successful internationally broadening experience for our students that owes much of its initiation to Rüdiger Ahrens' administrative and organizational skills. Over the years, he has kept his eye on the changes that have swept over education in terms of global exchanges, the women's movement, political correctness, and the relevance of literary education to the postmodern condition. In our last venture together, I contributed an essay to his edited book on *Why Literature Matters* (1995). I would like this essay to answer the concern of that title with special reference to his function as the educator in charge of English teacher preparation for Franconia in upper Bavaria.

I

One serious problem that has arisen in teaching literature is the confusing proliferation of stances or points-of-view in the interpretation of literature. The ever expanding self-reflexivity that continually announces further emancipations in diverse modes shows no sign of abating. I regularly teach a literary theory course either on the graduate or undergraduate level. My last effort was an undergraduate course: English 494: The Interpretive Turn. For most of my students this was their first theory course. When they read the case book introducing them to deconstruction, hermeneutics, reader-response, psychoanalysis, structural/semiological, Neo-Marxist, New Historicist, feminist, gender and queer theory, cultural studies, race/ethnic, and multicultural approaches, they retreated into stunned disbelief or dropped the course in panic. I tried to reassure them that despite this proliferating diversity, there was a similarity that these approaches all shared labelled "postmodernism." This common denominator, which amounts to an excruciating self-awareness or self-reflexivity, motivates, structures, and helps create these different approaches. By clarifying this reflexivity historically, I hoped to show its theoretical relevance to the student's own situation. I wanted to simplify the confusion and reveal to the student - who stood bereft of any widely accepted authority but bewildered by the many substitute authorities each offering emancipation and escape from mystification - that literature ultimately could still matter. To offset the stupifying effects of these centrifugal tendencies in literary theory, I presented them with a short intellectual history of how we got here (my version).

BACKGROUND TO POSTMODERNISM

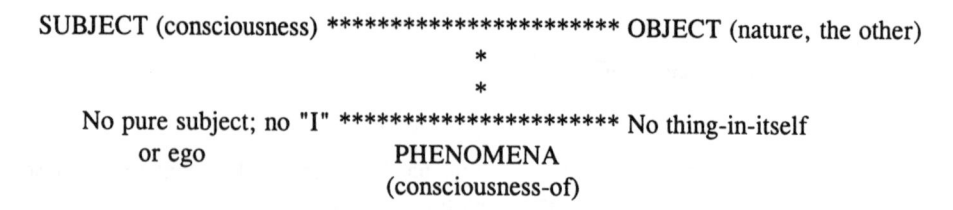

SUBJECT (consciousness) ********************* OBJECT (nature, the other)
```
                              *
                              *
```
No pure subject; no "I" ********************* No thing-in-itself
or ego   PHENOMENA
                         (consciousness-of)

Early in this century, Edmund Husserl followed by his student, Martin Heidegger, established phenomenology as the way through the impasse of trying to ground philosophical systems on either one or the other of the two poles above. The Subject centered systems produced the reductionism of Idealism while the Object centered systems that of Materialism. Phenomenlogy was a meditation on and description of experience understood always as a field wherein the subject and the object contribute equally. Thus, the perceptual field became an "active receiving" process that always included both the subject and the object as complementary poles. Husserl expressed this new understanding of experience in the term "intentionality." Consciousness is never an empty *I think*, a *cogito* without content. This *consciousness-of* relationship, Husserl made the starting point of all philosophy and insisted one could not successfully get behind it.

Phenomenology was an antidote to our habitual natural responses. It wished to displace the "natural attitude," our usual acceptance of things as existing independently in-themselves, by making us aware that things do not so exist but come into existence by and for a subject. An object always exists as a meaning for a subject. Thus, a degree of subjectivity is inescapable.[1]

LANGUAGE

Martin Heidegger changed phenomenology in two important ways: first, he temporalized it and secondly, he shifted from his earlier Daseinsanalysis of *Being and Time* to Language. According to Heidegger, man originates or "founds" the world he occupies with other things by projecting a future on the basis of an inherited past, one that gives meaning to the things-that-are in the present. Such temporalizing of intentionality leads to more awareness of history. If meaning-giving is a temporal process, then truth itself (the meaning of Being) becomes an open-ended, unfinished, historical affair. If there is no escape from having to work at truth from within time and history, the quest may become an absolute, but the truths so found must remain partial and relative. However much it is desired, an absolute vantage, or God's point of view, becomes an impossibility. This insight was to have a direct influence on literature and literary theory

---

[1] See my "Phenomenology and Literature," in *Encyclopedia of World Literature in the 20th Century*, Revised ed., 4 vols. (New York: Frederick Ungar, 1983) for a more detailed discussion of the influence of phenomenology on literature.

throughout the rest of the century. In addition to temporalizing the subject/object correlation, the later Heidegger replaced Daseinsanalysis with Language as mediator. The antithesis between subject and object is overcome in a language conceived not as an instrumentality operating upon pre-linguistic objects of the world but as constituting those objects into a familiar cultural horizon out of which new worlds will be produced which further reveal Being. Language, now "the house of Being," becomes both access and hindrance to Being, in any event an inescapable mediator. Hans-Georg Gadamer, Michel Foucault, and Jacques Derrida, all follow Heidegger in making language (culture) central to any understanding of human existence. Since then all of the human sciences have become interpretive not of "phenomena" but of "language" defined as cultural products whose existence have their beginnings and continuation in an ongoing dialogue of socially shared conventions or traditions.

CULTURE

Literary studies in Europe and later in the U.S. became cultural or discourse analysis replacing existential or consciousness analysis. Because of the denial of the availability of absolutes or foundations derived from either the Subject or Object poles, "truths" of theoretical standpoints also become inescapably historical. Similarly, rules, criteria, and rationality itself become contingent, conventional, and in view of many incommensurable and untranslateable.[2] Foundations disappear. The vertical dimension whether God, Plato's Ideas, elan vital, collective unconscious, or human nature drops out of postmodern discourse. One is left with the horizontal dimension, e.g. dialogical movement or process in which the present reinterprets the past out of which comes the future. One will never cross the culture/nature barrier to encounter Reality, Truth, or any other changeless Absolute or Transcendental Signified. Because of this embargo on referentiality, rational or cognitive claims for language are denigrated. In place of the pursuit of knowledge, language is now seen as motivated by Freudian desire (Lacan/Kristeva), Marxian materialism (with the help of Althusser's "interpellation" and Gramsci's "hegemony"), and Nietzschean will to power (using Foucault's micro-analytics). These irrational desires contribute more powerfully to the meaning-giving process than intellectual cognition. Critiques, when informed by such irrational premises, utilize a hermeneutics of suspicion which moves from surface values of a text to a subtext whose pragmatic interests control the surface or manifest content.

Because of this "loss of center" and with it a growing conviction that what fuels the production of meaning (culture) is never innocent but always motivated, most literary theory and especially cultural studies have become investigations of the social unconscious. Emancipation from the hegemony or dominance of our middle class, capitalistic, white, male, Western discourses has become the common goal of the majority of critics

---

[2] See Alasdair MacIntyre, *Three Rival Theories of Moral Enquiry* (South Bend: Notre Dame University Press, 1990) for how difficult it is to continue the Gifford Lectures before audiences that embrace incommensurability in rational and moral standards.

who speak from the margins. Roland Barthes in "Myth Today" gives a brilliant performance of how cultural critics should expose social discourses (myth).[3] Myth (culture) essentializes. It turns history into nature, it embalms a value or ideology as fact. What is always a motivated intention becomes naturalized into "the way things are." It is up to the critic to demythologize this essentializing process to reveal its rhetorical/ semiological basis. From Barthes' perspective there is only denotative language whose motivations historical situations supply. Language does not reveal nature; it is a process of projecting human desire through "the other" to give it purchase.

The benefits and shortcomings of these many demythologizing interpretations have by now become evident. Unlike studying the natural world, interpreting human beings must have ever changing parameters, at least more open to change than those of physics. The natural world provides a resistance to theory. It has a stability that makes testing out hypotheses possible. The human sciences have no such stability. As self-interpreting beings we are constantly underway, so it is necessary that we change our perspective, enrich our potentialities with imaginative alternatives and more adequate visions. More adequate visions and enrichment of the human potential for women, non-whites, manual workers, gays, and non-western peoples motivates most of the literary/cultural criticism of today. To the degree that traditional values found expression in stifling, even demeaning definitions and attitudes of some against others, such emancipation was and is necessary and salutary.

But there is a deficiency in most of these emancipatory programs. They are based on negative premises. They wish to demystify, deconstruct, and demythologize existing conditions and out of these negative actions, good somehow will make an appearance. At this point, we should sketch in the two main philosophies of language under whose auspices (models) culture (and literature) is analyzed and interpreted:

PRAXIS/PHRONESIS	SEMIOLOGY/RHETORIC
SPEECH ACT THEORY	SAUSSUREAN POSTSTRUCTURALISM
John Austin, J. Searle, H.G. Gadamer,	R. Barthes, J. Derrida, J. Lacan
M. Bakhtin, S.Fish, W. Iser, Charles	M. Foucault, Yale School of Critics.
Taylor, R. Rorty, A. MacIntyre,	Deconstructive feminists, e.g.
M. Nussbaum, Susan Bordo	Judith Butler, Sandra Harding

The two language orientations of the literary and cultural critics above need each other very much like the relation of *parole/ langue* need each other and on which the separation above is loosely based. From my viewpoint, this fork in the road is fundamental for the student to understand. The strengths and weaknesses of the two positions should be clarified in order that students perceive why literature can still matter. I choose the left hand road and encourage my students also to take it because it can operate dialogically with the right side while those critics on the right side find it difficult to incorporate the left without committing a performative contradiction. Those on the right dissolve the subject, the individual agent, into a site where various discourses meet. According to the

---

[3] Roland Barthes, *Mythologies* (New York: Hill and Wang, 1973), 109–59.

deconstructionists, author, work, determinate interpretations are at best momentary points in the eternal flux of intertexuality.

As neither truth, goodness, or beauty exist in the referential mode, textuality (the meaning-giving process) finds its motivation in irrational and unconscious drives which deconstructive procedures can bring to the surface. The denial of traditional values as having any objective existence has been one powerful contributory cause to the collapse of disciplinary boundaries in the Humanities. Instead of self-creating agents pursuing chosen intentions, goals, and values, behavior is determined by social discourses. Culture operates like some vast superorganic which inhabits individuals and controls their acts unconsciously and deterministically. The individual agent becomes merely the place or site where discourses meet. It is the decentered concept of subjectivity that makes it impossible for those on the right (poststructuralists) to account for the future adequately. They are guilty of a performative contradiction because they insist on the impossibility of agency while their own activity of writing, emancipating, and attacking rival perspectives has to presuppose self-determination and choice. In other words, their intention to free readers assumes an agency for both readers and writers that contradicts their description of the prevailing bondage, their specific version of the inherited social unconscious.

Even if one allows the poststructuralists the freedom to deconstruct or say no, they cannot provide any guidance into the future. On what criteria do they choose "b" over "a"? And not the alternative "c"? For some this is easy. They choose their criteria on the basis of what they happen to be, e.g. female, black, gay, non-Western. They assume a political identity based on the contingencies of their birth and upbringing and proceed to fight for their group interests. A laughable irony lies in having them demand emancipation from all systemic closure because truth issues as a precipitate from a point of view - then, watch them essentialize their points of view into a politics of identity. Incommensurability and untranslateablility of positions based on such political identity has become quite widespread. It has become intellectually quite virulent in academic conflicts between cultures, races, and even sexes. Of course, some conflict in viewpoint is inescapable (there is no God's point of view). But total flight from rational criteria in judging value reveals a bankrupt future. Here are some examples of implausibilities (often nonsense) that accrue to those who repudiate reason and embrace the irrationalities of some kind of social unconscious. Edward Said gives both a disturbing and hilarious example of a black female historian taking him to task at a conference for not mentioning living, non-European, non-males in his paper on imperialism. She did not make obvious to him "what their pertinence might have been." But she seemed to imply that merely affirming "the existence of non-European 'others' took the place of evidence, argument, discussion."[4] One has the feeling too often that individual agency and public evidence, argument, and discussion have become victims of incommensurableness and untranslateability pushed to ridiculous lengths.

---

[4] Edward Said, "The Politics of Knowledge," in David Richter, ed., *Falling into Theory* (New York: St. Martin's Press, 1994), 193-203, here 194.

Both Sandra Harding and Judith Butler champion a feminist point of view, but they countermand their purpose by linking it up with deconstructive postmodernism.[5] Sandra Harding divides feminist critiques of science into three classifications: feminist empiricism, feminist standpoint epistemologies, and feminist postmodernism. While she agrees with Susan Bordo that feminist standpoint epistemologies must be embedded in an historical account, she opts for postmodern *jouissance* and that there are no ultimate facts of the matter. Neither does Judith Butler move beyond emancipation. She brilliantly deconstructs the gender/sex relationship in which she proves their arbitrary and conventional connection, that what constitutes being a woman or man has no intrinsic connection with biology or sex at all. In fact, sex itself doesn't escape deconstruction. It is mediated by power relationships like everything else. She, of course, ends where deconstruction has to take her: sex can't be a controlling essence. Remember that for a deconstructionist everything is created out of rhetoric. A woman is what she does; she has no inherent bodily limitations that differentiate her from a man. Masculine and feminine categories are always social and historical constructs and, when substantialized, in need of deconstruction. In her version of feminism, Butler dissolves the body and makes it disappear. Or rather woman is liberated into infinite semeosis; she could assume a certain kind of corporeal style, to live or wear her body a certain way seemingly unhindered by any intrinsic bodily considerations. Considering what patriarchal rhetoric had done to women, Butler's liberation of feminine possibilities is most admirable. But to deny the body so totally seems counterintuitive somehow.

To Harding and Butler, the future seems open to any possibility but neither of them can articulate what a distinctly feminist agenda could be. Both seem to embrace freedom and fragmentation, a joyous disjuncture with the past, made possible by a deconstructive emancipation from patriarchal discourse. I prefer Susan Bordo because she does articulate a possible feminist agenda by contrasting a feminist way of thinking against the masculinist heritage sired by Descartes.[6] She does for feminism what Alasdair MacIntyre did for virtue ethics.[7] She provides an historical narrative which articulates an alternate and compensatory feminist epistemology against the dominant masculine orientation in science and philosophy. She sources this compensation in metaphors derived from the female body and female practices. Her intellectual/cultural history sees Cartesianism as "a reaction-formation to the loss of 'being-in-the-world' brought about by the disintegration of the organic, centered, female cosmos of the Middle Ages and renaissance" (Bordo, *Flight to Objectivity*, 106). And with the death of that world came the death of feminine epistemological values such as sympathy, participation, union with the object rather than Descartes' clarity and distinctness based on separation. All through her historical account, Bordo makes it clear, she is not describing some reified "eternal feminine" or "essential masculine" but giving a partial history of the social construction

---

[5] Sandra Harding, *The Science Question in Feminism* (Ithaca, NY: Cornell University Press, 1986) and Judith Butler, *Gender Trouble* (New York: Routledge, 1990).

[6] Susan Bordo, *The Flight to Objectivity: Essays on Cartesianism and Culture* (Albany: SUNY Press, 1987).

[7] Alasdair MacIntyre, *After Virtue* (Notre Dame, IN.: University of Notre Dame Press, 1984).

of gender (not all forms). Her dialoguing with the dominant other is her effort to establish "the scientific and philosophical legitimacy of alternative modes of knowing in the *public* arena (rather than glorifying them in their own special sphere of family relations)" because only then "do we present a real alternative to Cartesianism" (Bordo, *Flight to Objectivity*,115).

By historically revealing a suppressed feminine way of knowing, Bordo also strengthens two contemporary trends: ecology and literary ethics. The qualities that inhere in feminist thinking - holistic, participatory, embodied - have also found their use in ecology and an aestheticized ethics. With the scientific ideal (stemming from Descartes) of detached objectivity and the purely neutral observer shown to be a mystification, the parallel disenchantment of the world viewed until now as "required by science itself" also comes to an end.[8] The powerful image of the mother as giver and nurturer of life has never departed. Even under the suppression of Judeo-Christianity, she returns as Holy Mother, primary intercessor, and countless churches named "Our Lady." The ecology movement has done quite well in clustering the newly emerging feminine values around itself. Mother Earth deserves a neo-pagan comeback to its primary and earliest glory. Our religious aspirations need revitalization because traditional, patriarchal religions have become irrelevant and unearthly. Science and our planet need to have spirit, mind, and feelings restored to them. The forging of an environmental ethics, treating animate and inanimate "others" not as exploitable commodities but as fellow travelers united together for both a short and long journey, has much in common with literary ethics.

Now comes the climax for those students seeking in literature some relevance to their own rudderless condition. Literature viewed as praxis or phronesis, as the artistic creation of self and world, provides ethical support for our historical, foundationless, postmodern existence. Once again, those critics on the right above have little to offer in terms of ethics. One can't make something positive out of an absolutized negative. I have dealt with the deadend of poststructural ethics elsewhere.[9] But this quote from Zygmunt Bauman renders both the affect and limits of an ethics based on emancipation:

> If modernity, as Jean-Francois Lyotard suggests, sought legitimacy not in the myth of origins, not in a 'foundational act,' but in the future, if living with 'a project' was the characteristic mode of modern existence - that project, that Grand Idea at the heart of modern restlessness, that guiding lantern perched on the prow of modernity's ship, was the idea of *emancipation*: an idea which draws its meaning from what it negates and against which it rebels [...] and owes its allure to the promise of negation [...]. We are kept in flight by the force of repulsion, not the force of attraction [...]. What we want is to get away from here.[10]

The deconstructionists, of course, have gone even further by absolutizing emancipation within the operation of language itself. Language itself forbids leaping the gap between

---

[8] David Ray Griffin, ed., *The Re-enchantment of Science* (Albany: SUNY Press, 1988). See his introduction.

[9] See my "The Recent Ethical Turn in Literary Studies," in *Mitteilungen des Verbandes Deutscher Anglisten* (September, 1993): 30-41.

[10] Zygmunt Bauman, *Postmodern Ethics* (Oxford: Blackwell Publications, 1993): 224-5.

culture and nature. For Derrida and Lyotard, there seems little further use for reason once it has exercised its emancipatory function. The rational progress of the human animal ends with complete freedom from "objectivity," a joyful play that feeds off a total scepticism of any revelatory relationship between culture and nature.

While those theorists who embrace praxis and phronesis accept the impossibility of identifying the cultural with the Real, they do not believe, ethically speaking, that rationality is a lost cause. So, how to ground values rationally when an essentialistic platform is not available? Obviously, we have to be able to discriminate and choose. Where choices cannot be derived from universals, they need to be an embedded self-responsible procedure within historical limits propelled by searching out the better because it is rationally and emotionally available and because it is out there. That is the claim of those theorists (philosophical and literary) who base ethics on virtue and practical reason. Once universal foundations give way to historical standards that eventually will also face replacement, a ubiquitous dialogism emerges that privileges process over product. A greater value is placed on the making of self/world than to arrive at some founding Presence. If historical change and temporality become inescapable, then we must be willing to muddle through without certainties. Gadamer, Taylor, and Rorty all call for a model of meaning-giving that resembles an ongoing conversation or open-ended dialogue.

Used in literary theory, this dialogism turns literature into an aestheticized ethics. Taylor describes art as epiphanic, as "the locus of a manifestation which brings us into the presence of something which is otherwise inaccessible, and which is of the highest moral or spiritual significance; a manifestation, moreover, which also defines or completes something even as it reveals."[11] It is the function of art to articulate, clarify, and shape the not yet known, or dimly perceived, or only vaguely sensed. Getting clear about our identity calls for the articulation of our personal experiences. Literature does this better than any philosophical essay, according to Taylor and Martha Nussbaum. For her, the novel especially, has an intimate connection with ethics. Where philosophy lacks the particularity, emotive appeal, absorbing plottedness, variety and indeterminacy of good fiction, the novel involves the reader as participant and friend. These structural (narrative) characteristics allow fiction to play an ethical role in our reflective lives. They "show the mystery and indeterminancy of our actual adventure."[12] Because experiential living requires the cultivation of perception and responsiveness, the ability to read a situation, to single out what is important -- novels, by exemplifying and offering such lived experience, cultivate in the reader a finer perception and richer responsibility to life. Our moral self-understanding must take form not as a theory but as an ongoing practice of interpretive and critical engagement in concrete situations. If ethical knowledge is a matter of perspicuous articulations, the fine awareness and discriminations needed to pursue this quest for the good find in literary exemplars frequent and necessary re-evaluations of what that goal should be. Under the aegis of postmodernism, our journey

---

[11] Charles Taylor, *Sources of the Self: The Making of the Modern Identity* (Cambridge, MA.: Harvard University Press, 1989), 419.

[12] Martha Nussbaum, *Love's Knowledge* (New York: Oxford University Press, 1990), 44, 47.

will never arrive at the good, at completion. But an aestheticized ethics finds this a great attraction in that "the good life for man is the life spent in seeking for the good life for man, and the virtues necessary for the seeking are those which will enable us to understand what more and what else the good life for man is" (MacIntyre, *Three Rival Theories*, 220).

I hope that this, albeit personal, pedagogical offering will be taken as a further contribution to our international exchange of students, to their ongoing *Bildung* which in the coming generation will broaden and create new selves and worlds.

The Language of Poetry and the Untranslatability of Cultures

MURRAY KRIEGER (Irvine)

I have frequently argued elsewhere, in the face of increasing opposition, that it is important for us still to treat literature as a special mode of discourse.[1] If we should accept the claim that - despite the widely pursued arguments on the other side - there remain good reasons to look upon literary texts as distinctive linguistic artifacts, capable of making an extraordinary thematic impact upon their cultures, what are the consequences for the comparisons among literary cultures today?

As the world of transportation and commerce and international politics has been radically contracted in recent years, academicians in the West have become very conscious of the need to enlarge the realm of their literary subjects and cultures beyond those few interrelated languages to which their competence had for centuries been restricted. For example, most programs or departments of comparative literature have limited their considerations to the major Western, literatures (English, French, German, Italian, and Spanish). Now, under the pressures of a newly constituted global village, these programs, whether prepared for it or not, have been pressed to expand the number and kind of literatures now required to enter the pool of comparison. The major question to be asked is whether they can reasonably expect to be ready for such an expansion, and what readiness would consist of.

I am currently serving as a Principal Investigator of a multi-year project, sponsored by a German foundation and my own university, which is dedicated precisely to this subject and its attendant problems, aiming especially at East Asian cultures and literatures and the difficulties of bringing them into the range of comparative considerations. No one seems to doubt the high priority such newly inclusive studies deserve, in view of the multi-ethnic explosion both within and beyond the collection of cultures that nations today find combined both inside their borders and beckoning from outside. As our project proceeds (we are now at the end of our third year) we find the problems that call for resolution to be only multiplying.

At this early stage of the multi-cultural explosion, Western scholars may well ask, how, with some expert knowledge of the best writings of only a single family of language cultures, they can usefully have the sought-for interchange with other cultures. Robert Frost once defined poetry as that which cannot be translated. Such a notion suggests enormous difficulties in making the highest verbal art of one language system and culture accessible to another. But such difficulties must be confronted, and even partial solutions to them proposed, at a time when the communication and information revolution has, through its technological advances, made the intimate interaction

---

[1] This essay was originally delivered at the Chinese University of Hong Kong as a follow-up lecture to my essay, "The 'Literary' vs. the Political, or the 'Literary' *as* the Political." There I argued for the special function of literature within a cultural politics.

among radically different language systems and the cultures that largely determine them not only desirable but necessary. So we must press the determination of the degree to which texts in the verbal arts are translatable, and with what loss in the fullness of their power.

In other words, as with fine wine, we must worry more than ever about how well a culture's literature can "travel," and with what spoilage or loss of flavor. In apparently alien cultures, whose language systems are totally unrelated to one another and are only now in the process of new claims to relevance to one another (as in the case, for example, of the West and East Asia), one must face up to what can be translated and what cannot be translated without great loss; for we have to choose between the relatively easy task of reading translations, however inadequate, and the much harder task of learning a very foreign language and culture in order to savor the original version of the text.

Western literary theorists, concerned about literary commentary as well as translation, have, within their own cultures, been worrying for some time about what is "unrepresentable" except in the representations somehow set forth in literary texts. The question of what is untranslatable between cultures very unlike one another is a far more daunting version of this problem. Are we talking only of literary texts? What about theoretical texts that have been developed within our diverse cultures, partly in response to the workings of their literary texts? Are our theoretical and critical writings any more likely than our poetry to travel without spoilage? So, even as we discuss the difficulty, if not impossibility, of "faithful" translation, we must wonder about how many, and which variety, of our texts we are talking about?

Behind these questions lies the question about the nature of literary language and whether it differs essentially from what we used to call ordinary or normal or everyday language, in short, from "prose " - meaning by that just about everything that is not "poetry," in the Aristotelian sense of the word as covering all self-conscious verbal fictions. In short, is poetry best treated within the study of other sorts of language or within the study of the other arts? Within Western cultures this has always been a troublesome issue, and, as I tried to show in my first lecture, literary theorists have debated it for centuries, if not for millennia. The pendulum has swung back and forth between those moments in which poetry was taken to be a distinct and aesthetically privileged form of discourse, as an art, and those moments in which it was merged, without being essentially differentiated, into treatments of discourse generally.

I think it is worth tracing the history of this debate, beginning with its early versions in the heyday of rhetoric in late antiquity. There were innumerable handbooks - actually rulebooks - for rhetoricians written by those who followed in the discipline founded by Aristotle's *Rhetoric*, which defined the art of persuasion as it should operate in the real world of action. It was a discipline that could be viewed in distinction from Aristotle's definition of *Poetics,* which was to govern the art of moving audiences through the structure of a created fiction. But for the Hellenistic handbook writers, with their endless lists of instructions for the employment of figures, rhetoric was the only game in town and subsumed poetry.

Longinus, resisting the idolatry of rules in the proliferation of detailed rhetoric handbooks written to tell speakers and writers how to obey them, appears to have written the influential treatise *On the Sublime* in order to insist on the need for an internal spirit that would transcend the rules of rhetoric. He showed examples of the false sublime, mere "amplication" or bombast, when uninspirited verbal formulas took the place of what he called "greatness of soul" or "the power of forming great conceptions," producers of the true sublime.

Central to Longinus´ effort was his pioneering distinction between rhetoric and poetry, establishing for the latter a power to elicit awe in the reader, to make the reader marvel at the representation, instead of - as in rhetoric - merely admiring its correctness. According to Longinus, rhetoric had only to be "credible" (a term not altogether unrelated to Aristotle´s "probable"), while poetry had to arouse in the reader a wonder that would "in every way transcend the merely credible." Here was an early theoretical attempt to separate out and privilege the special capacities and powers of poetry, one that would be taken up, in somewhat similar terms, in the Renaissance by Jacopo Mazzoni.

In most Renaissance and Enlightenment writers (with Julius Caesar Scaliger as the most blatant, and yet perhaps most influential, example), the interest in a didactic aim for poetry allowed the missions of poetry and rhetoric to be joined, since both, seen as equally didactic, were to be devoted to persuading the reader to one sort of behavior or another: rhetoric was to persuade and poetry was to persuade by fictional example. Aristotle´s "fable," a free-standing fiction, was to be transformed into Aesop´s fable, a didactically controlled moral allegory. In this conception poetry was *not* seen as a special form of discourse. There were also exceptions among Renaissance theorists: I have mentioned Mazzoni, and another would be Castelvetro, both of whom, in different ways, argued for poetry´s special role, and hence poetry´s special character. But these represented minority voices.

I skip to the latter half of the 18th Century, when writers appeared who not only argued for a special role for poetry but, for the first time, for a special way of using language in poetry that would differentiate it from other, non-poetic uses. The remarkable Denis Diderot argued for what he termed the "syllabic hieroglyph" and the verbal emblem - notions that, I believe, should not be altogether alien to East Asian cultures, many of whose languages consist of written characters that have some relation to pictures. Here is a quotation from Diderot´s "Letter on the Deaf and Dumb for the Use of Those Who Hear and Speak," in which he distinguishes poetry from the two other major non-poetic uses of language:

> In all discourse in general we must distinguish between the thought and the expression: if the thought is rendered with clarity, purity, and precision, that is enough for ordinary conversation; join to these qualities the selection of words with rhythm and harmony, and you will have the style that is suited to the pulpit [that is, rhetoric]; but you will still be a long way from poetry [...]. In poetic discourse there is a moving spirit that gives life to every syllable [.... through that spirit] things are said and represented all at once: at the same time as the hearing seizes them, the mind is moved by them, the imagination sees them and the ear hears them, so that the discourse is no longer only a string of energetic

terms that expose the thought with force and nobility, but it is a tissue of hieroglyphs heaped up one on the other that pictures it. I would be able to say, in this sense, that all poetry is emblematic.[2]

A bit later the German critic Herder explicitly classified poetry as one of the "sensuous" arts by insisting upon the primacy of its aural character, and consequently its aural effect, which can modify, if not transform, the dictionary meanings of its words and phrases. Another German contemporary, Lessing, argued, in language that should now sound like echoes of Longinus and Mazzoni, that, unlike the writer of "prose" who merely wanted to be clear, it was the poet´s task - even if by some obfuscation, some clouding of the matter at hand - to bring us again into the land of wonder.

I use theorists like Diderot and Herder, followed by German romantics and their English mouthpiece, Coleridge, to mark the final rise of the poetic or the literary to its highest, separatist moment. This notion of poetry as a special kind of language continues and is theoretically deepened up to the middle of the 20th century as we move from Coleridge to Croce to the New Critics in the development of the opposition between symbol and allegory, between metaphor and analogy. This formalist opposition leads to an increasingly contemptuous, minimalizing view of *non*-literary discourse, from Mallarme´s dismissal of it as "newspaper language" to Cleanth Brooks´s definition of non-poetic discourse as restricted to a one-to-one reference between signifier and signified, both of them accompanied on the other side by an increasingly idolatrous view of poetic language in all its internal complexities.

From late 18th-century theorists to those who have been taking this position with greater and greater commitment through the middle of our century, we have an attempt to take poetry out of the common family of language, as just one among many kinds of discourse (history, philosophy, science, and just everyday language) that function as communication by virtue of the meaning of words, and to let it join the family of the arts (painting, sculpture, music, etc. - all the arts that have a sensuous medium to be manipulated). For poetry too, because of the influence of its aural character, now was conceded to have a sensuous medium. Still, of course, it retains its fundamentally linguistic character as well.

Poetry, then, is seen as a discourse that stands in the middle, between language and the arts, partaking of both. Its aural dimension allows poetry to share the sensuous appeal of the visual and auditory - the sensuous - arts while its linguistic dimension allows it to share the intelligible (rather than sensuous) appeal of other uses of language. But since the language of poetry, in view of its aural - and hence sensuous - character that helps shape its meanings, is to be a very special language indeed, among all the other kinds of discourse it now would stand alone, and privileged. And among the other arts it is also distinguished because it *is* language; that is, apart from its sensuous appeal, poetry alone has as its medium words that function primarily

---

[2] Denis Diderot, "Lettre sur les sourds et muets à l´usage de ceux qui entendent and qui parlent," in Assézat, ed., *Oevres complètes de Diderot* (Paris: Gamier-Frères, 1875), Vol.1, 374.

through meanings with which they come laden, meanings derived from other contexts, although they must be transformed in the poem if the verbal sequence is to be converted into poetic art.

Should there then to be a special language for poetry, apart from "normal" language? The claims of these critics should not be confused with the claims that 18th-century English neo-classicism made for a "poetic diction," a special vocabulary reserved solely for the use of the poet. These were standardized poetic phrases, formulaic epithets, many of them found in Pope´s translations from Homer, in which Dr. Johnson claimed to find just about every happy phrase that the English language was capable of yielding. As William Wordsworth was to remind us, Thomas Gray and many poets past mid-century exaggerated this tendency in poetry that was, from Wordsworth on, set aside as stilted and unnatural, the language of books rather than of living beings, not at all what Diderot or Herder had in mind. It was thus important for Wordsworth to insist "that between the language of prose and metrical composition there neither is nor should be any essential difference."

But this outlawing of "poetic diction" did not mean a return to the complete closing of the distance between poetry and prose, the leveling of discourse. For what Wordsworth scornfully termed "poetic diction" - just a fancy substitute for plain talk - was not at all what transitional thinkers like Diderot and Herder had meant by their distinctions between poetry and prose, based on the power of the poetic syllable to transform meanings beyond the ostensible references of words. To these Coleridge, following German theorists in some ways inherited from Herder, added another distinction in his argument with Wordsworth, conceding that, in their diction (the actual words used), poetry and prose might not differ from one another (that is, there need be no separate vocabulary fit only for poetry); but the intensity of the internal relations among words in poems - the additional dimensions of meaning that the poetic context forces upon its words - was such as would add to the possibilities for meaning in a way that is unavailable to a flat prose, whose words are meant to function only via their dictionary meanings. The latter is what Mallarmé called "newspaper language." (We must of course remind ourselves that recent theory has taught us that prose may never be quite "flat," that the sorts of play we have been taught to find in poems may await us wherever we look in discourse. But that is to close the gap again between poetry and the rest of discourse, though this time on grounds consistent with an aesthetics of language.)

It was the introduction of new dimensions of potential effect in the poetic word that came to control the distinction between the language of poetry and of so-called prose. We were moving toward the distinction, enunciated systematically in the earlier part of our century, between language that was used primarily to lead transparently beyond itself - to refer (presumably prose) - and a closed verbal system of internal relations (in poems) that was used both to complete itself and to break through to the complexities of our inner experience. The poetic was to be a verbal system that emphasized the special role of metaphor in poetry and that could thus press toward achieving a symbolic identity, distinguishing poetic metaphor from mere prosaic analogy. From Henri Bergson to John Crowe Ransom, this critical tradition distinguished poetry from "normal" discourse by means of the difference between the approximate and the precise, between the skeleton of the world and the fullness of its experienced body, between the universal and the particularity of the particular.

We recognize a similar theoretical pattern in the terms we commonly find in the attempt of Russian and Prague School formalists to define the effect of poetic, as distinguished from normal, discourse: "defamiliarization," "estrangement" or "making strange," "deviation from the norm" - in short, the violation of how words "normally" are presumed to work. I repeat that, unlike the old "poetic diction," these manipulations of language occur right in the midst of what, until we read it closely, appears to be "normal" discourse. Thus we need critics of poetry, acute readers all, to point out these deviations, these extra dimensions, which create the literariness of the literary, the poeticity of the poetic, for the less acute reader who has been reading prose— Mallarmé's newspaper language - all his or her life. If this were a longer essay, I might pause here to cite examples of ways in which poets used their distortions of the way words work in their attempt to create what we can read as special systems of verbal fictions.

Recent decades have seen yet another swing - this one perhaps the most violent yet - away from literature as an art and back to the assimilation of the literary into the generic domain of language, indeed of all culture, high and low. But the most exciting of these postmodern readers have not undone the specialness of literary ways of playing with language so much as they have been discovering those ways operating everywhere in discourse. This imperializing expansion of the tropological and narratological way of reading only makes any project of translation - the carrying of texts between widely separated languages and cultures - the more intimidating. For now almost no area of textuality seems eligible for uncomplicated transportation. In a theory of language from which, as in the New-Critical analysis of poems, synonyms have been precluded, the old "heresy of paraphrase" is now coextensive with language itself. So locked is each text within its particular verbal formulation, without a neutral substance that can be carried from one verbal formula to another, that the very word *trans-lation* is belied, even if for the words at issue we substitute other words within the same language.

We can ask whether this renewed and radical attempt to reduce all texts to an egalitarian sameness can account for the characteristics of those verbal sequences that, as self-conscious fictions, seem dedicated to the play among their many dimensions of conflicting meanings, all functioning together and at once. But we should defer this question until the next swing of the pendulum back toward poetic privilege. As my survey indicated, history does seem to produce oscillations between periods when poetry and prose are confounded and periods when poetry is given unique properties. It may very well swing back again as the oscillations continue.

It may be too late for most of those in my generation or even the next to work toward the comprehension of what we may think of as exotically unfamiliar languages, but it must be a goal for those who follow us. Surely we all have to acknowledge with some embarrassment that East Asian scholars do much better with our Western languages than Western scholars do with theirs, and this gives them a considerable advantage in *their* attempts at an inclusive comparative literature. They have been doing it while we in the United States are still struggling with the question of *how* to do it.

More than ever now, as more and more texts - and kinds of texts - are being read with an intensity that locks them into their language, our efforts at cultural interchange require original language study to go hand in hand with translation, as we increasingly recognize that a culture lives in and through its language, often in the most delicate and sensitive manipulations of words that create that culture's special vision, its hold on its "reality" - which is what those outside should most want to grasp. Comparative studies of literature are most valuable as they open us beyond ourselves to share those visions, hard as it will be to do so without those languages. Comparatists must not yield to the temptation, in their comparative zeal, of underplaying such distinctness in their desire to bridge differences by the use of easy translations. All of which leaves the special problems with which I began, given our situation in which languages now entering the comparative pool multiply and the distances between them widen immeasurably.

In dealing with each language culture, at the least we must try to learn how their several kinds of writings, poems and non-poems, relate to the language that shapes them and the other uses of that language. Then we may begin the comparative study of the role of language in constituting our respective discourses in their variety and in their sameness. And translation is a highly inadequate instrument for such studies.

What becomes apparent in our attempt to use translation for comparative studies, is that any serious translation of a text in that very act points up the untranslatable as it translates. Thus there are dialectical relations that control the co-existing need both for translation (of cultures as of the language of texts) and for our recognition of the inevitable persistence of that which is untranslatable. We must find a productive tension between these irreconcilables, the translated and the untranslatable, both of which simultaneously exert their control over our efforts.

Indeed it is precisely the inevitable presence of the untranslatable at every moment that makes the project of translation possible and necessary, though as a project whose failure is built into its justification. For it may well be the untranslatable elements that, by virtue of their untranslatability, can direct us to the heart of the culture out of which they issue. Yet how, except by knowing the language, can we direct ourselves to these delicate points? What I have been claiming about poetry's untranslatables projects outward to those intimate cultural ways and experiences - primarily those yielded up by the precious manipulation of language by the culture's poets - that remain beyond our capacities to translate into our own terms. It leads toward, though unhappily not *to*, our understanding of what must remain "other" to us; and thus it leads also to our greater understanding of ourselves.

Riddles of Interdisciplinarity: A Reply to Stanley Fish

GEORGE ROUSSEAU (Aberdeen)

Post-Foucaldian disciplines alter — the more recently and under the sway of virtual and cyber realities, the more discontinuously. Old professional allegiances die off and what was stable a few decades ago is now no longer palatable. This is not to deny continuities of many types, many extending back to the European Renaissance and Enlightenment, but the question about allegiances in the "new English departments" at the millennium and the nature of English studies themselves is rarely asked. When it is, the diaspora of replies is ambiguous, even disturbing. A group of responses — virtual set-replies — proves standard: including the conventional ripostes about the unstable canon, the diversity of a faculty's intellectual approaches, and the so-called disparate ideologies and methodologies of the discipline still oddly known all over the world as "English."[1]

During philosophical conjectures about generations of faculties, patronage and professionalism, self-interest and faith sometimes enter the debate, as do concerns about collective allegiances to any unifying or binding center no matter what the institutional labels: English, English Studies, English and American Studies, and — in the country in which I now reside, Scotland — English and Scottish Studies. The inevitable consequence appears to be a diminishing degree of bonding among younger members of departments, especially recent recruits, who find themselves confused and alienated in a sea of plurality while trying to carve a niche for themselves. A plurality of issues face these disputing and disputatious cadres — too many to be addressed adequately in private rooms, let alone in open departmental chambers. However, among these alienating topics few have been more unsettling to those who reflect on them in our time than that of *interdisciplinarity* : a hotbed of debate among scholars of all types, the darling of professional administrators who fund these scholars and their programs, and the taxpayers who empower the administrators to fund the scholars. The word itself — *interdisciplinary* — is perplexing: the rhetoric and sign of a new wave of English studies ranging from culture and media to 'English and other disciplines' (anthropology, philosophy, science, technology), 'English and computer studies,' as well as

---

[1] The resonances and textures of words *interdisciplinary*, *transdisciplinary* and *multidisciplinary* would make a chapter in themselves; here I merely note the obvious: that interdisciplinarity occurs only when the border between *two* disciplines is crossed, i.e., astronomy and physics (which already has a name: astrophysics); biology and chemistry (biochemistry); literature and medicine (lacking any institutional endorsement except as a vague and homeless *medical humanities* it has no single name as do the others). Alternatively, an approach to Shakespeare that draws on disparate materials but which remains firmly grounded within a Faculty or Department of Literature is in this usage not interdisciplinary. The condition then for interdisciplinarity is that the investigator-researcher must cross the border into another department or faculty - the widely accepted usage throughout North America.

literary applications in the realms of hypertext and virtual reality. English scholars, however diversely trained now and loosely organized, differ from other academics in one monolithic way: a very large number believe they can teach *other* disciplines, as in 'English and other disciplines,' and display little reticence in so doing. Few in other fields would. Even historians, who may be vulnerable to the same charge, continue to adhere to the principle that archival research is essential; and few historians anywhere would stake out the claim that they had genuinely unearthed an area unless they had uncovered its archival traces. Only the so-called historians of ideas, now usually classified as philosophers or theorists, would be so daring.

I

No one has written more insightfully and cautiously, if also more skeptically, than Stanley Fish about the implications of contemporary interdisciplinarity.[2] Not about a specific historical version or national variety or school within its applications, nor as the result of Fish himself having generated a unique approach; but rather about its epistemological profile, its so-called plurality of meanings, practices, and implications for those claiming to perform it, as well as those already professing to have been converted to its methods and codes. This Fish has accomplished in one crucial section of *There's No Such Thing as Free Speech*.

Fish's section title denotes his main assumption: "Being Interdisciplinary Is So Very Hard To Do."[3] In fact he seeks to demonstrate that it is "impossible," for reasons that are logical and epistemological, rather than inherently ideological or professional. The paradox, however, lies in the way in which Fish's professional career seems to endorse interdisciplinarity, to such an extent that one would have expected him to be one of its most ardent champions. Thirty years ago he began professional life as a traditional critic of seventeenth-century literature exploring the works of Milton, Herbert and the metaphysical poets, and has now, after many moves and career migrations, become Professor of Literature and Law at Duke University, occupying much of his time with the nature and ramifications of legal evidence rather more than seventeenth-century English texts. However, Fish is not a trained lawyer or attorney and has never, to my knowledge, tried a case, although he may have served as

---

[2] Stanley Fish, "'Being Interdisciplinary Is So Very Hard to Do,'" *There's No Such Thing as Free Speech* (Oxford: Oxford University Press, 1994), 231-42, which originally appeared with the same title in *Profession* (1989): 15-22.

[3] The weight of the subtitle gathers force in the ambiguity of "hard;" nevertheless it is crucial to recollect that at the time Fish was gathering his thoughts about this matter in 1985-88 the leading American universities were charging ahead with the making of interdisciplinary-based appointments to senior professorships and it appeared as if the *traditional* disciplines (English, modern languages, philosophy, etc.) were coming under the threat not of extinction but challenge from the new interdisciplinary methodologies. A decade later, in c. 1998-99, there now exists such a vast literature on this subject it is virtually impossible to document it or even list in major bibliographical works.

an expert witness. Yet he claims competence in the law and obviously believes he can teach it in the Duke University School of Law. Such filiation may seem inconsequential: what after all is the difference between teaching in one school or several? Why does the variety even matter? It would not matter if Fish had accounted for his migration from English (institutionally) to English *and* Law as the result of either two *discrete* interests (i. e., 1. literature, 2. law) or as a spilling over from the one to the other, hence an interdisciplinary move, or at least interdisciplinary gesture. But Fish has never claimed the former and has recently made the paradoxical claim (regarding the latter) that he is *not* an interdisciplinary scholar despite his coverage of two fields (literature and the law) and professorship in two faculties. Indeed, his main purpose here lies in demolition of the interdisciplinary prerogative and its shabby epistemological foundation. But by "very hard to do" Fish means "hard to bring off" on logical and epistemological grounds, rather than as the result of any fundamental crack inherent in the approach itself. He denigrates neither its apparent professional gains — contemporary theory, after all, is innately and necessarily *interdisciplinary* merely by virtue of its stratospheric philosophical threshold of argument — nor the dramatic, even comic, posture of assuming another academic type, say the English scholar as dilettante or *anti*-professional.

Nor is Fish interested in interdisciplinarity's historical trajectory: the *longue durée* so pivotal to understanding what it has been, and why it continues to be so charged and controversial. Even in recent history, it was an essential core of the whole Enlightenment agenda for understanding man and his progress in relation to their global Others. More recently it has been the American academic brand *par excellence*: virtually synonymous with the best of America's trailblazing scientific and humanistic research; the national insignia of its cutting edge of recognized new knowledge. Nowhere else in the world do so many scholars in more fields continue to claim that *single* disciplines — discrete fields — cannot solve their hardest problems. The fact, then, that late nineteenth-century German philosophies of education, which were inherently interdisciplinary, formed the basis of the modern American university, or provided it with the models for development, has no interest for Fish. Instead, he wants to demonstrate the hurdles of interdisciplinary activity. Impediment rather than natural step, treachery rather than easy passage, is his subject.

Fish's hypothesis about sheer "difficulty" can be expanded to take in other areas of knowledge, a desirable state of affairs in my view if we are to put what he means, or at least thinks he means, to the test. It can be extended not merely to fields within the humanities but to the applied and natural sciences, such as biochemistry, sociobiology and astrophysics (all inherently interdisciplinary), as well as to the new areas of computer engineering and broadly based biomedical technology. Fish's argument about sheer "difficulty," moreover, can, and should, be widely applied to those who work in any historical epoch, whatever the subject. In this sense, his argument is unfettered to historical scholars who toil in one era rather than another. But his specific caveats and their necessary consequences are made more acutely in reference to particular subjects of knowledge: literature, law, ethics; less so to history or philosophy, for reasons I discuss below. And I propose to explore his reasons locally within English studies because he himself began there, so to speak, and to attempt thereby to understand exactly what he intends by describing interdisciplinarity as "so very hard to do."

II

Fish claims that all "interdisciplinarians" are dissatisfied with the status quo and keen to topple it:

> It is fair to say that they are all alike — *all hostile* to the current arrangement of things as represented by 1) the social structures by means of which the lines of political authority are maintained and 2) the *institutional* structures by means of which the various academic disciplines establish and extend their territorial claims [italics mine][4].

Thus Fish rhetorically reduces the entire tribe — already politically tainted — to an odious similitude: "they are all alike." But who are *they*? Within the context of the contemporary research university this implied authority and territory extends (downwards) from president, provost, vice-chancellor and assistant vice-chancellor, through the hierarchy to deans, professors, junior and part time faculty. The hierarchical ladder and its authoritative zones are perhaps self-evident, as is the pervasive sign of the territory or border in Fish's mindset about interdisciplinarity. But Fish then claims that "often this hostility takes the form of antiprofessionalism, an indictment of the narrowly special interests that stake out a field of inquiry and then *colonize* it with a view towards nothing more than serving their own selfish ends" (Fish, 231). This imperialistic gesture articulated in ideological code language ("serving their own selfish ends") is understandable given that specialization within the academy has had such an extraordinary history over the last century, and insofar as contemporary "colonization" is today more self-righteous and less abashed than it has ever been in English studies. Besides, the colonizing tendency has infiltrated our entire culture (ponder all the varieties of hostile takeover in corporate America and Europe), and can thus hardly be accounted as a designatory, let alone unique, feature of academia. Many businesses, even national charities and nonprofit organizations, are also "colonizers" in Fish's sense. Why should those living by their intellects be immune from such tendencies? Much post-colonial theory publicly vaunts its goal to graft itself onto other fields; to aggrandize itself not merely in the name of national policy-making, as in North American and Western European national science and education policy, but also at the level of governmental social reform. When governments legislate national higher education policies they colonize their citizens by deciding what they (the government) will receive in return for subsidy. To discover — for instance — that "thick-description" (in anthropologist Clifford Geertz's phrase as deep-layered discursive explanation) is a fundamentally *interdisciplinary* concept is hardly an indication of its

---

[4] Unless otherwise noted all passages in quotations are Fish's; my own emphasized words appear in italics and are not designated in every case as they are here.

ontological status *apart from* contemporary culture, let alone the basis for any kind of condemnation. It is merely interdisciplinary by virtue of its applicability and spill-over. Its ontological status has nothing to do with spill-over.

Fish next extends his argument from social authority to the realms of the natural and ideological:

> At the heart of that argument is the assumption that the lines currently demarcating one field of study from another are not natural but constructed by interested parties who have a stake in preserving the boundaries that sustain their claims to authority (Fish 232).

His argument from nature and natural domains, in the old Puffendorfian sense of the evolution of natural law as inherently the most satisfactory of all available systems or bodies of law, is less well developed than that on the social construction of the disciplines. On the latter — the historical development of the disciplines — Fish's case can be better demonstrated. Historically the disciplines have evolved in proximity to the needs of the sources of social power, as even Foucault demonstrated. No one needs to roam further afield than to the origins of the university institutionalization of history as a playing field for the making of European, and especially English, gentlemen. Still, disciplinary history and (more generally) post-disciplinary knowledge in our time have rarely asked whether, and in precisely what sense, the trivium and quadrivium were "natural" arrangements. Even casual observers, like Fish, continue to claim that the boundaries of disciplines are drawn and framed without indicating on what authority — hence Fish's social construction - *merely* to sustain authority. Has there been no natural curiosity? Has there never been pleasure in education? Is there no personal maturation and growth? Is there not an aesthetic and even symmetrical rationale in the evolutionary formation of the Medieval trivium and Renaissance quadrivium? Whether or not, Fish resists the tampering with "boundaries" or "borders" on grounds that it disturbs the natural order.[5] But the "authority" to which he refers derives entirely from individuals having been trained *in* subjects; having been given a union card, so to speak, to practice the subject and teach it to others. Fish responds not to beauty or form, but to power. Hence the logic of the method by which one is trained *in* a subject

---

[5] The 1990s immersion in the border or boundary as a critical category and its implied margins (places lying on or near borders and thereby extremely worthwhile for exploration as the contested sites of dispute), has infiltrated virtually every aspect of literary theory and interpretation and will eventually be the subject of historical inquiry of the sort: why this generation? why this decade? why this signal feature of postmodernism? It requires no profundity of insight to recognize that the drive is the result, in part, of a late scientifico-technological era that has become disenchanted with the normal processes of collecting, classifying, organizing, labelling, and then, based on these prior activities, spinning hypotheses: the normal route of science. Our critical theory since c. 1970 is as scientific as it has ever been. See for example the obsessive role of these metaphors of borders and boundaries in the recent generation of the concept of metafiction; M. Currie, ed., *Metafiction* (Longman: London, 1995), or, alternatively, theoretical explorations such as R. Markley, "Boundaries: Mathematics, Alienation, and the Metaphysics of Cyberspace," *Configurations* 2:3 (Fall 1994): 485-507.

and then said to have mastered it naturally: because power condones authority. This "authority" constitutes the basis for jobs, of course; sustains posts in higher education especially in the contemporary tenured-in university where appointments are made for life and from which posts it is almost impossible to be deposed or made redundant on grounds other than economic ones.

Still, Fish proceeds much further than this. "The structure of the university and the curriculum," he continues, "is a political achievement that is always in the business of denying its origins in a repressive agenda" (Fish, 232). Historically the claim is spurious. It may be a "political achievement" *in part*, but it is also much more than that. Even the modern post-1950 curriculum reflects more than local politics and power. Its interdisciplinarity responds to genuine intellectual need (as in biochemistry or sociobiology) and mirrors much more than monolithic repression. Indeed, it inscribes global knowledge as that knowledge evolves in social institutions *larger* than the academy of higher education, even if admittedly carved up in academic specialties. Fish's point can only be substantiated by consulting the relation between knowledge within and without the university — that is, an artificial boundary demarcating knowledge *in* society *apart from* universities. However, this accomplished, it would be evident that disciplinary classifications exist there as well: medicine, theology, the law, mathematics, botany, linguistics, etc.

Fish's anti-ontologism, as it were, permeates his mindset. He refuses to acknowledge differentiations in the natural world: that astronomy and oceanography exist, for example, because a galaxy is not a star fish. And he takes less care than any competent philosopher of science would in distinguishing between the natural and the man-made universe. Precisely because the humanities are man-made, it is easier to deny their objectivity. Even so, a poem is not a philosophical treatise, and the consequence of the difference ought to be of tremendous interest to Fish. For it is preeminently in the humanities — in the loose, soft, and in our time highly ideological and thereby vulnerable arts — that Fish's point gains momentum. His angle of vision is also determined by a late twentieth-century notion of the North American university as a metonymy for the humanities; an odd position for one who apparently moves as easily among lawyers and law schools as among writers and literati.

Fish turns next to modern interdisciplinarity in the light of self-reflexivity. What do we *think* about what we now know? What do we *think* of those who do not reflect on what they know? The issue is reflection in relation to jobs and economy yet Fish pronounces from on high; far above those who must work within the system. Fish chastises:

> One who uncritically accepts the autonomy of his or her 'home enterprise' and remains unaware of the system of forces that supports and is supported by that enterprise will never be able to address those forces and thereby take part in the alteration of that system (Fish 232).

This is true: academia is permeated with the passive and unknowing types Fish describes. But why assume that those who "understand them" will address these forces? It is one thing to understand the forces historically and intellectually, quite another to attempt to alter them by placing one's job and source of economy in jeopardy. The contemporary academy, like the contemporary corporate sector, is permeated with yes-men — and now yes-women — who understand but will not act. For Fish to make self-reflection *qua* reflection an end in itself appears misdirected unless further conditions are to come.

Furthermore, "the system of forces that supports" the individual disciplines was not always lodged in the authoritarian and — according to Fish — "repressive" precincts of the university. Monasteries and clerical orders predate the rise of the medieval university. To deny, or neglect, the consequences of these origins is to seriously misconstrue the toll of history in the shaping of the contemporary university. Much more recently (and many of us forget just how recent English *is*), the subject now vexedly known as "English" offers another case in point. A recent discipline in its current incarnation as separate from rhetoric, logic, *belles lettres*, and philology, English fought hard to establish hegemonic departments for the study of language and literature barely one century ago. The detailed and differentiated "histories" of these departments and their relation to their universities has never been adequately reconstructed, although much work is now in progress: in part because English departments have only recently recognized (in the 1980s) the importance of their local histories; in part because the primary documents on which authoritative histories could be compiled have sometimes been withheld by the institutions themselves on grounds of confidentiality. The archival material is generally difficult to assemble or nonexistent owing to oral decision making. Finally, because the reconstructive historical task necessarily deals with the interdisciplinary dimension of institutional history, a field most literary scholars as distinct from historians of institutions such as universities consider peripheral and even irrelevant to themselves.[6]

Yet English studies are not alone in their plight. The social sciences possess a disciplinary history in the last century even more fraught and charged. The institutional opposition to their incorporation was fierce by any mode of comparison. Unlike the allegedly character-building discipline of history, they produced no "gentlemen" — their enemies said — and could not even claim to be "repressive" of anything. But if we succumb to Fish's version of history, we have in sociologists and anthropologists today mere passive and ignorant puppets because they do not "self-reflect" about the disciplinary possibilities of their subject. Are we really to think that a mainline sociologist or anthropologist today, satisfied to work within his primary discipline, is some type of non self-reflecting conservative, when so recently this noncanonical parvenu (sociology) could not be admitted into the university's curricular framework?

I think not. Other cases could be cited but, if anything, my critique of Fish may be too generous to the degree that it confers special value on the act of self-reflexivity

---

[6] The point is that the context has been too narrow and needs to view the history of this institution (i. e., the university) in a larger sweep than, for example, Jacques Derrida does in "The Principle of Reason: The University in the Eyes of its Pupils," *Diacritics* 13:3 (Fall 1983): 3-20, insightful as he is there. Furthermore, in North America race, religion and gender have occupied new positions of central authority in these debates about the internal content of disciplines.

itself without requiring the reflector to convert that wisdom into action. All manner of *non*-interdisciplinary scholars are profoundly "self-reflective" about their monodisciplinary allegiances without wanting to build bridges among disciplines. Their deep-layer psychological reasons, if analyzed, would embrace work-related and non work-related reasons. But Fish overlooks or dispraises missionary zeal and challenge; or (to change the metaphor) underestimates the bonding that occurs among researchers cemented by, and through, interdisciplinary gestures. Instead, he views the interdisciplinary approach within the terms of *defect*: as lack of self-reflexivity, as unquestioning of the true centers of power and authority, and, in his last and deadliest caveat, as a transgression (an act of defiance) within the realm of professional boundaries. Boundaries intellectual, economic, social, even inviolable borders of class and sex, as in radical feminist contemporary interdisciplinarity.

III

The metaphor of the boundary or border has become one of the insignias of our generation: a concept now so vibrant that conferences are devoted to its significations. The dissolving of boundaries has now taken on a life of its own — evolved into something more than a dominant trope of the contemporary academic mindset: it has become that mindset *itself*, bursting out of the chains of disciplinary arrangements and imagined academic expectations. Eventually the historians will explain what this boundary movement amounts to and why it appeared at the end of the twentieth century as part of its *fin-de-siècle* culture; will account for its chief anxiety lodged in the role of history within cultural representation. This last — history within cultural representation — has become both its energized plaything and feared Leviathan. But all its energy is monodirectional: towards dissolution, the *breaking down of borders*, never their construction or resurrection. Ours is a borderless age tortured by peripheries of every type, with most of us living on the edge.

In the 1980s Baudrillard claimed that the 'simulacrum' (or copy) is both the benchmark and hallmark of postmodernism: in its cities and especially in millennial, super-technological America where the copy is defined by, and measured on, the borders.[7] Postmodern suburbs — the mall, the desert, all the city limits whose attractions rival and even exceed the lure of the city's insides. The decay of inner cities had much to do with this perception, and urban renewal has no doubt altered the perception of city center and city limit.

Even so, a new kind of life exists today on the peripheries. Life on the edge (the metaphor as well as the geographical reality) privileges peripheries and borders as never before. Applied to postdisciplinary intellectual life, however, the same postulate holds water: postmodern institutional life, as well as natural curiosity, thrives on bor-

---

[7] J. Baudrillard, *The Mirror of Production*, trans. M. Poster (St. Louis, MO: Telos Press, 1975); J. Baudrillard, *America* (London: Verso, 1989); J. Baudrillard, *Simulations*, trans. Paul Foss et al. (New York: Semiotext(e), 1983).

ders and boundaries in ways it could not if it were to exist solidly within the center of the disciplines. This is why civic administrators and government ministers who decide funding are so crazed about, and predisposed to, a type of social interdisciplinarity: they perceive that "action" lies "out there" on the border. Our collective social flight to IT virtual reality — the radical extreme of interdisciplinarity in an informatics society, as MIT's Sherry Turkle has recently shown[8] — is but one example among many. Baudrillard and his derivative postmodernist theorists have provided less spectacular illustrations drawn from technological realms and radical forms of town planning, as in architect Frank Gerry's postmodern configurations of a twenty-first century Los Angeles.[9]

But what is the reconstructed interdisciplinary postmodern city if not life lived on the edge — on the boundaries — of the traditional disciplines? Such literally are its daily diversities, pluralities, tempi, blends, boundaries, city limits, that it is folly to claim these are mere metaphors: the shadowy chimera of armchair theorists or university scholars. They are metaphors as well as something else. Those who actually *dwell* in postmodern cities like Los Angeles or London, Singapore or San Francisco, New York or Sidney — postmodern as the result of their sheer degree of cultural diversity and the heightened intensity of their simulacra (copies) indistinguishable from originals — know they are not merely metaphors.[10] Yet postmodern geographical "boundaries" (especially within the contemporary workplace) are often mistakenly confined to abstract realms or at least to things knowable, despite their physical extension beyond the borders of the intellect.

An excursus makes the point. For example, no society in history has ever been more concerned than ours with notions of, or equivalents to, the *appropriate*. The appropriate gesture today exceeds any domain of mere manners; extends far beyond Enlightenment notions of decorum capable of being satirized, for example, by a contemporary Jane Austen in domestic comedies of manners. The new trend incorporates *limits* given its widespread usage to designate an unknown strain of action in public in a psychologically desolate (and depressed?) postmodern world unable to cope with strains and stresses.

In this sense the *appropriate* has profound affinities with the dissolving of boundaries. Curiously though, almost nothing substantial has been written about its recent striking appearance and wide acceptance especially in view of the swift legal trans

---

[8] Sherry Turkle, *Life on the Screen: Identity in the Age of the Internet* (New York: Simon & Schuster, 1995). For the informatics and literary theory see *Configurations* 5:1 (Winter 1997).

[9] Mike Davis, *City of Quartz* (New York: Vintage, 1993).

[10] See Edward Soja, *Postmodern Geographies : the Reassertion of Space in Critical Social Theory* (London: Verso, 1989); idem, *Thirdspace: Journeys to Los Angeles and Other Real-and-Imagined Places* (Oxford: Blackwell, 1996); S. Watson and K. Gibson, eds., *Postmodern Cities and Spaces* (Oxford: Blackwell, 1995). This choice of cities is problematic for smaller cities only. No one will dispute Los Angeles or Singapore but smaller European all exists on a continuum of postmodernism.

formation of America in just one generation from Watergate to Clintongate. The *appropriate* and its opposite, the *inappropriate*, seem to have sprung full-blown from nowhere like a fully mature virus.[11]

The word itself bears the most curious recent dictionary history and political geography.[12] Only recently has its usage moved almost entirely into the moral realm; hence the new colloquial *appropriate* behavior, *appropriate* designation, *appropriate* decision, and already partaking of legal teeth. Indeed, the *appropriate* frame of mind invades and haunts every space within the postmodern ethos because the law always remains a step behind it. If it had caught up, the *appropriate* would be unnecessary. *Au fin* the contemporary "appropriate" is not a metaphor (although it is that too) but a geographical and psychological reality. North American political correctness, for instance, dies without it, because the appropriate gesture always assumes an *unwritten* code of acceptable social behavior *before* it can be legislated into written codes. Once written and tested the limits of the appropriate are less relevant. The law cannot catch up, so to speak, with its boundaries and legislate their (the norms') centers. The salutary consequence within the new category of the "appropriate" lies principally in the public, even political, domain, without effect behind the bedroom door or under toilet seat. Moreover, the appropriate public gesture can be objectively gauged, it seems, by marketplace consent. It captures the bleak postmodern sense that human relations have been strained to a breaking point that has finally mandated this new radical version of respite. All of this profoundly bears on Fish's transgressive interdisciplinarians.

Yet the "appropriate" must not be confused with the "normative," for which there have always been standards based on values throughout history, elusive as they are to reconstruct, and only a naif would construe the new amplification and energization of *the appropriate* as the reification of the old norms now gone sour. One might as well configure the internet as a three-dimensional telephone. On the contrary, the "appropriate" action or behavior as a new psychological space exists *despite* the continuance of the old norms. It exists because they have been stressed and thereby enervated to the point of moribundity. Psychological space, like other geographical borders, is not a figurative construct: when people who work ten feet apart will only communicate by electronic mail in workplaces where free centrex telephones operate, one must inquire about the "borders" of postmodern human relations — and even the human voice. The *appropriate* is now an internal barometer by which — for example — half the English people would be adjudged *in*appropriate, if not patently or dangerously eccentric by virtue of their disobedience to its unwritten codes. Eccentricity in Britain, especially among intellectuals, retains positive valence: something exotic worthy of cultivation. The *appropriate* gesture in America now also represents a contraction of territory construed symbolically and psychologically, in order to curtail freedom within public spaces. Yet here specifically lies its untested double standard: that it had to be in-

---

[11] See n. 16.

[12] The closest definition of "appropriate" offered by the *Oxford English Dictionary* to our discussion is "specially fitted or suitable, proper." The word's transformations up to 1989 do not recognize this more recent legalistic meaning, which is doubtlessly a phenomenon of the 1990s.

vented precisely because postmodern norms — boundaries — have been pushed to such limits, as in Fish's transgressive interdisciplinary programs that are allegedly so "very hard to do."

The social practices of *appropriateness* that follow from these perceptions of "centers" and "borders" are far flung. Psychologists, for instance, have now generated entire systems of clinical therapy based on their clients' tight or loose sense of boundaries.[13] Again, borders or boundaries in relation to the *appropriate*. Even nations now debate their geographical "boundaries" with renewed vigor, to a degree not witnessed since Sarajevo exploded into war on that fateful night in the summer of 1914. Ethnic cleansing in the same Balkan geography today overtly admits the dispute over borders while sacrificing entire societies in the name of well-drawn boundaries. These examples are diverse, even far-flung. Elsewhere, marriage counselors and social workers are demonstrating that at no previous time in history have more people lived in solitary accommodations as *families of one* — anthropologically a new and almost unimaginable passion for the tightest drawn boundary of all: the solitary hearth. The best examples lie in virtual reality and cyberspace where the "appropriate relationship" has already merged with the simulacrum (copy): a shadow of the real relationship but nevertheless fulfilling because it is processed *through appropriateness* to substitute for originals.

The excursus has not been digressive for Fish exploits these tensions between boundaries and their limits within professional-disciplinary contexts. He taps into the new frenzy for "the appropriate center" (without naming it as such) by claiming that interdisciplinarians, like disturbed patients or deviant nations, "refuse to respect boundaries." He writes:

> By definition interdisciplinary studies do exactly that — refuse to respect the boundaries that disciplines want always to draw — and thus encourage a widening of perspectives that will make possible the fullness education is supposed to confer (Fish 233).

This statement about "education" and "fullness" appears promising but remains oppositional, as its context reveals. The indictment is odious enough in the specific terms it draws — a language of refusal and disrespect: as if there were agreed bodies of authority and codes of rules universally to be venerated. But is also suspect in attributing to "disciplines" the very "boundaries" they allegedly "always want to draw." Draw according to who? The preeminent force of the last decade has been in an oppo-

---

[13] For samples of the different discourses invoked for boundaries see the structuralist work of G. Anzaldua, *Borderlands/La Frontera* (San Francisco: Aunt Lute, 1987); Hector Calderon and Jose Saldivar, eds., *Criticism in the Borderlands: Studies in Chicano Literature, Culture, and Ideology* (Durham: Duke University Press, 1991); the work of historian Robert Kargon, especially in "Imagined Boundaries: Princeton, Stanford, and the Boundaries of Useful Knowledge in Post-War America," *Minerva* 32 (Summer 1994): 121-43; Gerald J. Larson and E. Deutsch, eds., *Interpreting Across Boundaries: New Essays in Comparative Philosophy* (Princeton: Princeton University Press, 1988); G. S. Rousseau, *Enlightenment Borders* (Manchester: Manchester University Press, 1990).

site direction, as discipline after discipline claims in one rhetoric or another that postinterdisciplinary life entails breaking loose from the straitjackets of disciplinary and departmental chains. Deans offices and government funding bodies are not the only agencies demanding that funded programs and projects be *interdisciplinary*; if they were, the term would be vapid and departmental members and grant applicants would merely be regurgitating the profession's favorite buzzword (interdisciplinary) without ascribing substantive energy to it. And why this word rather than others? The choice and range of possibility is wide. Why should *interdisciplinarity* have won out among its competitors (multidisciplinarity, etc.) if it were not the fittest to survive? The facts paradoxically prove otherwise than Fish suggests, though the riddle he erects is more complex than the facts imply. Anyone who sits on governmental review boards knows that interdisciplinary candidates for posts and interdisciplinary projects for funding remain far more difficult to obtain than traditional disciplinary work. The most reliable recent evidence suggests that this state of affairs has slowly been changing in the last decade but the battle is far from won even in North America. Fish complains (speaking of repression) about refusals and disrespect for boundaries; but the fact is that his so-called renegades constitute a minority within the profession *despite* all the current rhetoric of interdisciplinarity, and there is no evidence of their ranks significantly increasing in the near future. Governments may claim they desire these ranks to swell, but the aspiration and the reality continue to remain far apart. Furthermore *quant a* Fish, are we to believe that everyone has suddenly grown disrespectful and rebellious? Despite the strategies of consolidation among university administrators in the 1990s are academics everywhere holding up in their offices pondering the shackles of the departmental/disciplinary straitjacket? It is an implausible scenario despite the increasingly salubrious administrative tendency to consolidate humanities departments into single units as one means of repairing the tensions bred by "disrespect," as well as to cut costs.

IV

Having interlinked this alleged disrespect for boundaries with the deviance of those who trample appropriate borders, it remains for Fish to cast them as political radicals intent on disrupting normal everyday life in the contemporary, hierarchical university. Then his politically conservative task will have been done; his *tractatus logicus Fishiensis contra interdisciplinariorum* as a proof of "difficulty" — "it is very hard to do" — evidentially substantiated. And this is exactly what the very *logical* Fish does, claiming as the protector of the disciplinary status quo that ultimately interdisciplinarians commit "assault and attack on authority." They are but earlier or latter-day Foucaults. "In short," Fish writes, "for those more radical voices, interdisciplinary study is more than a device for prodding students to cross boundaries they would otherwise timidly respect; it is an assault on those boundaries and on the entire edifice of hierarchy and power they reflect and sustain" (Fish 234). Putatively then the various forms of dissidence coalesce: radicalism, timidity, assault, hierarchy, power.

Even the helpless student is comically cast as being "timidly prodded," as if some dimwit incapable of imaginatively crossing boundaries by himself. Finally, after all these logical twists and turns, there can no longer be any doubt about Fish's agenda: demolition of all those opposing authority and hierarchy in the name of something else. The rebellious Fish of the Sixties has thus refashioned himself now as one of the first-born conservatives (academically speaking and insofar as the development of knowledge is concerned) of the Nineties.[14]

Still, and however biographically coherent, it is an odd view of "assault" that violates the very best "Vanity of Human Wishes" history that Fish knows so well. For a large part of the edifice of Western knowledge has been bravely earned in the Temple of Opposition by those dissidents willing to go against the grain of Fish's "authority and hierarchy." Figures from Socrates to Galileo, Bacon to Nietzsche and Marx and Freud, are merely the most radical examples. The entire basis for Reformation humanism — as every sentence in Thomas More's quintessential *In Defence of Humanism: Letters to Dorp, Oxford, Lee, and a Monk* proclaims, and as Fish, the self-consuming exegete of Milton and Herbert, must have read — was articulated as an interdisciplinary revolt against the old disciplinary straitjacket of Catholic and casuistic piety: classicism *grafted on to* clericalism.[15] The essence of virtually all national brands of European Enlightenment was a new interdisciplinarity of approaches. What else are all those constructed and reconstructed "sciences of man" by David Hume, Adam Ferguson, Adam Smith and company, if not the *new* human sciences cross-fertilized by the disparate discourses of the Cartesians, Newtonians, Lockeans and so forth? And what was post-Kantian Romanticism *au fond* if not a new interdisciplinary engagement with German *Naturphilosophie* in a way thoroughly unknown to the worlds of Newton and Priestley? Are these not also (whether pre- or post-Foucaldian is irrelevant) "assaults on boundaries" and interrogations of the "entire edifice of hierarchy and power they reflect and sustain?" It is an odd view of assault for someone whose intellectual origins lie in the seventeenth-century world of the Copernican Revolution and the revolutionary New Science, and who would presumably be attuned (even without the assistance of Kuhnian and Foucaldian theory) to the degree to which

---

[14] The point requires abundant context. Fish is hardly alone in this transformation, it having been noted in large segments of the most successful members of his (and my) generation. A pattern seems to have developed: the more daringly radical and subversive in the Sixties, now the more retrenching and intractable; the more cautious and self-righteous, especially among the fundamentalist religious Right, even moreso now; middle-grounders in the Sixties seem to have veered the least and remain, more or less, middle-grounders. See, from the same university press directed by Fish, J. K. Wilson, *The Conservative Attack on Higher Education* (Durham: Duke University Press, 1996).

[15] Thomas More, *In Defense of Humanism: Letter to Martin Dorp; Letter to the University of Oxford; Letter to Edward Lee; Letter to a Monk*, with a new text and translation of *Historia Richardi Tertii*, ed., Daniel Kinney (New Haven: Yale University Press, 1986); for the interdisciplinary basis of modern humanism, Richard Etlin, *In Defence of Humanism: Value in Art and Letters* (Cambridge: Cambridge University Press, 1996), with his prolific arguments *pro* interdisciplinary scholarship in the early modern period.

disparate discourses and disciplines then overlapped to produce this revolution in scientific knowledge.[16] But it is perfectly coherent and contingent when the radical Child of the Sixties is followed professionally by the Conservative Adult of the Nineties.

Fish gives with the left hand what he removes with the right. Eager to appear poised in his denigration of the anti-authoritarian interdisciplinarians, he generously grants them a certain rationality and professional verve. Hence, "in the classical liberal paradigm, interdisciplinary studies seek only to transform the academy while maintaining the wall between it and the larger field of social action [...]" (Fish, 235). Thus the interdisciplinarians are misguided and this "larger field of social action" remains the one to avoid lest it pollute by its miasma of anti-authoritarianism. That is, any curricular deviation has a consequential ripple effect in social action if the connection will be made by those who have the eyes to ponder where to look. These are the bonds of "social action" Fish would destroy on grounds of their subversion. For the contemporary university is a place — according to Fish — where preexisting bonds now terminate at the front door, so far has interdisciplinary (i. e., read politically subversive) plurality progressed. Cross that boundary — to return to his favorite nemesis: the boundary crossers — and an inferno of envy and resentment explodes. Reside within its territory and remain safe. Such tensions must have been conceived at the juncture of ambivalence and crisis about his *own* biographical interdisciplinarity, although it would be revelatory to know what perspectives Fish brings to his own biographical interdisciplinarity.[17] For Fish, moreover, the divide of the public and private are monolithic: no bridge can be built because there is something, as we shall see, to hide. Even if it were not so, the desire to cross over from the one (public) to the other (private) is as deviant, in Fish's notion, as any wish to break out of the confines of the disciplines. It would seem to follow that the bonds that unite us within the university are entirely intellectual and cannot be social or private. All of which construes the contemporary university as an institution for the preservation of tradition and the proprietor of specialized, privileged forms of discourse. It is, adamantly, no place where general knowledge can be interrogated because that adumbrates the human condition; no site to improve our social and political lot, not even as intellectuals. The university *is* professional — even *professionally* certifying — but entirely irrelevant to the concerns of ordinary postmodern life.

Fish is too intelligent to demur from the logical consequences of this epistemological and ontological position:

> In short, if we take seriously the epistemological argument in the context of which the gospel of interdisciplinary study is often preached, we will come to the conclusion that

---

[16] See David C. Lindberg et al., eds., *Reappraisals of the Scientific Revolution*, (Cambridge: Cambridge University Press, 1990). For an even stronger case of the interdisciplinary bases of revolutionary transformations in knowledge see Bruce Mazlish, *A New Science: the Breakdown of Connections and the Birth of Sociology* (Oxford: Oxford University Press, 1989).

[17] Much rests, as is suggested in the opening note, on the definitions, disparities and paradoxes of inside and outside: what Fish thinks of his interdisciplinarity will not be what others do.

being interdisciplinary — breaking out of the prison house of our various specialities to the open range first of a general human knowledge and then of the employment of that knowledge in the great struggles of social and political life — is not a possible human achievement. Being interdisciplinary is more than a hard thing to do; it is impossible to do (Fish 237-8).

Here then is the final verdict. Hard becomes impossible — the reason contemporary departmental life permits no space for "revolutionary projects." It is a polarized view: of projects and research as *either* revolutionary or reactionary without a common middle. Then Fish stipulates in his shrillest and gloomiest pronouncement of all: "The epistemological argument deprives the political argument of any force, because it leaves *no room for a revolutionary project*" (Fish, 238). Logic and epistemology have triumphed over politics and ideology. In other words, all university scholarship is necessarily derivative, all pedagogy repetitive, all knowledge reductive, all teaching necessarily rotelike in an endless and unbroken chain. The revolutionary project is thus reduced to a metacritique of a few sentences.

At this point in his argument Fish charitably asks whether there is any way to salvage their impoverished position. "Needless to say, this is a conclusion many [one wonders who the many *are* in this utterance] are loath to reach" (Fish, 238). Granting this point Fish declares the only remaining imperative: "But in order to avoid it, the proponents of radical pedagogy must negotiate an impasse produced by one of their own first principles, the unavailability of a perspective that is not culturally determined" (Fish, 238). The moment of such cultural determination, apparently reducible to the raging constructionist-essentialist debates of the 1980s, is precisely the point where the very clever Fish wants to emerge. Yet the logic of moving from radical pedagogy to all culturally determined developments is less than clear — the first logical lapse in his otherwise astute condemnation of interdisciplinarity. He himself rejects radical pedagogy while recognizing cultural determination. Yet their incommensurability is hardly contrary. Besides, one would think interdisciplinary pedagogues and their interdisciplinary research programmes have more pressing concerns than radical pedagogy. But Fish has by this point in the argument become a staunch conservative-essentialist eager to smash the social constructionist argument. This is not the constructionist Fish of "self-consuming artifacts" and "textbooks in the classroom," but the recently converted Fish of literature and the law, literature and ethics, conservative tort and criminal law as the only mirrors to be held up instructively for literary evidence — all of which have paradoxically served to transform him into a hardened conservative neo-essentialist. Had it been the other way around, one could understand: the originally rebellious Child of the Sixties — an *enfant terrible* of literary studies — now championing more fiercely than ever an interdisciplinary approach to literature and the law. But even in David Lodge's ironic world nothing comes to academics in predictable sequence.

V

Yet again Fish imbricates the logical status of his argument by inserting a metaphor of performance into the ongoing debates about disciplinarity. He announces: "Once you turn, for example, from actually *performing* literary criticism to examining the 'network of forces and factors' that underlie the performance, literary criticism is no longer what you are performing" (Fish 240).[18] This approach to the humanities as performance is appealing and enticing. For one thing, performance means several things according to the *OED*, the first of which is the moral fulfillment of a promise: the performance of something entails retention of a promise.[19] If we are performing the humanities, or, as Fish suggests, "performing literary criticism," knowingly or not we are fulfilling a promise. The other dictionary meanings of perform embrace enactment, dramatization, excitement and expertise but normatively without the moral dimension implicit in the keeping of promises. Even more tantalizing, however, is Fish's claim that if we turn from the performance of literary criticism to understanding those "forces and factors" that underlie it, we necessarily cease performing it and perform something *else*. Fish does not name this "something else," this Other — nor is it evident what precisely it could be — but it presumably entails some fashionable contemporary impulse to revolt against authoritarian codes and norms over which we have no control. And that is why, à la Fish, we must not stop "performing literary criticism." It suppresses the rebel in every one of us and reifies our commitment to privilege imaginative canonical literature over noncanonical (and thereby possibly subversive) types.

It is unclear what logical advantage this performative notion bears for Fish's argument. It does nothing, for example, to alter his sense of the phylogeny of interdisciplinarians, for Fish never denies that interdisciplinarians *exist*. Indeed, he suggests that they abound, are ubiquitous, proliferating under our noses at every moment: "The obvious response to this conclusion is to point out that interdisciplinary studies are all around us. What is it that all these people are doing?" (Fish, 242). What indeed? In his answers Fish either diminishes their claim to effect radical change or soft-pedals the consequences of the work produced. The fact that they might stimulate otherwise enervated students or bored readers of specialized monographs is irrelevant to him. Specifically, he dispraises the proliferators in three primary ways, by claiming that they are importers, colonizers, or — in the most flattering taxonomy permitted — heuristic innovators:

1. borrowing or importing information from others
2. colonizing other fields
3. constructing a new discipline which is itself based on a history of disciplines

---

[18] For an eloquent contemporary statement of the problem see James Winn, *The Humanities as Performance* (New Haven: Yale University Press, 1998).

[19] This meaning was current in the seventeenth century as is evident from this translation of the Bible, quoted in the *Oxford English Dictionary*: "There shall be a performance of those things which were told her from the Lord" (Luke i. 45).

It is crucial that Fish absorbs the consequences of such reduction of interdisciplinarity to these three forms — importation, colonization, and construction of new discipline. Nevertheless, here Fish is unambiguous and his division provides examples of the form taken by each:

> The answer has already been given; either they are engaging in straightforwardly disciplinary tasks [1: the *importers*] that require for their completion information and techniques on loan from other disciplines, or they are working within a particular discipline at a moment when it is expanding into territories [2: the *colonizers*] hitherto marked as belonging to someone else — participating, that is, in the annexation by English departments of philosophy, psychoanalysis, anthropology, social history, and now, legal theory; or they are in the process of establishing a new discipline [3: the *heuristic innovators*], taking as its primary task the analysis of disciplines, the charting of their history and of their ambitions. Typically the members of this new discipline will represent themselves as antidisciplinary, that is, as interdisciplinary, but as Daniel Schön comments, 'they will constitute a "new breed" of "counter professionals/experts"'(Fish, 242).

Long ago Susan Sontag defended these "counter-professionals," and there is neither time nor space to repeat her reasons here or rebuild new ones now. Suffice it to say that the "counter professional" remains Fish's apocalyptic nightmare: specifically, the possibility that general enquiry and general critique could lead to the undoing of the entrenched mandarins and their six-digit salaries. This is the root of the matter. General critique could lead to educational reform by the *general* (i.e., interdisciplinary) enquiry of the counter-professionals. For the "importers and colonizers" Fish bears an almost dispassionate sympathy or condolence: why should they *not* import and colonize when everyone else in society at large is? It is the homology of the cultural whole that counts. But the undoing of specialization and its possible *fiscal* discontents is more than even Fish can imagine. If the "new breed" were content merely to "establish new disciplines," that would be one thing. But their "new breed" antidisciplinary agenda is revolutionary and threatening precisely because it unravels canonical discourse and enquires anew into the general nature of words and things. It leads thus not to the palace of wisdom but to anarchy and the potential disappearance — at least for starred professors in North America like Fish — of a whole yuppie class, now slowly becoming extinct, who drove BMWs and Mercedes in the aftermath of 1968 during the greatest known wave of university expansion.

VI

Interdisciplinarity may indeed be "very hard" to achieve but it is virtually "impossible" to perform if we are to believe Fish. But it is not globally dying or dead and whether hard or impossible, or in whichever version or phylogeny, its practitioners ought not — according to Fish — to ask too many questions, or raise points capable of dislodging the hard won economic effects of specialization. Mumbo-jumbo remains the rub and it was the crusade for which the Sontag camp, for example, fought so hard in the 1970s. Hence, for Fish, the villain remains the interdisciplinary "trespasser" who crosses boundaries between fields or discourses because this gesture leads to the "new breed of counter experts" who ask too *general* questions.

What sort of concrete threat does this new breed pose? This is the last question we must ask to comprehend why the counter-professionals represent such unequivocal menaces for Fish. The new breed of generalists might ask — for example — what are "departments" anyway, and where are the corridors of allegiance within "departments?" Foucault asked what an author is.[20] He might as well have enquired into the origins of departments and their internal codes and tessellated discourses. The "counter-professional expert" — to retain Fish's tripartite phylogeny in *There's No Such Thing as Free Speech* — might be one who wonders whether in view of the radical recent changes in subjects like "English Studies," it is possible that "the department" is itself an antediluvian structure or entity that ought to be reviewed or even abolished. Or that university academics ought to have more general allegiances: to faculties, as in broadly construed faculties of arts and sciences, or to colleges, as in the Oxbridge system in England and the Harvard and Yale colleges in America.

After all, it has now been several decades since "departments" — within the current canonical and noncanonical analogy — were constructively reviewed at all. In themselves they are not, and have never been, isomorphic organisms capable of facile or even accurate monolithic representation. Their histories and hegemonies, at least in America, have been deeply troubled and hardly congruent; their convergencies and internal loyalties far more haphazardly random than the disparate discourses of the French theorists so loathed by Fish and his cohorts. And what about divided or polarized "departments" of the byzantine varieties that now rack the great North American research establishments? Have they too become places in which loyalties can only be surrendered to some biased faction or self-interested clique within the larger entity but never to the organism as a whole? Precincts to patrol as if they were badlands on the borders? If so, no wonder that so many academics have left them in droves for the less factious departments of the American sunbelt from Florida to California? The day when any American academic would have toiled away for two decades in the hope of a phone call from the Ivy League may be over.

If members of such typically *divided* "departments" are no longer bonded by their disciplinary filiations but by other "histories" — generational, political, ethnic, national, racial, sexual — then what indeed are postmodern "departments" anyway? And where is their social responsibility: to their students and the community beyond departmental walls? Have they too (the departments and the entrenched views they harbor) become the precincts of academic life on the edge: "departmental city limits" on the badland-borders? The sites of new and as yet unwritten "academic *appropriateness*" ensuring that Fish's "revolutionary projects" in scholarship do not occur? These, I suspect, are merely the types of *general* questions Fish would prefer his "new breed

---

[20] M. Foucault, "What is an author?" in David Lodge, ed., *Modern Criticism and Theory* (London: Longman, 1988), 197-210, originally published in French in 1969 and first in English in 1979.

of counter-professional interdisciplinarians" not to ask. Generalists and empowered departmental ghettoes do not mix well.

In a generation there may well be *no* departments in the shape we have known them at the end of the twentieth century, and the critic's, as well as the cultural historian's, responsibility will have changed, as will the source and focus of professional loyalty. The guarantees of change are such that the matter of loyalty to departments, which appears pressing to us, may not be a concern at all in 2025 or 2050. Human beings will remain soulful, of course, but Fish's local caveats made contra interdisciplinarity (allegiance to departments, loyalty to groups) will vastly alter in the aftermath of the informatics society. And so too will subjects like English Literature and English Studies.

Universal Truths or Ethnic Peculiarities? On Tensions Inherent in the Reception of Post-Colonial and Minority Literature

LAURENZ VOLKMANN (Würzburg)

If a reader is not a member of an ethnic minority represented in a literary text, is he or she guilty of bourgeois self-indulgance if he or she seeks for 'universal truths' in this text? Or worse, does one — unwittingly or not — domesticate, appropriate, or even subjugate such a literary text? Is one's reading flawed from the beginning as one will never understand, possibly only misunderstand the complex value-systems of different cultural identities?[1] In literary theory, those critics insisting that texts can and may be read as revealing some transcendent truth about human existence are on the wane, while those demanding that any reading should stress the particular ethnicity of such a text are on the rise. Such a tendency towards authenticity and contextualization is not completely new; it has existed ever since minority literature made its first inroads into the mainstream of the Western canon. Yet the recent deluge of 'authors from the (former) margin' has swept aside many of the classic male authors who traditionally were given the role of providing profound insights into the human psyche and the *conditia humana*.

In discussing recent changes in the canonical hierarchy and in literary theories of postmodernism and post-colonialism, this article argues for a new privileged status for literature — especially minority/post-colonial literature — because of its exemplary staging of the current human condition and the insights it offers into the evolving new value-systems of the ethical turn of postmodernism. It argues for teaching post-colonial/minority literature in the EFL-classroom as a means of achieving cross-cultural or dialogic competence needed in an ever shrinking global village. Such competence entails, as I will point out, in great part an understanding of the recent theoretical debates on post-colonialism and *Fremdverstehen,* the intricacies of cross-cultural understanding. To exemplify these prevalent theoretical discussions, we may best begin with an early instance of how a text by a minority writer was able successfully to cross racial and cultural boundaries — Ralph Ellison's *Invisible Man* from 1952.

---

[1] On this dilemma compare especially Lothar Bredella's publications, for example "Ist das Verstehen fremder Kulturen wünschenswert?" in Lothar Bredella and Herbert Christ, eds., *Zugänge zum Fremden* (Gießener Diskurse, vol. 10. Gießen, 1993), 11-36, "Intercultural Understanding between Relativism, Ethnocentrism and Universalism: Preliminary Considerations for a Theory of Intercultural Understanding," in Günther Blaicher and Brigitte Glaser, eds., *Anglistentag 1993 Eichstätt. Proceedings* (Tübingen: Niemeyer, 1994), 287-306, "How Can Literary Texts Matter?" in Rüdiger Ahrens and Laurenz Volkmann, eds., *Why Literature Matters. Theories and Functions of Literature* (Heidelberg: Winter, 1996), 117-34; also Heinz Antor, "The Ethics of Criticism in the Age After Value," in Ahrens and Volkmann, *Why Literature Matters,* 65-85.

I. 'I Speak for You' — The Appeal of the Other's Voice

An early example of a minority writer praised by white (male) critics was Ralph Ellison (1914-1994), whose most impressive novel *Invisible Man* has in numerous ways proved to be paradigmatic in its appeal to the general reader. Charting the quest for racial identity of an unnamed Afro-American male from a Negro College in the Deep South to the mean streets of a Harlem riven by race riots, this novel of development offered a harsh message to white America. Rejected and abused by white racists, patronized by white philanthropists and ultimately tricked into killing another black character during a racial upheaval clandestinely instigated by whites, the protagonist is turned into a recluse. At the end he grotesquely hides from the real world in a subterranean place. Indeed, this is the symbolic racial history of black America summed up by the interlocutor as he relates his story of black invisibility to white America — he feels cast into a non-entity "because people refuse to see me."[2] Recollecting his tale from a position of self-induced hibernation, the protagonist offers a plea for common survival and co-existence. Not a melting pot is envisioned here, but rather a cultural mosaic of different identities.

> Whence all this passion towards conformity anyway? - diversity is the word. Let man keep his many parts and you'll have no tyrant states. [...] America is woven of many strands; I would recognize them and let it so remain. [...] Our fate is to become one, and yet many - This is not prophecy, but description. Thus one of the greatest jokes in the world is the spectacle of the whites busy escaping blackness and becoming blacker every day, and the blacks striving towards whiteness, becoming quite dull and grey. None of us seems to know who he is or where he's going. (Ellison, 465)

With his prophetic words the protagonist clearly aims at a general readership, even apostrophizing them in the last lines of the novel:

> [W]hat else could I do? What else but try to tell you what was really happening when your eyes were looking through? And it is this which frightens me:
> Who knows but that, on the lower frequencies, I speak for you? (Ellison, 468f.)

"I speak for you" - Ellison consciously constructed his novel with a view to a white audience's established framework of reception. The complex narrative structure of *Invisible Man*, embedded in the retrospective autobiography of an isolated soul; its effortless shifting from gritty naturalism in the first part to surreal phantasmagoric satire in the second; a wide range of intertextual references to the classics of European and American 'confessional literature', including Poe, Melville, Dostoevsky and Kafka — all these narrative devices put the novel firmly into the tradition of the great classics of modernist and pre-modernist European and American literature. It was not

---

[2] Ralph Ellison, *Invisible Man* (Harmondsworth: Penguin, 1981), 7.

only this adherence to an already familiar 'modernist' way of narrating that facilitated readings and interpretations by the established (white) interpretive community. The novel's appeal was furthered by authorial and textual strategies to foreground a universal meaning of the protagonist's sufferings. As the post-war climate of economic prosperity and moral stasis gave way to the inexorable growth of political and civil rights movements, of first hidden and then open political agendas of feminism, gay and lesbian rights, ethnicity and post-colonialism, Ellison's novel seemed to outline a blueprint of future developments. Its prophetic fostering of alternative universal values — multiculturalism, tolerance etc. — and the promise of authenticity in its portrayal of life on the margins of America proved to be an exciting literary formula for establishing it as a set text in the literature departments of both the U.S. and abroad. Entertaining as well as instructing to its educated readers, *Invisible Man* as literature of the social periphery promised the capacity to make its readers aware of the universal nature of suffering, of timeless mechanism of discrimination and suppression. It challenged moral assumptions by implying that its white readers, too, were turning a blind eye to the Other, merely perceiving him or her as "figments of [the] imagination." (Ellison, 7)

More recently, postmodern notions of hybridity may have perceived a mirror image in the novel. For among many possible solutions to the invisible man's erratic quest for ethnic and cultural identity a 'postmodern' sense of liberation of all the restraints of the self is hinted at. In one passage of the novel during which the narrator poses as a trickster-character (the Rev. Rinehart) he weighs the options of slipping in and out of racial and social roles. As he surmises without further elaboration, "multiple personalities" offer an unprecedented world of possibilities "too vast and confusing to contemplate." (Ellison 401f.) In such passages of the novel, 'blackness' is ultimately perceived not as a stable category, but rather as a racial identity so far constructed and imposed upon mainly by whites.[3]

Alternative readings of the novel are possible, if the specific ethnic identity of the main character and the sociocultural context of mid-twentieth century America is foregrounded. According to a more radical stance, any interpretation along the lines of universal values and timeless truths (or possibly any attempt by a non-black reader to interpret the character's plight) should be dismantled for wrestling the novel out of context. Any such domesticating and naturalizing of the African-American protagonist would be considered a severe act of interpretative violence.[4] A politically correct reading would emphasize the particular sociocultural framework of discrimination, suppression and torment which is so peculiar to the novel's world. Such an interpreta-

---

[3] Compare the recent debate on race, ethnicity and culture as categories of variable definitions. Henry Louis Gates Jr. has been most prominent with his notion of the biological category of race as an arbitrary construct (see H.L. Gates Jr., ed., *'Race', Writing, and Difference* [Chicago: University of Chicago Press, 1986]).

[4] On writing and interpreting as a form of violence in its own right by stabilizing or producing unjust power structures compare the New Historicist approaches of Nancy Armstrong and Leonard Tennenhouse, eds., *The Violence of Representation: Literature and the History of Violence* (London/New York: Routledge, 1989).

tion would define the text as a cultural site 'negotiating' the sociocultural energies of a Harlem marred by racial struggles. A much more radical textual meaning could be uncovered underneath the protagonist's confused search for identity — the ominous signs of racial frictions and upheavals; not the non-conflictual ideal of a cultural salad-bowl, but rather the writings on the wall for a society riven by racial tensions. As a result of this reading, the novel could be interrelated with other, more radical voices of its context, such as with the poem "Harlem" published in 1951 by Ellison's contemporary Langston Hughes (1902-1967). Exposing the festering black wound of white America, the poem asks what happened to "a dream deferred" — the dream of racial justice and equality. Its ominous last line — "*Or does it explode?*"[5] — hints at the racial subtext of *Invisible Man*, a subtext of a volatile precariousness threatening to disrupt any complacent universalist reading of the novel with a vengeance.

Ellison's elaborate effort to appeal to a common future of multiculturalism ("to become one, and yet many", Ellison, 465), was fated to be relegated to the background. "In the '60s, when the American civil rights sing-along gave way to Black Power shock therapy, Ellison found himself overshadowed by more urgent novelists, such as Richard Wright (*Native Son*), who played Malcolm X to Ellison's Martin Luther King Jr.",[6] as Ellison's obituary in *Time* reads. Denouncing integration and multicultural values as white sops, more pressing pushes for ethnic identity have been based on difference to or even separation from white America.[7] Simultaneously, in the current atmosphere of difference and diversity, universalist values have been declared as obsolete metaphysical chimaera or white imperialist tools of suppression, which need to be dismantled and consigned to the historical dustbin.[8]

II. From Discarding Universal Truths to the 'Ethical Turn of Postmodernism'

It seems a blatantly trivial observation that any notion of universal and timeless ethical or aesthetical norms is always — in spite of its claims — grounded in its sociocultural moment in history. Yet such postmodern truisms in the Age after Value too easily discard the existence of human demands for moral certainties and longing for fixed aesthetic norms as obsolete — to be deconstructed with grand gestures as an anachronism at the current state of progress of the human consciousness. With the superior vision of historical hindsight it seems easy to jettison such relics of the past. However, far from effecting a radical transformation of cultural consciousness in the direction of relativism and contextualism, postmodernism has failed to tamp down reader demand for transcendant truths. Additionally, it has failed to explain why the very cultures that

---

[5] Langston Hughes, "Harlem," (1951) in *The Heath Anthology of American Literature*. 2nd edition. Vol. 2. Gen. ed. Paul Lauter (Lexington, Mass./Totonto: Heath, 1994), 1620.

[6] Richard Corliss, "Invincible Man. Ralph Ellison 1914 - 1994," in *Time* April 25 (1994): 73.

[7] Cf. Alfred Hornung, "Postmoderne bis zur Gegenwart," in Hubert Zapf, ed., *Amerikanische Literaturgeschichte* (Stuttgart: Metzler, 1997), 304-75, 317.

[8] Cf. Lothar Bredella's discussion of the battle of the "universalists" versus the "leftists" in "How Can Literary Texts Matter?", 145.

it valorizes and even glamorizes persist in demanding transpersonal and transcultural values, the very reified values that it itself condemns.

When did this function of literature as a provider of truth and certainties begin? Historically, the focus on morality and values has been described as originating with the institutionalization of literature as an academic subject at a crucial point in Western cultural history. This happened "when religious faith was declining and when there was pressure to open up areas of study for those who had been previously excluded from formal education (i.e. women and the working classes)."[9] By means of establishing canons and emphasizing morality and values, the study of literature equalled a secularized quest for meaning and certainty amidst the "naked shingles of the world."[10] Prominent in this endeavour were Matthew Arnold and T.S. Eliot, of course, and F.R. Leavis, who was most outspoken in his preferences for certain authors over others. His list of "major novelists" with universal appeal consisted of Jane Austen, George Eliot, Henry James and Joseph Conrad, later augmented by D.H. Lawrence (a risky choice then) and Charles Dickens. For him this comprised *The Great Tradition* (1948). To justify his eclecticism he offered the motto that "they are significant in terms of the human awareness they promote; awareness of the possibilities of life."[11] Besides being somewhat oblique in the definition of his criteria and his version of humanism, he sold arbitrariness as aesthetic or moral parameters. Leavisite randomness has been much vituperated — and quite rightly so — for epitomizing an Oxbridge aloofness that saw no reason for justifying its literary tastes. What was hidden below such preferences was the allocation of superior aesthetic and ethical qualities to authors that were considered to be both universal and very English in their appeal.[12] Timeless values were to be found with a covey of authors representing a timeless *Englishness* — a prodigious *tour de force* in excluding other voices.

A similar pattern of exclusion on the one hand and preferential treatment of certain authors on the other evolved in the United States, as Theo D'Haen has shown convincingly.[13] Prominent American critics such as F.O. Matthiessen, Leslie Fiedler or Leo Marx all shared the tacid assumption that the hallmark of good literature was its representation of essential *Americanness* as well as transcendental and transhistorical values. In other words, in praising texts as repositories of ageless wisdom, critics also, and quite consciously so, aimed at producing a national identity. Major texts served as treasured repertoires of shared cultural archetypes. Erasing the differences between national and universal values by implying them to be coterminus, literary critics elevated texts to the status of national "identity-machine[s]"[14] which would

---

[9] Sara Mills, *Discourse* (London/New York: Routledge, 1997), 25.

[10] Matthew Arnold, "Dover Beach," (1867): 1.28.

[11] F.R. Leavis, *The Great Tradition* (London: Chatto and Windus, 1948), 10.

[12] On the convergence of universal with English or American values in the main tradition of Western literary criticism see Theo D'Haen, "American Identities and Postcolonial Theories," in Ahrens and Volkmann, eds., *Why Literature Matters*, 183-95.

[13] Theo D'Haen, "American Identities and Postcolonial Theories".

[14] Theo D'Haen, "American Identities and Postcolonial Theories," 185.

bolster up national cohesion. Intrinsic criticism (which focus on the text as an autonomous entity) became privileged — whether in the tradition of the Russian formalists or the New Criticism or grounded in formalist structuralism or even deconstruction. In the vain hope of establishing ever more objective aesthetic standards for literature, short shrift was given to the specific socioeconomic or cultural contexts in which texts are embedded. On the contrary, by foregrounding literature as a self-contained universe to be treated according to its own, purely aesthetic qualities, it was given a privileged transhistorical status. In retrospect, such formalist interpreters have been disparaged as adequate bedfellows of humanist *bourgeois* literary scholars. Together they are held responsible for a fossilized canon of *Dead White Male Poets*. As worshippers of literary "touchstones" of great "truth and seriousness"[15] (M. Arnold) the doyens of literary criticism as Matthew Arnold, E.M. Tillyard and F.R. Leavis have been utterly debunked. If Arnold, according to his much-quoted definition, regarded as the critic's task "[...] a disinterested endeavour to learn and propagate the best that is known and thought in the world,"[16] such grandiose gestures have been derided at best as naive self-delusion peddling the middle-class critic's whim as the measure of all perfection, at worst as a deliberate bourgeois ploy to stabilize or support an unjust status quo.

The tables have been turned on those critics obsessed with the text and its humanist message. In a true interpretative paradigm-shift a plethora of new literary theories has encouraged the disappearance of the text as an autonomous entity. With its emphasis on textual indeterminacy and historically varying concretizations of the text as a skeletal structure reader-response critism opened a first window on the historically situated reader and on history in general. French poststructuralists such as Derrida and Foucault simultaneously destabilized notions of texts, authors and readers as parts of a textualized universe in which texts become political and cultural gravitational fields, constituted by contradictory and competing sets of 'epistemes', i.e. constellations of a multi-facetted *zeitgeist*. The status of literature as an aesthetic foil to reality has finally been challenged by the New Historicism, which perceives all cultural products to be *always already* embedded in their sociocultural contexts. Congeneric texts such as pamphlets, legal documents, broadsheets, cookery books etc. are juxtaposed with literary texts in order to discover in the minutiae and niceties, preferably in the marginal practices of a culture its driving and determining forces. Such "thick descriptions" (Cl. Geertz) reveal contemporary fascinations with historically grounded constructions of identities along the lines of 'class, gender, and race'; they explore the intricate configurations of power and knowledge, the all-pervasive mechanisms of suppression and marginalization. In taking both a semantic and cognitive step out of the text as the elusive locus of eddying and swirling social energies, the New Historicist elevates himself or herself to a superior vantage point. From this position, traditional literary studies have been redefined fundamentally. Not only has the traditional

---

[15] Quoted in Hubert Zapf, *Kurze Geschichte der anglo-amerikanischen Literaturtheorie* (Munich: Fink, 1991), 125.

[16] Quoted in Zapf, *Kurze Geschichte,* 124.

canon been reexamined in the light of the repressed and marginalized, but the whole of literary history has been rewritten and is wide open to numerous expansions, drastic revisions and new formations. A new "centrality of marginality"[17] has been the result of the forceful 'return of the repressed'. Women's studies, gender studies, minority studies and post-colonial literature studies have emerged as the victorious challengers in this struggle for dominance.

With the shift in literary criticism from New Criticism and Old Historicism (a term coined for any nostalgic, naive idealization of the past) to the New Historicism, from majority to minority writers etc., a dynamic process of probing and establishing tentative new value systems has evolved. Postmodernism's giddy days of initial iconoclasm have gone. During its first phase of the liberating step from modernist preoccupation with suffering and a deep sense of loss, early postmodernism diagnosed and propagated the "breaking up of the grand Narratives"[18] in our society. However, its early project of demystifying, destabilizing, decentering, unsettling and dismantling accepted conventions, traditions and hierarchies was only a beginning. Its vision was that of an age of unlimited possibilities and individual freedom — liberated "from various encroachments or subjugations to bogus superior principles or authorities."[19] Initially, the visonary project of postmodernism aimed at the blurring or transgression of old dichotomies such as ethics versus aesthetics, fact versus fiction, high culture versus low culture. Such dissolutions were declared as the foreplay needed to rebuild the better, more humane foundations of future societies. The argument here was that the binary oppositions so fatally inherent in all Western thinking before post-modernism had been the cause of a history of suppression and marginalization. A moral dilemma inherent in this project became apparent, though. If, after all, all moral and aesthical decisions are merely part of 'language games', if individuals are *bricoleurs*, piecing together their identities from any number of 'identi-kits' (Z. Bauman) or choosing from 'a wardrobe of selves' to be supplied with ever new or different layers of identities to cover an empty (or rather 'open') kernel — why then should one commit oneself to any values or cause? Following a diagnosis of this stasis or even paralysis, recently a cure has been found — in the "ethical turn of postmodernism." Such a moral shift avoids all the possible pitfalls of a mindless 'anything goes'-attitude accompanied by moral indifference and aloofness which has all too often been accompanied by cynical gestures of the relativity of all notions.[20] While establishing a clearly defined set of new values and norms, the new ethical postmodernism has to face a paradox. Although it is deeply rooted in the postmodern notion that there are no ob-

---

[17] Guyatri Spivak, *Outside the Teaching Machine* (New York/London, 1993), 18.

[18] Jean-Francois Lyotard, *The Postmodern Condition: A Report on Knowledge.* Trans. Geoff Bennington and Brian Massumi (Manchester: Manchester University Press, 1986), 15.

[19] Vernon W. Grass, "The Recent Ethical Turn in Literary Studies," *Mitteilungen des Verbandes deutscher Anglisten* 4/2 (1993): 33.

[20] On the ethical turn of postmodernism see Grass, "The Recent Ethical Turn," and Heinz Antor, "The Ethics of Criticism in the Age After Value," in Ahrens and Volkmann, eds., *Why Literature Matters,* 65-85.

jective norms (and no universal and timeless truths), it has established a number of moral and aesthetic guidelines that reflect pre-postmodern norms — albeit often in inversion. For all the new values of ethical postmodernism share two common denominators: First, they establish values that are grounded in late twentieth-century European and American societies and use these as moral and aesthetic parameters in the observation of any other age or society. Second, these parameters, as true inversions of former preferences, are — even if they are not declared as transgressing all times and all borders — implicitly assumed to do so. Such — often exacting — new postmodern guidelines include, among others: the affirmation of freedom, liberty and individual choice; the praise of a multi-culturalism based on fragmentation, difference and diversity; acceptance of the conflictual nature of any social and aesthetic discourse which should enhance mutual respect, tolerance and acceptance; the 'negative capability' (J. Keats) to live without eternal truths, rather to live with contradictions, frictions and disharmony; a preference of the weak, marginalized or oppressed over strong, established and dominating forces. This list of the values of the recent ethical turn of postmodernism covers only a segment of the intricate panorama of postmodern ethics. Translated into real life, it engenders a practical commitment to environmental issues, to defending the politically oppressed, to supporting minorities and the disadvantaged. As worthy as such causes may appear, they engender a new universalism. At second glance, the ostentatious dichotomy of universal values versus specific contextualizations of texts is a false one. The true dialectic is that of old universalities versus new universalities. For a new universalism which can best be summed up by the fashionable term 'political correctness' has evolved as a complex, exacting system with many rules and constraints. This is a bourgeoisization of postmodernism which may itself be the object of scrutiny by future generations of critics who — archeologists like the apostle of postmodernism, Foucault — may unearth the grand apparatus of culturally fashioned support mechanisms which keep postmodernism in place; they may discover postmodernism's "prodigious machinery designed to exclude."[21]

III. Changes in the German Curriculum: from 'Literature as Cultural Capital' to 'Teaching the Conflicts'

There is a long way from the cutting edge of criticism to the routine of everyday teaching in the EFL-classroom at German grammar schools. To be sure, the radical changes in literary theory and university canons have not permeated the German classroom yet. This is partly due to a long traditon of teaching literature within a well-established formalist and humanist framework. The teaching of *Höhenkammliteratur* (literary texts representing the peak of aesthetic achievement) has always been an integral part of the EFL-classroom in Germany. Deeply imbued in the long-standing tradition of Greek and Latin, foreign languages, when they were first introduced at

---

[21] Michel Foucault, "The Order of Discourse," in Robert Young, ed., *Untying the Text: A Poststructuralist Reader* (London: RKP, 1981), 56.

German grammar schools at the end of the nineteenth century, imitated the grammar-translation method of the classics.[22] Their educational goals were the product of both formalist and universalist approaches. The idea of the reader as a philologist entailed a scrupulous command of grammar and vocabulary, a 'love of the word' that favoured meticulous analyses and translations of 'great' texts. This ideal of the philologist considered the knowledge of canonical works as a prerequisite to forming an educated adult well prepared to fit into his or her class-system. Such *Bildung* meant both the ability to appreciate great works of art and the development of a 'virtuous personality' — in the Greek tradition of the *kalos kai agathos* (the morally good also being the aesthetically pleasing). Teaching literature meant providing pupils with 'cultural capital' as the admission-ticket to the middle or upper class, where knowledge of high culture was deemed necessitous. Accordingly the cultural key to the English-speaking world was foremost defined as acquainting oneself with great works of art representing the cultural heritage of England; hence the great enchantment with Shakespeare, especially with his tragedies. The Bard of Avon was seen as representing the best of British culture as well as being the great propagator of metaphysical values. With the focus on Shakespeare as the thinker and philosopher an icon evolved that seemed to present the traditions of German Romanticism, Idealism and serious philosophizing — here was *our* national Shakespeare. Even if Wilhelm Vietor published his pamphlet *Der Sprachunterricht muß umkehren* in 1882 under the pen name Quosque Tandem, decrying the lack of practical command of English and recommending a more oral approach, the humanist approach to literature has remained highly influential up to now.

After the barbarous excesses of Hitler's reign, during which one (mostly modern) part of English literature was declared to be decadent and debased (*entartet*), the other part instrumentalized for political indoctrination (with Shakespeare as the true 'Aryan artist'), the process of re-education initiated between 1945 and 1949 meant a (re-)turn to humanist values — those of democracy and pluralism, tolerance and openness. A new, alternative dimension to this alliance of formalism and humanitarianism was added after the students' revolt of 1968. The generation which went to university in that period comprises the majority of grammar-school teachers at the moment. To a certain degree, they have been instilling in their pupils a sense of subversive resistance to the capitalist consumer society. Reared with Brechtian concepts of the political functions of literature, they subscribe to a sometimes muted, sometimes overt political agenda which determines the everyday practices of teaching literature. But has the old humanist/formalist tradition ceased to be of importance? On the contrary, the new classroom-practice seems to embody the essence of the old tradition, as summed up by Peter Weiss's famous demand for *[d]ie Ästhetik des Widerstands* (the title of a 1975 novel) which praises the aesthetics of subversion and opposition to established authorities — a final congruence of morals and form. But post-revolutionary fatigue or

---

[22] On the history of teaching literature in the German EFL-classroom see Wilfried Brusch, "Contextualizing Literary Texts. The Reception Process in English Language Teaching," in Ahrens and Volkmann, eds., *Why Literature Matters*, 135-45.

indifference has also somehow strengthened pragmatic approaches to language and literature teaching. The emphasis on moral tales has remained, with an important imperative for the right choice of texts gaining momentum. It is the ability of a text to create a fictional context that is either close to the every-day experiences and problems of pupils or that serves as a sociocultural lesson of the Anglo-Saxon world. In practice, texts are valued that encompass both potentialities. By creating stimulating contexts, literary texts provide vicarious experiences; learning to put themselves into the place of fictional (native) characters, pupils are teased into lively discussions and into an "interpretative dialogue" (E. Werlich). Both practical communicative skills and a sense of Anglo-Saxon values and habits are enhanced by this.

Unfortunately, only a slim body of established texts has stood the test of teaching during the last decades. Shakespeare remains the unchallenged champion. His great tragedies *Hamlet* and *Macbeth* have spawned a string of Teachers' Notes praising the bard and his plays for insights into the human mind and for being most stimulating in classroom discussions. Other time-honored stalwarts of the canon for advanced learners are George Orwell and William Golding. While the former's *Nineteen Eighty-Four* is favoured as a warning of totalitarian tendencies and forces, the latter's *Lord of the Flies* is revered as a profound probing of metaphysical evil. It also shows a close affinity to the questions which are of paramount psychological and moral interest to pupils of the protagonists' age group. Such tales of growing up to maturity through the painful ordeals of adolescent rites of passage are among the classroom favorites. As with Golding's novel and with Jerome Salinger's *Catcher in the Rye,* these stories of initiation sometimes turn out to deal with the refusal to turn adult — a true reference to *schülernahe Themen* (topics germaine to the experiences of childhood or adolescence). As a result of this well-established canon, minority and New English Literatures texts so far are just on the verge of leaving the position of token representatives of new directions in writing. Collections such as *Stories from the Black Experience* or *Native American Short Stories* (both Klett Publishers) and *Short Stories by Women from Different Cultures* or *Short Stories from Australia and New Zealand* (Cornelsen) are featured in the 1998 brochures of prominent publishing houses.

In spite of these new collections, discourses of alterity, cultural difference and diversity have only just begun to percolate from the university level to that of grammar schools. The average German classroom has so far been little affected by the debates which were programmatically summed up in two articles by Gerald Graff on the teaching of literature in the United States. From the title of the first article, "What Should We Be Teaching — When There's No 'We'"[23] readers may infer that in an age of multiculturalism and diversity there can be no more fixed canon. The title of the second article suggests a turn from the text to theory, to the reflection of competing critical stances: "Teach the Conflicts."[24] Such staging in the classroom of cultural conflicts — that we can only agree to disagree — seems unrealistic in Germany, given

---

[23] Gerald Graff, "What Should We Be Teaching - When There's No 'We'," *Yale Journal of Criticism* 1 (1987): 189-211.

[24] Gerald Graff, "Teach the Conflicts," *The South Atlantic Quarterly* 89/1 (1990): esp. 53.

the comparatively homogenious nature of privileged grammar-school students. Yet apart from engaging in theoretical discussions quite unpopular in a foreign language, the conflictual nature of texts can be highlighted. This means avoiding the dangers inherent in perusing post-colonial/minority texts solely to cater to the pupils' taste for exotic places and atmospheres. Rather than encouraging interpretations in the vein of this tourist mentality, teachers in the EFL-classroom should regard these texts as challenges. To follow Braj B. Kachru's observation could be a step in the right direction — that the wide range and international status of New English Literature offers unique chances of opening "a window onto other Western and non-Western cultures. The medium is familiar, but it is used in entirely different semiotic and cultural systems."[25] As with literature in general, here we have a "semantic vessel for the communication of foreign cultural meaning" (R. Ahrens),[26] offering insights into different cultures that cannot be found access to otherwise. Literature should no longer be seen as self-referential, but as an exemplary discourse constantly staging sociocultural conflicts and exchanges, thus participating in a complex give-and-take of sociocultural meaning-creation. As the Bakhtinian critic Michael Holquist puts it, this happens "at the price of reducing the world's variety and endlessness."[27] A truly polyphonic text does so by refraining from any monologic muting of counter-voices, but rather by celebrating the world's variety and its unbounded heteroglossia:

> In a literary text, the normal activity of perception, of giving order to chaos, is performed at a heightened degree. [...] Every time we talk we give order to the world; every time we write or read a literary text we give the greatest degree of (possible) order to the world. [...][Literary utterances] reduc[e] and (relatively, always relatively) finaliz[e] the roiling chaos of the world outside language into categories inside language.[28]

Hence the function of literature as a sematic key to other cultures, as our major source of the other. Reading equals travelling into a foreign world, as Heinz Antor puts it in his plea for exposure to alterity and for broadening the reader's horizon.[29] Rather than just transporting us into the world of other cultures, fictions can impose their own imaginary maps on our minds, shaping our perception of alterity. A look into Malcolm Bradbury's *Atlas of Literature* will convince the reader of the truth of the editorial comment that

> [...] our maps of the world have been shaped by literary writings: America, the New World, was imagined in European books long before Europeans ever explored, conquered or settled there. In our modern world, the globe has both shrunk and widened. Now im-

---

[25] Quoted in Rüdiger Ahrens, "The International Development of English and Cross-cultural Competence," in Rüdiger Ahrens and Heinz Antor, eds., *Text - Culture – Reception: Cross-cultural Aspects of English Studies* (Heidelberg: Winter, 1992), 14f.

[26] Ahrens, "The International Development", 20.

[27] Michael Holquist, *Dialogism: Bakhtin and his World* (London/New York: Routledge, 1994), 84.

[28] Holquist, *Dialogism*, 85.

[29] Antor, "Ethical Plurivocity", esp. 71ff.

portant books and great writers come and go between many regions, continents and cultures. In consequence our own mental and imaginary maps of the world have been transformed.[30]

IV. The Pluricentricity of New English Literatures: Why We should Teach Them, and What We can Learn from Them

The rise of English from a national language to a *lingua franca*, a 'link language' on the global scale, is the result of a historical development dating back to the Elizabethan Age. This transformation, giving much cause to anxieties of a corruption of the 'original' idiom, can be characterized as rooted in England's world-wide expansion resultative of individual desire for profit-making, state-supported mercantile enterprise and state-directed imperial conquests. The dissolution of former imperial power in the process of de-colonization and the establishing of a Commonwealth of Nations has historically been paralleled and finally superseded by the establishment of the true super-power at the end of the twentieth century, the USA. It is not only Western imperialism and neo-imperialism (as some would call it) or economic dominance that has helped to secure the global reign of English as the language of the international community. Additionally linguistic properties have facilitated this. As Peter Strevens has observed, English is "a *borrowing* and *incorporating* language."[31] Historically, it has absorbed a large number of foreign linguistic influences, from Latin, Celtic and Scandinavian terms to those from non-European languages. Furthermore, as a "diversifying language" it has established itself in dialectic and regional variations in many former colonies. Its usage in international aviation, for example, and the predominance of English pop music and Hollywood movies have fostered its status as a communicative tool. And, finally, its phonetic flexibility and replacement of grammatical by natural gender have furthered its international growth. Today its command is considered a prerequisite for social advancement and individual success, in some countries as instrumental to gaining access to international communication standards. From a national discourse English has shifted to a 'pluralistic discourse'. This historical and linguistical development has been accompanied by the growth and establishment of various ethnic literary voices in all nooks and crannies of the world, not just in the former centre of its expansion.

It seems quite self-evident that to disregard these tendencies when teaching literature in the EFL-classroom would be a sign of blind ignorance of the major sociocultural as well a economic currents of the English-speaking world. For European readers these new literatures allow access to a wealth of stimulating cultural sources of the Other, a wide range of possibilities to engage in negotiations of meaning which can challenge the very foundations of one's own cultured identity. As any literature these new fictions can open windows on other individuals, ethnic groups or nations which we

---

[30] Malcolm Bradbury, ed., *The Atlas of Literature* (London: De Agostini, 1996), 8.
[31] Strevens is quoted and discussed in Ahrens, "The International Development", 6f.

may find difficult to understand otherwise. Glances through these windows afford insights into the global functions of literature as an international discourse today. Whether one calls them post-colonial literatures, New English Literatures or uses any other term, these literatures have the status of world literature in various senses of the term: they are popular with an international readership, and they appeal to modern readers with a critical global awareness.

Such awareness reflects the current state of what is read and taught world-wide in university courses. As Bart Moore-Gilbert observed in a recent article on the state of the art of post-colonial criticism,[32] after their irrepressible growth since the early 1980s postcolonial studies — and, we may add, many other *return-of-the-repressed* studies — have not only consolidated their position, but have lost their momentum recently. What is more, with the diminished energy and the regrouping of old positions a new skepticism has arisen. Indeed, old dichotomies of the authentic indigenous culture on the one hand and the monolithic dominant culture on the other have crumbled. If old dualisms are no longer taken for granted, then a less static picture of former opposites emerges, a less uniform interpretation of historical relationships between the oppressor and the oppressed. For many critics, a new paradigm has been created — that of cultural and personal 'hybridity'.

To return to the beginnings of this rise, post-colonialism as an academic force to be reckoned with can be traced back to the 1970s, when in its initial thrust models of assimilation or acculturation in international cultural relations inherent in Commonwealth Literary Studies were rejected. This happened at a time when national and ethnic identities as well as the concept of post-coloniality as a counter-discourse evolved. However, it was only in 1989 that the seminal study that charted the map of post-colonial studies, Ashcroft, Griffiths and Tiffin's *The Empire Writes Back: Theory and Practice in Post-Colonial Literatures,* firmly established post-colonialism as a literary field worthy of major attention. During a preceding phase, critical scrutiny of the representation of otherness paved the ground for this. To a large degree this early phase was influenced by theoretical publications about 'Othering'. It was mainly Edward Said's *Orientalism* from 1968 which offered a powerful heuristic and interpretative tool to re-evaluate much of Western literature.[33] The Orient, and accordingly all

---

[32] Bart Moore-Gilbert, "Crises of Identity? Current Problems and Possibilities in Postcolonial Criticism," *The European English Messenger* 6/2 (1997): 35-43; also compare Hena Maes-Jelinek, "Postmodernism and Its Others: Cross-cultural Counterpoints in British Fiction," *Anglistik* 8/1 (1997): 61-73, Mills, *Discourse*, 105-30, and Ania Loomba, *Colonialism/Postcolonialism* (London/New York: Routledge, 1998) on the state of the art of postcolonial criticism.

[33] Of course, Said (*Orientalism*. London: Penguin, 1987 [¹1978]; also *Culture and Imperialism,* London: Chatto & Windus, 1993) is mentioned here as representative of a number of other critics tackling representations of the colonial or post-colonial situation. Another influential study is, for example, D.O. Mannoni's *Prospero and Calliban: The Psychology of Colonization* (New York: Praeger, 1964), and — as a critique of Mannoni — Frantz Fanon's *Black Skin, White Masks* (trans. Charles Lam Markmann, London: Pluto Press: 1986). All enforce the notion of white 'Othering'.

alien cultures, as Said and those arguing in his tradition have it, was produced in textual representations to reinforce and perpetuate Western myths and stereotypes about other cultures. Rather than as individuals or as societies functioning on their own terms, non-European individuals and countries were viewed as a repository of Western knowledge. By means of 'Othering' foreign characters in literary texts, indigenous people were perceived as a uniform mass, faceless and without specific traits. The East became an exotic pageant; its individuals were reified to become, according to the psychology of colonialism, objects of longing or loathing. Following such theoretical stances on petrified habits of Western perception, in a first step the old canon was re-examined with a view on how representations of the Other did or did not reveal the author's incrimination in the imperial enterprise.

Additionally, the constructing of the colonizer's identity was revealed as being on the back of the colonized or marginalized Other. With a view that colonial discourse was mainly organized around practices of exclusion, the classics of British colonial literature such as novels by Haggard, Kipling, Conrad or Forster became the focus of much controversy. Increasingly, reinterpretations were and have been marked and superseded by the shift towards post-coloniality in literature and criticism. 'Writing back' as a political project has been a product of this critical stance towards Eurocentric values embedded in colonial literature. Thus 'writing back' has always had at its heart the rewriting of (post-)colonial history. Feelings ranging from anger to resistance are behind the production of literary texts that give a different, sometimes inverse angle to dominant tales about the Other. Classical texts of the Imperialist epoch such as Conrad's *Heart of Darkness* have been given counter-voices.[34] As a tale about a native African village, Chinua Achebe's *Things Fall Apart* was hailed as an early example of an intertextual eye-opener. Other reinterpretations of Conrad's colonial story include Francis Ford Coppola's film *Apocalypse Now* (the stress is again on how whites go to pieces, this time during the Vietnam war), Margaret Atwood's *Surfacing* (Canadian context), V.S. Naipaul's *A Bend in the River* (Asian-Carribean frame) and Patrick White's *A Fringe of Leaves* (Australian soil). These are just some of the many examples of retelling a European story within a different context or from a different perspective.

Recently more prominence has been gained by a number of post-colonial authors conquering the literary scene. No longer is it just the token post-colonial author that is included in the mainstream of literary studies. Rather, powerful new writing, 'fresh fictions' are to be found in non-European countries today, or they are written by authors with a Commonwealth background. Their most prominent proponent is, of course, Salman Rushdie, whose ingenious straddling of national and ethnic identies and whose international consciousness in *Midnight's Children* was awarded the prestigious Booker Prize in 1981. Much public exposure has been given not only to this Indian-English author due to the infamous death threat brought upon him for alleged blasphemy in *The Satanic Verses*. The unfortunate *fatwa* has also moved a number of

---

[34] All further examples of recycling Conrad's story are from Keith Green and Jill LeBihan, *Critical Theory & Practice: A Coursebook* (London/New York: Routledge, 1996), 277.

other authors of similar 'cultural hybridity' into the literary limelight. These are authors whose writings and identies are rooted in both a non-Western country and in the West. Among authors of celebrated international renown are Vikram Seth, an Indian, whose novel *A Suitable Boy* brought him acclaim both by the critics and the reading public; Michael Ondaatje, born in Sri Lanka and raised in Canada, whose *The English Patient* proved to be the lucrative basis for an Oscar-grossing filmscript; Kazuo Ishiguro, raised in England and Japan, whose *Remains of the Day* was adapted for a star-studded movie. Apart from the grand old masters of the polyglott tale V.S. Naipaul, other authors with divided backgrounds and loyalties have turned former hierarchies upside down to the point that it seems almost uncommon for a traditional white European or American author to gain coveted literary awards.To name just a few more recent examples, Derek Walcott, of mixed African, Dutch and English ancestry, a native Carribean writer, but also an academic in the USA, was awarded the Nobel Prize for Literature in 1992; most recently Arundhati Roy with her novel *The God of Small Things* about a love story straddling different castes in a small village in India gained the 1997 Booker Prize. Not the first citizen of the British Commonwealth to win the award, she has shown the continuous infatuation of both the common reader and the critical establishment with literature from the former colonies.

There is indeed an ongoing enchantment of Western readers with these international fictions: the taste of the exotic; the appeal of magic realism which seems to have found its congenial setting on foreign soil. Moreover, they offer a freshness and authenticity that to some tastes has been knocked out of the body of the all too consciously self-reflexive mainstream of high-brow European literature. This breath of fresh air is treasured by readers and critics alike. A shift of the centres of 'great writing' to the former periphery has been observed both by conservative critics like George Steiner and by members of the post-colonial community of writers and critics, such as Yasmine Gooneratne. She was not the first to observe that the true descendents of Swiftean satire and of irony and humour in the vein of Austen can be found not at the heart of the former empire, but on its fringes — Naipaul is declared to be Swift's heir, Jhabvala and Atwood (and, we may add, Gooneratne herself) are seen as the new talented masters of 'British' irony.[35] The collected articles of *Text - Culture - Reception* (1992, edited by Ahrens and Antor) bear witness to multifacetted journeys of texts across cultural boundaries and how in this process entrenched prejudices and cliches are constantly being challenged and undermined. In the reception of reading and discussing literature from the (former) fringes, readers are lured into taking alternative views into consideration. By means of an ongoing negotiation our own preconceived notions are destabilized and contested. Such vivid tackling of alterity can provide us with the much-propagated 'cultural-competence' as we will discuss at the end of this article. To describe it in terms of discourse theory: as our 'meaning systems' are changed by the new and different cultural codes while counter-discourses compete with our established cultural discourse, the old master discourses are subverted and

---

[35] From "Yasmine Gooneratne, Sydney, in Interview with Rudolf Bader," *Anglistik* 5/1 (1994): 15-23, esp. 23.

demystified. We may recognize the limitations of our own discoursive framework and its construction by means of exclusion. As a possible result of this unhinging of old thought patterns a new, more humane and more holistic approach to both life and literature may evolve.

Such broadening of horizons may not just mean a gain in tolerance and an acceptance of diversity. Moreover, it can result in a less Eurocentric view that encompasses thoughts and philosophies once alien to us and now enriching our lives. It may in fact be, as some authors from non-Western countries have observed, that values and philosophies of a non-European tradition could prove to be more in demand in the future global village of constant change.[36] These are often indigenous philosophies and religious beliefs that emphasize holistic values. Former oppositions are dissolved, such as those of the mind versus the body, the individual versus the community, ecology versus economics. Indeed, a universal acceptance of these values could encourage a sounder, more integrating acceptance of the 'natural' parts of human life that have become stigmatized or a taboo in Western culture such as death, sexuality, the bodily functions etc. In general, these 'new' international values stemming from a closer observance of once muted voices can add to the recent ethical turn in postmodernism by contributing to the shift towards more humane virtues based on holistic concepts rather than on those of exclusion.

V. Post-coloniality's Pyrrhic Victory; or, the Mutability of Consumer Capitalism

If the West was won in the proliferation of minority and post-colonial studies and if we all agree that one of the pleasures of this conquest can only be the evolution of a better, more caring and less one-sided society and personality, why is there at the heart of the current debate about post-colonialism such a sense of uneasiness, even of "crisis of identity"?[37] After all, as Moore-Gilbert describes it, there are signs galore of post-colonialism's success: numerous conferences on the subject; an abundance of series by major publishing houses; the establishment of new courses, from undergraduate introductions to the 'New Literatures in English' to postgraduate programmes on any aspect of post-colonial literature; the consolidation of theoretical viewpoints, with the great postcolonial theorists Said, Spivak and Bhabha now having achieved canonization by being invoked, if tongue-in-cheek, as 'the Holy Trinity'. Why then are there the nagging doubts of having achieved a Pyrrhic victory? It is not that post-colonial studies or authors have 'sold out' to the old enemy, the West. Rather, a sense of bereavement is brought about by the propensity of consumer capitalism (the market economy or consumerist society — whatever critical or neutral term one may use for the system of free enterprise and competition mainly unrestricted by

---

[36] For example, Gooneratne suggests that the Buddhist concept of constant change and impermanence can be most valuable in a globalized future. Cf. her recent novel *The Pleasures of Conquest* (Sydney: Vintage, 1996).

[37] Moore-Gilbert, "Crises of Identity", passim. Some of the following examples of the establishing of post-colonialism as an academic subject are also taken from this article.

state-interference) to embrace all its enemies from without or within, to contain subversive voices in the dynamic maelstrom of internationalization. Far from being toppled by alternative and critical positions, market economies have tended to thrive on competing products; emerging challengers to sclerotic and fossilized systems have always been welcomed. Ironically, capitalism and the attached internationalization have proved to be inherently and methodologically diverse and indeed productive of dissent. Far from merely coopting diverging voices capitalism has been providing a meta-vehicle for plurivocal expressions.

What is even more ironic, the new products of post-colonialism have helped to re-create an energetic climate of rivaly perpetuating the machinery of globalization instead of serving as a spanner in the works of Western economic progress. The powerful trend of globalization — which seems to be analogous to the spread of Western (to be exact, US-American) consumerism and pop culture — is hand in glove with multinational conglomerations and a global communications systems in creating a homogenized contemporary world-culture. As a result, a sense of loss and deception has become pertinent in post-colonial studies — that all the polyglot, multi-cultural exchanges are clandestinely the ploy or just the symptoms of an irresistible encroachment of consumer capitalism, of McDonald's and Coca-Cola, on any remaining traditional societies. In much of post-colonial criticism a Marxist terminology and eschatology is the subtext of angry and frustrated rejections of such unifying world-wide trends. They appear as thinly veiled strategies of the neo-colonial system which is actually casting its net of exploitation ever wider. The 'new world order' once propagated by Americans as a synonym for the end of history as a struggle of capitalism against competing systems is today dreaded as the last stage in the Westernization of the globe.[38]

Against these all-pervasive tendencies new concepts are pitted. It is the new sense of place, of belonging to a certain region or of exploring a deeply rooted regional or ethnic identity that asserts its counter-position. Such strong affiliations intensify a sense of belonging and create communal as well as individual identity. Of course, they can harbour the danger of a new radical essentialism or parochial self-sufficiency which, again, constructs its identity mainly by means of exclusion. For a capitalist world-order such identities, however, do not primarily function as destabilizing pockets of resistance; rather, they create dynamic disturbances and function as vibrant sources of regeneration. They produce friction and thus energy and new challenges.

The ability, or even the very nature of the dominant capitalist order not just to absorb other voices (or products) like a sponge, or — if that cannot be achieved — to live with inherent contradictions and to contain them has been underestimated by its critics. This propensity of the ever expanding, ever diversifying Moloch may also be

---

[38] Such sentiments reject the concepts of multiculturalism, postmodernism and post-colonialism as sly guises for the values of late capitalism, consumer society, Western dominance etc. Cf. the positions of Gayatri Chakravorty Spivak, Homi K. Bhabha or Helen Tiffin, to name just the most prominent critics (cf., for example, their articles in Bill Ashcroft, Gareth Griffiths and Helen Tiffin, eds., *The Post-colonial Studies Reader* [London/New York: Routledge, 1995]).

at the centre of the success of post-colonial literature and theory. This success is also based on two anologous concepts of the human condition and of human identity both in postmodernism and in post-colonialism.

The question raised by Kwame Anthony Appiah as to the similarities of "[t]he Postcolonial and the Postmodern"[39] are of fundamental importance to an understanding of this partly symbiotic relationship. Ashcroft, Griffiths and Tiffin detect parallels in both projects:

> [T]he major project of postmodernism — the deconstruction of the centralised, logocentric master narratives of European culture, is very similar to the post-colonial project of dismantling the Center/Margin binarism of imperial discourse. The decentering of discourse, the focus on the significance of language and writing in the construction of experience, the use of the subversive strategies of mimicry, parody and irony — all these concerns overlap those of postmodernism and so a conflation of the two discourses has often occured.[40]

The resistance to a dominant discourse, destabilized notions of truth and certainty, the problematization of meaning, the stress of different viewpoints and competing voices —all these are further similarities of the two discourses. This 'co-mingling' effect appeals especially to existing habits of reading and analyzing post-colonial texts. Novels by migrant writers of mixed national backgrounds like Rushdie or Ondaatje seem to reflect the postmodern condition. Playfully celebrating the absence of centre, they sustain the laws of causality and progress in non-linear plots and, most importantly, in the exploration of the multiple ethnic layers of identity the post-colonial situation entails. The artful juxtaposition of different lifestyles and utterances in the polyphony of post-modern narratives entices the Western reader into an open-ended dialogue. It is exactly this reason for the popularity of post-colonial narratives that has been at the centre of radical criticism of those condemning Western co-optation and appropriation. Here seems to be the last turn of the screw of American-style capitalism. As an outspoken critic of these tendencies, the African-American feminist bell hooks (!) comments on the appropriation of the other's voice:

> In a white-supremacist, capitalist, patriarchal state where the mechanisms of co-optation are so advanced, much that is potentially radical is undermined, turned into commodity, fashionable speech as in 'black women writers are in right now.'[41]

As mentioned above, a disturbing sense of frustration, even despair runs through the recent writings of those who consider post-colonialism "a broad anti-imperialist emancipatory project."[42] In a world of increasingly globalized commerce and culture the term "post-colonial" — be it in literature or criticism — has become an increasingly

---

[39] In Ashcroft et al., *The Post-colonial Studies Reader*, 119ff., repr. of 1992.
[40] In Ashcroft et al., *The Post-colonial Studies Reader*, 117.
[41] Quoted in Green and LeBihan, *Critical Theory & Practice*, 299.
[42] Linda Hutcheon, "Colonialism and the Post-colonial Condition: Complexities Abounding," *PMLA* 1 (1995), 8.

fashionable and marketable position to be jockeyed for by any new writer or critic. As one may observe almost cynically, it has lost its thrust of a counter-discourse and has gained "academic marketability"[43] instead - a privileged asset with which one can reach the international interpretive community.

Even when taking such a pessimistic vantage point one should not disregard the wealth of exciting cultural products emanating from the synergy of blending world culture in the arts. It is not just with writers such as Rushdie, Ondaatje, Naipaul and Ishiguro that this enriching effect is achieved. New syntheses are also being created in the sculptures, installations or performances by international artists such as Nam June Paik, Christo and Kunc, in the theatre experiments of Mnouchkine, Brook or Wilson and in the films of Kurosawa, Zhang Yimou and Jarmusch.[44] With the interwebbing of cultural styles other borders are dissolved as well. Entrenched dualisms of popular and serious art or gendered identities are blurred in avantgard "funky culture"[45], as the multi-talented musician and performer David Byrne has termed the transgression of ethnic, sexual and aesthetic distinctions. As he envisions it, such hybrid forms of art perforate old concepts of purity and separation. As with a chemical reaction of incongruent substances mixed up in an experiment, this crucible will yield ever new fleeting constellations of diversified cultures.

The conflictual emergence and establishment of new competing positions has created its new idols. If, like the sword of Damocles, the fear of Western dominance hovers above the recent debate in which some writers and critics are paralysed, others intent on circling the waggons against the encroaching enemy of globalization, celebrating difference and ethnic identity, out of the powerful and contradictory forces shaping international and national identities a new embodiment of this *zeitgeist* has emerged: cultural 'hybridity'. In a world of fast changes, authors from a wide variety of cultural origins who use English as their language to reach an international audience are seen as privileged in capturing the current climate of being torn between rootlessness and the exploration of ethnic identity. Straddling different worlds, novelists such as Naipaul or Rushdie have been likened to former 'hybrid' writers of the likes of Conrad, Nabokov or Beckett. Rather than feeling estranged and deracinated, these citizens of the world seem to have discovered the globe as their home. Be it in the less antagonistic model of Said (who stresses humankind's common history) or the conflictual model of Bhabha (who emphasizes the difference between the colonizer and the colonized), the new "paradigm of hybridity"[46] bears strong resemblance to the concept of the 'decentered self' which has been propagated by poststructuralism and deconstruction (namely Foucault, Barthes and Derrida) and Bakhtinian dialogism.

---

[43] A. McClintock in LeBihan and Green, *Critical Theory & Practice*, 290.

[44] Compare the international artists mentioned by Uwe Wittstock, "Geschmackssachen," *Süddeutsche Zeitung* 24/25 Feb. (1996): FI.

[45] Quoted in Wittstock, "Geschmackssachen".

[46] For a discussion of various positions on this "new paradigm" see Moore-Gilbert, "Crises of Identity?".

Postmodern assaults on the "egotism of the West"[47] (Bakhtin) — its bourgeois illusion of a unique, stable and autonomous Cartesian self — have found an ally in the postcolonial identity of the 'hyphenated status', of an identity that is 'this' and always also 'that'. As some strands of postmodernism have been happy to celebrate the loss of affiliations, offering an unprecedented sense of freedom of choice, where the individual can seemingly shift in and out of identities without effort, cultural hybridity for some critics has been interpreted as the chance to plunge into the pleasures of rootlessness with abandon, to explore ever newer dimensions of the multi-facetted self. But the decentering of identity has its darker, tragic elements, too. If the self has lost its stability, the experience of dislocation, displacement and alienation can be paramount. The literature of 'hybrid identities' does not just offer a liberation from the former 'crutches of the self' (i.e. of religion, nation, class etc.) but a sense of the fragility of new constructions of the self. After all, the world of post-colonialism is not just theoretic playfulness. It often involves the tragedy of human suffering and loss in the historical processes of colonialism, post-colonialism and globalization.

VI. The Dialogics of Reading as an Open-ended Hermeneutic Process

As a project of liberation from old authorities, postmodern theories have destabilized our notions of texts, interpretations and of the possibility of ever achieving meaning in our encounter with the Other — be it the text or somebody from a different background. How can we grasp the Other if we ourselves are just an amalgam of conscious and subconscious sociocultural forces, if (as Richard Rorty once caustically remarked) our acceptance of the relativity of everything has come to the point that "[w]e have become so open-minded that our brains have fallen out."[48] To understand the other — let alone to understand the self — has become impossible in a world of semiotics and deconstruction in which the arbitrary and culturally constructed character of any cultural practice is constantly exposed. It is not just the epistemological impossiblity to impose any order on the great chaos of life; any attempt to understand the Other has also been declared a failure from the beginning. To gain knowledge of the Other equals a struggle for domination. The will to understand is a thinly veiled striving for power, as Said and others[49] in the tradition of the Foucauldian view of the knowledge-power nexus have claimed. It is either unabashed Eurocentrism which uses the Other merely as a distant mirror onto which one's own desires and pathologies can be projected. Or it claims for a sham universalism which absorbs the alien nature of the other while establishing Western hegemony.

---

[47] Quoted in Holquist, *Dialogism*, 90.
[48] Richard Rorty, *Objectivism, Relativism, and Truth* (Cambridge: Cambridge University Press), 203.
[49] See the chapter "Othering" in Mills, *Discourse*, 106ff.

As Lothar Bredella and others have suggested,[50] these position of resistance to intercultural understanding may lead to lethargy and entropy. Given the view that all cultures are incommensurable and that we are always culturally and historically pre-conditioned never to properly understand another culture, even to potentially co-opt the Other, why should we read at all? The only secure vantage point outside and above this dilemma seems to be the pessimistic and frivolous position never to engage in any cross-cultural encounter at all. Apart from its moral implications, such smugness does not take into account, as Heinz Antor has shown, the anthropological dimension of "[m]an as a pattern-building animal."[51] For deeply engraved into our human make-up there is a need for establishing meaning out of the contingency of our existence. Our human identity is constructed as a hermeneutic process by means of constantly engaging in complex interactions with other beings. We cannot pursue this dialogic process of creating meaning without holding a number of norms, ideas etc. — in other words, prejudices. As H.-G. Gadamer has it, these preconceived notions of the self and the other are the prerequisite for any meaningful communication. Rather than indulging in ethical indifference and disregard for anthropological needs for pattern-building and thus becoming an easy victim of essentialist tendencies, the active participant in exchanges is quite conscious of all the dangers inherent in such encounters and makes deliberate ethical choices, carefully weighing positive and negative potentialities of such encounters.[52] Rüdiger Ahrens has summed up the necessity of and the problems inherent in cross-cultural exchanges as follows:

> D[a]s hermeneutische Bemühen des interpretierenden Ichs ist dialogisch angelegt, weil es bestrebt ist, das Fremde und Unbekannte in den eigenen Verstehenshorizont einzubeziehen und sich mit ihm bedeutungsstiftend auseinanderzusetzen. Auch beim Verstehen fremder Kulturen wird dieses dialogische Verhältnis in besonderer Weise aktiviert, da sich nun neben der Sprache noch weitere kulturelle Probleme und Hindernisse, die etwa durch die geographische Distanz, die ethnischen Ursprünge oder die religiösen Wurzeln hervorgerufen werden, einstellen, die den Verstehensprozeß erschweren.[53]

The key terms here are "bedeutungsstiftend" (*creating meaning*) and "dialogisches Verhältnis" (*dialogic relationship*). They are inextricably interconnected in recent theories of understanding the Other by such literary critics as Bredella, Antor and Ahrens himself. Of course, such theories pay homage to the grand old philosopher of hermeneutics, H.-G. Gadamer, and to the Russian critic, philosopher and visionary of dialogism, M. Bakhtin. The project of a dialogic, hermeneutic approach to cross-cul-

---

[50] Cf. Bredella and Antor (see footnote 1).
[51] Heinz Antor, "Ethical Plurivocity, or: The Pleasures and Rewards of Reading," in Ahrens and Antor, eds., *Text – Culture – Reception*, 40.
[52] For a discussion of Gadamer see Antor, "The Ethics of Criticism".
[53] Rüdiger Ahrens, "Die Herausforderung des Fremden im post-kolonialen Roman: Yasmine Gooneratne, *A Change of Skies*, 1991," in Herbert Christ and Michael K. Legutke, eds., *Fremde Texte verstehen. Festschrift für Lothar Bredella zum 60. Geburtstag* (Tübingen: Narr, 1996), 246.

tural exchanges takes into consideration both active and creative, both cognitive and emotional aspects. Unlike postmodernism as Buridan's donkey, (morally) starving due to its inability to decide on any position, this projected dialogic principle asks for constant interactions with the voices of the other. Meaning, if only temporal, is achieved in this conflictual model by constant self-reflexive repositioning. Therefore, like Bakhtin's dialogism, it is a "stern philosophy."[54] If in popular reception the principle of dialogism has sometimes too easily been associated with a celebration of the pleasure-principle in a subversive carnivalism, one should not forget that the art of living dialogically entails a strenuous effort. There are rewards for "being fated to the condition of dialogue"[55] — we are offered a way out of postmodern double-binds. The way to dialogic mastery is learning to live with openness, relativity, contingency — in short, to subscribe to the new universal values of the ethical turn of postmodernism which I described in the first part of this article. It is during this process of give and take, of challenge and response that we are wrestled out of our familiar values and norms without completely abandoning our own position and losing our way in the postmodern maze. In enabling this, a dialogic concept of intercultural understanding can indeed empower the reader to "become less one-sided, less stubborn and less provincial."[56]

Finally, the role of literature in this process can be seen in serving as a catalyst of cross-cultural understanding. In refuting any monologic interpretative closure, in its polyphony of equally valid (ethnic) voices it challenges the native and the non-native reader alike. For both readers are implicated in an asymmetrical process of reading — texts that straddle ethnic and national boundaries (and which text does not to some extent) — cannot be understood better by any group of readers. For in the reception of the plurivocity of fictions native and non-native readers alike have an "Erfahrungsvorsprung" (are ahead in experience) and an "Erfahrungsrückstand"[57] (lag behind in experience). It is the negotiation between contradictory but also overlapping horizons of expectation and reading that creates the tension needed to lure us out of entrenched positions. And in the distance we may perceive a utopian and egalitarian promise of the emancipation of human perception and creativity. It is the promise of a world which, in spite of all its fault-lines and barriers, always entails the possibilities of a better, less hierarchical and less racist global society.[58] Again, this may smack of old universal values, but in this respect the universalism of old humanist and new postmodern values offers a vision adequate to the contingent, indeterminate and diverse nature of the human condition.

---

[54] See Holquist, *Dialogism*, on Bakhtin's dialogism, 181.
[55] Holquist, *Dialogism*, 181.
[56] Bredella, "How Can Literary Texts Matter?", 113.
[57] Ahrens, "Die Herausforderung des Fremden", 255.
[58] See the Bakhtinian critic Michael Gardiner, *The Dialogics of Critiqu: M.M. Bakhtin and the Theory of Ideology* (London/New York: Routledge, 1992), esp. 41, 94.

Intercultural Developments in German EFL Teaching

KLAUS STIERSTORFER (Würzburg)

Europe is evolving from a conglomeration of frequently antagonistic nation states into a neighbourhood of multi-cultural societies. Workers' migrations and an increase in general mobility surely have been an important factor in this development, but perceptual changes due to an ongoing deconstruction of the myth of the nation, inherited from the nineteenth-century, with a corresponding monolithic culture are equally important. Although macro- and micro-regional variations in this pattern are undoubtedly significant, its general validity can no longer be denied.[1] What remains, however, open to question is the ways and means to react to this development. The choice of options starts, on the one side, from an outright denial of its importance, and indeed its existence, in the very face of facts, amounting to an attempt to re-establish or strengthen the myth of the homogeneous national culture and implying the exclusion or assimilation of so-defined 'alien' elements. At the other end of the scale, the centripetal movement can be enhanced by supporting pluricultural tendencies.

The battle to decide which options will eventually prevail is fought on many fronts, but education has traditionally been one of the most hotly contested areas. The classroom, it is rightly felt, is not only a mirror of society at large, but also one of its major formative instruments. And, to narrow the focus further, the subjects emerging at the fulcrum of the cultural debate will naturally be those dealing with a country's own language and literature on the one hand and those concerned with foreign cultures and languages on the other.

In the following, a historical review of the teaching of English as a foreign language (EFLT) in German schools over the past century will blend with a systematic survey of approaches in foreign language teaching and conclude by projecting possible ways forward as we enter the 21st century.

Granting the simplification always inherent in a systematic survey,[2] the changing

---

[1] As a very useful source of information on the situation in Germany see Cornelia Schmalz-Jacobsen and Georg Hansen, eds., *Kleines Lexikon der ethnischen Minderheiten in Deutschland* (Bonn: Beck, new ed. 1997).

[2] For detailed accounts of the historical development of EFLT in Germany since 1871 see Volker Raddatz, *Englandkunde im Wandel deutscher Erziehungsziele 1886-1945* (Kronberg/Ts.: Scriptor, 1977); Reiner Lehberger, *Englischunterricht im Nationalsozia-lismus* (Tübingen: Stauffenburg Verlag, 1986); Volker Raddatz, *Fremdsprachliche Landes-kunde in Unterricht und Forschung: Eine Bilanz seit 1945* (Augsburg: Universität Augsburg, 1989); but also the concise summaries by Reiner Lehberger, "Geschichte des Fremdspra-chenunterrichts bis 1945" and by Herbert Christ and Werner Hüllen, "Geschichte des Fremdsprachenunterrichts seit 1945" in Karl-Richard Bausch, Herbert Christ and Hans-Jürgen Krumm, eds., *Handbuch Fremdsprachenunterricht* (Tübingen and Basel: Francke, 3rd ed. 1995), 561-572. To all of these I am indebted for general information used in my historical survey.

concepts of EFLT in Germany since the late nineteenth century can be reduced to four basic models (see figures 1 to 4 below). One of these, it has to be stated with regret, emerges as the dominant concept for the entire period from the 1870s to the end of World War II.

Surely it is easy to identify significant variations and developments in EFLT guidelines in the passage of so many decades; crosscurrents, ambiguities and even strong and persistent dissent were not unknown. When it comes to generalizations and applying the broad brush, however, the remaining contours show an educational system which mirrored the national culture from 1871 to 1945 in its blatant self-centredness and recurrently crude chauvinism. Caught in the snag of having to serve a nationalistic educational ideal on the one hand and being by its nature concerned with a foreign culture on the other, the compromises found in EFLT at the time were always uneasy ones and unfailingly ended with a kowtow to the former. In making English part of the educational agenda the nationalist interest could be couched in the terms of a wary "know thine enemy," first understood in a mercantile, but then an increasingly martial sense; it could also be declared in the wish for a darkling foreign foil to increase the luminescence of the 'superior' German culture in its brightness.

When in the first decades after the founding of the German Empire in 1871 patriotic sentiments ran high, EFLT did not only have to accomodate these, but was involved in a struggle for a position in higher education in the first place. The *Gymnasium* as the key institution of school education at the secondary level was still entirely centred on the classics and inimical to modern languages. It was only in a very slow process that EFLT was able to encroach on its curriculum. Initially, it had only found its niche at the so-called *Realschule* and similar, practical-minded institutions, where pupils were to be given expertise seen as directly conducive to their success in trade and business. The teaching was encyclopedic and utilitarian, that is to say, pupils were expected to learn to speak the language and at the same time get to know the foreign country by learning as many facts about it as possible. With the British Empire as the dominant economic power, speaking its language appeared a reasonable aim in this context. Given a patriotic twist, knowledge about the British might also be helpful in the attempt to emulate their success. At the same time, it could reveal their weaknesses and thus point out ways to compete with them in the international market place. Thus, when the Dresden society of modern philologists met in 1903 to celebrate their 25th anniversary, they called on German teachers 'to win the victory for the German people against other nations of long-standing traditions in trade and industry.'[3]

The *Realienkunde*, as this approach is usually referred to, was abandoned for a very different concept after World War I. Now, the cramming of facts about the foreign nation was replaced by the aim to instill an insight into the central characteristics of its culture. This *Wesens-* or *Kulturkunde* opposed all attempts at encyclopedic, compre-

---

[3] [My translation of:] "[...] um im Wettstreit mit den alten Handels- und Industrievölkern dem deutschen Volke den Sieg zu erstreiten;" quoted by Wilhelm Scheffler, "Fünfundzwanzigjährige Jubelfeier der Dresdner Gesellschaft für neuere Philologie," *Die Neueren Sprachen* 11 (1903/4): 28-36, here 34.

hensive knowlegde. In the wake of ideas propounded by Eduard Spranger and Wilhelm Dilthey, its exponents sought for characteristic examples, for the typical feature to lead them to a grasp of the gist, soul or core of a culture. The knowledge of that centre of a nation's being itself could, however, only be intuited, caught sight of in a creative act. It cannot, as Spranger was to point out in a later essay, be achieved by any methodology that could be taught, but depends on a quasi-artistic act of synopsis.[4] Although the movement to adopt a pan-European perspective was strong, nationalistic notes soon grew in volume once again. Thus, K. Schwedtke defined "the ultimate aim of our secondary schools" in 1930 "to work out the being and value of our national German culture from the counterfoils of the two great West European cultures and to illuminate their interpenetration and mutual influences."[5] Similarly, the *Curricular Guidelines for Secondary Schools in Prussia* of 1925 opposed the teaching of "mere knowledge of individual cultural facts" in favour of "guiding the pupil by means of a comparison between the foreign and the German natures [*Wesen*] towards an ever profounder understanding of the character peculiar to his own people."[6]

In a further turn of the screw, the most chauvinist aspects of *Kulturkunde* mutated into what then was dubbed *Volkstumskunde*. Representative of many, the change is clearly marked by M. Deutschbein in 1933. "It was a great error," he avers, "to believe that a consciousness of our German culture could be reached via the foreign culture." The recognition of "the enormous differences between the individual cultures" leads him to the conclusion "that peculiarity [*das Eigenwertige*] cannot be developed out of contraries, but that the contrasting and foreign nature of the other culture must be accepted as a fact."[7] Cultural self-definition by comparison with other cultures was thus vilified as below the dignity of the German people, not least, it has to be added, because of an apprehension that comparisons do not, of course, only show differences but can also point out similarities and interdependencies. To avoid this, German culture set up as an incomparable, original absolute, which was not

---

[4] Eduard Spranger, "Wie erfaßt man einen Nationalcharakter?," *Die Erziehung* 15 (1939/40): 41-62, esp. 62.

[5] [My translation of:] "[...] letztes Ziel unserer höheren Schulen [...], das Dasein und den Wert unserer nationalen deutschen Kultur aus den Gegenbildern der beiden großen west-europäischen Kulturen herauszuarbeiten und ihre wechselseitige Durchdringung und Beeinflussung zu beleuchten," K. Schwedtke, "Der Gedanke der Konzentration in seiner Bedeutung für die Auswahl der Lektüre im deutschen und neusprachlichen Unterricht," *Neusprachliche Mitteilungen* 1 (1930): 541.

[6] [My translation of:] "[...] kein bloßes Wissen von kulturellen Einzeltatsachen;" "vielmehr [...] soll dieser [i.e. der Schüler] durch den Vergleich des fremden mit dem deutschen Wesen zu einem vertieften Verständnis für die Eigenart seines Volkes geführt werden," in Hans Richert, ed., *Richtlinien für die Lehrpläne Preußens*, (Berlin: Weidemann, 1925), 113.

[7] [My translation of:] "Es ist ein großer Irrtum gewesen zu glauben, über die fremde Kultur zu einem deutschen Kulturbewußtsein zu gelangen. [...], daß man an dem Gegensätzlichen nicht das Eigenwertige entwickeln kann, sondern die Gegensätzlichkeit und Fremdheit der anderen Kultur als Tatsache hinnehmen muß." Max Deutschbein, "Die Aufgaben der englischen Philologie im neuen Staat," *Die Neueren Sprachen* 41 (1933): 321-9, here 328-9.

compared to other cultures to define it or understand it better, but, if it was compared at all, simply to make the division more clearly visible.

In this summary review, the entire period from 1871 to 1945 emerges as a time of extreme self-centredness and self-reflexivity in German EFLT. Among many things, this shows the insecurity and instability of what tried to define itself as German 'culture,' as its continual pre-occupation with 'the foreign' ironically undercuts all its vociferous isolationist claims to independence and self-sufficiency. In my graphic generalization of the period, therefore, the arrow aimed at the target culture is diverted half-way back to its origin. It never really reaches, and was not really meant to reach, its mark.[8]

fig.1

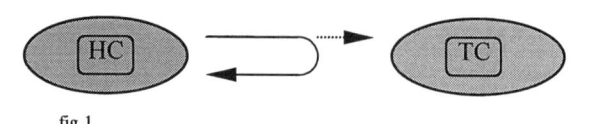

This instrumentalization of FLT had, of course, not been propounded without attracting fierce criticism even at the time.[9] Thus, Th. Litt deplored the utilization of FLT for chauvinistic purposes as "an unheard-of impoverishment, even voiding, of our entire educational effort" and called for the abandonment of "any other end but the understanding" of the foreign culture.[10] After 1945, it can be argued, Litt's demand was fulfilled in various ways. For obvious reasons, the years before the foundation of the Federal Republic of Germany in 1949, and for some years after, there was little cause for reflecting on any kind of German identity. FLT was seen as directly useful to communicate with the occupying forces and later, the major political allies and partners. English attained a clear dominance over other languages in FLT, but its educational concepts essentially retained, albeit with changing methodology, a narrow focus on 'pure' language teaching throughout the 1960s and 70s. *Landeskunde*, as the teaching and learning of knowlegde about the foreign country was now generally called, was relegated to a distant second rank of educational priorities and only admitted where it was seen to be helpful or even necessary to communicating with speakers of the target culture. Although the idea, much mooted from the 1950s onwards, that FLT should contribute to *Völkerverständigung*, the mutual understanding and harmony between nations, was strongly endorsed by all concerned, it remained vaguely defined and uncertain when it came to translate it into clear educational and didactic strategies. The link, therefore, between *Völkerverständigung* as a pedagogic principle and as a classroom practice was not at all clear.[11] The attention was fundamentally directed at

---

[8] Key to abbreviations used in this and subsequent figures: 'HC' = 'Host Culture,' 'TC' = 'Target Culture,' 'IC' = 'Intermediary Culture,' 'SC' = 'Subculture.' The direction of the arrows indicates the main direction of hermeneutic efforts.

[9] See for example Raddatz, *Englandkunde*, 43-5.

[10] Theodor Litt, "Gedanken zum 'kulturkundlichen' Unterrichtsprinzip," *Die Erziehung* 1 (1925/6): 105.

[11] For a critical perspective on the principle of *Völkerverständigung* see Dietmar Fricke, "Völkerver-ständigung statt Nationalstereotypen?" in Horst Arndt and Franz-Rudolf Weller,

the target culture with little reflection bestowed on the observer's premises (fig.2); a circumstance also to be seen in the emphasis on the unilingual method which called for the exclusive or at least predominant use of the foreign language in its instruction.

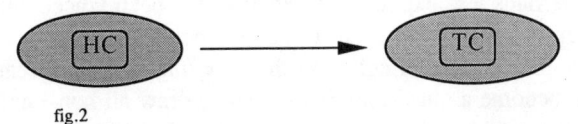

HC ──→ TC

fig.2

Since the early 1980s, several new and divers influences have made themselves felt in EFLT. They have raised a number of important issues which are a long way from being settled even today. One field of discussion was opened by the growing insight that the aim of endowing the pupils with 'communicative competence' as defined in the 1970s involved more than a mechanistic or structuralist concept of language seemed to imply. As new developments in linguistics in the wake of ordinary language philosophy and pragmalinguistics appeared to suggest, language never exists in a free communicative space, but is always inextricably bound up with a specific culture. Indeed, it was soon added, culture can only constitute itself in language. As this construct, culture had become, albeit variously defined, the object of study in an ever growing and increasingly confident discipline: cultural studies.[12] As the more comprehensive term, absorbing not only the strictly circumscribed field of *Landes-kunde*, but also language and literature, culture has been developing into a new paradigm of research and teaching. With their focus on 'the study of values' (Inglis, *Cultural Studies*, ix) and the ideologies, power structures and social negotiations which establish them, cultural studies also fitted nicely with new political and pedagogic objectives introduced into school curricula. In Germany, demands came from a wide political spectrum in the face of socio-political problems, of which the intermittent emergence of neo-Nazism is one of the most recent causes of national heartburn, that schools be given a much weightier portfolio in the general education of the nation's youth, including a renewed emphasis on the instillation of basic social and moral values.[13] With regard to the classroom practice of EFLT, a reappraisal of the relationship between the teaching of *Landeskunde* and language skills was the consequence. As the study of English cultures,[14] *Landeskunde* elements now moved from an ancillary function to the

---

eds., *Landeskunde und Fremdsprachenunterricht* (Frankfurt: Diesterweg, 1978), 179-206.

[12] For a survey of the 'cultural origins' of 'cultural studies' see for example Fred Inglis, *Cultural Studies* (Oxford and Cambridge, MA.: Blackwell, 1993), 25-106.

[13] In Bavaria, for example, "the clarification of the educational mission of the *Gymnasium* in our time" ("den erzieherischen Auftrag des Gymnasiums für unsere Zeit zu verdeutlichen") was one of the two major issues fomulated by the secretary for education and culture as guidelines for the revision of the curricula of the Bavarian *Gymnasium*. Hans Zehetmair, "Zum Geleit," *Lehrplan für das bayerische Gymnasium*, Bekanntmachung des Bayerischen Staatsministeriums für Unterricht und Kultus vom 2. August 1990 Nr. II/9, 3.

[14] See for example Michael Byram, *Cultural Studies in Foreign Language Education* (Clevedon, PA: Multilingual Matters, 1989), esp. 39-79, and Jürgen Kramer, "Cultural Studies. A New Paradigm in Teaching and Research" in *Cultural and Intercultural Studies* (Frankfurt a.M. et al.: Lang, 1990), 3-12.

centre of the pedagogues' interest by providing the forum where speech acts are embedded, values negotiated and pupils' as well as teachers' preconceptions could be put to the test.

Fierce criticism, perhaps less explicit in Germany, has been voiced against loading FLT with values alien or even detrimental to the host culture. Particularly in the face of the current hegemonic power of English as the new *lingua franca*, fears are growing that EFLT might become a quasi-imperialist tool to draw all non-English-speaking countries onto the victim side of a kind of neo-colonialist development. After all, Swinburne, in a semi-biographical reminiscence, had already noted in *Lesbia Brandon* that young Herbert, given "a few stray lessons in holiday" by Lady Wariston's Italian teacher, "learnt the language rapidly and roughly enough, and his politics in much the same fashion; as fast as he picked up words, he gathered up opinions."[15] In the face of this potential influence, Cem and Margaret Alptekin today warn that, "being at the receiving end of a virtually one-way flow of information from Anglo-American centers, the host country runs the risk of having its own culture totally submerged." They maintain that, despite their desire to learn English, the students are often unwilling to receive the cultural load of the target language. Hence, it is not uncommon for many who do not want to be 'culturally assimilated' to give up learning the target language.

What is more, students' possible compliance with this "cultural assimilation" would, in the Alptekins' eyes, just be the other prong of a cleft stick. In that case, as they demonstrate by A. Goke-Pariola's observations on the Nigerian situation, "it is not surprising [...] to see students alienated from their own social setting as they become adjusted to the values of the Anglo-American world." They accordingly point to exemplary practices in China, Japan, Venezuela and Kuwait "to 'de-Anglo-Americanize' English, both in linguistic and in cultural respects, in order for the language to be in tune with the needs of the EFL learners" in the host countries; or, in other words, to promote "bilingualism without biculturalism."[16] The way to achieve this, they argue, is, first to dismiss native speakers as EFL teachers and replace them by bilingually successful persons from the host country as models for the students to emulate. Second, their vision for suitable curricula tallies with the "culturally neutral, non-élitist, and learner-oriented" EFL programmes advocated by H. V. George.[17] The suggestion also corresponds to what Gillian Brown, in 1990, identified as a "recent trend:"

> It is noticeable that much modern published [EFLT] material has moved out of [...] any domain which is distinctively related to one particular country. So we find a great deal of language situated in travelling - at international airports, customs posts, at large international railway stations, on fast international trains, or in international hotels, where the

---

[15] Randolph Hughes, ed., *Lesbia Brandon by Algernon Charles Swinburne* (London: Falcon Press, 1952), 106.

[16] Cem and Margaret Alptekin, "The Question of Culture: EFL Teaching in non-English-speaking Countries," *ELT Journal* 38 (1984): 15-17.

[17] H.V. George, "Unhappy Professionalism," *World Language English* 1 (1981): 9-14 and C. and M. Alptekin, "Question of Culture," 18.

topic of conversation may be expected to refer to the location, or to expanding areas of leisure activity - sports, photography, pop music, and fashion. Such topics do not require a knowledge of any particular culture to understand but simply some acquaintance with westernized cosmopolitan culture which you are quite likely to encounter on television all over the world.[18]

In this concept, host and target culture do not directly intermingle, but converge on a kind of neutral territory which might be called an 'intermediary culture.'

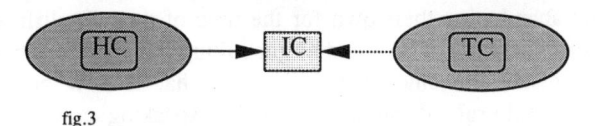

fig.3

The closest the German educational debate has come to this model was perhaps the suggestion to base the exemplary communicative situations in EFLT on everyday shared human experiences like eating and sleeping, love and hate. Taking up ideas from American cultural studies projects,[19] classroom discussion was to be restricted to these 'universals' to bridge the intercultural gap. Pupils were to be introduced to the foreign culture by pointing out its familiar elements and downplaying the differences. However, as Robert Picht concisely summarizes, the programme does not stand up to scrutiny:

> At a closer look, everyday life is by no means quotidian. Precisely because it happens spontaneously and is not preconceived, it contains the whole complexity of mainly subconscious cultural relationships. It is therefore, the less these are sublimated, much less universal than science, literature and the arts.[20]

Similarly, Gillian Brown goes on to answer her own question: "Are there contexts of language use which are value-free, quite independent of any cultural background?" I am writing as though what I have called 'cosmopolitan English' were value-free, but of course this is not so. That kind of English assumes a materialistic set of values in which international travel, not being bored, positively being entertained, having leisure, and, above all, spending money casually and without consideration of the sum involved in the pursuit of these ends, are the norm (Brown, "Cultural Values," 13).

---

[18] Gillian Brown, "Cultural Values: the Interpretation of Discourse," *ELT Journal* 44 (1990): 11-17, here 12.

[19] See Paul Mog and Hans-Joachim Althaus, eds., *Die Deutschen in ihrer Welt* (Berlin: Langenscheidt, 1992).

[20] [My translation of:] "Bei näherer Betrachtung ist Alltag also keineswegs alltäglich. Gerade weil er spontan und nicht durchdacht verläuft, enthält er die ganze Komplexität weitgehend unbewußter kultureller Beziehungsgeflechte, ist also, je weniger diese sublimiert sind, wesentlich weniger universal als Wissenschaft, Literatur und Kunst." Robert Picht, "Kultur- und Landeswissenschaften," in Karl-Richard Bausch, Herbert Christ and Hans-Jürgen Krumm, eds., *Handbuch Fremdsprachenunterricht* (Tübingen and Basel: Francke, 3rd ed., 1995), 66-73, here 69-70.

Against such convincing opposition, the concept of an intermediary culture for the purposes of EFLT seems bound to fail as a kind of cultural Esperanto, for reasons very similar to those that have prevented the introduction of Esperanto itself from ever becoming a success as an 'intermediary,' neutral language.

As a result, we remain stuck with two cultures facing each other, but divided by a cultural gap which somehow needs to be bridged to achieve successful inter-communication. The debate about intermediary cultures has also elucidated the impossibility, and indeed the perils of the notion that EFL teachers might simply lead pupils to enter another culture while abandoning their own for the time of their English lessons. The emphasis on this interrelatedness of host and target culture has therefore been a central aspect of the entire discussion since the 1970s on what is now generally called 'intercultural' or 'multicultural education' in English-speaking countries, *inter-kulturelle Erziehung* or *interkulturelle Bildung* in German and *éducation interculturelle* in French-speaking countries.[21]

fig.4

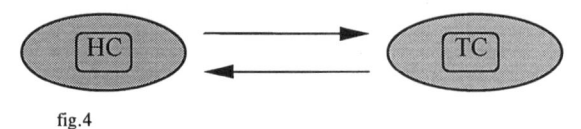

As the dialogic structure of figure 4 indicates, the issue of mutual understanding between cultures, and hence also its educational variant, is clearly a special case of the cluster of problems discussed in hermeneutics in general. Here, Hans-Georg Gadamer's seminal work *Wahrheit und Methode* (1960) has perhaps been the single most fruitful philosophical analysis for both literary and cultural studies to build on. Although Gadamer primarily investigated problems of historical understanding, his concepts (as well as the points for which they have been criticised) can equally be discussed in the context of different cultures. In his key phrase of the 'merging of horizons' (*Horizontverschmelzung*) Gadamer emphasizes, in a specification of the hermeneutic circle, that we cannot leave our own horizon behind to enter another one formerly alien to us, just as, so to speak, we pass from one room into another. Horizons are never static but in permanent flux, merging and reshaping as we pass through time. Our own horizon travels with us, both as we ourselves constantly develop and move along in our own time and as we try to go back in time to understand the past or as we try to leave our own cultural sphere and cross a cultural divide. Thus we communicate with another culture by bringing our own preconcep-tions to it, which in turn are changed by the new impressions and so forth.

Applied to the EFL classroom, Gadamer's hermeneutics underpin the importance of taking into consideration the pupil's own culture as a point of departure, which, however far they can be led to grasp the foreign sphere they enter, can never be entirely left behind. A true exchange between host and target culture includes constant and progressive reflection on the pupils' own cultural premises and how these affect, are affected by, the new insights gathered in learning another culture. Through Gada-

---

[21] For the details of terminology see for example Georg Auernheimer, *Einführung in die interkulturelle Erziehung* (Darmstadt: Primur Verlag, 2nd ed. 1996), 1-3.

mer's hermeneutics, the undeniable existence of prejudices (*Vorurteil*) and stereotypes has acquired much more positive connotations, as they emerge not only as falsifying interferences in an otherwise clear-sighted epistemological process, but its ineluctible constitutents.[22]

This intercommunicative dialogism of mutual preconceptions found also its expression in social psychology, notably in the work of Laing, Phillipson and Lee. As co-authors of *Interpersonal Perception* (1966) they described a 'spiral of reciprocal perspectives.' The model builds on the insight that our interpersonal relationships are not only affected by the image we have of them, but also by the image we think they have of us; by the image we think they think we have of them; by the image they think we think they have of us, and so forth. The spiral is only limited, one might say, by our brains' restricted processing capacity, and usually stops at the second or third meta-level. Their concept is of major importance for interpersonal as well as inter-cultural studies as it helps to see the sophistication of the interrelationship and thus can provide much more powerful diagnostic instruments in isolating the trouble spot when things go wrong. Let us take one of Laing, Phillipson and Lee's examples in a somewhat abbreviated form.[23] Jill and Jack truely and sincerely love each other as a granted fact. Jack, for reasons we do not further explore, is nevertheless prone to distrust Jill. If Jill now strives to show her love to reassure him, he may simply conclude that she is merely being ostentatious about it to cover up her real feelings which are quite on the opposite side. Should Jill then choose to tone down the expression of her love, she will incur Jack's censure as being cold towards him and again confirm his preconception that she does not love him. The important inference, say for a marriage counsellor, would be that it is completely useless to advise Jill on any type of behaviour. No matter how she tries, she will always lose. It is Jack's misguided image, what he thinks Jill thinks of him, that causes the troubles. The sore point is on the first meta-level, and it would be pointless to try to adjust behavioral patterns on the primary level, i.e. Jack's feelings towards Jill or Jill's feelings towards Jack, as here both sides completely agree.

Transferred to the intercultural context of FLT, it immediately becomes clear that the conceptions that, for example, German pupils form of England, are quite as relevant as the coneptions they have of what English pupils think of a) them, the German pupils, as well as b), themselves, as English pupils and so forth. Following studies by Gottfried Keller done during the mid-1960s, Manfred Erdmenger[24] summarizes a

---

[22] Hans-Georg Gadamer, *Gesammelte Werke*, Bd. 1 (Tübingen: Mohr, 1960; 6th ed. 1990), 270-295; Gordon Allport's classic *The Nature of Prejudice* (Reading, MA: Addison-Wesley, 1979) applies this positive view of prejudice to the field of multicultural education. His specific approach has, however, also been strongly criticised; see Christine I. Bennett, *Comprehensive Multicultural Education: Theory and Practice* (Boston et al.: Allyn and Bacon, 1986, 3rd ed. 1995), 21-4.

[23] Ronald David Laing, Herbert Phillipson and A. Robert Lee, *Interpersonal Perception. A Theory and a Method of Research* (London and New York: Tavistock Publications., 1966), 22-6.

[24] Manfred Erdmenger, *Landeskunde im Fremdsprachenunterricht*. Forum Sprache (Ismaning:

similar concept, albeit without identifying its roots in social psychology. He defines as two educational goals of FLT the reduction of *Autodistanz* (auto-distance), which is the difference between the pupils' image of themselves and the image they think members of the foreign culture form of them, and the reduction of *Heterodistanz* (heterodistance), that is the difference between the image the pupils have of the foreign culture and the image which they think members of the foreign culture entertain of themselves. The latter could, for example, be reduced by giving detailed information about the image with which the foreign culture actually identifies itself. Thus, misunderstandings can be avoided.

Behind these approaches, Gadamer's ideas remain clearly visible in the background; nor are they, as a consequence, left unscathed by the fire Gadamer's model drew from critics. Most famously, perhaps, Gadamer was attacked by Jürgen Habermas[25] for the supposed lack of reflective and indeed defensive instruments in his system to identify and eliminate wilful distortions in the communicative process motivated by authority and power. "Authority and knowledge do not converge," as Habermas put it at one point.[26] In short, Gadamer does not take ideology into account. Of course the question would have to be returned to Habermas whether his 'ideal speech situation' was at all attainable, even thinkable, since all human communication can be conceived as ineluctably warped by ideology, be it only in a subconscious, Lacanian sense. With regard to the EFLT situation, however, it will not be necessary to pursue the debate further here, since some aspects of Habermas' point remains valid however far we want to agree with his train of thought. The 'fusion of horizons' that happens according to Gadamer's model in the classroom when the pupils are introduced to a foreign culture is never innocent in a political, social and ideological sense. If, according to Fred Inglis' definition (*Cultural Studies*, ix) specific values and value judgments consitute a culture, the pupil's own values will come under scrutiny and are exposed to a literally 'foreign' influence in the course of intercultural hermeneutic processes which require careful attention. Here the circle is closed and the points of pre-war discussions in *Realienkunde* and *Kulturkunde* seem to be revisited, albeit on a different note. The assimilation, it must now be acknowledged, works both ways. The foreign culture's as well as the host culture's values are equally at peril to be lost in a potentially homogenizing process, the dialectic of which is inevitably inscribed with ideologies and power structures we can only try to make visible. We can

---

Hueber, 1996), 49-51; see also, to give an earlier major example, Lothar Bredella, "Zielsetzungen der Landeskunde im Fremdsprachenunterricht" in *Landeskunde und fiktionale Literatur, anglistik & englischunterricht* 10 (Trier: VWT, 1980): 9-34, esp. 18-21.

[25] On the Gadamer-Habermas debate see for example Martin Jay, "Should Intellectual History Take a Linguistic Turn? Reflections on the Habermas-Gadamer Debate" in Dominick LaCapra, ed., *Modern European Intellectual History: Reappraisals and New Perspectives* (Ithaca and London: Cornell University Press, 1982), 86-110, and Michael Pusey, *Jürgen Habermas*. (Chichester et al.: Ellis Horwood, 1987), 60-65.

[26] Jürgen Habermas, "A Review of Gadamer's Truth and Method" in Fred R. Dallmayr and Thomas A. McCarthy, eds., *Understanding and Social Inquiry* (Notre Dame, IN.: University of Notre Dame Press, 1977), 360.

never wholly grasp or eliminate them, however, since there is no archimedian point outside them. Politicians, educational theorists and teachers alike are inextricably caught up in them.

While Habermas ultimately perceived in the warping of the communicative process a reflection of the warping of the social structure which produced it, there are other critical approaches which do not as directly lead back to specific and hence potentially remediable causes in society. It is equally possible to see the communicative process itself as irremediably fraught with a tendency to violent assimilation. Emmanuel Lévinas,[27] for example, posits an abolute otherness of the other (*autrui*) to deconstruct the entire occidental Socratic ontology as a system of violence, which always pictures the other as an *alter ego* and consequently finds only sameness even in pluralistic concepts. Translated into grammatical terms, so Lévinas, we must not reach the 3rd through the 1st person, but both 1st and 3rd person are to be explored in the 2nd, the other, who is their measure and yard-stick.[28] How, then, are we to relate with him or her at all under these circumstances? In its ultimate consequence, Lévinas' thought leaves only the vocative as a form of address, since it does not say anything about the other but remains pure address, a language without predication. As Derrida aptly replies, "A speech produced without the least violence would determine nothing, would say nothing, would offer nothing to the other; it would not be *history* and it would *show* nothing [...]."[29]

Discourse, Derrida concludes from Lévinas, must always be violent by nature; but we are caught in the paradox "that the philosophical logos, the only one in which peace may be declared, is inhabited by war:"

> The distinction between discourse and violence always will be an inaccessible horizon. Nonviolence would be the telos, and not the essence of discourse. [...] [This is why] language can only indefinitely tend toward justice by acknowledging and practicing the violence within it. Violence against violence. *Economy* of violence (Derrida, *Writing and Difference*, 117).

Thus, "the irreducible violence of the relation to the other, is at the same time nonviolence, since it opens the relation to the other" (Derrida, *Writing and Difference*, 128-9). All the discourse can do is "*do itself violence*, can only negate itself in order to affirm itself, make war upon the war which institutes it without ever *being able* to reappropriate this negativity, to the extent that it is discourse" (Derrida, *Writing and Difference*, 130). In Derrida's view, discourse is the way of the smallest possible violence, for the kind of silence which would ensue as its fearsome alternative is "the worst violence," "the violence of primitive and prelogical silence, of an unimaginable night which would not even be the opposite of day, an absolute violence which would not even be the opposite of nonviolence: nothingness or pure non-sense" (Derrida,

---

[27] Emmanuel Lévinas, *Totalité et infini: Essay sur l'extériorité* (Den Haag: Nijhoff, 1961).

[28] For further reference see Bernhard Taureck's concise summary in his *Lévinas zur Einführung* (Hamburg: Junius, 1991), 44-61.

[29] Jacques Derrida, *Writing and Difference*, tr. Alan Bass (London: Routledge, 1978), 147.

Writing and Difference, 130). "Peace," as Derrida puts it in a nutshell, "is made only in a *certain silence*, which is determined and protected by the violence of speech" (Derrida, *Writing and Difference*, 148).

What separates Lévinas and Derrida from Gadamer, then, is their different estimation of the chasm between the communicating parties. While Gadamer remains optimistic about actual communion happening in the fusion of horizons, Derrida sticks to Lévinas' concept of the other's absolute otherness. It cannot be familiarized but only accepted and highlighted in its alterity, which ineluctably includes a violent appropriation in discourse.

It is certainly not easy to translate these philosophical insights into strategies of intercultural communication in EFLT. A postmodernist pedagogy of FLT is a long way from being developed or, indeed, universally desired, not least because postmodernism is so diverse and difficult to channel into didactic approaches. Nevertheless, the basic situation of two contrasting spheres caught in the paradox of being forced to enter a communication which will always be warped by violent appropriation as outlined above is a common feature in a number of postmodern discourses, such as Foucault's opposition of madness and sanity, the relationship of colonizer and colonized in post-colonial theory or between the sexes in feminist and gender studies. These individual discourses have come up with a host of very sophisticated ways to deal with this paradoxical situation in their various fields. They could therefore continue to prove a fertile soil to sift for seeds to plant in the pedagogics of intercultural education. However, this search will not be further pursued here except for one issue which appears to be particularly pressing in the development of EFLT in Germany and elsewhere in Europe as we enter the next century.

Hermeneutic problems have so far been discussed in a framework where interpersonal relationships were treated as analogous to those between different cultures or different historical periods. The procedure is indeed helpful but it also needs differentiation. To effect it, however, another analogy will serve as a starting point. It is one of the salient features of postmodern discourses that they do no longer accept the concept of the subject as an organic entity. As in some post-structuralist approaches the subject has completely dissolved into a more or less arbitrary intersection of contending and variously incompatible discourses of will, power, or desire, it has at least become "fundamentally de-centred" in others, as Lacan called it with reference to child development as early as 1936.[30] Bypassing an interesting line of inquiry leading from here to the individual pupil's psyche with reference to multicultural education, the interest here is with possible inferences for the social and hermeneutic aspects of the intercultural context.

Figures 1 to 4 above seem to suggest that the cultures involved were self-contained, Spenglerian monads, or that they have at least a clearly defined identity as they enter the hermeneutic process. That is of course an illusion. What is more, it is an illusion

---

[30] Jacques Lacan, "The Looking-glass Phase" (1936); first reference to it in *The International Journal of Psychoanalysis* 18 (1937): 78; later esp. in "Subversion du sujet et dialectique du désir dans l'inconscient freudien" (1960) in *Écrits* (Paris: Ed. du Seuil, 1966), 793-827.

which it is increasingly difficult to uphold for two reasons. First, the postmodernist rift in conceiving nations or cultures as integral organisms which are at least united in a *discordia concors*, has exerted an eminently deconstructive force. General sensitivities to areas where jarring notes had been suppressed by discursive power structures are greatly increased and cultural critics' heuristic instrumentaries to ferret them out has become rather sophisticated. The decentralization of cultural identities this produced is further enhanced by recent developments in most Western societies themselves.

Migrating workers, and then a long line of asylum seekers from all over the world, notably from the countries' former colonies, have drastically altered the ethnic landscape in Europe. In the specific case of (West) Germany, workers were in short supply but high demand as the so-called *Wirtschaftswunder* was beginning to take off in the 1950s. This led to large numbers of *Gastarbeiter*, 'guest workers,' as they were called, to be invited from Southern Europe and the Balkans where there was a surplus of hands and a shortness of well-paid work. The first idea was to have them stay in Germany for a limited period of time, usually even without their families. Not all of them returned to their home countries and stayed on with their families. Their children who were then born in Germany, found themselves in a cultural limbo. Often considering Germany as their home country where they were born, had their friends and received their schooling, their parents' home had usually remained a cultural enclave of their country of origin.

The problems which ensued in the educational sector were considerable. The approaches to solutions can, as Georg Auernheimer does,[31] be generalized into three stages. Beginning in the early 1970s, what was called *Ausländerpädagogik* aimed at compensating disadvantages which children of foreign descent might face in German schools. Their 'differences' were treated as handicaps, and indeed an interdisciplinary overlap was acknowledged between the pedagogics for foreigners and that for the handicapped. By helping them overcome these handicaps, such as an imperfect command of the German language or lack of other vital knowledge about the German culture, it was hoped they would assimilate quickly to become 'normal' German citizens. About 1980 the beginning of a second phase can be identified in a surge of criticism against this type of assimilationist pedagogics. The search for educational solutions to these problems, it was argued, was in reality an attempt to veil their structural and political roots. "Über die Unmöglichkeit, Politk durch Pädagogik zu ersetzen" (On the impossibility of substituting pedagogics for politics) was the title of a programmatic article by Hamburger, Seus and Wolter in 1981.[32] There was a growing awareness, that these were not ephemeral phenomena on the sidelines of society. The entire concept of the nation, the way Germans understood their own culture, was at

---

[31] Auernheimer, *Einführung*, 5-11. In his categorization, Auernheimer follows Wolfgang Nieke, "Multikulturelle Gesellschaft und interkulturelle Erziehung - Zur Theoriebildung in der Ausländerpädagogik," *Die deutsche Schule* 4 (1986): 462-473.

[32] Franz Hamburger, Lydia Seus and Otto Wolter, "Über die Unmöglichkeit, Politik durch Pädagogik zu ersetzen," *Unterrichtswissenschaft* 9 (1981): 158-67.

issue. Germany was on its way to realizing that it had become a multi-cultural society and that the diversity of its subcultures would yet be growing for the foreseeable future. This is where the beginning of a third phase is discernible which W. Nieke summarizes under the motto "Interkulturelle Erziehung für eine multikulturelle Gesellschaft" (intercultural education for a multicultural society)[33]. The situation was not substantially changed by German re-unification in 1989, except perhaps for the fact that the centripetal forces towards an integrative national culture have been somewhat revitalized. The pedagogic and political preoccupation with the problems created by the rising number of criminal offences perpetrated by right-wing extremists has not, as Auernheimer points out (*Einführung*, 11), been connected with the debate on multicultural education.

While the general educational issues of multiculturalism have been extensively explored by now,[34] there seems to be a deficit in realizing both its difficulties and potentials in FLT. The debate has been opened, however, by such contributions as Maria Felberbauer's investigation of the advantages for a multicultural Austrian class[35] to be derived from the fact that all pupils start from scratch in the new language to be acquired,[36] or by Michael Byram's comprehensive exploration of FLT with respect to minority languages in the multi-ethnic context of Britain (see Byram, *Cultural Studies*, esp. 25-38). What has to come under consideration, however, is the entire complexity involved in FLT's mediating no longer simply between a host and target culture as these two entities have broken down into multi-ethnic and multi-cultural systems of great heterogeneity. If the terms host and target culture in the singular are still maintained, therefore, they now must be pictured as consisting of a variety of quite distinct subcultures (see fig. 5). These subcultures are of course interrelated, and often problematically so, within the national 'umbrella' culture, but they may also have strong links, or indeed form a cultural unit, with subcultures in the target 'umbrella' culture. Allowing for much reductionist simplification, figure 5 tries to express this new situation.

---

[33] Quoted in Auernheimer, *Einführung*, 9.

[34] See Auernheimer's introduction and substantial bibliography.

[35] This model's possibly fruitful similarites with Eric Rothstein's concept of 'relational dispersion' cannot be further persued here. Rothstein's aim is to replace, in the vein of Lyotard's 'fabric of relations,' the holistic and antagonistic models to describe textual as well as social and intercultural relationsships in a new and more flexible way. Eric Rothstein, 'Diversity and Change in Literary History' in Jay Clayton and Eric Rothstein, eds., *Influence and Intertextuality in Literary History* (Madison: University of Wisconsin Press, 1991), 114-45, esp. 135-6.

[36] Maria Felberbauer, "Englischunterricht an der Grundschule: Ein Beitrag zum interkulturellen Lernen," *Der Fremdsprachliche Unterricht Englisch* 25 (1991): 10-14.

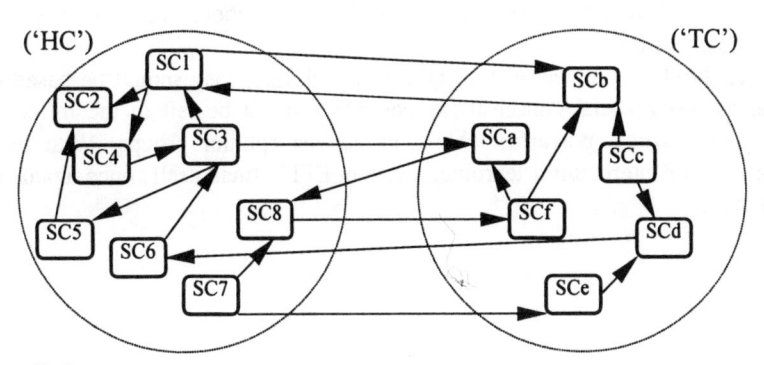

fig.5

While some may find this new complexity chaotic and confusing and thus adding to the heavy load of both teachers and pupils, it opens new opportunities for FLT which must be investigated and utilized. First, and most obviously, it corresponds to the 'facts' as shown by statistics and prognostics: all Western societies already are multicultural with a tendency towards further diversification in the near future. Therefore the only issue remaining open to debate is the way to deal with the situation. Second, FLT staff and theorists are, one might say, veterans in the battle for intercultural understanding. They could be ranked among the first authorities to ask for help with multicultural issues within the host culture. It is very likely that the hermeneutic principles developed for the intercultural understanding between the German and British cultures might also prove helpful to mediate between, for instance, Muslims and Christians in Germany. Third, to give a last example, the concept does not only bring further complication but can also have a facilitating effect. Intercultural experiences between German subcultures may be used to understand the target culture. What is more, pupils of one subculture may have closer links to particular subcultures in the target culture than others and could therefore help their classmates to understand them. Thus, members of a minority group in the class could very readily sketch the situation of a minority group in the target culture. Muslim pupils may be called on to assist their classmates with understanding Pakistani cultures in Britain, or pupils of Italian descent could explain the mentality of the community in New York's 'Little Italy.'

It is obvious that political and educational decisions will be necessary as to the extent and the ways to deal with the issue. A discussion of the social and cultural future of Western societies is necessary and changes to the curriculum could be incisive. Would, for example, the holiday visit of a young native German couple of Turkish descent professing to the Islamic faith to Nigeria where they meet Nigerian friends and exchange their views make a desirable background for an English lesson in a German school book? How would the German pupil of Zinti extraction be accepted as the hero of an adventure story in the American mid-West where she or he is helped by Roma emigrants? How different would the second-year EFL story become when, instead of the two 'normal' German friends on a visit to the southern states of the USA were explored by two grandsons of Spanish immigrants to Germany who meet members of the Hispanic community there and are told about immigration problems on the Mexican border?

Whatever the decisions we wish to take will look like; they should be based on as broad and as just a social consensus as possible and not be left to the influence of single political parties, powerful lobbies or activist splinter groups. With its very mixed tradition of intercultural learning, German EFLT finds itself, once again, at the cross-roads.

An Aspect of Tragedy: A Comparative View of Displaced Heroes in Medieval Literature

SHINSUKE ANDO (Tokyo)

Chaucer's *The Monk's Tale* presents a series of short histories of famous men and women who suffered terrible downfalls. It is a series of medieval 'tragedies'. The Monk offers his audience the following definition of tragedy:

> Tragedie is to seyn a certeyn storie,
> As olde bookes maken us memorie,
> Of hym that stood in greet prosperitee,
> And is yfallen out of heigh degree
> Into myserie, and endeth wrecchedly.
> And they ben versified communely
> Of six feet, which men clepen *exametron*.
> In prose eek been endited many oon,
> And eek in meetre in many a sondry wyse.
> Lo, this declaryng oghte ynogh suffise.
> 'Now herkneth, if you liketh for to heere.
> But first I yow biseeke in this mateere,
> Though I by ordre telle nat thise thynges,
> Be it of popes, emperours, or kynges,
> After hir ages, as men writen fynde,
> But tellen hem som bifore and som bihynde,
> As it now comth unto my remembraunce,
> Have me excused of myn ignoraunce.'
> *(The Monk's Tale, 1973-90)*[1]

The Monk goes back to this theme at the beginning of his Tale, adding that the stories he is going to tell are 'ensamples trewe and old', that is, 'traditional and authoritative *exampla*:'

> I wol biwaille in manere of tragedie
> The harm of hem that stoode in heigh degree,
> And fillen so that ther nas no remedie
> To brynge hem out of hir adversitee.
> For certein, whan that Fortune list to flee,
> Ther may no man the cours of hire withholde.

---

[1] All the quotations from Chaucer are from Larry D. Benson, ed., *The Riverside Chaucer* (Oxford: Oxford University Press, 1988).

> Lat no man truste on blynd prosperitee;
> Be war by thise ensamples trewe and olde.
> (1991-8)

Even after having touched on this same subject twice, the Monk repeats it once more at the end of the story of Croesus,--the last story of the *Tale*, just before he is interrupted by the knight:

> Trageiës noon oother maner thing
> Ne kan in singyng crie ne biwaille
> But that Fortune alwey wole assaille
> With unwar strook the regnes that been proude;
> For whan men trusteth hire, thanne wol she faille,
> And covere hir brighte face with a clowde.
> (2761-6)

The word 'tragedy' had thus entered the English language by later years of the 14th century. In Chaucer's definition, there is no implication of dramatic form. A tragedy is a narrative which narrates the life of some distinguished personage who underwent a decline of fortune toward a disastrous end.

It is clear that this definition of 'tragedy' corresponds to that given by Boethius:

> What other thynge bywaylen the cryinges of tragedyes but oonly the dedes of Fortune, that with an unwar strook overturneth the realmes of greet nobleye?
> (*Boece* II, pr. 2, 67-70)

In this way, medieval tragedy is centred on the concept of the goddess Fortune--*Fortuna* in Roman antiquity. Two instances of the repeated formula, in which the Monk describes the goddess Fortune's power over human destiny, would be enough to show the fundamental sentiment prevailing in *The Monk's Tale*.

> a. At Lucifer, though he an angel were
> And nat a man, at hym wol I bigynne.
> For though Fortune may noon angel dere,
> From heigh degree yet fel he for his synne
> Down into helle, where he yet is inne.
> (*MkT, Lucifer*; 2000-2004)

> b. For whan Fortune wole a man forsake,
> She bereth awey his regne and his richesse,
> And eek his freendes, bothe moore and lesse.
> For what man that hath freendes thurgh Fortune,
> Mishap wol maken hem enemys, I gesse;
> This proverbe is ful sooth and ful commune.
> (*MkT, Balthazar*, 2241-6)

George Steiner, in his splendid discussion of tragedy, *The Death of Tragedy,* points out as follows:

Chaucer's definition derives its force from contemporary awareness of sudden reversals of political and dynastic fortune. To the medieval eye, the heavens of state were filled with portentous stars, dazzling in their ascent but fiery in their decline. The fall of great personages from high place (*casus virorum illustrium*) gave to medieval politics their festive and brutal character. Sweeping over men with cruel frequency, the quarrels of princes implicated the lives and fortunes of the entire community. But the rise and fall of him that stood in high degree was the incarnation of the tragic sense for a much deeper reason: it made explicit the universal drama of the fall of man. Lords and captains perished through exceeding ambition, through the hatred and cunning of their adversaries, or by mischance. But even where the moralist could point to a particular crime or occasion of disaster, a more general law was at work. By virtue of original sin, each man was destined to suffer in his own experience, however private or obscure, some part of the tragedy of death. The Monk's lament 'in manere of tragedie' begins with Lucifer and Adam, for the prologue to the tragic condition of man is set in Heaven and in the Garden of Eden. There the arrow of creation started on its downward flight. It is in a garden also that the symmetry of divine intent places the act of fortunate reversal. At Gethsemane the arrow changes its course, and the morality play of history alters from tragedy to *commedia*. Finally, and in precise counterpart to the prologue of disobedience, there is the promise of a celestial epilogue where man will be restored to more than his first glory. Of this great parable of God's design, the recital of the tragic destinies of illustrious men are a gloss and reminder.[2]

The reason why I have dared to quote this rather long passage by Steiner is that, in my opinion, this is the most serious and judicious evaluation of *The Monk's Tale*, which is often treated by the specialist Chaucerians as merely a boring collection of threads and patches.

It is certain that Chaucer's idea of 'tragedy', as far as the lexical meaning of this word is concerned in Chaucer's works, is alien to us today. It is rather difficult for us to accept as tragic the mere 'fall' of people in 'high degree' or of 'regnes that been proude'. It also seems difficult for us to accept the 'downfall as being determined only by the 'unwar strook' of Fortune. Indeed, as Piero Boitani points out:

> [S]ince at least 1789, the year of the French Revolution, such 'falls' would most likely fit in with the modern idea of justice or of social movements rather than that of fortune. For us, tragedy is inevitably linked to the names of Orestes, Oedipus, Philoctetes, Macbeth, Hamlet, King Lear, or, in a different realm, to Christ's Passion, to the sufferings of the Karamazovs and of Prince Myshkin. Our idea of tragedy involves the fallibility of man, his errors and sins, power and justice, ignorance and knowledge, madness and death.[3]

Boitani is right. No one would regard Ceausescu's fall as the result of the whimsical stroke of the goddess fortune. Many would even refuse to accept it as a tragedy. It is

---

[2] George Steiner, *The Death of Tragedy* (New York, 1961; reprint, New York: Oxford University Press, 1980), 12-13.

[3] Piero Boitani, *The Tragic and Sublime in Medieval Literature* (Cambridge: Cambridge University Press, 1989), 42.

also true that Chaucer himself holds a different, more complex, mature, and sophisticated idea of tragedy. We have only to refer to the 'litel tragedye' of *Troilus and Criseyde*.

Moreover, the company of pilgrims in *The Canterbury Tales*, the audience of *The Monk´s Tale* does not seem to be satisfied with the stories of the downfall of glorious men and women. The Knight interrupts the Monk and complains as follows:

> 'Hoo!' quod the Knyght, 'good sire, namoore of this!
> That ye han seyd is right ynought, ywis,
> And muchel moore; for litel hevynesse
> Is right ynough to muche folk, I gesse.
> I seye for me, it is a greet disese,
> Whereas men han been in greet welthe and ese,
> To heeren of sodeyn fal, allas!
> And the contrarie is joye and greet solas,
> As whan a man hath been in povre estaat,
> And clymbeth up and wexeth fortunat,
> And there abideth in prosperitee.
> Swich thyng is gladsom, as it thynketh me [...].'
> (*The Prologue of the Nun´s Priest´s Tale*, 2757-78)

The Host is even more brutal. He accuses the Monk of bothering the whole company and putting it to sleep. At this point there is a trap which the modern readers of Chaucer should be careful to avoid. The two severe critics of *The Monk´s Tale*, (the Knight and the Host) may well lead us to the conclusion that the Monk´s stories are badly written. However, they were not badly written. Chaucer´s intention of locating the Monk´s stories within the framework of *The Canterbury Tales* was certainly a serious one. And we must clearly take *The Monk´s Tale* seriously. Also it should be noted that Chaucer was able to take advantage of the particular structure of *The Canterbury Tales* in implying some criticism of its form. Undoubtedly this is the same kind of criticism as was offered by the Host when he was bored with the 'rym doggerel' of Chaucer´s *Rime of Sir Thopas*. As Donaldson points out: "If the tragedies are to be read at all they must be read seriously, but the reader is at liberty to accept the Knight´s and Host´s opinion as authoritative, and skip them".[4] But George Steiner did not skip them. Nor did he fail to grasp the meaning of Chaucer´s suggestion, expressed by the Knight, of the possibility of turning from tragedy to comedy. If it is difficult for us today to accept Chaucer´s idea of tragedy as serious, it may be because we have lost the sense of tragedy, and this loss of the tragic sense on the part of the moderns, Steiner may say, is undoubtedly what led to the death of tragedy, or to the 'displacement' of tragedy.

Meanwhile, the fundamental tragic motif, or tragic feeling in classical and medieval Japanese literature seems to be thoroughly imbued with the idea of 'the legends of exiled nobles' [*Kishuryūritan*]. There are many Japanese tales and legends in which

---

[4] E. T. Donaldson, ed., *Chaucer´s Poetry: An Anthology for the Modern Reader*, (New York: Ronald Press Co., 1958), 940.

an infant god comes from the 'other world' to undergo various hardships in the human world before being restored to the other world, or otherwise a young man and woman of high birth are banished from the prosperous city and obliged to live a wandering life. It was round about 1920 that Origuchi Shinobu, eminent scholar of ancient Japanese literature, coined this new word '*Kishuryūritan*' as a technical term for this prominent folkloric and literary tradition. Origuchi examined how this tradition had come to foster the tragic temperament of the Japanese people, giving rise to various tragedies.[5]

The archetype of 'the legends of exiled nobles' is a story recounting the wandering life of a hero or heroine. The hero is often a divine being or such a noble personage as can be compared to a god. The cause of the hero´s wandering is attributed to a certain crime or sinful act--very often related to amorous affairs. The hero is displaced from his sovereign position and begins a painful wandering. Wandering is an ordeal for the sinner-hero to be redeemed from sin. Once the redemption or expiation is accomplished, the hero is allowed to return to his former position. The paradise lost is regained in the end. However, the story of the 'wanderer' is really a sad one full of pathos. The wanderer suffers a succession of hardships in the human world and laments the loss of his fortune. The tone is that of lyric rather than epic. Aristotelian '*eleos*', that is 'pity' [the Monk´s 'pitee' in Chaucer], is the effect of his tragic autobiography. The literary tradition of the 'legend of exiled nobles' is clearly based on the folkloric archetype of tragic feeling. After the eleventh century, the story of a wandering exile came to receive continental influences and grew much more complex and sophisticated. The narrator even applied this traditional pattern to historical facts to create a literary work. The narrator´s intention in this case may be regarded as corresponding to that of Chaucer in adding modern instances to *The Monk´s Tale* to show the contemporary relevance of the theme. The tradition of the 'legends of exiled nobles' finally attains its culmination in two books of *The Tale of Genji* 'Suma' and 'Akashi'. The hero of the *Tale*, Hikaru Genji, commits religious and political crimes by getting married to his mother-in-law and having an affair with the empress. This prince is displaced from the palace for redemption and lives as an exile in Suma, a dilapidated district away from the capital. According to the traditional pattern he is supposed to be able to return to his former life in happiness and comfort. Separation and restoration are again the characteristic elements of this tradition, but the description of his life in displacement is full of pathos. 'Suma' begins as follows:

> For Genji life had become an unbroken succession of reverses and afflictions. He must consider what to do next. If he went on pretending that nothing was amiss, then even worse things might lie ahead. He thought of the Suma coast. People of worth had once lived there, he was told, but now it was deserted save for the huts of fishermen, and even they were few. The alternative was worse, to go on living his public life, so to speak, with people streaming in and out of his house. Yet he would hate to leave, and affairs at

---

[5] As regards my knowledge of the literary theory of '*Kishuryuritan*', I owe very much to my colleagues at the Department of Japanese Literature of Keio University, Profs. Toru Nishimura and Tatsuo Iguchi.

court would continue to be much on his mind if he did leave. This irresolution was making life difficult for his people.

Unsettling thoughts of the past and the future chased one another through his mind. The thought of leaving the city aroused a train of regrets [...].[6]

In this passage one can not fail to recognize the sense of mutability, the tragic sense of displacement which is characteristic of the literary tradition I have been discussing. It is extremely interesting to find the theme of the 'displaced hero' also playing a crucially important role in the tradition of Japanese literature.

---

[6] Murasaki Shikibu, *The Tale of Genji*, translated by Edward G. Seidenstecker, (Tokyo: Charles E. Tuttle Company, 1976), Vol. I, 219.

A Portrait of the Artist as a Young Man: Henry VIII's Early Songs

THEO STEMMLER (Mannheim)

> Youth will have needs dalliance,
> Of good or ill some pastance...

I

Henry VIII provides us with a striking example of the general observation that tough guys may be excellent artists — or at least would-be artists. Above all the death sentences against two of his wives (Anne Boleyn and Catherine Howard) and Thomas More, ruthlessly promoted or even inspired by him, are apt to obscure the fact that he was an ardent lover and patron of the fine arts, a talented musician, and a gifted songwriter.[1]

Fig. 1. Henry VIII playing the harp. Royal Psalter, c.1534.

---

[1] On the bewildering complexity of his character see my *Heinrich VIII. Ansichten eines Königs* (Frankfurt/Main: Insel, 1991).

Henry VIII played several musical instruments (lute, virginals, flute) with considerable skill if we may trust the testimonials of diverse contemporaries. Moreover, he was able to sing "from book at sight." In view of his musical talent it is not astonishing that he went out of his way to enlarge and improve *The King's Musick*, which already consisted of several ensembles. Whilst his father, Henry VII, was content with approximately sixteen musicians, he finally employed no less than almost sixty recruited above all from Italy and Flanders.

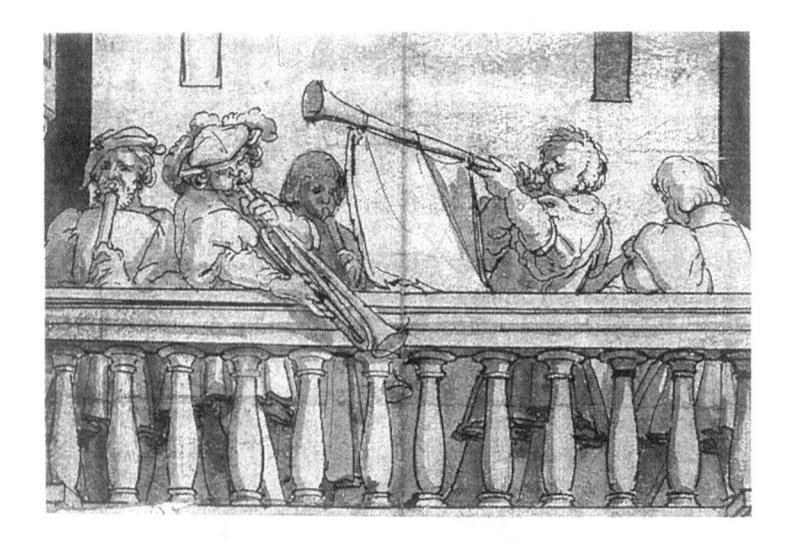

Fig. 2. Musicians at the court of Henry VIII (drawing by Hans Holbein).

And Henry's huge collection of musical instruments testifies to his musical inclinations, too: 147 flutes, 25 viols, 26 lutes, 18 portative organs were, inter alia, in his possession.

II

That His Royal Highness was more interested in songs and instrumental music than in poetry is well reflected in the inventory of his artistic legacy: not a single poem from his pen is extant, but about three dozen of his songs, compositions and arrangements have been preserved. The vast majority of these items — about two-thirds — are songs whose lyrics and music were provided by King Henry, the rest being instrumental pieces. Interestingly enough, only one of Henry's songs — the three-part motet "Quam pulchra es" — treats a religious theme. The other twenty vocal pieces deal with secular subjects: mostly erotic ones. This worldly bias is not an outcome of an idiosyncratic predilection on the part of King Henry but corresponds to the production of Tudor songs in general: *Amor vincit omnia*.

Nearly all of Henry's songs and instrumental pieces are preserved in one single manuscript: Additional MS 31922 (British Library, London). Only the motet "Quam pulchra es," the song "Pastime with Good Company" (two versions), and a pavane are contained in other manuscripts (Royal Appendix 58, Additional MS 5665, Stowe MS 389 respectively). For the very reason that it contains almost all of Henry's thirty-five compositions Additional MS 31922 is usually called "Henry VIII's Manuscript" — a misleading term, however, since this book never belonged to the King. In all probability it was written for Sir Henry Guildford, Controller of the Royal Household and

Fig. 3. Portrait of Sir Henry Guildford by Hans Holbein.

Master of the Revels. It is one of those three Tudor songbooks whose importance for the history of English songs - and of English culture in general - cannot be overestimated: "These song-books [...] are documents of social activity at court, records of the noble life."² It was compiled c. 1515 - at a time when King Henry was in his early twenties: still happily married to Catherine of Aragon, still vital and exuberant, not yet the intimidating and suspicious colossus of later years.

Fig. 4. Medal of Henry VIII as a young man (c. 1525).

III

The most striking feature of the songs contained in "King Henry VIII's Manuscript" is what John Stevens rightly calls "the continuity of the courtly world:"

> [...] Chaucer and Wyatt, Charles of Orleans and Henry VIII can be said to have been playing the same game and obeying the same rules. It may be that by the time of Wyatt's

---

2   John Stevens, *Music and Poetry in the Early Tudor Court* (London: Methuen, 1961; 2nd, revised edition, Cambridge, 1979), 329. This volume contains not only a brilliant monograph on the subject but a complete edition of all texts contained in the three Tudor songbooks; I shall quote from this edition. Another important work by John Stevens provides us with a complete edition of "King Henry's Manuscript" (both of the music and the lyrics): *Music at the Court of Henry VIII*, Musica Britannica, XVIII (London: Stainer and Bell, 1962; 2nd, revised edition, 1969).

death the tradition was in a state of rapid disintegration. But *Henry VIII's MS* and *The Devonshire MS*, to name no others, assure us that it was still a force - alive, if not kicking - in the early sixteenth century (Stevens, *Music and Poetry*, 156).

It is indeed astonishing how long-lived many elements of that poetic genre are and which had of course already characterized the earliest courtly love-poems written in Occitan and French during the 12th and 13th centuries, i.e. three or even four hundred years before the compilation of "King Henry VIII's Manuscript."

Thus the courtly lover in Henry's songs poses as the lady's servant, e.g. in H 10:

> Helas, madam, cel que i'eme tant,
> Soffré que soie voutre humble seruant.
> Voutre umble seruant ie [se]ray a tousiours
> E tant que ie viueray altre n'aimeray que vous [...]

The central idea that courtly love has an ennobling effect on the lover recurs in several of Henry's songs. In H 34:

> For love enforcyth all nobyle kynd,
> And dysdayne dyscorages all gentyl mynd.
> [...]
> Love encoragith and makyth on bold;
> Dysdayne abattyth and makith hym colde.

In H 51 Henry makes use of the traditional opposition between the lover ennobled by courtly love and the loveless "disdainer" reduced to the status of a "villein:"

> Love maynteynyth all noble courage;
> Who love dysdaynyth ys all of the village.

Again and again the lover's heart - aching or not - is mentioned by Henry. In H 15:

> O my hart and O my hart!
>   My hart it is so sore,
> Sens I must nedys from my love depart
>   And know no cause wherefore.

Similarly in H 30:

> Alac, alac, what shall I do,
> For care is cast into my hart,
> And trew love lokked therto?

In H51 Henry uses the medieval concept of love reaching the lover's heart via his eyes:

> Wyth ee and mynd doth both agre,
> There is no bote, ther must it be.

> The ee doth loke and represent,
> But mynd aftormyth with full consent.
> Thus am I fyxed without gruge,
> Myne ey with hart doth me so juge.

Finally, by proposing the union of the lover's and the lady's hearts, Henry again follows a centuries-old tradition (H 64):

> Without discord
> And both acorde
>   Now let us be;
> Both hartes alone
> To set in one
>   Best semyth me.

This *entente cordiale* is, by the way, pictorially evoked in one of the love-letters written by Henry to Anne Boleyn. At the end of letter 7 he drew the outlines of a heart inscribing the initials AB of his beloved in its centre:

> [...] vostre loyal et plus assuré serviteure -
> Henry aultre AB ne cherse [...][3]

IV

Whilst the majority of Henry's song-texts follows the well-known stereotypes of medieval love-poetry, a handful of them leaves the beaten track, introduces individualizing personal remarks and mingles them with traditional formulas. Five songs belong to this small group: only one love-song (H 33:"Green Grows the Holly") and four songs which all deal with - in Henry's own words - "the pastimes of youth." These songs (H 7, 23, 66, 92), as a matter of fact, share the same key-words: "pastime," "youth," "company," "dalliance," "sport;" in them love is only of minor importance.

The carol "Green Grows the Holly" is perhaps Henry's finest song-text. Here he succeeds in giving the old symbolism of the holly and the ivy a new meaning. Henry does not in the traditional way hint at the antagonism between the male principle (holly) and the female (ivy) but compares his ever-lasting love to the evergreen holly:

> As the holy growth grene,
>   And never changyth hew,
> So I am, ever hath bene,
>   Unto my lady trew.

---

[3] See my edition: *Die Liebesbriefe Heinrichs VIII. an Anna Boleyn* (Zürich: Belser, 1988) and my essay "The Songs and Love-Letters of Henry VIII: On the Flexibility of Literary Genres," in Uwe Baumann, ed., *Henry VIII in History, Historiography and Literature* (Frankfurt/Main: Lang, 1992), 97-111.

This new comparison is followed by the age-old promise:

> Now unto my lady
> > Promyse to her I make,
> Frome all other only
> > To her I me betake.

The last two of these lines strongly remind the reader of so many medieval love-poems — a passage in the famous "Alysoun" - poem for instance:

> From alle wymmen mi loue is lent
> And lyht on Alysoun.[4]

Compared with "Green Grows the Holly" the above-mentioned four songs of the "youth and pastimes" - group are written in a still more original, at times even personal tone. Within the textual corpus of King Henry's songs they stand apart and form a homogeneous group. They are, it is true, secular songs but do not deal with courtly love - in contrast to Henry's other sixteen worldly songs which have been preserved. In these four songs the King makes himself the mouthpiece of the aristocratic leisure-class: only members of this social class are entitled to — and can afford — enough spare time to indulge in pastimes. Henry does, of course, not plead for idleness but for pastime activities, as he expressly states in H 7:

> For idlenes
> Ys chieff mastres
> > Of vices all;
> Than who can say
> But passe-the-day
> > Ys best of all?

By the way, two and a half centuries later Samuel Johnson will make the same distinction by wittily remarking (Letter to Mrs. Thrale of 25 August 1780): "I am not grown, I am afraid, less idle; and of idleness I am now paying the fine by having no leisure."

The four songs in question are indeed a kind of manifesto proclaiming and ethically justifying the entitlement of the King and his "minions," as they were called, to leisure, pastime, "sport." Since these claims are brought forward in such a personal tone and many details specifically refer to the King, we may by way of exception equate the lyrical *persona* of the songs with the historical person of the King. It goes without saying, however, that this approach is not comparable to the questionable efforts of nineteenth-century scholars to reconstruct a poet's life by assembling passages from his works into a pseudo-biographical mosaic. (Above all, many a notorious "life" of a troubadour is a case in point.)

---

[4] G.L. Brook, ed., *The Harley Lyrics: The Middle English Lyrics of Ms. Harley 2253*, (Manchester: Manchester University Press, 4th ed. 1968), 33.

182   Theo Stemmler

Henry's best known song "Pastime with Good Company" is also the most conspicuous text of our "group of four." Its early popularity can be deduced from the fact that only this song by Henry is preserved in several manuscripts and referred to in a contemporary sermon (Stevens, Music and Poetry, 143 and 389).[5] From its first line to the last stanza the royal author leaves no doubt about his intentions and about his firm determination to push them through - nobody will "let" (= hinder) him:

Fig. 5. "Pastime with Good Company" in "Henry VIII's Manuscript."

---

[5] I quote from the second version contained in the Ritson MS edited by John Stevens (R 12).

> Passetyme with good cumpanye
> I love and shall unto I dye;
> Grugge so woll, but noon denye.
> So God be plecyd, this lyve woll I:
> > For my pastaunce
> > Hunte, syng and daunce;
> > My hert ys sett
> > All godely sport
> > To my cumfort:
> > Who shall me lett?

The almost threatening tone of Henry's statements is clearly perceptible and fits his personality. At the end of the song the expressions become a bit softer but nevertheless remain unmistakable:

> The best insew,
> The worst eschew,
> My mynde shall be;
> Vertu to use,
> Vyce to reffuse,
> Y shall use me.

And what is all this royal fuss about? In no other text Henry is more outspoken - in no other song does he drive his point home more persistently. The most important keywords "pastime" ("pastance," "pass-the-day") and "company" are repeated four times. Moreover, the usual word-order is inverted in the first two lines so that the central word "pastime" moves to the very beginning of the song. Henry precisely specifies the activities he will indulge in during his leisure time: hunting, singing, dancing — pastimes he was actually fond of. Above all, hunting was the aristocratic pastime *par excellence*. In one of his sermons Bishop Latimer (ca. 1550) comments on this activity and expressly refers to Henry's song "Pastime with Good Company:"

> Yet a king may take his pastime in hawking or hunting, or such like pleasures. But he must use them for recreation, when he is weary of weighty affairs, that he may return to them more lusty; and this is called *Pastime with good company*.[6]

Not only the plain proclamation of aristocratic pastimes is the theme of this song but also their moral justification. Again and again Henry juxtaposes good and evil pastimes. On the one hand he simply pleads for "good companye" (line 1) and "godely sport" (line 8), on the other hand he antithetically yokes vices and virtues together — in lines 11 to 12:

> Yowth woll have nedes dalyaunce,
> Of good or yll some pastaunce.

---

[6] Quoted by J. William Hebel and Hoyt H. Hudson, eds., *Poetry of the English Renaissance 1509-1660* (New York: Appleton-Century-Crofts, 1929; repr. 1957), 911.

and in all lines of the last stanza:

> Cumpany with honeste
> Ys vertu, and vyce to flee.
> Cumpany ys gode or yll,
> But every man hath hys frewyll.
>> The best insew,
>> The worst eschew,
>> My mynde shall be.
>> Vertu to use,
>> Vyce to reffuse,
>> Y shall use me.

All motifs used by Henry in this song recur in the other song-texts of our "group of four" - to a lesser or greater degree. Thus these songs may be called variations on various themes. That the young King speaks on behalf of youth is only casually mentioned in "Pastime with Good Company" (line 11). This motif is much more prominent in the other three songs. Especially in H 66 and H 92 this aspect is hammered home somewhat crudely.

H 66 is definitely the most personal of Henry's songs — not simply because of the jovial *ipse dixit* at the end of the text: "Thus sayth the kyng, the eighth Harry." The whole song is permeated by the King's own references to himself as a young man in a clinch with his critics who reproach him for being "ruled by youth." As to be expected from "King Harry" he goes on the offensive attacking his elderly detractors by asking:

> I pray you all that aged be:
> How well dyd ye your yough carry?

— and by sarcastically giving the answer himself:

> I thynk sum wars [= worse][7] of yche degree:
> Therin a wager lay dar I.

He proclaims the general prerogative of the young to pursue morally irreproachable pastimes and — as to himself — his right to do so since he is not interested in erotic frivolities but loves his wife:

> Pastymes of yough sumtyme among,
>> None can sey but necessary.
> I hurt no man, I do no wrong:
>> I love trew wher I dyd mary.

This message of a young, vital, sociable king is effectively stressed by the refrain: "Though sum saith that yough rulyth me..."

---

[7] Here I do not follow Stevens' gloss "wars: was (pl.)," (Stevens, *Music and Poetry*, 412). The form "wars" is a not infrequent variant of "worse" in Early Modern English.

In "Lusty Youth Should Us Ensue" (H 92) the motif of "honest mirth in youth" is again of prime importance — though with a difference: handled less personally than in H 66, at times almost sententiously. The pleasing effect of this song is due to the dramatic structure of its text: the permanent altercation between the King (taking sides with the young) and the "disdainers" (keeping aloof from "merry company" and blaming "lusty youth" for their fondness of pastimes). This text is a striking example of how argumentative and "un-lyrical" the lyrics of a song may be. In the first four stanzas the King attacks the "disdainers." He reproaches them for trying to curtail the "liberty" of the young and criticizes their mainly materialistic interests: "to purchase riches." Perhaps one might interpret this outlook as aristocratic contempt for the baser concerns of the bourgeois world — the haughty perspective of the leisure class. Henry states his position in a similarly authoritative way as in H 7:

> For they wold have hym hys libertye refrayne
> And all mery company for to dysdayne.
> But I wyll not so whatsoever thay say
> But follow hys mynd in all that we may.

The tone of the royal statement is all the more contemptuous as the King calls the "disdainers" only twice by their name; more often he refers to them in an oblique way as "they."

As in the other songs of the "group of four" Henry emphasizes the honesty of these aristocratic pastimes: he speaks of "honest mirth" and of "virtuous pastance." Moreover, this motif is elaborated in the second part of song H 92. Young Henry is self-critically aware of the temptations besetting the young:

> With goode order, councell and equite,
> Goode Lord, graunt us our mancyon to be!
> For withowt ther goode gydaunce
> Yough shuld fall in grett myschaunce.
>
> For yough ys frayle and prompt to doo,
> As well vices as vertuus to ensew.
> Wherfor be thes he must be gydyd
> And vertuus pastaunce must be theryn usyd.

In this song the King not only appears as the advocate of "merry company" but quite unexpectedly poses as a sermonizer giving advice to morally endangered young men - to misuse E.M. Forster's words: Henry VIII is "a round character" still "capable of surprising" his readers.

Poetically more successful is "The Time of Youth Is To Be Spent" (H 23), where Henry uses the same motif. In this short song of only twelve lines he renounces lengthy sermonizing in favour of a few succinct remarks arranged in a rhetorically convincing manner. The antithesis of vices and virtues forms the structural frame of the song as presented in the first and in the last stanza:

> The tyme of youthe is to be spent,
> But vice in it shuld be forfent.
> [...]
> Vertue it is then youth for to spend
> In goode dysporttys whych it dothe fend.

This frame is easily recognizable since Henry uses the same rhyme-words for these lines. Moreover, the structure of the whole text is perfectly symmetrical. The recommendable "pastimes" mentioned at the beginning and at the end ("goode dysporttys") are precisely described in the middle of the song:

> As featys of armys, and suche other
> Wherby actyvenesse oon may utter.

Here we listen to His Majesty's original voice: "Feats of arms" (tournaments) were among his favourite pastimes. This finely structured and formulated text shows that King Henry was not only capable of moral acumen but also of writing excellent songs.[8] Perhaps this is the real surprise.

---

[8] On his music see David Fallows, "Henry VIII as a Composer," in Chris Banks, Arthur Searle and Malcom Turner, eds., *Sundry Sorts of Music Books: Essays on the British Library Collections* (London: British Lib., 1993).

'... *and tyranny tremble at patience*': Patience and Impatience in Shakespeare's Plays[1]

ERWIN WOLFF (Erlangen)

If there is one theme which fascinated Shakespeare all his life long, it is the kind of attitude and behaviour we refer to as patience or impatience. In his plays the theme of patience comes up again and again and only a small selection of the numerous references can be considered here.

We modern people are used to associating patience with old age and impatience with youth, so we are immediately ready to assume that it was the ageing Shakespeare who was specially interested in this theme. But we would be mistaken. In Shakespeare's earliest comedy, *The Comedy of Errors*, the theme of patience is already of central importance, and of his thirty and more comedies, tragedies and histories there is not one in which Shakespeare does not use this theme to a greater or lesser extent. Of course his treatment of the theme in his later works is of a very different nature from his treatment of it before 1600, but this has less to do with the author growing older than with the radical changes in the general way of thinking that were taking place on the threshold of the modern era and that Shakespeare was both affected by and party to.

In order to understand this change in his treatment of the patience theme, we must remember that, for Shakespeare and his contemporaries, patience represented not a quality one possessed as a characteristic, but rather an ideal of virtue, a moral value that everyone, whether old or young, male or female, rich or poor had to strive towards. The idea of patience had its roots to a more or less equal extent in Judaism, in classical philosophy and in the New Testament, but it was Christianity that gave it its special stamp. The Old Testament linked patience as a moral principle, in the sense of long-suffering endurance, to the eschatological and messianic prophecies. The towering example of this kind of patience was Job, and in Psalm 37,7, we find one of the many references to the subject:

'Rest in the Lord and wait patiently for Him'[2]

In the ethical code of heathen antiquity, the virtue of patience had more of an active content, representing bravery, independence and manly virtue, as exemplified in the Nicomachian Ethics of Aristotle (III.10 & II.2) and in the Stoic philosophy of Seneca. This view of patience also found its way into Christian ethics, as can be seen in the work of writers like Thomas Aquinus (*Summa Theologiae*, 2/II, q.1366a.4 and I),

---

[1] Unabridged version of the author's farewell lecture on his retirement in February 1992.
[2] Biblical quotations from the Authorised Version.

who defines patience as 'pars fortitudinis quasi potentialis'. Calvin was still using it with this meaning, with Seneca as his authority (*Institutio*, III, 8, 4, 10f.).

In the New Testament, especially in the letters of St. Paul, the virtue of patience appears in a very different guise. Patience is linked with the three "divine virtues" of faith, hope and charity, and in particular with hope. Paul writes to the Thessalonians:

> We give thanks to God always for you all, making mention of you in our prayers; Remembering without ceasing your work of faith, and labour of love, and patience of hope in our Lord Jesus Christ, in the sight of God and our Father [...] (1Th, 1, 2-3)

We still find this basic pattern of Christian virtues in the work of Goethe, who made a pretty mythological picture of it in his *Maximen und Reflexionen* where he pointed out that Faith, Charity and Hope were once sitting quietly together when they felt a powerful urge to create something substantial. They set to work busily and created a beautiful creature, a Pandora on a higher plane.

However, the letters of St. Paul teach us even more about the moral values that were certainly still alive in Shakespeare's consciousness:

> And not only so, but we glory in tribulations also: knowing that tribulation worketh patience; and patience, experience; and experience, hope [...] (Rom, 5, 3-4)

Accordingly, it is patience that is the mother of experience and not, as one might think, experience that is the mother of patience. And Paul goes on:

> But thou, O man of God, flee these things; and follow after righteousness, godliness, faith, love, patience, meekness. (1Ti, 6, 11)

Besides faith, hope and charity, then, the virtues listed alongside patience are also righteousness, godliness and meekness. Meekness is a quality that Shakespeare often gives to his positive female characters. And finally we read in the Titus letter:

> That the aged men be sober, grave, temperate, sound in faith, in charity, in patience. (Tit 2, 2)

Thus patience is seen not as a quality that comes with old age but as a virtue that the elderly in particular are expected to attain.

Let us turn to Shakespeare's early work. *The Comedy of Errors* (1593) takes us to the half-heathen, half-Christian world of Ephesus, where the people have not yet abandoned their old beliefs in magic and witchcraft. They fall prey to banal instances of mistaken identity and deception, because they are not capable of being patient enough to use love and meekness to get to the bottom of things in a gentle and loving way. If the play did not have at least some characters, both young and old, both male and female (especially female) who, again and again, urge others to be patient, it would end up as a tragedy of errors rather than a comedy of errors.

Luciana is the unmarried sister of the wife of Antipholus of Ephesus, who wrongly believes her husband is deceiving her. In Act I, Scene 2 Luciana speaks of a husband being lord over his wife and master of his own time, while a wife must practise patience and meekness. Luciana has to listen as her sister retorts that this is easier said than done. Nevertheless, in the given situation in the play, she is not so far from the truth. In the end it is Emilia, the aged mother of the two Antipholi and now the abbess of a nunnery, who saves all those involved from a dreadful fate. It is her obstinate refusal to act hastily that saves them. Already in this early play it is the women who bring events to a happy conclusion by means of their patience and long suffering.

Shakespeare had already provided his audience with a vivid example of youthful, manly impatience in his earliest history play, *Henry VI Part I* (1593), in the young Talbot, whose "rough deeds and stern impatience" (IV,7, l.8, p.490)[3] lead not only to his own death but also to that of his father, and contribute to the loss of Bordeaux as well. Here we see a pattern emerging of how the capacity for suffering and the willingness to be patient are distributed between the sexes.

But already in Part II of *Henry VI* (1593),[4] we are treated to a completely different type of call for patience, made by the wizard Bolingbroke. It is directed towards Eleanor, the wife of the Lord Protector, Humphrey of Gloucester, who like Lady Macbeth in the later play, also "unwomans" herself in order to help her well-meaning but ineffectual husband:

> Patience, good lady - wizards know their times.
> Deep night, dark night, the silent of the night,
> The time of night when Troy was set on fire,
> The time when screech-owls cry and bandogs howl,
> And spirits walk, and ghosts break up their graves -
> That time best fits the work we have in hand.
> (2 *HVI*, I,4, ll.15-19)

This is a devilish sort of patience which puts its trust not in faith, hope and charity but in the "ripeness" of time. We shall meet it again, for it is from this view of patience that the new, modern capacity to wait and watch for the favourable moment (Machiavelli's "occasione") is to grow.

In *The Taming of the Shrew* (1593) Petruchio prophesies, not without a touch of irony, that, once tamed, the wildcat Kate will become a second Griseldis, a paragon of patience:

> For patience she will prove a second Grissel [...] (II,1, l.287)

Here we meet the female personification of the virtue of patience given to literature by Boccaccio (*Decameron*, 10th day, X) and Petrarch, and introduced into English literature by Chaucer in *The Clerkes Tale*. She is a female Job, whose patience is to be understood as a limitless capacity for suffering. But that is the very core of the Chris-

---

[3] The text and page numbers of the Shakespeare quotations are all from the Norton Shakespeare (based on the Oxford Edition), ed. Stephen Greenblatt, W.Cohen, J.E. Howard. K Eisaman Maus (Oxford: OUP 1997).

[4] *The First Part of the Contention of the Two Famous Houses of York and Lancaster.*

tian notion of virtue anyway: "Patentia vero a patiendo nomen acceperit", it says in St. Augustine's *De Patentia*.

The character of Julia in *The Two Gentlemen of Verona* (1594) is also based on the Griseldis type of paragon. The young woman persists in her love for the hot-headed and changeable Proteus to the point of self-sacrifice. It is love and hope which give her the power to do so, and not an extraordinary strength of character. When Proteus takes leave of her (II,2, .l. 1-2) with the words, "Have patience, gentle Julia!" she answers with a sigh, "I must where is no remedy." Female patience in matters of the heart is what will lead to her victory over the tyrannical, Protean nature of the male:

> I'll be as patient as a gentle stream,
> And make a pastime of each weary step
> Till the last step have brought me to my love.
> And there I'll rest as after much turmoil
> As a blessed soul doth in Elysium.
> (II,7, l.34-38)

Let us not be unjust and accuse her of being pragmatic and calculating. She is following the ideal of love that Shakespeare has the shepherd Sylvius define so well:

> It is to be all made of fantasy,
> All made of passion, and all made of wishes,
> All adoration, duty, and observance,
> All humbleness, all patience and impatience,
> All purity, all trial, all obedience,
> (V,2, l.84-87)

In *Romeo and Juliet* (1595), we come upon a tragic treatment of the theme of impatience. It was only by moving the emphasis to this theme, which is not of much import in the sources, that Shakespeare was able to make out of a tale of tragic lovers, with all its attendant strokes of fate and fortune, a tragedy of character. Nevertheless it would not be right to speak indiscriminately of a tragedy of youthful rashness or of impatience in love as described by Sylvius four years later in *As You Like It*. When Romeo is banished form Verona, Friar Laurence admonishes him to be patient:

> Hence from Verona art thou banished.
> Be patient, for the world is broad and wide.
> (III,3, l.16-16)

Romeo's impatiently dismissive reply to this admonition is characteristic of him, and at the same time provides a key to the drama as a whole:

> There is no world without Verona walls
> But purgatory, torture, hell itself.
> Hence banished is banished from the world,
> And world's exile is death.
> (III,3, l.17-19)

Friar Laurence calls the attitude of the young man "deadly sin" and "rude unthankfulness", and it is in fact Romeo's manly impatience that is the cause of his and Juliet's tragic end. It is not the impatience of love which leads to the tragedy, love which paradoxically is to be paired with patience, according to Sylvius. It is with Romeo that all the reponsibility for the course of events lies, a responsibility that he is on several occasions not up to bearing. This becomes fatally obvious in Act VI, Scene 1, ll.24 ff. when he ignores Balthasar's admonition to him to be patient, and rushes off back to Verona. If this first tragedy of Shakespeare's had a moral it might be expressed in the words of the Prince in Act V, Scene 3, 1.220: "Let mischance be slave to patience!".

In the man's world of *Richard II* (1595), which starts off the Lancaster cycle and, with Richard's abdication, depicts the "Fall" of the English nation, the virtue of patience is shown in a patently negative light. In Act 1, Scene 1, 1.52, Mowbray speaks scornfully of that "tame patience" he can lay no claim to. And the Duchess of Gloucester, who in Act I, Scene 2 tries to persuade John of Gaunt to raise his hand against "the annointed of the Lord," the King, and to avenge the death of his brother, Thomas Woodstock, counters his refusal with the words:

> Call it not patience, Gaunt, it is despair.
> In suff'ring thus thy brother to be slaughtered
> Thou show'st the naked pathway to thy life,
> Teaching stern murder how to butcher thee.
> That which in mean men we entitle patience
> Is pale cold cowardice in noble breasts.
> (I,2, l.29-34)

Here we see the beginnings of the new way of seeing patience, we are coming to that turning-point in the way patience is used that we spoke of earlier: Bolingbroke, who is later to become Henry IV, is Shakespeare's first royal example of a machiavellian politician in the modern, non-judgemental sense of the word. He acts from "necessity" and waits for the "right moment", "the occasion" to seize the throne. Here we meet a more modern understanding of the idea of patience, which is no longer identical with the "Job's patience" that the deposed Richard seemed to show when in Act V, Scene 2 he was pelted with dirt by the mob, as York reports:

> His face still combating with tears and smiles,
> The badges of his grief and patience [...]
> (V,2, l.33-4,)

But York is wrong: Richard, even when imprisoned and faced with death, has not really learned the Christian virtue of patience either. His last words on the subject make this clear:

> Patience is stale, and I am weary of it.
> (V,5, l.103)

On the other hand, in another play which dates from the same time, *A Midsummer Night's Dream*, there is much talk of "maiden's patience," the patience of young girls (III,2, 1.66), which is sorely tried by the fickleness of the young men. It sounds like a manifesto for patient endurance when Hermia says in Act I ,Scene 1:

> If then true lovers have been ever crossed,
> It stands as an edict in destiny.
> Then let us teach our trial patience,
> Because it is a customary cross,
> As due to love as thoughts, and dreams, and sighs,
> Wishes, and tears, poor fancy's followers.
> (I,1, ll.150-155)

A year later , in *The Merchant of Venice*, Shylock declares patience a virtue born of necessity and characteristic of the Jews living in a Christian environment:

> In the Rialto you have rated me
> About my moneys and my usances.
> Still have I borne it with a patient shrug,
> For suff'rance is the badge of all our tribe.
> (I,3, 1.107-10)

But this no longer has anything to do with the proverbial patience of Job in the Old Testament. This is more the pragmatic, waitful type of patience that can be used for good or ill, and that we have already met once before. This patience is biding its time, waiting to take its revenge. Shakespeare sets it against the long-suffering, Christian virtue of patience with the words of Antonio in Act IV, Scene 1:

> And that no lawful means can carry me
> Out of his [the Duke's] envy's reach, I do oppose
> My patience to his fury, and am armed
> To suffer with a quietness of spirit
> The very tyranny and rage of his.
> (IV,1, 1.8-12)

In *Henry IV* Parts 1 and 2 and in *Henry V*, however, the plays which bring the Lancaster Tetralogy to a close between 1597 and 1599, Shakespeare shows us in the figure of Henry Bolingbroke, and even more so in that of his son, the development of a machiavellian politician - machiavellian in the value-free sense - for whom what once was a Christian virtue becomes a necessity. The notion of virtue breaks away from the notions of suffering and eternity and becomes joined with those of time in this world and the ability to wait till that time is ripe. Impatience is no longer a sin, but a rash deed, like that of Prince Hal, when he tries to grasp the crown while his father is on his sick-bed and dying, but not yet dead. The simple soldier Nym in *Henry V* Act II, Scene 1 shows an instinctive if hazy comprehension of things when he comments:

I cannot tell. Things must be as they may. Men may sleep, and they may have their throats about them at that time, and some say knives have edges. It must be as it may. Though Patience be a tired mare, yet she will plod. There must be conclusions. Well, I cannot tell. (II,1, l.18-22)

One gets the impression that the old, Christian virtue of patience is in retreat and now only to be found in the world of the comedies, and that is a woman's world. More and more it is the men who are the impatient ones, especially the old men, for patience requires strength and stamina, which they no longer have, as the ancient philosophers knew. In *Much Ado About Nothing*, Hero's aged father Leonato rejects an admonition that he should be patient with the words:

> No, no, 'tis all men's office to speak patience
> To those that wring under the load of sorrow,
> But no man's virtue nor sufficiency
> To be so moral when he shall endure
> The like himself. Therefore give me no counsel.
> (V,1, l.27-31)

And he adds sagely:

> For there was never yet philosopher
> That could endure the toothache patiently,
> (V,1, l.35-6)

In the series of tragedies that begins with *Julius Caesar* in 1599, the theme of patience versus impatience is overlaid by the motif of hesitation versus over-hasty action ("rashness"), or perhaps we should say the new theme grows out of the old one. Brutus holds back, unwilling to join the conspiracy against Caesar so long as it is not yet clear whether Caesar is really after the crown or not. In Brutus the two themes come together. In the expectation of certain defeat at Philippi, he behaves with stoical equanimity. On being told of Portia's death (Act IV, Scene 2) he says:

> Why, farewell, Portia. We must die, Messala.
> With meditating that she must die once,
> I have the patience to endure it now.
> (IV,2, l.242-4)

Strengthened by his stoic philosophy he rejects suicide as a way out:

> [...] arming myself with patience
> To stay the providence of some high powers
> That govern us below.
> (V,1, l.105-7)

Hamlet is another character who wants to be sure of things before he takes action to get his revenge. In his hubris he lets the opportunity to strike go by, when he misses his chance in the bed-chamber scene. From then on he decides to vacillate no longer and go for "rashness", which is what makes him kill Polonius. Unlike Brustus, he seems to know nothing of the virtue of patience either in the old or in the new sense, neither as the wavering scholar of Acts I and II, nor as the nobleman braced for action of Acts IV and V. There is only a faint hint of the old, Christian, female call for patience in the ravings of Ophelia, rendered mad by Hamlet's murder of her father:

> I hope all will be well. We must be patient.
> (IV,5, 1.66)

Blinded by jealousy, the hot-blooded Othello, who stems from a non-Christian background, is incapable of patience, unlike the devilish Iago, who is. Iago's two-edged, cynical remark in Act II, Scene 3 is meant to be taken seriously:

> How poor are they that ha' not patience!
> (II,3, 1.343)

In Act II, Scene 3 he takes the liberty of warning his master, Othello, now mad with jealousy, to wait and be patient. But Othello does not possess the devilish capacity for patiently biding his time that Iago has, as he makes desperately clear when he says in Act IV, Scene 1:

> Dost thou hear, Iago?
> I will be found most cunning in my patience,
> (IV,1, ll.88-9)

In one of the great "patience" speeches in Act IV, Scene 2, Othello compares himself to Job. If God had subjected him to the kind of trials that He made Job suffer, so goes his reasoning, he would surely have been able to find "a drop of patience" somewhere in his soul. He could even bear the ignomy of being branded a cuckold. But for him to be cut off from the very source of his life, his love for Desdemona, is death to him. Defiantly he apostrophises patience personified:

> Patience, thou young and rose-lipped cherubin,
> Ay, here look grim as hell.
> (IV,2, ll.65-6)

In *Macbeth* (1605) there is a surprise waiting for us. In Act IV, Scene 3, patience turns up in the catalogue of royal virtues presented by young Malcolm, Macbeth's designated successor:

> The king-becoming graces,
> As justice, verity, temp'rance, stableness,
>
> Bounty, perseverance, mercy, lowliness,
> Devotion, patience, courage, fortitude [...]
> (IV,3, ll.92-5)

Whether it is the Christian, the classical-stoic or the modern-pragmatic kind of patience that is meant we do not know. If we think of *Henry V,* then it is probably more the new, pragmatic type of patience that we have here. When we remember *King Lear,* written at the same time (1605), we may be confirmed in our assumption, for the old king in his hastiness is the very incarnation of 'rashness', the new version of impatience. Although he belongs to the older generation, like Gloucester he too has been corrupted by the spirit of the new era, the era of science, "naturalism" and selfishness. In the midst of his Job-like trials, when he is wandering "houseless" and naked on the heath, he begs to be given patience ("you heavens, give me that patience, patience I need", l. 424) and even promises in Act III, Scene 9 (QT) that he will be "the pattern of all patience" (l. 36). In his madness he even admonishes his fellow-sufferer Gloucester to patience, but even if patience were granted to Lear and to Gloucester at this stage, it would be too late. In the godless world in which he lives there is no eschatological perspective for patience anymore, there is only the here and now.

In Shakespeare's later works, it seems as if the Christian virtue of patience has retreated and taken up residence in the world of women. We have the wonderful Rosalind of *As You Like It,* of whom Duke Frederick can say in Act I, Scene 3:

> Her very silence, and her patience
> Speak to the people, and they pity her.
> (I,3, ll.73-4)

We also have a character almost beyond the comprehension of the modern mind, the Griseldis-like character of Helena in *All's Well That Ends Well,* and we have Paulina, the lady-in-waiting in *The Winter's Tale,* whose wisdom and patience help Queen Hermione survive the "long winter" of jealousy and tyranny. She it is who speaks the words we have used as a title for this paper:

> I doubt not then but innocence shall make
> False accusation blush, and tyranny
> Tremble at patience.
> (III,2, ll.29-31)

The "winter" is the modern age where there is no longer a cosmic perspective to life. In this world, the Christian virtue of patience is no more than a faint memory kept alive by the women. Not by all of them, of course. For we also have Cleopatra, who in *Antony and Cleopatra* masterfully plays up and down the scale of patience and impatience. Her slave, Charmian, finds it extremely amusing when Cleopatra tells her how she has treated Antony:

> I laughed him out of patience, and that night
> I laughed him into patience [...]
> (II,5, ll.19-20)

What she thinks of patience is brutally clear:

> Patience is sottish, and impatience does
> Become a dog that's mad.
> (IV,16, ll.81-2

But there is some comfort for the men of today, nevertheless: In Shakespeare's later work there are also some men, mostly old ones, who still remember the Christian virtue of patience and try to pass it on to the younger generation. There is Prospero, of course, in *The Tempest*, who tries to school the impatient young lovers, Ferdinand and Miranda, in the virtue of patience before he lays down his magic wand. And finally in *Pericles* (1608), the patience theme is absolutely central to the plot of this dramatic romance in which the passage of time causes the heinous crimes of the fathers and mothers to be forgotten. But there would be no life worth living for the young people in the world of *Pericles* if it were not for the old men who keep urging them to be patient. I should like to give one of these old men the opportunity to say a final word and quote Helicanus, the old counsellor of the prince. Pericles is in dire straits and asks him: "What wouldst thou have me do?" His advice is:

> To bear with patience
> Such griefs as you do lay upon yourself.
> (Sc.2, ll.69-70)

And yet: in the end it is not an old man who is to have the last word, but a young girl. Pericles has grown old and sees his daughter, Marina, who has been restored to him, as the very incarnation of patience. He asks her to tell the story of her trials and tribulations.

> Tell thy story.
> If thine considered prove the thousandth part
> Of my endurance, thou art a man, and I
> Have suffered like a girl. Yet thou dost look
> Like patience gazing on kings' graves, and smiling
> Extremity out of act.
> (Sc.21, ll.123-28)

Thus we can see, if we only look carefully, that there is a message in Shakespeare's plays that may still be relevant to us today in our "impatient" modern times.

Don Quijote and Eighteenth-Century English Literature

HEINZ-JOACHIM MÜLLENBROCK (Göttingen)

From the European perspective, England can claim to have pioneered the reception of *Don Quijote*,[1] and it was in the eighteenth century that a new approach was taken which finally led to a different, more constructive and altogether deeper view of Cervantes's novel. This change will be my topic today. The logic inherent in this process of England's understanding of Cervantes's *chef-d'oeuvre* is what my article is concerned with — it was a process that gradually intensified throughout the eighteenth century, and that can be studied best by looking at how some of the novel's prominent features were taken up in English literature, first and foremost in English novels. It is not, therefore, an interpretation of specific passages or a (nearly) complete collection of references to Cervantes in English novels that I want to present. My interest lies in elucidating this literary grappling, as it were, with Cervantes by taking a close look at how it developed, and by trying to show what discursive order can be established in the views that people held towards *Don Quijote*. To the best of my knowledge, this approach has never been consistently followed in the existing studies of Cervantes in English literature.[2]

The *Oxford English Dictionary* defines *Quixote* as "an enthusiastic visionary person like Don Quixote, inspired by lofty and chivalrous but false or unrealizable ideals." It is easy to forget that it took a long way to arrive at this Romantic view, and England played a major role throughout it. In fact, England was the first foreign nation to honour *Don Quijote* extensively and intensively: The first English as well as the first foreign translation ever was Thomas Shelton's,[3] which appeared in 1616 and 1620 respectively. Later, the first biography and the first annotated edition of *Don Quijote* were published first in England. In addition, literary references to Cervantes's novel appeared remarkably early; those in the fourth acts of Ben Jonson's *Epicoene* (1609) and *The Alchemist* (1610) are only two examples. Moreover, it was in England that we find a radically new interpretation of *Don Quijote*. I would now like to show the dynamic process which, in the end, produced new readings of *Don Quijote*.

---

[1] Compare especially James Fitzmaurice-Kelly's impressive conclusion "Cervantes in England," *Proceedings of the British Academy* 2 (London, 1905-1906): 11-29, especially 29.

[2] Compare especially Susan Staves' synopsis in her article on "Don Quixote in Eighteenth-Century England," *Comparative Literature* 24 (1972): 193-215.

[3] Compare Edgar Allison Peers, "Cervantes in England," *Bulletin of Spanish Studies* 24 (1947): 226-38, here 227-9; the same article appeared in *Homenaje a Cervantes*, 2 vols. (Valencia: Vives Mora, 1950), II, 272-5 under the title "Cervantes en Inglaterra."

I

In seventeenth-century England, most people considered Cervantes's novel to be a farce. They regarded it mainly as good entertainment, even fit to impress children. In fact, *Don Quijote* was often judged like one of the romances parodied by Cervantes. One example for the negative, farce-like interpretation of *Don Quijote* is Samuel Butler's satire on Puritans, *Hudibras*, which was published at the beginning of the Restoration period and saw Don Quijote as a quarrelsome crank. Criticizing his egocentric distortion of reality, Butler even made him the butt of his satire. Towards the end of the seventeenth century this interpretation could still be found in John Phillips' *Don Quixote* (1687) and in Thomas D'Urfeys stage-adaptation of the novel, *The Comicall History of Don Quixote* (1694 - 96).

In the eighteenth century, men of letters still regarded Cervantes's protagonist as an eminently humorous figure, but at a very early stage the verdicts on his extravagant behaviour became more lenient. In the *Spectator* no. 30 (4 April 1711), for example, Oxford students elect Don Quijote patron of the "Amorous Club" because of his "Phrenzy." Although comments like "that gentle Knight" already point towards a less severe opinion of Don Quijote's behaviour, Steele still regards him mainly from an ironic distance. In Addison's *Guardian* no. 135 (15 August 1713), we find little more than a slightly condescending appraisal, although he had classified both *Hudibras* and *Don Quijote* as the same kind of satire in *Spectator* no. 227 (20 November 1711).

The interest in *Don Quijote* as burlesque, inherited from the Restoration period, can still be found in *The Memoirs of Martinus Scriblerus*, which is typical of the first phase of the reception of *Don Quijote* in eighteenth-century England. Although published only in 1741, the satirical work was written much earlier, a large part even as early as 1714, in the reign of Queen Anne. Martinus Scriblerus and his father Cornelius Scriblerus are characterized as being quixotic scholars, so that, in accordance with the authors' satirical aim, a kind of intellectual horseplay is being staged, exposing the scholarly absurdities of the main characters. Already in the introduction, the similarities between Martinus Scriblerus and Don Quijote are pointed out, beginning with Scriblerus's appearance:

> [...] By the Gravity of his Deportment and Habit, [he] was generally taken for a decay'd Gentleman of Spain. His Stature was tall, his Visage long, his complexion olive, his brows were black and even, his eyes hollow yet piercing, his nose inclin'd to aquiline, his beard neglected and mix'd with grey: All this contributed to spread a solemn Melancholy over his countenance.[4]

The following is a collection of curios where one scientific eccentricity, one scholarly pedantry succeeds the other, throwing the reader into fits of laughter. Cornelius Scriblerus's love of antiquity, for example, is shown in all its absurdity by the revelation that he is ever so happy about the wart in his son's face because Cicero, too, had one.

---

[4] Charles Kerby-Miller, ed., *The Memoirs of the Extraordinary Life, Works, and Discoveries of Martinus Scriblerus* (New York and Oxford: Oxford University Press, 1988), 91.

Unlike Don Quijote, the *Memoirs'* heroes meet with only few adventures; but there is one episode with more 'action' and a certain quixotic flavour. It is entitled "The Double Mistress," and tells how Martinus Scriblerus, induced by his predilection for all things curious, falls in love with a virgin whose body is joined with that of her twin sister. This adventure undoubtedly mirrors Don Quijote's fantastic character and his stiff-necked insistence on doing things his own way; the comic effect of this adventure is enhanced by a counter-plot instigated by Martinus's enemies, who are angered by his behaviour.

However, comparing Don Quijote and the two Scribleruses, we find that unlike Cervantes's hero they are not ambivalent characters, i. e. possessing noble and foolish traits at the same time, although both Martinus and his father strive after higher ideals. Nowhere is there any tension discernible between ideality and reality. Instead of throwing a critical light on reality from a quixotic point of view — as later authors do — the *Memoirs'*[5] authors use their protagonists — who ludicrously fail to see reality as it is because of their scholarly pedantry — as victims of satire.

II

It was Henry Fielding who took the decisive step towards a new interpretation of Don Quijote, regarding him not only as a ridiculous madcap but also as a good-hearted star-gazer, thus creating tension between reality and ideality. He deserves the credit for having read Cervantes's novel from a completely different angle, and the shift towards a new assessment of Don Quijote is forever connected with his name. The first approach to this new reading was, of course, still rather crude, which comes as no surprise given the fact that it was introduced by a coarse comedy: Fielding's *Don Quixote in England* (1734), written when he was still a young man.

Here is a short summary of the play which ushered in the second phase of the reception of Cervantes.[6] Sir Thomas Loveland's daughter Dorothea is to be married against her will to the rich Squire Badger; she, on her part, is in love with the poor Mr. Fairlove, with whom she has a rendezvous at Mr. Guzzle's inn. By sheer coincidence, Don Quijote and his squire Sancho Panza have just arrived there, and Don Quijote meets with similar difficulties as in Cervantes's novel. Here, too, he mistakenly believes that he has arrived at a castle, and thus he refuses to pay for his food and lodging. First and foremost, however, he follows his vocation of relieving people in need or in otherwise dire straits, and as a result of his meddling Loveland finally

---

[5] Concerning this satirical work compare Gustav Becker's detailed study *Die Aufnahme des Don Quijote in die englische Literatur (1605 - c. 1770)* (Berlin: Mayer & Müller, 1906), 99-111.

[6] For a detailed interpretation of the play compare Rita Gnutzmann, "*Don Quixote in England*, de Henry Fielding, con relación al *Don Quijote*, de Cervantes," in Manuel Criado de Val, *Cervantes: Su obra y su mundo: Actas del I congreso internacional sobre Cervantes*, (Madrid: EDI-6, 1981), 1115-35; the article was reprinted in *Anales Cervantinos* 22 (1984): 77-101.

agrees to his daughter's marrying Fairlove.

At first sight, Fielding's Don Quijote still seems rather traditional, and there is no doubt that he does belong to the group of anti-romance Don Quijotes of English literature. Yet this is only one side of his character, and by no means the prominent. Compared with the other figures, his position becomes more important as he is turned into a well-meaning idealist with certain moral values, used as a yardstick to measure contemporary society, which reveals grave shortcomings. To these Fielding reacts in different ways in his play, including poking fun at some of the minor deficiencies and harshly criticizing the more severe ones. The mayor, for example, suggests that Don Quijote stand for Parliament because he thinks that he will then be able to fleece him. Less critical and more funny are Don Quijote's remarks in act II, scene 5, when, addressing himself to Squire Badger — whose chief delight is the fox-hunt — he states: "Hunting is a manly exercise, and therefore a proper recreation. But it is the business of a knight-errant to rid the world of other sorts of animals than foxes."[7]

Usually, however, Don Quijote's critique of English society reaches far deeper. Already his first longer passage contains a kind of declaration of sociocritical principles; turning to Sancho he says: "Virtue, Sancho, is too bright for their eyes, and they dare not behold her. Hypocrisy is the deity they worship."[8] This shows that Fielding uses Don Quijote as his mouthpiece; and this is by no means the only instance. At the end of the play we find another good example of this re-definition of Don Quijote.[9] The hero himself discovers the 'madness' — which of course everybody believes him to be possessed of — in the representatives of the different professions. Thus, Don Quijote, supposed to be ill himself, plays the (traditional) role of the doctor in this play, which turns out to be a satire on English society, especially on the corruption of public life. In the end, it is Don Quijote's common sense and goodheartedness that bring about the marriage for love between Fairlove and Dorothea instead of the marriage for economic reasons planned by Sir Thomas. In this play, Don Quijote does not only possess foolish as well as noble traits, which was to become quite normal in future times; in moral respects, he even acts as an example to everybody else.

However, Fielding's painting of Don Quijote's character is not altogether without flaws. The way he introduces his character does not prepare the reader for Don Quijote's function as a mouthpiece of humane common sense. It even comes as something of a surprise as Don Quijote is never given the chance of proving his common sense in everyday situations before his sudden comments on the state of English society. In this respect, Fielding's play is quite different from Cervantes's novel. There, the protagonist again and again bridges "la discreción y la locura;"[10] here, in Fielding's play, we

---

[7] James P. Browne, ed., *The Works of Henry Fielding, Esq. With an Essay on his Life and Genius by Arthur Murphy, Esq.*, a new edition, III (London: Bickers, 1905), 94.
[8] *Works of Henry Fielding*, III, 85.
[9] Gnutzmann ("*Don Quixote in England*," 1126) emphasizes that Don Quijote's opinions are accepted by all characters in the concluding song.
[10] Miguel de Cervantes Saavedra, *Don Quijote de la Mancha*, texto y notas de Martín de Riquer (duodécima edición, Barcelona: Planeta, 1990), 970 (part II, chapter 59).

have two different sides of Don Quijote — one representing the traditional humorous interpretation, and the other presenting serious insights — that are not moulded into one consistent character.

Still, in spite of this lack of psychological plausibility, *Don Quixote in England* pointed towards the future reception of Cervantes's novel. It created a precedent by using Don Quijote as a background for judging society, following the principle of contrast common to satire. It is quite interesting, by the way, to notice how from the very beginning the ever more serious and constructive reading of *Don Quijote* went hand in hand with an increasingly one-sided interpretation. In some respect, less ambitious adaptations like *The Memoirs of Martinus Scriblerus* are closer to the original message of the Spanish novel. In his *Don Quixote in England*, Fielding had to idealize the protagonist in order to use him in the way I have pointed out. This straightforward idealization is missing in the original as Cervantes never openly takes sides.

The decisive change, therefore, with regard to Don Quijote's function is the hero's radical mutation from being the butt of the satire, in Restoration times and well into the eighteenth century, into setting an example of normative correct behaviour and at the same time exposing aberrations. In this context, one should perhaps not forget that the play was dedicated to Lord Chesterfield, who then was a member of the opposition.

In his first novel, *The History of the Adventures of Joseph Andrews and his Friend Mr. Abraham Adams* (1742), Fielding transferred this idealization to the character of Parson Adams, who is generally considered the proper embodiment of Cervantine influences on Fielding. It seems that it was only by firmly rooting this perception of Don Quijote in the genre of the novel that Fielding was able to establish a new tradition because it was only here that he was on an equal footing with the Spanish author and could therefore live up to (or rather write up to) his model. Significantly, Fielding's first novel is subtitled "written in imitation of the manner of Cervantes, author of *Don Quixote*." Further evidence for Cervantes's influence on Fielding is found in the programmatic first chapter of book III of *Joseph Andrews*, in a passage full of admiration for the Spaniard's novel: "[...] the achievements of the renowned Don Quixote [are] more worthy the name of a history than even Mariana's."[11] "History," one of Fielding's key-terms of course, is used to show his disapproval both of the romance tradition and of historiography to the extent as it is dedicated to delivering facts only.[12]

However, in spite of these seemingly convincing references it is not easy to assess the range of Cervantes's influence on *Joseph Andrews*. Looking at the main characteristics of *Don Quijote*, it seems that it is its prevailing mood, its cheerfulness, that Fielding managed to imitate most authentically in his picaresque novel; Parson Adams, Don Quijote's successor, and his adventures never leave any feeling of

---

[11] Henry Fielding, *Joseph Andrews* (London and New York: Everyman's Library, 1970), 143.
[12] Compare Wolfgang G. Deppe, *History versus Romance: Ein Beitrag zur Entwicklungsgeschichte und zum Verständnis der Literaturtheorie Henry Fieldings* (Münster: Aschendorff, 1965).

pessimism or a sense of tragedy behind, in spite of all the obstacles the Parson encounters. In the eighteenth century, people hardly ever saw Don Quijote as a tragic hero anyway; this view was to be propagated only later by the Romantics.

Several other aspects of the novel seem to have been taken directly from Cervantes. One is the confrontation of reality and ideality which I will return to later. Another aspect concerns the novel's structure. Fielding's "comic epic poem in prose" also shows a shift in locality from "camino/posada" to "camino/casa."[13] Moreover, there are similarities with regard to the inserted stories and reports of the Golden Age, which occur in both novels.[14] The narrator, too, seems to come directly from *Don Quijote*: Time and again he makes metafictional comments, and this strongly points towards Cervantes as the origin of Fielding's satire against contemporary English authors. There is yet another similarity: Parson Adams and Joseph Andrews enjoy a companionship which is modelled on that of Don Quijote and Sancho Panza. While they travel together, their friendship becomes richer and more intense; and yet, to what extent there really is a "sanchificación de Don Quijote" and a "quijotización de Sancho," as Salvador de Madariaga has put it, is a matter open to discussion.

The touchstone, however, for assessing the quixotic contents of *Joseph Andrews* is Fielding's characterization of Parson Adams and his views of the world. In the third chapter, Parson Adams is introduced as follows: "He was, besides, a man of good sense, good parts, and good nature; but was at the same time as entirely ignorant of the ways of this world as an infant just entered into it could possibly be."[15] Although he is, strictly speaking, no imitation of Don Quijote — in fact, he rather resembles Sancho Panza in his dedication to food and drink[16] — it is his idealism that makes him a true heir to Don Quijote. Without being mad like the Spanish knight, yet similar to him in his naiveté (compare Gilman, "Henry Fielding's Reception," 33), Parson Adams again and again finds himself in dire straits because he is so very unsuspecting. Once, for example, intending to sell his sermons because of his financial embarrassment, he frankly talks about his situation to the bookseller and is somewhat surprised about the ungenerous offer he gets (compare Fielding, *Joseph Andrews*, book I, chapter 17). Such ignorance of worldly matters recalls Fielding's by no means uncritical verdict from his play *The Coffee-House Politician* (1730): "Good nature is Quixotism, and every Princess Micomicona will lead her deliverer into a cage" (compare act III, scene 2). However, the way Fielding made use of Don Quijote can be seen much more clearly in one of his later reviews in the *Covent Garden Journal* (1752), where he deals with the main characters of *Don Quijote* and *The Female Quixote*, Charlotte

---

[13] For a discussion of this aspect compare Santiago Acosta Aide, "El influjo del *Quijote* en *Joseph Andrews*," *Revista Canaria de Estudios Ingleses* 11 (1985): 69-80, here 70-75.

[14] For Fielding's adaptation of these elements of Cervantes's novel compare Homer Goldberg, "The Interpolated Stories in *Joseph Andrews* or 'The History of the World in General' Satirically Revised," *Modern Philology* 63 (1965-66): 295-310.

[15] Fielding, *Joseph Andrews*, 5.

[16] This is correctly pointed out by Stephen Gilman, "On Henry Fielding's Reception of *Don Quijote*," in Ian Michael and Richard A. Cardwell, eds., *Medieval and Renaissance Studies in Honour of Robert Brian Tate* (Oxford: Dolphin, 1986), 27-38, here 34.

Lennox's recently published novel. Part of his review can easily be applied to Parson Adams: "Both Characters are accordingly represented as Persons of good Sense, and of great natural Parts, and in all Cases, except one, of a very sound Judgement, and what is much more endearing, as Persons of great Innocence, Integrity and Honour, and of the highest Benevolence."[17] In spite of his folly, Parson Adams, just like Don Quijote, retains his natural dignity and superiority, which all those many mishaps cannot destroy.[18]

However, in his characterization of Parson Adams, Fielding goes well beyond Cervantes. "Benevolence" — the last word in the above quotation — is a character trait that has no equivalent in Don Quijote, who is rather stoical with little emotion to support his reason. Parson Adams, on the other hand, is benevolence personified, thus embodying the contemporary role model that Fielding as an enlightened Christian chose as the centre of his novel. Although "Prudence" is one of the aims that Fielding wants Parson Adams to reach, he is, compared to Cervantes's protagonist, made much less responsible for the predicaments he finds himself in.

The role Fielding assigns to Parson Adams is free of ambivalences and therefore quite different from Don Quijote's role. Cervantes accepts reality, the world as it is, and shows Don Quijote to be positively mad. Fielding, in contrast, firmly supports Parson Adam's exaggerated altruism. The Parson's rather child-like lack of knowledge about the ways of the world sometimes even proves an advantage: Although his extreme goodness of character is slightly ridiculed, it triumphs in the end over those in society that make fun of him without any reason.

Divine providence, too, is interpreted differently in the two novels, although it carries a positive connotation in both. Cervantes's novel seems to leave the impression that everybody knows his place in a well-ordered society, with the only exception of Don Quijote. Fielding, in turn, uses Parson Adams as a mouthpiece to demand that man's behaviour in society be perfect, though he believes even more explicitly than Cervantes that the world is well-ordered by God's benevolent providence. While in *Don Quijote* there are only few passages where satire is aimed at society, Parson Adam's idealism is used again and again to satirically highlight the imperfection of reality. It is true that whenever the Parson deviates from Fielding's enlightened course, which follows reason and balance, such extremist behaviour appears to be a flaw in his character;[19] and yet such flaws are described as something amiable and forgivable — noble weaknesses, as it were — not as ridiculous vices.[20] What Una-

---

[17] Ioan Williams, ed., *The Criticism of Henry Fielding* (London: Routledge and Kegan Paul, 1970), 192. Compare also Staves, "Don Quixote in Eighteenth-Century England," 205-6.

[18] With reference to Don Quijote Menéndez Pelayo writes: "[...] su derrota no es más que aparente, porque su aspiración generosa permanece íntegra, y se verá cumplida en un mundo mejor [...]" (Marcelino Menéndez y Pelayo, *Discursos* (Madrid: Espasa-Calpe, 1956), 158).

[19] Although Gerhard Buck usually plays down the affinity between Parson Adams and Don Quijote too much, he is certainly right in considering this as Fielding's "Warnung vor dem Nicht-Maß-Halten" ("'Written in Imitation of the Manner of Cervantes,'" *Germanisch-Romanische Monatsschrift* 29 (1941): 53-61, here 57).

[20] This is why Parson Adams is not at all "half-way between the two possible extremes of the

muno wrote about Don Quijote in his essay "El Sepulcro de Don Quijote" can also be applied to Parson Adams: "Caballero que hizo reír a todo el mundo, pero que nunca soltó un chiste. Tenía el alma demasiado grande para parir chistes. Hizo reír con su seriedad."[21] The 'publicity campaign' for Cervantes's protagonist is quite obvious in *Joseph Andrews*. In the end, goodness, as embodied in Parson Adams, is intended to prove that badness is ridiculous. Fielding's reading of Don Quijote in *Joseph Andrews*, therefore, already shows signs of an interpretation which later was to be taken up by German Idealism.

At the beginning of the eighteenth century, Cervantes had been read and imitated in a superficial and mainly burlesque manner — even in *The Memoirs of Martinus Scriblerus* comic situations are described for comedy's sake alone. Now, in the second phase of the reception of *Don Quijote*, the attitude towards the novel changed. It was increasingly often used as an opportunity to show the author's commitment to moral standards.

There was no mistaking Fielding's commitment: *Joseph Andrews* illustrated the thesis that "affectation" characterizes human behaviour. However, this led to an overemphasis of stage-like situations, intended to expose hypocrisy and vanity, but which at the same time reduces the wealth of nuances typical of Cervantes's novel. *Don Quijote* is ambivalent and possesses far more different perspectives.[22] Where Cervantes is neutral or reserved on moral matters — he hardly ever goes beyond 'sophisticated understatements' — Fielding explicitly takes sides, thereby moulding Cervantes's hero to serve his own purpose, namely to criticize human behaviour in society. It was on account of the centrality of the contrast between reality and ideality that Fielding's way of upgrading and reassessing quixotism constituted a milestone in the history of the interpretation of *Don Quijote*.

III

That Fielding used Cervantes's novel for his serious criticism of society did not only initiate the second phase in the reception of *Don Quijote*, but deeply influenced the eighteenth century as a whole: It is precisely the novels that followed Fielding's satire-oriented interpretation which characterize this second phase of continuing Cervantine impulses.

Charlotte Lennox's *The Female Quixote or the Adventures of Arabella* (1752) used the Spanish novel's theme to describe the world in which women lived in the eighteenth century: The heroine is fond of reading romances mostly of French origin. At first sight, the novel seems to be a setback as the heroine's one-sided characterization in the manner of the comedy of humour strongly reminds us of the customary view of

---

    quixote figure" (Staves, "Don Quixote in Eighteenth-Century England," 206).
[21] Miguel de Unamuno, *Obras Completas*, tomo IV: *Ensayo II* (Madrid: Aguado, 1958), 74.
[22] Gilman ("On Henry Fielding's Reception of *Don Quijote*," 31) remarks about Fielding: "[...] he converted sly Cervantine understatement into deadpan over-statement."

Don Quijote. Although Arabella, too, misunderstands reality because of her reading habits and therefore does recall the simple interpretation of *Don Quijote* that asks for ridicule on the part of the reader, she is by no means only — not even primarily — a ridiculous figure. Lennox actually upgrades her heroine:[23] Arabella's extravagant behaviour is not only eccentric, it also expresses a particular attitude which she takes very seriously, claiming it to be morally correct. Thanks to her naturalness and naiveté — both of which are traits that recall Fielding's interpretation of Cervantes — she has internalized standards that strongly suggest a critical view of society, although, in this respect, *The Female Quixote* is not as transparent as *Joseph Andrews*. There is, in other words, a connection between her character and the way she imitates the lives of literary figures. The seemingly 'normal' behaviour of the other figures sets off Arabella's foolishness; Arabella's integrity, however, which can be glimpsed behind her eccentricities, points out the foolishness and weakness of the other characters. Lennox even uses her heroine as the mouthpiece for her own moral convictions,[24] and this correspondence of moral values does indeed justify the comment that "[...] Lennox [...] enlists the reader's sympathies on what the novel formally designates as the wrong side."[25] In the case of Lennox's *The Female Quixote*, too, the structure and the theme of Cervantes's novel are at least partly utilized to throw a critical light on the author's contemporary reality.

This is even more true of Tobias Smollett's *The Life and Adventures of Sir Launcelot Greaves* (1762). It rounds off the second phase in the reception of Cervantes, characterized by taking an increasingly favourable, even idealized view of the characters in imitation of Don Quijote, who are used in a satirical context as positive role models and mouthpieces for social criticism.

Smollett is rightly regarded as the second great satirist, next to Fielding, among the English novelists of the eighteenth century. In his earlier experiments with quixotic figures in *The Adventures of Roderick Random* (1748), *The Adventures of Peregrine Pickle* (1751) and *The Adventures of Ferdinand Count Fathom* (1753), and with his translation of *Don Quijote* (1755) he had shown his interest in Cervantes. *Sir Launcelot Greaves*, however, "the most extensive effort of any major eighteenth-century novelist to imitate *Don Quijote*,"[26] is, I think, not a very felicitous continuation of Cervantes because the character of Smollett's protagonist is too different from that of

---

[23] Compare especially Theodor Wolpers, "Der weibliche Quijote in England: Charlotte Lennox' *The Female Quixote* und die literarische Tradition," in: Theodor Wolpers, ed., *Gelebte Literatur in der Literatur: Studien zu Erscheinungsformen und Geschichte eines literarischen Motivs, Bericht über Kolloquien der Kommission für literaturwissenschaftliche Motiv- und Themenforschung 1983 - 1985* (Göttingen: Vandenhoeck & Ruprecht, 1986), 134-62, here 157.

[24] Compare Arno Löffler, "Die wahnsinnige Heldin: Charlotte Lennox' *The Female Quixote*," *Arbeiten aus Anglistik und Amerikanistik* 11 (1986): 63-81, here 75.

[25] Debora Ross, "Mirror, Mirror: The Didactic Dilemma of *The Female Quixote*," *Studies in English Literature* 27 (1987): 455-73, here 461.

[26] Edward L. Niehus, "Quixote Figures in the Novels of Smollett," *The Durham University Journal* 71 (1978-79): 233-43, here 237.

Don Quijote as far as his mentality is concerned. Smollet characterizes Sir Launcelot Greaves as a "satirist-errant,"[27] setting out to fight injustice that really exists, not merely imagined. This is why large parts of the novel turn into a biting satire directed at the situation in contemporary England, especially at the corruption of public life in town and country. Slightly varying Ortega y Gasset,[28] Smollett might have asked: "Dios mío, ¿qué es Inglaterra?" Smollett, however, does not imitate Cervantes very closely as Sir Launcelot remains quite sensible and acts neither unreasonably nor in a foolhardy manner. At the beginning of the novel, when Sir Launcelot introduces himself, he declares unmistakably: "I see and distinguish objects as they are discerned and described by other men."[29] Why he disguises himself as a knight-errant, succumbing among other things to a grotesque ceremony of dubbing, remains unexplained; besides, in spite of his odd appearance he never draws any ridicule upon himself, quite in contrast to Don Quijote. The mad and eccentric Captain Crowe, a minor figure designed simply to be comic, is in comparison much more like the Spanish original; he even experiences more setbacks than Sir Launcelot. Smollett makes his hero wisely and energetically stand up for justice and point out the flaws in society, always guided by the contemporary concept of benevolence; but there is no real affinity between Don Quijote and Sir Launcelot. The latter quite lacks Don Quijote's 'mental bond' to the Middle Ages, the evocation of which appears as a somewhat artificial device.

Yet — and this is the important point here — the increasingly positive interpretation of Don Quijote within a satirical context logically culminated in *The Life and Adventures of Sir Launcelot Greaves*. Smollett's high regard for Cervantes, by the way, was not only based on *Don Quijote* but also on Cervantes's biography: In his "Life of Cervantes," which precedes his translation of *Don Quijote*, Smollett is full of admiration for the Spanish author's character.[30] By concentrating all the traditional weaknesses of the Quijote figure in his own figure of Captain Crowe, Smollett relieved Sir Launcelot of these character flaws and at the same time avoided the problem of having to create a round figure. As a consequence, the reader's sympathies could be directed entirely at the noble Sir Launcelot, who is near perfect in his role of the critic of society, albeit one-dimensional. After Smollett's novel, the positive utilization of Don Quijote could not be taken further; the reception of Cervantes would henceforth have to follow different paths.

---

[27] Compare Ronald Paulson, *Satire and the Novel in Eighteenth-Century England* (New Haven and London: Yale University Press, 1967), 189-90 and 199-200.

[28] The Spanish quotation runs: "Dios mío, ¿qué es España?" (*Meditaciones del Quijote con un apéndice inédito* (Madrid: Alianza, 1987), 72).

[29] Tobias Smollett, *The Life and Adventures of Sir Launcelot Greaves*, ed. Peter Wagner (Harmondsworth: Penguin, 1988), 50.

[30] Compare A. P. Burton, "Cervantes the Man Seen through English Eyes in the Seventeenth and Eighteenth Centuries," *Bulletin of Hispanic Studies* 45 (1968): 1-15, here 11.

IV

The third phase in the reception of Cervantes in the eighteenth century was ushered in by the publication of Laurence Sterne's revolutionary novel *The Life and Opinions of Tristram Shandy, Gent.* (first complete edition 1767). It is no coincidence that the novel was written in the 1760s, a time of change regarding literature and taste. Sterne's approach to Cervantes can best be illustrated by a quotation from one of his letters from the summer of 1759: "[...] the happiness of the Cervantic humour arises from this very thing — of describing silly and trifling Events, with the Circumstantial Pomp of great Ones."[31] This verdict, which does not do justice to Cervantes's intentions, is reminiscent of a similar passage in Pope's postscript to his translation of Homer's *Odyssey*: "The use of pompous expression for low actions or thoughts is the *true Sublime* of *Don Quixote*."[32] These two quotations appear to be akin, firstly because they seem to contain similar views, and secondly because they point towards a satirical or burlesque reading of Cervantes. In reality, however, there is no such similarity as satire is only superficial in Sterne's novel; for example, when Walter Shandy, openly parodying Don Quijote, holds forth in a highly erudite manner on his theory of the importance of names and of the form of noses for success in life. The novel is full of similar passages; but the barbs of satire are few and comparatively blunt from the beginning.

Making the reader laugh about such follies is not Sterne's proper concern. He is far more interested in teaching the reader to smile with his characters; he wants him to like their eccentricities. In the end, Sterne does not use the original mock-heroic method any more with its sharp separation of the important from the less important and with its ridiculing the vain: In Sterne, we have integration instead of separation. Comic and sublime elements are inextricably intertwined in *Tristram Shandy*, and what is small, insignificant and trivial is increasingly often endowed with a quality that points to the innermost of man and does him credit. Sterne's redefinition of eccentricity as a person's idiosyncratic and unfathomable hobby-horse marks a new view of man, which is characterized by sentiment. The move from sense to sentiment also explains the narrator's spontaneous preference in book III, chapter 19: "[...] my dear *Rabelais*, and dearer *Cervantes!*"[33] It was no doubt easier to sentimentalize the Spanish author than the French.[34]

Yet, it is only Sterne's very subjective re-reading of *Don Quijote* that can explain the godfather-like function of Cervantes in *Tristram Shandy*. In contrast to most

---

[31] Lewis Perry Curtis, ed., *Letters of Laurence Sterne* (Oxford: The Claredon Press, 1935), 77.

[32] Alexander Pope, *The Odyssey of Homer (Books XIII-XXIV)*, in Maynard Mack, ed., *The Twickenham Edition of the Poems of Alexander Pope*, x (London: Methuen and New Haven: Yale University Press, 1967), 388.

[33] Laurence Sterne, *Tristram Shandy* (London and New York: Everyman's Library, 1967), 137.

[34] Compare a remark of Alan B. Howes in his "Laurence Sterne, Rabelais and Cervantes: The Two Kinds of Laughter in *Tristram Shandy*," in: Valery Grosvenor Myer, ed., *Laurence Sterne: Riddles and Mysteries* (London: Vision Press, 1984), 39-56, here 55.

earlier authors, Sterne shows that he has an unusually personal relationship with Cervantes,[35] whom he addresses several times. The key to this approach can be found in a highly suggestive phrase in "The Invocation" towards the end of the novel: "Gentle Spirit of sweetest humour, who erst did sit upon the easy pen of my beloved *Cervantes*" Sterne, *Tristram Shandy*, 464). The emotional "sweet" will, by the way, later also be used by Coleridge with reference to Cervantes.[36] The quotation shows that Sterne sentimentalizes and trivializes Cervantes; he seems to notice mainly the absurd naiveté together with the simplicity and sentimentality of the Cervantine figures. Yorick, for example, is to remind the reader of Don Quijote because of his purity of heart. Interestingly, Sancho Panza, mostly ignored or debased by earlier English authors, is highly appreciated in *Tristram Shandy*: His words, not Don Quijote's, are quoted! In book VII, chapter 32 Tristram Shandy embraces his donkey, talks to him and shields him from being beaten (compare Sterne, *Tristram Shandy*, 382), just like Sancho Panza does in Cervantes's novel. That Sterne felt especially attracted to Cervantes because the latter seemingly preferred sentiment to sense — at least that is how Sterne read it — is convincingly proved by a passage in *A Sentimental Journey* (1768). The narrator is about to pay a visit to the mad Maria, and comments: "'Tis going, I own, like the Knight of the Woeful Countenance, in quest of melancholy adventures."[37]

In Sterne's novel we find a shift of interest from the public sphere — which found literary expression in the criticism of society with reference to *Don Quijote* — to the private sphere: 'inwardness' or 'nobility of heart.' The contrast between ideal and reality, which was the essential element in the second phase, is turned into a kind of idealization of reality, corresponding to the amiably eccentric side of man. By reducing the comic and satirical elements in favour of the novel's sentimental and sublime potential, Sterne opened the way for the interpretations in the ages of Sentimentalism and Romanticism.

All in all, Sterne's reception of Cervantes is characterized by a remarkably mixed quality. On the one side, Sterne can be regarded as the most congenial of Cervantes's followers: Firstly in his ingenious development of the narrative metareflexion, and secondly in the subtle mixture of comic, satirical and sublime elements and their interdependence. Unlike the earlier and straightforward adaptations of the Spanish novel which concentrated on one aspect only, Sterne gave expression to the paradoxically complex nature of man.[38] On the other side, though, Sterne reduced the stature of Cervantes's noble and militant protagonist by endowing all his figures, also and especially average persons, with quixotic traits,[39] and by ascribing motives to them that are

---

[35] Burton remarks quite rightly: "Sterne knew Cervantes within *Don Quixote*, and knew of him as a man in his own right" ("Cervantes the Man," 15).

[36] Compare "Lecture VIII: Don Quixote-Cervantes," in Thomas Middleton Raysor, ed., *Coleridge's Miscellaneous Criticism* (London: Constable and Co., 1936), 99.

[37] Laurence Sterne, *A Sentimental Journey - The Journal to Eliza* (London and New York: Everyman's Library, 1969), 121.

[38] This achievement of Sterne's is especially stressed by Edward L. Niehus, "Quixote Figures in the Novels of Sterne," *Essays in Literature* 12 (1985): 41-60, here 43-4.

[39] Compare Staves, "Don Quixote in Eighteenth-Century England," 202.

by no means as pure as those of Don Quijote.[40] Besides, the greatness of the Spanish knight's conflict with the world around him has been scaled down to a series of mere trifles. The price that had to be paid for Sterne's 'philanthropic' transformation of Cervantes was the loss of Don Quijote's heroic aura.

V

Sterne did not only prepare the way for contemporary sentimental authors but also for the Romantic reading of Cervantes. His far-reaching influence can also be discerned in a novel like Richard Graves' *The Spiritual Quixote* (1773), which satirizes ideological extravaganza, thus following an older reading of *Don Quijote*, but which by tolerating eccentricity also contains elements of Sterne's perspective.[41] Incidentally, Smollett's last novel, *The Expedition of Humphry Clinker* (1771), shows similar traces of Sterne's influence. Much in Sterne already pointed towards the Romantic reading of Cervantes: the emotional identification with Cervantes, which shows the Spanish author as worthy of veneration; blending the rational with the irrational; characters as wise fools.

The Romantic authors, vindicating among other things the elements of romance in *Don Quijote*, in particular discovered the tragic potential[42] of the novel, which they often read as an autobiographic confession; as they saw it, the most important quality of *Don Quijote* did not lie in exposing human weakness to ridicule, but — and this was especially true of the German movement — in a refined sense of humour, exploring the metaphysical depths of human existence.[43]

---

[40] Compare also Laurence Sterne, *A Sentimental Journey through France and Italy by Mr. Yorick*, ed. Gardner D. Stout, Jr. (Berkeley and Los Angeles: University of California Press, 1967), 40 ("Introduction").

[41] Compare especially book II, chapter 4: "Essay on Quixotism."

[42] Compare Walter F. Starkie, "Miguel de Cervantes and the English Novel," *Essays by Diverse Hands. Being the Transactions of the Royal Society of Literature*, New Series, xxxiv (London: Periodical Publisher H. Milford, 1966), 159-79, here 177.

[43] As to the Romantic reception of Cervantes cf. esp. Anthony Close, *The Romantic Approach to 'Don Quixote:' A Critical History of the Romantic Tradition in 'Quixote' Criticism* (Cambridge: Cambridge University Press, 1978) and Werner Brüggemann, *Cervantes und die Figur des Don Quijote in Kunstanschauung und Dichtung der deutschen Romantik* (Münster: Aschendorff, 1958).

Intercultural Conflicts: Godwin and his Counter-Revolutionary Reviewers

KENNETH W. GRAHAM (Guelph)

In the 1790s, an intercultural conflict was taking place in Britain that has not yet received a full assessment, partly because its nature and effects have not been effectively measured. That major ideological changes were taking place in the 1790s can be substantiated by a study of British literary reviews. The broad nature of the change is revealed in a contrasting perspective. Our studies of the British romantic poets furnished us with an awareness, perhaps obscure, perhaps vivid, of reviewers and their power. We encountered Shelley's white-hot condemnation of Keats's reviewers as "herded wolves," "obscene ravens" and "vultures."[1] We may have inclined to Byron's skeptical "`Tis strange the mind, that very fiery particle,/Should let itself be snuffed out by an article."[2] Still, a study of romantic reviewing reveals the dark dimension characterized by William Hazlitt during slightly calmer post-Waterloo days.

> It was pious and loyal to substitute abuse for argument [...] [T]o belie a Whig, a Jacobin, a Republican, or a Dissenter, was doing God and the king good service; at any rate, whether true or false, detected or not, the imputation left a stain behind it, and would be ever after coupled with the name of the individual, so as to disable him, and deter others from doing farther mischief [...] Prejudice and power [...] felt that reason was against them - and therefore it was necessary that they should be against reason [...] Conscious that they were no match for modern philosophers and reformers in abstract reasoning, they paid off their dread of their talents and principles by a proportionable contempt for their persons, for which no epithets could be too mean or hateful.[3]

The press of the period of British romanticism deserved such condemnations. Reviewing was highly partisan and aggressively unethical.

How it became so is revealed by changes in reviewing practices in the 1790s when notions of piety and loyalty became distorted by perceived threats. Reviews of the 1780s are less partisan. Generally they let a work speak for itself; they provide a digest with copious excerpts and, usually at the conclusion, a brief paragraph or two of opinion. The responses of Shelley and Hazlitt tell us that reviewing changed. We need to know more about the nature of the change. In such collections as Donald Reiman's *The Romantics Reviewed*, we have access to reviews that *our* century finds most inter-

---

[1] "Adonais," in Thomas Hutchinson, ed., *The Complete Poetical Works of Percy Bysshe Shelley* (London: Oxford University, 1934, rpt 1947 Press), 438, ll. 244-6.

[2] Lord Byron, *Don Juan*, ed. T.G. Steffan, E. Steffan and W.W. Pratt (Harmondsworth: Penguin, 1982), XI:60, 412.

[3] William Hazlitt, „The Periodical Press," in P.P. Howe, ed., *Complete Works* (New York: AMS Press, 1967), 16: 233-4.

esting. What we need is a coherent collection of reviews more representative of their own times, a collection of reviews considerable enough to demonstrate the ideological shifts that precipitated changes in the styles and purposes of reviewing.

A collection of reviews of the books of a single person extending over a fixed period should supply that need. A valid and significant sample of one kind of discourse can afford us specific evidence of changes in cultural attitudes. The review is a particularly sensitive yet conservative indicator of its times since its loyalties are divided between the work under review and the satisfaction of the readers. Thus the times are served both by the work under review and the expectations of the audience. I have gathered all the reviews of William Godwin's works published in Britain during a working life that extended from 1783 to 1834. A focus on the 1790s shows how reviews signal subtle movements in ideas and attitudes. Increasingly the world of the review reveals the ideological forces being exerted in the 1790s to define with growing clarity a cultural divide separating one element of the British population, the reformers, from another, the loyalists.

In this context, the word *ideology* is emphatically not anachronistic. It was coined[4] by Destutt de Tracy in France and echoed almost immediately in the 1796 *Monthly Review* and the 1797 *Monthly Magazine*. Godwin did not use the word, but he was certainly aware of the process by which opinions, beliefs, and impressions form a cultural environment out of which our thoughts articulate themselves. Godwin was a thorough empiricist. He speaks of individuals as *imbibing* beliefs as if we were living in a fluid of significances, breathing and drinking in the impressions and ideas which influence the shaping of our very thought processes.[5] Anthropology teaches us that cultures are in a constant flux of self-definition, that a useful approach to the understanding of cultures is through the signs it generates, and that one useful way of analysing change is through the shifting antitheses of competing perspectives.[6] *Piety* and *loyalty* stand firmly at one side of sets of antitheses that increasingly exclude expressions of dissatisfaction with political and social establishments.

Because of their sensitivity to their times, reviews reveal and respond to changes in notions of what squares with British culture during this period. In particular, they reveal the shifting margins enclosing notions of piety and loyalty and discover the conceptual boundary beyond which exclusions are defined. It is a measure of his importance and influence that Edmund Burke established in his *Reflections on the Revolution in France* the basic paradigm of British cultural self-definition during this period of tension. He affirms the Britishness of piety and loyalty and associates them

---

[4] Raymond Williams traces the term, *ideologie*, to Destutt de Tracy and ist first appearance in English as *ideology* in 1796. Cf. Raymond Williams, *Keywords: A Vocabulary of Culture and Society* (London: Fontana, 1976, rpt 1988), 153-4.

[5] A prominent use of the *imbibe* metaphor is found in the second-to-last paragraph of *Caleb Williams*. *Political Justice* uses various metaphors of influence – infect, impress, insinuate – in the empiricist arguments of the prefaces and four opening chapters.

[6] Clifford Geertz, for example, argues the semiotic conception of culture and the importance of determining the import of structures of signification. Cf. Clifford Geertz, *The Interpretation of Cultures* (New York: Basic Books), 5-9.

with those who are moved by the reverend metonymies of the political and social structure - "our state, our hearths, our sepulchres, and our altars." Excluded from the category of the true Briton are "literary caballers," "political theologians," and, of course, a "swinish multitude." The paradigm emerges from a discourse that welcomes stability and suspects change, that mystifies the sources and sinews of power and authority by surrounding them with expressions of veneration. That same discourse demonizes reform: reformers are plotters with foreign ideas undermining religion, common sense, and social order by sowing confusion.

William Godwin sought to subvert the Burkean paradigm. Throughout his working life he expressed skepticism of a social order based on monarchy, aristocracy, property, and an established church. Godwin projects an egalitarian society of responsible individuals. His negative vision is of tyranny perpetuated by mysteries, pious lies and secrets, a continuation of a huge and corrupt system of institutions and prejudices that is, to him, the real heritage from the past. Changing attitudes to Godwin's writings in reviews signal changes in the cultural milieu.

Histories of British reviewing point out that in 1790 the four major reviews were liberal, a term that generally connotes Whiggish in politics and dissenting or at least latitudinarian in religion. They were, the *Analytical, Critical, English,* and *Monthly Reviews*. In the course of the decade they were joined by two prominent Tory reviews, the staunchly Church of England *British Critic*, founded with a government subsidy in 1793, and the xenophobic *AntiJacobin Review*, established in 1798 with extreme and narrow notions of loyalty. The extremism of the latter two reviews moved the margins of loyalty towards a narrower denotation. These and other changes in the cultural environment affected the liberal reviews. The extent to which they inclined to Burkean ideas of loyalty and piety is revealed in their reception of three related works.

Two works published by Godwin under his own name, *Political Justice* (1793) and *The Enquirer* (1797) and an anonymous work of 1798, *Essay on the Principle of Population*, reveal the character of this *fin de siècle*. The shifting opinions and fates of the four liberal reviews in about half a decade tell us a great deal about the changes toward styles of reviewing that Hazlitt and Shelley condemn. The relevant reviews, with summaries and excerpts edited out, are supplied in the appendix.

Political Justice was published in the same month (January, 1793) that Louis 16th was condemned and executed. Perhaps, the time was not ripe for a condemnation of monarchy as "a system of universal corruption." Still, Godwin's book was greeted by fair and balanced reviews, even by reviewers philosophically and ideologically opposed to the arguments of *Political Justice*. The *British Critic* disliked the work but had the justice to offer grudging respect for "a long work of connected subtilty and argument"[7] and give the first volume a thorough summary, before condemning it as extravagant nonsense and associating the work with Helvétius and Rousseau.

The liberal reviews, *Analytical, Critical,* and *Monthly*, were more sympathetic. They delivered lengthy digests extending over two or more numbers. All offer ac-

---

[7] *British Critic* 1 (July 1793), 307-18.

counts that balance strengths and weaknesses. The terms of the balance express antitheses that grow in ideological significance with the passing decade.

> *Analytical Review*: "[...] among several extravagant and Utopian ideas, we have found much close argument, judicious observation, and profound thought."[8]

> *Critical Review*: "[...] some valuable matter, but with much alloy of error and absurdity."[9]

> *Monthly Review* [the most sympathetic and the most sensitive to changes in the political environment]: "[...] he has rather chosen to encounter all the effects of [deep-rooted] prejudices, than to conceal truths in which the happiness of the whole may be involved."[10]

The fourth liberal review, the *English*, did not examine the first edition for reasons to be discussed.

The *Monthly* is unique for expressing antitheses wholly sympathetic to *Political Justice*: they balance truth and happiness against deep-rooted prejudices. *Political Justice* is on the positive side of the antithesis and a prejudiced society on the negative. The negative terms in the antitheses of the *Analytical* and *Critical* condemn *Political Justice* with "extravagant" in the *Analytical Review* and "absurdity" in the *Critical*, echoing the Burkean antithesis between visionary theory and practical politics.[11] In those two reviews, Godwin is distanced from "normal" discourse and opinion. We experience the culture defining itself through exclusions.

In the 1780s, Godwin himself had written for the fourth review, the *English*. Its proprietor, John Murray, died before a review of *Political Justice* could be published. *The English Review* chose the appearance of the second edition in 1796 to review the work and, in the course of three wildly-contrasting installments, to take three giant steps towards a new ideological purpose. The first installment appeared in February; with extensive quotations, it summarizes in considerable detail Books 1 and 2 but offers no opinions. The continuation, after an unusual delay of seven months, is openly opinionated and thoroughly Burkean. Like Burke, it denominates political theory as "foreign" and praises establishments for their growth over time. It calls Godwin "a disciple of the French school" [who would] "emancipate men from all real reverence and respect for established powers." The third installment takes its antithe-

---

[8] *Analytical Review* XVI (June 1793): 121-30; XVI (August 1793): 388-404.

[9] *Critical Review* 2nd Series VII (April 1793): 361-72.

[10] *Monthly Review* NS 10 (March and April 1793): 311-20, 435-45; NS 11 (May 1793): 187-96.

[11] This antithesis echoes through Burke's *Rflections*. A particular instance would be: "The pretended rights of these theorists are all extremes; and in proportion as they are metaphysically true, they are morally and politically false [...] Political reason is a computing principle: adding, subtracting, multiplying, and dividing, morally and not metaphysically, or mathematically, true moral denominations." Edmund Burke, *Reflections on the Revolution in France*, ed. Thomas H.D. Mahoney (New York: Bobbs-Merrill, 1955), 70-71.

ses beyond Burke and beyond the restrictions of good manners. It is virulent to the author it contemptuously denominates "Mr Dogwin" and terms *Political Justice* a "chaos of crude and cold abstractions," "wild and wrong-headed," and, finally, "wicked" for questioning some of the teachings of Jesus. Piety and loyalty outweigh objectivity. The antitheses are meant to be militant: a term like "wicked" is positively coercive.[12]

This is the first review in my collection that repudiates the prevailing practice of reviews of providing an honest digest of the work under review. It begins on that pattern, but the last two parts of the review are almost wholly given over to refutation. They omit to mention, let alone summarize, the work's damning examination of institutions and practices productive of social and political injustice - which for Godwin include monarchy, hereditary aristocracy, the political superintendence of opinion, and crime and punishment. This style of reviewing is normally attributed to the influence of the *Edinburgh Review*, which was not to begin publication for another six years, a style that inflates the opinions of the reviewer over fidelity to the work reviewed. Its omissions are blatant and symptomatic of a commitment to loyalty that embraces silence on subjects that must not be spoken of. It also foreshadows the coming century in a hostility that extends from ideas to the personal. There is no civility in the final number. The *English Review* suggests the direction a review might take with a change of proprietor: managerial uncertainty means a move to the right.

Two acts of parliament may bear some responsibility for the deepening hatred and threat in the second and third installments of the review of *Political Justice* in the *English Review*. Passed into law in late December 1795, the two acts, The Treasonable and Seditious Practices Act (36 Geo.III, c.7) and The Seditious Meetings Act (36 Geo.III, c.8), restricted freedoms with extended definitions of treason and sedition. The first act, sponsored by Lord Grenville, defined utterances as seditious that encouraged "contempt"[13] of "the established government and constitution [...]" The offense applied to "writing, printing, preaching, or other speaking."[14] The second act, sponsored by Pitt, severely restricted what Godwin in protest called "the fundamental provision of the bill of rights, the right of the subject to consult respecting grievances, and to demand redress."[15] The liabilities for offenses were severe: Pitt's Act was punishable by heavy fines; Grenville's by transportation for seven years for a second offense. Since disease and hard labour made transportation generally fatal to reformers so punished, Grenville's Act represented a major enlargement in governmental terror. Both acts gave official sanction to the victimization of anyone who made dis

---

[12] *English Review* 27 (1796): 138-43; 28 (1796): 314-19, 437-43.

[13] The term "dislike" is used in the bill. Before passage, the word was changed to "contempt."

[14] A. Aspinall and E. Anthony Smith, *English Historical Documents 1783-1832* (London: Eyre and Spottiswoode, 1959), 319.

[15] *Considerations on Lord Grenville's and Mr Pitt's Bills, concerning treasonable and seditious practices, and unlawful assemblies* in *Political and Philosophical Writings of William Godwin*, ed. Mark Philip (London: William Pickering, 1993), Political Writings II, 134.

satisfaction with the government and constitution a topic of meetings or writings. *Political Justice* and its author were fair game for symptomatic silences and calculated abuse.

Godwin's *Enquirer* of 1797 is a two-volume collection of essays, chiefly on education, manners, and literature. It appeared in a year full of fears of invasion from France and insurrection at home, fears exacerbated by mutinies at Spithead, the Nore, and Yarmouth. Godwin's discussions are in the main unexceptionable, but some of his essays offer opinions - especially one condemning Christianity for fomenting bigotry - that raised hackles. Nevertheless, the ideas developed are not nearly as disturbing as those introduced in *Political Justice*, nor as painfully close to contemporary events. Still, the liberal reviews are not as hospitable as the content of the volumes seem to merit.

The *Analytical Review* is sympathetic to the "bold and manly independence of [Godwin's] opinions: to several of them we cannot, indeed, assent; but to all of them we would pay that attention, which they are authorized to claim from the firmness and ability with which they are supported."[16] The *Monthly Review*, warmest in praise of *Political Justice*, is cool to the *Enquirer*. It opens with reservations about "innovation" and dogmatism. It closes with some equivocal praise and warning: "[...] with all its faults, it is a production of great merit, and [...], if perused with caution, it cannot fail of being perused with profit."[17] The *Critical Review*, while friendly to the *Enquirer*, opens with an extended characterization of *Political Justice* from the perspective of 1797 that uses the terms *singular, eccentric, dogmatism, innovation*.[18] Within the culture of the Burkean paradigm, these are terms of disapproval. The reader begins the review of the *Enquirer* predisposed to suspect Godwin's loyalty.

By 1797 there were only three liberal reviews (the English having been taken over by the *Analytical Review*), and they seem nervous. The language in which they couch their reservations - "bold," "singular," "eccentric," "innovation," "dogmatism" - is a language that inclines to exclude innovative thinking from the affirmed world of collective sentiments.

The reception of a third work offers further evidence of change. In 1798 was published anonymously a work entitled *Essay on the Principle of Population, as it affects the Future Improvement of Society, with remarks on the Speculations of Mr. Godwin, M. Condorcet, and Other Writers*. The work - by Thomas Malthus - undercuts Godwin's arguments in *Political Justice* in favour of egalitarianism and perfectibility. About a third of its 400 pages is devoted to Godwin's philosophy, which Malthus presents as a beautiful fiction but contrary to the "fixed [...] laws of human nature" regarding food and sex. Its central argument propounds the notorious ratios: food production increases arithmetically: 2,4,6,8,10; and population increases exponentially: 2,4,8,16,32. Population will always outstrip food supply unless controlled by vice and misery.

---

[16] *Analytical Review* 25 (1797): 395-404; 27 (1798): 481-90.
[17] Monthly Review 2nd Series XXIII (July 1797): 291-302.
[18] *Critical Review* 2nd Series XX (May 1797): 58-64.

Let me quote the passage that most intensely assails Godwin's agrarian dream.

> Let us imagine for a moment, Mr. Godwin's system of equality realised [...] let us suppose all the causes of vice and misery in this island removed [He describes the exponential growth in population overwhelming the arithmetical growth in food production and offers this tableau:] The spirit of benevolence, cherished and invigorated by *plenty*, is repressed by the chilling breath of want. [...] the mighty law of self-preservation expels all the softer, and more exalted emotions of the soul. [...] Benevolence [...] makes some faint expiring struggles, till at length self-love resumes his wonted empire, and lords it triumphant over the world. [...] In these ages want indeed would be triumphant, and rapine and murder must reign at large [...][19]

The essay not only refutes *Political Justice*; it is completely antithetical to its social vision of justice and benevolence.

The *Monthly* and *Critical Reviews* don't assess the essay but the *Analytical* does, and, surprisingly, with warm echoes of the Burkean paradigm. It begins by associating Godwin's philosophy with the French Revolution that "destroyed the distinctions which generations have held in veneration" and admits, "We are glad to see a refutation of the new philosophy."[20] It gives a thorough and charitable summary of Malthus's essay, pausing from time to time to enjoy particular disparagements of *Political Justice*.

Coming from the *Analytical*, a journal renowned for its moderation and liberalism, the response is surprising. The cool but open praise of the *Enquirer* has been replaced by a hardened conservatism. That Burkean perspective, however, can be traced to events. The review of Malthus appears in the August 1798 issue. On July 17th of that year Joseph Johnson, the *Analytical*'s proprietor, was caught up in the wake of Grenville's bill on seditious utterances.[21] He was tried and convicted for selling a work by Gilbert Wakefield that dared to argue that the poor and wretched of England might welcome a French invasion.[22] For a man aged 61, a second offense would be fatal. Johnson ceased publishing the *Analytical Review* after December 1798.[23]

The last years of the eighteenth century experienced terrifying changes. An extensive collection of reviews reveals adjustments to public events and to a changing emotional and intellectual environment in the language of hardening allegiances. The movement to a more rigid and selfish nationalism was prompted by war, mutiny, censorship. It was prompted as well by threats to owners and managers that opened

---

[19] *Essay on the Principle of Population, as it affects the Future Improvement of Society, with remarks on the Speculations of Mr. Godwin, M. Condorcet, and Other Writers* (1798), 189-92.

[20] *Analytical Review* 28 (1798): 119-25.

[21] The offenses had been extended to include printing and publishing in 38 Geo. III, c. 78 passed in May 1798.

[22] Gerald P. Tyson, *Joseph Johnson: A Liberal Publisher* (Iowa City: University of Iowa Press, 1979), 159. The work was Gilbert Wakefield's *Reply to ... the Bishop of Landaff's Address*.

[23] A review of the same name continued for another six months, but it was not published by Johnson. Cf. *Joseph Johnson: A Liberal Publisher*, 169.

opportunities for adjustments in editorial policy that, almost invariably, meant conformity to collective sentiments. But in the details, in subtle variations in tone and language, we perceive the substance of change.

In an extensive collection of reviews we can see the influence of larger events signified in the language of shifting loyalties. The liberal reviews of the 1790s responded to a political climate increasingly intolerant of dissent. The same intolerance encouraged departures from objectivity that one seldom sees in reviews of the 1780s but which are characteristic of reviews in the first two decades of the nineteenth century. Developments in ideology and language promoted fear and hatred of ideas that challenge comfortable prejudices. Such fear and hatred excused an ethical laxness and encouraged the intolerance and distortion that prompted Shelley's anger and Hazlitt's disgust twenty years later.

Appendix: Intercultural Conflicts - A Selection of Reviews

William Godwin, *Enquiry Concerning Political Justice* (1793)

Analytical Review 16 (June 1793), 121-130; (Aug. 1793), 388-404.

Of all the subjects, which can occupy the attention of a philosophic mind, moral and political science may justly be pronounced to be incomparably the most important. Pure morals unquestionably constitute the basis of individual happiness and public prosperity; - it is equally certain, from reason and experience, that a well-constituted polity is highly favourable to the promotion of truth, and the advancement of virtue. Where the constitution of a state, and the administration of its government are repugnant to the principles of wisdom and equity, *there* it is impossible for virtue to exist in any considerable degree. In vain does the moralist labour to promote the improvement of mankind if his efforts be counteracted by a system of laws, that either in their immediate or direct operation, exasperate [sic] the evils, which *he* strives to correct. - We deem it therefore our duty to encourage every attempt, the object of which is, to illustrate the principles of sound and rational morality, and to establish the theory of a wise and equitable government. And we conceive, that the politician or the philosopher, whose labours are directed to this end, possesses a just claim to our most grateful acknowledgements.

Mr. G., desirous to present the public with a work, which, instead of being merely elementary, should embrace the 'larger views of political science;' and persuaded at the same time, that politics form no improper 'vehicle of a liberal morality,' was hence led to undertake the present inquiry. These volumes, comprising a variety of matter not a little condensed, it will not be in our power to give a complete detail of the very numerous topics which come under his discussion, much less to enter into a particular examination of the truth of his positions, or the validity of his arguments. The utmost we can attempt, is to present the reader with as full an accurate analysis of the 'Enquiry,' as is consistent with the narrow limits of a periodical Review.

[For a full column, summarizes and quotes from Book I.]

The benefits of political justice, or a wise and equitable form of civil government, next engage the attention of the author. After briefly enumerating these, he proceeds to show, that robbery and fraud, two of the greatest vices which prevail in society, originate, first, 'in extreme poverty; secondly, in the ostentation of the great; and thirdly, in their tyranny;' and that these vices are confirmed, first, by 'legislation,' which is in almost every country partial to the rich; secondly, 'by the administration of law;' and thirdly, 'by the inequality of conditions.' - His observations on this part of his subject, we are sorry to say, are too amply attested by daily experience.

[Quotes Godwin on property inequalities and introduces his notions of perfectibility.] In answer to the objections which may be offered to his principles, he proves, from reason and experience, that all nations are capable of liberty; and affirms that physical causes, particularly climate, operate but little in fixing the national character of a people. His observations on this subject are exceedingly pertinent, and his reasoning is, in our judgment, incontrovertibly conclusive. - That physical causes have *some* influence in fixing the national character, we readily admit; but that moral causes operate far more powerfully, we are fully convinced.

[Twenty-three pages of careful summary and detailed excerpts extend through the June and August numbers]

We have now presented our readers with as accurate an analysis of Mr. G.'s Enquiry, as our limits would permit: before we dismiss it, we would offer a few observations on what we conceive to be it's general character.

The plan of this multifarious inquiry Mr. G. seems to have sufficiently digested, and the execution is, on the whole, entitled to approbation. A few subjects are indeed introduced, which are but remotely connected with the great scope of the inquiry: but, as they tend to illustrate the operations of the mind, to the philosophical reader they will not be unacceptable. [...] The arrangement of his ideas is, in general, methodical and perspicuous; and his arguments are, with a very few exceptions, stated with force, succinctness, and accuracy. The language is, on the whole, clear and energetic, but sometimes incorrect - a few phraseologies occasionally occurring, which are sanctioned neither by colloquial nor written usage. The value of the sentiments will be variously appreciated. For our part, we bear this testimony, that among several extravagant and Utopian ideas, we have found much close argument, judicious observation, and profound thought. If his ardent enthusiasm in favour of truth and liberty, with a sanguine anticipation of the perfection of human nature, have betrayed Mr. G. into a few extraordinary and chimerical positions, though we may be disposed to smile at their singularity and extravagance, we can scarce censure the principle in which they originate. His morality is bold and imperious: if in any instance it be either impracticable or inconsistent, it seems to be in his doctrine of sincerity - While we thus cheerfully bestow on Mr. G.'s Enquiry that praise which we conceive it deserves, we are sorry to add, that we observed one or two insinuations, with respect to public worship and a future state, which we scruple not to pronounce highly offensive and improper. If Mr. G have aught against our religion; if he believe all social worship to be superstition, or that a futurity is inconceivable and its existence false; let him come forward into the open field of discussion and argument; but let him not unnecessarily and wantonly introduce, with an air of derision, either truths or practices which mankind have justly held in veneration. Contemptuous insinuations, without argument, are impertinent and illiberal. - We conclude our remarks with observing, that the author discovers considerable talents, a clear intellect, and an ardent mind in the pursuit of truth.

British Critic 1 (July 1793), 307-318.

[The opening two columns of general comments associate Godwin with self-important metaphysicians who put forward novel theories without considering their consequences.]

[...] we would not be so dishonest as to say, or to imply, that the author is deficient in natural powers. His malady is surely not imbecility of nature, but that which imbecility has been said completely to prevent. A weak man cannot produce a long work of connected subtilty and argument. It is the property of a very different state of mind to take for granted one or two extravagant absurdities, and then to reason justly and correctly from them, as if they were undoubted truths. Such is the origin and conduct of this book, which affords a striking example to what excesses of extravagance a man may proceed, who discards all revealed truth, to adopt the reveries of writers like the author of *Système de la Nature, Helvetius, and Rousseau.* Beyond these, who are his professed teachers, Mr. Godwin has taken an unmeasurable flight, on the waxen wings which they instructed him to fabricate; and before the conclusion of his book is perfectly in the clouds, to fall, like Icarus, as we shall show when we consider the last chapters.

Nothing can be more easy, for a person who has read a book of this nature, than to convey a full and just notion of it in a very few pages. Detached extracts alone, in the greatest number, could not do it; and could only serve to disseminate the poison, without conveying the antidote, which is, the knowledge of the unsubstantial basis on which the whole is founded. But as the whole is clearly enough deduced from a very few principles, to show what they are, and in what manner pursued, with a very few specimens of the mode of execution, will put every reader in possession of the real merits of the case, without the toil, which, we confess, is not a small one, of going through the volumes.

The principles then, taken for granted as axioms, on which the whole is founded, are these; 1. The omnipotence of truth; 2. The *perfectibility* (as it is expressed) of man; probably by means of this omnipotent truth; 3. That man is a mere machine; and, 4. That his actions, as well as every thing that happens in the universe, are the result of *absolute necessity*. Granting these things, there is certainly much acuteness and consistency in the mode of drawing the deductions from them; denying any one of them, - and what reasonable man will not strenuously deny them all? - the whole fabric crumbles into dust, or vanishes into less than air [...]

[The review proceeds to present and rebut its versions of each of the four principles. It offers no thorough and accurate reflection of *Political Justice*.]

Now, reader, be pleased to recollect what was said in the beginning of this article, on the empty vanity of the present times; and consider fairly what there is in all this, either in the conception of the author, or the authorities on which he rests, that can give a reasonable man any idea, that the work is the production of an enlightened age. Let us endeavour, if we can, to make it enlightened; but since those of its writers, who have by some been held the teachers of wisdom, have published doctrines that lead to such absurdities as these, let us not, with idle flattery to ourselves, call it *wise*, for alas! it must appear, to sober reason, a very foolish age! What is there in the *entelechia*, or *occult qualities* of Aristotle, the *Ideal System* of Plato, the *fatalism* of the stoics, the *atomism* of Democritus and Epicurus, or even the wildest conjectures of the most barbarous sects, that is not quite as rational and as intelligible as these *omnipotences*, and *pefectibilities*, and *necessities*? The true light, therefore, in which we ought to regard this book is, as a complete refutation of Helvetius, Rousseau, the author of *Système de la Nature*, and some English writers of equal extravagance, by a fair *reductio ad absurdum*; by showing demonstratively, to what nonsense and extravagance their doctrines, when pursued, must lead.

As to the style of the book, it is in general good; some few words are used affectedly, but on the whole it is perspicuous and clear; nor is there anything that demands notice, in the way of censure, very particularly. The method of the author, as his object was to conceal his real grounds as long as possible, is very different from that which is here stated; and from that which propriety demanded. He begins with the importance of political science; proceeds in Book ii. to the principles of society; in Book iii, to the principles of government. Book iv. contains miscellaneous principles, many of which should have been prefixed. Book v. is on legislative and executive power. Book vi. On opinion as a subject of political institution. Book vii. On crimes and punishments. Book viii. On property. The marrow of the whole we have already given in our own method; and if any one of the those who shall peruse this account should feel any inclination to gain further acquaintance with the book itself, it is a feeling in which the writer of this article is not likely to participate. He takes leave of it finally, careless whether he shall ever view it again; certainly neither willing or expecting to behold another like it.

Critical Review S2, 7 (April 1793), 361-372.

In his Preface Mr. Godwin seems to express some degree of apprehension, that the freedom of his sentiments may draw upon him the resentment of the executive government in this country. - For our own parts we cannot for a moment admit the supposition. We cannot for a moment believe that a British minister would attempt to fix shackles on the freedom of philosophical speculation, or that the nation would endure such an attempt. The only fair reason that can be urged for the prosecution of any publication is, that it is calculated to excite insurrection, and to render the mass of the people bad subjects. This reasoning can never apply to a speculative work like the present; a work in which particular men and particular measures are rarely animadverted on; a work which from its nature and bulk can never circulate among the inferior classes of society; and a work which expressly condemns violent alterations, violent measures, and the aim of which is to change the system of opinion and sentiment, rather than to effect any sudden change in government.

In this view, while we reserve to ourselves the right of private judgment, and profess to differ on some points from Mr. Godwin, we have yet the candour to say that we have been pleased and instructed with many parts of the work. - Science does not arrive at maturity at once, nor can it be expected that any human powers should produce a treatise which embraces such a variety of matter, and which should yet implicitly command in every page the approbation of every reader.

Mr. Godwin adopts as a leading principle, the opinion that the nature of a government must greatly influence the morals of a people, and that a government well constructed might frame and mould the manners of its subjects to every point of virtue and excellence; a principle which we believe true in some degree, but which we doubt of in the extent in which he appears to pursue it. Government can undoubtedly do much either in reforming or corrupting the morals of a people; but that any thing like perfection in this or any human institution is to be attained we hesitate to believe.

Our author proceeds to analyze with much acuteness the objects and the conduct of most governments which have existed, and particularly the monarchical governments; and we cannot help feeling too much truth in the melancholy inference which he seems to draw, that to increase the stock of virtue, to improve the real happiness of the nation, has seldom been the primary object in any state. War has hitherto been the great business of statesmen, and has been considered as inseparable from every political institution. - And yet what is *war*, but an accumulation of all the vices and all the calamities that can pervert and afflict mankind!

[The reviewer then quotes Godwin at length for over nine columns on wars, on penal laws, on luxury, on legislation, on the administration of the law, and on the use of argument to change government.]

In treating of morals our author most laudably condemns every appearance of falsehood, every habit of insincerity, even those which universal custom seems to have authorized, such as the custom of ordering the servants to deny the master or mistress of a house when they are really at home. In this principle we cordially agree with him.

The metaphysics of Mr. Godwin are entirely in the modern style, and he is a strong assertor of the doctrine of necessity. For our own parts, we will venture to prophecy that this doctrine cannot be long-lived. A doctrine which brings after it a train of such monstrous absurdities, which destroys at one blow all the moral attributes of God, and the responsibility of man, cannot long be popular among thinking and religious beings.

Independent, however, of this circumstance, Mr. Godwin's work is well deserving the perusal of every philosophical politician, of every man indeed who considers politics as a science. It also contains many important practical hints, which may be useful in the highest degree to the legislators of France, of America, and of Great Britain.

Critical Review S2, 8 (1793), 290-296.

[The review continues.]

Whatever may be the political heresies of our author, there is one article of his faith which has completely exempted him from our censure; and that is, 'that no revolution, no change of government, no innovation should be attempted, which is not preceded and called for by a radical and universal change of sentiment in the people' - Indeed we almost incline to the opinion of Rousseau, that scarcely any reform in government is worth the life of a single citizen.

While Mr. Godwin lays down so safe a principle as this, as the basis of his speculations, he is entitled to lenity, and even respect, from those who differ from him on particular topics; and we cannot but compliment his sagacity, which has been so amply justified by the unhappy situation of France, even since the publication of his volumes. Other writers on the side of democracy have been less cautious, and we have therefore treated them with less reserve, as we shall ever do those whose writings are calculated to produce disorder or discontent in this country.

We return, therefore, with pleasure to this entertaining production, (for even the errors of Mr. Godwin are entertaining) and shall endeavour, for the gratification of our readers, to exhibit a few impartial remarks on the contents of his second volume.

It was the observation of our venerable friend and coadjutor Dr. Johnson - That a too ardent zeal for liberty is the common error of young and ingenious minds. This observation certainly applies to our author, whose predelection for republican government is supported through all the first chapters of the present volume.

On this subject we are sorry that we cannot at all agree with Mr. Godwin, notwithstanding the ingenuity which he evinces in pointing out the defects of monarchy; for we are not such enthusiasts as to deny that this form of government has its defects, as well as every other; and nothing is in our opinion more evident than that, even in a limited monarchy, a great degree of vigilance is necessary in the people to guard their privileges from encroachment. This, however, does not prove that the institution itself is bad, and with all its defects the evidence of history decidedly proves that liberty itself is preserved (if the people are not culpably remiss themselves) better and more safely under this form than any other; and for this plain reason, that one tyrant is more easily resisted than many.

Though, however, we may not implicitly assent to Mr. Godwin's doctrines, yet his observations are far from being destitute of utility, even to those who substantially differ from him. In his chapter, On the Education of Princes, he very accurately points out the causes which combine to deprave their morals. - He is of opinion, that the hypothesis which makes adversity essential to virtue, has been commonly carried too far by moralists, and cannot see any reason why virtue may not be matured without previously undergoing the discipline of injustice or oppression.

. . . . .

[The review quotes excerpts discussing the political consequences of prosperity, misery, and honours.]

That there is truth in these observations, it would be absurdity to deny, and still more in the horrible and striking picture which he afterwards draws of a despotic government; but the conclusion which we should draw from them is very different from that of Mr. Godwin. - Not that a republic is the only remedy for these evils; not that a democracy will eradicate all the bad passions from the human breast; but that power is generally a corrupter of human nature, and that *without the controlling influence of public opinion*, most men who are entrusted with it, will be led to abuse it.

[The review accepts *Political Justice*'s objections to elective monarchy and the sycophantic education of the nobility.]

We join heartily with Mr. Godwin in deprecating so fatal and humiliating a distinction among individuals of the human species, as that between a Polish prince and a manorial serf, between a West India planter and a Creolian negro; but the objections do not apply to a nobility possessed of no odious or oppressive privileges; a nobility distinguished rather by their titles than their power. - From such an institution we see many advantages resulting to this country; and it is perhaps not the least that it operates as a salutary check upon the insolence of overgrown wealth, upon the purse-proud upstart, who has filled his coffers by the unlawful commerce of human flesh, by successful gambling in the national funds, or by plunder and extortion in the character of an agent or a commissary. The multitude must ever have some idol to worship, and we think the innocent vanity of birth and title a less dangerous object of adoration, than that already too general one, the love of gold.

Mr. Godwin has fairly pointed out the objections to democratical government, viz. the ascendancy of the ignorant, and the crafty; the inconstant character of such governments, the rash confidence, and the groundless suspicions by which they are actuated - These objections he has answered ingeniously, but we think not decisively; at least his arguments have not been sufficient to remove all *our* prejudices on the side of monarchy.

In treating of offensive war, Mr. Godwin is very powerful indeed; and we fear we must give it up as one of the defects of monarchical government, that it is (at least in modern times) more prone to interrupt the tranquillity of the people in this way, than democratical institutions.

[The review concludes with excerpts from Godwin's discussion of unjustifiable causes of war.]

Critical Review S2, 9 (1793), 149-54.

[The review concludes.]

From the several extracts which we have presented to our readers from the work before us, it must be evident that the man who would deny to our author the praise of both ingenuity and information, must be destitute of common sense or of common honesty. On the other hand, we have been more than once reduced to the unpleasant necessity of censuring the wild and visionary principles which occur in different parts of the work, and which we are sorry to see multiply as we draw towards a conclusion. The principle indeed upon which the modern democratic writers ground their theory of government, appears necessarily to lead into error, and has produced some of the most glaring into which Mr. Godwin has fallen. - This principle seems to be, that political wisdom and moral perfection are as reasonably to be expected in whole communities, as in individuals: the fact, we fear, is otherwise; and that the more numerous the association, the greater in general is the aggregate of error and fallibility. The affairs of an empire, like those of a family, must be conducted by a few persons, and the great use of popular assemblies is to form a bulwark against gross oppression and malversation. Mr. Godwin indeed seems to be aware of this objection, and allows that 'national assemblies should be employed as sparingly as the nature of the case will admit.' - But if wisdom and integrity are not to be expected from a representative body, how should we possibly look for them in a large society, and in a government, such as our author seems to recommend, where every man would do 'that which is right in his own eyes?'

Mr. Godwin reasons, in general, best, when he reasons from himself, and is not warped by the visionary and absurd philosophy which is, at present, floating about the superficial part of the literary world. On the subject of sumptuary and agrarian laws, he is deserving both of commendation and of attention.

[An excerpt follows on the dangers of governmental interference in the lives of the citizens.]

Mr. Godwin might have added, that nothing promotes the welfare of society and the happiness of the individual, like general industry; and an agrarian law must infallibly annihilate the principle of industry, and all the best and most active powers of the mind.

On the subject of religious establishments, our author is again misled by the dreams of those men who are fonder of speculation than of study, and would rather follow the fictions of their own imaginations, than labour up the steep of truth through the arduous paths of history and experience. Regarding ecclesiastical establishments in the light of a national education, which is the most simple and plainest point of view in which they can be placed, nothing can be clearer to us than the position, - that no system of education can be good without the sanctions of religion, and the belief of a future state [...]

The same reasoning will apply to the subject of tests. To us nothing is more clear, than that the man who occupies a superior office in the state, should not be hostile to the religion of the state. How far the obligation ought to descend in the scale of subordinate offices, is another question, and must in all cases be regulated by the particular expediency of the times.

[There follows a lengthy excerpt on the nature of libel.]

We agree with our author, that all social decisions are better determined by open vote than by ballot. We also concur with him in the opinion, that the most salutary species of punishment for offenses, and perhaps the most salutary mode of punishment, is that of sending the convicts to unsettled countries. We however see many things to disapprove in our author's notions of crimes and punishments.

Mr. Godwin's opinions concerning property are certainly impracticable; and favour too much of the modern *mania*, which has been misnamed philosophy; and his sentiments on marriage must incur the reprobation of every good and well-informed man. We hope, indeed, that if ever the work should arrive at another edition, our author will expunge this and many other disgraceful eccentricities.

The *acme*, however, of Mr. Godwin's speculations, are his extraordinary reasonings concerning the prolongation of human life, even to 'immortality.' Such an hypothesis requires only to be mentioned to be refuted, as totally inconsistent with the scheme of Providence in every thing that respects this world [...]

To conclude, we have endeavoured to exhibit as fair and impartial a sketch as possible of this singular, and, we must add, very unequal performance. It certainly contains some good information, and much interesting and entertaining dissertation. The mind of the author is evidently warped by the false philosophy of the times, and, however *free* he may fancy himself, writes more in fetters than any author we have lately perused. Where he disengages himself from these prejudices, and reasons with coolness and candour, we frequently discern the efforts of a vigorous mind, and have generally to admire his ingenuity, even where we cannot applaud his judgment [...]

The style of Mr. Godwin is fluent and pleasing; in general, chaste, and not prolix or redundant. In a very few instances we discovered something like affectation, but it is not such as to disgust, and we may say, upon the whole, that we have seldom met with better composition in any similar publication.

Monthly Review NS10 (March 1793), 311-20.

It may well be doubted whether, at any period, since the fatal contest between Charles I and his parliament, the minds of men have been so much awakened to political inquiry, as they are at this moment. If the well-being of society may be said to depend on the progress of political knowledge, it will follow that nothing is so desirable as the earnest pursuit of this inquiry; and what indeed can so effectually promote the peace and welfare of society, as knowledge? Wherefore do men dispute, quarrel, and make war on each other, but in consequence of their mistakes? Who will affirm that devastation and slaughter are good? - and why do these happen, but because of individual and general *ignorance*? Hence, too, arises all the oppression that exists among mankind; from which no system of government, nor of legislation, can free them; though, by unwise legislation and misgovernment, evils may be perpetuated. A general diffusion of knowledge is the only remedy for these evils; and he, who increases its stores, is the most useful of citizens, and the best of benefactors to mankind.

For these reasons, we have no small degree of pleasure in announcing the present work to our readers; as one, which, from the freedom of its inquiry, the grandeur of its views, and the fortitude of its principles, is eminently deserving of attention. - By this eulogium, we would by no means be understood to subscribe to all the principles which these volumes contain. Knowledge is not yet arrived at that degree of certainty, which is requisite for any two men to think alike on all subjects; neither has language attained that consistent accuracy, which can enable them to convey their thoughts, even when they do think alike, in a manner perfectly correct and intelligible to both. These difficulties are only to be overcome by a patient, incessant, and benevolent investigation.

Many of the opinions, which this work contains, are bold; some of them are novel; and some, doubtless, are erroneous: - but that which ought to endear it even to those whose principles it may offend, is the strength of argument adduced in it to prove, that peace and order most effectually promote the happiness after which political reformers are panting; - that, as the progress of knowledge is gradual, political reform ought not to be precipitate; - and that convulsive violence is dangerous, not only to individuals, (for *that* result, comparatively, would be of small account,) but to the general cause of truth. It is the opposite of this principle that inspires the enemies of political inquiry with so much terror; it is the supposition that change must inevitably be attended by the turbulence and injustice of commotion; and that innovation cannot be made, without the intervention of evils more destructive than those which are intended to be reformed. Under the conviction of this philanthropic sentiment, of calm and gradual reform, (which, in its proper place, he has fully illustrated,) Mr. Godwin proceeds, without scruple, first to inquire into present evil, through its essential branches, and next to demonstrates future good.

Dividing his work into eight books, and making the IMPORTANCE OF POLITICAL INSTITUTIONS the subject of the first, he begins by an attempt to prove the omnipotence of government over the moral habits of mankind; and that, on these moral habits, their wisdom, virtue, and felicity, depend. We must here remark, that, as he proceeds, and as the subject opens on him, he in part changes his opinion, and considers government rather as a necessary restraint on ignorance, than as an instrument for the promulgation of truth. While men continue to have vices, the coercion of government is an inevitable consequence: but in proportion as they acquire virtue, restraint and coercion become pernicious. Taken, however, in either point of view, government, and its effects on general happiness, are most important subjects of discussion. In proof of this, he states, that war, penal laws, and acts of despotism, are destructive operations; that the moral characters of men originate in their perceptions; that literature, education, and political justice, are the three principal causes of moral improvement; that mind is progressive; and that moral are superior to physical causes [...]

. . . . .

[Quotes I, 2 on the causes of war the the benefits of literature.]
Among other instances, contained in this first book, of the influence which political institutions have on society, the characteristic marks of the priesthood are animated, but severe; though far more liberal than the general sentiments of the declared enemies of hierarchy. For these, and for numerous other particulars, on which we have not time to expatiate, we must refer to the work itself.

BOOK II. treats of the principles of the society; of the distinction between society and government; of justice, including suicide, and duelling; of duty; of the equality of mankind; of the rights of man; and of the exercise of private judgment. The first book may be considered as introductory, and the subject is fully discussed in the second. An opponent, not only of divine right and patriarchal power, but even of the favourite and famed social contract, our author makes justice the foundation of his system [...]

. . . . .

[Provides excerpts from II, 2 on the discussion of justice.]
Building all his arguments on these immutable principles of justice, the author proceeds to define duty, and equality, and afterward that very popular subject, the rights of man; his reasonings on which, because of their originality and force, we think it our duty to state [...]

. . . . .

[Quotes from II, 5 Godwin's denial of the rights of man and the rights of society; and his affirmation of the duties of plain speaking.]
The third book treats of the principles of government; containing the systems of political writers; an examination of the social contract; of promises; of political authority; of legislation; of obedience; and of forms of government. We shall select

the question of promises, as likely to afford, from the solution which is given to it, pleasure and information to the lover of truth [...]

[In the excerpt from III, 3, Godwin expresses greater confidence in the compulsions of justice and reason than in promises and other declarations of intent.]

Monthly Review NS10 (April 1793) 435-45.

[The review continues.]

The farther we proceed in our examination of this bold and original work, the more we are convinced that it is proper, at this particular period, to present our readers with as clear an analysis of its contents as the nature of our publication will allow, rather than to obtrude any decided opinion of our own. The minds of men are at present so agitated, and their principles are unfortunately so opposite, that we think it *our duty* thus to limit ourselves, and to suffer each reader to draw his own conclusions. Under this conviction, we proceed.

Book IV. treats of miscellaneous principles; that is, of resistance; revolutions; duties of a citizen; mode of effecting revolutions; political associations; the species of reform to be desired; tyrannicide; the cultivation of truth; of abstract truth and sincerity; of necessity and its inferences; of the mechanism of mind; and of the principle and tendency of virtue.

[Quotes from IV, 1 the argument that government must not interfere with the individual's exercise of judgment.]

Mr. G. next examines whether it be the duty of a citizen to support the constitution of his country, and tells us that the claim of such support must either be made because the constitution is good, or because it is British. After proving the absurdity of the latter motive, he inquires into the mode of effecting revolutions [...]

[The excerpt from IV, 2 advocates the revolution of opinion through argument and persuasion.]

Political associations are next considered, of the good tendency of which Mr. Godwin doubts [...]

[The excerpt from IV, 3 prefers patience and argument of individuals to the zeal and passion of parties.]

Though persuaded of the inefficacy, as well as the evil consequences, of endeavouring to enforce truth by numbers, or by vote, the author is still a friend to discussion in small societies, and to the most unlimited communication and inquiry.

Of reform, his doctrine is, that it ought to be deliberate, sober, and gradual.

To tyrannicide he is a declared enemy [...]

[The excerpt from IV, 4 rejects all violence.]

The author then proceeds to the consideration of truth; and the tendency of his arguments is, that truth, wisdom, virtue, and happiness, are properly but one and the same thing. He then examines the consequences of sincerity, which prove, as he insists, that sincerity ought to be unequivocal and entire. The doctrine of necessity he next discusses and asserts. On this subject his arguments are acute, cogent, and some of them, perhaps, original: of this kind is the following passage:

[Quotes IV, 8 on virtue and necessity.]

On the mechanism of the human mind, and on the principle and tendency of virtue, he suggests many ingenious and profound ideas, but which are so connected with and dependent on each other, that we rather refer the reader to the work itself than offer him a partial and inadequate abstract on them. With these subjects, the first volume concludes.

[The review lists the subjects covered in Book V.]

After premising his intended method of inquiry, the author makes the education of a prince his first subject of discussion. Adversity he holds to be salutary, though perhaps not indispensable, to virtue; and the prosperity of effeminate superfluity he deems pernicious [...]

[Excerpts from V, 2 and 3 lament the distortions and lies inherent in the education and private life of a prince.]

In chapter iv, the author examines the assertion which has frequently been made, "that absolute monarchy or despotism is the best and most desirable of all forms of government under a good and virtuous prince." This dangerous doctrine, after allowing all that its advocates can demand, he with little difficulty refutes.

After his observations on monarchs, he inquires into the characters of courts and ministers [...]

[The excerpt from V, 5 attacks a system of administration that functions on "hollowness, duplicity, and falsehood."]

Continuing to portray the venality of courts with great energy, Mr. Godwin gives the following animated detail of absolute monarchy; particularly as it existed among the French [...]

[The excerpt from V, 5 describes a system of spies and prisons that enforces obedience through fear.]

The relative situation between subject and king is next examined, and again we find many severe animadversions on despotism, and the monarchical character [...]

[The quoted passage from V, 6 enumerates some of the fictions on which monarchic government is founded.]

After stating that monarchy generates indifference to merit and truth, false wants, pusillanimity, and a disbelief of virtue, he adds the following, pointed, and in part original, observations, on the effects of luxury and wealth [...]

[The passage from V, 6 attacks of system that rewards money and makes it a primary object of pursuit.]

Mr. Godwin next attacks the systems of hereditary and limited monarchy, and of dictator, protector, or president with regal powers. To hereditary distinctions, and their consequences, he is likewise an enemy [...]

[The review quotes three passages from V, 9 demonstrating the injustice of a class system, the absurdity of titles, and the enmity of the aristocracy to the claims of justice and reform.]

The remainder of this book is dedicated to the subject of democracy, which the author considers as the least exceptionable form of government. This part contains many opinions which, if true, are indeed highly interesting to society; at least they deserve a serious and deep investigation, since the conclusions, to which they lead, are fascinatingly attractive; and, if false, deserve to be clearly, fully, and immediately exposed. On this task, did the nature of our publication permit, we should enter with cheerful alacrity: but it is too unweildy and mighty for our narrow limits. We must, therefore, content ourselves with recommending it to others, as a subject that truly merits attention.

Monthly Review NS11 (May 1793), 187-96.

[The review continues.]

. . . . .

[The review lists the topics of the sixth book.]
Here again, as we proceed, we frequently find the author in direct opposition to many of the received opinions and common practices of mankind; and, however his readers may be led to doubt, the arguments which he adduces are frequently advanced with such appearance of cogency, that we cannot do better than bring forward such passages as our limits will admit, and earnestly recommend it, as a labour worthy of all inquiring minds, to examine the work itself; in order that they may confute these new doctrines, if in opposition to virtue and truth; or, in agreement with them, that they may farther elucidate, strengthen, and expand the writer's principles [...]

[The review devotes six pages to excerpts from Book VI and almost three pages to Book VII.]

For the satisfaction of our readers, and in order to enable them to judge, we have thus far made copious extracts from this work; which, be its principles what they may, treats on subjects the most interesting to the human race. Our limits will admit no more selections, and we must therefore satisfy ourselves with repeating the heads of the eighth book, the subject of which is *property* [...]

Desirous that the public should form their own opinions, on subjects concerning which the world is so much divided, we have generally abstained from obtruding our sentiments on this work. In fact, the singularity and novelty of many of its doctrines, beside those which our limits would permit us to cite, are so great, that, if we would deliver opinions well founded and instructive, an intensity of labour would be required which our most sanguine readers cannot reasonably expect us to bestow: - but, whether the author's opinions prove to be truths, which time and severe scrutiny shall establish, or the visions of an over-zealous mind, which strict examination shall dissipate, it is certain that his intentions are friendly to man. The tone of virtue is uniform, and predominates throughout the work; so that the reader, who may take offence at the writer's doctrines, cannot but applaud his motives. Convinced that he should rouse and offend many of the most deeply-rooted prejudices of mankind, he has rather chosen to encounter all the effects of those prejudices, than to conceal truths in which the happiness of the whole may be involved.

Had we time, we could point out some occasional errors of style; though, in general, Mr. Godwin's diction is simple, clear, and logical. There are passages, likewise, in which we discovered inconsistencies, either in the language or in the sentiments, as opposed to the opinions of the author in general: but these are so few as scarcely to require animadversion.

New Annual Register for 1793 14 (1794), 218-19.

. . . . .

[The first two-thirds of the review lists and summarizes the subjects and chapter titles of the eight books comprising *Political Justice*.]

[...] We have been the more full in our account of the subjects which are discussed in this work, as it has greatly excited the public attention, and is likely to give rise to numerous interesting disquisitions in morals, jurisprudence, and politics. The author possesses a well informed, bold, and vigorous mind, and has delivered, without concealment, the result of his reflections, after a liberal and unrestricted enquiry. Unfettered by system, and fearless of offending the prejudices of mankind, he contends for what appears to him to be truth, with an ardour, which is would be doing him injustice not to ascribe to the best and most praise-worthy motives. In discussing the numerous important subjects which he has selected, he has advanced much valuable and instructive matter, which is recommended by great ingenuity of argument, energy of diction, and perspicuity and correctness of language. We do not, however, subscribe, without exception, to Mr. Godwin's opinions. Many of them differ widely from the principles which we have imbibed, which we consider to be of importance, and which we have not been led to change by his very acute and plausible reasonings. Some of his positions and projects we consider to be fanciful and extravagant. His work, however, is highly deserving of the attention of philosophical politicians: and we conceive Mr. Godwin to be entitled to the thanks of the public, for his endeavour to illustrate the principles of morals, and the theory of government, on grounds which appear to him to be more rational and consonant with truth than the disquisitions of preceding writers, and more favourable to the permanent establishment of human happiness.

English Review 27 (February 1796), 138-43.

[The five pages of volume 27 are devoted to a summary of Books 1 and 2, substantiated with extensive quotations. No opinions are offered.

English Review 28 (Sept. 1796), 314-19.

[The review continues.]

It would be useless to give a detail of the circumstances that have so long interrupted the account begun in a former Number, of Mr. Godwin's Political Justice. Suffice it to say, that the interruption was not designed, but merely accidental. - Our readers may, perhaps, retain some impression of our analysis of this book, so far as we carried it on. Mr. Godwin avows, that he was determined to bring forth his system by the French revolution, 'by which only he was reconciled to the desirableness of a government of the simplest construction. To the same event he owes the determination of mind which gave existence to this work.' - He forms, in his imagination, a standard of excellence and virtue, and considers the relations and duties of mankind to each other in such an ideal state. But he is obliged, when he descends to the actual state of society, so mixed, imperfect, and vicious, to make a great variety of exceptions, and to enter into a kind of political casuistry, and make great and frequent use of the faculty of discretion. He finds that there are many, very many, cases or predicaments to which his laws, simple and sublime, do not descend. While he carries his head above the clouds, he is obliged to walk on the ground. He frequently stumbles into ruts and holes; but, by a dexterity of political tactics, he maintains or recovers his erect mien, and maintains his system with much address. He is a nimble walker, but he is wrongly directed. He possesses more subtlety of mind, than soundness of sense, or comprehension of views. He has lively parts, but false principles - as we shall endeavour to shew, after we have completed the analysis, which we had begun, of the work before us.

It will not appear surprising that a disciple of the French school should teach and preach liberty and equality. The liberty and equality that Mr. Godwin would establish is more unbounded, more chimerical, and more inconsistent with the existence of society, than any of all the innumerable systems of political economy and jurisprudence to which the French revolution has given birth. His system could not be realised even among savages. He would emancipate men from all real reverence and respect for established powers; although, in the present rude and imperfect state of society, it may be prudent and necessary to shew an outward obedience, contrarily to the inward dictates of our understanding. In all things we are to consider what it is that we owe to what is right and just; that is, what we owe to political society, which, 'being nothing more than an aggregation of individuals,' its claims and duties must be the aggregate of their claims and duties. He considers, in fact, all the individual members of a state as independent and sovereign princes, whose duty it is to judge concerning what is most fit and convenient for the whole society; and on all occasions to advise, reason, and expostulate, and, as much as possible, to act accordingly. The sovereign, then, or supreme power, ought to be the representative of the general understanding and will, the very genius and soul of the society. The chiefs who went to war against Troy were independent princes, though Agamemnon was king over all; and then only did the subordinate chiefs yield him obedience and respect when they thought it proper to do so. Mr. Godwin has not made this comparison: but the case we have stated comes the nearest of any thing we know, in real history, to the ideal government of our author. Achilles withdrew his men, and reviled Agamemnon to his face, because he was a powerful chief, and could do it with safety. Others, of inferior note, might not, and did not. Since it is, according to our author, the duty of everyone to worship and obey the king of his own creation; that is, the system of laws and conduct that he may think best for the whole community. If such a subject as Achilles should be ordered to do one thing by the existing government, and another by the *genius* or *representative* of the public judgment and will, i.e. his own individual judgment and will (for it is the private judgment of individuals that must determine what the public must and would recommend if duly exercised and fairly represented): - in such a case, such a powerful subject ought, undoubtedly, according to our author, to disobey the real, and pay homage to the ideal and internal government of his own creation. To mark out the cases and circumstances when disobedience and resistance are just, practicable, and prudent, and when not, is impossible, on principles so abstracted as those assumed by this writer. He is, therefore, frequently aground and non-plushed [sic], though he is never at a loss for a distinction. He is not, indeed, silenced, but he ought to be silenced. In many, nay most cases, the proselytes to this system, and the whole nation, if proselyted [sic], must, according to a common proverb, *be looking one way and drawing another*; reverencing their *metaphysical*, and yielding a reluctant obedience to their *living* king. The apostle Paul exhorts the Romans 'to be subject to the higher powers, not only for wrath, but also for conscience sake:' certes, the political system under review is in quite a different spirit.

We have judged it proper to exhibit this general outline of Mr. Godwin's system, that the reader, bearing in his mind the chief points and general result of his philosophy, may not be bewildered and lost while he endeavours to follow him through all the traverses, windings, and subterraneous passages, by which he attempts to lead mankind to a state of the highest possible felicity and perfection. - We shall now follow Mr. Godwin somewhat closer at the heels, and, as is fit and just, make him speak for himself.

. . . . .

[The review summarizes Book 3 for 2½ pages using extensive quotation.]

In opposition to those who maintain, that one form of government may be best for one people, and a different form for another, Mr. Godwin contends, that there is one *best form* of government for all; and this he endeavours to prove from the unity of truth, and the nature of man. Since government, even it its best state, is an evil, the object to be principally aimed at, is, that we should have as little of it as the general peace of human society will permit. Less and less restraint or constraint will be necessary, in proportion as mankind advance in the improvement of the mind; the grand instrument in the promotion of which, is, the publication of truth. Political renovation may strictly be considered as one of the stages in intellectual improvement. Literature and disquisition cannot, *of themselves*, be rendered sufficiently general. Those abstract and bold speculations, in which the value of literature principally consists, must necessarily continue the portion of the favoured few. As soon as any important truth has become established to a sufficient extent in the minds of the enterprising and the wise, it may, tranquilly and with ease, be rendered a part of the general system.

Thus our author's system is shortly this, there is no authority but reason; and no legislators but philosophers and propagators of truth; that is, writers of pamphlets and books. But, as he admits that the great mass of the people must necessarily be directed by the *wise few*, a question arises, How are the people, amidst such an inundation of political writers, to distinguish who are the *wise*, and who the foolish? The only standard by which they could judge would be, the size of their volumes (in which case our author would have a good chance of being chosen a representative); and, to say truth, this would be just as good a criterion for judging of men, as the long-winded speeches in parliament.

English Review 28 (October 1796), 437-43.

[The review concludes.]

Having in the last, and in another number of our Review, stated the principles on which Mr. Godwin builds his system, and having also briefly recapitulated the spirit of that system, we will readily be excused by our readers if we decline the talk of following our author, in his details on the subjects of political institution, and the different subjects of government. The grand point at which he aims, as the practical inference to be drawn from the whole of his reasonings, is, the EQUALISATION of PROPERTY; which reform, however, he readily admits, is not to be effected until men shall have made much greater progress in intelligence; although he thinks, that the earlier and the more we indulge presages of such improvement, the better. By cutting off luxury and industry, he would cut off many artificial wants, and many crimes, and elevate human nature to the dignity of Diogenes, who, retrenching his enjoyments with his wants, gloried in his independence. He is a kind of little Lycurgus: but he has the prudence not to prescribe iron money and soup meagre to his countrymen, until they shall, by progress in philosophy, be weaned from their taste for turtle soup, and all the luxuries that can be commanded by gold. In return for the excision of many gratifications, he would free society from many restraints, particularly that of marriage. As to the education of youth, this would be left to the operation of government, or a general arrangements of political and moral causes, and indeed of accidental circumstances.

. . . . .

[The review quotes from Book 8 on individualism and social duty.]

Mr. Godwin possesses great vigour, independence, and originality of mind. Had his learning, and acquaintance with civil and political history, been greater, and his temper less sanguineous and ardent, he would not have dreamt that it could ever be possible for mankind, constituted as they are by nature, ever to arrive at such a state as he holds up to their view, and as the end of their noblest ambition. Nor is the condition he holds up to our contemplation, in every respect, to be desired, were it possible to reduce it to practice. After all that he has urged in defence of his system, it would harden the heart, it would cut off the most endearing charities of life, it would weaken the social band, and exhibit the whole of mankind as a kind of philosophical savages: even men and women, resting, as he says, *on their own centre*, sending one another *to Coventry*. His system is so far removed from all appearance of either profit or practicability, that there are a thousand objections to its utility, as well as to the possibility of realising it. These he had acuteness enough to foresee, and address enough to combat with much plausibility. But still, so arduous is his task that he resembles an ambitious mole, labouring to overturn a mountain, and, after all his labyrinthical labours, only throwing up a heap of mud.

Mr. Godwin hopes that men may one day be governed by the purity of their own minds, and the moderation of their own desires, without all external coercion [...]

[The review quotes at length dissenting opinions from Hindu law and Paul's Epistle to the Romans.]

[...] Mr. Godwin and his disciples, if he has any, which he not unlikely may have among malcontents and malefactors, must be in a similar situation and disposition to those political powers, who, humbled by the events of war, are fain to make peace, but who, retaining a grudge against the victorious party, are ready to recommence hostilities on the first favourable opportunity.

The conjuncture that led Mr. Dogwin [sic] to publish the volumes under review, was, the French revolution; that is, as appears from dates, the commencement of the French revolution; an era that seemed auspicious to the interests of mankind, also to Dr. Price, who seemed actually to think that the *millennium* had commenced. But Satan, far from being in chains, seems to be more rampant than ever. When our author reflects on what has passed in France, sanguine as he is in his hopes, and bold in his reforms, he will acknowledge the extreme uncertainty and danger of political innovation. He supposes the science of government to be as capable of improvement and demonstration, as mathematics. This is a fatal error, common to our author, and many other orators as well as writers. There are different kinds of truth; metaphysical, moral, and political: and also different kinds of GOOD; physical, moral, and political. Political good is that which is good to tribes, and nations of men, in certain determinate circumstances and situations. Were men set down upon the world, without appetites, passions, habits, and manners, then might the political projector move them about, and place them in any new situation, with as little ceremony as the men of a chess-board. But, rivetted and intertwined as the nature and happiness of men are with a thousand circumstances, physical and moral, these are to be consulted in every political movement; and, consequently, political reformations, of any great extent, must be the work of much time. Our reformers, for the most part, follow analogies taken from some system of inanimated matter; and seem to conceive, that they should set to work in the same manner with house-builders, smiths, potters, staymakers, taylors, and so on. But there is a closer analogy, which they would do well to keep in their eye; an analogy between societies or governments, and plants and animals; which require particular soils, food, and culture. No man, in his senses, thinks of making a seed or a plant - he digs around it, he waters it, but never thinks of creating such another, on an improved plan, by any mechanical or chemical process of his own.

But there is much in the power of government

'What cannot active government perform?
New-moulding man.' - THOMSON'S SEASONS.

In the first place, as already observed, Mr. Godwin's plan does not appear to be a desirable one, even if it could be realised by any powers of legislation. But to effect such an order of human affairs as is held up by Godwin, exceeds the powers of legislation; since nothing so completely repugnant to nature, as his system is, in many parts, can be established, or, if established, could possibly be lasting.

What our author asserts concerning the omnipotence of government, is not altogether consistent with his observations, in different parts of his work, that the moral qualities of men depend on the impressions that happen to have been made on their minds. There are sensible impressions and perceptions, and there are moral impressions and perceptions. For the strength and importance of the former (not certainly within the province of government) we refer our author to one of his three masters, Helvetius. The moral impressions that may be made on men are, in great measure, under the power of government; but still, in spite of laws and education, the moral characters of men will be diversified by contingent circumstances, not to be commanded or controlled, in every instance, by any government; while enough of nature will always remain to expose the impracticability as well as the inexpediency of the chimeras of our little Lycurgus. - The empire of sensation and perception is somewhat stronger, and that of opinion and reflection somewhat less, than Mr. Godwin seems to imagine. The fortitude of SCÆVOLA, and of the Indians under torment, prove, indeed, the incredible power of the mind, firmly collected within itself, for a time, over even sensation. But it is downright insanity to suppose, with Mr. Godwin, that any effort of the mind can triumph not only over disease, but over death itself. Nor is there much more sense in the supposition, that any measures of government, or exertions of philosophy, could long maintain, we do not say dominion, but even a struggle, with some of the strongest propensities of human nature; with which Mr. Godwin is very imperfectly acquainted. - The wise economy of nature has strengthened every emotion, passion, and principle of action, necessary to the being, and the well-being, of both the individual and the community, by the *impetus* and warmth of sensation. General ideas or abstractions are too cold and inefficient for those grand purposes. It is the recollection, or, according to the brief lexicon of a gentleman of distinguished genius and knowledge as well as virtue, it is the *resensation* of the most ardent and generous passion in nature, that is at the bottom of the tenderness of parents to the pledges of their mutual love. It is the experience of kindness and fostering care that so warmly attaches the infant and child to its mother and nurse, inviting and rewarding numberless good offices by the most unbounded confidence, and cordial return of love for love. A period arrives when attachment and love, for the same gracious end, are drawn to new objects. Yet even in the midst of courtship, the tender parent is remembered with reverence and grateful affection. The fruits of matrimony, by new feelings, powerfully recall, how much we owe to our own parents. And, O wise and divine beneficence! the love of grandfathers and grandmothers passes on, undiminished, to their grandchildren: and thus the mutual affection of parents to children is reunited and strengthened by common love and concern for the same kindred objects! In like manner, by a thousand recollections or associations or tender and pleasing ideas, we are attached to the companions of our early years, to our native home, fields, and neighbouring villages. And this is the germ if patriotism - according to universal consent from Cicero, who considers one's country as dear on account of such endearments, to Mr. Burke, who traces patriotism to the little plat and neighbourhood, or circle, by which our affections are exercised. Agreeably to this doctrine of love and attachment being connected with sensation, is the following position, involved in the form of a question, by the apostle John: 'He that loveth not his brother whom he hath seen, how can he love God whom he hath not seen?' I John iv. 20. Not so Mr. Godwin! All this order he would reverse, and arrange all ideas of attachment and duty around the centre of a most complicated chaos of crude and cold abstractions! We could point out many other extravagances and ravings in Godwin's Political Justice; but we have insisted too much on so wild and wrong-headed a system. We shall only say, that he resembles a mountebank teaching the boys whom he destines for his assistants, to walk on their hands and heads.

But he is not only wrong-headed (though he really possesses great subtlety of genius, as well as vigour or fancy); we are afraid he is a wicked body; for he speaks against that most merciful institution, the sabbath; and cavils against the divine precept of our Saviour, 'Whatsoever you would that men should do unto you, do ye even the same unto them; for this is the law and the prophets.' This Mr. Godwin considers as vague and *indefinite*. It is in its being indefinite that its great excellence consists. Truly, no one can hesitate long to choose between the morality of *William Godwin* and that of JESUS CHRIST!!

William Godwin, *The Enquirer* (1797)

Analytical Review 25 (1797), 395-404.

The most rare, and, under the direction of reason, the most excellent quality in a writer, is originality. Many people can make books from materials already furnished; but there are few who possess the power of creating the matter for a book, from the unassisted efforts of their own genius. In works of fancy, new production appears with the greatest brilliancy, and most irresistibly captivates applause: in philosophy, however, it is most important, because most likely to be useful.

Mr. Godwin has, unquestionably, the merit of being an original thinker. Perhaps few authors have produced so large a work as his 'Political Justice,' with fewer supplies from foreign sources. Whatever different readers may be disposed to think of the solidity of some of his speculations, it will, we believe, be generally allowed, that he has formed a habit of close and deep reflection; and that he is capable of exhibiting to the world, in a masterly way, a connected chain of thoughts. This plan was pursued with great success in his former work; in which a few simple principles are developed, applied to a number of points, and followed into a variety of inferences, in a manner which entitles the treatise to the name of a system.

In the present publication Mr. G. pursues a different method. The less ostentatious, but safer mode of investigating truth, by a continual appeal to experiment and actual observation, is adopted in these essays: which, though not altogether independent of each other, are not digested in a systematic form. Their relation does not so much arise from arrangement, as from the leading principles, and general views, to which they all, more or less, refer, and of which the author seldom loses sight. If the appeal here made to experience have rendered this performance less eccentric than the former, it will be found to contain much new, as well as useful matter, expressed with the author's accustomed correctness and energy.

The work is divided into two parts. The first part, though not a regular treatise on education, chiefly adverts to that most interesting subject; and offers to the reader's consideration some singularities perhaps - but many things, which may well deserve the attention of parents and preceptors.

. . . . .

[The review excerpts and summarizes, for nine pages, each essay in the first volume.]

We must defer our account of the second part of this instructive and valuable work to a subsequent article; and shall, for the present, only add, that though in a few particulars Mr. G.'s ideas on education may be liable to objection, they will in general be found just, solid and useful; the result of accurate observation, and deep reflection; and calculated to improve the important art.

Analytical Review 27 (1798), 481-490.

Scarcely any thing impresses us more favorably concerning a man, than his unsolicited acknowledgement of error, either in practice or speculation: a general and vague declaration, indeed, of openness to conviction, and so on, is the most common and unmeaning thing imaginable; obstinacy itself is ashamed to *appear* obstinate; but an avowal of explicit error is somewhat rare, and is the undeceiving index of an ingenuous mind. In the second edition of Mr. G.'s 'Political Justice' were omitted or modified several of the extravagances which appeared in the first, and the preface to the present performance affords additional and abundant evidence, that the author is not to be accused of an unreasonable tenacity in his opinions; several of them, indeed, are of so eccentric a nature, that such tenacity would argue a very uncommon share of self-conceit, and of disrespect to the opinion of many a sagacious and unprejudiced observer.

The first part of the Enquirer relates chiefly to the subject of education; the latter, which comes under our present consideration, though somewhat more miscellaneous, treats (with the exception of the twelfth essay, on English style) of questions connected with political economy and morals.

'Riches' and their correlative 'poverty,' form the subject of the first essay. It is contended, in contradiction to the decision 'of what may be styled an intemperate spirit of philosophy,' that poverty is an enormous evil. We feel no inclination to dispute the proposition: but how is this 'enormous evil' to be remedied? We have no instance upon record of an equality in point of property, which equality, by the by, would be tantamount to its annihilation, so far as domestic commerce was concerned, among the members of any civilized society; and every refinement of society, according to the common acceptation of the term, has a direct tendency to increase the inequality between the loftiest and the lowest members; rather, we are disposed to believe, by exalting the former than depressing the latter, for no set of people can possibly be *more* ignorant and brutal, than the boors of a half-civilized country. From the connection, therefore, between civil society and the division of its members into rich and poor, lazy and laborious, having hitherto remained from the remotest ages undissolved, we may almost regard this connection, however to be lamented, as indissoluble, and perhaps necessary to its existence. The alternative is obvious.

Essay the second. 'Of avarice and profusion.' If the preface of Mr. G. had not prepared us for some dissonance among his positions, we should have been surprised at the inconsistency of two neighbour assertions; one, in support of the opinion that poverty is an enormous evil, states the mistake of those persons, 'who affirm, that the wants which are of the first necessity are inconsiderable, and are easily supplied.' 'No,' says Mr. G.; 'that is not inconsiderable, which cannot be purchased but by the sacrifice of the best part of my time, and the first fruit of my labours;' (p. 166) and the other, to facilitate the reception of a favourite measure, namely, the equal division of labour, directly contradicts it: 'the commodities that substantially contribute to the subsistence of the human species, form a very short catalogue; they demand from us but a slender portion of industry' (p. 174). We suspect, moreover, that our author is somewhat incorrect in other parts of his reasoning on avarice and profusion; we fully acquit Mr. G. of the slightest intention to delude, but the inaccuracies of so fascinating a writer should not be concealed. In trying the question, which character deserves the preference, the man of avaricious habits, or he who spends his income with spirit and liberality, Mr. G. decides in favour of the former. 'Every man,' says he, 'who invents a new luxury, *adds* so much to the quantity of labour entailed on the lower orders of society;' on this principle, it is contended, that, if a rich man employ the poor in breaking up land, and cultivating its useful productions, he may be their benefactor;

yet, 'if he employ them in erecting palaces, in sinking canals, in laying out his parks, and modelling his pleasure-grounds, he will be found, when rightly considered, their enemy.' (p. 178). The invention of a new luxury is not to be regarded as an *addition* to the quantity of labour, but rather as the exchange of one species of labour for another; or is it true, 'that the poor are paid no more now for the work of ten hours, than before for the work of eight.' Mr. G. would find it difficult to prove, that the hours of diurnal labour among the artizans and peasants of this kingdom, have at all increased within the last hundred years, and a very little knowledge of the subsisting relation between the labourer and his master, would have informed him, that wages are *generally* proportionate to the quantity of work done. Mr. G. has overlooked a circumstance in his estimate of the avaricious and profuse character, which, even on his own principles, should detract from the superior utility which he ascribes so decidedly to the former; this circumstance is, that it is the nature of avarice to generate profusion; the massy coffers of the miser descend to his heir, and the *salutary* penuriousness of the father, is counterbalanced by the riot, the debauchery, and extravagance of the son.

The third essay treats 'on beggars.' Here we find much to admire; Mr. Godwin's observations on the duty of relieving beggars evidently flow from a feeling and compassionate heart.

The fourth and fifth essays, the former on 'servants,' and the latter 'on trades and professions,' though certainly not destitute of some just reflections, are in our estimation extremely exceptionable. It is impossible, surely, to read the following passages, without disgust at the wanton and extravagant misrepresentation of the general state of servants, and their relative situation with their respective masters.

. . . . .

[Quotes for a page Godwin's opinion that the contrasting living conditions of masters and servants creates envy and discontent in servants.]

If features be an index of the mind, we are authorized to contend, in opposition to this piteous tale, that a more comfortable class of people does not exist among us than domestic servants: their countenance is suffused with a serenity and cheerfulness, to which the master of them is frequently a stranger; so far as our observation has extended, their food is usually plentiful, their clothing good, and their labour light. On the score of intellectual acquirement, they rise but little, indeed, above the labourers of the day; but their leisure for improvement is past comparison greater [...] [For $1^1/_2$ pages, summarizes and excerpts the essay "Of Trades and Professions."]

. . . . .

On the subject of 'self-denial,' (essay six) we find a great deal of sound, good sense: how far the pleasures of sense are to be cultivated, and wherein the gratification of them becomes inconsistent with intellectual enjoyments, or endangers the relish for them, are clearly pointed out, and elegantly illustrated. The compatibility of sensible and intellectual pleasures is argued from the dependance of the latter upon the existence of the former; from our animal sensations is derived a large portion of the materials of our knowledge.

. . . . .

[Quotes the opinion that a healthy body nourishes a healthy mind.]

In this essay Mr. G.'s scepticism is evinced, not to say his disbelief of a future state, (see page 243): we pass it over - not with the sneer of anger or contempt; far from it; belief is not a matter of choice: it is in no man's power, by the utmost exercise of his volition, to make any proposition appear more or less probable to him, than if his mind is sanctioned by its evidence: as well may he by volition determine, that the colour of blue shall appear green to his eyes. We pass it over in silence and in sorrow.

. . . . .

[For 1½ pages, summarizes and excerpts the essays on personal reputation and on posthumous fame]

There are few essays wherein we find more to admire than that which treats 'of difference in opinion,' (Essay IX); it abounds in sagacious and salutary reflection, and breathes the purest spirit of liberality: 'one of the best practical rules of morality, that ever was delivered,' says our author, 'is that of putting ourselves in the place of another, before we act or decide any thing respecting him.' This admirable essay must have been written subsequently to that on trades and professions; the latter could never have been penned by the hand which had written the former.

. . . . .

[Quotes two paragraphs of the discussion of partisanship.]

It is necessary to remark, that *one page* of this essay is devoted to an attack on that maxim of christianity, which says, 'he that believeth shall be saved; he that believeth not shall be damned.' (Mark, chapter xvi, verse 16.)

Scarcely any thing is of more difficult definition than 'true politeness,' the subject of the tenth essay: it is very properly denominated by our author, 'one of the lesser moralities': actions in which a man may consult the transitory feelings of his neighbour, and to which he can seldom be prompted by a lofty spirit of ambition; "actions which the heart can record, but which the tongue is rarely comptetent to relate." Under the greater moralities, are ranged those actions of a man's life, adapted to purposes of beneficence, which are fraught with energy, and cannot be practised but in an exalted temper of mind. The following observations are not to be overlooked [...]

. . . . .

[Quotes three paragraphs on the importance of small politenesses in daily living.]

It is unnecessary to mention, that the politeness, which stands thus high in Mr. Godwin's estimation, is very different from that mockery of fine feeling, that hollow, insidious, and unmeaning courtesy, which is practised in some fashionable circles, with so much assiduity and success: far from it, 'without habits of entire unqualified sincerity, the human character can never be raised to its true eminence. It gives what nothing else can so effectually give, an assured, unembarrassed, and ingenuous manner. Is it the true progenitor of contentment, and of the complacency with which a virtuous man should be able to advert to his modes of proceeding. Insincerity corrupts and empoisons the soul of the actor, and is of pernicious example to every spectator.' It will naturally be asked, "does Mr. Godwin's politeness prompt him to tell every man abruptly to his face the precise impression, unfavourable, perhaps disgusting, which he feels concerning him?" by no means, 'when I refuse to vent the feeling of bodily anguish in piercing cries, as the first impulse would prompt me to do, I am not therefore a hypocrite. In the same manner, if I refuse to treat any person with pointed contempt for every petty dislike, and prefer the keeping my mind always free for the reception of new and opposite evidence; this is no breach of sincerity.' Though it is inconsistent with our limits to state the precise mode, in which Mr. G. has made the strictest sincerity accord with the most perfect politeness, such is in fact the case; and we do not recollect to have seen this difficult subject any where treated in so unexceptionable and masterly a manner, as in the essay before us.

. . . . .

[The review then summarizes and quotes, for two pages, the last two essays of *The Enquirer*.]

We rise from the perusal of Mr. Godwin's Enquirer, impressed with a sense of the bold and manly independence of his opinions: to several of them we cannot, indeed, assent; but to all of them we would pay that attention, which they are authorized to claim from the firmness and ability with which they are supported.

Critical Review S2, 20 (May 1797), 58-64.

It is somewhat out of order, we believe, in the critical senate, to refer to the former productions of an author, in examining his present claims to merit: - indeed, it is unquestionably the fairest mode of proceeding, to let every literary production stand upon its own basis, and to decide upon its character only from its contents. As a former production of Mr. Godwin, however, from the singular tenor of its doctrines, and the eccentric character of some of the sentiments, necessarily extorted some strictures from us in a former review, it is necessary to state that the present collection of essays are materially different from his Political Justice. The boldness and even the degree of dogmatism with which some of his schemes of innovation were advanced, are in this publication very properly avoided; and the subjects are of a more familiar nature, and many of them are better adapted to practice and utility.

Our review of Mr. Godwin's Political Justice sufficiently evinced that we were not actuated (as we can truly aver we never are) by any principle of personal hostility. On many topics we differed widely from our author; we expressed our dissent in plain but unprejudiced terms; while, on the contrary, we evinced that truth is acceptable to us from whatever quarter it comes; and though we may lament that it sometimes appears mingled with a considerable alloy of error, yet we are ever happy to draw the line of discrimination, and to avoid the uncandid practice of condemning in the mass, because we cannot uniformly approve.

Some of Mr. Godwin's opinions we considered then as the exuberances and eccentricities of an ingenious mind; such as candid disquisition would refute, and such as his own riper judgment would correct. Some of his former notions he seems already to have discarded: and in the publication before us, he in general appears rather in the character of a sceptic than of a dogmatist. Like his former production, the present is of a mixed character; there is in it much ingenuity, and some excellent remarks: there are also some passages and opinions which we cannot approve.

. . . . .

[The review lists the titles of the chapters of Part I dealing with education.]

In the third essay Mr. Godwin observes, in treating of genius, 'that some differences (in point of talent) are born with children, cannot be denied;' and indeed much of his reasoning in the subsequent essays is built upon the fact, that there is such a thing as natural genius, in opposition to the absurd fancy of Helvetius, that the talents of all men are naturally on an equality. In the sixteenth essay in particular, which treats on 'the early Indications of Character,' this topic is enlarged on with much ingenuity.

The author, however, though he admits a difference in point of natural talent, yet with much truth attributes a considerable effect to education in forming the character.- 'That man brings a certain character with him (says he) into the world, is a point that must readily be conceded. The mistake is, that he brings an immutable character.' Natural genius, he observes, may be greatly quickened by cultivation, and it may also be blunted by neglect. 'The children of peasants have often a quickness of observation, an ingenuousness of character, and a delicacy of taste, at the age of seven years, the very traces of which are obliterated at fourteen.'

Mr. Godwin, in the fourth essay, very properly blames the temerity and conceit of modern philosophers -

'There is' (says he) 'an insanity among philosophers, that has brought philosophy itself into discredit. There is nothing in which this insanity more evidently displays itself, than in the rage of accounting for every thing.'

. . . . .

'But there is a regularity and system in the speculations of philosophers, exceeding any that is to be found in the operations of nature. We are too confident in our own skill, and imagine our science to be greater than it is.'

To this kind of 'insanity' may be justly attributed the atheism and infidelity so prevalent in this superficial age. Because revelation has not explained every thing to these soi-disant philosophers, they hastily conclude that it explains nothing; and, because they would willingly appear to their gaping admirers to know every thing, and yet cannot comprehend the nature of God, they as impudently as absurdly deny his existence. It was the advice of honest Bentley to a writer of this description – 'Since by a little learning, and a huge conceit of himself, he hath lost his religion, let him try to find it again by harder study with a humbler mind.' (Bentley Phileuth. Lips.) We were pleased to find Mr. Godwin unite in reproving this dangerous quality.

Our author condemns, with some reason, the austere and slavish mode of inculcating knowledge by the severity of punishment; yet we have great doubts whether children can possibly be induced to apply without some degree of coercion, particularly if classical learning is to be acquired, which, according to his own principles (see essay vi.), is a necessary branch of liberal education.

On the vicious and destructive practice of accustoming children from their earlier years to a series of falsehood and deception, our author's sentiments are pointed and good -

'The practice of deception is one of those vices of education that are most early introduced into the treatment of youth.

'If the nurse find a difficulty in persuading the child to go to sleep, she will pretend to go to sleep along with it. If the parent wish his youngest son to go to bed before his brothers, he will order the elder ones upstairs, with a permission to return as soon as they can do it unobserved. If the mother is going out for a walk or a visit, she will order the child upon some pretended occasion to a distant part of the house, till she has made her escape.

'It is a deception too gross to be insisted on, to threaten children with pretended punishments, that you will cut off their ears; that you will put them into the well; that you will give them to the old man; that there is somebody coming down the chimney to take them away.' P. 102.

The paragraph which succeeds, contains a piece of criticism very unworthy of the taste which Mr. Godwin has evinced on other occasions. The passage in the book of Proverbs – 'The eye that mocketh at his father, and despiseth to obey his mother, the ravens of the valley shall pick it out, and the young eagles shall eat it,' was never certainly meant to be held out in a literal sense as a bug-bear to children, but is a most beautiful poetical expression, denoting the calamities that generally attend wicked and undutiful children. In Shakespeare this passage would have been admired.

The system of Rousseau is justly condemned by our author as a system of deception-

. . . . .

[Quotes Essays 12 and 14 condemning Rousseau's as "a system of incessant hypocrisy and lying."]

There is much ingenuity in the following observations on the mistakes which are often fallen into, concerning the moral tendency of particular books

. . . . .

[Quotes from Essay 15 that the tendency of a book may contradict its explicit moral.]

We do not, however, agree in opinion with our author respecting that system of indiscriminate reading, in which he seems to think young persons may be indulged.

. . . . .

[The review lists the titles of essays in Part 2 and quotes from the essay "Of Avarice and Profusion" the anti-Mandevillian argument that demands for new luxuries are additional burdens on the labour of the poor and seldom benefit them.]

The essay 'on Servants' contains some good cautions to the rich, against encouraging the increase of a race of beings who in too many instances are in the condition, and retain too many of the ill qualities, of slaves. Of the succeeding essay, we cannot speak in so favourable terms. It is full of liberal insinuations, and contains some direct aspersions. It is a foul calumny to characterize every tradesman, as a 'cold-hearted liar,' as one 'whose whole mind is buried in the sordid care of adding another guinea to his income,' as 'a supple, fawning, cringing creature,' who is 'so much in the habit of exhibiting a bended body, that he scarcely knows how to stand upright.' We have lived among tradesmen; and, as we can only judge from what we know, we aver that the great majority of those whom we have known, were at least as abhorrent of falsehood as Mr. Godwin, and that a more honourable and independent race of men does not exist than the traders of Great Britain. Whether they are of that sordid character or not, which Mr. Godwin would insinuate, let their liberality and generosity in the support of every charitable institution determine, upon the only solid basis of argument, - fact, and experience. In speaking of the physician, Mr. Godwin observes, that 'pain, sickness, and anguish, are his harvest. He rejoices that they have fallen upon any of his acquaintance' - ergo, there ought to be no person whose province and study should be to relieve pain, sickness, and anguish; but there is no man who is acquainted with the liberal spirit of that truly respectable and scientific body of men, the medical profession, who will not, from his own knowledge, repel with indignation the base aspersion contained in the last sentence of the quotation. Against the lawyers, the old objection, so ably refuted by Dr. Johnson, is revived, that they must do the best for their client, whether his case be good or bad; and that they are men 'who have nothing to do with general and impartial reason.' With equal force of argument, our author divides the divines into two classes, viz. a set of cunning impostors, who only 'play a solemn farce of hypocrisy;' or a stupid and illiterate race, on whom 'not a doubt ever ventures to obtrude itself.'

There is a similar spirit of illiberality evinced in the ninth essay: and Mr. Godwin's own example might be quoted to prove that a man may be 'a bigot,' and an intolerant bigot, without being a Christian; indeed the greatest and the blindest bigots we have the misfortune to know, are among unbelievers. Mr. Godwin will do well, if his book should reach a second edition, to expunge from it the trite and pointless sarcasms against religion, with which he has injudiciously interlarded it: they create disgust, without producing conviction. - If he wishes to attack religion, let him write a work purposely on the subject. - He will then either convince or be refuted; he will either have answerers or disciples; in the present case his fanaticism (for fanaticism it certainly is) will only serve to discourage serious persons from a perusal of his publication; and what is really worthy of attention in it, will be disregarded, from a suspicion that the whole is meant as a vehicle for the abuse of what the majority of this nation consider, and we trust ever will consider, as their ultimate and best consolation.

The best essay in the volume is unquestionably the twelfth and last, 'Of English Style.' Indeed we have always been of opinion, that Mr. Godwin's forte is polite literature. - His reading in the departments of politics and theology is not sufficiently extensive to qualify him for assuming the professor's chair on either of those sciences; but he is a man of taste and genius, whose studies have evidently been chiefly directed to the modern languages and modern publications, and to those in particular which are termed works of imagination. As a novelist, as a critic in the belles letters, probably as a dramatic writer, Mr. Godwin will excel; and if he regards his own reputation, and rightly estimates his own talents, he will quit the barren track of polemics, and cultivate an imagination which is certainly capable of great and vigorous exertions, and of producing works of taste and fancy that may amuse and delight not only his contemporaries but posterity.

The Monthly Magazine 4 (August 1797), 119.

The improvement of morals, in many important branches, is the principal object of one of the most interesting publications of the period before us, Mr. Godwin's "Enquirer; Reflections on Education, Manners, and Literature." Mr. G. wishes to make all men, children of reason. The corrections and improvements which he proposes in education, all tend to exercise the intellect, and form a habit of thinking: the reformations which he would produce in manners, are adapted to emancipate men from the dominion of passion, fancy, and fashion, and make them rational beings. The work would, probably, have produced more effect, had the author indulged himself less in excentricity [sic]. Mr. G. as a philosopher is capable of reasoning logically; and he should never, from the vanity of being admired as a fine writer, condescend to become a declaimer. The critical part of the work discovers a correct taste. No excentricity will be charged upon another moralist, Mr. Gisborne, who has written a very useful "Enquiry into the Duties of the Female Sex," in which, in strict, and, perhaps, somewhat too rigorous, adherence to established principles and rules, the author gives the female world a great abundance of wholesome counsel, expressed in correct and elegant language. We must not overlook the moral [...] instruction provided for the poor in [...] "The Cheap Repository."

Monthly Review S2 XXIII (July 1797), 291-302.

. . . . .

[Opens with general remarks on philosophy.]

In the class of benevolent philosophers and enlightened reformers we are willing to rank Mr. Godwin, and we readily give him credit for good intentions, as well as for great talents. We have no doubt that the public has been instructed as well as entertained by his writings; and we are not without hope that they may contribute essentially to the correction and improvement of established systems. In proportion, however, to the height of our opinion of this writer's qualifications for being a public instructor and monitor, must be our solicitude to examine every innovation which he proposes; and to appreciate, as accurately as we are able, the value of his leading suggestions.

The present Essays, we are told in the preface, are principally the result of conversations, some of which passed many years ago: but they have nothing colloquial in their structure. They exhibit the writer's specimens rather with the confidence of a dogmatist, than with the modesty of an *Enquirer*: our principal concern, however, is with the opinions themselves; which are properly classed in the title under the heads of Education, Manners, and Literature.

In the observations on Education which Mr. G. has here offered, we find much to approve, some things to admire, and a few subjects of animadversion. We shall attempt to throw our account of the essays into an arrangement somewhat more regular than that of the author.

Concerning the *subject* of Education, the human mind, two papers are employed in an ingenious discussion of the question whether genius be natural or acquired. Genius was, many years ago, judiciously and elaborately analyzed by Dr. Gerard. The subject is here treated in a more desultory way, but with more vivacity; and it is, we think, fairly established that, though divers causes may produce constitutional varieties, favourable or unfavourable to mental exertions, genius is to be considered as chiefly generated by circumstances which happen in the course of infancy and childhood. It is reasonably admitted that every man brings a certain character, or, more properly, a tendency towards a certain character, into the world with him: but it is denied that he brings an immutable character. Yet there are extraordinary cases of apparent genius, for which is would be difficult to account on any mechanical or chemical principles, or even on the theory of the association of ideas. By what generative process did one human being become the admirable Chrichton, another the musical Crotch, and a third the idiot-arithmetician Jedediah Buxton? - The progress of talent is beautifully described in the following passage:

. . . . .

[Quotes the last paragraph of the essay "Of the Sources of Genius."]

We entirely agree with Mr. G. in his opinion concerning the values and utility of talents: a greater vulgar error does not exist, than a notion that a lad may have too much genius: for what is genius, but an enlarged capacity of action, enjoyment, and usefulness?

On the *End* of education, - the subject of the first Essay, - we differ in opinion essentially from the Enquirer. To awaken the mind, to excite the faculties, to exercise them in various directions, we acknowledge to be one object in education: but we cannot admit that it is either the sole or the principal object. A better answer cannot, we think, be given to the question, *what should a boy be taught*, than that which is said to have been given by Aristippus; *What he will want when he becomes a man.* We cannot, therefore, agree with Mr. G. in the remark that 'he who should affirm, that the true object of juvenile education was to teach no one thing in particular, but to provide against the age of five-and-twenty a mind well regulated, active, and prepared to learn, would certainly not obtrude on us the absurdest of paradoxes.'

With respect to *modes* of education, our Enquirer makes some just observations on the comparative advantages of public and private instruction. There can be little doubt that the society of a school is of great use in awakening the faculties, in producing a vigorous and active mind, and in preparing the young citizen for the world, by enuring him to preparatory scenes, similar to those which lie before him in life: - but some material objections lie against our great schools, which Mr. G. has not encountered. The course of instruction, though excellently adapted to form great scholars, is little suited to the present state of knowledge and of society, and has little relation to the future duties, occupations, or even amusements, of the man: the mode of correction is brutal and savage, a disgrace to civilized life; and the state of manners is so depraved and licentious, that these seminaries may, with too much truth be regarded as initiatory schools of vice. Our philosopher, however, has new projects with respect to the mode of communicating knowledge, which, if adapted, would supersede the public schools, and model anew the private academics. According to these, the customary order of things is to be inverted, the pupil is to lead, and the master to follow: young people are to enjoy perfect liberty, and to be led to knowledge, not by authority, but by inclination: the preceptor's business is only to present motives to inquiry, to furnish necessary helps, to give information, and to solve difficulties; the scholar is to be stimulated by a sense of the value of knowledge, and, in short, is to study for himself. This plan may seem promising, but is, we fear, impracticable. It might save the master the trouble of teaching, but would, perhaps, also deprive the scholar of the benefit of learning: for how shall the various branches of learning be made so interesting, as to furnish a motive superior to the strong love of amusement and exercise implanted in every young mind? In classical learning, for example, to which so much importance is justly given in these essays, by what means shall young minds be so deeply impressed with its value, as to encounter voluntarily all the drudgery of the rudiments of language for several years, in the period in which so many other things have more powerful attractions than books? We admit the utility of the study of classics, on the various grounds here stated: but we are of opinion that leisure and inclination would very seldom be found together sufficiently for this purpose, without some degree of compulsion.

On that useful *auxiliary* of education, an Early Taste for Reading, Mr. G. writes eloquently; and he suggests many good hints concerning the method by which the tutor, or parent, should guide the miscellaneous reading of his scholar. We must, however, object *in toto* to the latitude which he gives to children in the choice of books, without allowing parents at all to interpose their authority. Books are, in effect, companions; and parents might almost as safely trust their children to gather up any straggler whom they may find in the streets for an associate, as, before their judgment is in some degree matured, to read any book that falls in their way. Precaution should, as much as possible, prevent the necessity of prohibition: but, at all events, children must be kept out of bad company.

Concerning *discipline* in education, the reader will find in this volume several valuable suggestions, mixed with some eccentricities. One very important point here discussed is, how far parents, or preceptors, should reason or contend with children. The common practice of arguing with them, without giving them a chance of victory, is justly condemned; and the following admirable lesson may well deserve the attention of parents:

. . . . .

[Quotes from Essay 11, "Of Reasoning and Contention," that parents must distinguish clearly in their own minds principles from which they will not deviate and positions that are open to discussion. The former they must maintain with resolution and the latter they must be ready to consider with an open mind.]

Other useful precepts and observations, the result of sound sense occupied in a diligent attention to interesting facts in domestic life, are presented to the reader, on the topics of *deception and frankness*; on *manly treatment and behaviour*; and on *obtaining the confidence of young people*. We are less pleased with what is offered on the subject of the familiarity arising between the master and pupil from dwelling together, or, what Mr. G. calls, cohabitation. There may be truth in the adage that familiarity breeds contempt, but it may with equal truth be said that familiarity breeds affection. In education, with due caution, more advantages than inconveniences will arise from the circumstances of the tutor and pupil residing under the same roof; and, if it be Mr. G.'s intention to extend his doctrine on this subject to other relations in domestic life, it is fraught with consequences destructive of social happiness.

The Essay on Early Indications of Character is judicious and candid. Concerning the happiness of the state of childhood and youth, Mr. G. we think, judges too unfavourably, from the want of allowing enough, in the estimate, to the pleasures arising from novelty, and from a lively flow of animal spirits.

The Essays in the second part, on *Manners*, we shall more rapidly notice; not because we think them inferior to the former in merit, but because they offer fewer occasions of animadversion. - We do not follow, to its utmost extent, Mr. G's notion concerning the practicability, or the desirableness, of enabling mankind to pass the greater part of their working hours in a perfect freedom from labour: yet we agree with him in thinking that inordinate labour is a great evil, and that a daily command of some portion of leisure is a great blessing. We therefore admit that those luxuries, and that profusion, which cause an unprofitable waste of labour, are enormous evils; and that the character of the avaricious man is less injurious to society than that of the profuse spendthrift. - The difficulties, which, on each side, attend the question concerning the relief of beggars, are very fairly stated; a due allowance being made on the one hand for the indisputable right of every human being to support, and, on the other, for the moral mischiefs which necessarily arise from the condition of the beggar. Some material objections appear to us to lie against the Essay on Servants. The picture which Mr. G. draws of the house of a rich man is striking, though certainly overcharged: it is as follows:

. . . . .

[Quotes three pages describing the extreme contrasts between the learning and wealth of masters and the ignorance and poverty of servants. That the master will voluntarily live in such extremes demonstrates to Godwin how custom renders us callous.]

All this is in the main true, as well as what follows concerning the different appearance of the respective apartments of the master and the servant: yet we cannot admit that the character of voluntary servitude is unnatural, or its condition wretched. Servants in general, especially among the opulent, live better, are subject to fewer contingencies, have less care, less anxiety, and less labour, than would fall to their lot in any other situation. If they are subject to commands, and their actions and time are at the disposal of another, this is true of every mechanic whose labour is hired. Those who make our shoes are as truly our servants as those who make our fires. Many servants have much more leisure for amusement or improvement, than the common people in other stations.

Mr. G. lashes too indiscriminately and severely the several professions. On this subject, he plays the orator with greater latitude than in any other part of his book: yet he has not convinced us that there is no trade nor profession in which a young man has a tolerable chance of remaining honest. There is an illiberality in general professional as well as national censures, which is scarcely consistent with, and is certainly unworthy of, the character of a philosopher. We are inclined to hope that the lying, cheating tradesman, the dishonest lawyer, the unfeeling physician, the hypocritical clergyman, are rather the exceptions to the general character, than the true representatives of the body. If any of Mr. Godwin's portraits be drawn without the caricature pencil, it is that of the soldier: which we shall present to our readers at some length.

. . . . .

[The reviewer quotes from "of Trades and Professions" Godwin's damning sketch of a soldier's profession as a killer and a martyr to the inequities of kings and ministers of state.]

On the importance of restraining the Appetite for Sensible Pleasure, for the sake of contributing to the improvement of the mind, Mr. G. preaches orthodox morality. The subject of General Reputation is largely and very judiciously discussed. The real value of reputation is well estimated; and the cases in which it coincides with merit, or recedes from it, are distinctly and accurately pointed out. Concerning Posthumous Fame, we admire the apposite illustrations which the author has given of its uncertainty; and we acknowledge that the expectation of it is for the most part a delusive dream; yet, it is an expectation so gratifying to an ingenuous mind, that we are inclined to say concerning it, as Cicero said of the hope of a future state, "If it be a dream, let me not be undeceived." The argument for Candour, from the consideration that diversity of opinion is the unavoidable consequence of different situations and modes of education, was never more happily unfolded, than in the Essay before us upon this subject:

. . . . .

[Quotes two paragraphs from "On Differences of Opinion" describing human readiness to hold opinions without testing them.]

From this Essay, all parties, at the present time so much inflamed with mutual animosity, might learn mutual forbearance. We must not, however, pass over without censure the unnecessary, and we will add the unreasonable attack on Christianity, which is in this Essay abruptly introduced. Mr. G. ought to have studied the language of the New Testament enough to know that the faith, which it requires as the condition of salvation, is not an implicit subjection of the understanding to authority, but a rational conviction grounded on evidence, and a practical principle influencing the disposition and manners; and, consequently, that its doctrine of faith cannot be fairly brought as a proof that its spirit is intolerant.

The grand principle of universal benevolence, which is Mr. Godwin's pole-star in all his moral speculations, is employed with admirable effect in explaining the nature and determining the value of *Politeness*, in an Essay on that subject. By means of this guiding principle, sincerity and politeness, which are so often at variance in real life, are brought into perfect amity.

'Sincerity (Mr. G. beautifully as well as justly remarks) in its principle is nearer, and in more direct communication with, the root of virtue, utility, than politeness can ever be. The original purpose of sincerity, without which it is no more than idle rant and mysticism, is to provide for the cardinal interests of a human being, the great stamina of his happiness. The purpose of politeness is of a humble nature. It follows in the same direction, like a gleaner in a cornfield, and picks up and husbands those smaller and scattered ears of happiness, which the pride of Stoicism, like the pride of wealth, condescended not to observe.'

Here, according to the division expressed in the title-page, the second part of the Enquirer ought to have terminated; and the remaining two Essays, which are properly literary, should have formed a third part. The first of these, or the 11th of the second part, treats of *Learning*, and suggests and unfolds an obvious but important argument in favour of learning, that it gives to a man the advantage of the labours of others; an advantage of which the self-educated man, who investigates his own thoughts, with little attention to those of others, purposely divests himself. If our limits would permit, we could with pleasure cite an excellent passage from this Essay on the true mode of reading.

The last Essay, divided into seven sections, which takes an historical review of the progress of English style, and cites examples from celebrated writers, from the age of Queen Elizabeth to that of King George the Second, both inclusive, might afford occasion for much minute discussion: but we must content ourselves with general remarks. Mr. Godwin has here made use of a new method of criticism. Asterisms, placed before words or phrases, which this critic thinks objectionable, are left, without any remarks, to suggest the objections to the reader. This may, in some cases, be assuming too much on one side, and expecting too much on the other. Let our readers judge for themselves. A short but famous passage from Swift's Tale of a Tub is given as a curious example of negligent and disjointed composition, and the supposed faults are, in the author's peculiar manner, *stigmatized*.

. . . . .

[He quotes one of a series of passages in which Godwin makes use of asterisks to signal stylistic lapses from his basic principle of style, that it "should be the transparent envelope of our thoughts [...]"]

Few compositions could stand the test of such minute yet summary criticism. We doubt whether the language of the censor himself would pass unhurt through this ordeal: but, on the principle of retaliation, we had designed to stretch Procrustes on his own bed. We desist, however, lest we should provoke the wrath of this modern Aristarchus; who is as formidable with his asterism, as the ancient censor was with his obelisk. To his own style we allow the praise of general accuracy, perspicuity, terseness, and vigour: but we must add - and that remark may be extended to a numerous list of modern writers - that, in order to avoid the looseness of expression which he censures in our old English writers, he frequently falls into a dissolution of thought; exhibiting conceptions in a succession of short sentences, which would have appeared with more advantage in one flowing period, after the Greek model, so justly admired by Lord Monboddo. Tendencies towards this fault, and towards others that are destructive of ease and simplicity, it would not be difficult to remark in the style of the age of George the Third: but it is necessary for us to terminate this article, and to take our leave of the present work; after having observed that, with all its faults, it is a production of great merit, and that, if perused with caution, it cannot fail of being perused with profit.

[T.R. Malthus], *Essay on the Principle of Population, as it affects the Future Improvement of Society, with remarks on the Speculations of Mr. Godwin, M. Condorcet, and other Writers* **(1798)**

Analytical Review 28 (1798), 119-25

The french revolution, which has broken up the established forms of society, and destroyed the distinctions which generations had held in veneration, has very naturally called the attention of all men to the study of the social relations of life, and to the investigation of the powers and expectations of man. The imaginations of men, which are ever soaring able the reality of things, and prepared to take wing upon every remarkable occasion, have conceived, that a new era is about to commence, and that the future history of our species will resemble the past in nothing. Mr. Condorcet, Mr. Godwin, and Mr. Brothers have, indeed, been differently affected by the astonishing events which have lately occurred; but it would be difficult to say of the three which has reasoned and prophesied with most extravagance. It appears to us more probable, that Brothers is the appointed king of the jews, commissioned to collect that extraordinary people from the four winds of Heaven, and to replace them in their father's land, than that every man upon this globe shall be able to sustain himself and the helpless who depend upon him, by the labour of half an hour in every day; that intellectual vigour shall destroy the sexual appetite; or that man shall no longer be subject to death, but live for ever, without suffering from the wastings of age, or the ravages of disease. Such are the pleasing dreams of Condorcet and Godwin.

The author of the essay before us undertakes to examine the reasons which have been adduced by these gentlemen in favour of their opinions, and he has well performed his task, for he has men them with infinite acuteness, and in the true spirit of candour and philosophy. He is not one of those who rail when they should reason, and laugh when they should refute their antagonists. He is not one of these unfeeling enemies of mankind, who ridicule all ideas of the melioration of the condition of man. He thinks the condition of mankind may be improved, and that an improvement of it ought to be attempted. The question therefore, between the family of the visionaries and this philosopher is, to what extent this improvement can be carried, and what degree of felicity man has reason to expect in this world. "He has read," he says, "the fanciful speculations of Condorcet and Godwin, with a wish to find them true; but to him does not belong the power of concluding all the wishes to be fact, and of thus subduing the understanding to the will." We are glad to see a refutation of the new philosophy, if it, indeed, merit the name of philosophy, and more especially by such a man, by a man inclined to admit whatever is admissible in its favour, and to embrace with eagerness whatever promises benefit to mankind. The speculations of Condorcet, in one sense, belong to another country, and we have a right to look to France for a refutation of them. Mr. Godwin belongs to us, and we have long expected some english philosopher to examine critically what he has so confidently advanced. Whether his hypotheses were esteemed too visionary even to deserve animadversion, or whether his acknowledged acuteness deterred our countrymen from the undertaking, we know not; but the fact is, that the essay before us is the first performance, which professedly treats upon the fundamental principles of his book, and touches the inquiries, which are the basis of all his superstructure, concerning the perfectibility of man. It is not now necessary, that other labourers should enter the field, for we are much mistaken, if this essay will not be considered as a full and fair confutation of this extravagant philosophy.

Our author makes two postulata, on which he bottoms all the observations he offers in refutation of Mr. Godwin's hypotheses. They are the following:

First, That food is necessary to the existence of man.

Secondly, That the passion between the sexes is necessary, and will remain nearly in its present state.

Mr Godwin has not attempted to prove, neither has he suggested, that it is probable, that food will not continue to be necessary to the existence of man: yet, as he had ranged so far in the field of conjecture, we wonder he has not told us, that the vigour of improving intellect will, in time, overcome the desire for food, and be, of itself, without the vulgar aid of ordinary diet, equal to the support and the health of the human being. He has found it more easy, however, to dispose of the sexual appetite; yet, as far as facts are concerned, we have as little reason to think, that man will cease to marry and to be given in marriage, like the angels of heaven, as that he will cease to need, for the support of life, the bread which perisheth. Men, the most intellectual, as our author has well observed, have hitherto been much disposed to sexual indulgences; and, we find by daily observation, that the pressure of no difficulties, the experience of no want, deter man from gratifying this impetuous and imperious appetite. Our author is therefore warranted in making this second postulatum by the currency of all experience, which establishes his second, as firmly as it does his first, postulatum. It is really astonishing, that Mr. Godwin did not attempt to show the probability of the extinction of the desire and the necessity of food, when he wanted to prove that half an hour, of every day, devoted to labour, by every human being, would be equal to the supply of the wants of all that live.

The postulata of our author being admitted, let us now attempt to analyse his deductions. He observes, that the increase of mankind, when all obstructions to population are removed, would be in a geometrical ratio; whereas the ratio of the increase of the produce of the earth, upon the most romantic supposition, can be only arithmetical [...] Our author gives his opponent every advantage, and bottoms his calculations upon indisputable data, that his conclusions may admit of no doubt. Mr. Godwin, admits that there is a principle, which proportions the population to the means of subsistence; but seems not at all to comprehend what the principle is, or how it operates. He will find this well illustrated in the following paragraph [...]

. . . . .

[The review quotes liberally from Malthus's essay for more than a page to the effect that increases in wages do not increase the sources of subsistence.]

Admitting the validity of the argument, from the principle of population, against the practicability of Godwin's scheme of equality, and the perfectibility and happiness of men in society, Mr. Godwin thinks the objection contemplates a very distant evil. Myriads of centuries of still increasing population may pass away, says he, and the earth be still found sufficient for the subsistence of its inhabitants. This, which is the common reply to this overwhelming argument, of all the family of visionaries, our author has very seriously considered, and, we think we may add, very satisfactorily refuted.

. . . . .

[Summary and excerpts for another page show the Godwinian dream of equality becoming a nightmare with an increase in population and, inevitably, in vice and misery.]

Our author then draws the picture of society after its attempt to realize the scheme of benevolence and equality, returning again, from dire necessity, to the scheme of private property, monopoly, and selfishness. No hope now is left for man, and we have not yet disposed of one hundred years, much less of myriads of centuries, but what arises from the energy of mind extinguishing the sexual passion. This our author fully examines in the eleventh chapter, and shows, that no experience or probability exists to encourage any such hope.

The sixteenth chapter examines an important part of Dr. Adam Smith's work on the Wealth of Nations; and shows, that every increase of wealth does not better the condition of the labouring poor. We think much of this chapter worthy to be quoted; but the nature of our work forbids us to indulge too freely our feelings on this very important and elaborate essay.

The latter part of this essay is spent in an attempt to show the probability, that man is not placed here in a state of trial, according to the vulgar notion of that term, but for the purpose of awakening and forming his mind; or, to speak more generally, for the purpose of working matter into mind. This view leads the author to conclude in favour of a future state, adapted for the residence of great and noble minds; an that minds, not formed by this process to excellence, will be again extinguished in their parent clay, and lose all conscious existence. Such is the essay to which we invite the reader's attention. It is written with great animation and eloquence, and although we have remarked some instances of inattention and carelessness in the style, yet, in this respect, upon the whole, it is entitled to great praise. Perhaps, too, it might have been compressed into a narrower compass, and we think the arrangement is not always happy; but we have received so much pleasure from the perusal of it, that we are ready to pardon the faults we have mentioned, for they are, indeed, venial. The view it gives us of human life is not the most flattering; neither is it such as affords any pleasure to the author, who appears to feel warmly for the interests of humanity. But, if it be a true view, we must submit to the painful necessity of receiving it. Without intending it, however, we think the author, in this essay, has furnished the best apology for prostitution, that has ever been written. Miserable man seems, according to this system, to be doomed to make his choice between prostitution and infanticide; and the philosophy of Hobbes thus appears to be established, which states the natural state of man to be a state of warfare. We cannot doubt that this essay will receive much of the public attention. The subjects on which it treats are so important, and it is written with so much ability, that we need not invite the metaphysician and philosopher to consider it attentively.

Making Sense: Jane Austen on the Screen

YASMINE GOONERATNE (Sidney)

> "Tai and I don't make sense. You and I make sense."[1]

> "I thank you; but I assure you you are quite mistaken. Mr Elton and I are very good friends, and nothing more;" and [Emma] walked on, amusing herself in the consideration of the blunders which often arise from a partial knowledge of circumstances, of the mistakes which people of high pretensions to judgment are for ever falling into; and not very well pleased with her brother for imagining her blind and ignorant, and in want of counsel. He said no more.[2]

At the heart of every novel Jane Austen ever wrote are three linked concepts relating to the art of living: belief in the need to 'make sense' of the world into which one is born; belief in accommodating oneself to that world's requirements without sacrificing intelligence, sensibility or honour; and conviction that an ability to accomplish the first two can (though often with difficulty) be learned.

The film-maker who translates an Austen novel to the cinema or TV screen cannot escape the pressure of these ideas, which were so deeply held by the author that every turn of plot and every scrap of dialogue in her novels are saturated by them. The temptation to escape ideas altogether must be strong in film-makers of our times - how else can we explain the huge quantities of films made and successfully distributed worldwide every year, whose directors cheerfully admit to abandoning the main themes of a difficult novel in favour of 'developing' (they do not say 'exploiting') one aspect of it, that aspect usually being an emphasis on sex or violence? Since Jane Austen's novels famously refuse to dwell on 'guilt or misery,' the recent craze for making cinematic versions of her books is a phenomenon that must interest not only the heterogeneous audiences such versions are designed to attract, but that long established international community of single-minded literates, Jane Austen's readers.

In the following essay, which focuses on an unusual screen version of *Emma* titled *Clueless*, made in 1995, we might begin with some observations about that novel and its suitability to cinematic adaptation, particularly in comparison with *Pride and Prejudice*, Austen's best-known and most popular book (now more popular than ever before, probably, following the BBC TV adaptation starring Jennifer Erle and Colin Firth). *Emma* is Jane Austen's longest novel (nearly a hundred pages longer than *Pride*

---

[1] Elton to Cher Horowitz in *Clueless* (1995), produced by Scott Rudin and Robert Lawrence, written and directed by Amy Heckerling for Paramount Pictures, featuring Alicia Silverstone as Cher Horowitz (Emma).

[2] Jane Austen, *Emma*, eds., James Kinsley and David Lodge (Oxford: Oxford University Press, 1980), 5. All subsequent references are to this edition.

and Prejudice). It was for many years the least popular among younger readers (due to the snobbishness of its heroine), but now rivals *Pride and Prejudice* in terms of book sales. This, say booksellers, is largely due to the success of its screen adaptation, *Clueless*, which has become something of a 'teen cult' movie and has spawned a TV series involving characters from the film.

With the exception of movies that focus on pre-meditated crime, popular films, as everyone knows, tend to emphasize action. Characters in films do not devote time to philosophizing, they go places and do things, preferably on impulse, moved by passions that impel them towards lust, murder, self-sacrifice or joining the French Foreign Legion. The major characters of *Pride and Prejudice* and *Emma* do none of these things. The former, however, does offer a film-maker several changes of scene, and a large cast of varied characters. Elizabeth Bennet visits Hunsford, and later tours Derbyshire with her aunt and uncle Gardiner, Jane Bennet visits the Gardiners in London, while Lydia Bennet goes to Brighton, and elopes with George Wickham, causing both Mr Darcy and Mr Bennet to make hasty journeys to London to find her. Lady Catherine de Bourgh and Mr Collins travel from Hunsford to Longbourn, while the Bingleys move between Meryton, London and Derbyshire. In comparison, the characters of *Emma* are practically immobile. Elton, Frank Churchill and George Knightley make moves beyond Highbury, Elton to have Emma's portrait of Harriet Smith framed and later, to find a wife; Churchill to buy a piano for Jane Fairfax; and Knightley to put Emma out of his mind. But we do not accompany any of them. The furthest Emma Woodhouse travels is on an expedition to nearby Box Hill. In short, *Emma* remains fixed in the 'large and populous village' of Highbury (*Emma*, 5) and its chief characters are the small group of people who are relations or friends of Emma Woodhouse and her father.

As regards any crisis events related, however distantly, to 'sex and violence' that contribute to the plot, *Pride and Prejudice* offers us one elopement (Lydia and Wickham), one near-elopement (Georgiana Darcy and Wickham), and three situations comparable to duels, in which Elizabeth confronts in turn Mr Collins, Mr Darcy, and Lady Catherine, while fending off side-attacks from Caroline Bingley and Mrs Bennet. In contrast, the only near-sexual event in *Emma* is Mr Elton's proposal to Emma in the carriage, following the Westons' dinner party, and the only 'violent' incidents are a cruelly witty remark made by Emma to Miss Bates, and Harriet's meeting with the gypsies.

Since *Emma* has hardly any plot, and its characters hardly go anywhere, what use does Austen make of those extra hundred pages? The short answer to that is, that the plot, while hardly sensational, is extremely complicated, such complications being related, not to sensational events, but to errors and mistakes made by the heroine, while the 'journeys' undertaken by the characters, especially Emma herself, are not quick visits to specified locations, but journeys of the mind which take place over the period of a full year. They are part of the learning process which reflects Austen's emphasis on moral education, and the reader is with Emma every step of the way, as she progresses along a twisting road each bend of which leads her towards maturity and better judgment of herself and of society.

As Dr Saw-Choo Teo has recently pointed out in a recent socio-linguistic analysis of the opening conversation between Mr and Mrs Bennet in Chapter 1 of *Pride and Prejudice*, the dialogue between selected characters undoubtedly provides the basis for one of Jane Austen's many claims to pre-eminence as a writer of fiction.

> Much of the power of Jane Austen's story-telling lies in her ability to draw the reader into [...] becoming a participant in the events unravelling through the pages of her novel [...]. It is the conversations that the novelist so skilfully inserts into the crucial points of the novel that invite you to step in and listen to what is happening.[3]

Yet, films are notorious for cutting out speech in favour of action, an exercise that is regarded as one of the most important skills to be developed by an aspiring screen writer. How does a screen-writer deal with *Emma*, a novel rich in dialogue, providing plenty of evidence that Jane Austen very carefully observed, listened to, thought about, and recorded the relationships of people around her?

Chapter V of *Emma* provides an excellent example of Austen's mature skill. Here Mr Knightley has a long and private discussion with Mrs Weston on a subject that concerns them both: the present and future welfare of her former pupil and his sister-in-law, Emma Woodhouse. Mr Knightley has called on Mrs Weston in her husband's absence, and it is he who introduces the topic (two indicators to the fact that the subject concerns him closely). Analysis breaks this conversation down as follows:

1. Mr Knightley: (Introduces the topic) Emma: He thinks the friendship between Emma and Harriet Smith is 'a bad thing' (for Emma).
2. Mrs Weston: (Supports the topic, but opposes Knightley's viewpoint) She thinks it will be a good thing for Emma, encouraging her to read more in order to educate Harriet Smith.
3. Mr Knightley: (Introduces the topic) Emma: her intentions are better than her execution. Having known her from the time she was a child, he does not expect her to abide by any systematic course of study.
4. Mrs Weston: (Supports the topic, but opposes Knightley's viewpoint) Emma never omits doing anything she asks her to do.
5. Mr Knightley: (Continues the topic) Emma: her gifts of mind, her wish to control affairs, and her self-assured confidence in her own judgment.
6. Mrs Weston: (Supports the topic, but implicitly opposes Knightley's viewpoint) Is Mr Knightley implying that she was unable herself, though she was employed as a mother-substitute, to 'cope with' Emma's tendency to dominate and control?
7. Mr Knightley: (Continues topic) Emma: Living with Emma has inculcated in her governess a willingness to submit to another person's will that is an essential qualification for marriage.
8. Mrs Weston: (Introduces topic) Her husband's easy-going nature.
9. Mr Knightley: (Introduces topic) Frank Churchill may give Mr Weston cause for

---

[3] Saw-Choo Teo, "The art of conversation in *Pride and Prejudice*," in *Sensibilities* 15 (December 1997): 34 - 40.

worry.
10. Mr Knightley: (Introduces topic) Emma: Her 'genius for foretelling and guessing.'
11. Mr Knightley: (Reversion to Topic 1): Emma: The Emma/Harriet friendship will injure and hurt both young women.
12. Mrs Weston: (Change of subject): Emma: Her pleasing appearance.
13. Mr Knightley: (Supports the topic, but opposes Mrs Weston's viewpoint) Emma: He regards Emma from the viewpoint of 'a partial old friend.'
14. Mrs Weston: (Continues topic) Emma's loveliness and wholesome, healthy appearance.
15. Mr Knightley: (Supports topic, but opposes Mrs Weston's viewpoint) Emma: Her pleasing lack of personal vanity - but 'her vanity lies another way.'
16. Mr Knightley: (Reversion to Topic 1): Emma: The Emma/Harriet friendship will injure and hurt both young women.
17. Mrs Weston: (Supports topic, but opposes Mr Knightley's viewpoint) Emma's qualities may be trusted.
18. Mr Knightley: (Introduces topic) Emma: He will discuss the matter at Christmastime with John Knightley and Emma's sister Isabella.
19. Mrs Weston: (Supports topic, but opposes Mr Knightley's viewpoint) Advises him that it will be counter-productive for him to discuss the matter with the John Knightleys.
20. Mr Knightley: (Introduces topic) Emma: While accepting Mrs Weston's advice in good part, wonders what Emma's future will be.
21. Mrs Weston: (Supports topic) Agrees.
22. Mr Knightley: (Continues topic) Emma: Thinks it would do Emma good to fall in love and be 'in doubt of a return.'
23. Mrs Weston: (opposes Mr Knightley's viewpoint) Emma falling in love would greatly disrupt her father's comfort and peace of mind.
24. Mr Knightley: (Change of subject) The weather.

Of the twentyfour contributions listed above, fourteen are Knightley's, of which twelve focus directly or indirectly on Emma. Of the remaining two, one indicates a problem that concerns him, and which is indirectly related to Emma: Frank Churchill's tendency to worry his father. This is the only criticism we hear of Churchill, and it is an early indication that Knightley will not welcome an attachment between Churchill and Emma. The other signals a change of subject to the weather.

Eight of Mrs Weston's ten contributions are in the nature of Topic Support, either by agreement with or by polite opposition to a statement of Mr Knightley's. The remaining two tactfully introduce new (if related) topics on which they are in agreement: Emma's beauty, and Mr Woodhouse's fear of change. The conversation as a whole illustrates Mrs Weston's tactful diplomacy, her respect for Knightley, her affection for her former employer, and her loyalty to Emma, based on genuine, if one-eyed, affection. It indicates Mr Knightley's directness, his personal respect for Mrs Weston, his high standards of critical judgment (as regards Emma), and (an unconscious revelation, this) a long-standing and very deep affection and admiration for Emma. The fact that two persons of such integrity take opposed views on Emma while agreeing to love her and be concerned for her future happiness indicates that Emma's is a complex character worthy of their concern, which will be explored by the reader and developed in the course of the novel (*Emma*, 31-6).

The example above shows Austen's remarkable ability to direct a conversation between two people in such a way that, while still seeming to 'go nowhere' in terms of place, she can explore her themes while advancing her plot and developing her characters. In comparison with Mr Knightley and Mrs Weston, who have complicated and unconfessed agendas (Mr Knightley loves Emma and secretly fears the advent of Churchill, while Mrs Weston secretly hopes Churchill and Emma will make a match of it when he does appear), Mr and Mrs Bennett of *Pride and Prejudice* are simple, one-note characters, he cynical, witty, irresponsible, and somewhat cruel, she mercenary, stupid and self-centred. While Austen herself knew *Pride and Prejudice* to be rapid in the pace of its events, with plenty of coming and going among its characters to provide a lively, changing scene, it is in detailed, leisurely exploration of complex character that the strength of *Emma* lies.

That exploration is effected through conversation, and here lies a problem for the film-maker who wants to translate *Emma* to the screen. It is not surprising that the 1996 Miramax International film version omits this important and beautifully detailed conversation between Mr Knightley and Mrs Weston in its entirety.[4] Most of the book's essence lies in speech, and it is lively action, not speech, that the 90-minute time-limit cinema requires and invariably emphasizes. Also omitted are the monologues of Miss Bates and Mrs Elton. The Austen reader must regret this omission, since the Bates/Elton monologues are among the glories of the novel: Miss Bates because she sketches for us in a series of quick impressions the everyday life of a country town, while unconsciously scattering cunningly hidden clues to the secret relationship between Jane Fairfax and Frank Churchill;[5] Mrs Elton, because she provides an awful warning of what Emma could quite easily become if she doesn't check herself: a control freak.

"I am Lady Patroness, you know," Mrs Elton tells Mr Knightley.[6] It is a line that reminds the reader of Lady Catherine de Bourgh, another loud-voiced, domineering specialist in attention-demanding monologue. Vol. 2, chapter 18, 275-82 has a good example of Mrs Elton in full flow. See also Vol. 3, chapter 6, 324 for Mrs Elton "in all her apparatus of happiness," picking strawberries at Donwell. Here Austen uses Mrs Elton's characteristic habits of speech to describe the action and the weather.

As these remarks indicate, while Emma Woodhouse and her progress towards humility and good sense is the central concern of the book, she is surrounded by other

---

[4] *Emma*, written and directed by Douglas McGrath, a 1996 Miramax International film, featuring Gwyneth Paltrow as Emma Woodhouse, Toni Collette as Harriet Smith, Alan Cumming as George Knightley, and Greta Scacchi as Mrs Weston.
[5] See *Emma*, Vol. 2, chapter 9, 212-16, for a superb example of this technique.
[6] *Emma*, Vol. 3, chapter 6, 320.

figures who are developed fully in speech, thought and action, to become living personalities in their own right. Obviously, it is beyond any film-maker to use *all* such rich material. A conversation that *is* included in the Miramax International film, and is treated there to good effect, is the social exchange in Volume 1, chapter 6, 41-3, as Emma's Highbury circle give their opinions on her picture of Harriet Smith. Also well done, within the limitations of cinema, is Mr Elton's proposal to Emma in the carriage returning from Christmas dinner at the Westons'.

The relation of *Clueless* to Austen's *Emma* is by no means apparent at first sight, since the film is set, not in Regency England, but in contemporary '90s America. The world of the heroine, Cher Horowitz who delightfully resembles Emma Woodhouse in being "handsome, clever, and rich, with a comfortable home and happy disposition"[7] is not the country town of Highbury but Beverly Hills High. English Highbury-speak of the early nineteenth century has been replaced by American teenager-speak of our own day. Advising Tai on ways to increase her popularity, Cher informs Tai that her social status has already risen steeply "due to the fact that you hang with Dionne and I."

The actors in *Clueless* play characters who replicate (with some additions and omissions) the principal characters of Austen's novel, as follows: Alicia Silverstone (Cher Horowitz / Emma Woodhouse), Brittany Murphy (Tai / Harriet Smith), Paul Rudd (Josh / George Knightley), Dan Hedaya (Lawyer Horowitz / Mr Woodhouse), Justin Walker (Christian / Frank Churchill), and Jeremy Sisto (Elton/ Rev. Elton).

Despite this, the presence of sex and drugs on campus camouflages the connections well, and it is not until the film is well under way, and Cher undertakes to engineer a romance between two of her teachers, and follows up this supposed 'success' by undertaking a makeover of a dowdy friend, that the viewer perceives the plot's link with Emma's matchmaking between Mr Weston and Miss Taylor and her 'education' of Harriet Smith. Cher being fifteen years old (and not twenty-one), and her close companions being not her father's contemporaries but her own High School classmates, lead to important differences as well, among which an important one is, that while Emma at twenty-one is not given to personal vanity, Cher at fifteen glories in her own style and good looks, and spends some of her most fulfilling moments (and a lot of her father's money) shopping for clothes and accessories in the mall.

On the other hand, while Emma shows genuine concern for the welfare of the Highbury poor, Cher too puts energy and compassion into collecting for the environment. Like Mr Woodhouse, Cher's father appreciates her thoughtfulness and hard work on behalf of his health and comfort. The appearance of a 'Knightley' figure in the form of 'Josh,' Cher's protective step-brother, clinches our perception of a link between the two plots. Like Mr Knightley, Josh is not so blinded by his young relative's charm that he cannot see her faults. Also like Knightley, he is not interested in dancing, but he wins Cher's lasting admiration by coming to the aid of her dowdy friend Tai in her moment of humiliation.

---

[7] *Emma*, Vol. 1, Chapter 1, 3.

The connections between the novel and its innovative and witty screen adaptation in terms of characterization and action are close, and carefully developed. "Both of the main characters are spoiled, high class snobs who, after undergoing a crisis brought on by their own pride and [the] repression of their feelings, are transformed from callowness to mental and emotional maturity." The comment I have just quoted is taken from an admirably detailed essay by an undergraduate reading English in the USA that has been made available, like a considerable amount of material from a variety of 'non-traditional' sources, on Internet.[8]

This fact alone might indicate some of the changes that are taking place in Jane Austen's relationship with her 'public.' Once that public consisted of the small circle of her family, her friends, and a small band of literary admirers, from which point it extended and diversified rapidly, assisted by the enthusiasm of Kipling and the 'Janeites.' Through the tendency of readers to seek escape from the frightfulness of two world wars in her eighteenth century world of tranquillity and order, and the magisterial judgment of Leavis which awarded her a central place in 'The Great Tradition' of English literature, Jane Austen achieved the unusual distinction in the 1950s of becoming at once universally 'popular' and critically respected (not to say revered). In our own day there is hardly a TV channel that is entirely free of bonnets and breeches, and cinemas are filled to overflowing by people who have never in their entire lives read a novel, Jane Austen's or anyone else's, but flock to see movies adapted from her works.

Some people regard the current craze for making films based on Jane Austen's novels as ample proof, if proof were needed, that you can't keep a good woman down. Others query the implications of the so-called 'revival' for feminists in today's context. Some argue that such marked public interest - which amounts to a kind of cult in some countries, reflects a nostalgia for the traditional family, and for family values. Others see a flight from prurience and violence: as the male party-goer in a *New Yorker* cartoon says, "I'm reading a lot of Jane Austen these days, just to cleanse my palate." Some see the emotional power of the books, now given greater emphasis through translation to the screen in a period which has seen the cinema leave little to the imagination, as a sign of the author's repressed and thinly veiled sexuality. (The late J.W. Taylor expressed this well when he implied in a cartoon that the novels we admire so much have been heavily censored. "We like the plot, Miss Austen," says a shocked looking publisher to a little lady with a sharp nose, a poke bonnet, and a dolly bag who sits primly before him. "We like the plot, but all this effing and blinding will have to go.") Others argue that Austen's women are lively, determined rebels who

---

[8] Jordie Margison, 'Character Transformation in *Emma* and *Clueless*, December 3 1996, in Karen P. 'Some Reactions from Janeites.' Clueless and Jane Austen's *Emma* Website - *http://uts.cc.utexas. edu/˜churchh/ clueless. html*, 16 August 1996. See also: Internet Movie Database - http://www.imdb.com; Jane Austen Information page - http://www.pemberley.com/janeinfo/clueless/html; *Clueless. The Script* written by Amy Heckerling, 1995 - Internet at pacey 578@rocketmail.com; Stern, Lesley. 'Emma in Los Angeles: *Clueless* as a remake of the book and the city.' *AHR*, http://www.lib.latrobe.edu.au/AHR/archive/Issue - August 1997/stern.html.

manage to tread the fine line between social conformity and private integrity, and that they represent positive feminine values, among them the responsibility to nurture, protect and defend friends and families.

The more cynical view is that Darcymania is merely the result of Hollywood hype, a constructed popular fantasy controlled by image makers. 'Darcymania' swept Britain (and later the world) a few years ago, with the BBC adaptation of *Pride and Prejudice*. The audience that once fell in love with Olivier in the Hollywood version of that novel contained the mothers and grandmothers of the scores of young women who now, as Libby Greig put it in a recent piece for the *Sydney Morning Herald*, 'quiver in their muslins' before the passionately smouldering gaze of Colin Firth. Students tell me they find the films useful as extensions of the novels which happen to be current set texts: one can only hope they do not ever imagine that they can serve as substitutes for them! It is no surprise, these days, to read an article in *The New Yorker* that begins: "Currently, it seems, Jane Austen is hotter than Quentin Tarantino."[9]

As I have suggested in this essay, the film versions of Jane Austen's novels certainly have many good points, but even the best of them are, in the end, no substitute for the fiction. At the same time, there appears to be plenty of room for adaptations such as *Clueless* that translate the Austen concern for moral education into contemporary terms. It is possible to watch *Clueless* in much the same way that one reads Emma, many times over, each time finding something new to admire, some new detail that sharpens perception of some aspect of Austen's fiction.

One very good thing that can be said for good Austen adaptations is, that the best among them lead people back to the novels. An enterprising bookseller in Colombo has been quick to grasp this important fact. Announcing an offer of 39% off the price of copies from a new stock of *Sense & Sensibility*, the ad reads:

LATEST BOOKS

Sense and Sensibility by Jane Austen. Published price Rs. 237.50. Our price Rs. 145.00. Read the book of the award-winning film.

---

[9] Martin Amis, "Jane's World," in *The New Yorker*, 8 January 1996, 31-5.

Of the Origin of Images According to Yeats

JACQUELINE GENET (Caen)

Yeats distinguishes two kinds of imagination: on the one hand the imagination calling on the "images of desire" and therefore using the mask, on the other hand, visionary imagination. The poet gives primacy now to one imagination, now to the other. His aesthetic principles are marked by a deep ambiguity, resulting from these two conceptions.

At the same time, he wonders about the origin of images. Well-versed in the Platonic philosophy of the Anima Mundi, he is convinced that the poet must look for inspiration in some Memory or Universal Tradition, peopled with imaginary characters and experiences: "I had as yet no clear answer, but knew myself face to face with the Anima Mundi described by Platonic philosophers."[1] The fundamental question is to know whether this memory or Tradition creates the poet or is created by him. Is the first creator the human mind, or is it the divine? Is imagination submitted to a transcendantal truth beyond the human psyche, or is the imaginary instinct immanent? Does not the Great Memory, inspired by Platonic philosophy, finally fuse with Jung's collective Unconscious?

"Image of desire"[2]

In his *Autobiographies*, Yeats first refers to the images formed in accordance with desire, assimilated to the mask or anti-self which is a natural complement of the self. The fusion of the mask and the ordinary self allows the fulfillment of personality--the Unity of Being. For his study of the mask in its relations with artistic creation, Yeats borrows from Blake - "Without contraries is no progression" - from Goethe and from Henry More. As early as 1909, he questions himself: "Is not one's art made out of the struggle in one's soul? Is not beauty a victory over oneself?"[3] "The more I tried to make my art deliberately beautiful, the more did I follow the opposite of myself."[4] The conflict of the self and the mask is an aspect of this quarrel with ourselves which is a source of poetry. The artist, divided between his daily self and his mask, uses art to reach his identity. The great poets create by imitating this mask which includes whatever is missing in the daily self; the work is the anti-self of the life of the artist, a necessary complement if he wants to fulfill himself.

---

[1] William Butler Yeats, *Autobiographies* (London: Macmillan, 1966), 262.
[2] *Autobiographies*, 247.
[3] William Butler Yeats, *Memoirs* (London: Macmillan, 1974),157.
[4] William Butler Yeats, *Essays and Introductions* (London: Macmillan 1961),271

The debate of "Ego Dominus Tuus"[5] the poem which opens *Per Amica*, first entitled "The Self and the Antiself" is central in Yeats's career. A dialogue between Hic, the primary self, that of the mirror, and Ille, the anti-self, the mask, it expounds the idea that each man possesses an anti-self, the opposite of what he is. Ille attracts Yeats's sympathy. The imaginative intensity of the poets comes from their struggle to convey a vision of this mask in their poems. The works of Dante and Keats are the contrary of what they were in real life. Dante celebrates the pure Beatrice and divine justice "because he had to struggle in his own heart with his unjust anger and his lust"[6] Keats in his poetry satisfies the thirst for luxury that life refuses to quench. Literary creation becomes a compensating dream, even a therapeutic one. In the modern world where man no longer seeks his anti-self but is satisfied with looking at himself in a mirror, like Hic in "Ego Dominus Tuus", there is no real creation: we are but critics. For creation is not the imitation of the world as it appears to us but the representation of a world as it could be. Images can be explained as dramatic antitheses, since Yeats believes that no mind can create without being divided into two. Notice that the interest of Yeats for the masks on the stage coincides with the elaboration of his philosophy. In his literary history, Yeats symbolizes the moment of creative inspiration by phase 15 which solves antinomies.

"Images of...vision"[7]

This Romantic imagination made up of will and desire does not account for the whole Yeatsian conception. Images are also inspired by a visionary sacred imagination, in other words, imagination appears now as a power-game playing with what is alien to the self, i.e. the mask, now as subordinate to a power or truth different from itself - the "images of vision". Yeats grasps the "images of vision" either through his wife's trances and automatic writing, or directly, for he tries to control his imagination, to detach himself from the daily world, to empty his mind until he fills it with the images of the world beyond ours. He asserts that, during the seances with Mathers and Mme Blavatsky, uncontrollable mental images appeared; this he confirms in the following sentence: "[...] my imagination began to move of itself and to bring before me vivid images. Then images loom up suddenly."[8] The adverb "suddenly" is the typical marker of the vision. The bedazzling instant when this vision occurs prevents the intellectual processes from reaching their ends ("before I had well finished"[9]).

Ecstatic imagination is recognized by Plato in the mystic dialogues: the *Phaedrus*, the *Timaeus*, the *Philebus*. For Yeats, it is the imagination of the seer. In this perspective, the poet receives images rather than creates them; he seems to be the recep-

---

[5] William Butler Yeats, *Poems: Variorum edition* (New York: Macmillan, 1957), 367.
[6] William Butler Yeats, *Mythologies* (London: Macmillan, 1959), 330.
[7] *Autobiographies*, 248
[8] *Essays and Introductions*, 29.
[9] *Variorum*, 322.

tacle of transcendental visions. Visionary imagination seeks "a unity with a life beyond individual being"[10] It is sacred: "Any one who has any experience of any mystical state of the soul knows how there float up in the mind profound symbols."[11]

Among the seers, Yeats reckons Saint Simeon on his column and Saint Anthony in his cavern. In a whole lineage of writers, he finds an evidence of this visionary imagination which rejects the grip of the will and of personality in favour of a submissive attitude towards ancient images. His survey of the mystic visionaries ranges from Swedenborg and Boehme to AE. and Synge. Blake is one of these exceptional poets, sensitive to this timeless memory which reveals events and symbols of far-off centuries. Yeats glorifies the imagination of his master whom he quotes in *Essays and Introductions*. According to Yeats, a poet as typically Romantic as Shelley, on privileged occasions, would have known the religious ecstasy of the saint when the self indulges in a truth transcending his own creative will. "Images of vision" also inspired the poetry of George Herbert, Francis Thompson, George Russell.[12]

Similarities between the ecstatic imagination of the poet and that of the saint are not rare. In the holy city of Byzantium, the artist and the saint are one; the sages "in God's holy fire" serve as "singing masters" and so turn the heart "sick with desire" into "the artifice of eternity" ("Sailing to Byzantium"[13]). When he understands the Irish tradition as the expression of visionary imagination, Yeats sees in it a specific collection of images, similar to the archetypes appearing to visionary poets. This conception of imagination urged him to found a mystic order of contemplation at Castle Rock where he wanted to create mysteries like those of Eleusis and Samothrace. The rhythms of "All Souls' Night"[14] for instance are hypnotic; the very poem is a ritual taking the reader beyond himself.

These collective images, according to the poet, form a "Unity of Image" which could be the founding symbol of a national literature[15] and allow the achievement of a Unity of Culture, as opposed to Romantic imagination which aims at the Unity of Being. Thus Yeats seeks primordial mythological images preceding the subsequent divisions into different religious, political or philosophical beliefs. Some images of Irish folklore are decisive and the poet turns to the past:

> [...] the images of the past -
> The unperturbed and courtly images.[16]

As soon as visionary imagination forgets its passive bent, as happens with Morris and Henley, then, according to Yeats, art degenerates. Even AE. seems to have deceived him sometimes, as far as his visionary imagination has been misled into "mod-

---

[10] *Autobiographies*, 331.
[11] *Essays and Introductions*, 78-9.
[12] *Autobiographies*, 248.
[13] *Variorum*, 407.
[14] *Variorum*, 470.
[15] *Autobiographies*, 263.
[16] "The People", *Variorum*, 351-2.

ern subjective romanticism" which deprived him of "some form of traditional belief."[17] Yeats's criticism here does not concern either of the two imaginations, but the attempts to blur this distinction, to betray the imagination to which one feels attracted by contaminating it by its contrary.

Vacillation between the two imaginations

If there is a gap between the two imaginations, Yeats's Romantic self cannot be completely separated from his visionary self. So, in "First Principles", he recommends the two kinds of art. One gets a glimpse of this ambiguity through his criticism of Blake. Now he approves of his conception according to which vision is the revelation of some "invisible essence;" and he opposes the "word of imagination" as "the world of eternity" to the more fleeting one created by fancy for the sake of "amusement."[18] Now, in another passage, he criticizes Blake who prefers vision - which he has previously praised - to style.[19]

This vacillation seems to indicate the incompatibility of these two forms of imagination, a reading confirmed by the passage of "Anima Mundi" where Yeats states that if the saint or the sage reaches truth when following the straight line, the artist and the poet must follow the winding path of the serpent, going from desire to weariness, to come back to desire. In this perspective, the sacred vision could be obtained only by renouncing the circular self of desire.

In actual fact, the virtues of the two imaginations very often appear not as rival or contradictory powers but complementary ones. They can come one after the other. In his *Autobiographies*, Yeats writes: "Does not all art come when a nature, that never ceases to judge itself, exhausts personal emotion in action or desire so completely that something impersonal, something that has nothing to do with action or desire, suddenly starts into its place, something which is unforseen, as completely organized, even as unique, as the images that pass before the mind between sleeping and waking?"[20] In "Discoveries" (1906), Yeats suggests that the great artist always has his share of "the sadness that the Saints have known" and of the "Promethean fire"[21] creating the energies of active life. Therefore he seems to think that these two imaginations must work together in order to reach artistic perfection. Consequently, if he can assert that the poet "may not stand within the sacred house, but lives amid the whirlwinds that beset its threshold", he can also state at the same time that "in all great poetical styles there is (a) saint"[22] thereby achieving a dialectical union of contraries.

---

[17] *Autobiographies*, 248.
[18] *Essays and Introductions*, 116.
[19] *Essays and Introductions*, 119-21. *Mythologies*, 361.
[20] *Autobiographies*, 332.
[21] *Essays and Introductions*, 278.
[22] "Per Amica", "Anima Hominis" V et VI, *Mythologies*, 333.

The Great Memory

The reciprocal exclusion of the two imaginations becomes problematic as soon as Yeats confesses that he does not know "whether it is we or the vision that create the pattern, who set the wheel turning."[23] He questions himself: "What certainty had I that (these images) which had taken me by surprise could be from my own thought?"[24] He reaches the conclusion that there is only one source of images, a universal storehouse which he calls Anima Mundi or Great Memory, transmitting to the poets a body of universal images or at least images shared by a community. Like visionary images, those of the mask also resort to the Anima Mundi: "My mind began drifting vaguely towards that doctrine of the mask which has convinced me that every passionate man is, as it were, linked with another age, historical or imaginary, where alone he finds images that rouse his energy."[25] Each human soul partakes of this general soul"[26] and in "The Philosophy of Shelley's poetry", he expresses his convictions that "our little memories are but a part of some great Memory that renews the world and men's thoughts age after age."[27] The principles ruling the imagination are the following ones: 1) That the borders of our mind are ever shifting, and that many minds can flow into one another and create or reveal a single mind, a single energy. 2) That the borders of our memories are as shifting, and that our memories are a part of one great memory, the memory of Nature herself. 3) That this great mind and great memory can be evoked by symbols."[28]

Plato and the Soul of the World

One has often spoken of the influence of the Platonic thinkers on Yeats; for Plato, a narrow union exists between human nature and universal nature, between microcosm and macrocosm. The sensible world is created after an eternal model including the forms or eternal essences of all living creatures, under the law of Good. The Demiurge organizes the visible world, his eyes fixed on the ideal model. It is its reflection, as the myth of the cavern explains. Most of the interpreters identify the Demiurge and the idea of Good, the aim towards which all souls tend; others state that the Demiurge is himself a compound of ideas, that he is not one with the idea of Good. If sometimes the world of Ideas, God and the Soul of the world appear as distinct, elsewhere they are different names for a single suprasensible reality that we can apprehend through dialectics. Besides, are ideas realities entirely distinct from sensible objects, constituting a separate world, without communication with our universe? Or do we pass,

---

[23] "Anima Hominis" XII, *Mythologies* 341.
[24] William Butler Yeats, *Selected Prose* (London: Macmillan, 19), 77.
[25] *Autobiographies*, 152.
[26] *Mythologies*, 345.
[27] *Essays and Introductions*, 79.
[28] *Essays and Introductions*, 28.

through imperceptible transitions, from the highest and most immutable Idea down to the inferior forms of the world of appearances? The two interpretations are possible according to the texts. However that may be, the Soul of the World is divine. If Plato generally seems to place himself from the transcendental viewpoint, in other texts he seems to make concessions to the doctrine of immanence, altering the pattern of his philosophy: the sensible world no longer seems a copy of the intelligible world; Form descends into matter to order it directly. As to the human soul, its immortal element is similar to the Soul of the World. The *Phaedo*, the *Phaedrus*, the *Republic* imply the eternity of the souls, the condition of reminiscence; the doctrine of the *Phaedrus* includes an original union of the soul with the divine, then a separation resulting from sin. What prevails is the impression that, thanks to its superior functions, man's thought is directly united to the divine.

From his perfect city, Plato banishes poetry as imitation which concerns only appearances and not the nature of things. The artist is unworthy for he copies a copy: to hold a mirror before nature is foolish since nature itself is a mirror. Greek myths dealing with inspiration however state that, in certain circumstances, we can find back the lost knowledge of the universal spirit, through reminiscence. According to Plato, there are three kinds of souls who remember: the philosophers who possess knowledge, the lovers who, admiring the object of their love, have access to Beauty, and the "musical souls", i.e. the artists who in this world create copies of eternal originals. Art requires anamnesis, the memory of eternity.

Yeats as a Platonist

The Yeatsian tradition is Platonism. Yeats quotes Blake who does nothing but expound Platonic philosophy: "There exist in that eternal world the eternal realities of everything which we see reflected in the vegetable glass of Nature."[29] As a good platonist, Yeats maintains: "[...] all our mental images no less than apparitions (and I see no reason to distinguish) are forms existing in the general vehicle of Anima Mundi, and mirrored in our particular vehicle."[30]

Yeats juggles with Platonic terminology in "A Bronze Head" for instance

[...] who can tell
Which of her forms has shown her substance right?"[31]

The ideal beauty which was Maud's, though destroyed by time, will recover its prenatal perfection after death:

But in the grave, all, all, shall be renewed.[32]

---

[29] *Essays and Introductions*, 150-151.
[30] *Mythologies*, 352.
[31] *Variorum*,. 618.
[32] "Broken Dreams", *Variorum*, 356.

It is this archetype of beauty that Yeats beholds in his moments of vision:

> [...] always when I look death in the face,
> When I clamber to the heights of sleep,
> Or when I grow excited with wine,
> Suddenly I meet your face.[33])

Such is Maud's face, the Form of her Beauty.

A fair number of Yeats's poems follows the movement of Plato's most famous dialogues which, from the corporeal world, that of flux and multiplicity, accedes, through a dialectical ascent, to the world of ideal form, myth and unity. The poems opening on the word "I" or including it in the first line, progressively turn the personal into the impersonal, the ego into eidos: "I was soon to write many poems where an always personal emotion was woven into a general pattern of myth and symbol."[34] From the temporal world of "casual comedy," one rises to the eternal universe thanks to memory and anamnesis. From "I have met them at close of day," one passes to "A terrible beauty is born,"[35] from "I have heard that hysterical women say " to "Their ancient, glittering eyes are gay;"[36] from "walk through the long schoolroom questioning" to "How can we know the dancer from the dance?"[37] All these poems begin by the ephemeral world of bustle and social daily routine, described by the tense of the verbs: "I have met", "I have heard", by the language of conversation and the informal rhythm -"polite meaningless words." In contrast, the last lines which expound eternal truths use a timeless present. The Chinese who partake of art – "I delight to imagine them seated there"[38] -stay in a state of happy eternity like the melodies imagined on the Grecian Urn of Keats which have much in common with the Music of the Spheres. The rhythms which first are familiar, become ritual and incantatory and carry us to the moment between waking and sleeping which is that of creation and whose plenitude Yeats conveys in "Vacillation" section IV.[39] If Augustus John's painting for instance "is a powerful but prosaic art, celebrating the 'fall into division',"[40] "Lapis Lazuli," a poem on creative energy and on the gaiety of the artist, achieves the "resurrection into unity."[41] In the same way, "Among School-Children" turns the common world of the first stanza into a Platonic world. Accomplishing an act of anamnesis of which they are unaware, the nuns and the mothers remember the eternal Forms, in our world ruled by time. It is Plato's metaphysics with a middle world of "images or "Presences" as a link between them.

---

[33] "A Deep-Sworn Vow", *Variorum*, 357.
[34] *Autobiographies*, 151.
[35] "Easter 1916", *Variorum*, 391.
[36] "Lapis Lazuli", *Variorum*, 565.
[37] "Among School-Children", *Variorum*, 443.
[38] *Variorum*, 565.
[39] *Variorum*, 501.
[40] *Autobiographies*, 502.
[41] *Autobiographies*, 502.

Yeats also knows Plato's anamnesis who writes that to seek and learn is nothing other than remembering. One reads in *Explorations*: "[I] value all I have seen or heard [...] because of something they remind me of, that exists, as I believe, beyond the world."[42] Yeats's drama and poetry are often rituals of anamnesis, a glimpse at the eternal from the temporal, a movement from multiplicity to unity.

Yeats's defence of the artist, directed against Plato but ironically derived from him, consists in saying that the artist, during his vision and creation, can apprehend Forms:

> Quattrocento put in paint
> On backgrounds for a God or Saint
> Gardens where a soul's at ease;
> Where everything that meets the eye,
> Flowers and grass and cloudless sky,
> Resemble forms that are or seem
> When sleepers wake and yet still dream,
> And when it's vanished still declare,
> With only bed and bedstead there,
> That heavens had opened.[43]

In 1916, in a letter to his father, Yeats says that if art imitates, it does so in a Platonic way, in the same way as time imitates eternity. In art, there is " an intensity of pattern that we have never seen with our eyes."[44]" The little ritual "of verse resembles "the great ritual of Nature," because both are "copied from the same eternal model."[45]

The images of the Yeatsian Anima Mundi have an involuntary and transpersonal character as testified by this passage from *Hodos Chameliontos*: "When a man writes any work of genius, or invents some creative action, is it not because some knowledge or power has come into his mind from beyond his mind? It is called up by an image [...] but our images must be given to us, we cannot choose them deliberately."[46]

Through a repeated meditation on the work of sacred poets, he becomes bold enough to formulate the idea of "a supernatural artist"[47] revealing himself in the images. Yeats, as it seems, endorses the Platonic doctrine of the imagination as the first vehicle of a transcendental truth. The Anima Mundi is a house where images live, existing as "living souls" - "an image that has transcended particular time and place becomes a symbol, passes beyond death, as it were, and becomes a living soul."[48] A passage from *Essays and Introductions* explains: "[...] there is a memory of Nature

---

[42] William Butler Yeats, *Explorations* (London: Macmillan, 1962), 254.
[43] *Variorum*, 639.
[44] A Wade, Rupert Hart-Davis, eds., *The Letters of W.B. Yeats* (London: Macmillan, 1954), 607.
[45] *Essays and Introductions*, 202.
[46] *Autobiographies*, 272.
[47] "Magic" in *Essays and Introductions*, 36.
[48] *Essays and Introductions*, 80.

that reveals events and symbols of distant centuries. Mystics of many countries and many centuries have spoken of this memory; the honest men and charlatans, who keep the magical traditions which will some day be studied as a part of folklore, base most that is of importance in their claims upon this memory. I have read of it in Paracelsus and in some Indian book that describes the people of past days as still living with it [...] And I have found it in the "Prophetic Books" of William Blake who calls its images "the bright sculptures of Los's Hall."[49] In the visionary states which, according to Yeats, Russell, Blake and Synge experienced - and which he also experienced-- these living images which have transcended time and space enter imagination. They are in no way created by it. Yeats subscribes to the description that Shelley gives of images; for him they are "'gleams of a remoter world which visit us in sleep,' spiritual essences whose shadows are the delights of all the senses."[50] Yeats explicitly borrows from Plato the notion of ecstasy to explain this mystic meeting with images which emerge from a source beyond the self. He compares it to that of the saint, implying self-abnegation: "For ecstasy is a kind of death."[51]

But even in his essay "Magic," Yeats is sometimes sceptical when he wonders whether the supernatural artist who grants visions is really transcendental. Admitting that the primordial importance of all mystical, poetical or magic vision is the proof of the supremacy of imagination and the power that several minds have to fuse in one, he leaves the question in abeyance. When, he writes in "Ideas of Good and Evil": "Goethe has said 'Art is art, because it is not nature', it brings us near to the archetypal ideas themselves, and away from nature, which is but their looking-glass,"[52] it is not easy to determine whether Yeats insists more on the adjective "archetypal" - thus turning towards the Jungian notion of a deposit left by centuries of psychic life - or on the word "idea", turning towards Plato's paradigmatic Forms. This does not matter. Yeats would probably have liked to reconcile the two trends, because of the balance that the artist must keep between vision and creation. Jung also felt very close to Plato: "[...] within the limits of psychic experience," he writes, "the collective unconscious takes the place of the Platonic realm of eternal ideas."[53] The archetype becomes a synonym of the Platonic idea.

---

[49] *Essays and Introductions*, 46.
[50] *Essays and Introductions*, 75.
[51] *Essays and Introductions*, 71.
[52] *Essays and Introductions*, 101-2.
[53] ,Carl Gustav Jung, *The Collected Works* trans. R.F.C.Hull (Princeton: Princeton University Press Bollingen Series XX; London: Routledge & Kegan Paul, 1953-1978). The quotations mention volume and paragraph.XIV, par. 101.

The Jungian collective unconscious

One has compared Yeats's anima hominis to the personal unconscious and his Anima Mundi - sometimes called "the mind of the race"[54] -to Jung's collective unconscious, even though the two men did not know each other. Jung distinguishes on the one hand the personal unconscious, belonging to each individual and compounded of repressed impulses and infant-desires, as well as numberless forgotten experiences, and on the other hand the collective unconscious, the part of the psyche common to all humanity and lying in a deeper stratum than the personal unconscious. Defining the collective unconscious, Jung explains: "The collective unconscious is [...] the mighty deposit of ancestral experience accumulated over millions of years [...] Because the collective unconscious is [...] a deposit of world processes embedded in the structure of the brain and the sympathetic nervous system, it constitutes in its totality a sort of timeless and eternal world-image"[55] and "I have chosen the term 'collective' because this part of the unconscious is not individual but universal; in contrast to the personal psyche, it has contents and modes of behaviour that are more or less the same everywhere and in all individuals. It is, in other words, identical in all men and thus constitutes a common psychic substrate of a supra-personal nature which is present in every one of us."[56] And again: "This collective unconscious does not develop individually but is inherited."[57] Its existence is partly revealed from the observation of instinctive behaviour - the instincts being impulses with no conscious motivation. The unconscious unites men, the conscious differentiates them.

The creative mind draws from the collective unconscious which, as Jung writes, "corresponds to the mythic land of the dead, the land of the ancestors."[58] We have the impression of listening to Yeats saying: "[...] there is a memory of Nature that reveals events and symbols of distant centuries,"[59] and "All spirits inhabit our unconsciousness, or, as Swedenborg said, are the Dramatis Personae of our dreams."[60] It is from the deepest recesses of the soul that Jung elaborates his theory of a collective unconscious with its archetypal figures. It is also from the same abyss - "Where only body's laid asleep" - that Yeats discovers the "elemental things" he conjures up in "To Ireland in the Coming Times."[61]

---

[54] *Autobiographies*, 372.
[55] Jung *Collected Works*, VIII, par. 729.
[56] Jung *Collected Works*, IX, par. 3.
[57] Jung *Collected Works*, IX, par. 90.
[58] Carl Gustav Jung, *Memories, Dreams, Reflections*, ed. Aniela Jaffé, trans. Richard and Clara Winston (New York: Pantheon Books (Random House), 1961, 1962, 1963; London: Collins and Routledge & Kegan Paul, 1963). The quotations refer first to the American edition, then to the British one, 191, 183.
[59] *Essays and Introductions*, 46.
[60] William Butler Yeats, *A Vision* (London: Macmillan, 1962), 227.
[61] *Variorum*, 137.

Yeats: from the tradition to the unconscious

When Yeats says he lives in the past, he means the unconscious, with his dead ancestors, and this past is not only a personal past but a collective, universal one. "Now that I am old and live in the past, I often think of those ancestors of whom I have some detailed information [...] Then, as my mood deepens, I discover all these men in my single mind [...] Vico was the first modern philosopher to discover in his own mind, and in the European Past, all human destiny."[62] If we look for our ancestors beyond Blake, Vico, Swedenborg, Boehme, Paracelsus and Plotinus, we will find them in the unconscious of mankind.

For Yeats, the source of the images is one with the unconscious. "The Tower" mocks at the transcendental vision of Plato and Plotinus:

> I mock Plotinus' thought
> And cry in Plato's teeth

and concludes:

> Death and life were not
> Till man made up the whole.[63]

About this poem Yeats writes: "When I wrote the lines about Plato and Plotinus I forgot that it is something in our own eyes that makes us see them as all transcendence."[64] As for him, does he not choose immanence? He mentions that, for his friends the occultists, "the dark portion of the mind - the subconscious - had an incalculable power."[65] In certain texts, he clearly states that imagination is a product of the unconscious: "I know now that revelation is from the self, but from that age-long memoried self that shapes the elaborate shell of the mollusc and the child in the womb, that teaches the birds to make their nest; and that genius is a crisis that joins that buried self for certain moments to our trivial daily mind,"[66] and also: "[...] the creative energy of men depends upon their believing that they have, within themselves, something immortal and imperishable."[67] He likens the images of poetic creation to those of a dream. It is in this condition when "we are lured to the threshold of sleep"[68] that we behold visions. That is what Jung calls "active imagination" and the poet "the one moment of creation."[69]. *Per Amica* states the kinship between the muse and the unconscious.

---

[62] "On the Boiler", *Explorations*, 429.
[63] *Variorum*, 415.
[64] *Variorum*, 826
[65] *Autobiographies*, 372.
[66] *Autobiographies*, 272.
[67] "The First Principles" Samhain 1904, *Explorations*, 151.
[68] *Essays and Introductions*, 160.
[69] *Essays and Introductions*, 159

For more than from the subconscious, it is from the unconscious that the images emerge: concerning Mathers, Yeats writes: "It was through him that I began certain studies and experiences that were to convince me that images well up before the mind's eye from a deeper source than conscious or subconscious memory."[70] "The Double Vision of Michael Robartes"[71] celebrates the birth of an image. After having been held back ("hold fast") by the blind memory of dream, it frees itself and becomes accessible to consciousness ("I knew"). The representation of the dancer no longer belongs only to night but appears in full daylight and becomes a vision. In his poems, Yeats questions himself on the origin of images: the problem is raised in "Fragments":

> Where got I that truth?
> Out of a medium's mouth,
> Out of nothing it came,
> Out of the forest loam,
> Out of dark night where lay
> The crowns of Nineveh.[72]

"The Circus Animals' Desertion " is more explicit:

> Those masterful images because complete
> Grew in pure mind, but out of what began?
> A mound of refuse or the sweepings of a street,
> [...]
> Now that my ladder's gone,
> I must lie down where all the ladders start,
> In the foul rag-and-bone shop of the heart.[73]

Can we assimilate the impure, though fruitful vision, of "A Circus Animals' Desertion" - the rough materials which are the very stuff of the poet - to the unconscious? As to the growth of images, the process is represented by the rungs of this ladder which reaches the summits of art. Yeats thinks that, through the great poets' work, the Anima Mundi, the "general cistern of form," as he puts it in *Mythologies*,[74] can spread its images and he even wonders whether works such as Keats's "Ode to a Nightingale" pre-exist in the Anima Mundi, whether Keats was only the instrument through which the poem came to daylight.[75] This origin of images in the collective unconscious concerns images of desire as well as images of vision. This unconscious is transmitted throughout the ages. Of the mythological battle of "The Valley of the

---

[70] *Autobiographies*, 183.
[71] *Variorum*, 384.
[72] *Variorum*, 439.
[73] *Variorum*, 630.
[74] *Mythologies*, 351.
[75] Harper, *The Making of Yeats's "A Vision" A study of the automatic script* (London: Macmillan, 1986), II, 356.

Black Pig" and many others which are alike, Yeats writes: "All these battles are one, the battle of all things with shadowy decay. Once a symbolism has possessed the imagination of large numbers of men, it becomes, as I believe, an embodiment of disembodied powers, and repeats itself in dreams and visions, age after age."[76]

His philosophy also emerges from the unconscious. In *A Vision*, the Instructors come from it and the paradox of the unconscious becoming conscious comes true: "I am finishing my belated pamphlet," Yeats writes about *On the Boiler*, "and will watch with amusement the emergence of the philosophy of my own poetry, the unconscious becoming conscious. It seems to me to increase the force of my poetry."[77] Mythos turns into logos and contributes to poetry: "I wished for a system of thought that would leave my imagination free to create as it chose and yet make all that it created, or could create, part of the one history, and that the soul's. The Greeks certainly had such a system."[78] He confesses in "All Souls' Night": "I have mummy truths to tell."[79] His "mummy truths", he draws from the writers who were his masters - Swedenborg, Blake, the Neo-Platonists, but also among the mediums or near his Instructors, or also in his dreams or his visions and in myths.

The archetypes

The Jungian unconscious which represents the hoarding of the millenary experiences of mankind, expresses itself through the archetypes - first called "primordial images" - which are forms of representation. "The collective unconscious consists of the sum of the instincts and their correlates, the archetypes," Jung writes.[80] They are "the inherited possibilities of human imagination as it was from time immemorial."[81] Unconscious, they can only be postulated, but we become aware of them through certain typical images which recur in the psyche. Jung calls "inflation" the possession by the archetypes, indicating that the possessed person has been, as it were, inflated by something which is beyond him,or her, something collective and not personal; it is the poet's inspiration. For it is in the creative imagination that the "primordial images" become visible.

If Jung describes the archetypes as "deposits of the constantly repeated experiences of humanity,"[82] Yeats, condemning "all that is not tradition" explains: "[...] there is a subject-matter which has descended like the 'deposit' certain philosophers speak of"[83] and he goes on: "[...] this subject-matter is something I have received from the gen-

---

[76] *Variorum*, 810.
[77] *Letters*, 904.
[78] Dedication of *A Vision* (1925) to Vestigia XI.
[79] *Variorum*, 474.
[80] Jung, *Collected Works*, VIII, par. 281.
[81] Jung, *Collected Works*, VII, par. 101.
[82] Jung, *Collected Works*, VII, par. 109.
[83] *Essays and Introductions*, VIII.

erations, part of that compact with my fellow men made in my name before I was born." The poet gets in touch with this deposit in the "supernormal experience" and he ends: "I have met with ancient myths in my dreams, brightly lit; and I think it allied to the wisdom or instinct that guides a migratory bird."[84] There we have Yeats's theory on instincts, myths or archetypes and the Anima Mundi, or collective unconscious.

In the same way as we tried to know if the Anima Mundi was transcendental or immanent, we hesitate on the genesis of archetypal figures: do they come from a spiritual world, from pre-existing models suddenly remembered or revealed, or are they the fruit of ancestral experience stored in the memory? Are not these interpretations one and the same explanation? Yeats seems to believe so. For him, at certain moments, Jung's archetypes are identical to Plato's Forms.

Some Jungian archetypes appear under an abstract or geometrical form, the gyre, cycle, circle or sphere. They are already present in Pythagoras, Heraclites, Parmenides, Empedocles and Plato among whom all the circular movements are imperfect reflections of the immutable Sphere. For Jung: "God is an intelligible sphere whose centre is everywhere and whose circumference is nowhere."[85] Yeats uses this symbol of absolute perfection in *A Vision*. From a structural point of view, his myth "that was itself a reply to a myth"[86] is "centric,"[87] as he put it, circles within circles. The process of the human soul and that of history are both circular: "All circles are but a single archetypal circle seen according to different measures or time."[88] The geometric skeletons of *A Vision*, primordial images, are used in the poems which describe gyres, such as "A Dialogue of Self and Soul"[89] where the antithetical element grows stronger when the primary one weakens. The poet even succeeds in settling in a gyre for, as "Blood and the Moon" testifies,[90] the tower where he lived possessed a winding stair, a reification of the gyre. Yeats wanted to make the transfer of images easy - using domestic architecture as well as philosophy and poetry.

Other archetypes appear under a human or semi-human form, as gods and goddesses, or in any other aspects of which we find numberless examples in mythology. Jung devoted much time to the study of myths which he considered as fundamental expressions of the psyche. They appear under similar forms among all the peoples and through all the ages. Yeats, perhaps because he was a poet, sometimes gave an autonomous life to the images of the Anima Mundi: then they are faeries or the souls of the dead. In ancient Irish literature, he appreciates the superhuman abundance; in his poetry he tries to create ubris, the inordinate, intense passion, the everlasting:

---

[84] *Essays and Introductions*, VIII.
[85] Jung, *Collected Works*, XIV, 47.
[86] *Explorations*, 392.
[87] *Letters*, 829.
[88] *A Vision*, 140.
[89] *Variorum*, 477.
[90] *Variorum*, 480.

> [...] certain men-at-arms there were
> Whose images, in the Great Memory stored,
> Come with loud cry and panting breast
> To break upon a sleeper's rest.[91]

One of these warriors can fight against a demon for a hundred years (*The Wanderings of Oisin*); ideal lovers are changed into swans, eternally united by a golden chain ("Baile and Aillinn"); a man in love with the infinite leads his boat out of the world (*The Shadowy Waters*). Fantastic creatures also come from the Great Memory:

> The Second Coming! hardly are those words out
> When a vast image out of Spiritus Mundi
> Troubles my sight.[92]

Spiritus Mundi, which he defines in his notes to his poems as "a general storehouse of images which have ceased to be a property of any personality or spirit"[93] is the other name of the Anima Mundi, the store of images. The history of religions, in the broader sense, including mythology and folklore, constitutes a rich mine of archetypes. Folklore helped him to define the relations between sleeping and waking. He delighted in the stories where faeries kidnap new brides or children and keep them in an extraterrestrial realm. Life in faery-land is characterized by its intensity: "A woman, said still to be living, was taken, from near a village called Ballisodare, and when she came home after seven years, she had no toes - she had danced them all off."[94] Faeries have kept something of the splendour of the gods of ancient myths and one notices everywhere the combined presence of the physical and the spiritual: "Is Eden far away."[95] The Theosophical and Rosicrucian societies, which Yeats joined between 1887 and 1890, taught him that the material world is an emanation of the spiritual world. In the Society of Psychic Research, in the same way as in the beliefs of Irish country-people, he found the confirmation of the existence of an anti-world, the invisible complement of the earth.

For Jung, the Self can appear in dreams in the guise of a hermaphrodite figure - a symbol of totality, or be represented by a treasure which it is difficult to reach, or by geometrical figures, circle, wheel, square, set in a concentric manner, "mandalas", i.e. in Sanskrit magic circles. Jung notices that the symbolism of the mandala spontaneously arises in dreams and visions, accompanied by a feeling of harmony and peace: "[...] this symbol is not only to be found all through the East, but also among us."[96]

---

[91] „The Tower", *Variorum*, 412.

[92] "The Second Coming", *Variorum*, 402.

[93] *Variorum*, 822.

[94] William Butler Yeats, *Uncollected Prose*, ed. John P.Frayne (London: Macmillan, 1970), I, 177; Cf. also *Mythologies*, 76.

[95] *The Shadowy Waters*, *Variorum*, 745.

[96] Carl Gustav Jung, *Psyche and Symbol: A selection from the writings of C.G. Jung*, ed. Violet S. de Laszelo (New York: Doubleday Anchor Books, 1958), 318.

Yeats's *Secret Rose Stories*, also make use of mandalas. In "The Heart of the Spring," a monastery stands in the heart of the island; around it, the landscape describes concentric circles: lilies and roses protect the sanctuary; they are Spring flowers, symbolizing resurrection. "Rosa Alchemica" is set in a Temple, a "square building,"[97] in a vast circular room. A circle inscribed within a square enclosure, this mandala is the representative of divine powers and the psychagogic image which leads to illumination. The rose orders space. It is above and reflected below, in keeping with Hermes Trismegistes' famous formula: "What is below is like what is above." Such is the case in "Rosa Alchemica": "Upon the ceiling was an immense rose wrought in mosaic,"[98] and the dance is the reflection of this rose.

These archetypes often follow an antithetical pattern. Jung's animus and anima find their poetic equivalents in the tower - a masculine symbol - and the winding stair -a feminine symbol -, the lion and the virgin, Apollo and Dionysos etc. For Yeats and for Jung, one pole implies the other: body/soul, conscious/unconscious, good/evil. In "Blood and the Moon," Yeats identifies himself both with the tower and the stair. The first lines of "Vacillation" state the problem:

> Between extremities
> Man runs his course.[99]

And Yeats adds in his letters: "To me all things are made of the conflict of two states of consciousness, beings or persons which die each other's life, live each other's death. This is true of life and death themselves. Two cones (or whirls), the apex of each in the other's base."[100] This configuration of the double cones is an archetype. Nothing is more striking in the evolution of Yeats's poetry than the progressive replacement of a simple dialectics - the opposition of two terms - by a dialectics accompanied by a synthesis. If the structure of the first poems is based on binary contrasts - the human and the faery land, the temporal and the eternal - later, Yeats solves these "antinomies of day and night" in a third element or by the interpenetration of opposites:

> 'Fair and foul are near of kin,
> And fair needs foul', I cried.[101]

The poem "There" makes us enter the Great Memory directly:

> There all the barrel-hoops are knit,
> There all the serpent-tails are bit,

---

[97] *Mythologies*, 281.
[98] *Mythologies*, 287.
[99] *Variorum*, 499.
[100] *Letters*, 918.
[101] "Crazy Jane talks with the Bishop", *Variorum*,. 513.

>   There all the gyres converge as one,
>   There all the planets drop into the Sun.[102]

In each line, the images are those of the complete circle, the ouroboros.

Finally, the effort that the elaboration of the mask requires conjures up the individuation process as described by Jacobi: "[...] the individuation process represents a dialectical interaction between the contents of the unconscious and of consciousness: symbols provide the necessary bridges, linking and reconciling the often seemingly irreconcilable contradictions between the two 'sides'."[103]

The Yeatsian archetypes are, like Jung's, impersonal images. In 1921, the poet enumerates his main symbols to T.Sturge Moore: "Sun and Moon (in all phases), Tower, Mask, Trees (Trees with Mask hanging on the trunk)."[104] One could add a few others like the rose and the golden bird or like the harmonious chestnut-tree or the dancer that cannot be distinguished from the dance ("Among School-Children"). Yeatsian poetry borrows images from folklore, ancient Irish myths, the visionary poetry of Blake or Shelley, seances, alchemical research, spiritualist societies, philosophy - from Plato and Berkeley and the Upanishads. When he went from cottage to cottage with Lady Gregory, collecting the stories of the Irish country-people, he had the impression he was descending "into some fibrous darkness, into some matrix out of which everything had come."[105] Jung uses the same terms: " The unconscious is the matrix of all metaphysical statements, of all mythology, of all philosophy."[106]. When Yeats climbed to the top floor of a house in Soho or Holloway, in quest of "the wisdom of some fat old medium,"[107] or when he read Swedenborg, he found everywhere "an ancient system of belief:" "[...] like Paracelsus who claimed to have collected his knowledge from midwife and hangman, I was discovering a philosophy"[108] -a philosophy as old as human thought. Mythic tales, the spirits in the seances, visions and dreams, all of them emerge from the unconscious. "I have always sought to bring my mind close to the mind of Indian and Japanese poets, old women in Connacht, mediums in Soho [...]; to immerse it in the general mind where that mind is scare separable from what we have begun to call 'the subconscious'."[109]

It seems that Yeats's final position is that the greatest literature issues from a dialectic alliance of the antithetical imagination of the mask and of visionary imagination. Whatever may be the images in use, art is symbolic and symbols link the temporal and eternal worlds, either in the Platonic perspective or in the Jungian one. To account for

---

[102] *Variorum*, 557.

[103] Jolande Jacobi, *Complex, Archetype, Symbol in the Pyschology of C.G.Jung*, transl. Ralph Manheim (Princeton: Princeton University Press, 1959), 115.

[104] W.B.Yeats and T.Sturge Moore, *Their Correspondence 1901-37*, ed. Ursula Bridge (New York: Oxford University Pres, 1953), 38.

[105] *Essays and Introductions*, 429.

[106] Jung, *Collected Works*, XI, par. 899.

[107] *Explorations*, 30.

[108] *Explorations*, 31.

[109] *Mythologies*, 343.

the origin of images, Yeats who uses Platonic terminology, like Jung, calls on the archetypes of the Anima Mundi: "I cannot now think symbols less than the greatest of all powers whether they are used consciously by the masters of magic, or half unconsciously by their successors, the poet, the musician and the artist."[110] Yeats and Jung, though the second was born ten years after the poet, follow the same roads. Jung was interested in symbols and myths when exploring the dreams of his patients, as revealing the work of the unconscious. Yeats discovered a fair number of the same symbols through the study of folklore, philosophies and heterodox mysticism, even if he first wanted "metaphors for poetry."[111] Both looked for a confirmation of their ideas in Plato and the Neo-Platonists and in alchemical or gnostic texts.

One could wonder whether Yeats, who believes in the existence of a Great Memory, is not an imitator rather than a creator in so far as he only brings back to the surface images which have preceded him. This would ignore the poetical context in which he took care to insert the image. The impact of "Byzantium" or of "The Second Coming" for instance is felt by the reader who focusses on the poem and not by him who looks for the keys in *A Vision*, even if it can be useful. To take up archetypes is not enough to create a poetical work. Yeats knew it who, having conjured up "a naked woman of incredible beauty, standing upon a pedestal, and shooting an arrow at a star," gathered connected symbols drawn from folklore, archeology, Greek mythology, dreams [...] to complete his partial vision, then worked on the verse, the syntax, the words, the rhythm - "the purpose of rhythm is to prolong the moment of contemplation:"[112]

> God guard me from those thoughts men think
> In the mind alone;
> He that sings a lasting song
> Thinks in a marrow-bone.[113]

So poetry gives a new dimension to myth by using conscious literary devices, fruit of the creator's labour, of Adam's curse. The poet's creative life is spent between the unconscious which unites and the conscious which separates, between the universal and the personal. So tragic art is the product of the meeting of the natural and the supernatural in the conscious unconsciousness which allows the revelation of "mummy truths" which the conscious alone could never perceive but which, in an unconscious state would remain uncompleted. The poet has conceived devices to hold back the vision which fades by daylight. He needs both this "old mummy wheat" that he draws "in the mad abstract dark" and "wholesome food" ripened by the sun ("On a Picture of a Black Centaur by Edmund Dulac")[114] - the unconscious and the conscious. Yeats valued his art too much to let himself be submerged by the flow of

---

[110] *Essays and Introductions*, 50.
[111] *A Vision*, 8.
[112] *Essays and Introductions*, 159.
[113] "A Prayer for Old Age", *Variorum*, 553.
[114] *Variorum*, 442.

images from the unconscious. It was his wife who practised automatic writing. As to him, he said: "I am awake and asleep, at my moment of revelation, self-possessed in self-surrender."[115] He tries to reproduce some of this state of conscious unconsciousness which is that of the poet at the moment of creation. As to Jung, he says: "The Unconscious can realize itself only with the help of consciousness and under its constant control."[116] Yet the effort of writing must open on its contrary and give the impression of being done on the spur of the moment, in a dazzling instant. The poet is the conjurer of illusion:

> [...] A line will take us hours maybe;
> Yet, if it does not seem a moment's thought,
> Our stitching and unstitching has been naught.[117]

---

[115] *Essays and Introductions*, 524.
[116] Jung, *Letters*, I, 240.
[117] "Adam's Curse", *Variorum*, 204.

Modernism and the Magazines

MALCOLM BRADBURY (Norwich)

1.

In the early 1950s, a young research student intending to write a thesis on the subject of British Modernism, I decided to pursue the role that was played in its promotion and development by magazines and 'little reviews' - the many and various *avant garde* journals that functioned somewhere between the offices of manifesto and discoverer of new talent. At this time the study of Modernism, which today flourishes so extensively, was just beginning, even as Modernism itself was just ending. It was still possible to interview some of the most interesting participants. I talked to T.S. Eliot, in his office at Faber and Faber in Russell Square, from which *The Criterion* was published. He sent me to see Ezra Pound, who had been active with *The Egoist*, during his confinement in a mental ward in St. Elizabeth´s Hospital, Washington, DC, after he had been put there to avoid a charge of treason. I had help from Edgell Rickword, editor of *The Calendar of Modern Letters*, from F.R. Leavis and some of the other contributors to *Scrutiny*, from John Lehmann, editor of *New Writing*, and from a good number of other editorial performers or magazine contributors who had been involved with a vast variety of literary magazines through from the years before the Great War to the 1950s.

My notion was that by studying the magazines (not hard to do now, but a difficult task then, since many periodicals were difficult to trace, despite the archives of the British Museum) from the 1890s to 1950 it was possible to follow out the day-to-day - or rather the month to month, quarter to quarter, year to year - development of arguments, ideas and personalities that shaped the literary debate and formed the aesthetic perceptions and quarrels that guided the onward movement of modern writing in Britain. It was in the periodicals that the growth of new movements and intellectual themes, the lines of influence and the critical judgements on past and present, could be most clearly be seen unfolding. As is usual in these matters, simple presumptions I had about the development of modern British writing and its cultural debate and institutions soon gave way to more complicated ones. Old arguments, forgotten personalities and confused allegiances emerged afresh from the many pages I was turning. I´ve always been grateful for lighting on this particular theme, for two reasons. One is that it gave a detailed, vivid history of modern writing and its personalities which was indeed day to day, and not always consistent with the textbooks. The other was that magazines are the real frontage of writing, the battlefront of literary culture, the maximum and most topical point of encounter with reader. They argue the case for writers, ways of writing, movements. We can usually trace their sales, how they were received, the impact they had on a given moment of cultural interaction, the difference they made.[1]

What I aimed to show was that literary magazines are a significant cultural institution, which deserve attention in their own right. Like so much else in the cultural transformation of the late nineteenth century, with its growth of print and periodical, they went, as a genre, through a great change. In the first half of the nineteenth century, the "Great Reviews" of general educated opinion, like the *Edinburgh* and the *Quarterly* had heavily dominated literary debate and argument, shaped the reputations of writers, poets and movements, and been a major place for the publication of new work in serial form. That situation was often to be looked back upon with considerable nostalgia in the pages of their early twentieth century successors, in a period of magazine fragmentation and far less cultural consensus.[2] By the mid-Victorian years magazine culture was already greatly changing. According to Matthew Arnold in his essay "The Function of Criticism at the Present Time," by his time it was already necessary to turn to France to find examples of the serious review at its true work, the pursuit of the best that is known and thought in the world (his great example was the *Revue des deux mondes*), whereas in Britain "our organs of criticism are organs of men and parties having practical ends to serve, and with them those practical ends are the first thing and the play of mind the second." Many of the Victorian novelists found publication in the household magazines of the popular marketplace, in which Dickens, Thackeray and other contemporaries became formidable editors. By the end of the nineteenth century the growth of the commercial magazine and the growth of a mass reading public had more or less dissolved the equation whereby the review of general

---

[1] An important and indeed pioneering study is Frederick J. Hoffman, Charles Allen and Carolyn F. Ulrich, *The Little Magazine: A History and Bibliography* (Princeton: Princeton University Press, 1946), to which my own work was indebted. In that volume, which is particularly concerned with little magazines in the USA, Charles Allen comments, reasonably, that the magazines studied "have stood, from 1912 to the present, defiantly in the front ranks of the battle for a mature literature. They have helped fight this battle by being the first to present such writers as Sherwood Anderson, Ernest Hemingway, William Faulkner, Erskine Caldwell, T.S. Eliot -- by first publishing, in fact, about 80% of our most important, post-1912 critics, novelists, poets and storytellers. Further, they have introduced and sponsored every noteworthy literary movement or school that has made its appearance in American during the last thirty years."

[2] One of the strong achievements of *Scrutiny* was its studies of the institutions of literary culture, and it ran a fair number of articles on periodicals. A notable series was by R.G. Cox, "The Great Reviews," *Scrutiny*, 4, 1 & 2 (June and September 1937), which challenged the familiar view that their claim to fame was that they had excoriated the Romantic poets, and argued that "with their extraordinary influence and authority [they] played a major part in creating for the writers of their age that informed, intelligent and critical public without which no literature can survive for very long, and which is so conspicuously lacking today." "At their best, the Great Reviews provided [...] criticism of the general tendencies and the particular writers of their age which is often better than anything else on the same subjects throughout the century that followed," Denys Thompson observed in another article, "A Hundred Years of the Higher Journalism," *Scrutiny*, 4, 1 (June 1935).

affairs was also the major journal of criticism, and probably also the chief outlet for significant new literary publication.

So, by the turn of the century, gloom on the periodicals question was the order of the day. When in 1908 Ford Madox Hueffer founded *The English Review* - which under his editorship was a notable enterprise in attempting to link the old review format with the new "critical attitude" consequent on Modernism, and introduce a new generation of experimental writers - he confessed the risky absurdity of his task: "To imagine that a magazine devoted to imaginative literature and technical criticism alone would find more than a hundred readers was a delusion that I in no way had," he later reflected.[3] Through most of the magazine ventures of the twentieth century, this note of gloom would become a familiar feature of the periodicals, that associated themselves with new writing and the modern movement. They were forever hunting angels, patrons, subscribers; they were constantly, and no doubt sensibly, anticipating their own demise; they were ephemeral, episodic, unreliable, always going through phoenix-like deaths and rebirths. When T.S. Eliot finally had to close down *The Criterion* with the issue for January 1939 (down to 300 subscribers), he struck with finality the note that went with the task of trying to run the modern literary and intellectual periodical:

> For the immediate future, perhaps for a long way ahead, the continuity of culture may have to be maintained by a very small number of people indeed [...]. It will not be the large organs of opinion, or the old periodicals, it must be the small and obscure papers and reviews, those who are hardly read by anyone but their own contributors, that will keep critical thought alive, and encourage authors of original talent.[4]

The papers Eliot refers to are, of course, the "little magazines," the marginal papers that, as the nineteenth century died, started to emerge, in a wide variety of forms, and campaign for new literary publication, *avant garde* adventure, critical and aesthetic debate. It took a whole series of new and modern "cultural" institutions to provide the foundations for their activities: the growth of "Bohemian" movements and groupings (on the "French" model), the emergence of a cultural war between the artists and the philistines, a new degree of political indifference among writers committed to high aesthetic doctrines, the fading of a socially dominant educated reading public and the downward drift of "general" taste, and the various other forces that led to the development of what by the end of the nineteenth century was already being called an *avant garde*. We can early find British origins for the "little magazines" in various ventures from the mid-Victorian period, starting roughly with the age of "movements" that developed in the wake of the revolutions of 1848. This was at a time when "bohemia" first began to be systematically talked of (Henri Murger's *Scènes de la vie de bohême* appeared in 1851), and alliance between painterly and literary movements intensified. A classic example was the Pre-Raphaelite monthly *The Germ*, which published four issues in 1850. Uniting the verbal and the visual, founded in the spirit of a coterie or

---

[3] Ford Madox Ford (Hueffer), *Return to Yesterday* (London: Liveright, 1931), 378.
[4] T.S. Eliot, "Last Words," *The Criterion* 18, 71 (January 1939).

"movement," fighting a war to establish a new style, it provided a useful model for the magazinists of the Decadent 1890s.

The 1890s saw a great flourishing of small magazines. Most emphasized the link between new writing and new art (painting, design, illustration), announced their alliance with an aesthetic campaign or coterie, and displayed the growing fragmentation and privatization of the publishing process. There was the *Century Guild Hobby Horse* (1884-94), edited by A.H. Mackmurdo and Herbert Horne, a periodical which was first and foremost concerned with *art nouveau* and architecture. Through the participation of Selwyn Image, it also printed contributions from members of the Rhymers' Club. In its last phase, as a coterie magazine selling around 500 copies of an issue, it was taken over by two important publishers, Elkin Matthews and John Lane, who were seeking their place in the changing marketplace. This made it an antecedent of another John Lane venture, *The Yellow Book* (1894-97), perhaps the best remembered magazine to come out of the magaziney 1890s. "And it´s not even yellow," complained Oscar Wilde, who, despite all the folklore that associated him with it, did not contribute. It was the "Yellow Dwarf" personality of the editor Henry Harland, the American bohemian who had served the requisite period stint in Paris bohemia ("Ah, you're not mad about style, but I am. Why doesn't everyone live in Paris?"), and Aubrey Beardsley who created its distinctive dandyish character. Of course it caused public offence, and some thought it should be prosecuted by Act of Parliament. "So far as literature can be lynched, I was," Max Beerbohm said, after his article "A Defence of Cosmetics" appeared in the magazine.

Published by John Lane in Vigo Street, an original new publisher, *The Yellow Book* was, naturally, yellow-bound and expensively produced. Its volumes clearly shaped or set period taste, and added art, style and high amusement to the idea of the "New" or "Modern," which the paper much cultivated. Thus the "New Woman" and her male counterpart the "New Dandy," the "New Hedonism" and the "New Cosmetics," as well as the new Paris movements and the new dance, preoccupied its fashion-conscious pages. Evanescence was part of the mood; there were deliberately no bulky items, no sections of novels, essentially "glimpses" and "impressions." As the Nineties survivor Holbrook Jackson said in his evocative book *The Eighteen Nineties* (1913), *The Yellow Book* was in its way an upmarket equivalent of the *Daily Mail*. They were contrasting forms of Nineties sensationalism; *The Yellow Book* and the Yellow Press virtually coincided. "The one was unique, individual, a little weird, often exotic, demanding the right to *be* - in its own way even to waywardness; but this one was really an abnormal minority, and in no sense national. The other was broad, general, popular; it was the majority, the man-in-the-street awaiting a new medium of expression." As he also noted, *The Yellow Book* was the one that passed away, while the *Daily Mail* sailed successfully on into the mass market future.[5]

---

[5] Holbrook Jackson, *The Eighteen Nineties* (1913; reissued with an introduction by Malcolm Bradbury, London: Harvill, 1988), 61-2. There is an interesting article on the mixture of "new writing" and "new journalism" in the 1890s in John Stokes, *In the Nineties* (London: Harvester, 1989). On the whole topic of 1890s little magazines, see Ian Fletcher, "Deca-

The 1890s was a true magazining period, in part because all the conventions of publication, the costs of printing, and means of distribution were changing in response to a new marketplace. It saw many other adventures in ephemeral papers, most appealing to the claims of the "aesthetic." Their character generally resembled a manifesto, their contents usually professed some manner of distinctive and flamboyant artistic allegiance. When *The Savoy* (1895-96) started, selling at 2s 6d., expensive but still half the price of *The Yellow Book*, it claimed to reject the going movements ("decadence," "naturalism"), for "good art" in general. Yet this was yet another declaration of "aestheticism," which had in effect become a movement itself. From Anglo-French and painterly origins, *The Savoy* printed the familiar Nineties experimentalists: Beardsley, Arthur Symonds, George Moore, Bernard Shaw, Havelock Ellis and the French symbolists. It was, effectively, succeeded by *The Dome* (1897-), "a quarterly containing examples of all the arts" (it later became a monthly, and sold at the yet more modest price of one shilling). Another "aesthetic" magazine, its eclectic policy let it publish the work of the London symbolists, the poetry of the Celtic Twilight. All these magazine adventures were versions of the Bohemian Chap-Books that appeared round this date in many cities, not least New York (where Harland learned his trade) and Chicago, where "bohemia" became the rage (it still is).

But the lesson, as well as the spirit, of *fin de siècle* was precisely that all to do with style, art and their novelties are by nature evanescent, fleeting glimpses and impressions captured for their instant, then let go on the river of time. And, by the turn of the century, in times rendered sober by the Boer War and the advent of many forms of technological modernity, the magazine scene changed again. The old order of magazines - the magisterial, general "great reviews" - was beginning to die, giving way to more specialist journals generally concerned with new politics and world affairs. The small coterie magazines, committed to the "new" in everything, had also passed their butterfly season. The question of the character of serious literary publication still had to be settled, in the unstable world of magazines as in that of book publishing. In the last Victorian years, there was also a lull in movements themselves, the chief source of the newer magazines. As the century dawned, it already seemed that the modern writer was essentially commercial, an H.G. Wells or Arnold Bennett, writing not for the small journal but for a growing popular book market and the new daily newspapers. Hence there was presumably no room for the small and experimental magazines of aesthetic "modernity." They were, like the *fin de siècle* itself, ephemeral.

2.

Fortunately this aesthetic, elusive dismay proved premature. The great revival of new magazines was still to come - though not until the years shortly before the Great War, when there was a sudden and massive multiplication of movements and artistic cam-

---

dence and the Little Magazines," in Malcolm Bradbury, David Palmer and Ian Fletcher, eds., *Decadence and the 1890s* (London: Edward Arnold, 1979), 172-202.

paigns, many of them as a result of the new radiation from Paris. Those who believed, as most *bien-pensants* did, that Britain was eternally and incorrigibly the land of the Philistine took the age of the Edwardian bookman as the normal condition of things. But there were those, like Ford Madox Hueffer (with impeccable origins in the Pre-Raphaelites and the Germano-French heritage), who believed in the need for a periodical forum for cultural debate and the advancement of a modernist literature. Hueffer also believed in all the things that went with this: the need for writers and artists to associate in groups or movements, the need for a new "critical attitude," the conviction of a true *refuse* that talent was always denied by the dominant cultural outlets, and that the daring Young were always at risk from the Establishment Old. The venture where he hoped to act was *The English Review*, which he conceived in 1908. There were signs of change in the cultural climate; his friends Joseph Conrad and Henry James were producing some of their most experimental work. As one observant American commentator explained in 1930 about this climate:

> The advance of the little magazine in England was not hastened by any such need for national expression as existed in the United States. But the body of dead tradition that had accumulated was even more formidable. There were the older reviews, basking in a tyrannous senility; Mr [Robert] Bridges had just succeeded Alfred Austin as poet laureate; and the lending libraries [...] did what they could to prolong the Victorian epoch.[6]

The English Review - described on the title page as "a periodical devoted to the arts, to letter and ideas" - appeared in December 1908, a bulky monthly in a blue paper cover. Hueffer was an original: a writer's writer, a man deeply committed to the encouraging other writers. But he was not a good businessman, and had borrowed half the £5,000 capital from a politician friend. Despite its dignified frontage and grand name, the fate of *The English Review* was always precarious, but he did succeed in keeping it in his hands until 1910, when it passed to others. The *English Review* has (rightly) been much honoured in retrospect. As Hueffer's one-time assistant editor Douglas Goldring put it:

> In 1909 there were distinct signs of a revival [in literature] and Mr Hueffer - a critic of discernment and courage, possessed by a distinguished passion for good writing - made his choice of all the best work that was available. Quality was the sole criterion; and among the then 'unknown' he discovered almost everyone who was worth discovering. There was something gallant about Mr Hueffer's editorial adventure, I believe it had rarely had its equal before or since, and that adequate thanks have never been accorded to him for it.[7]

Ezra Pound gave a yet more impassioned assessment:

---

[6] William Troy, "The Story of the Little Magazines," *The Bookman* 70, 5 (January 1930): 476.

[7] Douglas Goldring, "Modern Critical Prose," *The Chapbook* 2, 8 (February 1920): 10.

the EVENT of 1909-1910 was Ford Madox (Hueffer) Ford's ENGLISH REVIEW, and no greater condemnation of the utter filth of the whole social system of that time can be dug up than the fact of that review's passing out of his hands.[8]

Hueffer's chief aim in *The English Review's* stout pages was to bring together the best of the old guard - Thomas Hardy, W.B. Yeats, Henry James, Joseph Conrad (with whom Hueffer collaborated on three novels) - with the new, or as Hueffer called them in *grand maitre* style, "Les Jeunes:"

> Les Jeunes, as they chronologically presented themselves to us, were Mr Pound, Mr D.H. Lawrence, Mr Norman Douglas, Mr [F.S.] Flint, 'H.D.,' Richard Aldington, Mr T.S. Eliot [...] in our Editorial Salons they found chaises longues and sofas on which to stretch themselves while they discussed the fate of already fermenting Europe,

Hueffer reported, adding "A Movement in the Arts - any movement - leavens a whole Nation with astonishing rapidity."[9] Hueffer always claimed that what first roused him to action was the rejection by other literary papers of Thomas Hardy's poem "A Sunday Morning Tragedy," and he did great justice by the older literary writers. But the aim was no less to bring in new writers: "We aimed at founding an *aube de siècle Yellow Book*," he said. And the score of achievement is remarkably high - doubtless helped by the appearance in London of the young Ezra Pound, who was quickly running his own 'movement' in Frith Street. May Sinclair introduced the two: "the greatest writer to the greatest editor" of the day, she said. And the magazine is to be seen against the background of a newly alive literary life, filled with youthful and confident geniuses like Pound, Wyndham Lewis and D.H. Lawrence, a fair number of whom first found print in his pages.

Though it was *avant garde* publication, the actual format of *The English Review* - one of the starting magazines of serious literary publication in Britain this century - was staid, dignified, traditional. Political articles of considerable consequence appeared; the little magazine was set within the case of the great public review. Hueffer's editorials, later republished as *The Critical Attitude*, discussed the writers of the day, his own Flaubertian standards, the prevailing philistinisim of readers. The first issue had Hardy's "suppressed" poem, Henry James' "The Jolly Comer," and the serialization of H.G. Wells' (best) novel, *Tonobungay*, as well as pieces on politics and international affairs. When Ezra Pound's "Provencal" poem "Sestina: Altaforte" appeared, squeezed between Eden Philpotts and an article in French on peace and war in Europe, the signs of new American influences were clear. Lawrence gained his first national publication here in November 1909 (the poem "A Still Afternoon"), and Hueffer promoted him with publishers ("He introduced me to Edward Garnett, who introduced me to the world," Lawrence explained). Money troubles grew, and the paper was losing £120 a month. At the end of 1910 Sir Alfred Mond bought it and installed a new editor from the *Daily Mail*. Some key contributors -

---

[8] Ezra Pound, "This Hulme Business," *Townsman*, 2, 5 (January 1939).
[9] Ford Madox Hueffer, *Thus to Revisit* (London: Chapman and Hall, 1921), 59-64.

Joseph Conrad, Lawrence, Hardy, Bridges, E.M. Forster - stuck with the paper, which went on through various editors and political standpoints, but with declining literary standards, until it merged in 1937 with the conservative *National Review*. But its lasting importance was in providing, during the two Hueffer years, the outlets, chaises longues and sofas that allowed a complex and lively literary community to form.

The *English Review* restored the magazine climate; from it came many smaller spin-offs. A number of *Enlish Review* contributors published in a new small poetry magazine called *The Thrush* (1909-10). One was Hueffer himself, who was so overwhelmed by the quality and daring of "Les Jeunes" that he published here a highly premature farewell to literature (happily he was still writing furiously when he died in 1939). Douglas Goldring started another little magazine, *The Tramp* (1910-11), hoping, he said somewhat oddly, to blend the literary distinction of the *English Review* with the commercial success of *Country Life*. While it conveyed the Georgian "nature poetry" tone of the period, it is chiefly noted (unlike *Country Life*) for publishing the Futurist Manifesto by Marinetti ("We will destroy museums, libraries, and fight against moralism, feminism and all utilitarian cowardice [...]. The essential elements of our poetry will be courage, audacity and revolt"). Futurism was also the interest of Michael Sadler, who with the young John Middleton Murry started another, much more important venture, *Rhythm*, a quarterly of art, music and literature, which produced its first number in Summer 1911. This ambitiously announced itself as "a magazine with a purpose. Its title is the ideal of a new art to which it will endeavour to give expression in England." The magazine was advised by the Scots painter J.D. Fergusson, living in Paris, who promoted "Fauveiste" ideals. The now very familiar comparison was drawn; this would be, said Murry, *The Yellow Book* of the modern movement. This time the link is more appropriate, not least because of the close allegiance forged between writing and painting, the high quality of illustration, and the close attention that was paid to new movements and tendencies, especially in Europe. Murry, a serious and solemn critic, wrote on Bergson´s and Croce´s philosophy. There were articles on Fauveism, reproductions of Picasso, Derain, Augustus John, Jessie Dismorr. Katherine Mansfield appeared, first in Murry´s personal life, then in print, often under pseudonyms. She joined the editorial team, and the two lived together in the *Rhythm* flat at 57 Chancery Lane.

Following the golden rule of these things, the magazine was ever in financial trouble. When the sponsor, Stephen Swift, went bankrupt, Mansfield and Murry found themselves carrying heavy debts. However friends, including Edward Marsh, rallied with helpful financial or literary contributions. The intervention of Marsh gave *Rhythm* a link with the 'Georgian Poetry' movement. Also, through the magazine Murry and Mansfield met D.H. Lawrence and Frieda ("it´s a daft paper, but the folk seem rather nice"), founding a crucial association that would have many consequences later. The magazine printed Lawrence´s story "The Soiled Rose" in the May 1913 issue, and he then reviewed for it. By now the paper had just been reconstructed under a new name, *The Blue Review*. Of this only three monthly issues appeared - containing striking stories by Mansfield, poetry by W.W. Gibson, James Elroy Flecker, articles by Hugh Walpole and Frank Swinnterton, and Lawrence on German books - before it died with the issue for July 1913. Crucially, though, its period of publication covered a major period of adventure in British writing, during which a variety of new movements - Georgianism, Fauvisme, Futurism, Imagism - declared themselves.

By now the smaller magazines were culturally important chiefly for their campaigning support for this burst of movements, which were in fact the founding movements of early British Modernism. Much of the energy had moved into poetry. Now, fortunately, the very seemly Poetry Society asked Harold Monro to reorganize their small publication *The Poetry Gazette*, which he re-started as the quarterly *The Poetry Review* in January 1912, while in 1913 he opened the Poetry Bookshop (38 Great Russell Street) for readings, events and book publications. It published the five volumes of *Georgian Poetry* edited by Edward Marsh, and *Des Imagistes*, the key anthology edited (anonymously) by Ezra Pound. By virtue of its Poetry Society funding, *Poetry Review* had an open and easy-going policy, but it succeeded in advancing several new and crucial *avant garde* campaigns. F.S. Flint contributed articles on French poetry which started the campaign for *vers libre*. Ezra Pound announced his credo in an essay "Prologomena" ("the trampling down of every convention that impedes or obscures the determination of the law, or the precise rendering of the impulse"). Rupert Brooke´s "The Old Vicarage, Grantchester," appeared here, and won the prize for the best poem. There were inevitable struggles with the tireless conservatism of the Poetry Society, till eventually Monro broke loose to found the quarterly *Poetry and Drama*. (The title *Poetry Review* stayed with the Poetry Society, and it ran as a very middlebrow and anti-modernist journal for many years, with some strong episodes of revival.) *Poetry and Drama* continued Monro´s eclectic and open door policy. However it followed out the fortunes of Imagism, flirted with Futurism (printing the new Futurist manifesto of 1913), and printed Rupert Brooke, Robert Frost (then living in London), and Ezra Pound ("Albatre"). With the December 1914 issue the magazine was suspended for a year, because of the national situation (the war had not after all been over by Christmas). It didn't return until 1919, in the very different form of the manifesto-like *The Chapbook*.

3.

In the years just before the Great War, then, small magazines, ranging from a public review (*English Review* to the small and elegant magazine of art and literature (*Rhythm*) to the poetry magazine (*Poetry Review*) became important outlets for the cultural and artistic transformation sweeping through the Western arts at this time. This was the period which Hueffer called "the opening world," which Virginia Woolf saw as the era when human character and the arts all changed ("In or about December 1910 human character changed"), and Wyndham Lewis saw as the time of "a new art coming to flower to celebrate or to announce a 'new age'." The magazines displayed not just the change and excitement but the chaotic multiplicity of directions, the crossover of the generations, the constant confused trading of allegiances and alliances.

Lawrence saw himself for a time as a Georgian, then as an Imagist. Ezra Pound was for a time the foremost, most doctrinal Imagist, then a Vorticist. Lewis identified himself with the Omega Workshops of Roger Fry, before falling out with "Mr Fry´s curtain and pincushion factory in Fitzroy Square" and going on to found Vorticism and the Rebel Art Centre. The magazines chart the transformation of a cultural scene in active motion. One thing was becoming clear: small-manifesto-like magazines with specialist and 'advanced' readerships were now one of the chief weapons of artistic transformation - providing an environment for work that could not win publication in the conventional magazines or with most established publishers, encouraging radical experiment, opening up urgent debate about the character of modern writing. More, it was through the magazines that the important new writers of the time - the Lawrences and Lewises, Eliots and Pounds - first found their way.

Perhaps the most conspicuous example of the active role of the new magazines was the way Ezra Pound self-consciously manipulated the periodical and publishing scene to establish his transatlantic *avant garde* world of "Make It New." Pound marked an important new stage in the whole affair, systematically linking together British, European and American modernism. Arriving in London from the Middle West via Venice in 1908, he soon became an active impresario within the movement, magazine and publishing scene, acting as European editor for various magazines now starting up in parallel on the further side of the Atlantic - above all Harriet Monroe´s *Poetry (Chicago)*, founded in 1912, and later Margaret Anderson´s *Little Review*. In 1912, in a Kensington teashop, he came up with the idea of a 'mouvemong' on the French model, called "Imagisme," and persuaded his friend Hilda Doolittle to begin signing her poems "H.D. Imagiste." Imagisme first laid out its manifesto in the transatlantic pages of *Poetry (Chicago)*. But Pound´s ambition was both to bridge the Atlantic and to have a magazine of his own, which he could steer as he wished. He did this on the cuckoo principle, becoming involved with a feminist magazine *The New Freewoman* (formerly *The Freewoman*), "an individualist review" in newspaper format which published its first number on 15 June, 1913. The editor was Dora Marsden, the backer Harriet Shaw Weaver, who would prove one of the great patrons of a time when Modernism depended greatly on the kindness of strangers, mostly ladies of means. Pound met both, and offered to supply them with advanced literary contributions. In Paris he also met a fellow American, the poet John Gould Fletcher, and suggested he should finance a literary review under his, Pound´s, editorship. When Fletcher agreed, Pound then suggested that, if he became literary editor of *The New Freewoman*, Fletcher put up a monthly sum to pay his contributors. By the end of the year, Pound had stamped the paper with a distinct Poundian character, and was already negotiating a less gender-specific title. On 1 January 1914 the paper became *The Egoist*, and Pound passed on the literary editorship to his friend Richard Aldington.

From the first, Pound meant the paper to have an Anglo-American dimension, writing to Harriet Monroe: "I am sending you our left wing, *The [New] Freewoman*. I've taken charge of the literature dept. It will be convenient for things whereof one wants the Eng. copyright held. I pay a dmd. low rate, but it might be worth while as a supplement for some of your darlings." Since these darlings included such powerful new poets as Wallace Stevens, William Carlos Williams, Amy Lowell and Marianne Moore, it was an important bridge, and Pound was at the same time placing his British friends and contributors (Aldington, Yeats, Lawrence, Hueffer, etc.) in the American magazines. At various points he also attempted to get the rich Amy Lowell to take over the paper, and even edit it from Boston. After Aldington became literary editor, Pound yielded direct but not indirect control, exerting considerable influence. Famously he introduced James Joyce's work to Harriet Shaw Weaver, and got her to pay him a capital sum. Thus *The Egoist* was to publish *A Portrait of the Artist as a Young Man*, which appeared in 25 instalments between 2 February 1914, Joyce's 32nd birthday, and 1 September 1915. At Pound's instigation it also brought out the British edition in book form in 1917. Writing to Margaret Anderson, he described *The Egoist* as "an official organ" in which, "I and T.S. Eliot can appear once a month [...] and where Joyce can appear when he likes, and Wyndham Lewis can appear if he comes back from the war." He engineered the appointment of the young expatriate Eliot, another protege, as assistant editor in June 1917, with considerable consequences for the magazine future. Besides ensuring fruitful contacts with the USA, he took care to have equal contact with Paris and the French movements, poets, critics and philosophers, laying particular emphasis on Remy de Gourmont and Henri Bergson.

Above all the paper was the British outlet for Imagism and the broader tendencies and writers associated with it. The 15 August, 1913, issue of *The New Freewoman* has Rebecca West publishing an article on "Imagisme," no doubt at Pound's instigation. This is followed by the influential reprinting, from *Poetry (Chicago)*, of Flint's essay on the same subject, Pound's "A Few Don'ts By an Imagiste," and seven of Pound's Imagiste poems, the last being the famous "A Station in the Metro." Soon the paper was systematically promoting what it called "The Newer School," who included H.D., William Carlos Williams, Richard Aldington, D.H. Lawrence, Charlotte Mew, Marianne Moore, Robert Frost, and many more. By June 1914 the final 'e' of Imagism was dropped, the definitions have changed somewhat. May 1915 saw a special Imagist number, with an article by Flint giving its history back to the cafes of 1909; there were various discussions of the major poets and tenets. In 1915 the fortnightly became a monthly, and printed some of Wyndham Lewis's Vorticist novel *Tarr*, though he had not yet come back from the War. In 1917, after Eliot joined, major critical articles by the most interesting critic of the day started appearing regularly. January 1918 also saw a striking Henry James number, with excellent essays by Eliot and Pound, while the issue for September 1919 contained Eliot's influential essay "Tradition and the Individual Talent." In 1918 perhaps the most daring venture began, when extracts from Joyce's *Ulysses* began appearing. In December 1919 the *Egoist* ended, with, according to Pound, only 153 subscribers. It has justly been called the first of the British "little magazines" - marked by its firm commitment to generation, movement and tendency, by its critical energy and impassioned aesthetic debate, and its continuing publication of the most exciting work in progress. It was the paper where Pound carried out his well-planned "Make It New" programme, and effectively established the idea of a British *avant garde* that was part of a truly international movement, which reached from Paris and Trieste to New York, Chicago and Saint Louis.

The other major adventure of this time - as much a manifesto as it was a magazine - was *Blast*, "a review of the great English Vortex," whose first number is dated 20 June 1914, though it appeared somewhat later, close to the outbreak of war. Published by John Lane, it was edited by Wyndham Lewis and addressed from the Rebel Art Centre in Great Ormond Street, as well as the flat in Church Walk, Kensington, which accommodated Ezra Pound. It was concerned with art, literature, drama, music, sculpture, and the great anti-Victorian revolution: "there must be no echo of a former age, or of a former manner," Lewis pronounced. Though Pound was again an active figure, disillusioned by the descent of Imagism into Amygism after Amy Lowell highjacked it, Lewis did not regard him as a full practising Vorticist, and later on called him a "revolutionary simpleton." There was nonetheless a kind of truce or transition that linked Imagism and Vorticism, and so Pound, Aldington and Eliot all appeared in *Blast*. The paper's crucial feature was its long manifesto list of "Blasts" and "Blesses" ("BLAST the years 1837 to 1900," etc.). The look of the magazine was as crucial as its contents.

> With a page area of 12 inches by 91/2, this publication was a bright puce colour. In general appearance it was not unlike a telephone book. It contained manifestoes, poems, plays, stories and outbursts of one sort of another,

wrote Lewis.[10] It had 160 pages, and the cover, variously called puce or magenta, had the title BLAST printed across it in heavy black type three inches high, with interior sans-serif type up to an inch high. The manifestoes ran to forty pages, beginning with "Long Live the Vortex," and declaring:

> We stand for the Reality of the Present - not for the sentimental Future, or the sacripant past [...] BLAST sets out to be an avenue for all those vivid and violent ideas that could reach the Public in no other way.

Though England, John Galsworthy and Cod Liver Oil were all blasted, England (again), James Joyce and Castor Oil were all blessed. This issue had twelve poems by Pound, Lewis's play "The Enemy of the Stars," and a section of Hueffer's wonderful novel *The Good Soldier*, as well as plentiful illustration from Lewis, Edward Wadsworth, Gaudier-Brzeska and Epstein. In July 1915 a second number appeared. By now the blasts were real, and it was announced in its pages that Gaudier-Brzeska had been killed in action, after having written an article at the front on Vorticism, which was printed. Lewis himself was in France, and Hueffer, who contributed a poem, shortly would be. This issue contained T.S. Eliot's "Preludes" and "Rhapsody on a Windy Night." But Vorticisin was over, or rather it had transformed into something else: war art.

The War was scarcely a lively time for the production of new literature; and it

---

[10] Wyndham Lewis, *Blasting and Bombardiering* (London: Eyre and Spottiswood, 1937), 41.

changed and darkened the whole character of the emerging *avant garde*. Perhaps the most significant wartime magazine was *The Signature*, which essentially represented D.H. Lawrence's bitter, apocalyptic response to the conflict. He wrote to Cynthia Asquith:

> we are thinking - Murry and Mrs Murry [Katherine Mansfield] and I, primarily, of issuing a little paper, fortnightly, to private subscribers [...]. Perhaps Bertie Russell and Gilbert Cannan will come in [...]. The persistent nothingness of the war makes me feel like a paralytic convulsed with rage.

He made a similar appeal to Lady Ottoline Morrell, asking for subscribers: "I only want the people who care." Soon he announces that he has already written six papers for the magazine, but only has 27 subscriptions (there were probably not many more later). Later on, when he was in virtually permanent exile abroad, Lawrence would explain this small but important paper as a "little escapade" of Murry's. Murry would say the first suggestion had come from Lawrence, as it probably did. Only three numbers of the venture appeared, dated 4 October, 18 October and 1 November, 1915. It was Lawrence's bitterest time; he felt hounded by the authorities for his pacifism, and over this period his new novel *The Rainbow* was prosecuted and destroyed. In *The Signature*'s pages Lawrence published his apocalyptic wartime essay *The Crown*, Murry *There Was a Little Man...* and Katherine Mansfield contributed several stories. There were no other contributors. A few other magazines started over the wartime period, some preparing the way for the mood of the Twenties. One was *The Palatine Review* (1916-17), run by T.W. Earp and the young Aldous Huxley in an Oxford where there were virtually no undergraduates. But Robert Graves was invalided back, and became one of the contributors; and the magazine helped to clear the ground for the livelier scene after 1918, when the Brideshead Generation, then the Auden Group appeared. But, as Wyndham Lewis later said, the excitement and experiment of the prewar years was snuffed out by the war, and "We are the first men of a future that has not materialized."

4.

By the time civilian cultural operations resumed after 1918, it was evident that a great deal had changed. The era of the Edwardian bookman had quietly faded; poets who a few years earlier had written lyric nature poetry for magazines like Lascelles Abercrombie's *New Numbers* now seemed a whole lost world away. The buoyant mood of "Georgianism" which had delighted D.H. Lawrence had turned into something darker and more troubled, as later war-pained anthologies of *Georgian Poetry* themselves revealed. Many writers had encountered, and many had not survived, the horrors of the trenches, and the shattering of dreams of heroism and patriotism. If the first stage of the Modern movement had been a lively war with the Philistines, now the war was more likely to be with those in power who had destroyed the cultural and historial idea of Europe, and brought the destruction of a generation. In many respects, however, the "Modern movement" had triumphed, and its former outrages had become the norms of expression in a dark and fragmentary age. Its art no longer expressed a joy in new forms nor a protest against Victorian values; it was rather a revolt against that world of falling cities, wounded spirits and shattered lives that Eliot emblemized in "The Waste Land," the exemplary poem of the decade. By 1919 Eliot in *The Egoist*, Middleton Murry in *The Athenaeum*, were already asserting the age of Georgianism was over, and calling for a new irony, wit and vision in modern poetry, a different voice and consciousness in the novel. The postwar generation shared the common experience of war and the feeling of cultural transition and human fragility it engendered. At the same time, an analytical sobriety entered literary experiment; if the prewar years had been the era of excitement what now emerged was the era of analysis. What was happening was that Modernism was becoming magisterial and respectable.

The extent to which the war changed the mood of the culture, and opened it to a new generation of writers, can be seen from two other important magazines that began during wartime and carried on into the early postwar period. One was Holbrook Jackson's *Today*, which appeared from March 1917 to December 1923: a thoughtful popular monthly, which printed Yeats, Hardy, Eliot, Pound and Robert Graves, and carried serious critical articles on Joyce, Lawrence and Katherine Mansfield. The other and more significant was *Art and Letters*, "an illustrated quarterly," which started in June 1917 and lapsed for a while in 1918. Then it was redesigned as a postwar magazine deliberately devoted to young writers and artists, continuing until the issue for Spring 1920. Its editors were Frank Rutter, Herbert Read and Osbert Sitwell, and it systematically affirmed the importance of the Modern movement, about which it attempted to create a serious critical debate. An article by Charles Ginner, "Modern Painting and Teaching" (June 1917), commented thoughtfully on the importance of Cubism and Vorticism, and drawings by Picasso, Matisse, Modigliani, and Wyndham Lewis appeared regularly in the magazine. Herbert Read's article "Definitions Toward a New Theory of Poetry" (January 1918), stressed the significance for a new poetry of Imagism and Clive Bell's doctrine of "significant form," "achieved by unity, vitality, exactness, concentration and decoration." This started a powerful critical debate where Read was answered, in an early appearance, by I.A. Richards. Unsurprisingly war was a central subject matter, in such poems as Read's own "Kneeshaw Goes To War" and Wyndham Lewis's story "The War Baby." The magazine also printed posthumous war poetry by Isaac Rosenberg and Wilfred Owen, drawing attention to their importance. T.S. Eliot gave editorial advice and contributed regularly, writing influentially and powerfully as critic on the blank verse of Marlowe, Webster and Euripedes, and as a poet with "Burbank With A Baedeker, Bleistein With a Cigar" and "Sweeney Erect." Herbert Read suggested that it was the disappearance of *Art and Letters* which led Eliot to go on and found *The Criterion* in 1922. He also fairly adds:

if in the future the two decades between 1920 and 1939 seem to achieve a certain homogeneity in the history of literature, the explanation should be sought in the direction and cohesion provided, first and tentatively by *Art and Letters*, and then clearly and confidently by *The Criterion*.[11]

The "Modern Movement" had indeed left behind its more flamboyant and spectacular period, and was a matter for sober reflection, serious critical debate and analysis. The new centrality of literary criticism (at a time when English was becoming an important university subject, and more analytical debate was thus made possible) is nowhere more evident than in the postwar pages of that well-established reviewing paper *The Athenaeum*. It had appeared as a drab monthly in wartime, but with the issue for 4 April, 1919, it was restructured and reverted to weekly reviewing format. The new editor was John Middleton Murry; the assistant editorship was first offered to Eliot and, when he refused it, to Aldous Huxley, who served for a year. A new generation of magazinists, among them some of the best literary writers of the day, many now depending on the magazines for a career, had emerged from the pre-war reviews. For the two-year period of Murry´s editorship, *The Athenaeum*, which covered literature British and foreign, fine arts, music, drama, history and science, was to be a major journal for criticism and reviewing; its files still offer a basic and powerful record of new critical opinion. For his critical essays, and reviews of the burst of "modern" publication that occurred in the immediate postwar period (Virginia Woolf´s fiction and criticism, Eliot´s criticism and verse, Conrad´s later fiction, etc.), Murry brilliantly commissioned a fresh, responsive, topical generation of critics and reviewers, and let them write at length. They included Eliot, Woolf, Vanessa Bell, George Santayana, E.M. Forster, Lytton Strachey, Edward Muir, D.H. Lawrence (writing under the pen-name "Grantorto"), Aldous Huxley (writing as "Auctolycus"), Katherine Mansfield, Edmund Blunden and Conrad Aiken: a generation on display. Out of these pages came some of the finest critical essays of the Twenties, the material of volumes like Eliot´s *The Sacred Wood*, Murry´s *Aspects of Literature*, and Woolf´s *The Common Reader*. This regime continued until the issue for 18 February, 1921, when the paper merged with *The Nation*, to become *The Nation and Athenaeum*. Later, when this too merged with the leftwing *New Statesman* the name *Athenaeum* went out of the title - though for several generations after the paper sustained the tradition of a strong and independent critical section Murry had established.

Other magazines captured a similar mood, uniting new experimental writing with a campaign in modern criticism. *Coterie*, an advanced quarterly of art, prose and poetry, which started in May 1919 and ended in Winter 1920/21, was edited by Chaman Lall, and had Eliot on the editorial board, as well as other growingly familiar names: Richard Aldington, Wyndham Lewis, T.W. Earp, Conrad Aiken. Eliot´s "A Cooking Egg" appeared, Edith Sitwell made a sprightly appearance, Aldous Huxley contributed poetry and prose. (It was later revived as *New Coterie*.) There was *The Owl*, very probably edited by Robert Graves, which printed three expensive and

---

[11] Herbert Read, *Annals of Innocence and Experience* (London: Faber and Faber, 1940), 199.

splendidly illustrated issues in 1919, and introduced some significant American poetry by Vachel Lindsay and John Crowe Ransom; American and British poetry were going through a time of close alliance. Harold Monro returned to the fray with *The Chapbook* (1919-1925), a series of small monthly pamphlets (forty in all) devoted to some single aspect of poetry or drama. The first contained 23 three new poems by contemporary poets, the fourth was devoted to F.S. Flint on contemporary French poetry, another given over to "Three Critical Essays on Modern English Poetry," by Eliot, Flint and Aldous Huxley, and another, in May 1920, to contemporary American poetry. Overall these publications amount to a remarkable sequence, displaying important reactions to such matters as the appearance of "The Waste Land" and the emergence of the new generation of experimental American poets.

These were the *avant garde* magazines, but they made their way against the middlebrow literary climate represented by more popular and larger circulation literary publications, some of considerable quality. The most notable was *The London Mercury*, a monthly for the general reader, founded in November 1919. Edited by J.C. Squire, it soon reached a circulation of 20,000. It published an eclectic range of poetry, including much that was notable (the "Crazy Jane" poems of W.B. Yeats, etc.), had a fair share of important essays, and printed a number of significant short stories (Sherwood Anderson, Liam O'Flaherty, D.H. Lawrence, Graham Greene, etc.). In 1934 R.A. Scott-James took over; in 1935 it merged with *The Bookman*; during the later 1930s it increasingly represented the "Auden Generation." Finally in April 1939, as the troubled political climate made its economics ever more difficult, its owners (*The New Statesman*) sold it to *Life and Letters Today*, and it ceased as a separate publication. Often seen as drearily middlebrow, the *London Mercury* displayed the fact that there was a vigorous general book culture in Britain, with eclectic interests. It took its place with the generally good reviewing standards of the weekly reviews (*The Nation*, etc.) and the *Times Literary Supplement* (founded 1902), whose record in covering Modernism is displayed, in all its variety, in a recent anthology.[12]

By the dawn of the Twenties, an increasing number of journals were concerned to define and capture the postwar mood. The most flamboyant was Wyndham Lewis´ *The Tyro*, "a review of the arts of painting and design, to be produced at intervals of two or three months." Only two issues appeared, both undated, but published in April 1921 and March 1922. "No time has ever been more carefully demarcated from the one it succeeds than the time we have entered on has been by the Great War of 1914-18 [...]," it announced, explaining that "we, then, are the creatures of a new state of human life," "immense novices," "tyros." Again T.S. Eliot was involved; he wrote essays reflecting on the Baudelaire and the Dada movement, and published a

---

[12] John Gross, ed., *The Modern Movement: A TLS Companion* (London: Harvill, 1992). As John Gross remarks in his introduction, it has generally been said that, as Harry Levin once put it, the *TLS*, "took a dim view" of Modernism, but the story was rather more chequered. Modern titles did tend to be assigned to "old reliables," but it employed the services of Pound, Eliot, Murry and Virginia Woolf, was strong in its reviews of foreign literature, and did, behind the facade of donnish anonymity, offer some very striking recognitions and interpretations.

poem, "Song to the Opherian," under the odd and playful pseudonym of Gus Krutzsch. Lewis returned polemically to the fray later, in his magazine *The Enemy* (1927-28), announcing: "there is no 'movement' gathered here (thank heaven!) merely a person; a solitary outlaw and not a gang." It was virtually a single-headed critical campaign, though once more Eliot was involved.

Indeed Eliot was now becoming a crucial figure in the magazine scene, and in 1921-22 he was in process of becoming the most important magazinist of the day. He had been negotiating with Lady Rothermere (an American with whom he had been at school) to found a new British periodical that might serve as successor to the *Egoist* and *Art and Letters*, with a modern perspective and a strong European, and international dimension: a truly ambitious review. The model they agreed on was the American magazine *The Dial*, to which Eliot was already a contributor. As he was an employee of Lloyd's Bank, which would not allow its staff to take paid outside employment, Eliot's role as editor was necessarily part-time and amateur. That helped dictate that it would be a quarterly, though there was a paid assistant editor, Richard Aldington (another line of continuity with *The Egoist*). The review was to be called *The Criterion*, an apparently magisterial title, though story has it that it was named by Vivien Eliot after a restaurant where she met a lover. Various departments were set up - J.B. Trend looked after the "Music Chronicle," and so on. Weekly luncheon discussions started around aesthetic, philosophical and critical topics, and Eliot soon set up a brilliant network of international contacts and correspondents, who included George Santayana, Paul Valery, Valery Larbaud, Jacques Maritain and Luigi Pirandello. Eliot himself reflected in the new paper, a bulky and dignified quarterly in a dull yellow cover, that the times were not so much now an age of creation as an age of criticism, and that the Modern movement had come of age.

5.

The new review published its first issue in October 1922, a timely moment. 1922 was a key year of Modernism. Joyce's *Ulysses* had appeared in Paris earlier in the year, and Eliot's own "The Waste Land" appeared in the review's very first issue. This had an important essay on *Ulysses* by Valery Larbaud, and Eliot also acknowledged the book as a major achievement, capturing the age's panorama of "futility and anarchy." Soon there were key contributions from Ezra Pound ("The Malatesta Cantos"), Yeats, Virginia Woolf, Wyndham Lewis, Marcel Proust, D.H. Lawrence, Benedetto Croce and more. Before the decade was over, the magazine - following a contemporary internationalist policy - had printed creative work or criticism by Paul Valery, Luigi Pirandello, Hermann Hesse, Wilhelm Worringer, C.P. Cavafy, Jean Cocteau, Charles Maurras and Ernst Robert Curtius, in many of these cases introducing them to Britain. Eliot was closely involved in the modern experiment, but no less preoccupied with the idea of the "European mind" as a vital centre of humanism and culture. That culture was acknowledgedly in crisis, political and metaphysical, and Eliot made that an abiding theme. In 1925 he finally left the bank (something his friends had long been raising money for him to do) to join the publishing firm of Faber and Gwyer. They took over the costs, meaning Eliot could now devote himself more thoroughly to the enterprise, which for a time began to appear monthly, as *The New Criterion*, then *The Monthly Criterion*, and also ask himself public questions about the task of such a review.

He proposed that this was surely to illustrate a tendency, or rather, as he put it, reveal, within limits the time and the tendencies of the time, so that it had a value over and above the individual contributions. The "tendency" represented by *The Criterion* was shaped by the cultural dilemmas and bitter political debates of the postwar period, but also by the personal crises, marital and philosophical, through which Eliot was passing. About this time he committed himself to the Anglo-Catholic Church and took British nationality. He subsequently remarked on his reasoning, saying it was only after 1926 (the year of the General Strike) that the features of the postwar world began clearly to emerge, and "from about that date one began slowly to realise that the intellectual and artistic output of the last seven years had been rather the last efforts of an old world than the first efforts of a new." He introduced a series of editorial commentaries, signed "Crites," to discuss the intellectual, moral and metaphysical climate, and argued the case for "classicism," a commitment to reason and order, an argument part-based on the pre-war speculations of T.E. Hulme and on his own doctrine of "impersonality." There was a key debate about the "New Humanism," involving his American mentors Irving Babbitt and Paul Elmer More, and a wealth of discussion, involving French writers like Charles Maurras, on communism and fascism, part of an endeavour in contemporary political and social circumstances to achieve "a definition of culture."

Meantime the magazine contained some of the best writing of the time: new poetry, prose, drama, and criticism. Poetry included Yeats´ "The Tower," Hart Crane´s "The Tunnel," and excerpts from *Finnegans Wake* and Pound´s *Cantos* appeared. Major critical essays were regularly printed: Herbert Read on metaphysical poetry, the prolific Eliot himself on Elizabethan dramatists and, fascinatingly, on detective fiction, J.M. Robertson on English blank verse, Stephen Spender on Yeats, Montgomery Belgion on Gide and Kafka, E.M. Forster on Virginia Woolf, Virginia Woolf on character in fiction, and so on. There were regular letters from America and France, as well as a "Fiction Chronicle," a "Music Chronicle," and a "Verse Chronicle." There were excellent accounts of the contents of foreign reviews worldwide, singling out exciting new talents. And from 1924 onward there was regular reviewing of the highest standard, using I.A. Richards, Bonamy Dobree, Paul Elmore More, L.C. Knights, Marianne Moore, William Empson, W.H. Auden, Edwin Muir and many more. *The Criterion* represented nothing less than a 'definition of culture,' which embraced poetry, fiction and drama; literary criticism, music, politics, philosophy and religion; the debates of Britain and America, Paris, Berlin and Rome. Eliot used his office magisterially, and the review created a distinctive sense of history and culture that was steered, often very explicitly, by his own preoccupations, but also of the many critics and intellectuals who gathered around the magazine.

For reasons clearly explored in the biographical records,[13] his own poetry now tended to lapse - though he did publish his "Fragment of a Prologue" (October 1926) and "Fragment of an Agon," From "Wanna Go Home, Baby?" (January 1927), which became *Sweeney Agonistes*. But he was in fact writing formidably as a critic, both for his own review and many others. And the crucial fact was that he was an excellent editor, large in his aims and interests, and ever generous to new writing. As a result, the writing of the "new world" after 1926, when in fact there was a fundamental changeover of literary generations in Britain, appeared prominently in his pages. Eliot encouraged Auden's early work, and his "Paid on Both Sides" appeared in January 1930, followed by book reviewing in later numbers. Over the next two years verse by William Empson, Stephen Spender, Hugh McDiarmid, Louis MacNeice, Ronald Bottrall, Charles Madge, George Barker, and Dylan Thomas, was printed, and the review did much to relate the Thirties movement to a larger culture. *The Criterion* became the most desirable outlet for modern writing; to appear there was to win international recognition as a serious writer. The new writing that appeared carried forward the general critical, cultural and political argument (the succession of controversies over economics and religion, classicism and romanticism, aesthetic detachment and political engagement), giving a sense of the best minds at work on the increasingly intractable problems of the time. These, though, finally provoked Eliot to end the magazine, in profound depression, with the issue for January 1939.

Inevitably, given the central role it played despite its small circulation (800 at its highest, around 300 at the end), *The Criterion* provoked resistance. A significant example was a small, often quirky literary monthly, *The Adelphi*, edited by John Middleton Murry, which began in June 1923. Mansfield had died earlier in the year, so the new magazine was partly meant as a memorial to her (her photograph appeared as frontispiece, and there were many personal references to her). It was no less meant as a homage to D.H. Lawrence, on whose support Murry counted, and he promoted it as a vehicle of Lawrentian ideas, describing himself in the first editorial as *"locum tenens* for a better man." Other supporters were A.R. Orage, who edited the formidable *The New Age*, and Vivian Locke-Ellis. An essential motive for this weirdly personal project was Murry's "instinctive" resistance to "classicism," and what he called "the search after truth."

> As far as I can remember, the decisive impulse was one of rebellion against the combination of rationalism and aestheticism which was (or seemed to me) in danger of becoming dominant in literature in 1923,

he recollected in the paper in 1950, when the magazine was still going, though in a revived form and under different editorship.

"Frankly I have no interest in editing what the critics would call a good magazine [...]," Murry was already announcing to a body of obviously sympathetic readers in 1924, "I am interested now, not in 'good writing,' or in 'attractive articles,' but in

---

[13] See Peter Ackroyd, *T.S. Eliot* (London: Hamish Hamilton, 1984) for a detailed account.

truth." So were most other contributors; the paper retained this personal tone and impassioned concern with romanticism, atheism, deism, socialism, and communism, for most of its existence. Still it carried many significant contributions: posthumous stories by Katherine Mansfield, stories by Liam O'Flaherty, A.E. Coppard, poetry by Lawrence, Hardy, Graves, Yeats. Lawrence kept his distance, even indicated his embarrassment, but did contribute essays that would appear in *Fantasia of the Unconscious* and *Mornings in Mexico*. In 1927 it became a quarterly, *The New Adelphi*, and went through a vigorous period, printing Capek, Edwin Muir, Santayana, Herbert Read, and Jung, as well as (at great length) Murry himself. A particularly notable issue mourned Lawrence's death in 1930. In 1930 Max Plowman and Sir Richard Rees became editors, the paper reverted to monthly format, and began to print many newer writers from the "Auden Generation." By 1932 it was firmly identified with the Independent Labour Party. Later Murry, who had always been the major contributor, resumed the editorship. In 1936 it largely dropped its literary dimension, but continued, uncertainly, to survive. In 1948 Henry Williamson took over, and it went on under him, then George Godwin and B. Ifor Evans, till its death in the 1950s.

From its "romantic" and then socialist position, *The Adelphi* consistently challenged *The Criterion*. A different, more specifically critical kind of challenge came in March 1925, when *The Calendar of Modern Letters* appeared as a monthly literary review, with Edgell Rickword (later to be editor of the avowedly Marxist *Left Review)* as editor. A year on it became a quarterly and survived until July 1927, printing some of the most important criticism of the decade. Declaring the value of a review must be judged by its attitude to the living literature of the time, it instituted a series of articles, "Scrutinies," designed to pursue serious critical judgement. In 1926 it firmly rebuked both *The Criterion* and *The Adelphi*, the classic and the romantic, the intellectualist's abstraction and "the intuitionalist debauch." The "Scrutinies" series (from which F.R. Leavis's *Scrutiny* would take its name and attitudes) attacked its subjects with vigour and rigour, and was the main achievement. Edgell Rickword discussed J.M. Barrie, Douglas Garman (assistant editor) Walter de la Mare, Bertrand Higgins (also assistant editor) John Masefield and so on. Other critical articles of distinction appeared, and for the first time a rigorous and considered New Criticism afforded the serious basis for a magazine. John Crowe Ransom published his "Thoughts on Poetic Discontent," establishing 'irony' as a judgemental principle), Edwin Muir wrote on "The Zeitgeist" and "*Ulysses*," Wyndham Lewis on "The Dithyrambic Spectator," and D.H. Lawrence on "Morality and the Novel." In an article "A Short Note on Fiction," C.H. Rickword established what was in effect a new "New Critical" approach to the novel as genre. The reviewing of new books was equally determined and rigorous. Rickword wrote a considered review of T.S. Eliot's *Poems 1909-1925* which interestingly praised "the urgency of his personality," and D.H. Lawrence wrote on Hemingway's collection of stories *In Our Time*. *The Criterion* praised the achievement; H.P. Collins recognized a group of critics, most unknown, "who possess a detachment and a capacity for subtle differentiation and analysis which would have been incomprehensible a dozen years ago," though he also noted that "it is not easy to recognize in them a criticism that is fruitful or, in the true sense, creative." The creative side of the paper was also distinguished; fiction by Lawrence ("The Princess"), T.F. Powys, Kay Boyle, Pirandello, and Leonid Leonov, poetry by Graves, Sassoon, Edmund Blunden, Hart Crane, Allen Tate, Roy Campbell, and John Crowe Ransom. By the time *The Calendar of Modern Letters* died, magazine criticism and the serious literary essay had acquired a new authority.[14]

6.

By the mid-1920s, another generation - the "Brideshead Generation," as Humphrey Carpenter has it[15] - was becoming evident. Oxbridge magazines were an established convention, an important training ground for neophyte literary styles and manners. Eliot cast a strong influence everywhere: "Cautiously received amongst dons, Eliot was read, learned, discussed and above all imitated by undergraduates with competitive eagerness," recalls James Reeve, of 1920s Cambridge. At Oxford, as Evelyn Waugh´s *Brideshead Revisited* recalls, "The Waste Land" was read out through a megaphone, and various magazines reflect that impact. *Oxford Outlook*, started in 1919, printed the work of C. Day Lewis (1924), Christopher Isherwood (1925), W.H. Auden and Louis MacNeice (1926), as well as Stephen Spender, Isaiah Berlin and Enid Starkie. Revived as *The New Oxford Outlook* in 1933, it would carry a good deal of the work of the "Auden Generation." In 1923 Harold Acton started his neo-modernist *Oxford Broom*, to which Waugh contributed design and a story. In Cambridge, with its growing commitment to literary criticism and Communism, two new magazines appeared in the same month in 1928: *Venture*, edited by Anthony Blunt, H. R. Fedden and Michael Redgrave, and carrying young writers like William Empson, Louis MacNeice, Julian Bell and John Lehmann; and *Experiment*, edited by J. Bronowski, William Empson and Hugh Sykes Davies. As its name foretold, this was the more modernist, with stills from films, an unpublished extract from Joyce´s *Work in Progress*, articles on Hemingway, Joyce and Eliot, and early Empson poetry in some quantity, as well as sections from his key critical book *Seven Types of Ambiguity* (1930). Later issues had Boris Pasternak, Malcolm Lowry, and a discussion by Empson of Auden´s *Paid On Both Sides*. Round this date F.R. Leavis published an article approving of Eliot in *The Cambridge Review*, causing, he said, much offence and controversy. Oxford produced *Farrago* in 1930, by which time the climate was already beginning to grow political. There was *Cambridge Left* in 1933, which printed John Cornford and much socially concerned poetry, and other university magazines reflected the greater politicisation of the next literary generation.

The most important review to emerge from the university climate was undoubtedly *Scrutiny*, started in Cambridge in May 1932, continuing until October 1953. It was

---

[14] The *Calendar of Modern Letters* was reprinted in 3 volumes in 1966 (London: Frank Cass), with an introduction, "A Review in Retrospect," by the present author.

[15] Humphrey Carpenter, *The Brideshead Generation: Evelyn Waugh and His Generation* (London: Faber, 1989).

founded by a group of young collaborators, most of them teaching fellows and research students, who remembered the ideal of the "common pursuit of true judgment" Eliot had written of in his essay "The Function of Criticism," and I.A. Richards' account of literature as the "storehouse of recorded values." Two closer and more immediate influences were Q.D. Leavis's *Fiction and the Reading Public* and her husband F.R. Leavis's *New Bearings in English Poetry*, both published that year. Though the masthead of the first issues bore other names - L.C. Knights and Donald Culver - it was these two who proved to be the essential editors, and their books set out most of the underlying presumptions. The first editorial struck the firm *Scrutiny* note:

> The general dissolution of standards is a commonplace [...]. Those who are aware of the situation will be concerned to cultivate awareness and will be actively concerned for standards. A review is necessary that will combine criticism of literature with criticism of extra-literary activities. We take it as axiomatic that concern for standards of living implies concern for standards in the arts.

Leavis was from the beginning an energetic contributor, much exercised about the question of the critical guardians. And that was the role to be performed, often formidably, by the Scrutineers themselves. The Leavises were fortunate in having around them a group of figures - Knights and Culver, D.W. Harding, Denys Thompson, H.A. Mason, John Speirs, R.G. Cox and more - who were able to make the *Scrutiny* campaign collective and systematic. Knights wrote on Shakespeare, Speirs on Middle English, Martin Turnell on French literature, Henri Fluchere on French literary papers, Marius Bewley on American literature. There were important occasional contributors: Muriel Bradbrook, I.A. Richards, Michael Oakshott, William Empson, Edmund Blunden, Edgell Rickword, W.H. Audenm George Santayana, Arthur Humphreys. At first *Scrutiny* professed a strong commitment to printing creative work, but most of what it had to offer in this respect appeared in early numbers: poetry by Ronald Bottrall and Richard Eberhart, fiction from G.H. Peacock (from his novel *Coolstone Park*) in December 1932. There can be little doubt of the reason for the shortfall: the aroma of critical scrutiny that came from the magazine was no encouragement to the submission of original writing.

Scrutiny's strength lay elsewhere. Leavis had his heroes, who came from both sides of the classic/romantic divide: Eliot in poetry and criticism, Lawrence in the novel. He and most fellow contributors also shared the certainty that the culture was going through a period of fundamental decline, destructive to the creation of serious literature. Even so, especially in earlier days, *Scrutiny* offered a strong and powerful analysis of contemporary work as it appeared: Pound's essays and poetry, Eliot's criticism and drama, Empson's criticism, Virginia Woolf's fiction, Auden's verse and that of his contemporaries. The essential achievement was the creation of a distinctive critical voice. When Empson left Cambridge in some scandal, and Richards began to withdraw, the *Scrutiny* group represented - at least to many in the outside world - the spirit of "New Criticism" as practised in the Cambridge English School. Its tone was rigorous, its demands of writing testy and precise, its insistence on the centrality of literature as the test of a civilization appealing to more than one generation, its rejection of Bloomsbury and the dominant literary climate explicit. Leavis was concerned with literature's definitive existence at the centre of a mature culture; it was not a politics, not a mode of religion, but a moral act of the imagination. As Eliot grew more religious in *The Criterion*, and youthful Marxists took charge in the new upcoming reviews, *Scrutiny* founded its position in a formidable defence of judgemental literary values, not on aesthetic but on moral and interpretative grounds, "designs for living."

In the final days Leavis had no doubt of the importance of what it had achieved:

> this sober claim can be made: the volumes offer an incomparable literary history of the period, and at the same time, in such consonance as to be an organic part of the whole coherent critical achievement, what will be recognized to amount to a major revaluation of English literature,

he wrote in the magazine in Spring 1953,

> That is because *Scrutiny* was concerned to determine the significant points in the contemporary field and to make, with due analysis, the necessary judgment, and because these judgments have invariably turned out to be right.

Scrutiny was born in the critical and intellectual wars of the early Thirties, and, despite its militancy and its sense of representing a minority culture, the sole saving remnant, it owed much to them. But it well outlasted all rivals, and its period of greatest influence was in the 1950s - when the university system expanded, English acquired a new centrality in the academic curriculum, and rigorous modern revaluations were the order of the day. By now, though, the critical energy was tiring, and the review running dry of contributions - and *Scrutiny* expired with the issue for October 1953.[16] It was, perhaps, the last seriously critical and high-minded literary magazine. For the 'dissolution of standards' - the collapse of an elite and select modernism into the universal mush - was soon to be under way in the years after its demise, and its prophecy was exact.

7.

The 1930s saw a whole new body of other significant magazines, their direction greatly shaped by the appearance, in 1932, of Michael Roberts' Hogarth Press anthology *New Signatures*, followed a year on by *New Country*, stressing the political engagement and bias of the new generation. The best were Geoffrey Grigson's *New Verse* (1933-37), heavily devoted to the Auden Group, famous for publishing a mock obituary of Eliot, later very attentive to surrealism; *The Left Review* (1924-38), pro-

---

[16] Much of the background to the Scrutiny story is recorded in Ian MacKillop, *F.R. Leavis: A Life in Criticism* (London: Penguin Press, 1995).

duced by the "Writers' International," edited by T.H. Wintringham and then Edgell Rickword; and above all *New Writing*, founded by John Lehmann in Spring 1936 and appearing twice yearly until Christmas 1939 - when it went through a magic transition to become the wartime monthly *Penguin New Writing*. There were also Roger Roughton's *Contemporary Poetry and Prose*, started in May 1936, particularly devoted to Surrealism, and Julian Symonds' *Twentieth Century Verse* (January 1937-July 1939). However, like *The Criterion*, most of these magazines (along with their political attitude) died in or around 1939. By the 1940s, when the two dominant magazines were the new format *Penguin New Writing* and Cyril Connolly's *Horizon*, the graceful and quirky cheap monthly started in January, 1940, the periodical had begun to have a different meaning. It reported on wartime, captured the twilight mood and profound cultural uncertainty, sustained new immediate writing in a time of chaos, gave imaginative relief to fighting soldiers or blitzed civilians. By the Thirties the War for Modernism was in effect over; most writers had imbibed some aspect of its influence and styles, and it was a digested tradition. By the beginning of the 1940s many of its founding figures - Virginia Woolf, James Joyce - were dead, or had fled into American exile. An era was complete, leaving the periodical, once peace resumed, with a different future.

Yet much of the construction of a serious twentieth century literature had been first done in the magazines and literary reviews (in many more, indeed, that can be considered here). For all their marginal existence, their minority sense of themselves, their shaky finances and small readerships, they represented the front edge of writing, the changing styles and arguments of literature, the new voices and the needed campaigns. They were the places where most of the movements announced themselves, the grounds on which or between which aesthetic and critical battles were constantly fought. Here new writers generally had their first access, and won their first acceptance, moving from this magazine to the other, this flag of convenience to that. Starting on magazines or in literary journalism, and depending on them both for modest income as well as a place in the artistic debate, they then moved on to books, which were, in turn, very often essentially the products of original periodical publication. The magazines were the essential meeting place of new writing and criticism, and criticism itself was largely the self-examining practice of writers, though the academy became gradually more important. But by the 1950s the pattern began to transform considerably. The two dominant magazines of wartime, *Horizon* and *Penguin New Writing*, both closed in 1950, with the conviction that the literary culture was declining (as Cyril Connolly put it, it was "closing time in the gardens of the West"), and *Scrutiny* collapsed shortly after. Printing costs were rising, and the reliable audience disappearing; the shape of the postwar literary generation was slow to form.

Today, our periodical literary culture is fundamentally different from the one that carried the Modernist campaign into the centre of culture. We have significant literary journals, not least the reviewing papers *The London Review of Books* and the revived *Times Literary Supplement*. But books are trade, writers a commodity. The common pursuit of true judgment has dissolved into a reviewing traffic in factions, generation and gender wars or other agendas, while the more abstract aspects of critical scrutiny have turned into theory and deconstructive enterprise. Criticism has become either a specialized academic discourse concerned not with standards but theories; reviewing is essentially a self-flaunting branch of contemporary journalism, given to celebrity gossip or the pursuit of target reader-groups. The pursuit of standards or definitions of culture has given way to culture in its postmodern sense: the eclectic contents of a Sunday supplement, where books are part of the same spread as film, pop music, food, wine, fashion, alternative life-styles and other designer chic. Style is no longer the form of an aesthetic knowledge, but an aspect of design and marketing. Modernism, and the critical enterprise that developed out of it, was by definition an elitist or coterie enterprise. Making it new depended not simply on a deconstruction but a reconstruction of the canon, on learning how to read, again. The postmodern norm is pluricultural, pluri-generic eclecticism; culture is all that is the case. Writers are no longer experimental explorers, cultural movers and shakers, formers of values; they are sub-atomic particles and individualized celebrities. The periodical, like the book has been enveloped in the new age of communications conglomerates. It is not about the shaping of the "critical attitude" or the "saving remnant;" it is another signifying commodity, competing in the marketplace. If the story of the magazines of Modernism is one of an enterprise in moving from an era of *fin de siècle* cultural ephemerality to a kind of permanence, the postmodern process is the reverse: the ephemeralisation, randomization and commodification of "culture" and "art" is the impermanent triumph of the postmodern condition.

Some Important British Literary and Little Magazines

ADAM (Bucharest, London). Ed: Miron Grindea. Irreg. 1932-present?.
ADELPHI (later NEW ADELPHI). Ed: J.M. Murry, others. M, Q. June 1923-195?.
ARENA. Ed: Jack Lindsay. Bi-M. 1949-June 1951.
ART AND LETTERS. Ed: Frank Rutter, Herbert Read, Osbert Sitwell, others. Q. June 1917-Spring 1920.
BLAST. Ed: Wyndham Lewis. June 1914, July 1915.
BOLERO (later KINGDOM COME) (Oxford). Ed: John Waller. Irreg. 1938-9.
CALENDAR OF MODERN LETTERS. Ed: Edgell Rickword, others. M, Q. March 1925-July 1927.
CAMBRIDGE LEFT. Ed: H.V. Kemp, others. Q. Summer 1933-Autumn 1934.
CAMBRIDGE WRITING. Ed: William Watson. Irreg. Easter 1948-1951.
THE CHAPBOOK (later MONTHLY CHAPBOOK). Ed: Harold Monro. M. 1919-1925.
CONTEMPORARY POETRY AND PROSE. Ed: Roger Roughton. Irreg. May 1936-Autumn 1937.
COTERIE (Oxford). Ed: Chaman Lall. Q. May 1919-Winter 1920.
CRITERION (later NEW CRITERION, MONTHLY CRITERION). Ed: T.S. Eliot. Q, M. Oct 1922-Jan 1939.
CRITIC (Mistley, Essex). Ed: Raymond Williams, others. Q. Spring 1947- ?.

DAYLIGHT. Ed: John Lehmann, others. 1 only. 1941.
THE ENEMY. Ed: Wyndham Lewis. Irreg. Jan 1927-1929.
ENGLISH REVIEW. Ed: Ford Madox Hueffer, others. M. Dec 1908-1937.
EPILOGUE (Deya, Majorca; London). Ed: Robert Graves, Laura Riding. Annual. 1935-1938.
EUROPEAN QUARTERLY. Ed: Edwin Muir, Janko Lavrin. Q. May 1934-Feb 1935.
EXPERIMENT (later NEW EXPERIMENT) (Cambridge). Ed: Jacob Bronowski, others. Irreg. Nov 1928-Oct 1930.
FARRAGO (Oxford). Ed: Peter Burra, others. Feb 1930-June 1931.
FORM. Ed: Austin Spare, others. Q, M. April 1916-1917; Oct 1921-Jan 1922.
HORIZON. Ed: Cyril Connolly. M. Jan 1940-Dec 1949.
LEFT REVIEW. Ed: T.E. Wintringham, E. Rickword, others. M. Oct 1934-MAY 1938.
LIFE AND LETTERS. Ed: T. Earle Welby, Violet Hunt. M. Nov 1923-Jan 1924.
LIFE AND LETTERS (later LIFE AND LETTERS TODAY). Ed: Desmond MacCarthy, others. Q, M. June 1928-June 1950.
LONDON APHRODITE. Ed: Jack Lindsay, others. Bi-M. Aug 1928-July 1929.
LONDON BULLETIN. Ed: E.L.T. Messens. M. April 1938-1940.
LONDON MERCURY. Ed: J.C. Squire, others. M. 1919-1939.
MANDRAKE (Oxford, London). Ed: John Wain, Arthur Boyars. Irreg. 1945-?.
THE MINT. Ed: Geoffrey Grigson. 2 only. 1946, 1948.
NEW FREEWOMAN (later THE EGOIST). Ed: Dora Marsden, others. Fort., M. 15 June-Dec 1919.
NEW NUMBERS (Ryton, Dymock, Glos.) Ed: Lascelles Abercrombie. Q. 1914.
NEW ROAD (Billericay). Ed: Alex Comfort, others. Annual. 1943-1947.
NEW STORIES (Oxford). Ed: H.E. Bates, others. Bi-M. Feb 1934-April 1936.
NEW VERSE. Ed: Geoffrey Grigson, others. Bi-M. Jan 1933-May 1939.
NEW WRITING (also FOLIOS OF NEW WRITING, NEW WRITING AND DAYLIGHT). Ed: John Lehmann. Irreg. 1938-1947.
NINE. Ed: Peter Russell. Q. Autumn 1949-?.
NOW (Maidenhead). Ed: George Woodcock. Irreg. 1941-1947.
OPUS (Tring, Herts). Ed: Denys Val Baker. Q. 1939-Spring 1943.
ORION. Ed: D. Kilham Roberts, others. Irreg. 1945.
OXFORD OUTLOOK (later NEW OXFORD OUTLOOK). Ed: Beverley Nichols, L.P. Hartley, others. Irreg. May 1919-May 1932.
OXFORD BROOM. Ed: Harold Acton. Irreg. 1923.
PALATINE REVIEW (Oxford). Ed: T.W. Earp. Q. Jan 1916-May 1917.
PENGUIN NEW WRITING. Ed: John Lehmann. Irreg. M. 1940-1950.
POETRY AND DRAMA. Ed: Harold Monro. Q. Spring 1914-Autumn 1915.
POETRY LONDON. Ed: Tambimuttu. Irreg. Feb 1939-?.
POETRY REVIEW. Ed: Harold Monro, others. M. Jan 1913-present.
PROGRAMME (Oxford). Ed: Kenneth Allott, others. Irreg. 1935-1937.
REJECTED MSS (Oxford). Ed: N.F. Hidden, others. 2 only. June, Dec 1934.

RHYTHM (later BLUE REVIEW). Ed: Michael Sadler, J.M. Murry, Katherine Mansfield. Q, M. Summer 1911-July 1913.
SCRUTINY (Cambridge). Ed: F.R. Leavis, Denys Thompson, others. Q. Jan 1932-Oct 1953.
SIGNATURE. Ed: D.H. Lawrence, others. Fortnightly. 4 Oct-1 Nov, 1915.
TODAY. Ed: Holbrook Jackson. M. 1917-1923.
TOWNSMAN (also THE SCYTHE). Ed: Ronald Duncan. Irreg. Jan 1938-Feb 1944.
THE TRAMP. Ed: Douglas Goldring. M. 1910.
THE TYRO. Ed: Wyndham Lewis. Two only. 1921-1922.
TWENTIETH CENTURY VERSE. Ed: Julian Symons. 8 p.a. Jan 1937-July 1939.
THE VENTURE (Cambridge). Ed: H.R. Fedden, others. Irreg. Nov 1928-June 1930.
VOICES Ed: Thomas Moult. Q. 1919.
WALES (Llangadock). Ed: Keidrych Rhys, others. Irreg. Summer 1937-1948.
WANDERER. Ed: J.M. Murry. M. Dec 1933-Nov 1934.
WELSH REVIEW (Cardiff). Ed: Glyn Jones. Bi-M. Feb 1939-?.
WHEELS: AN ANTHOLOGY OF VERSE (Oxford). Ed: Edith Sitwell. Annual. 1916-1921.
THE WIND AND THE RAIN. Ed: M. Allmand, N. Braybrooke. Irreg. 1941.

Inter- and Intracultural Antinomies in Aldous Huxley

LUCIEN LE BOUILLE (Caen)

What remains of Aldous Huxley at the turn of the millennium, a few years after a number of celebrations of the centenary of his birth? The question may seem impertinent, but moralists always call for provocation, and Huxley, first and foremost, *was* a moralist. The song goes that Monsieur de la Palice was still alive a quarter of an hour before he died, and he lives on because of the common obviousness of his condition. One is tempted to say that Huxley would now be forgotten if it were not for the obvious uncommonness of his, just as his death passed unnoticed because J.F.Kennedy had been assassinated the day before. Some are born with a silver spoon in their mouth, he was born with an encyclopaedia in his hands and a library in his cot. Without his formidable family, his formidable *Brave New World*, and his formidable body of writing - in all literary genres - and the formidable erudition it displays, *of course* there would be little justification in considering him as one of the major figures of the twentieth century. Are these enough, however, to ensure lasting literary fame, which, in his case, could conceivably have been restricted to a circle of scholars outside of which only his futuristic fantasy might have seemed likely to catch the lasting attention of the myth-making public, with, perhaps, his farewell spiritual allegory of *Island*, and his tentative explorations of drug induced ecstasy. Who, apart from a circle of specialists and a respectable number of adepts of Eastern philosophy and moksha medicine, would think, as Conrad's Marlowe keeps reminding us about Lord Jim, that what matters about Huxley is that he is and has always been one of us, whoever that "us" may be?

In spite of the odds against a form of Alexandrianism - an encyclopaedic culture and the multifocal interests of the *honnête homme* more readily associated with his grandfather's age than with his own - Huxley is inescapable for anyone interested in the history of literature and ideas in the twentieth century, though his importance as a novelist, as a poet, as a religious thinker, does not bear comparison with the great novelists, poets, or philosophers of his time. Or to put it another way, none of his many assets separately can make a great writer, yet he *is* a great writer and his books sell all over the world, many of them in paperbacks. Though public access to Internet came a quarter of a century after his death, Huxley is as representative of the age of the web, perhaps even more, as he is of the roaring twenties, of the anti-nuke fifties and of American Vedanta of the sixties. Huxley has survived and will survive because he was a mesh of cultural encounters. His was the age of the knowledge explosion which prepared the communication explosion of our days. The omnivorous bookworm gnawed the walls of the library and his children are the webcrawlers that browse continents at the speed of light, fostering the exponential growth of worlds within worlds, an invisible nest of intercultural nets which contain the best and the unmentionable of total freedom. If he had lived to see this he might have written an edifying essay on the moral problem.

Reduced to essentials, Huxley was what he always *appeared*: a knot of contradictions and ambiguities, an all-round paradox in that he was at once one of the least self-consciously conspicuous and - like all great writers - one of the most significant mirrors of the century. He was British to the bone and yet a thoroughly Americanized melting-pot of ideas, his work is marked by the passing of time and yet germane to the electronic world-culture of the space age, and to our misgivings about bioethics. Strictly, and even narrowly conditioned by his birth, his cultural milieu and his social environment represent what contemporary critics rather loosely called British intellectual aristocracy, whose nursery was Bloomsbury, circumstances and his protean psychological malleability turned him, between the first World War and the beginning of the sixties, into a kaleidoscope of intercultural encounters. He had a sense of mystery, but was without mystery, except on one point: the workings of that splendid intellect caught in a Faustian dilemma between knowing and loving; a perfect connection machine interested in the only connections that matter, bridges between othernesses, forever seeking union between opposites. This, more than anything else, was at the heart of his curious affinity with a personality so unlike his own, D.H.Lawrence.

For Huxley, as for many men of his generation, the second World War was the great divide, though historically the real split occurred in 1914, when he was eighteen, a little too young to have been close to the first conflict, and unfit to take part in the second, but ideally placed to see them both in the larger context of the history of Europe since the seventeenth century. Yet, here again, Huxley's commitment was paradoxical, since it was characterized by distance from, not proximity to its object. The First World War he knew at several removes and in 1937 he took the decisive choice which T.S.Eliot had taken the other way round a decade earlier, and Henry James sixty years before: expatriation. What was Europe for Huxley the expatriate? Was he ever a European? This seems doubtful, though European countries were slowly and painfully moving towards union throughout those years during which Huxley the moralist, the philosopher, the historian, the observer of the state of the world, reflected on the ravages of nationalism on the Old Continent since Richelieu. Huxley's intellectual galaxy was organized around cultural antinomies which were appreciably different before and after that sea change of 1937. As long as he lived in the European context Huxley bore testimony to attitudes which placed Europe and, within Europe, Britain at the centre of the universe, much as Rome and Athens once were. In his works at that time intercultural encounters took the well-known, reassuring form of the discovery of exotic lands, cities and beliefs. Before 1937 Huxley's approach was not very different from Rousseau's, even if his natives were just the opposite of *nobles sauvages*. It took all the complicity with D.H.Lawrence and a youthful, albeit fast waning enthusiasm for the cult of life, to make him yearn for the primitive. It was indeed sad tropics that he found in his disenchanted journey round the world, which took him to Asia in 1925 and 1926, and then in his dark encounter with South and Central America, which he visited in 1933. Depression and a sense that all civilisations, modern or primitive, are mortally boring, prepared him for that definitive leap across the Atlantic which brought a new perspective to a European tradition that he himself embodied and whose failings he felt as his own. Just before his departure, 1936 was the year when this most uncommitted of writers, this debunker of politics, came nearest to a form of political commitment, in his lectures in favour of pacifism under the banner of Dick Sheppard's Peace Pledge Union.

Then, after eventually retiring *au-dessus de la mêlée*, in the westernmost part of the USA, on that margin of the Mojave desert which was fast becoming a crowded tryst of new-age hermits, golden boys of dream technologies and eternally young film stars, he suddenly turned from his theoretical and rather laborious militant work for pacifism to a lucid diagnosis of the deeper causes of European wars. As in all his endeavours, however sceptical, however liable to ironical criticism he may have been, Huxley was absolutely candid in his attempt. Even as he was tracing the roots of evil at least to the beginning of the seventeenth century he maintained that, in the field of politics, nothing or very little could be done by people of good will to bring about the desired changes. About Richelieu's Grey Eminence he wrote in 1941:

> I have developed a great feeling of compassion for my poor Father Joseph, who started out to become a saint, then imagined that there was a short cut to the kingdom of heaven through politics, and got more and more deeply involved in more and more frightful power policies, which resulted in the destruction of a third of the population of Central Europe, guaranteed the rise of Prussia as the head of the German confederation and paved the way for Louis XIV, the Revolution, Napoleon and all the rest. Plain utilitarian considerations demonstrate that anyone who has any desire for sanctity, any gift for the knowledge of ultimate reality, can do far more good by sticking to his curious activities on the margin of society than by going to the centre and trying to improve matters there. Instead of raising politics to his level, he will always be pulled down to the level of politics.[1]

In 1952, when witch hunting was becoming rampant, he returned to a similar biographico-historical subject, which he had already had in mind at the time he was writing *Grey Eminence*: the frightening intracultural encounter between superstition and reason, innocence and "fraud, hysteria, malicious plotting [resulting in] the commission of a monstrous judicial crime, the burning of Urbain Grandier"[2] at Loundun, in France, also in Richelieu's time. In this Huxley continued the work begun centuries earlier by the pioneers of the Enlightenment, as though for him the definition of history were not that it explains the past, but that it describes the eternal. The paradox is that, unawares, he thus gave history a function which naturally belongs to religion. In these books there was also something of a retrospective Zola, which became attenuated and diluted in the later Huxley, when the mystic preacher eclipsed and all but devoured the moralist, till the final defeat of the good boys in *Island* came almost as a

---

[1] Letter to Julian Huxley, 13 March 1941, in Grover Smith, ed., *Letters of Aldous Huxley* (London: Chatto & Windus, 1969).
[2] Letter to Harold Raymond, 12 July 1942.

relief and the image of evil triumphant left a feeling that all hope might not be lost in the land that had made that priceless gift to the world: the western. Such a reading of his spiritual testament may of course appear as heretic to ecologist or mystic readers, but Huxley himself might not have disagreed with it, considering his manichean view of evil, for his mind worked constantly in close action-reaction to the cultural currents of the time and to the ambience created by intra-and-intercultural antinomies. Those who heralded him as the prophet of a new relationship between man and the cosmos tended to forget that, however sincere Huxley always was, he also tended to remain critical of the evolutions he announced or reflected or fostered. Philip Thody even holds that between the idea of unity and the reality of separateness, between the motion towards a "perennial philosophy" and the act of writing fell the shadow of "mystical disbelief," or, as the critic puts it bluntly, that, fortunately for his readers, Huxley did not really believe in certain ideas on whose uniqueness and truth he insisted so stridently.[3]

The successive works in which these antinomies appeared show how they evolved and they reveal some of his blind spots. Naturally enough intracultural antinomies conditioned his attitudes towards his immediate environment, the British intellectual milieu in which he was brought up; but they also had a lasting effect on his response to foreign, if not to say totally alien cultures. There too Huxley epitomised modern man's growing difficulties in trying to reconcile old and new, the near and the far, and in coming to terms with the distaste and fear inherent in the dizzying multiplication of contacts in an open universe: with what could be called the adaptation syndrome. Huxley's serious reflection on contemporary problems was the continuation of debates whose sources can be traced to the origins of Western societies, and whose developments are found in the works of many other writers. These antinomies are as inescapable as time itself because they are part of our history, and perhaps, for some of them, of our intellectual build, though the forms they take may vary from author to author. For Huxley they had a peculiar urgency, for they had been in the family, as it were, at least since the famous grandfather Thomas Henry chose to defend Darwin. One of the most important debates, as reflected in Aldous, was between Science and Religion, but it extended and ramified into the religious controversies which were echoed in his mother's successive conversions and reconversions to and from the Church of Rome. The debate also included the post Romantic questioning about God and the cult of Nature. It revealed a more general quest which by and by became obsessive : that for a common ground not only between Science and Religion, but also between action and contemplation, as well as between all the forms of knowledge and all the forms of being. A passing reference to the debate on the two cultures may be included in this chart of a divided mind in search of unity.

---

[3] Philip Thody "Huxley and Religion: From Agnosticism to Mystical Disbelief," in Bernfried Nugel ed., *Now More Than Ever: Proceedings of the Aldous Huxley Centenary Symposium, Münster 1994.* (Frankfurt a. M.: Lang, 1995), 271-281.

In spite of his surprising oversight about the atom bomb in 1932[4] science was on Huxley's mind from the beginning of the 1920's. In his memoirs Julian Huxley recalls the heated discussions they had with D.H.Lawrence at Les Diablerets about the promises and dangers of science. Aldous Huxley could not accept Lawrence's downright rejection of scientific knowledge as such, but he also rejected his brother's belief in human progress through science. Julian Huxley belonged to H.G.Well's camp[5] against which Aldous fought constantly. His hope that a perfect balance between two extremes could be achieved proved delusive: caught between primitivism, which he would have liked to accept wholeheartedly, but which went against the grain with him, and the fascination he felt towards science, which he wished to condemn on ethical grounds, Huxley was perpetually trying to find a firm hold on a third term, actually no less delusive and self-contradictory than the other two: religion. But instead of clarifying the issues it introduced further antinomies which complicated the moral duty of choice. Religion went with sin and fanaticism, as exemplified by the Inquisition and fundamentalism. The savage in *Brave New World* showed the hopelessness of a guilt-ridden life. So, little by little, as we get deeper into the mechanism of Huxley's tight-rope-walking we see that he borrowed and adapted Stein's secret, the advice given to Lord Jim: "In the destructive element immerse." Aldous Huxley's unity rests on the multiple contradictions which remained unresolved to the end. He drew largely from those he attacked. Viewed from this relativistic vantage point it is knowledge itself that turns out to be intrinsically antinomic and provocative.

Huxley's religious attitude may be defined by that curious word invented by his grandfather: agnosticism. The word is a jack of all trades which, in its pointed Hellenistic quaintness does not reject gnosis but implies a regret: the loss of a bridge to the Gods. It sums up Huxley perfectly because in his case it applies beyond the strictly religious as an object of knowledge and becomes a mode of being. One suspects that in *Brave New World* this most lucid debunker of the dangers of science was unwittingly of the devil's party, for he protested so much that the denunciation of Frankenstein revealed that he could not shake off the mirage of the creature. Much in the same way his agnosticism reflected the whole spectrum of colours which the term may evoke, from downright atheism to a willing suspension of disbelief that left room for all beliefs. The difference between Huxley and others on this point is that in him the various attitudes coexisted and he could be Voltaire and Pascal rolled into one, he could deride religion and advocate it simultaneously. Just as, for him, the human comedy was also the human vomedy, the magic lantern of his agnosticism displayed the flitting images of a world without God, a Wordsworthian pantheistic ecologism, a collection of eastern philosophies, all dancing a merry syncretism and chanting a perennial faith in the universal everything. To charge him with inconsistency would be beside the point: Huxley's coherence rested on his insatiable curiosity. His agnosti-

---

[4] Huxley tried to explain this oversight in his foreword to the 1946 edition of *Brave New World*. Yet, as André Dommergues pointed out, Harold Nicolson published a novel about atomic warfare as early as 1932, the very year Huxley's dystopia was first published.

[5] *The Science of Life* was written in collaboration with H. G. Wells and his son G.P. Wells.

cism covered religion *and* science: he was ready to inquire into the paranormal, into the most exotic manifestations of ecstasy, into the chemistry of God. In his psyche intracultural encounters were ruled by the most absolute principles of intellectual democracy. God, science, belief and disbelief, saints and charlatans, all were facts with an equal right to exist and to speak. This is one of the fundamentals on which Huxley and his century meet.

The antinomy between Science and Religion was certainly stronger at the start in Aldous Huxley than in most of his contemporaries because his grandfather had helped set up a landmark in Western cultural history. But he did not think Science was right against Religion or Religion against Science. Curiously, until the beginning of the 1930's he thought both were wrong:

> About these scientists - it really is amazing the way they go on imagining that they are telling the truth, the whole truth and nothing but the truth. Their lack of realism is quite astonishing [...]. The habit of scientists was and still is to assert that the theories which work in the particular category of phenomena which they have chosen, arbitrarily, to consider, must work in *all* categories and conversely that the phenomenal categories in which these theories don't, as a matter of observed fact, work are for that reason illusory, non-existent. Hence the science-religion dispute, hence all the stoical despair of such professional scientific despairers as Bertrand Russell. I can only find it all rather comic - though also tiresome. Being an unmetaphysically-minded person preoccupied with phenomenal appearances, not ultimate reality, I think mostly of the diverse Many and not much of the final One (Letter to Scudder Klyce, 6 January 1930).

In *Do What You Will* Huxley's attacks against Christianity coexisted with Laurentian pantheistic echoes: "[A]ll the manifestations of life are godlike,"[6] heralding the mystic swing perceptible in *Eyeless in Gaza*, that goodbye to Europe. Once the change was made Huxley found himself in a position which seemed to be exactly opposite to the views at one time thought to be those of T.H.Huxley and Darwin himself. Nobody seriously thinks now that Darwin's theory, and science in general were a menace to religion. After 1936 Aldous Huxley broadly agreed with many famous scientists and theologians who thought that there was a convergence between science and religion: Eddington, Heisenberg, Bohr, Einstein, Pauli, de Broglie ; some even sharing Huxley's partiality for Eastern mysticism, like Schrödinger and Oppenheimer.[7]

If Aldous Huxley had stopped at that point he would merely have reflected the complete integration of science, especially of its apparently most irrational tenets, within the mental frame of twentieth century man, its coming to terms with faith. But, following and fostering a movement of opinion that is still gaining ground he went beyond and tipped the scales back against science, perpetuating that intracultural antinomy which has fuelled the dialectic motor of intellectual and social evolution. The question now is not simply, as in 1932, that scientific utopias are feasible, but that a host of religious utopias are too, whatever form they may take, from the mildest to the

---

[6] Aldous Huxley, "Spinoza´s Worm," in *Do What You Will: Twelve Essays* (London: Chatto and Windus, 1970), 62-92, here 78.

[7] Cf. June Deery, *Aldous Huxley and the Mysticism of Science* (London: Macmillan, 1996).

most fanatic. Huxley does not seem to have been fully aware of the risks inherent in advocating the setting up of modern mystic communities or in the pre-eminence given to the religious in secular matters, whereas he never failed to denounce the aberrations science could lead to. Except perhaps in his last work the later Huxley can even be suspected of naïveté on the supposed intrinsic harmlessness of the remedies he advised to contemporary problems: transcendental or ecological forms of utopianism also have their lobbies.

Were it feasible it would be needlessly tiresome to analyse all the sets of oppositions in which Huxley was caught, because they are the fabric of our civilisation, and the controversies they gave rise to have gone on to this day. The Sokal affair has recently shown that the debate on the two cultures is not closed. One East-West antinomy has become obsolete with the fall of the Berlin wall, but this was never a central concern of Aldous Huxley's. On the contrary, the other antinomy between "Eastern wisdom" and "Western thought" is still topical. Similarly Protestant or Catholic issues were never as determining for Aldous Huxley as they were for his mother, but his epistemological inconsistencies are those of many of our contemporaries: pseudo-science mistaken for science and used in support of mystical views; religious or pseudo-religious beliefs adduced to erode the hard edges of scientific pragmatism; action for ever at odds with non-attachment. Conversely, just as to Western eyes colonial attitudes and prejudices now seem to belong to another age, Huxley's reaction to the Far East and to Central America appears as die-hard nineteenth century chauvinism.

Intercultural antinomies were illustrated mainly in his travel books, published during his pre-mystic period. Superficiality is the reproach most commonly made concerning his approach to other cultures.

> All his judgements on the East expressed in *Jesting Pilate* seemed hopelessly immature and adolescent, the result of a deliberate evasion of social issues, a blindness towards the fierce revolutionary fervour which had taken Asia by the throat long before the time came for him to skim so delicately over the Asiatic landscape [...].[8]

In short Huxley, as a traveller, is the product of a double tradition: that of the Grand Tour and that of British Imperialism which fostered an unprecedented vogue of travelling round the world, reflected in the foreign, exotic, alien settings of many works of fiction and in the numerous travel books published in the last 150 years.[9] The fact that Huxley was commissioned by *The Nation* and *The Bookman* to write the articles that make up *Jesting Pilate* proves that the market for this intercultural commodity was as flourishing then as it is today.

Like the students in Erasmus's days Huxley began travelling through Europe in his teens, but unlike them he never studied abroad. There was nothing of the initiatic or

---

[8] Robert Payne, "Aldous Huxley," in Bernfried Nugel ed., *Now More Than Ever: Proceedings of the Aldous Huxley Centenary Symposium, Münster 1994*. (Frankfurt a. M.: Lang, 1995), 1-6, here 1-2.

[9] Cf. David Lodge. *The Art of Fiction* (London: Secker and Warburg, 1992).

the self-formative in his discoveries, only a democratised version of the Grand Tour, often reduced to some of the most fashionable spots, without necessarily including all those that were most significant from a cultural point of view. The first foreign country he went to was Germany, in 1912. Then in his Citroen he travelled extensively through France, Belgium, Holland and Italy. He went several times to Spain, but visited Greece only in 1954, when he was sixty. He saw Tunisia, India and Indonesia in 1925, and Central America in 1933. Huxley's attitude to European countries was at first that of a northern tourist happy to find sunshine and a change of scene in a not too unfamiliar environment. He quickly became partial to three countries which he eventually came to know in depth: Belgium, for obvious reasons, since it was there he found his first wife; France, because he admired French culture and loved the south; and Italy, the land of colour and artists.

Before his expatriation he settled in each of the three countries successively. His impressions appeared in *Along the Road*, in 1925. Even when he dealt with those countries he knew best his comments remained strangely detached. It seems he could like people only when they were at a distance. What he liked in France was the solitude of the underpopulated Massif Central; in Italy the anonymity of tourist resorts. He had "no interest in the political future of France." He might have added "or Italy." In his encounter with Europe Huxley thus exemplified an attitude often unjustly associated with British particularity: a curiosity for everything foreign provided it did not fundamentally call one's certainties into question. In Huxley's case the curiosity was real and the challenge to the stiff upper lip soon followed in his comments, as it did in Forster's fiction. Huxley's subsequent travels round the world were conditioned by that antinomic reaction he first showed towards his immediate neighbours, the French and the Italians. When, in Borneo or Bombay, he remarked that the world was owned by the whites and the natives were just good enough to bring the whisky, he at once reproduced and criticised the old colonial prejudices. His reaction was not protest, but a faint adumbration of that ironical complaint, by a South African celebrity, who said, before Mandela's return to political life, that he passed for an Englishman in New York while he was an alien in Africa his homeland. There was always something of an E.T. about Huxley in Britain, because he represented the old and the seed of the new at one and the same time.

"The Pierian Spring" in *Along the Road* is a striking illustration of Huxley's ambivalent attitude to modernity, with its corollary of unlimited intercultural contacts. It is named after the sacred water of knowledge which the Muses, daughters of Memory, made Dionysos drink: a striking emblem of the intercultural heritage of Europe.[10]

> The history of these two centuries, and especially of the last fifty years, has proved that, so far as the artist is concerned, much learning is quite as dangerous as little learning. It is, in fact, a great deal more dangerous [...]. In time, no doubt, the artists will have inured themselves to the poison of the Pierian spring. The immense mass of knowledge which, in our minds, is still crude, will gradually be digested [...]. To Voltaire and Dr. Johnson even Gothic art seemed a barbarism. What would they have said if we had asked

---

[10] The reference is to Michael Drayton and to Alexander Pope.

them to admire the plastic beauties of a Polynesian statue, or the painting of an animal by an artist who lived millenniums before the dawn of history?[11]

In 1925 this question, for Huxley, opened up the debate about how to redefine values "in an age of dissipated energies, of experiment and pastiche, of restlessness and hopeless uncertainty;" and for us, several decades later, it eventually raises the additional issue of the democratisation of knowledge in a world society, and that of the consequences of cultural imperialism.

Jesting Pilate, with its ambiguous title pointing both ways like Janus, to derision of any commitment and to derision of derision itself, was above all a testimony to Huxley's uneasiness in front of everything really foreign. Europe before the fall of the Eagles was the extended Victorian family, a close tribe in which the intercultural was immediately translated into the intracultural, because it did not include what lay beyond the family's grounds. Just as western Papua was considered by the Dutch as their property, even though most of them had never seen a Papuan and many did not even suspect that such a creature existed,[12] India was annexed to the British mental geography wholesale. There was indeed a striking contrast between Huxley's insensitivity when he was there to India's inner evolution, to the problems and expectations of a country seething with the ferments of change, and his subsequent devotion to "Eastern Wisdom" when the real East had safely receded to the antipodes: "To my mind 'spirituality' (ultimately, I suppose, the product of the climate) is the primal curse of India and the cause of all her misfortunes." The only perceptive comments on Indian civilisation in *Jesting Pilate* concern music.

In the Philippines, Java and Borneo, however, we see him faintly beginning to become interested in native realities:

> [T]he world into which you have stepped [in the Philippines ...] is unlike anything of which you have yet had experience in the equatorial orient. It is Spain—diluted, indeed, distorted, based on Malayan savagery and overlaid with Americanism, but still indubitably Spain. The Dutch have been in Java for more than three centuries [...]. But Java remains Javanese. The people have retained their clothes, their language, their religion; even in the towns, at the cosmopolitan ports, they are totally un-Dutch, just as the Malays of the peninsula, the Dyaks and Dusuns of Sarawak and North Borneo are totally un-English.[13]

At the end of his journey he might have added: "so are the Americans."

Huxley's failure in *Jesting Pilate* was all the more unaccountable as *A Passage to India* had been published two years before and had a considerable impact. His failure in *Beyond the Mexique Bay* was not due to the same reasons, for there could not be any mistaking Guatemala or Mexico with an exotic cricket ground. But just as the

---

[11] Aldous Huxley, "The Pieran Spring," in *Along the Road: Notes and Essays of a Tourist* (London: Chatto and Windus, 1974), 190-201, here 191, 197-8.

[12] Gabriel Defert, *L'Indonésie et la Nouvelle-Guinée-Occidentale* (Paris: L'Harmattan, 1996).

[13] Aldous Huxley, *Jesting Pilate: The Diary of a Journey* (London: Chatto and Windus, 1957), 231.

India he visited was haunted by the ghost of Victoria, in the land beyond the Mexique Bay hovered the shade of D.H.Lawrence and the obsessive image of Quetzalcoatl, that is to say a Western allegory of primitivism, a twentieth century romantic illusion. More than intercultural the encounter reflected the intracultural questioning of a time in which the cult of Life and of Blood and of the Dark God could not be innocent of political implications, though D.H.Lawrence and Huxley himself were never fully unaware of their ultimate consequences outside the field of art and literature.

The dissociation between what the artist thought he was doing and what he was actually doing saved Huxley's fiction. But the laws of fiction do not necessarily apply in travel books, which are devoid of plot and characters with a life of their own. This is why *Beyond the Mexique Bay* and *Jesting Pilate* are so disappointing. If Huxley had written what he had set out to write: an account of his experience in foreign lands, the books would have been different, and much more interesting. He would have included what we find only in his letters or in his biography by Sybil Bedford. We would have been thrilled by the adventurous episodes, for travelling in those days was not what it is today. Central America was largely impenetrable, Indonesia, and even some parts of India were far from safe. Huxley, instead, offered the ruminations of an introspective misanthrope who relished the curious but abhorred the picturesque. Refusing to behave like a tourist he eventually reacted like the worst of tourists who find fault with everything and carry around the cloak of the West with them. His novels narrowly escaped didacticism, but in his travel books the pontifex had lost the know-how of bridge building. The antinomies stood like useless pillars on either side of a stream of discovery which should have united rather than divided cultures.

If the avid traveller was clearly unable to establish direct contact with the traditions he sought to meet, the situation changed completely when he encountered the East dressed to Western tastes and when he saw differences from a safe distance. Even the foreign culture which he knew best, the French, was significantly more present in his works after his emigration from Europe. True, his literary beginnings were marked by Laforgue, but he never wrote so fully and perceptively about French culture as in the books published after 1937. The greatest change in this respect concerned the influence which Eastern doctrines, or rather Western versions of these doctrines exerted on his thinking. He confessed that in his student days he was interested in Buddhism, like T.S. Eliot, but this interest remained theoretical. The so called "conversion to mysticism" announced in *Eyeless in Gaza* was actually less a continuation of this early interest or a rejection of his former attitude of indifference, not to say downright hostility to Indian "spirituality" manifested in *Jesting Pilate*, than a sudden acceptance of the basic tenets of American transcendentalism, concomitant with his adoption of a new homeland. This would be unaccountable without the considerable influence Gerald Heard came to have over him. At times this influence verged on mimetism, some pages by Aldous Huxley reading as though they had been written by Heard. The soul brotherhood which differences in temperament had hindered with D.H.Lawrence Huxley now found in Gerald. Unfortunately, this went with a difference in stature too.

Huxley's intercultural syncretism after the Second World War was a utopian collage of elements that had been present in the American melting pot since the 19th century at least: miscellaneous elements stemming from the World Parliament of Religions, in Chicago in 1893,[14] a wealth of oriental studies that had been accumulating, and the fast developing sectarian movement. Huxley's main contribution appeared in *Vedanta and the West*, the organ of the Vedanta Society of Southern California. Huxley advocated the constitution of a world culture associating a moralised form of Western technology with a rationalised mysticism mainly of Hinduist inspiration. Needless to say criticism came from all sides. But the main paradox attached to this supposed vocation to universality of a model which, after all, was fundamentally American, both in its form and in its aspiration, was that the projection into a rosy future of cultural reconciliation between East and West of Eden was actually a nostalgic looking backwards. This "discovery" of world harmony was a rediscovery, a romantic avatar of the One by an author distrustful of romanticism.

As in Huxley's days the hill towers above Chichicastenango, in Guatemala and the pagan altars among the pines are still attended to by the chanting shamans. Children dance the *conquista* for a few quetzals at the foot of the hill as they did over half a century ago. Huxley would have been surprised by that unflagging vitality of the old cults. Owing to his Western prejudice he could no more have read the Aztec icons which Diego Rivera was inscribing all over his frescoes in Mexico than he could penetrate the unblinking impassiveness of the Indian soul. It is significant that he never mentioned Zapatta and that he accepted the simplistic view of Mexico as a land of unceasing light opera revolution. He did not suspect that Mayan culture was far from dying and that Quetzalcoatl had been slowly digesting Spanish Catholicism as it is now in the process of digesting the innumerable Protestant sects that have been flourishing since then in Central America, as they have been all over the world. The sixty odd years elapsed since Huxley's visit make us realise that the arrow of change was not directed towards the disappearance of the old civilisation, but, as the dancing children hinted, towards a reviviscence. When he went there the pagan rites were performed within hearing distance of the church. Nowadays the Catholic priest is barely tolerated in the church of Chichicastenango and is totally barred entrance in San Juan Chamula and many other churches. Huxley noted that the incumbent was in charge of 30, 000 souls in the early 30's. Catholics will see this as a shocking decadence, forgetting the systematic destruction of the old codices and the cultural persecution.

In Tikal the overgrown pyramids have been cleared and rebuilt for the tourists. Curiously there were next to no pyramids in his picture of Central America, perhaps because he saw few of them at the time, and above all because he did not go there to discover and decipher the traces of his own past in the Indian heritage. He was not out to find reasons to admire man, but to despair. It is a comforting thought that, lost in the jungle, a pre-classical heap of stones still awaited discovery. Mundo Perdido is the entrance to a vast subterranean city with, some say, kilometres of frescoes depicting Mayan civilisation, carefully preserved from indiscreet visits and from destruction.

---

[14] Stephen N. Hay, *Asian Ideas of East and West* (Cambridge MA.: Harvard University Press, 1970), 25. The American response to Swami Vivekananda's exposition of Sri Ramakrishna's teachings was enthusiastic.

From the few evanescent figures seen in other sites we can imagine that Huxley would have been as fascinated and repulsed by the wealth of their colours as he was by the exuberance of the Baroque and of Eastern art. He hated and relished what he considered as gesticulation in art and his tastes, in the monumental, went to Piranesi's *Prisons*, with their staircases that lead nowhere, rather than to the sacred steps of pyramids. Although a cultured man he could sometimes be blind to the force of culture against the modern barbarian's machine gun. The explanation may be that at the time he reflected the despair of twentieth century man. He was one who had eyes and saw only sorrow.

What saves the later Huxley from banality is his integration of the 18th and 19th century clichés of cultural universality within the frame of his creative imagination. Most of his fiction was published before his emigration, but after it Huxley's manner remained that of a novelist even in his non fiction. His intercultural landscape from 1936 onward was a dream landscape, a desert mirage reflecting his own generosity and benevolence, a form of illusion against which the hard facts of our world may eventually crumble. Amid the jetsam of innumerable subsequent catastrophes, it is hope which survives in Huxley's works, a blind man's hope, but still a reason to live. For, in that world culture which, like André Malraux, he helped bring forth, antinomy is now the condition of freedom, even as all intercultural encounters are becoming intracultural. By a strange reversal his very shortcomings and vulnerability lead us to discover the strength below, the ground for confidence, everybody's Mundo Perdido, the old missing links which make meaning.

Silence in Pinter: Regression from the Everyday to the Poetry of Memory

NORBERT GREINER (Heidelberg)

The "inadequacy of language" has been a prominent theme in 20th century literature both within the wider context of the Theatre of the Absurd and within the global context of the general decline of language.[1] These may at times provide meaningful approaches to Pinter, yet in his drama silence has different strategic tasks in the context of everyday verbosity. Surprising as it may seem, there are relatively few instances of silence as a gesture of inferiority or submission. In *The Birthday Party*, Stanley's speechlessness can from a certain stage be interpreted as intimidated silence, but I suggest that his is a far more radical form of falling silent which never finds words again and which indicates the final disintegration of figural identity.[2] Intimidated silence is almost restricted to the immediate context of another's verbosity, when a character puts up with the antagonist's displays:[3] McCann's relationship with Goldberg, Hirst's with Spooner in Act One of *No Man's Land*,[4] Spooner's quiet waiting after Brigg's and Foster's appearance (35-39). But apart from McCann's clearly secondary role, all the gestures of inferiority are deceptive and often transitory, designed to deflect and blunt the weapon of verbosity.

Forms of silence as gestures of superiority are in fact more frequent and more effective.[5] Hesitations, pauses, silences and total blackouts are familiar and characteristic features of Pinter's dramaturgy. Hesitant, stammering speech as a sincere attempt at (self?)-communication contrasts positively with copious wordiness; silence in Pinter is chiefly marked by conceited self-certainty, as in Foster's "What am I talking to

---

[1] On the general approach and literary history context see Hans Mayer, "Sprechen und Verstummen der Dichter" in Günther Patzig, Peter Hartmann, Hans Mayer et al., *Die deutsche Sprache im 20. Jahrhundert* (Göttingen: Vandenhoeck & Ruprecht, 1969), 64-78. See also Susan Sontag, "On Silence," *Aspen Magazine* 5-6 Sect. 3 (XIII) (1968); Ihab Hassan, *The Literature of Silence* (New York: Knopf, 1968).

[2] Cf. Norbert Greiner et al., *Einführung ins Drama*, 2 vols. (München: Hanser, 1982), vol.2, 67.

[3] With reference to individual dramas and Pinter's oeuvre, critics deal frequently with the phenomenon of hesitations and silences. Within the extensive literature, attention is drawn particularly to John Dawick's study "Punctuation and Patterning in *The Homecoming*," *Modern Drama* 14 (1971): 37-46; and for Pinter's work as a whole to Max Melius Wycisk, *Language and Silence in the Stage Plays of Harold Pinter* (Phil. Diss. Univ. of Colorado, 1972).

[4] Harold Pinter, *No Man's Land* (London: Methuen, 1975).

[5] This phenomenon still seemed paradoxical to Rüdiger Imhof, *Harold Pinters Dramentechnik* (Bonn: Bouvier, 1976), 187 but is in fact the rule rather than the exception when seen retrospectively and with regard to the function of verbosity.

him? ... I don't usually talk. I don't have to. Normally I keep quiet" (*No Man's Land*, 49). Verbose aggressivity may be advantageous for characters in particular situations, but it arises above all from a situational compulsion to attack. The character initiating a confrontation is actually or imagines himself to be at a disadvantage. He has to bring himself into play, establish or display his position or at least demonstrate his claim to superiority. In most cases this is the first sign of weakness, and in the long term the tactical advantage proves illusory. Silence communicates superiority, expressing itself as bored lack of interest in another's offer of communication and as demonstrative indifference to another's exhibitionism. The intense final scene of *The Caretaker*, when first Mick and then Aston make their escape from Davies' verbiage by quietly leaving or turning away, is frequently modified in Pinter's later dramas. A similar situation is found in the opening scene of *The Homecoming*, where Lenny undermines Max' repeated and varied discourse tactics (abuse, direct question, stories from the past, register and further measures designed to initiate conversation, to be accepted as a dialogue partner and to be affirmed in his role as head of the household). Lenny simply goes on reading his newspaper or ignores the topics Max offers and defines those that interest him. Max readily takes up these topics. Situations like this show how blunt the weapon of verbosity can become when faced with superior silence, and how ineffective verbal strategies are when the essential prerequisite of any phatic conversation is lacking, namely mutual willingness (for details see Dawick, "Punctuation," 39-40). This structural motif is copied in the final scene of *No Man's Land* when Hirst triumphs over Spooner. Here verbosity that draws substantially on the reservoir of everyday language is contrasted with indifferent silence. Aston's ambivalent behaviour is quite different however from Hirst's resigned and cynical "Let us change the subject" (91) and "I'll drink to that" (95). In this play with its parodistic and metaliterary elements that even extend to selfquotation, ordinary speech patterns and non-ordinary ways of speaking that have taken on ordinariness are dealt with indirectly and their contrivance is exposed. In this way the conflict is followed not only by the witnesses in the outer communication system, i.e. the audience, but also by the participants in the fictional stage situation, observing with cold and scornful detachment the character who fails to realise that his tactics have been seen through and his weapon has been blunted. His verbal sparring lacks a sparring partner.

The poet Hirst has at this moment long since recognised, for himself and with regard to Spooner, that both the poetic and fictional creation of the world through language and a "meaningful" construction of everyday life as a meaningful form of life directed at least towards some social purpose are futile. A language which, apart from the many non-referential functions indicated, can also be used in the context of everyday social small talk to reduce the monstrosities of our century to the level of banal party chat, treating them as phatic topics like the weather or sport ("You did say you had a good war, didn't you?" - "A rather good one, yes." - "How splendid...," 71), can no longer be the material of poetic vision. Only at rare moments, such as in an alcoholic haze, can language hesitantly and almost stutteringly be bold to give utterance.

In *Old Times*[6] as well, silence underscores the action. Here, however, the development proceeds almost reciprocally. During the course of nearly the entire drama, in which Deeley and Anna battle for Kate's affections, the two are reticent and silent. When they do speak, their brief utterances refer to tangible matters, and emphasize their untouched position. Only occasionally (see 42) does what they have to say betray any interest, and that is when the dialogues between the two rivals approach areas that have something to do with their solipsistic dreaming. Just once, at the very end, does Kate intervene, retaliating with the same weapons, ones which she however has much better control of than the other two. Yet this verbosity on Kate's part is not the end of Pinter's drama, despite the fact that it serves its purpose by shutting up the two rivals once and for all. The actual closing scene is underlined by silent play that keeps being interrupted - a total of seven times - by *silence* and *long silence*. It is a silence that, despite its ambiguity, underscores Deeley's defeat and Anna's partial defeat, as I see it. In addition, it also justifies Kate's success in defining her own world.

In moments such as these, silence can go so far as to pose an existential menace: "In the cracks of silence in Pinter's plays, some nameless and perhaps unnameable terror seeps in."[7] Yet apart from speculations as to its metaphysical significance, this terror has a social reason: It is the fear of one who has grown up believing in the power that language possesses to create reality. In this involuntary silence, the character does not see the yearned for final stage of a contemplative act which is directed toward things that are inexpressible. Instead, he or she can only see the loss of society and as a result, his or her loss of the world. Those characters who are the source for my silence do not share my fear. Terror is always - and it seems to me that this has always been overlooked in analyses of silence in Pinter's dramas - the condition of persons who are involuntarily confronted with the silence of others and not or only rarely of those persons who consciously choose to remain silent. And this occurs frequently, especially in Pinter's later dramas. Every time it does, Pinter critics interpret it to be the climax of a dissociation process of the character's personal identity and the dramatization of a terminal stage.

It is true that from the perspective of role concept theory, "those figures (are) the strongest, who either are completely taken over by their roles (Goldberg, McCann) and as a result actually do not possess their own ego-identity, or those who do not have any role or who reject every role (Matchseller, Kate)."[8] However, critics taking this perspective always consider the rejection of any and every role to be a loss or a defeat. The logical consequence for Kate, then, is that she experiences the fictitious world as "a being without identity, without roles, thus a non-person" (Mengel, *Harold Pinters Dramen*, 201). For the characters in *No Man's Land* and for Hirst in particular it is valid that they are "without any identity," and that they have lost "hope" and the

---

[6] Harold Pinter, *Old Times* (London: Methuen, 1971).
[7] Phoebe Wray, "Pinter's Dialogue: The Play on Words," *Modern Drama* 13 (1971): 418-22, here 421. Cf. John Lahr, " The Language of Silence," *Evergreen Review* 13 (1969): 53-5, 82-91.
[8] Ewald Mengel, *Harold Pinters Dramen im Spiegel der soziologischen Rollentheorie* (Frankfurt/M.: Lang, 1978), 201.

"access to reality normally guaranteed by the distribution of positions and roles." This perspective makes sense considering that it is consistent with a socio-psychological role concept model and that it excludes any identity constructions beyond the level of social reality such as in myths and metaphysics. Yet it must be possible to view the attempt to flee the world in another light. It is the character's attempt to flee from the world as it presents itself to him or her, from everyday life with its routine, utilitarian and power-oriented events that have taken on monstrous proportions, and from the hell that is posed by "the others." Especially considering that these attempts are accompanied by the conspicuous stylistic characteristics in the form of poetic language taking the place of monotonous everyday language. On the linguistic level, the character's poetic language provides a positive contrast to that of the other characters in the play.

The question should be raised as to whether Pinter's silent characters do not have a perfectly good reason for withdrawing from the world. There is no doubt that it is a matter of regression. Yet, it is the regression from a discourse world that not only was no longer able to guarantee the security of the character but by its very nature led him or her to an emotional breakdown. It is the regression from a discourse world whose thing-like blather created a social solidarity that was only short-lived and appeared to be much more suitable for aggression and provocation. Finally, it is the regressions from reality via memory into amorphousness (Mayer, "Sprechen und Verstummen," 65), which in our context should be interpreted as being a regression from everyday routine and its language.

Here, silence is still a concrete and poetic vision of an individual *Mysterium* that is linguistically inaccessible and not available to others yet does not necessarily betray any and every identity, but which prevents the character from disintegration into everyday conflict. We would like to interpret this as the attempt to work one's way through[9] an extremely subjective, radical asocial psychic reality that is beyond everyday reality and identity constructions that are defined by social context. This new reality serves as a refuge from everyday struggles, from the problems of alienation, from social or political compulsions or repression and effectively undermines the instrument of inauthentic verbosity.

It is probably no accident that Susan Sontag contrasts the self-forgetful contemplation of a landscape with rational, analytical "understanding" discourse, and that Pinter entitles his study in silences[10] *Landscape*. This regression to the subjective landscape of memory is imaginary in that it apparently selects from the past those "moments of

---

[9] Cf. Norman Oliver Brown, *Love's Body* (New York: Vintage Books, 1968), 257: "The doctrine of the unconscious, properly understood, is a doctrine of the falseness of all words, taken literally, at their face value, at the level of consciousness. The true psychic reality, which is the unconscious, cannot be put into words, cannot ever be translated into words" (cited in Lahr, "Language of Silence," 85).

[10] Lahr, "Language of Silence," 86; cf. Susan Sontag's apt comment: "A landscape doesn't demand from the spectator his 'understanding,' his imputations of significance [...] it demands, rather, his absence, that he does not add anything to it. Contemplation, strictly speaking, entails self-forgetfulness on the part of the spectator."

bliss" (Beth) (Dawick, "Punctuation," 42) which were not exposed to the daily process of disintegration or are quite obviously wishful thinking (Ellen).

These two cases of subjective, lost utopia are deliberately set apart from the ugly events of everyday life as enacted or remembered. This step is not simply into the "past" in the usual sense. It is a step into the more complex and unfathomable remembrance, almost indistinguishable from repressed yearnings. This step is the only conceivable way out of everyday life, when the usual step into the feast-day can no longer be taken. And this area also takes on another linguistic form, or at least seeks to do so.

In the context of a colloquial, pragmatic use of language this may well appear to be a loss. In abandoning the socially constituted role, and withdrawing from everyday action and speech, language also seems to have lost its function. Not only does instrumental action become impossible, but also meaningful linguistic action, since when people lose the access to reality guaranteed by their position and role-playing this also means losing their grip on the subjects they could still talk about (see Mengel, *Harold Pinters Dramen*, 22). This applies to the extent that the position of the figure is a pure negation, as in the case of Hirst's programmatic rejection of reality. But Hirst also has moments of yearning for another world, a world that can have its place only in the inner life of the character. It remains closed to him and his cynical rejection of the world denies him the saving regression into a world of remembered or projected alternatives. Yet associations of another kind meanwhile penetrate his timelessness, in which past and future jell into an eternal now, allowing no change of theme:

> I was dreaming of a waterfall. No, no, of a lake. I think it was ... just recently.
> [...] Something is depressing me. What is it? It was the dream, yes.
> Waterfalls. No, no, a lake. Water. Drowning (43-4).

Yet his dream gains no contours. The past remains a closed book and his memory fails or is deliberately blocked:

> I've forgotten. By all that's sacred and holy. The sounds stopped. It was freezing. There's a gap in me. I can't fill it. There's a flood running through me. I can't plug it. ... I remember nothing ... (46).

In these moments he finds another language, however, different from Spooner's mannered, elaborate style, and from other passages of his own. This language is deliberately verbose, and he uses it to engage in the everyday wordplay of phatic communion. Here short sentences do not give an impression of staccato tirades or aggressive tension; the diction is not one of tormented, strategic change of register; the phrase linkers, rhetorically unadorned, do not suggest he is speaking to impress. This is certainly not "meaningful language acts" - but perhaps it is more. Fragments of memory and associations are pieced together to make up a sub-picture, like a jigsaw puzzle of which most of the pieces are lost. Yet such passages in *No Man's Land* are rare and less in quantity than the social wordplay of the characters.

Kate in *Old Times* is similarly withdrawn. Not opening herself to either of the men fighting over her, she too is characterised by large-scale language abstinence, except for the above mentioned, last long speech of the play, the only time when she makes use of the linguistic weapon of her opponents. After that she only speaks at length one more time, in a passage of extraordinary language interest:

> Kate
> Thank you. I feel fresh. The water's very soft here. Much softer than London. I always find the water very hard in London. That's one reason I like living in the country. Everything's softer. The water, the light, the shapes, the sounds. There aren't such edges here. And living close to the sea too. You can't say where it begins or ends. That appeals to me. I don't care for harsh lines. I deplore that kind of urgency. I'd like to go to the East, or somewhere like that, somewhere very hot, where you can lie under a mosquito net and breathe quite slowly. And living close to the sea too. You can't say where it begins or ends. That appeals to me. I don't care for harsh lines. I deplore that kind of urgency. I'd like to go to the East, or soewhere like that, somewhere very hot, where you can lie under a mosquito net and breathe quite slowly. You know... somewhere where you can look through the flap of a tent and see sand, that kind of thing. The only nice thing about a big city is that when it rains it blurs everything, and it blurs the lights from the cars, doesn't it, and blurs your eyes, and you have rain on your lashes. That's the only nice thing about a big city (59).

This passage features a similar simplicity to the cited dialogues from *No Man's Land*, particularly as it clearly contrasts with the linguistic finesse otherwise typical of the other characters. What is interesting, however, is the central image complex of this monologue, tantamount to a self-characterisation, linking Kate with Hirst and above all to the much more closely drawn women's figures in *Landscape* and *Silence*. They are all quietly fascinated by water, rain and the sea (in Hirst's case, the lake and waterfall, the image of drowning). In all cases, as also in *Silence*, this imagery evokes the opposite to the restricted, hopeless, ugly life of the city - just compare Briggs' Bolsover Street speech (*No Man's Land*, 62-63) with Kate's rejection of urban, unnatural life[11] and with the city/country antinomy developed in such detail (crowd, dirt, noise: wind, horizon, solitude) in *Silence*. In perfect harmony with the complexities of chaos, ancient wisdom, rebirth and purification, conventionally symbolized by water, we may sense a yearning which - be it a matter of individual psychology, or social and cultural critique - dreams of a condition free of the "hellish" interpersonal pressure of everyday middle-class life and modern civilisation.

By formal analogy with the selected sphere of imagery, the memory making such withdrawal possible at all turns out to have no clear contour, shape or definition. Instead, it resembles the unlimitedness, inconceivability, indefinability and imponderability of the whole material.

---

[11] In a further, much shorter speech Kate asks Anna whether her home is paved with marble on which she can walk barefoot and whether she loves the local population - a question to which Anna responds with silence (41-3).

In *Landscape* and *Silence* only these complexes of theme and imagery are consistently related to one another. Thematically, dramatically and linguistically these two plays focus on the phenomena referred to above. A short final glance may indicate the new stylistic analogies Pinter is seeking in order to shift his motifs, although a more exact analysis could only follow from a general interpretation, which cannot be given here. The fact that the accents in the language sphere have shifted from strategic verbosity to a lyrical tone going beyond the above mentioned poetic features is clear in Pinter criticism, although not always pointed out in a sufficiently textured way.[12] And from these texts too it could be shown that the language conventions of the early work have not been totally abandoned, being used in thematic contexts similar to that of the early work. Yet the thematic context as a whole is different. Referring to our general theme of everyday action and reality, the characters have - successfully or not - been more radical in their inward regression than Kate and Hirst. This applies at least to the - in this sense - positive figures of Beth, Ellen and Rumsey. The need for other language dimensions and functions arises from this denial, in which Kate finds her strength vis-à-vis the two antagonists and Hirst his superior cynicism and acceptance of losing the world. As the characters no longer relate to one another in speech and action, seeking or projecting themselves in their memories, the speech situation resembles a lyrical self much more than a dramatic character. Such characters, who continue to speak and move in the present - it is mainly the male ones ("Beth: Lots of people ... *Pause* People move so easily. Men. Men move" [*Landscape*, p.91]) - possess all the features of linguistic aggression and everyday language action we have described. The differing worlds of memory and of practical, everyday life are somehow demarcated linguistically.[13] Kate, Hirst, Beth and Ellen are also related through their characteristic spheres of imagery. The water, waterfall, lake and sea symbolism of *No Man's Land* and *Old Times* corresponds to the cloud and wind symbols in *Silence* and the striking sea symbolism in *Landscape*. One might think that Kate's yearning for the formless, boundless depths and Hirst's dream of drowning is partially, even fully realized in Ellen's psychic state - her *floating* corresponds to the wonderful flying clouds (40, 48):

> Suddenly I stood. I walked to the shore and into the water. I didn't swim. I don't swim. I let the water billow me. I rested in the water. The waves were very light, delicate. They touched the back of my neck (*Landscape*, 16).[14]

---

[12] Cf. Ruth Milberg, "1+1=1: Dialogue and Character Splitting in Harold Pinter," *Die Neueren Sprachen* 73 (1974): 225-33, here 225: "[...] the conversation is lyric and poetic, not the clipped distinctive Pinter debate." This statement fits Beth, but Duff only to a limited degree (see below).

[13] Cf. Francis Gillen, "'All these bits and pieces:' Fragmentation and Choice in Pinter's Plays," *Modern Drama* 17 (1974): 477-87, here 481-2. Also Arthur Ganz, "Mixing Memory and Desire: Pinter's Vision in Landscape, Silence and Old Times," in Arthur Ganz, ed., *Pinter: A Collection of Critical Essays* (Englewood Cliffs: Prentice Hall, 1977), 161-9.

[14] *Floating* also characterizes Kate (*Old Times*, 54). Notice also the elaborate *wetness* metaphor around Beth in *Landscape*, 24-5.

In all these cases the yearnings for water signify dissolution processes, inadequately expressed in the sociological term of identity loss, particularly with its pejorative connotation. In all these cases there is the yearning for a raison d'être beyond rationality linked to identity-promising "everyday" forms of society and modern life,[15] indicated as contrasts in the antagonistic positions of each text, as the origin of threatening identity crises.

The dilemma of all Pinter characters must remain that everyday life and interaction represent both a condition for life and threat to the identity of the individual and their suffering through the existence of others. So the regression from everyday life into a memory so contourless and unfathomable as the water that symbolises it, and with which it is immaterial whether it is made up of authentic or imaginary particles,[16] is only possible as a dream or fiction, the language here reminiscent of the powerful lyric drama of Dylan Thomas.

> Beth
> ...So sweetly the sand over me. Tiny the sand on my skin.
> Pause.
> So silent the sky in my eyes. Gently the sound of the tide.
> Pause.
> Oh my true love I said (30).

Far from everyday forms and functions, far from the symptoms of linguistic disintegration, here the rhetorical repetitions, alliterations, euphonic assonances and simple but precise metaphors in dactylic metre form themselves into a theatrical poem[17] reflecting those natural rhythms that signify the yearning for a dissolution of everyday identity.

---

[15] The fragments of memory always present the opposite of what the characters experience in everyday life: idealisations of fundamental areas of life like love, social bonding, sense of identity and freedom. And only in the "positive" characters do water, rain etc. gain the mentioned symbolic significance. For Duff e.g. a shower of rain that seemed a blessing to Kate in *Old Times* is a nasty *downfall*, to be protected from and not enjoyed.

[16] Ellen also suffers isolation and withdrawal into memory, albeit more closed than Beth's.

[17] It remains to be shown in detail that through repetition, echoes of theme and motif, and carefully orchestrated sound patterns not only the monologue parts of the two characters are related to one another, but also the macrostructure of the whole text is woven in this way (cf. James Eigo, "Pinter's *Landscape*," *Modern Drama* 16 (1973): 197-83, here 179-81).

The Discourse of Radical Alterity: Reading Process and Cultural Meaning in William Faulkner's *The Sound and the Fury*

HUBERT ZAPF (Augsburg)

William Faulkner's *The Sound and the Fury* (1929), one of the greatest novels of American literature, poses to the reader a special hermeneutic challenge.[1] To the initial attempt of a coherent reading, it proves a highly resistant object of understanding, a barely decipherable labyrinth of linguistic signs, which nevertheless offers fragmentary glimpses of a fictional world suggesting a fascinating cosmos of language and meaning hidden beneath the chaotic surface, and enticing the reader to its imaginative exploration. I shall focus in the present essay on this aspect of the reader's experience in *The Sound and the Fury*, asking specifically in which way the problems of communication that the text presents are themselves part of its intended 'message,' and in which way the temporal sequence of perspectives, themes, and states of consciousness into which the reader is transposed in the novel's process contributes to its production of cultural meaning.

I will look at both micro- and macrostructural aspects of the reading process, whereby the difference of strangeness and familiarity serves as an interpretative frame which is relevant to both reception psychology and cultural hermeneutics. For it is in the difference of strangeness and familiarity that the reader-oriented process of communication and the cultural-critical production of textual meaning converge. The underlying methodological assumption is that the psychodynamics of the reading process itself, beyond the systemic quality of the text as a 'spatial' structure of meaning, gains an important function in the production of the text's cultural meanings in the temporal sequence of its successively unfolding fictional experiences. It goes without saying that I can sketch only the outlines of this process within the scope of this paper.

Literature can be considered, generally speaking, as a complex linguistic act of understanding one's self through understanding another, which by staging cultural borderline-situations defamiliarizes the familiar and confronts the dominant self-images of a cultural world with their neglected 'other.' *The Sound and the Fury* appears as a radicalization of this literary discourse of alterity. The extreme destabilization of the relationship between sign and referent, between signifier and signified in Faulkner's

---

[1] The role of the reader in Faulkner's fiction has been variously commented upon by critics, but has not received the kind of sustained and systematic critical attention it deserves. A pioneering study, however, was Wolfgang Iser's chapter on *The Sound and the Fury* in his book *The Implied Reader: Patterns of Communication in Prose Fiction from Bunyan to Beckett* (Baltimore: Johns Hopkins University Press, 1974). More recently, Irene Visser, *Compassion in Faulkner's Fiction* (Lewiston et al.: Mellen University Press, 1996), investigates the communicational structure of Faulkner's texts from the perspectives of hermeneutics and reception aesthetics.

novel opens up a semiotic space in which the perspectives of cultural outsider figures can be foregrounded and articulated in unprecedented scope and intensity. The text turns into a discourse of radical alterity, in which the familiar becomes strange and the apparently strange gains an irritating familiarity. By including the culturally excluded and repressed in the understanding of the self, the text suspends any binary opposition between self and other and involves the reader in a process of reception in which alterity is experienced as an irreducible element of difference within one's own subjectivity.

I

Faulkner's literary productivity -- besides poems and numerous short stories he wrote nineteen novels -- can be said to have developed out of a characteristic tension between provinciality and modernity, regionalism and universalism, the retreat into privacy and cosmopolitan openness. For all their close connection to biography and local history, his themes are at the same time transpersonal, transnational, and transhistorical. In the private microcosm of his fictional province of "Yoknapathawpha," world literature is always implicitly present.

Nowhere else in his work is this tension between the idiosyncratic proliferation of the private -- the 'idiotic' in the original, Greek sense of idiotes (=private individual) -- and the dimension of the universally human more obvious than in his first great novel, *The Sound and the Fury*. Nowhere else, too, is the aesthetic experiment conducted as uncompromisingly as in this book, which according to Faulkner marked his decisive breakthrough to his own characteristic style. In its four chapters, the novel relates from the different perspectives of three brothers and, finally, of an omniscient third-person narrator the fate of a once powerful, but now declining Southern family, the Compsons. In the famous first chapter of the novel, surely one of the most bizarre and at first glance confusing ones in literary history, the world is described literally from an idiot's point of view, through the eyes of the mentally retarded Benjamin, the youngest of the Compson brothers.

Faulkner in fact attempts the impossible here: he tries to transform into language what defies language, and it is precisely in this paradoxical task that he defines the function of literature. Let us look at the beginning of the novel:

> APRIL SEVENTH, 1928
> Through the fence, between the curling flower spaces, I could see them hitting. They were coming toward where the flag was and I went along the fence. Luster was hunting in the grass by the flower tree. They took the flag out, and they were hitting. Then they put the flag back and they went to the table, and he hit and the other hit. Then they went on, and I went along the fence. Luster came away from the flower tree and we went along the fence and they stopped and we stopped and I looked through the fence while Luster was hunting in the grass.
> "Here, caddie." He hit. They went away across the pasture. I held to the fence and watched them going away.

"Listen at you, now." Luster said. "Aint you something, thirty-three years old, going on that way. After I done went all the way to town to buy you that cake. Hush up that moaning. Aint you going to help me find that quarter so I can go to the show tonight"(3).[2]

The confusion of the first-time reader is considerable. To be sure, the choice of words is simple and the outward form of language is intact. But what is described remains blurred and shadowy. The perceptions that are registered in a paratactic-descriptive mode and in a highly restricted code appear to happen mechanically and are not connected in any logical way. Although there is a first-person narrator, he appears to be a subject without subjectivity, a merely passive medium recording movements and impressions, without the ability of ordering the unfiltered sensory material that streams through it.

Still, there are a few signals of orientation for the reader. The first sentence introduces the fence motif, which, like other words, is repeated several times, and which marks the boundary between the narrator and the world he is excluded from, a world which nevertheless appears to command his almost exclusive attention. The gaze through the fence, as if through the bars of a prison the narrator is locked into, falls on a world which contains flowers and in which strangers, for unknown reasons, are "hitting." This outside world is therefore at once attractive and threatening, and the inner world of the narrator is separated from it by the fence in a both protective and painfully isolating way. Furthermore, the reader is informed that the narrator is 33 years old and has been given a cake, and yet has started to cry. This incoherent reaction appears vaguely connected with the call "Here, caddie," whose relevance however cannot be accounted for at this stage.

This is about all that the reader can conclude from a first reading of this opening passage. It does, nevertheless, create a first impression of the characteristic atmosphere and motifs of the Benjy-chapter, which are developed and differentiated in the subsequent parts of the text. And although the meaning and coherence of what is being communicated remain unclear and chaotic at first, the form of its linguistic presentation is outwardly clear and well-ordered -- it is characterized by ortho-graphically and grammatically correct simple sentences structured by conventional punctuation. This is by no means always the case in the novel. On the contrary, Faulkner's style is distinguished by ultra-long sentences, often without punctuation, by the attempt "to force the whole cosmos into one sentence," as one critic aptly put it. What matters here, however, is that the verbal representation of the inner world of a mentally retarded man incapable of speech becomes recognizable as a fictional construct, as a bridge the author tries to build for the reader between the structures of language and the amorphous material of pre-linguistic experience. From the very beginning of the novel, then, Faulkner's stream-of-consciousness technique disclaims any character of 'immediacy,' and instead becomes visible as an always only secondary attempt of capturing in language the pre-linguistic origins of what literature tries to express.

---

[2] Page numbers refer to the following edition: William Faulkner, *The Sound and the Fury* (New York and Toronto: Vintage Books, 1974).

What Faulkner confronts here in its extreme form is the paradox of literature itself. For if literary language is marked, from the beginning of the novel, as a medium for staging the pre-linguistic origins of experience, it is at the same time marked as an insuperable boundary to what it tries to express. It becomes perceptible as a semiotic boundary drawn by the structure and the conventions of its own medium, illustrating an irredeemable rupture between the cultural signs and the experiences they represent, but also the inescapable interdependence of both poles in the process of human self-interpretation.

The justification for thus taking the extremely limited perspective of the Benjy-chapter as exemplifying the generally human problems of self and world, of language and experience, of life and literature, derives not least from the Shakespearean quote after which it is modeled. The novel's title, of course, refers to the passage in Macbeth, V, 5, in which Macbeth, confronted with the news of Lady Macbeth's death, reflects on human life in the following way:

> Life's but a walking shadow, a poor player
> That struts and frets his hour upon the stage,
> And then is heard no more: it is a tale
> Told by an idiot, full of sound and fury,
> Signifying nothing.

Life itself appears as an unreal shadow play in this *theatrum mundi*, as a 'text' originating from the mind of a fool, full of empty noise and aimless activity -- or, in the language of contemporary literary criticism, as a 'signifier' without a 'transcendental signified' ("Signifying nothing"). Faulkner takes this passage literally, and the Benjy-chapter is precisely in this sense a "tale told by an idiot," a narrative that at first appears as a chaotic process of signs without aim or meaning. On a closer look, however, it becomes clear that Faulkner moves beyond the semiotic nihilism of the Macbeth-quote. Even though the connection between language and world, sign and meaning is broken, it is not wholly abandoned or merely arbitrary in a postmodern sense. Rather, the process of the text is characterized by an extreme degree of tension between the poles of signifier and signified, between the promise and the denial of meaning.

It is the task of the reader to bridge this gap, and to transform the apparent chaos into order -- a task which can, however, never be fully achieved. As we have seen, the way the reader experiences the text at first converges more or less with the chaotic way Benjy experiences the world. What is created here is a hermeneutic borderline-situation, as it were, which by defamiliarizing the familiar, by withholding information, and by establishing a high degree of indeterminacy, raises and radicalizes the problem of understanding itself.

And the reader's initial bewilderment still increases in the course of the first chapter, because the narrator lacks any sense of time and moves back and forth between different time planes according to his associations. In Benjy's memory, all perceptions, scenes, and dialogues have been stored completely but without order, and are all simultaneously present. Scenes from the past can be recalled through the impulse of an impression, an image or a sound, and are indistinguishable from present events in their intensity. It has been calculated that the Benjy-chapter consists of 106 fragments that are related to 13 different scenes from 13 different time levels and merge into an effect of simultaneity. Traumatic experiences of the present and daydream-like scenes from the past form an indissoluble continuum that follows exclusively Benjy's tensions of pleasure and pain and thus additionally complicates the reception of this chapter.

At the same time, however, as the text progresses, it provides more and more clues to a possible interpretation of and an approximation to this hermetic inner world -- clues, which transgress the limitations of this experiential perspective and open up in retrospect ever new contexts for the comprehension of what has been radically alien at first. The seemingly inaccessible alterity of an extreme outsider position is thus brought back from cultural exclusion and becomes part of the process of meaning that the novel unfolds.

Looking back at the novel's beginning with this additional knowledge, the situation becomes far more clear and concrete. It is Easter Saturday 1928, Benjy's 33rd birthday, and, as every day, he is waiting at the gate of the garden fence for his sister Caddy to return from school. Caddy, the only one who has ever made Benjy feel loved and cared for, has in reality grown up long ago and, because of her ruined moral reputation, has not only moved away but has become a *persona non grata* in her own family. What is happening on the lawn on the other side of the fence is a game of golf taking place on a piece of land formerly belonging to the Compsons, which used to be the children's playground and which was later sold to enable the eldest son Quentin to go to Harvard. Luster is Benjy's young guard and a member of the family of black servants of the house. He is looking for a lost quarter in the grass, which he needs to be able to go to the show of a traveling theater company that evening. Benjy's crying, which seems to be unmotivated at first, can be explained with the golfer's call to his "caddie," which painfully calls back to Benjy his sister's absence, and in connection with this the loss of the children's playground, and possibly also his castration, with which he was punished after he once slipped through the open gate into the street and approached passing schoolgirls who reminded him of Caddy.

Thus, a closer look reveals that the situation is not at all abstract but, on the contrary, highly charged with emotions and psycho-biographical implications. For Benjy, Caddy is the absent center of meaning of his world, whose imaginative presence is continually evoked by his memories, but whose traumatically felt absence makes him all the more sharply suffer the pain of alienation. The key scenes which he remembers and which often supersede his present perception of reality are centered around her. They enable the reader to trace the outlines of Caddy's fate, from early childhood experiences to her adolescence and her first relationships with young men -- to which Benjy reacts with panic-like fears of loss --, to her pregnancy, her failed marriage, and especially her promiscuity which is in utter defiance of the Southern code of morality and provokes her banishment from the family.

Although Benjy can neither speak nor master the cultural rules of communication, he has developed an extraordinary ability to turn his sensory perception into a form of emotional perception -- an interpersonal sensitivity bordering on the parapsychological. He "smells" sickness and death, "hears" the darkness, and knows by instinct everything about the important moral and personal events and crises of the family. To Benjy, the moments in which Caddy took him in her arms and "smelled like trees," are the moments of perfect happiness in his childhood, and these are, within the stream of his associations, just as intensely present as the feelings of separation, alienation, and suffering.

As the reader is immersed into this inner world, other characters' opinions of Benjy which are merely based on outward perceptions appear all the more reductive - that of his whining, cold-hearted mother, who in her frequent bouts of self-pity calls him a curse laid upon her; that of the black servant, who fears him as a bad omen; and that of the cynical middle brother Jason, who regards him and his black guard merely as inferior, subhuman caricatures of the race: "Well at least I could come home one time without finding Ben and that nigger hanging on the gate like a bear and a monkey in the same cage"(291-92).

II

The novel's second chapter records the stream-of-consciousness of Quentin, the oldest of the Compson brothers and a Harvard student, and relates the day of his suicide, June 2, 1910. It is set 18 years before the first chapter, while the third chapter again moves 18 years forward in time and narrates the day before the first chapter. Through this alternation of time levels, the novel's narrative process itself conveys the presence of the past in the present which is one of Faulkner's chief concerns.

For Quentin, too, his sister Caddy is an absent center of meaning which nevertheless influences the events in a crucial way. The figure of Caddy was for Faulkner a central theme of the novel, which he tried to deal with in an indirect way through the different perspectives of her three brothers and, finally, of the omniscient narrator. In her omnipresent absence she stands for everything which is excluded and tabooed by the official family system and its anachronistic Southern code of morality, but which nevertheless subconsciously becomes an all the more powerful determining force in the text. She herself, however, remains vague and a figure of the imagination for the reader rather than a real character, and only indirectly, through the obsession with which she is evoked by the narrator figures, does she take shape for the reader. In the case of Quentin, this obsession with and fixation on Caddy as a symbol of the loss of an ideal world of values, of his internalized version of the Southern moral code, is one of the main reasons for his self-destructive melancholy.

At first sight, the contrast of this chapter to the preceding Benjy-chapter could not be any more striking. Its narrative perspective is easily recognizable as that of an intellectual. The vocabulary is richly differentiated, the sentences are far more complex, and the narrated events are subjected to an unceasing process of reflection. Perception and abstraction, matter-of-fact report and poetic-symbolic interpretation of the events interfuse and merge into a highly elaborate, semantically dense discourse. The narrating I watches itself continuously, and is fully aware of each of its activities. It is not a merely reactive and unconscious medium of perception like Benjy's, but a highly sophisticated medium of reflection that intensely and consciously relates to itself and the world.

And yet a closer look reveals some significant parallels as well. Quentin reacts in a hypersensitive way to all experiences, and he compulsively relates them to the problems of his family's history upon which he, no less than Benjy, is fixated. His memories, which constantly intrude into the story set outwardly at Harvard, focus on similar scenes as Benjy's. Quentin, too, does not appear free but strangely traumatized and as if under trance-like compulsion, always painfully trying to keep his external life under control, yet always threatened by the catastrophic loss of control, by the fear of moral and metaphysical chaos. Quentin has indeed a stronger affinity to Benjy than seems to be the case at first. But it is his particular problem that he is unable to come to terms with the discrepancy between consciousness and desire, between his idealistic value system and the disillusioning forces of reality. Whereas the first chapter is set on Benjy's birthday, the second chapter is set on the day of Quentin's death. Thus the two parts are related in terms of beginning and end, of (re-)birth and mortality, and form complementary rather than antithetical perspectives.

The contradictory doubling of Quentin's consciousness is mirrored in the manner of narration. On the one hand, it records in a controlled, matter-of-fact way the different stages of the last day of his life, but on the other hand, it keeps plunging into proliferating associations and phantasies from his past which, as in the Benjy-chapter, arbitrarily change time levels. Just as his plan of suicide is interrupted several times by unforeseen events, his narrating I keeps being flooded by dream-like images of his subconscious, and correspondingly, the coherence of language breaks down and dissolves at times into mere clusters of discursive shreds.

At least there is, in contrast to the Benjy-chapter, something like a recognizable plot here, even if it is limited to banal activities which are nonetheless carried out with ritual care by Quentin and which are interrupted by grotesque incidents. The narrative starts out in the morning in Quentin's room at Harvard, where he tears off the hands of the old watch his father gave him as a legacy and a *memento mori*. Instead of attending classes, Quentin dresses formally as if for a holiday and then goes to town with the ruined but continually ticking watch in his pocket. In a hardwareshop, he buys two heavy flat-irons which he is going to tie to himself when going into the water. Around noon he meets a little Italian girl in a bakery, who starts following him on his aimless walks and whom he cannot get rid of. When relatives in search of the child discover her in Quentin's company, they believe he's a kidnapper and get the sheriff to arrest him, and only after paying a small sum he is set free again. On his way back to college, Quentin, for no apparent reason, attacks a student who reminds him of Caddy's first seducer, but is severely beaten up by him. Back in his room by early evening, he tidies up his clothes, cleans his teeth, and puts on his freshly brushed hat before turning off the light.

As mentioned before, this is just the external course of tragicomic events which seem to occur as if on a surreal surface, and which are overshadowed by the all-pervading presence of Quentin's anguish-stricken inner world. He is like a sleepwalker hypnotized by his dreams of the past, whose pressure is so intense he can barely distinguish it from the present. His obsession with time is expressed by his quixotic battle with his shadow and the ticking watch. The little girl following him evokes associations of Caddy and, while being a symbol of innocence, nonetheless leads him into a morally ambivalent situation. His act of aggression against the student, as in earlier cases, just entails yet another humiliation of Quentin. All these highly symbolic incidents show that he merely acts out in the present the unresolved problems of his past.

Quentin's stream of associations seems to flow in an intermediary sphere between upper- and underworld, which is stressed throughout by symbols like twilight, shadow, water, or mirror. The part of the Macbeth-quote which likens life to a "walking shadow" applies particularly well to him, because Quentin is like a "walking shadow" himself, always acutely aware of his shadow, perceiving it everywhere with paranoid anxiety, and trying to fight and outwit it as if it were a sinister alter ego.

In one sense, Quentin's fixation on Southern morality and its cultural ideal of female innocence, which he sees destroyed by Caddy's promiscuity, makes him a moral idealist whose death becomes an act of self-sacrifice for a code of values threatened by historical annihilation. In another sense, however, the potentially tragic stature of the Quentin-figure is undermined by the unreal, paranoid character of his value system, which in its bizarre anachronism appears as a displaced cultural superego tyrannizing rather than providing moral guidance for his mind. His intellectual crisis reveals not only a hidden drama of jealousy and repressed desire, but a profoundly disturbed relationship to his own cultural identity. In his inner life, Quentin shows the same symptoms of the fanatic of order which also manifest themselves in his outward behavior and which on the last day of his life make him dress, with a ritual sense of formality, for his own funeral in the fashion of a Southern gentleman.

III

The third chapter again stands in sharp contrast to the preceding one in terms of tone and narrative attitude. It is set on Good Friday, April 6, 1928, 18 years after the Quentin-chapter and one day before the Benjy-chapter, and is narrated from the perspective of Jason, the middle one of the Compson brothers. In this part, too, the account is interspersed with the subjective reactions of the narrative I, which manifest themselves in memories and digressions of thought. But for the first time, the present clearly dominates the past, and the conscious gains predominance over the unconscious. There are hardly any abrupt changes of time levels, the focus is on action and dialogue, and the atmosphere is far more sober and realistic. The language becomes more direct and plain, and the presentation of events is easier to follow, so that in retrospect the preceding chapters, too, become more understandable. It seems as if a fog were lifting, finally opening up the view on a reality previously clouded by images of the subconscious.

The sense of relief the reader may feel because of this return to more easily recognizable, familiar patterns of language and experience, however, soon changes into new bewilderment about the view of the world with which the reader is confronted. The alleged common sense-perspective with its claim to social 'normality,' into which the reader enters in the Jason-chapter, turns out to be far more repulsive and absurd than those of the 'idiot' and the self-destructive romantic. The process of reception is reversed, as it were. If in the former chapters the apparently eccentric and 'abnormal' perspectives of cultural outsiders are brought closer to the reader's empathy and understanding, in the Jason-chapter the apparently familiar, normal perspective of an average citizen is made to appear increasingly strange, and indeed even monstrous and diabolical. The colloquial speech of the self-proclaimed 'common man' brings with it, instead of clarification, vulgar simplification and populistic ideology. The petty bourgeois claim of self-confident knowledge of the world which Jason cultivates turns out to be a continuous projection of prejudices and aggressive stereotypes. "Once a bitch always a bitch," he says right at the beginning of the chapter about Caddy's daughter Quentin, who grows up separated from her disowned mother in the Compson household and who develops similar ways of rebellion against the puritanical hypocrisy of the Compsons as Caddy did before. Jason's misogynist attitude keeps surfacing in the course of the chapter and so do his prejudices against blacks, intellectuals, and Jews - "'I have nothing against the jews as an individual,' I says. 'It's just the race. You'll admit that they produce nothing'"(219).

Jason's voice is the voice of resentment, which combines the feeling of universal injustice against his own person with envious hatred and self-righteous condemnation of others. He is a reactionary petty bourgeois who believes himself the victim of his familial and social environment while in reality it is he who unscrupulously exploits his own family members. He acts as the self-appointed keeper of moral law and order while in truth he is a fraud and a prime example of the sexual double morality he denounces in others. In comparison with the melancholy Quentin, who is psychologically bound to the past, Jason's character clearly has more 'modern' traits. He reflects a capitalistic mentality and a 'rugged individualism' which became especially influential in the American 1920s and which at that time had begun to transform Southern society and culture as well. Jason, as it were, combines the vices of both systems: the moral hypocrisy and the racism of the South, and the egotism, rootlessness and amoral ideology of the Northern self-made man.

The negative character traits associated with Jason's posture of common-sense-familiarity create a constant ironic tension, which has a strange, double effect on the reader. It mobilizes the reader's aggression against a fictional character to whom he or she, by the technique of the first-person narration and by the use of popular, colloquial speech, is at the same time brought uncomfortably close. The discrepancy between the character's positive self-image and his actual behavior incites the reader's moral indignation, but also creates a feeling of irritating unease. The reading process counteracts and undermines the self-confident assertions made on the textual surface, on whose questionable authority it nevertheless depends. The reader's position in this chapter is defined in a painfully ambivalent tension between the uncomfortable familiarity of and the critical distance to a perspective that the reader is temporarily forced to share in the act of radical cultural (self-)understanding that the novel performs.

Jason's actions, designed to secure control over his life, are not as self-determined, however, as he would like them to be. It is true that he has managed, by forging cheques and manipulating bank accounts, to obtain the money Caddy sends regularly for Quentin's support, and which, over the years, has amounted to forty thousand dollars. And after the death of the alcoholic father, he plays the role of the patriarch and tyrannizes the rest of the Compson household in a humiliating and even sadistic way to keep up the facade of bourgeois decency. Yet the day he tells about in his chapter shows how his lines of action keep being thwarted and how his attempts to force his own concepts of order onto the world keep drifting off into disorder and chaos. In his futile scramble for money and the protection of the family honor, he appears to be the pursued one himself, and the hectic acceleration of the narrative pace corresponds with the hectic and ultimately aimless course of events. Jason's world, like that of the Hamlet-figure Quentin, is "out of joint," and in his pose of one who claims to have it under control, he becomes a figure of ridicule, a caricature of his own exaggerated claim to authority. While the first chapters are dominated by a tragic tone, the novel here changes into the satirical and absurdly comical mode, as the fictional subject turns out to be the object of the actions it believes to dominate.

One climax in the plot is reached when Jason discovers Caddy's daughter, whom he believes to be in school, in the car of a member of the theater company that is in town, and at once starts chasing them. During the chase, he loses his way and finally has to leave behind his car to follow them on foot through terrain that becomes more and more impassable. When he finally finds their car, they drive away honking the horn, before he can get hold of his niece. And as he returns to his own car, he discovers that one of the tires is flat. The reader thus witnesses how Jason, in his own way, becomes a "poor player" on the stage of a petty farce, and how his story, too, is in this sense only "a tale told by an idiot," the story of a mad fool masquerading as a common man.

IV

In the fourth chapter, the portrayal of the Compson-world takes another sharp turn. The poetic element, which is completely missing in Jason's prosaic world-view, returns together with the reactivation of multiple registers of language. The first person narration is replaced by that of an omniscient third person narrator, who, however, is not placed above the narrated world, but remains close to the horizon of experience of the persons involved. For the first time, the monological inner view of the three Compson brothers is broken up, and the subjective distortion of the world through different "forms of reduced subjectivity" (Wolfgang Iser) is transcended and expanded towards a more intersubjective and communal view that moves beyond the nihilist materialism of the preceding Jason-chapter and at least hints at an alternative perspective of meaning.

The latter is represented, first and foremost, by the old black servant Dilsey, who emerges as another main character: "The day dawned bleak and chill, a moving wall of grey light out of the northeast [...] [Dilsey] stood in the door for a while with her myriad and sunken face lifted to the weather [...]" (306). Dilsey figures as a counterpart to the Compson-world, of which she has been a part from the beginning, but to whose decadent self-centeredness she represents a fundamental human alternative. As a representative of the subaltern, who is completely marginalized in the other chapters, she now becomes the bearer of an existential knowledge and a communicative attitude that overcomes the egocentrism dominating before, since it replaces the principle of individualism by that of the community, and a self-referential by a relational way of thinking.

At the same time, the relationship between black and white cultures moves into the foreground. It is embodied above all in the two poles of Dilsey and Jason, and unfolds contrapuntally in the chapter's double plot. One narrative line starts out with Dilsey's making preparations for Easter Sunday, which -- like any other day -- she has to organize for the whole Compson family, and it culminates in Dilsey's going to Easter service in a black church with her family and Benjy. The other strand of the plot starts out with Jason's discovering that his niece Quentin, Caddy's daughter, has broken into his room during the night and has stolen 3000 dollars, and it subsequently relates his frantic but ultimately failing attempts to find his niece, who has fled with her lover.

It is not until this chapter that we see Ben, the narrator of the first part, from the outside:

> [...] Luster entered, followed by a big man who appeared to have been shaped of some substance whose particles would not or did not cohere to one another or to the frame which supported it. His skin was dead-looking and hairless; dropsical too, he moved with a shambling gait like a trained bear. His hair was pale and fine. It had been brushed smoothly down upon his brow like that of children in daguerrotypes. His eyes were clear, of the pale sweet blue of cornflowers, his thick mouth hung open, drooling a little (317).

Dilsey is the only person who, in spite of being constantly overworked, also takes care of Ben, the outsider tolerated only grudgingly by the whites and hidden away from the world. The chapter shows to what extent Dilsey is not only an exploited servant but the bearer of the entire family life as well. Not only has she always done all of the housework and made possible the functioning of daily life, she has also raised the Compson children alongside her own. She is a fictional icon of that matriarchal subculture which increasingly came to characterize black family life in the South and infused it with a particular ability and power to survive.

This aspect is already stressed at the beginning of the chapter in the relationship between Dilsey and Mrs. Compson. Both their husbands have died, but while Mrs. Compson is a hypochondriac, who stays upstairs in bed most of the time like a *malade imaginaire* and imperiously commands Dilsey around, the latter, in spite of the almost unbearable physical and mental burden inflicted on her, has a stoical capacity for calmness and composure in the chaotic Compson household. Her joy of life has survived despite all exploitation and deprivation, and this links her to the creative vitality of African-American culture -- a vitality which has helped black culture to live through and beyond the darkest years of slavery.

This life-affirming joy is expressed in Dilsey's singing during work, and especially in the Easter service she attends, which culminates in a sermon that is a prime example of the African-American sermon culture as it developed in the South from folklore and anti-slavery traditions. While Jason's chase after his niece and the stolen money resembles a cheap action movie, Dilsey's experience is spiritually enlarging: with Ben and her children she goes to church in the black quarters and during the preacher's charismatic sermon she experiences a spiritual catharsis and an epiphanic insight into the deeper meaning of life, which remains inaccessible to the white Compsons. "I seed the beginnin, en now I sees the endin," she says, and this vision not only applies to her personal existence, but to the Southern culture under whose restrictions she has lived and whose decline she foresees.

The Easter service, which centers on the theme of resurrection and apocalypse, is clearly presented as a specifically African-American form of cultural-spiritual self-expression. The preacher, who at first seems to be cool and distanced and "sounded like a white man," soon changes over into a black idiom and, through the dialogic interchange with his audience in the hypnotizing rhythm of the call-and-response-pattern, initiates an ecstatic experience of self-abandonment, in which isolation is replaced by communication, and the "I" is transcended by the "we:"

> And the congregation watched with its own eyes while the voice consumed him, until he was nothing and they were nothing and there was not even a voice but instead their hearts were speaking to one another in chanting measures beyond the need for words [...] (340).

Again, the glimpse of possible meaning which the novel here provides stands in sharp contrast to the other strand of the chapter's plot dominated by Jason, who in his egomaniac self-aggrandizement is ironically associated with satanic features. He is caricatured as "cold and shrewd, with close-thatched brown hair curled into two stubborn hooks, one on either side of his forehead like a bartender in caricature"(323). And during his mad chase, while the distorted sounds of the Easter bells are ringing in his ears, he turns his search for his niece into a grotesque blasphemy, into a cosmic challenge of the divine power:

> "And damn You, too," he said. "See if You can stop me," thinking of himself, his file of soldiers with the manacled sheriff in the rear, dragging Omnipotence down from his throne, if necessary; of the embattled legions of both hell and heaven through which he tore his way and put his hands at last on his fleeing niece (354).

The corrupt petty bourgeois posing as promethean rebel, and the modern self-made man in his revolt against divine authority acting as the hero of his own cosmic apocalypse -- this is the burlesque parody of Dilsey's epiphanic revelation and at the same time an abysmally ironical comment on the kind of social order that Jason represents and that, at least outwardly, is restored at the end of the novel.

VI

I hope to have managed to convey an impression of the complexity of the reading process and of its implied cultural meanings in Faulkner's novel. By way of concluding this essay, I would like to mention just a few of the many possibilities and ways of interpreting the novel as a whole, some of which have already been hinted at before.

First it should have become clear that, despite the rather different and partially conflicting perspectives, and despite the open, polyphonic form of the novel's composition, there is nonetheless a strong overall sense of a multiple relatedness and interconnectedness of the various parts of the text, which is developed through recurring themes and motifs. Through paralleling and contrasting different types of outsider positions - that of the idiot, the suicide, the petty bourgeois ideologue, the exploited black servant - Faulkner manages to convey, within the narrowly confined world of the consciousness of a few characters and their private family relations, an extraordinarily broad range of general cultural and anthropological themes. In its experimental exploration of what remains excluded from the official cultural self-image, the novel demonstrates the function of literature as an imaginative balancing of the human deficits of its cultural world. It functions as symbolic counterdiscourse, as the medium of a cultural ecology which stages in its fictional scenarios the human realities that are neglected in the dominant cultural sign systems and self-interpretations. It articulates in language and makes accessible to the aesthetic experience of the reader that which otherwise remains amorphous and unarticulated in predominant discourses, but which nevertheless represents very real dimensions of concrete personal and anthropological experience. An implicit theme of the novel, therefore, are the possibilities and functions of literature itself, which are foregrounded in the interplay of the four changing narrative perspectives and of their different modes of narration, generic forms, and registers of speech.

In correspondence to this pluralization of representational codes, Faulkner constructs the meaning of his novel on a number of different levels, which are interrelated in multiple ways. One important level is that of the psychoanalytic model, which has shaped the stream-of-consciousness novel in general and which makes the tension between the conscious and the unconscious a shaping force of the text. The technique of free association, which is adopted to a large extent in the first two chapters, makes it possible to bring to the surface and articulate in language that which remains suppressed in the rationalizations of the conscious. If we try to apply the psychoanalytic model to the four chapters, we can relate the Benjy-chapter to the id as the location of instinctual drives, the Quentin-chapter to the superego as the site of social morality and critical self-monitoring, the Jason-chapter to an ego reduced to a mere utilitarian self-interest, and the Dilsey-chapter to a deeper, archetypal human self. In this light, the novel could be viewed as a progression from the instinctual subconscious to an ever increasing and deepening consciousness, as the successive transgression of lim ited horizons of experience -- a progress, however, which does not appear as a smooth ascension towards higher insights, but involves always new aberrations and new forms of blindness.

On an anthropological level, the four chapters may be considered as exemplifying different human systems of ordering experience, which are shown in a state of permanent crisis, as they are being radically questioned by forces beyond their control. In the chapters on Benjy, Quentin, Jason, and Dilsey, an emotional, moral, material, and spiritual system of order succeed one another. For all characters, the establishing of order appears as a fundamental human need, and the calling into question of their subjective systems of order triggers off the states of chaos by which each of them is threatened in different ways. Correspondingly, the four perspectives illustrate different basic forms of relating to the world: the first chapter, sensory perception; the second, reflection; the third, action; and the fourth, communication.

On a historical-sociological level, *The Sound and the Fury* is a critical depiction of Southern society and culture between a discredited tradition and a problematic process of modernization. On the one hand, it deals with the continuing impact of the Old South, the paralyzing shadow of the past which is cast over the lives of the characters, and which manifests itself in the inevitable decline of the once powerful and influential Compson-family. On the other hand, the alienating forces of modernization are embodied especially in the figure of Jason; and in their effects of isolation, aggression, and monstrous egotism, 'modern' society appears to be as deformed as the past on which the other Compsons are fixated.

As far as the relationship between black and white is concerned, there is a pervasive racism of the white characters, who believe in the natural supremacy of their race and accordingly behave towards blacks with a mixture of indifference, condescension, and oppression. At the same time, the process of the novel counteracts this ideology, not only insofar as it shows the inner desolation and spiritual emptiness of its representatives, but also because it is a black character who comes to personify the only meaningful alternative to the morbid Compson world.

On a mythical-religious level, the fact that the idiot Benjamin is 33 years old and is allocated the role of the victim in the novel lends him traits of a Christ-figure -- albeit the figure of a degenerate savior, who is condemned to impotence and speechlessness in the modern world. On the other hand, it seems significant that the temporal arrangement of the four chapters starts with Ben's birthday on Easter Saturday, followed by the day of Quentin's death long before, then succeeded by Jason's grotesque Good Friday blasphemy, and ending on Easter Sunday culminating in its climax, the resurrection service. The apocalyptic dimension which Faulkner associates with the Easter sermon and which is one of the key motifs of American literary and cultural history, may therefore anticipate the possibility at least of a new cultural beginning dawning over the ruins of the cultural past.

Apart from its contents, however, the text also may be regarded as a polyphonic structure of sound, as a linguistic composition between tonality and atonality, which consciously develops sound as an important aspect of the novel's title. Accompanied by the wailing of the idiot Benjy, which recurs as a leitmotif throughout the text and represents a kind of expressionistic keynote of the novel articulating the "grave hopeless sound of all voiceless misery under the sun" (366), the other figures, too, are associated with different kinds of sound: Quentin with the irritating ticking of his watch, Jason with the honking of car horns and the distant sounds of the theater company's brass band, and Dilsey with the songs and chants of the black community. Thus on this level of composition, too, the themes of the novel are communicated, in whose polyphonic dissonance the text's paradoxical (dis-)harmony is realized.

What these different possibilities of interpretation show is that the 'meaning' which the novel constructs and which counters the semiotic nihilism of the Macbeth-passage from which its title is taken, does not consist in one definitive, concretely identifiable content. Rather, it lies in the radical staging of 'alterity,' in the intense and complex experience of the culturally excluded, suppressed, and radically 'other' which the text so impressively conveys, and which may help lead its readers to a better understanding of themselves and their own culture.

I should like to thank Julia Grunenberg and Sabine Gust for their helpful assistance in the translation of this essay.

Cultural Interchange in Siouxland: An Approach to Frederick Manfred´s Buckskin Man and Woman Tales

IAN ROSS (Bardscroft, Gambier Island)

A herd of 3,000 pale-coloured Longhorn cattle drifts up the trail from south Texas to Montana: the Old West captured in the perspective of 1903, half a century before Manfred's time. In June 1882, the herd is more than two months out from Brownsville, and forty miles on from Doan's Crossing over the Red River. In the Indian Territory that became Oklahoma in 1907, "about a hundred mounted bucks and squaws sighted our herd and crossed the North Fork from their encampment." They are Comanche, and not understanding their language the cowboys communicate in Spanish with two Apache "renegades" accompanying them. Their leader, a "fine specimen of the Plains Indian," who looks "every inch a chief," begs for ten beeves to feed his people suffering from hunger and poverty caused by the white hidehunters slaughtering the buffalo. The civilized cowboy foreman replies he is taking the herd as a present from the white man's chief in Washington to the good Blackfeet Indians in Montana, who have "welcomed priests and teachers among them to teach them the ways of the white man." The Comanche are beaten down to three beeves to feed the "hungry squaws and little papooses," and the herd rolls on north.

In August, a month before delivery, the herd crosses the Montana line, and the cowboys have to take their damaged chuck wagon to be repaired at Frenchman's Ford on the Yellowstone, a "pretentious frontier village of the squatter type." Two thirds of it consists of tents, and it is a collection point for "immense quantities of buffalo hides [...] drying or already baled, and waiting transportation [...] to navigable points on the Missouri." There are many large ox trains camped round the village, and the drivers lounge in the streets or drink and gamble in the saloons with buffalo hunters and other plainsmen. The mixed population speaks "almost every language," and "typical specimens of northern Indians [grunt] their jargon amid the babel of others tongues," while their squaws wander the "irregular streets in gaudy blankets and red calico." The only "civilizing element" visible is the camp of engineers on a survey mission for the Northern Pacific Railroad. The young narrator of this cattle trail saga, Tom Quirk, son of a Confederate soldier who had taken his family from Georgia to Texas at the close of the civil war, goes with the other cowboys relieved from guarding the herd to drink in The Buffalo Bull saloon. He notes the "unrestrained freedom of the village," and the upholding of the "primitive law of self-preservation" evident in "every man in the place [wearing] the regulation six-shooter, and quite a number [wearing] two." In another saloon, Yellowstone Bob's, a frontier gambler with shoulder-length black hair, dressed in buckskin, "profusely ornamented with beadwork and fringes," tries to inveigle Tom's "bunkie" (partner), a Confederate veteran nicknamed The Rebel, into drinking a toast to the Northern victor, General Grant. The ensuing quarrel ends with a shoot-out back at The Buffalo Bull. There the gambler vaults on to the bar, curses the Texas cowboys, gets a warning that The Rebel is on his feet and is reaching for his gun. He blazes away at the Texans ineffectively, before The Rebel coolly hits him with two shots that make him reel backward, and he crashes heavily into the glassware on the back bar.[1]

Andy Adams (1859-1936), who included these episodes of cultural interchange in his first-person fictional narrative, *The Log of a Cowboy* (1903/1964), was a working cowhand in Texas for twelve years, and drove cattle up the northern trail before he turned to writing novels. He has earned praise from critics for the realism and authenticity of his details, also the vigour of the speech he recorded. As well, his book has been hailed as for 'setting the pattern and tone of the trail novel when it comes to the cowboy at work."[2] This genre has flowered subsequently into a more complex art form, most recently in Larry McMurtry's *Lonesome Dove* (1985/1986).[3]

The limitations of Adams" outlook, however, reveal clearly the ideology and values of his generation and working brotherhood. The Protestant work ethic dominates Tom Quirk and his outfit taking the Circle Dot herd to the Blackfeet Agency in Montana. In the interaction with the Comanche, no questions are asked about the justice of destroying the way of life of these native people--once hailed and feared in the West as the lords of the Plains, through the slaughter of the buffalo herds they hunted; and no interest is shown in how they are expected to survive on their reservation. A derisive handout permits the cowboys to pass on their way north. The violent outcome of the interaction of the cowboy known as The Rebel and the buckskin-clad gambler is endorsed and glorified without hesitation as an instance of upholding the code of the West. Civilization at the frontier site of Frenchman's Ford is represented by railroad surveyors. Regarding delivery of the cattle to the Blackfeet, Tom Quirk asks an Agency priest in a perfunctory way if the cows handed over to Indian families for domestication will survive the winter, and is given a reassuring answer. He shows no curiosity whatever about the difficulties of a nomadic, hunting and gathering people being goaded into cattle-raising, and reveals emotion only over parting with the horses assigned to him in the *remuda*, when it is sold *en bloc* to a Montana ranch.

The Plains Indians did succeed for a time running cattle, but by the 1890s the Federal government began to withdraw support from such ventures, and state and local governments showed more interest in manoeuvring Indians into leasing or selling land so that white ranchers could have bigger spreads. There was subsequent overgrazing on the grasslands, and they suffered from the drought and dust storms of the

---

[1] Andy Adams, *The Log of a Cowboy: A Narrative of the Old Trail Days* 1903. (Lincoln and London: University of Nebraska Press, 1964), 136-41; 334-44.

[2] J. Frank Dobie, *Cow People*, 1964. (Austin: University of Texas Press, 1990), 101; Richard W. Slatta, *Cowboys of the Americas* (New Haven and London: Yale University Press, 1990), 205-6; Alfred R. Shulz, "The Trail Drive Novel," *Studies in the Western* 3:1 (1995), 38.

[3] Larry McMurtry, *Lonesome Dove* (New York and London: Pocket Books, division of Simon & Schuster, 1985/1986).

era of the Great Depression in the 1930s.[4] With hindsight, it appears that Adams" enchantment with the work ethic and the code of the West produced a kind of cultural myopia. Getting the job in hand done, observing punctilio between white males, and expressing "unrestrained freedom" or resolving conflict through violence more or less sum up the mentality exposed in the novel.

The Old West fiction of Frederick Manfred (1912-94), which he covered with the title Buckskin Man Tales, has a much more troubled and heart-searching quality, taking up themes of complex interchange within a culture or between cultures. To do so, he adds further levels of meaning to the icon of the buckskin man, found in Adams as a picturesque detail of life on the plains, with the quarrelsome gambler of Frenchman's Ford given this dress to help paint him as a frontier swashbuckler.

Manfred seems to have kept in mind the problematic Biblical story of Esau the hunter, who dresses in skins and, though the elder born of twins, sells his birthright to his younger brother, Jacob the herder, for bread and a pottage of lentils. Also, Esau is tricked out of the blessing Isaac wishes to give his firstborn when Jacob assumes his brother's dress of skins (Genesis 25:27, 29-34; 27). Further, Esau is described as being red on emerging from Rebekah's womb (Gen. 25: 25). Thus he is an archetype of the so-called Red Indian hunters who were displaced by the trickery of the whites, first coming to the Plains as hunters, and then taking over as herders.

Inevitably, Manfred's readers will think also of James Fennimore Cooper's Leatherstocking Tales featuring the hunter and scout Natty Bumpo, who slays deer and wears their skins, fated to be tragically involved in the dispossession of the Indians, and the "[deranging] of the harmony of the wilderness."[5] Manfred further brings in his awareness of the emblematic, even heraldic, significance of the buckskin shirt in Plains culture worn by men of distinction such as the great chief of the Sioux, Crazy Horse,[6] and the white man's impoverished attitude to such garments. As well, Manfred's vision embraces the experience of Indian women who wore doeskin dresses, and even the nonconformist women who wished to wear men's buckskins.

Sprung from Saxon, Dutch, and Frisian ancestry, Manfred was born into the Feikema family that had farmed in Iowa for two generations. His mother wanted him to become a pastor in the Christian Reformed Church, but his intellectual growth and rebelliousness at Calvin College in Grand Rapids, Michigan, led him away from orthodox religion and confirmed a boyhood ambition to become a fulltime writer. In 1943, after a brief spell as a sports journalist in Minneapolis, and two years in a tuberculosis sanatorium, he was able to make writing his career. His first published novel, *The Golden Bowl* (1944), whose title alludes sardonically to the hopes dashed

---

[4] Betty and Ian Ballantine, eds., *The Native American: An Illustrated History* (Atlanta: Turner Publishing, Inc., 1993) — Peter Nabakov, "Long Threads," 363, and Philip J. Deloria, "The Twentieth Century and Beyond," 411; Sharman Apt Russell, *Kill the Cowboy: A Battle of Mythology in the New West.* (Reading, MA. and Menlo Park, CA.: Addison Wesley Publishing Co., 1993), 4-5.

[5] James Fennimore Cooper, *The Deerslayer* (Oxford and New York: Oxford University Press, 1987), 443.

[6] Colin F. Taylor, *The Plains Indians* (New York: Barnes & Noble Books, 1997), 178-98.

by the dust bowl years in the USA, attracted favourable critical attention. This included appreciation from Sinclair Lewis, who befriended Manfred, and whose memorial address he gave in 1951, referring to the older writer as his "friendly literary uncle--yes, even my father [...]."[7]

In a string of novels, all more or less autobiographical, he continued to focus on the recent past and contemporary life of the people of the farms and towns in the Midwest: *Boy Almighty* (1945), *This Is the Year* (1947), and *The Chokeberry Tree* (1948); also *The Primitive* (1949), *The Brother* (1950), and *The Giant* (1951), conceived as a trilogy. Criticism of his work, however, turned somewhat sour, especially that concocted by Eastern reviewers, who found the raw, Midwest subject matter, seriocomic flights, and the unconventional style increasingly disagreeable. His publisher Doubleday rejected manuscripts, five in all, on which he had relied to support his growing family, and would not give advances for new projects.

In these desperate circumstances, the novelist changed his name from the unfamiliar Frisian, Feike Feikema, to Frederick Manfred, which he believed would be more readily identified by his readers. In the case of each name, nevertheless, the elements are connected with the Old Germanic root words expressing "freedom" and "peace."[8] These are watchwords for this novelist, and the critic Robert Wright has divined correctly that Manfred's fictions "do get at universal truths and move people's hearts towards reconciliation. [His] books are to be cherished as instruments of peace" (Wright, *Frederick Manfred*, 76).

Perhaps it can be said with some justice, that Manfred's creative energies began to flow most strongly when he devoted them to the Old West, and assumed his new name. In 1953 an advance from his new publisher McGraw-Hill, together with a research grant, allowed him do field research in South Dakota on the amazing year of 1823 in the life of the mountain man, Hugh Glass, fugitive from white domesticity and cultural interchanger with Indians. He is the massive, hairy, hide-clad, hunter hero of the first of the Buckskin Man Tales to be published. This is *Lord Grizzly* (1954/1982),[9] which deals with the agony of Glass's need to take personal revenge on companions who leave him for dead after he has slain a giant female bear. Its considerable commercial and literary success encouraged Manfred to elaborate a polysemous historical series about the Old West, that works on historical, mythical, and figurative levels.

In part, Manfred's inspiration comes from Fennimore Cooper's five Leatherstocking Tales: *The Pioneers* (1823), *The Last of the Mohicans* (1826), *The Prairie* (1827), *The Pathfinder* (1840), and *The Deerslayer* (1841). They had not followed a

---

[7] Robert C. Wright, *Frederick Manfred* (Boston: Twayne Publishers, division of G.K. Hall & Co., 1979), 26.

[8] *Conversations with Frederick Manfred*, moderated by John R. Milton; foreword by Wallace Stegner (Salt Lake City: University of Utah Press, 1974), 13; Wright, *Frederick Manfred*, 165 n.9.

[9] Frederick Manfred, *Lord Grizzly*, 1954. (Harmondsworth and Middlesex: Signet/Penguin Books, 1982).

chronological order as published, and no more did Manfred's series. The second Tale to appear, *Riders of Judgment* (1957/1973),[10] deals with the range war times in Wyoming, specifically 1892, when the "big spread" operators seek to drive out the little herders who find a heroic defender in Cain Hammett, a character based on a historical figure, Nate Champion. The native people have been driven out, and Manfred demonstrates what the drastic end of white-Indian cultural interchange has brought. Greedy exploitation in the form of capitalism applied to herding has replaced Indian religious care for the land and its creatures. So often presented on horseback, Cain is both a centaur and something of a half-buckskin man in that he wears leather chaps. There is also an Esau-type of wildness in him, that the big bosses cannot overawe, though in the end their hired killers reduce him to a corpse red with blood from gunshot wounds.

Conquering Horse (1959/1965),[11] which is discussed more fully below, explores the era about 1800, before the Indians who are featured had contact with whites. *Scarlet Plume* (1964/1973)[12] is set in 1862, the time when the Sioux of Minnesota in a bloody uprising attacked the white settlers who were taking over their land. The settlers" viewpoint about cultural interchange is expressed early in the book: "It hain"t right fer an ignorant savage to own so much land, unplowed, while the better white man is forced to live in want. The Indian never did use the land for what the Lord intended it fer--raisin wheat" (Manfred, *Scarlet Plume*, 36).

The ostensible narrator of this novel is a white woman, Judith Raveling, who is captured by Yankton Sioux, falls in love with her rescuer, the hero-victim who gives his name to the novel. After his undeserved execution, she travels west to live with the Yanktons. In the course of their cultural interchanges, Scarlet Plume, a great hunter of deer for necessary food and clothing, explains to Judith after he has killed a doe, something of the holistic vision of the Sioux:

> [The doe] understands. The Yanktons were once animals before they were people. Her family and my family have been neighbours for many grandfathers. She and I are of one blood. Therefore the Yanktons are cousins to the deer and must apologize to her and ask her for the food and the doeskin. [...]. We only need the blood of one at a time (Manfred, *Scarlet Plume*, 250).

King of Spades (1966/1973)[13] is described in the author's "program" of the Buckskin Man Tales as developing the theme of "Black Hills justice in 1876." On one level it is an Oedipus-story of a lost son's rape of his unrecognized mother, and on another it depicts gold mining as the white man's rape of the Black Hills of South

---

[10] Frederick Manfred, *Riders of Judgment*, 1957. (Harmondsworth and Middlesex: Signet/Penguin Books, 1973).
[11] Frederick Manfred, *Conquering Horse*, 1959. (Harmondsworth and Middlesex: Signet/Penguin Books, 1965).
[12] Frederick Manfred, *Scarlet Plume*, 1964. (Harmondsworth and Middlesex: Signet/Penguin Books, 1973).
[13] Frederick Manfred, *King of Spades*, 1966. (New York: Signet, 1973).

Dakota, sacred to the Sioux as the home of *Wakantanka*, the Great Spirit, the 'sum of all that was powerful, sacred, and full of mystery."[14] The lost son is introduced to us as sixshooter-armed, buckskin-clad Earl Ransom, a 'swamper", low man on the totem pole whatever work he undertook, and a prospector (Manfred, *King of Spades*, 62-3). While exploring in the Black Hills, for a brief space he gives up prospecting to enjoy a love idyll with a native girl in an Edenic setting. In their cultural interchanges, she teaches him some of her Sioux language, but cannot awaken in him reverence for the earth. Heedless of her warnings reinforced by a lightning strike, he will not give up prospecting. The nymph vanishes carrying his child, Ransom takes up a claim successfully with other miners joining in, and his Eden becomes the gold mining centre of Deadwood, resembling something created by prairie-dogs: "What had once been a lovely dell was now suddenly a dusty hell of uprooted earth" (Manfred, *King of Spades*, 179). In this setting, he becomes as he thinks a devil, kills his wife-mother, and brings on the punishment of death by hanging, watched by his father. Learning about the Indian girl, the father sets off on a quest to find her and the grandchild.

Artistically speaking, *King of Spades* is the least successful of the Buckskin Man Tales, and perhaps unwilling to put an end to the series with it, Manfred added to his canon the short novel, *The Manly-Hearted Woman* (1975).[15] This explores sexual roles and deviance among the Sioux in the era when his series commences. Its circling back to the concept of the warrior hero and introduction of that of Buckskin Woman make it a fitting subject for the concluding part of this essay after the survey of *Conquering Horse*.

Each work in the series, we can now appreciate, deals with a nineteenth-century cultural or historical interchange of a crucial nature in the region he called Siouxland: Minnesota, South Dakota, Iowa, and Nebraska, in particular the locality where these states meet near the joining of the Big Sioux and Missouri rivers, but also extending westward to Wyoming and Montana (Wright, *Frederick Manfred*, 165 n.13). Pressed by the Chippewa who had been armed with guns by the French, the Sioux had moved from the eastern woodlands to the grassland beyond, and on acquiring horses in the late 1700s, roamed freely on the Great Plains to hunt buffalo. A major Indian linguistic stock, they were divided into seven tribes. The Mdewakanton, Wahpeton, Wahpekute, and Sisseton formed the Eastern division, known as the Santee or Dakota. The Yankton and Yanktonai were the middle division known as Nakota, and the largest of all the tribes, the Teton Sioux or Lakota, formed the Western division (Taylor, *Plains Indians*, 26, 28).

Manfred refers to the Seven Council Fires of the Sioux, but concentrates for the most part on the Yanktons. In 1960, he built his home outside Luverne, in southwest Minnesota, under the Blue Mounds, so named because blue-green lichen growing on their red Sioux quartzite gave it a bluish hue. For the most part, the action in *Conquering Hero* and *Manly-Hearted Woman* is set in the surroundings of Luverne.

---

[14] Edward Lazarus, *Black Hills / White Justice: The Sioux Nation v. The United Nations 1775 to the Present* (New York: Harper Collins Publishers, 1991), 7.

[15] Frederick Manfred, *The Manly-Hearted Woman* (New York: Crown Publishers, Inc., 1975).

The religious relationship between this land, also its creatures, and the Yanktons is explored by Manfred who came to know their region intimately. He was acutely sensitive to the Yanktons" experience of displacement by westward-pressing whites-- mountain men, soldiers, miners, settlers, and ranchers. Identifying strongly with his Frisian forebears, who were "never on the side of the majority," Manfred wrote sympathetically about the victims of the struggles in Siouxland.

Coming to terms with what Manfred offers us, this essay dwells now on the evocative literary qualities of certain episodes and passages in *Conquering Horse* and *Manly-Hearted Woman* to establish how he created the *genius loci* of Siouxland, dramatized its myths and ethos, and articulated differentiating languages for its contending dwellers and invaders in their cultural interchanges.

The bridge from Manfred's contemporary fictional world, or near-contemporary one, back to Siouxland dreamtime is to be found in *This Is the Year* (1947). This novel covers the period 1918-36 in northwestern Iowa (Manfred's birthplace), and a Frisian family's inner struggles and contention with weather cycles resulting in the humans and the land becoming barren. In an early episode, we get the outsider's view of Siouxland from the immigrant grandfather, Alde Romke, who has been pushed off the farm by his son, his ultimate fate after coming to America, "to drive the Indians out of the prairies of Iowa and set up a line of free Frixens." When he first came to his new home in Iowa, he had looked down from Red Bluff, gazing for hours "at the flowing grasses on the prairies beneath, to the east, to the south, to the west down by the Big Sioux banks." He had seen "to the north, across Blood Run Creek, rows of mounds on the land," one hundred and forty-three of them, and he had wondered: "What strange thing was this? Had a people as old as the ancient Free Frisians lived and worshipped here in the olden days?" He ponders on the heedless, irreligious and wasteful ways of the Frisian immigrants, and their disdain for the native people: "They should have observed the ways of Chief Yellow Smoke and his Sioux Indian bands, who killed only enough for the day's needs and then roved on." Sad at heart, cast out by his son, his speech evoking It Lân Fan Myn Aldfaers left so long ago, Romke stands weeping by a river in Siouxland, until a memory of his grandmother's folk being fishermen suggests to him a renewal of hope, that he can make a living, perhaps, netting the "catfish, pickerel, perch, carp in every bend" of the Big Sioux.[16]

In *Conquering Horse* (1959/1965), Manfred presents the dreamtime of the Sioux's heyday, perhaps about 1800. Certainly the action seems to occur before the Lewis and Clark Expedition encountered in 1804 the Brulé band led by Black Buffalo, and recorded the opinion these Lakotas or Western Teton Sioux were the "vilest miscreants of the savage race," who should be driven from the Missouri River country if the new American republic was ever to assert supremacy in the West.[17] Manfred's

---

[16] John Calvin Rezmerski, ed., *The Frederick Manfred Reader* (Duluth, MS: Holy Cow! Press, 1996), 195-9.

[17] Clyde A. Milner II et al., eds., *The Oxford History of the American West* (New York and Oxford: Oxford University Press, 1996)--Peter Iversen, "Native Peoples and Native Histories," 18-19.

Yankton Sioux inhabit a world that is unified and understood to be *wakan*, permeated with the numinous. As horticulturalists and hunters, they seek to live in balance with nature that is the gift of *Wakantanka*. Manfred's young protagonist--a Buckskin Man, normally dressed in breech clout, leggings, buckskin shirt, and moccasins--has the noble characteristics of bravery, physical prowess, and mental resourcefulness, but at first is identified as No Name. Outliving an older brother, who died after treating too lightly a place that was "greatly *wakan*," No Name aspires to succeed his father, Chief Redbird, but must go on a terrifying dream-vision quest to acquire adult status and be given a name suitable for his rank. Before he sets off, he offends against the code of *wakan* by insisting that Leaf, a virgin of his tribe whom he wishes to marry, have sexual intercourse with him. She disappears, and he fears she has taken her life, also that his transgression will thwart his vision quest. Reassured by his father that his action is a step towards maturity, and ritually prepared for his quest by his shaman uncle, Moon Dreamer, he sets off on horseback with a companion on his quest, travelling westward across the Missouri to the Butte of the Thunders, in present day South Dakota. On the fourth day of fasting on the top of the Butte, he experiences a first vision in which a phantom white mare becomes his helper and tells him that he must travel to the land of the Sioux's enemies, the Pawnees, and capture there a white stallion with a scarlet mane. On returning to his village, he shows he has leadership capacity through playing successfully the role of the hero-victim of the sun dance ordeal, but it is revealed to him that his father must die on his return with the stallion.

Setting off alone on foot, on the second part of his vision quest, he triumphs over terrifying physical and mental hardships, perhaps hallucinating about miraculous guides, perhaps actually receiving help from such agencies. Manfred cleverly leaves both options open. Among these guides for No Name are two round stones, painted red, about the size of buffalo testicles. They convey the message: "We are round. We have no beginning or end and no end. We are related to the sun and moon because they are also round" (Manfred, *Conquering Horse*, 184) As the critic Sanford E. Marovitz remarks in a perceptive essay about the Buckskin Man Tales,[18] the message of the stones is of the cyclical nature of life and the endless continuity of day, month, and year. Before No Name's eyes, they appear to shift position and point out for him the "true path" leading to Leaf, who has been buried to the neck by Pawnees outraged on finding she is pregnant, when they intended to sacrifice her as a virgin at corn-planting time, to ensure the protection of the Morning Star. This was a practice recorded among the Pawnee (Taylor, *Plains Indians*, 67).

Leaf recovers from her ordeal, and tells No Name about a compassionate Pawnee who directs him to the range of the white stallion he seeks. No Name captures the horse and names him Dancing Sun, but as in the legend of the Great White Pacer known in Texas,[19] the stallion seeks death rather endure captivity--a symbol of the untamable West. No Name sings the death song over the stallion and drinks from his

---

[18] Sanford E. Marovitz, "From Mythic Visions to the American Dream: Nature Expropriated in Frederick Manfred's Buckskin Man Tales," *Studies in the Western* 3:1 (1995), 6.

[19] J. Frank Dobie, *The Mustangs*, 1934. (Austin: University of Texas Press, 1984), 150-54.

heart's blood, also for his medicine he takes a part of the scarlet mane. Leaf gives birth to a son, and helps to rear a white colt, one of twins fathered by the stallion. No Name brings back the colt to his village together with Leaf and his son, and his identity as a true hero is disclosed through the ceremonial bestowal on him of a name of power, Conquering Horse.

There remains to be fulfilled the second, dreaded part of his vision about the necessity of the death of his father. Troubled deeply about this requirement, he brings the scarlet plume from Dancing Sun's mane to the shaman Moon Dreamer, who divides it into a fetish for Conquering Horse's hair braid and medicine to be hung in a bag in his lodge. He feels that the power of *Wakantanka* has entered into, and is available to him in, these objects, also under Moon Dreamer's prompting he feels that the power of his dream vision mare has entered him, assuring him of the strength to face the climactic test of his father's death next day at dusk. Moreover, he sees life as "one huge flow, with himself a streaming part of it [...]. One part of the flow was exactly like any other part of it. It was all one and the same. Therefore he no longer needed to think about how his father's life would end" (Manfred, *Conquering Horse*, 336). In the event, he does not slay his father: when Redbird clad in buckskins and armed calls upon the braves led by Conquering Horse to attack him, as the visionary white mare had commanded, the Thunders speak and a lightning flash strikes the old Chief's copper lancehead, pulverizing him amid a dazzling explosion. Conquering Horse accepts this as the command of *Wakantanka*, and he cuts off his left forefinger at the knuckle to commemorate the father he has now succeeded.

This is a demanding and disturbing Tale. Much of it, for example, cutting off a finger as a sign of commemoration of the dead, and sharpening generational conflict to the point of depicting ritual preparation for killing the son killing the father in order to succeed him, is sharply at odds with our present-day sensibilities. But Manfred's skill with prose rich in natural imagery, and haunting in rhythm, conjures the contemporary reader into accepting cultural interchange with the Yankton Buckskin Man of that long ago dreamtime, and thus plausibly sharing his sense of the unity and sacredness of life.

But what of Buckskin Woman? Conquering Hero's partner, Leaf, is a role model, we may believe, of a self-sacrificing Sioux wife and mother--she is even prepared to give suck to Dancing Son's colt so that he will survive to bring his sire's *wakan* seed to strengthen the line of Sioux horses. At the outset of his second quest journey, however, No Name remembers the tale of a bold and daring Yankton maiden who gave a feast for forty braves and accepted sex from them in turn before choosing one of the tallest to be her husband. She remained faithful and loving to him until death, as well as holding power over him and helping him in the "wise rule of the tribe" (Manfred, *Conquering Horse*, 167).

There is a link here to the later novel, *The Manly-Hearted Woman*, in which Manfred goes much further in exploring human nature through imaginative investigation of exchange of sexual roles, and plumbing greater depths of the mystical nature religion he ascribes to the Sioux. Taken back again to the dreamtime of the Yankton, though in this story white men have been heard of, associated with the violation far away of a Yankton woman who was carried off and then returned to her people, we learn first of a young male among The People of The Talking Water who is thought worthless. His sole feat has been to find clams in a tributary of the Big Sioux River, which would be harvested by women, and he wears a clamshell in his hair, so there is a suggestion he is effeminate. Manfred does not develop this character as one of the *winkta* known among the Lakota, men who dreamt of being women and then dressed as such, often specializing in women's activities such as beadwork, and getting important roles in ceremonies (Taylor, *Plains Indians*, 59, n.11). Rather we have the folklore motif of the despised youth, who finally achieves heroic stature.

Despite the scorn directed at the youth, he is included in a war party organized to help a sister band, The Nation of The Blue Mounds, whose buffalo jump has been usurped by the Omaha. He takes with him a strange weapon he has fashioned from an oak limb and honed down with a quartzite knife, which gives him his name Flat Warclub. In this weapon he has hidden his helper, a meteorite that fell from the clouds at his feet one day. He recognizes it is *wakan* and sent to him to be his helper. Moreover, this helper has announced his dead warrior father needs Flat Warclub in The Other Life, and *Wakantanka* has promised this will happen when the youth gives his people his most precious possession.

Meantime, among the Blue Mounds band, a unique female has been accepted by her people. As a child, she longed to play with her brother at male games, and finally persuades an uncle to teach her to handle a bow and arrow and mount a horse, though he refuses to tell her how a vision may be sought. She takes the lead in sex play with boys, but scandal is averted when she marries an old chief who is rejuvenated for a time by her vibrant sexuality. When he dies, she marries a widower who covets her first husband's horses. This husband turns out to be a sadist, and frightened off from his practices by his new wife, he is no good in bed. She determines to go on a buffalo hunt, sheds her woman's clothes, and dresses in those of her dead husband, the old chief, including his hunting shirt of buckskin. She has great success in the hunt, while her husband has very little, and she is accepted among the members of the Soldier Society, fully earning her name, Manly Heart, a designation, in fact, among the Sioux for women who broke away from restrictions on their sex (Taylor, *Plains Indians*, 151, 177 n.1). She speaks contemptuously of her husband in his presence and that of his brother and his wife. The husband strips off his buckskin shirt and drops his breechclout to cow her by showing her his genitals. Far from being overawed, she pulls off her leather skirt and exhibits her private parts also. She then demands to be carried home naked by the husband whom she proceeds to divorce by breaking a stick and throwing the pieces at him. In time, she has a vision in which an eagle speaks to her, telling her to wear the clothes of man, and that she will be given a *wakan* helper as a man might be. She is also told that her "people need a manly-hearted woman to save them" from nearby danger (Manfred, *Manly-Hearted Woman*, 52). Her helper, to which she is guided by two grass lizards, proves to be a flint spear point. It gives her direction in assuming the role of a man, including taking a "wife." When Flat Warclub arrives in her village with his band's war party, and is excluded from hospitality by the villagers, who are aware of his difference from other warriors, Manly Heart admits him into her tipi.

Flat Warclub thereafter begins to expand on his singularity. He insists that the lance bearers of the Soldiers" Society carry him on a buffalo robe to a war feast in the council lodge. Chief Seven Sticks asks him why he has to do things in a singular manner, and tells him how he was instructed always to look to a leader:

> This was done to teach my soul the habit of never thinking to do one single act apart from my fellows. This was done that I might make of my life here on these wide plains, to the uttermost, an unbroken circle, of circles within circles, of family, of band, of tribe, of nation. For the circle is *wakan*. That is why our tipis are built in a circle. That is why our encampments are always set in a circle. A wiser and better rule no man has ever discovered, nor ever will, nor a truer art of victory or happiness (Manfred, *Manly-Hearted Woman*, 73).

The other warriors sneer at Flat Warclub, to which he makes no direct response, but we are told that the clamshell in his hair gleams and glitters. This was a powerful symbol from the older times of the Plains Indians, seeming to combine the forces of the spirits below the waters with that of the life-originating and renewing sun, suggesting even the power behind the sun (Taylor, 1997: 194-5). Associated in this way with higher powers, and directed by his helper, Flat Warclub can and must act outside the circle to be the saviour of his people. He explains that to defeat the Omaha, he must throw his life away after bringing down seven of their braves with his mighty weapon. But in return for this sacrifice, the Nation of The Blue Mounds must accept something totally against their customs. Flat Warclub asks for license to have sexual intercourse with any woman he chooses in the four days before his death.

Handling this part of his story with great tact and considerable humour, Manfred recounts how seven Yankton maidens, one of them being Manly Heart's "wife," offer themselves to receive Flat Warclub's seed, which will renew their people. Manly Heart, reassuming her femininity, also desires Flat Warclub, but he resists her, and after a bloodcurdling battle dies the death fated for him. When Manly Heart's helper deserts her, she rejects her "wife," and takes it upon herself to receive the body of Flat Warclub, for whom she grieves like a bereft lover, lapsing thereafter into a silent and solitary life.

What on earth are we to make of these Buckskin Tales of Frederick Manfred, in particular *Conquering Horse* and *The Manly-Hearted Woman*? With their attention to the violence found in sexuality, as well as in hunting and war, can they "move people's hearts towards reconciliation," and be "cherished as instruments of peace," as Robert Wright claimed? Andy Adams" heedless cowboys forever ride away from the Comanche, and surrender their horses to the Montana rancher likely to appropriate Blackfeet hunting grounds for his range. But Manfred's art can shock us out of our buckskins and doeskins, and stir us into charged cultural interchange with the Yanktons in their heyday. It is just possible that, if receptive enough, we will be inspired by his vivid nature imagery and incantatory rhythms to accept the reconciling and peacemaking teaching of the Sioux:

All of this [creation] is sacred, and so do not forget. Every dawn as it comes is a holy event, and every day is holy, for the light comes from [the Great Spirit, *Wakantanka*], and you must always remember that the two-leggeds and all the other peoples who stand on this earth are sacred and should be treated as such.[20]

---

[20] White Buffalo Woman, Sioux Sacred Woman, quoted in *The Native Americans: An Illustrated History*, 207.

Decolonizing the Mind: Toni Morrison's *The Bluest Eye* and *Tar Baby*

LOTHAR BREDELLA (Giessen)

In his book *Decolonising the Mind*, Ngugi wa Thiong'o points out that the colonizers exercised not only physical but also social and psychological power over the colonized by viewing their language and culture as "inferior" and forcing them to adopt the language and culture of the colonial power as superior.[1] In some cases the colonized have even internalized the demeaning and degrading images the colonizers have imposed on them to such an extent that these images have become an essential instrument of their suppression. According to Charles Taylor, we have become aware of the destructive effects of these degrading images and protest against them:

> The politics of recognition is based on the insight that our identity is partly shaped by recognition or its absence, often by the *mis*recognition of others, and so a person or group of people can suffer real damage, real distortion, if the people or society around them mirror back to them a confining or demeaning or contemptible picture of themselves.[2]

In *The Bluest Eye*, Toni Morrison describes the degrading effect of the values of the dominant culture, especially its concept of beauty, on African-Americans. The novel, which appeared in 1970, was written during the Black Power movement, whose slogan "Black is beautiful" indicates the attempt to re-describe the demeaning images of the dominant culture.

Since African-Americans as a group have been treated as inferior, they must change the image of their group as a whole. Thus the collective identity gains a prominent significance in the politics of recognition. Yet this emphasis on the collective identity becomes problematic when it prescribes how individuals have to behave. Commenting on Taylor's essay "The Politics of Recognition," Kwame Anthony Appiah highlights the conflict between collective and personal identity. At first he stresses how important it is to fight for the recognition of one's collective identity. African-Americans must re-describe the negative script of self-hatred so that they can be proud of being African-Americans:

> An African-American after the Black-Power movement takes the old script of self-hatred, the script in which he or she is a nigger, and works, in community with others, to con

---

[1] Cf. Ngugi wa Thiong'o, *Decolonising the Mind. The Politics of Language in African Literature* (London et al.: Heinemann, 1986), 19ff.
[2] Charles Taylor, *Multiculturalism. Examining the Politics of Recognition*, ed. and intr. by Amy Gutman (Princeton: Princeton University Press, 1994), 25.

struct a series of positive Black-life scripts. In these life-scripts, being a Negro is recoded as being Black, and this requires, among other things, refusing to assimilate to white norms of speech and behaviour.[3]

African-Americans do not want to assimilate to the norms of the dominant culture, but what are the norms of the minority culture and who decides what they are? When the Black community claims the right to prescribe how the individual should act, then the minority culture repeats the violence of the dominant culture: "It is at this point that someone who takes autonomy seriously will ask whether we have not replaced one kind of tyranny with another" (Appiah, "Identity",162f.).

Steven C. Rockefeller argues in a similar way, but in addition highlights another aspect of the conflict between collective and personal identity. He also stresses that minorities must fight for the recognition of their collective or ethnic identity because the recognition of one's own identity depends on the recognition of one's racial or ethnic identity. Yet we do not only belong to our ethnic-racial group, but to larger, more comprehensive groups. The exclusive emphasis on the collective identity is problematic because it easily leads to intolerance against others. Rockefeller asks us not to lose sight of what he calls our universal identity:

> To elevate ethnic identity, to a position equal in significance to, or above, a person's universal identity is to weaken the foundations of liberalism and to open the door to intolerance."[4]

Decolonizing the mind, i.e. rewriting the negative scripts of self-contempt and self-hatred, is necessary, but what is the result of this process? Does it lead to the reconstruction of one's culture before colonization with a strong emphasis on the traditional way of life and the cultural heritage? Or does it lead to the recognition of several cultures in one and the same person? The first version will lead to a kind of cultural pluralism with an emphasis on distinct cultures which demand loyalty from their members. The second version will lead to a kind of cosmopolitanism which recognizes that people can live in-between cultures and develop multicultural identities. For the pluralists, cosmopolitanism leads to the loss of one's identity and to assimilation to the dominant culture, whereas for the cosmopolitanists, pluralism leads to ethnocentrism and intolerance. I have indicated here two possible responses to the politics of decolonizing the mind, which will play an important role in my interpretation of *Tar Baby*. This novel also raises the question of who decides what colonization and decolonization mean. According to the tar baby myth, Jadine is a colonized person; according to her own self-understanding, she is a self-reliant, independent young woman.

My approach to *Tar Baby* differs from my approach to *The Bluest Eye*. My interpretation of the first novel is close to the procedure we used in class, reading chapter by chapter and exploring our responses to them. The interpretation of the second one

---

[3] Kwame Anthony Appiah, "Identity, Authenticity, Survival: Multicultural Societies and Social Reproduction," in Charles Taylor, *Multiculturalism*, 149-163, here 161.
[4] Steven C. Rockefeller, "Comment," in Charles Taylor, *Multiculturalism*, 87-98, here 88.

concentrates on the relationship between Jadine and Son and examines it from different perspectives. While my interpretation of the *The Bluest Eye* is to a large extent affirmative and accepts Morrison's comments on her novel, the interpretation of *Tar Baby* suggests different readings and is critical of Morrison's comments on her novel.

I. The Bluest Eye *(1970) by Toni Morrison*

In *The Bluest Eye*, Pecola, an unattractive Black girl, wishes to have blue eyes. She wants to look like Shirley Temple in order to receive recognition and admiration from those around her. In the end, her wish is fulfilled. In a conversation with Charles Ruas, Morrison describes the novel's theme with the following words:

> I began to write about a girl who wanted blue eyes and the horror of having that wish fulfilled; and also about the whole business of what is physical beauty and the pain of that yearning and wanting to be somebody else, and how devastating that was and yet part of all females who were peripheral in other people's lives"[5]

While Morrison was attending elementary school, a girl told her of her wish to have blue eyes. Two decades later, Morrison explores the kind of self-contempt that underlies Pecola's wish: "Implicit in her desire was racial self-loathing. And twenty years later I was still wondering about how one learns that."[6] In trying to find out how people acquire such destructive views, Morrison uses a special situation, the ugly child of an unhappy family:

> In trying to dramatize the devastation that even casual racial contempt can cause, I chose a unique situation, not a representative one. The extremity of Pecola's case stemmed largely from a crippled and crippling family – unlike the average black family and unlike the narrator's. But singular as Pecola's life was, I believed some aspects of her woundability were lodged in all young girls." (Morrison, *Bluest Eye*, 210)

These words provide a hint as to how to read the novel. There is a tendency to read minority or post-colonial literary texts as though they portray typical experiences and typical characters. Morrison criticizes this tendency to read novels as sociological reports:

> This kind of sociological judgment is pervasive and pernicious. 'Novel A is better than Novel B or C because A is more like most black people really are.' Unforgivable. I am enchanted, personally, with people who are extraordinary because in them I can find what is applicable to the ordinary. (Morrison, *Conversations*, 125)

---

[5] Toni Morrison, *Conversations with Toni Morrison*, ed. Danille Taylor-Guthrie (Jackson: University Press of Mississippi, 1994), 95f.
[6] Toni Morrison, *The Bluest Eye* with "Afterword" (London et al.: Signet, 1994), 210.

In a different context she says that she finds it demoralizing to write about individuals "who are 'typically Black'" (Morrison, *Conversations*, 67). Does such an argument create a dilemma for minority and post-colonial literature? In the influential book *The Empire Writes Back*, the authors point out that in the writings of post-colonial authors "the day-to-day realities experienced by colonized peoples have been most powerfully encoded and so profoundly influential."[7] These words show that post-colonial and minority literary texts cannot be read as mere fiction which have no reference to reality, but we must also be aware of the fact that they are not sociological reports. Therefore they demand a special sensitivity from readers. This also raises the question of how we relate what is presented to our own world. A dialogue between Eva Hoffman and her American friend in *Lost in Translation* can highlight this problem:

> **My American Friend**: What did you think about that Hungarian movie last week?
> I: I thought it was quite powerful.
> M.A.F.: Me too. It was a very smart comment on how all of us can get co-opted by institutions.
> I: But it wasn't about all of us. It was about the Communist party in Hungary circa 1948.
> M.A.F.: Collaboration isn't the monopoly of the Communist party, you know. You can be bought and co-opted by Time, Inc., quite successfully.
> I: I think there may be just the tiniest difference between those two organizations.[8]

Hoffman's American friend reads the Hungarian film aesthetically. For her the events in the film can illuminate her own American reality. But Hoffman accuses her of levelling the differences between the Communist Party and Time, Inc. One can understand her anger about such a form of reading which plays down the terror of the Communist party, but an ethnocentric reading which uses the communist terror to glorify the United States would be as problematic. An ethnocentric reading which stresses the difference between the foreign and our own culture will prevent the work of art from challenging our concepts and attitudes. It is, however, one of the essential advantages of literary texts that they allow us to transcend boundaries. For the Chinese-American writer Maxine Hong Kingston the reading of literary texts makes it possible to identify with the mind of others:

> One of the first things I ever noticed and loved about reading is that words can get through all kinds of barriers; they can get through skin and culture. It's so easy to read and go through all kinds of struggles with an author. I love the way, when we read, we actually take on the mind of the person that we're reading about."[9]

For the anthropologist Anthony Cohen such a reading of a literary text can also be the model for understanding the members of other cultures because it acknowledges

---

[7] Bill Ashcroft, Gareth Griffiths and Helen Tiffin, *The Empire Writes Back. Theory and Practice in Post-colonial Literatures* (London & New York: Routledge, 1989), 1.

[8] Eva Hoffman, *Lost in Translation. A Life in a New Language* (London: Penguin, 1989), 205.

[9] Shelley Fisher Fishkin, "Interview with Maxine Hong Kingston," *American Literary History* 3:4 (1991), 782-791, here 787.

them as self-reflexive and creative human beings, whereas a sociological or anthropological approach tends to treat them as objects determined by social and economic conditions:

> [...] that is also how I begin to do fieldwork among others, others whom my own self-experience and introspection tell me cannot and must not be treated as mere ciphers of a collective social and cultural condition."[10]

This does not mean that Cohen believes that we are all the same under the skin, but he wants to make clear that we can only understand the differences between others and ourselves adequately if we do not forget what we have in common with them, namely that we have self-reflective and creative selves and therefore can distance ourselves from and transform our own culture.

As already indicated, my interpretation of *The Bluest Eye* is based on the procedure I chose for reading the novel in class. The students were asked to read the first few pages of the novel and to record their responses so that they could be discussed in class. Later we read the book chapter by chapter. The method of interpretation varied: Sometimes we directed our attention to certain themes, and discussed them in class, sometimes students selected a passage which they found interesting and reported their responses to it. This procedure encourages students to reflect on the difficulties they had in understanding the text and to come up with creative solutions for their difficulties, and it makes possible involvement and critical detachment. In the aesthetic experience, as D.W. Harding points out, we are not only guided by the text to create characters and events but also respond to and evaluate what we have created:

> It is an elementary form of onlooking merely to imagine what the situation seems like and react *with* the participant. The more complex observer imagines something of what the participant is experiencing and then reacts to him, for instance with pity or joy on his account."[11]

In the aesthetic experience we are involved, and at the same time we can step back and observe how we are involved. Wolfgang Iser describes this dialectic with the following words: "The ability to perceive oneself during the process of participation is an essential quality of the aesthetic experience; the observer finds himself in a strange, halfway position: he is involved, and he watches himself being involved."[12]

---

[10] Anthony P. Cohen, *Self Consciousness. An Alternative Anthropology of Identity* (London and New York: Routledge, 1994), 188.

[11] D.W. Harding, "Psychological Processes in the Reading of Fiction," *British Journal of Aesthetics* 2:2 (1962), 145.

[12] Wolfgang Iser, *The Act of Reading. A Theory of Aesthetic Response* (Baltimore and London: Johns Hopkins University Press, 1987), 134.

1. The Primer

Before the novel begins with the section "Autumn," the reader is confronted with two very short chapters. The first is taken from an elementary school reading primer and is repeated twice, once without punctuation and a second time without spaces between the words. Students wondered how they are supposed to understand the beginning of the novel. We recorded their initial responses and wanted to pursue how they underwent a change during the further reading of the novel. The chapter titles always refer back to the primer. In a conversation with Thomas LeClair, Morrison describes her intention in using the primer:

> In *The Bluest Eye* I used the primer story, with its picture of a happy family, as a frame acknowledging the outer civilization. The primer with white children was the way life was presented to the black people. As the novel proceeded I wanted that primer version broken up and confused, which explains the typographical running together of the words. (Morrison, *Conversation*, 127)

Morrison argues that Black children need Black characters to identify with. For her the expectation that Black children should recognize themselves in White characters is a form of colonization. Therefore she sees it as her obligation to write literary texts for Black readers in which they can recognize themselves as African-Americans. In this context, students asked the question of whether we as Germans can understand African-American literature and whether we should attempt at all to understand it. Some of the students were in favor of this attitude while others pointed to the racist consequences of such a view. If German literature can only be understood by Germans we exclude others. We create a kind of German essence which is regarded as inaccessible to others.

2. Autumn

The primer already indicates that Morrison asks for active participation of her readers. She not only wants to move them but to make them think and reflect critically on the situations presented. How the story is presented influences how we respond to it. Morrison says that she first wrote the story of Pecola and her family in the third person. But this version did not seem effective to her. There was a gap between the text and the reader. In order to overcome this gap, Morrison introduced Claudia and Frieda and let Pecola's story be told from Claudia's perspective, ."..so that there would be somebody to empathize with her at her age level. This also gave a playful quality to their lives, to relieve the grimness" (Morrison, *Conversations*, 97).

At the beginning of the novel, Claudia reports that she does not receive the pity she expects from her mother when she is sick. She vividly describes how she, as an eight-year-old girl, experiences her sickness and her mother's behavior. However, this is followed by a sentence which demonstrates the limited perspective of the child and relativizes what is being presented: "I do not know that she is not angry at me, but at my sickness. I believe she despises my weakness for letting the sickness 'take hold'" (11f.).[13] Such sentences remind us of the fact that many scenes are written from a limited perspective. The recognition of how literary texts "subjectivize" reality by presenting it from different perspectives and how they "subjunctivize" reality by making us wonder whether the characters understand their reality adequately is an important element of the aesthetic experience.[14]

With Claudia, Morrison introduces a character who instinctively rejects the Whites' ideal of beauty. She destroys dolls with blond hair and blue eyes, to the dismay of adults who do not understand her behavior: "I was physically revolted by and secretly frightened of those round moronic eyes, the pancake face, and orangeworms hair" (20). She cannot be happy about the kind of doll which others admire, but instead wants to tear it apart:

> To see of what it was made, to discover the dearness, to find the beauty, the desirability that had escaped me, but apparently only me. Adults, older girls, shops, magazines, newspapers, window-signs – all the world had agreed that a blue-eyed, yellow-haired, pink-skinned doll was what every girl child treasured. (20)

Claudia is shocked when she realizes that what she does to dolls, she could also do to White girls, and she wants to find out why she is ignored when she is next to White –or light-colored children: "To discover what eluded me: the secret of the magic they weaved on others. What made people look at them and say, 'Awwwww,' but not for me?" (22) As Claudia becomes aware of her sadistic tendencies towards White girls and cannot reconcile this sadism with her image of herself, she discovers a mechanism with which she can avoid being sadistic:

> The best hiding place was love. Thus the conversion from pristine sadism to fabricated hatred, to fraudulent love. It was a small step to Shirley Temple. I learned much later to worship her, just as I learned to delight in cleanliness, knowing, even as I learned, that the change was adjustment without improvement. (23)

Here Claudia, the narrator, gives an answer to the question of how one comes to the point of adopting White ideals and values although they lead to self-contempt and self-hatred. One adopts them in order to escape one's feeling of inferiority. Later we shall learn that Cholly identifies with those who are strong and turns against those who are weak. Claudia sees through this mechanism, which other characters like Pecola, Cholly, Pauline, and Soaphead succumb to in different ways.

In order to explain why Pecola wishes to have blue eyes, Morrison gives a detailed description of her parents, who are not only despised by the Whites, but who also live

---

[13] All page numbers in brackets in Section I refer to *The Bluest Eye*.
[14] Cf. Lothar Bredella, "The Anthropological and Pedagogical Significance of Aesthetic Reading in the Foreign Language Classroom," in Lothar Bredella and Werner Delanoy, eds., *Challenges of Literary Texts in the Foreign Language Classroom* (Tübingen: Narr, 1996), 1-29, esp. 14.

as outcasts in the "Black community" and torment each other (cf. 34ff.). Pecola suffers because of her parents' fighting and wishes that God would let her die or disappear. She wants to run away like her brother, but she is convinced that she cannot run away from her ugliness: "Long hours she sat looking in the mirror, trying to discover the secret of the ugliness, the ugliness that made her ignored or despised at school, by teachers and classmates alike" (45). Pecola believes that blue eyes would make her beautiful and that her beauty would make her parents stop fighting (cf. 46).

When Pecola buys candy at Mr. Yacobowski's, he doesn't look at her and she detects repulsion in his behavior towards her: "The distaste must be for her, her blackness" (49). Morrison herself talks about the horrifying experience of not being recognized for what one is. "You knew you were not the person they were looking at. And to know that and to see what you saw in those other people's eyes was devastating. Some people made it, some didn't. And I wanted to explore it myself" (Morrison, *Conversations*, 199).

3. Winter

Maureen Peale gets the attention Pecola cannot get because she comes from a relatively wealthy family and is good-looking. Claudia and Frieda are jealous of her and despise her in order to preserve their own self-respect. They feel threatened by Maureen, but they also understand that Maureen is not their enemy: "The *Thing* to fear was the *Thing* that made *her* beautiful, and not us" (74). In contrast to Maureen, who no one dares to attack, Pecola is the perfect scapegoat even for Black boys, who project their own self-hatred and hopelessness onto her (cf. 65).

The theme of conforming to the norms of the dominant culture is further pursued in the description of Geraldine. She represents the Black middle class, which has adopted Whites' norms, thereby disowning their own culture (cf. 83). The narrator describes Geraldine's world as a sterile one in which the *physical* needs of her son are met, but not his *emotional* ones. He gradually adopts his mother's ideals and values and comes to the conclusion that Black children are not good enough for him and begins to torment those who are weak. One of his victims is Pecola (cf. 88ff.). While Morrison gives most characters the chance to present the world as they see it, Geraldine is described in a sarcastic way only from the outside. What Morrison says about her portrayal of Maureen could also be said of her description of Geraldine:

> I was not good with her. She was too easy a shot. I wouldn't do that now with her. I mean we all know who she is. And everybody has one of those in his or her life, but I was unfair to her. I did not in that book look at anything from her point of view inside. I only showed the façade." (Morrison , *Conversations*, 203)

In *Tar Baby,* however, as we shall see, Morrison gives Jadine the chance to present the world from her point of view.

4. Spring

At the beginning of this chapter we experience one of the most depressing scenes of the novel. In the kitchen of the Fishers' house, where Pauline Breedlove works as a servant, her daughter Pecola accidently knocks over a hot pie and burns her skin. Pauline, however, does not comfort her but beats her and comforts the White child who is upset because of Pauline's anger. Pauline Breedlove views her role as servant as the fulfillment of her wishes: "She became what is known as an ideal servant, for such a role filled practically all of her needs" (127). As a Black, she must wait for Whites to be served in a store before it is her turn. As a servant, however, she is served immediately and can even make demands (cf. 128). Like Geraldine, Pauline adopts the values and ideals of the Whites in order to fulfill some of her needs: "Power, praise, and luxury were hers in this household" (128). Yet her acceptance of White norms leads to the destruction of her children's self-confidence:

> Them she bent toward respectability, and in so doing taught them fear: fear of being clumsy, fear of being like their father, fear of not being loved by God, fear of madness like Cholly's mother's. (128)

Seeking refuge in the role of the ideal servant is, however, only one element in Pauline's moving life story. At the age of two, she injured her foot and began to walk with a limp. This deformity, according to the narrator, "saved Pauline Williams from total anonymity" (110). Before the beginning of World War I, Pauline's parents moved from Alabama to Kentucky with the hope of finding work in the mines and factories. In Kentucky, Pauline meets Cholly. They marry and move to Ohio. In the north, Pauline feels isolated and lonely. During her pregnancy, she often goes to the movies, where she devotes herself to ideas of romantic love. The more Pauline allows her thoughts to be determined by ideas of romantic love, the more difficult it is for her to go back home to Cholly. For the narrator, Pauline's mind is colonized by the values of the dominant culture and alienated from her own culture. However, the critique of the concept of romantic love transcends the opposition between majority and minority culture:

> Along with the idea of romantic love, she [Pauline] was introduced to another – physical beauty. Probably the most destructive ideas in the history of human thought. Both originated in envy, thrived in insecurity, and ended in disillusion. In equating physical beauty with virtue, she stripped her mind, bound it, and collected self-contempt by the heap. (122)

Pauline's life story is followed by Cholly's. He was abandoned at birth by his mother and raised by his great aunt. After her death, he is all alone in the world. One of the experiences that shaped him takes place when he makes love to a girl for the first time. Two Whites surprise them in the act and force Cholly to continue. However, Cholly does not direct his hatred toward the two Whites who humiliated him, but instead toward the girl who witnesses his humiliation. He hates her so much that he could strangle her (cf. 149). The narrator explains Cholly's misplaced hatred by pointing out that Cholly, as a powerless Black boy, cannot direct it at the powerful Whites (cf. 150f.).

After the death of his aunt, he searches for his father. He only knows his name, Samson Fuller, and the place where he could be. When he finds himself standing in front of a man with this name, he loses his nerve to reveal his identity. This failure is connected with a destructive pain, which also leads to a kind of rebirth. Cholly becomes a person who feels completely free without any obligation to anyone: "Free to feel whatever he felt – fear, guilt, shame, love, grief, pity. [...] He was free to live his fantasies, and free even to die, the how and the when of which held no interest for him" (159). From now on he is only concerned with himself (cf. 160). For Morrison, Cholly is "lawless." He does whatever he wants to do and knows no self-control (cf. Morrison, *Conversations*, 19f.). Since he never experienced how parents deal with children, he is unable to deal with his own children and cannot even comprehend the relationship between parents and children (cf. 160).

When Cholly comes home drunk on a Sunday afternoon, he sees Pecola in the kitchen. To him, she appears ugly and unhappy. He feels that her ugliness and unhappiness condemn him: "He wanted to break her neck – but tenderly. Guilt and impotence rose in a bilious duet" (161). He sees her loving eyes and doesn't know how to respond: "What could his heavy arms and befuddled brain accomplish that would earn him his own respect, that would in turn allow him to accept her love?" (161f.). Then a gesture of his daughter reminds him of Pauline: "The tenderness welled up in him, ..." (162).

Most of the students in my class were confused by the portrayal of the rape. Since the rape is seen from Cholly's perspective, the students got the impression that they, as readers, are prevented from condemning the rape as they should. Morrison herself said about her presentation of Pecola's rape: "This most masculine act of aggression becomes feminized in my language, 'passive,' and, I think, most accurately repellent when deprived of the male 'glamour of shame' rape is (or once was) routinely given" (Morrison, *Bluest Eye*, 215). Morrison also wants to describe the pain of a love which can only be expressed destructively: "I want, here, to talk about how painful it is and what the painful consequences are of distortion, of love that isn't fructified, is held in, not expressed" (Morrison, *Conversations*, 41). Morrison is clearly not trying to downplay the rape, but she is also concerned with not dehumanizing Cholly: .".. I did not want to dehumanize the characters who trashed Pecola and contributed to her collapse" (Morrison, *Bluest Eye*, 211). In reality, says Morrison, we do not notice individuals like Cholly, but she wants us to face them in literature: "In order to look at them in fiction, you have to hook the reader, strike a certain posture as narrator, achieve some intimacy" (Morrison, *Conversations*, 123). While students were discussing their uneasiness about Morrison's description of the rape, one of them pointed out that we should not project our concept of rape into the novels of African-Americans. He had read several novels by African-American writers in which fathers rape their daughters and drew the conclusion that such an event, which obviously happens often in Black families, should not be evaluated by our standards. For him, our responses were ethnocentric. Yet he was severely attacked for being insensitive and accused of reading literary texts as "sociological reports." The relatively frequent presentations of rape in African-American texts do not indicate that rapes are a normal occurrence in Black families, but must be read as a symbol of the inflictions African-Americans have suffered.

5. *Summer*

The last section, "Summer," is the shortest. The Breedloves, who were outsiders already, have now become completely isolated since Cholly's rape of his daughter has become known. According to the judgment of the neighborhood, it would be best if Pecola's baby were to die at birth. Claudia, however, hopes that the baby will live. She and Frieda oppose the hatred toward the yet unborn life and want to offer God a sacrifice if He allows the baby to live. Claudia realizes that all of them have used Pecola as a scapegoat: "All of our waste which we dumped on her and which she absorbed. [...] We were so beautiful when we stood astride her ugliness. [...] we were not compassionate, we were polite; not good, but well behaved" (205). We discussed in class who this "we" might be. The Black community? American society? Is the reader also part of the "we"? Does this "we" level the difference between White and Black by making both Whites and Blacks responsible for Pecola going insane? This question makes explicit what has played a significant role from the beginning: How do we as students relate to what has been presented? Nandini Bhattacharya distinguishes between two different types of response, which could be loosely classified as "liberal" and "conservative" ways of reading. The liberal reader will tend to accept the guilt of the Whites toward African-Americans and see them as victims of slavery and the dominant culture. In this type of reading, African-Americans are good and Whites are evil. Conservatives accept the liberal reading but reject texts which make them feel guilty.[15] Bhattacharya argues that Morrison wants us to take a position beyond "liberal" and "conservative" ways of reading and points out that Morrison describes Blacks not only as victims but also as responsible agents. She asks her readers to take several perspectives into account when they answer the question of who is responsible for Pecola's insanity (cf. Morrison, *Bluest Eye*, 211). It was difficult for the students to find a position beyond a liberal reading. The novel describes how Pecola's, Pauline's, Cholly's, and Geraldine's consciousness is colonized and suggests that these people are victims. Is Pauline responsible when she beats Pecola who burned her legs? Is Cholly responsible for destroying Pecola? The students admitted that they were often insecure as to how to respond.

---

[15] Cf. Nandini Bhattacharya, "Postcolonial Agency in Teaching Toni Morrison," *Cultural Studies* 9:2 (1995), 226-246.

II. Tar Baby: *The Conflict between Pluralism and Cosmopolitanism*

In my interpretation of *Tar Baby*, I will concentrate on one aspect of the novel, the relationship between Jadine and Son and explore the topic of decolonizing the mind within the debate on pluralism and cosmopolitanism.

Jadine is a successful Black model who lives in New York, Paris and Rome. She went to famous universities and has a degree from the Sorbonne. Unlike Pauline Breedlove, who attempts to escape her depressing reality by accepting the values of the dominant culture, Jadine can feel at home in it. She is accepted:

> The handsome raucous men wanted to marry, live with, support, fund and promote her. Smart and beautiful women wanted to be her friend, confidante, lover, neighbour, guest, playmate, host, servant, student or simply near" (44).[16]

Yet Jadine – on "one of the happiest days of her life" (41), because she had just been chosen for the cover of *Elle* – has an unsettling encounter with a Black woman in a supermarket. This woman dressed in yellow spits at her and shatters her self-confidence:

> Turned those eyes too beautiful for eyelashes on Jadine and, with a small parting of her lips, shot an arrow of saliva between her teeth down to the pavement and the hearts below" (43).

This gesture makes Jadine flee from Paris to a Caribbean island, Isle des Chevaliers, to her uncle and aunt, who brought her up after her parents' death, and to her White patron, who financed her education. Jadine cannot understand why the encounter with this woman in yellow makes her lose her composure and attempts to rationalize it:

> The woman had made her feel lonely in a way. Lonely and inauthentic. Perhaps she was overreacting. The woman appeared simply at a time when she had a major decision to make" (45).

The major decision she refers to is whether she should marry Ryk, a white man. She wants to marry him, yet she fears that he just wants to marry a black girl, "any black girl who looks like me" (45). This is ironic because Jadine wants to escape her collective identity and be an autonomous person.

On the Isle des Chevaliers Jadine meets Son, a Black man who has hidden himself in the house and who, after being discovered, is not handed over to the police but accepted as a guest by Valerian, Jadine's patron. Son presents the opposite of Jadine's world. He identifies with Eloe, a Black community, and does not want to get involved

---

[16] All page numbers in brackets in Section II refer to Toni Morrison, *Tar Baby* (London: Triad/Panther, 1984).

with the White man's world. He scorns assimilation and speaks for segregation. But he cannot live in Eloe any longer because he killed his wife and her lover, a fourteen-year-old boy.

According to the title of the novel, Jadine's fight for independence and autonomy is devalued right from the start: "In the original story, the tar baby," writes Morrison, "is made by a white man – that has to be the case with Jadine. She has to have been almost 'constructed' by the Western thing, and grateful to it" (Morrison, *Conversations*, 134). Morrison herself pursues further the analogy between the tar baby story and her novel when she says:

> It's a love story, really: the tar baby is a black woman; the rabbit is a black man, the powerless, clever creature, who has to outwit his master. He is determined to live in that briar patch, even though he has the option to stay with her and live comfortably, securely, without magic, without touching the borders of his life. (Morrison, *Conversations*, 47)

If we follow Morrison's interpretation of her novel, Jadine is constructed by the White man in order to seduce Son to assimilate to the dominant society. Yet one might question this logic: Why should the White society, which has rejected African-Americans as "unassimilable," reward Son with a beautiful woman for his willingness to assimilate?

While Jadine wants Son to leave the Black community, he wants her to leave the White society, which for him represents evil and death: "He thought he was rescuing her from Valerian, meaning *them*, the aliens, the people who in a mere three hundred years, had killed a world millions of years old" (271). Therefore, Jadine should not feel grateful for her education at the best colleges and universities (cf. 265).

Son stresses that African-Americans must resist the temptation of assimilation: "They [white folks and black folks] should work together sometimes, but they should not eat together or live together or sleep together. Do any of those personal things in life" (211). Son tells Jadine that she will not be Ryk's wife if she marries him but only a nanny who takes care of his children. The following words are also reminiscent of Morrison's condemnation of Blacks who accept middle class White values in *The Bluest Eye*:

> Then you can do exactly what you bitches have always done: take care of white folks' children. Feed, love and care for white people's children. That's what you were born for; that's what you have waited for all your life [...] There are no 'mixed' marriages. It just looks that way. People don't mix races; they abandon them or pick them. But I want to tell you something: if you have a white man's baby, you have chosen to be just another mammy only you are the real mammy 'cause you had it in your womb and you are still taking care of white folks' children. (272)

How are we as readers supposed to take these words? According to the tar baby myth, Son is right, there cannot be mutual recognition between Black and White people but only the fight for hegemony. But he also confirms the racist's view that "there are no 'mixed' marriages" and attempts to destroy Jadine's self-respect and self-esteem. Or do we have to take into consideration that he is afraid of losing Jadine to another man and says things which he might regret later? It will probably depend on our presuppositions of how we interpret these words, whether they reveal the truth about Black-White relationships or whether they are the words of an egocentric young man who believes in an illusory concept of a pure Black community which cannot be realized in a multicultural society. But let us pursue further how Son and Jadine experience the dominant culture and the Black community and how the novel attempts to direct the reader's sympathy. For Son, New York resembles hell and destroys Black people's innocence and identity (cf. 216). Son encounters the same alienation of Black people on television. These Black people are not those he has been familiar with in Eloe (cf. 217f.). Son's experience of New York underscores the necessity of segregation and justifies his belief in Eloe. When Jadine arrives in New York, however, her experience of the city is quite different. What is depressing for him is exhilarating for her (cf. 223).

While New York is home for Jadine, it is a god-forsaken place for Son. Therefore he dreams of living with Jadine in Eloe, Florida: "Black people. No whites. No white people live in Eloe" (173). Yet for Jadine, Eloe is a great disappointment. After their arrival, Son asks her to stay with Ellen, the wife of his friend, so that he can meet his father alone. Son expects her to understand this, but she does not understand it: "[...] no more than she could understand (or accept) her being shunted off with Ellen and the children while the men grouped on the porch and, after a greeting, ignored her; ..." (248). For Jadine the Black community turns out to be a group of male intimates who like to be among themselves. The women in the community seem to approve of the men's behavior and treat Jadine as an outsider (cf. 257). In Eloe, Jadine has a dream which, like the encounter with the woman in yellow, unsettles her and seems to be a sign of her inauthenticity. Women assemble around her bed and show her their breasts. She tells them: "I have breasts too" but they do not seem to believe her. For them she is not a woman (cf. 264).

The image of the self-reliant woman is rejected by the Black community, and Jadine's dream seems to express her feelings of guilt. In the morning, however, Jadine attempts to liberate herself from the depressing feeling of her dream and criticizes the women who claimed to be superior: "The mamas who had seduced him and were trying to lay claim to her. It would be the fight of their lives to get away from that coven that had nothing to show but breasts" (265). Jadine fights for her self-reliance and independence by rejecting Eloe: "Eloe was rotten and more boring than ever. A burnt-out place. There was no life there. Maybe a past but definitely no future and finally there was no interest. All that Southern small-town country romanticism was a lie, a joke, kept secret by people who could not function elsewhere" (262). Yet Son gets furious when he feels that Jadine thinks that "living there [in Eloe] was child's play, easy" and that it only matters that you make it in the First Cities of the world. When Son stresses that he cannot live in New York, she asks him: "Is it because you're afraid? Because you can't make it in New York?" This accusation gives him the chance to attack the myth of making it in New York:

Make it in New York. Make it in New York. I'm tired of hearing that shit. What the fuck is it? If I make it in New York, then that's all I do: 'Make it in New York'. That's not life; that's making it. I don't want to *make* it. I want to *be* it. (268)

Son rejects her concept of success and points out to Jadine that he is unable "to get excited about money." But for her the refusal of money is "transcendental, Thoureau crap":

[...] stop making excuses about not having anything [...]. It's not romantic. And it's not being free. It's dumb. You think you're above it, above money, the rat race and all that. But you're not above it, you're just without it. It's a prison, poverty is. (172)

How are readers supposed to respond to Jadine's and Son's description of Eloe? Jadine seems to be arrogant when she thinks that life in Eloe is "child's play" and despises the women in Eloe. Yet she seems to be right when she defends her image of herself and criticizes Son's glorification of Eloe. She refuses to romanticize Son's poverty and low living standards. Therefore it might come as a surprise to many readers that for Morrison, Jadine's negative view of Eloe is a sign of her corruption. When Son is willing to see Eloe through Jadine's eyes, Morrison says about him:

[...] there is some complicity in him, also. He is derailed by his romantic passion and his sensibilities are distorted; he can't make judgments any more. When he looked at the photos that she took of his people, he saw what she saw and it could not revive what he had, and that's testimony of his frailty. (Morrison, *Conversations*, 107)

Morrison severely criticizes Jadine not only for her contempt of Eloe but also for her contempt of the women in Eloe (cf. Morrison, *Conversations*, 106).

Morrison's presentation of the relationship between Jadine and Son can be seen as a comment on the debate between pluralists and cosmopolitans. In his book *Postethnic America: Beyond Multiculturalism*, David A. Hollinger argues that in a multicultural society, as he envisions it, collective or ethnic identities should be recognized, but people should also be free to decide which group they want to belong to. Considering the increasing number of children from marriages between people from different racial and ethnic groups, one's ethnic identity can no longer be determined by birth. Therefore Hollinger's position "favors voluntary over involuntary affiliations ... and promotes solidarities of wide scope that incorporate people with different ethnic and racial backgrounds."[17] Hollinger distinguishes two kinds of multiculturalism, a pluralist and a cosmopolitan one:

Pluralism respects inherited boundaries and locates individuals within one or another of a series of ethno-racial groups to be protected and preserved. Cosmopolitanism is more wary of traditional enclosures and favors voluntary affiliations. Cosmopolitanism pro

---

[17] David A. Hollinger, *Postethnic America: Beyond Multiculturalism* (New York: Basic Books, 1995), 3.

motes multiple identities, emphasizes the dynamic and changing character of many groups, and is responsive to the potential for creating new cultural combinations. (Hollinger, *Postethnic America*, 3f.)

For Hollinger, ethnic and racial ties can no longer be binding. He mentions Ismael Reed who says about the author of *Roots*: "If Alex Haley had traced his father's bloodline, he would have traveled twelve generations back to, not Gambia, but *Ireland*," but he is aware of the fact that such a choice would not have been accepted by white Americans because of the "one-drop-rule" (cf. Hollinger, *Postethnic America*, 19ff.). Therefore, for Hollinger, it is not without irony that today Black politicians use the "'one-drop-rule' that was designed to serve slaveholders and white supremacists" (Hollinger, *Postethnic America*, 1) to keep the races apart and to secure the loyality of African-Americans.

In an essay entitled "Minority Cultures and the Cosmopolitan Alternative" Jeremy Waldron makes a plea for a cosmopolitan version of multiculturalism. He is afraid that the pluralist version with its emphasis on loyalty to one's racial- and ethnic-cultural group will lead to the persecution of those who develop multicultural identities. For him it is no accident that Salman Rushdie is persecuted by those who defend the purity of their culture, which he questions when he writes:

> *The Satanic Verses* celebrates hybridity, impurity, intermingling, the transformation that comes of new and unexpected combinations of human beings, cultures, ideas, politics, movies, songs. It rejoices in mongrelization and fears the absolutism of the Pure.[18]

Waldron draws the conclusion from Rushdie's description of the Cosmopolitan that "[i]t can no longer be said that all people *need* their rootedness in the particular culture in which they and their ancestors were reared in the way that they need food, clothing, and shelter" (Waldron, "Minority Cultures", 762).

Yet pluralists such as Molefi Kete Asante argue that Afro-Americans will lose their identity in such a cosmopolitan culture:

> To lose one's terms is to become a victim of the other's attitudes, models, disciplines and culture; and the ultimate effect of such a massive loss is the destruction of self-confidence, the distortion of history, and psychological marginality.[19]

For Asante, Afrocentrism has the obligation to maintain a distinct African-American perspective:

> If you are African American, placing yourself in the center of your analysis so that you are grounded in a historical and cultural context is to be Afrocentric. Without Afrocentricity, African Americans would not have a voice to add to multiculturalism. (Asante, "Afrocentrism", 7)

---

[18] Rushdie quoted in Jremy Waldron, "Minority Cultures and the Cosmopolitan Alternative," *University of Michigan Journal of Law Reform* 25:3 (1992), 751-793, here 751.

[19] Molefi Kete Asante, „Afrocentrism," *American Studies Newsletter* 36 (1995), 6-8, here 7.

Waldron would not deny that some people might need a homogeneous culture for self-realization, but he also stresses that there are people who prefer to live in-between cultures and develop multicultural identities. Therefore it is not a basic human right that one's own culture must be maintained: "At best, it leaves the right to culture roughly on the same footing as the right to religious freedom. We no longer think it true that everyone needs some religious faith or that everyone must be sustained in the faith in which he was brought up" (Waldron, "Minority Cultures", 762). We need culture but not our culture in order to survive and develop our potentials. The cosmopolitan, so Waldron, "refuses to think of himself as *defined* by his location or his ancestry or his citizenship or his language" (Waldron, "Minority Cultures", 754).

While for the pluralist the cosmopolitans are inauthentic because they have lost or betrayed their cultures, for the cosmopolitan the pluralists are inauthentic because their belief in a homogenous culture is an illusion: " ... to immerse oneself in the traditional practices of, say, an aboriginal culture might be a fascinating anthropological experiment, but it involves an artificial dislocation from what actually is going on in the world" (Waldron, "Minority Cultures", 763). Pluralists argue that it is our obligation to preserve the variety of cultures as it is our obligation to preserve the variety of animals and plants. Cosmopolitans, however, reject this equation as misleading because cultures do not exist for their own sake but for the people who live in them and who can change them.

Morrison takes sides with Son against Jadine, but she also criticizes his plea for a pure Black community because such a concept has no future: "He [Son] may identify totally and exclusively with the past, which is a kind of death, because it means you have no future, but a suspended place" (Morrison, *Conversations*, 112). On one occasion in the novel Morrison explicitly criticizes Jadine's and Son's position as one-sided:

> Each was pulling the other away from the maw of hell – its very ridge top. Each knew the world as it was meant or ought to be. One had a past, the other a future and each one bore the culture to save the race in his hands. Mama-spoiled black man, will you mature with me? Culture-bearing black woman, whose culture are you bearing? (272)

When we consider Jadine's self-reliance and independence and Son's emphasis on community, we can also interpret the conflict between these characters as a conflict between two concepts of the self. In his book *Dilemmas of the American Self*, John P. Hewitt points out that there are two basic strategies for the construction of the self in the American culture: "exclusivity" and "autonomy." Exclusivity means that one constructs one's self by an identification with one's group. "Exclusive identification with the quasi-organic ethnic, religious, or other enclave provides the rationale for decisions that affect the life course as a whole (whom to marry, for example) as well as less consequential matters, ..."[20] Yet there is a problem with such an identification in modern society. It is not "natural," but rather based on a choice: "The quasi-organic

---

[20] John P. Hewitt, *Dilemmas of the American Self* (Philadelphia: Temple University Press, 1989), 196.

community is not a spontaneous, natural world unto itself, but has a 'constructed' character that makes integration a more self-conscious and less automatic achievement" (Hewitt, *Dilemmas*, 196). In order to reduce self-doubts, one reconstructs the past as a quasi-organic community "in which there was a true generalized other" (Hewitt, *Dilemmas*, 197). But such a community probably never existed. As Stuart Hall points out: "The organic community was just always in the childhood you have left behind. [...] We always constructed them [the great collectives] more essentially, more homogeneously, more unified, less contradictory than they ever were, once you actually know everything about them."[21]

Yet, not only the communal but also the autonomous self is inherently ambivalent because it cannot avoid being dependent on others. It is true, the autonomists reject the community which they regard as threatening and "seek the freedom of society" (Hewitt, *Dilemmas*, 201), but they need a society which appreciates autonomy and self-realization. Therefore success plays an important role in the search for autonomy: "Just as 'success' is a measure of autonomy, the 'successful' provide models for the would-be autonomous person to emulate" (Hewitt, *Dilemmas*, 202). From this perspective Jadine's and Son's dispute about success gains a new significance (cf. Hewitt, *Dilemmas*, 203).

Morrison rejects the concept of success for African-Americans because it leads to a betrayal of their African-American identity. In an interview she confirms Son's resistance to Jadine's temptation: "There is a new, capitalistic, modern American black which is what everybody thought was the ultimate in integration. To produce Jadine, that's what it was for. I think there is some danger in the result of that production" (Morrison, *Conversations*, 105).

Yet, should Blacks not be interested in improving their socio-economic conditions? Appiah discusses this question in detail and comes to the conclusion that African-Americans should receive a better education which prepares them for better jobs, even if it means assimilation to the dominant culture to a certain extent. He also points out that assimilation does not mean that everybody would be the same as everybody else. It would, however, make racial identity less central to the self-concept of African-Americans:

> It would make African-American identity more like Irish-American identity is for most of those who care to keep the label. And that would allow us to resist one persistent feature of ethnoracial identities: that they risk becoming the obsessive focus, the be-all and end-all, of the lives of those who identify with them.[22]

---

[21] Stuart Hall, "Old and New Identities," in Anthony D. King, ed., *Culture, Globalization and The World System: Contemporary Conditions for the Representation of Identity* (London: Macmillan, 1991), 41-68, here 46.

[22] Kwame Anthony Appiah, "Race, Culture, Identity: Misunderstood Connections," in Kwame Anthony Appiah and Amy Gutman, *Color Conscious: The Political Morality of Race* (Princeton: Princeton University Press, 1996), 30-105, here 103.

According to Appiah the obsessive emphasis on racial identities makes African-Americans forget "that their individual identities are complex and multifarious – that they have enthusiasms that do not flow from their race or ethnicity, interests and tastes that cross ethnoracial boundaries, that they have occupations or professions, are fans of clubs and groups" (Appiah, "Race, Culture, Identity", 103). From this perspective Jadine's desire not to be defined by her collective identity gains a new significance. It is not necessarily a sign of inauthenticity. For Appiah collective identities tend to "go imperial" when they prescribe "too tightly" how their members should behave. He stresses "that we are not only simply black or white or yellow or brown, gay or straight or bisexual, Jewish, Christian, Moslem, Buddhist or Confucian" (Appiah, "Race, Culture, Identity", 103) but have personal identities.

For Son the personal identity should be subordinated to one's racial identity. His ideal is the pure Black community. For Appiah this ideal is an illusion: "African-American identity [...] is centrally shaped by American society and institutions: it cannot be seen as constructed solely within African-American communities" (Appiah, "Race, Culture, Identity", 103). Robert Allen also questions the belief in a pure black community as long as it is dependent on the outside society: "[...] black control of black communities will not mean freedom from oppression as long as black communities are subservient to an outside society which is exploitive."[23] And for Stephen Steinberg pluralism is problematic because of its "ignominious origins." The melting pot in the nineteenth and at the beginning of the twentieth century did not include non-European immigrants and former Black slaves. They were rejected as "unassimilable." The message of the melting pot to non-Europeans ran: "No matter how much like us you are you will remain apart" (Steinberg, *Ethnic Myth*, 42). For Steinberg pluralism has racist overtones and confirms economic and social inequalities. This is, Steinberg writes, "the pitfall – the fatal flaw – that robbed ethnic pluralism of its cultural innocence" (Steinberg, *Ethnic Myth*, 255). Yet the pluralists will point out that Steinberg is contradicting himself. If even the melting pot rejects non-Europeans as unassimilable, then pluralism is the only possible consequence. It is needed to change the economic and social inequalities, because assimilation allows only individuals to improve their economic and social status and thus hides the fact that Whites have better chances than people of other races. An effective change can only come about if group rights are acknowledged. The dominant ideology which makes individuals responsible for their success or failure stablizes the *status quo*.

The discussion about pluralism and cosmopolitanism allows us to see Jadine and Son in a new light. Yet Morrison is very explicit in her condemnation of Jadine as inauthentic. In an interview she says about her:

> She [the woman in yellow] is the original self – the self that we betray when we lie, the one that is always there. And whatever that self looks like – if one ever sees that thing, or

---

[23] Quoted in Stephen Steinberg, *Ethnic Myth. Race, Ethnicity, and Class in America* (Boston, Mass.: Beacon Press, 1989), 255.

> that image – one measures one's other self against it. So that with all of the good luck, and the good fortune, and the skill that Jadine has – the other is the authentic self. (Morrison, *Conversations*, 148)

This is not only a provocative statement for the cosmopolitan discourse but also for the postmodern one on the self. For postmodernists, the distinction between an authentic and inauthenitc self is untenable because it presupposes that there is a substantial self which exists independently of the individual experiences and decisions of the self. In his book *The Saturated Self: Dilemmas of Identity in Contemporary Life*, Kenneth Gergen writes that there is no self beyond socially saturated relations.[24] For Gergen, Jadine could represent the ideal postmodern self. She is not only the socially saturated self but as a model she also deconstructs the distinction between appearance and reality: "If all is style, the concept fails to signify difference; it is simply synonymous with what there is. At this point such terms as *style, superficiality*, and *self-presentation* may be abandoned, for they cease to be informative" (Gergen, *Saturated Self*, 155). Gergen is right. There is no fixed self independent of the individual's experiences. The self exists only through the mediations with the non-identical. But this dialectical relationship does not justify the abolition of the self. Post-colonialists who have suffered from the misrecognition of their selves will regard it as cynical if postmodernists tell them that they are mistaken in their struggle for recognition because there are no selves. Henry Louis Gates asks us to consider the irony "when we (and other Third World peoples) obtain the complex wherewithal to define our black subjectivity in the republic of Western letters, our theoretical colleagues declare that there is no such thing as a subject; so why should we be bothered with that?"[25] In his book *Selves at Risk* Ihab Hassan does not attempt to refute the postmodern theories but points out that the concept of the self is not so easily denied:

> Good enough. But we should not dazzle by a deconstruction that explodes all essentialist notions, leaving every urgent question hanging sullenly in the air. The self may rest on no ontological rock; yet as a functional concept, as historical construct, as a habit of existence, above all as an experienced or essential reality, it serves us all even as we deny it theoretically.[26]

Colonized people must rediscover their roots but, as Hall points out, there is no authentic past:

> The past is not waiting for us back there to recoup our identities against. It is always retold, rediscovered, reinvented [...] You are bringing new narratives into play but you

---

[24] Cf. Kenneth J. Gergen, *The Saturated Self. Dilemmas of Identity in Contemporary Life* (New York: Basic Books, 1991), 179.

[25] Henry Louis Gates Jr. "On the Rhetoric of Race in the Profession," in Betty Joan Craige, ed., *Literature, Language and Politics* (Athens and London: University of Georgia Press, 1988), 20-26, here 25.

[26] Ihab Hassan, *Selves at Risk* (Wisconsin: University of Wisconsin Press, 1990), 34.

cannot mistake them for the 'real' back there by which history can be measured. There is no guarantee of authenticity like that in history. (Hall, "Old and New Identities", 58).

This underscores how problematic the concept of authenticity is, but this does not mean that we should give it up altogether. We must rather consider that it means something different for pluralists and cosmopolitans. For pluralists "affiliations based on choice are somehow artificial and lacking in depth while those based on the ordinance of blood and history are more substantive and authentic ..." (Hollinger, *Postethnic America*, 119). Cosmopolitans do not reject authenticity and commitment but they do not base it on tradition and heritage but rather on choice: "The adopting of a child from a different 'race' than oneself is a very postethnic act by virtue of its refusal to allow the social bond to be determined by the genetic bond, but this act carries a lifetime commitment" (Hollinger, *Postethnic America*, 117). This emphasis on choice does not mean that we are completely free to decide about our identity: "One does not easily choose to be a Japanese American in the absence of an element of Japanese ancestry to begin with" (Hollinger, *Postethnic America*, 117).

According to the tar baby myth Jadine is a colonized, inauthentic person who betrays her African-American identity but such a characterization of Jadine prescribes "too tightly" what an African-American identity should be and leaves little room for the dialectic between personal and collective identity.

Conclusion

The Bluest Eye enables us to experience what colonization and decolonization of the mind means to various characters and stresses the necessity of constructing an African-American identity. If one gives up one's cultural heritage, one becomes a victim of the attitudes of others and loses one's identity. *Tar Baby*, as the title indicates, confirms the need for decolonizing the mind. The novel, however, gives a voice to Jadine, who does not want her life to be determined by a narrowly scripted African-American identity and experiences the Black community in Eloe as narrow-minded and oppressive.

For the cosmopolitanist the pluralist's belief in a homogeneous culture easily leads to intolerance and the exclusion and persecution of those whose attitudes and values differ from the dominant ones. Thus a collective identity "can go imperial" in the same way as a national one. Therefore the cosmopolitans argue that we should not attempt to define people by their descent, heritage, and roots but respect the influence of different cultures. Such an influence is not a threat to our identity but can enrich it. Therefore what can appear as colonization of the mind to the pluralist, can appear as an enrichment of the mind to the cosmopolitan. This complicates the politics of decolonizing the mind in a multicultural world.

The tension between pluralists and cosmopolitanists has far-reaching consequences of how we approach a foreign culture. If we follow the pluralists, we will stress the difference between the foreign culture and our own and make sure that we see others in their otherness. Yet the cosmopolitanists will argue that such a hermeneutics of contrast will exaggerate the differences between cultures and make the foreign culture as well as one's own appear more homogeneous than they really are and will not do justice to the commonalities between cultures and to the existence of bi- or multicultural identities. For the pluralist, cultures are separate units and understanding should highlight the differences between them, while for the cosmopolitanist, understanding has also a practical function. We not only have to work out the differences but also create a new language which allows us to do things together. These are challenging questions of a pedagogy for understanding foreign cultures.

The Colossus of New Roads, or, The Reconstruction of Gulliver: Mineral Drama and the Colloquial Supernatural from the Colonial Era to the Age of Encounters

KEVIN L. COPE (Baton Rouge)

If the history of multi-, poly-, and inter-culturalism is ever written, historical hindsight will reveal that neither the revisions of the Greenblatts nor the critiques of the Foucaults nor the heteroglossias of the Bakhtins initiated the "construction" of this "critical discourse." Credit will go to works in a less sober, more satiric, occasionally reactionary vein, especially to Jonathan Swift's *Gulliver's Travels*. Swift's famous send-up of travel literature--his critique of the mixture of literature with anthropology that we now call "interdisciplinarity"--includes a comical vignette in which the awkwardness of an intercultural encounter is intensified by incongruities of scale and improper selection of building materials.

> [The Emperor of Lilliput] desired I would stand like a colossus, with my legs as far asunder as I possibly could. He then commanded his general (who was an old experienced leader, and great patron of mine) to draw up the troops in close order, and march them under me, the foot by twenty-four in a breast, and the horse by sixteen, with drums beating, colours flying, and pikes advanced. This body consisted of three thousand foot, and a thousand horse. His Majesty gave orders, upon pain of death, that every soldier in his march should observe the strictest decency with regard to my person; which, however, could not prevent some of the younger officers from turning up their eyes as they passed under me. And, to confess the truth, my breeches at the time were in so ill a condition, that they afforded some opportunities for laughter and admiration.[1]

Gulliver's Travels has been adapted for a thousand different media, from animated cartoons to children's coloring books. Despite this diversity of media, the Lilliputians (like all the other races in the book) are always portrayed as white and European, albeit out of scale. This, even though Swift's imaginary map places Lilliput lies near Sumatra, suggesting that its inhabitants would have a Melanesian, Polynesian, or Asiatic "look."

Whether or not Gulliver meets genuine "persons of color," the foregoing passage makes a number of points about "intercultural encounters" in colonial-era literature. First, Gulliver perceives himself as a "colossus," as an instance of a genre of statuary. Among westerners, colossi are presumed to be fantastical, artificial, and inanimate; among Lilliputians, a miniature people living in a different, smaller ecosystem with a different, smaller organisms, colossi have a higher degree of reality, there being so many things in the world that could be significantly bigger than Lilliputians. Cultural relativism--here simplified into notion that apparent size is relative to the perceived average size of the

---

[1] Jonathan Swift, *Gullivers Travels*, in Louis A. Landa, ed., *Gulliver's Travels and other Writings* (Boston: Riverside [Houghton Mifflin]), 1960, p. 34.

members of a culture--ends up reifying rather than contextualizing colossism. For Lilliputians, a culture-relative art-historical concept becomes all too real.

Second, Gulliver's encounter with the Lilliputians is never primarily a matter of race, class, or gender. Rather, it is a matter of scale, of size rather than of hue, genetics, or customs. Swift takes a broader view of what constitutes "difference" than might such multiculturalists as Henry Louis Gates or Cornell West, who ignore the scalar (and other) distinctions between the tallest Watusi or the shortest Mongolian to focus exclusively on color.

Third, part of the absurdity in Gulliver's situation arises from a confusion about building materials. In Europe, colossi are made of inanimate stone. Setting up Gulliver as a real-life "colossus" crosses the boundary between animal and mineral, between frozen crystals and moving organic matter. This substitution of building materials problematizes the concept of heroism, for it destabilizes the grand "frozen moments" in history that are the typical topics of colossal artifacts and that only rocks, ores, girders, and gems can support.

This episode from *Gulliver's Travels* demonstrates that post-Enlightenment inter- and multi-culturalism has only come to grips with *some* aspects of the "encounters" that occur among colonial and post-colonial cultures. It is easy enough to talk about the clash of values or the discovery of peoples who look or think or act differently than westerners, but this culture-centered perspective omits from its polychromatic picture the array of paraphernalia and the many modes of being--mineral, gaseous, aqueous, plasma--that inform colonialism. Colonialism started in the quest for rough objects, for raw materials, from timber and tobacco to sugarcane and saltpeter. A fixation on "race" and "culture" reveals our postmodern narrowmindedness more than our breadth of view. It excludes the *stuff* that so fascinated our ancestors as to stimulate the undertaking of great risks and the committing of monstrous acts in its pursuit.

In an earlier study, I pointed out that most modern readers simply skip over those long spans of text in which eighteenth-century writers recounted endless details: restaurant menus, coach schedules, and just about every bit of junk in the British Isles. The Augustan audience, on the other hand, relished abundant particular data.[2] In this paper, I shall look in greater detail at the cultural and intercultural implications of "mineral drama," by which I mean not didactic plays on the wonders of geology, but cultural phenomena highlighting the most dramatic of all possible cultural encounters: that between sentient and insentient beings, between animals and minerals, between men or women and rocks. "Mineral" I shall use in a fairly general sense, one retaining its hard-headed crystallinity yet one pointing up the broad issues generated by this encounter: the semantical, emotional, literary, and cultural issues at the intersection between the animate and the inanimate, between the conceiving, the conceptionless, and the inconceivable (who can imagine what it is or is like to be a boulder?). In the course of this essay I shall focus on American popular culture, although I shall begin with a short historical introduction to *cultural minerality*. Drawing on the most marginal or neglected or

---

[2] Kevin L. Cope, "Richardson the Advisor," in Albert J. Rivero, ed., *New Essays on Samuel Richardson* (New York: St. Martin's, 1996), 17-33.

seemingly insignificant aspects of America's material-cultural *assemblage*, I shall attempt to broaden the idea of an "encounter," an idea that is fundamental to contemporary multiculturalist discourse. Contemporary studies of "popular" culture inadvertently tend to focus on a narrow spectrum of covertly high-cultural phenomena, whether the highly cerebral postmodern pop music of "The Talking Heads" or the high-tech innovations of music video makers. By probing "mineral drama," I hope to enlarge the purview of popular-cultural studies and to enhance its methodology--to make it more popular, more concerned with the stuff that real people encounter, and less obsessed with theoretical methodologies.

I. A BRIEF HISTORY OF ROCK(S)

A major motif in American "pop" culture is that, someday, someone will write a definitive "history of rock" (rock-and-roll music). Although few could provide even a provisional etymological for the word "rock" as used to describe this fusion of African, folk, and country-western musical elements, most everyone is confident that there *is* a real, objective history to this nominally mineral form. One reason that rock music has acquired so mythic and historic a stature despite its historical recency is its nominal association with everlasting substances. Few ideas could be historically deeper or more persistent than that of rocks. Two millennia ago, Jesus informed St. Peter that Peter was the rock on which Jesus would build his future church. Jesus uses mineral imagery to draw attention to the qualities of endurance and strength that will characterize the Apostolic succession, yet Jesus's metaphor is in some ways too artful to carry its seemingly obvious, "natural" meaning. Rocky ground, whether the Rocky Road to Dublin or the rough terrain of Alcatrez, is not a natural site for building a foundation. As the history of highway building suggests, rocky ground is a site for a tough encounter between construction contractors, who normally would build on more pliable ground, and the natural resistance of inanimate nature to reconfiguration. It was far easier to build the enormous palace of Versailles on ordinary soil than to rivet the tiny Drachenfels castle to the stone faces of the Rhine valley. From the Rock of Peter to the Rock-and-Roll of Elvis, literary rocks and rock imagery have thus imagistically juxtaposed cultural institutions against subtly hostile foundations or environments. Whenever there is a mineral on the literary scene, there is almost always some interesting incongruity or disproportion or *encounter* between its natural and allegorical, institutional and mineralogical meanings. Rocks always have been, and always will be, emblems not only of desireable permanence, but of the permanent recurrence of difficult encounters, intercultural or otherwise.

In America, the religious legacy of the rock metaphor has been polished so as to blunt this implicit conflict. In the predominantly Protestant American nation, popular religious music replaces the Rock of St. Peter with either "the Rock of Ages" (Jesus, as rendered in the famous song by pop singer Wayne Newton) or "the everlasting Rock" (a diffuse term from televanglism for God or for divine things generally). Peter-as-Other, as remote rock, as institution chartered by but different from God, is replaced by churchgoers-as-metonymy-for-God, by a discourse of personality and interpersonal continuity rather than a discourse of differentiation. The independent stone of church institutions becomes identified with flexible and accessible people in the clericy and congregation.

Although founded by Puritan extremists and later chartered by such Deists and Latitudinarians as Washington, Jefferson, and Hamilton, America is superficially a secular state. America was the first nation created through a non-denominational literary artifact, a Lockean social contract (the American Constitution). In our rush either to applaud their progressive political thought or decry their colonial imperialism, it is often forgotten that the American pilgrims, pioneers, and founders were technologically and scientifically minded. Puritan "mechanic" thinkers and freethinking, Whiggish virtuosi provided the liberal-positivist ideological basis and the preoccupation with "progress" that engendered American culture. Early American intellectuals were more likely to think in scientific terms, imagery, and metaphors than to deploy the specialized theoretical rhetoric of our day.

Understanding that American culture was defined by gentlemen-scientists or entrepreneurial technocrats makes it is easy to appreciate the juncture between American geopolitical concepts and minerality. America took its initial geographical form through a mixture of political and geographical accidents, through land grants bestowed in a hit-or-miss fashion on a strange mixture of dissidents, criminals, entrepreneurs, and adventurers. By the time of the Constitution, however, America was more organized than it might appear. The thirteen original colonies were the political equivalent of a *crystal*.

The defining characteristic of a crystal, mineral or otherwise, is its spontaneous--what scientists now call "chaotic"--emergence into regular form. Crystals suddenly emerge from a solution, spontaneously queuing up into familiar, recurring patterns. A variety of elements and atomic structures gives rise to a dependable yet highly varied internal patterns, patterns rhythmically enclosed by smooth planes. So with the first thirteen colonies: they defined their smooth mutual boundaries without any intervening open space, began emulating one another's internal constitutions in order, and then, as the Constitution has it, began "to form a more perfect Union" (or, as "politically correct" language has it nowadays, "to find unity within diversity"). Early America's crystalline integrity had no spaces between the borders of its states; despite its immensity, despite much of its territory remaining unexplored, America's first states were always stitched together into "Columbia, the *gem* of the ocean." The Civil War made no difference in this geopolitical crystallinity. With the victory of the Union and the gradual addition of states, the tendency toward the geopolitical imitation of crystalline structures increased. Rocky Mountain states such as Wyoming or Utah--appropriately, those with the most voluminous granite, crystal structures in their landscapes--are often perfectly square and smoothly rectilinear, their borders being determined by theodolites rather than natural barriers. Eighteenth-century scholars are often astounded or amused to discover that Thomas Jefferson so admired crystalline regularity that he intended to survey and gerrymander the states not according to natural geographical features but with graph paper, by dividing America into uniformly square parcels with equal degrees of political reprsentation.

The mineral vision politics and culture had many adherents in the old world as well as the new. The English Queen's astronomer, J. T. Desaguliers, a post-Newtonian with a Rosicrucian ideology, rebelled against conventional astrology and other forms of planetary allegory by arguing that the universe is not a symbolic, but an exact representation of proper social order. Politics and astronomy directly influence one another:

> What made the Planets in such order move,
> He [Pythagoras] said, was Harmony and Mutual Love.
> The Musick of his Spheres did represent
> That ancient Harmony of Government:
> When Kings were not ambitious yet to gain
> Other's Dominions, but their own maintain;
> When, to protect, they only bore the Sway,
> And Love, not Fear, taught Subjects to obey.
> But when the Lust of Pow'r and Gold began,
> With Fury, to invade the Breast of Man,
> Princes grew fond of Arbitrary Sway,
> And to each lawless Passion giving Way,
> Strove not to merit Heaven, but Earth posses'd,
> And crush'd the people whom they should have bless'd.
> Astronomy then took another Face,
> Perplex'd with new and false Hypotheses.
> Usurping Ptolemy depos'd the Sun,
> And fix'd the Earth unequal to the Throne.[3]

Desaguliers moves seamlessly back and forth between heaven and earth, astronomy and politics. Good astronomy creates good governments; bad princes produce the repugnancies of Ptolomaism. "Sol," the Sun, "holds a lasting Scepter in his Hand."[4] For Desaguliers, a great appeal of the Newtonian system is its crystalline conception. It permits the sun to bring various planets with various periods and properties under a uniform scientific law, into a single amalgamative structure, and into the single plane of the solar system. The sun adminsters a uniformitarian system that is not opposed to but rather depends upon diversity, much as granite or marble crystallizes according to uniform laws but acquires its aesthetic properties only through the preservation of the variety.

Desaguliers and others like him subscribe to a *constructivist* version of the mineral worldview. Admirable systems, whether political, solar, or crystalline, piece together countless disparate parts. Regularity emerges from the sophistication of structures rather than from the concealing of differences. For these thinkers, a nation like America, with all its disparate factions and groups, is in some ways more regular than an old-world nation with more pre-existing ethnic, religious, or cultural unity. The amplitude and

---

[3] J. T. Desaguliers, LL.D., FRS, *The Newtonian System of the World, The Best Model of Government: An Allegorical Poem. With a Plain and Intelligible Account of the System of the World, by Way of Annotations: With Copper Plates: To which is Added, Cambria's Complaint Against the Intercalary Day in the Leap-Year* (Westminster: 1728), pp. 3-4.

[4] Desaguliers, pp. 25-6.

complexity of the American political and cultural *structure*, its ability to hold together so many disparate parts, is more compelling than the predictable tendency of naturally affiliated groups to stick together in one place or under one government. Practical astronomers of the time were therefore obsessed with, of all things, the sundial. Although it seems like a simple instruments, the sundial is astonishingly complex. Different angular and spatial intervals between each of its hour lines mark out the complex trajectory of the sun. As Phillippe de La Hire exults,

> I have always considered the description of *Sun-Dials* as one of the most ingenious and useful Inventions derived from the study of *Mathematicks*. Also there is nothing that draws more Admiration from all Men, than to see Strait-lines drawn on a *Plane* at *Unequal Distances*, to measure exactly the equal Divisions of the time of the Continuance of a Day: and altho the *Sun* appears in different places of Heaven according to the different Seasons of the Year, yet the same Strait-lines do still determine the same hour at all these different Seasons.[5]

La Hire is certain to include a mineral, geological context for his rhapsody; although it is the sun that works these wondrous effects, it is nevertheless all the more amazing that the earth, a dull mineral orb, should be so cooperative as to provide so fine and regular a platform for a universally useful sundial. Sundial theorist Jacques Ozanam makes this reconciliation of equal and unequal divisions on the orbs of heaven and earth part of the sundial's essential definition:

> La Gnomonique est une Science, qui par la moyen de rayons de quelque astre, & principalement par la moyen des rayons du Soleil, divise let temps en parties égales, & represente sur un Plan la machine du premier Mobile.[6]

Ozanam refines the crystalline vision by enjoying the sight of fantastically complex, three-dimensional celestial and terrestrial motions being projected on the two-dimensional *plane* of the sundial. This capacity to appreciate amazingly complicated actions by non-sentient beings is taken as a sign and integral part of noble character. John Ray proved his worth as a Royal Society virtuoso by assembling heterogenous collections of sentient and insentient creatures and comments: for example, his *Collection of English Words Not Generally Used, with their Significations and Original, in two Alphabetical Catalogues, The One such as are Proper to the Northern, the other to the Southern Countries. With Catalogues of English Birds and Fishes: And an Account of the Preparing and Refining such Metals and Minerals as a Gotten in England*. Ray, of course, participates in the love of variety for its own sake, a love that animated all the other early empirical scientists, from Abraham Cowley to John Wilkins. Yet Ray, like Ozanam, goes one step further, time and again making it clear that minerality and character, sentience and insentience, chaos and crystalline order interact with one another.

---

[5] Phillipe de La Hire, *Gnomonicks, Or, The Art of Shadows Improved. Plainly Set forth in the Drawing of Sun-Dials on All Sorts of Planes by Different Methods* (London: 1709), signature A2r.

[6] Jacques Ozanam, *Traité de Gnomonique, Ou, De la Construction des Cadrans sur Toute Sorte de Plans* (Paris: 1773).

This account of the whole process of the Iron-work I had from one of the chief Iron-masters in *Sussex*, my friend *Walter Burrell* of *Cuckfield* Esquire deceased. And now that I have had occasion to mention this worthy Gentleman give me leave by the by to insert a few observations referring to Husbandry communicated by him in occasional discourse on those subjects.[7]

In two short paragraphs, Ray covers and links together metallurgy, human character, and husbandry, each of which empower, describe, and implement each other. Knowledge of iron smelting proves Mr. Burrell's character, which in turn lends credit to his reports regarding the technology of the barnyard.

It may seem odd or bold to assert that since the beginning of the Enlightenment matters mineral were also supernatural. What, after all, could be more deadeningly "natural" than rocks? It is, however, for this very reason, their stupidity, that minerals received an epistemic promotion during and after the seventeenth century. There are at least three ways of being supernatural: participating in some spiritual world; participating in an epiphenomenal or perceptual world in which dull matter is turned into cognized ideas; and, most literally, being above man's natural habitat, being up in the air or in outer space.

The modern period has been linked from its beginning with the elevation of rocks into at least two of these species of supernaturalism. Descartes, Leibniz, Locke, Spinoza, and their colleagues might be described as hyper-conscious persons, persons unusually concerned with the theory of knowledge and the manner of knowing things. In the twentieth-century classroom, Descartes' (and others') occasional concern with heavenly minerals--with comets, asteroids, and the formation of planets--is overlooked or dismissed as obsolete speculation or as crackpot cosmology. Cartesian respect for rocks, however, was an important step in the process of Enlightenment and modernization. It gave a new, literary vivacity to the old-fashioned "argument from design," the assertion that the existence of God (and the knowledge of the world and its right order) could be inferred from the intelligent arrangement of the universe. If rocks were knowable or organized, God must have some message that he wants to communicate by means of them. Additionally, because rocks were knowable, controlled by ordering intellect, or even marginally sentient, there might be more to say about them than meets the ear. Hence the profusion throughout the Enlightenment of geological tracts, epic geographical poems, and substance-oriented philosophical speculations like George Berkeley's later *Siris* or Emmanuel Swedenborg's visions. The desire to discover the order in the insentient, material creation also promoted the discovery of variety; the more extensive and complicated the cosmological scheme, the greater the need for and the more emotionally compelling its insinuation of an ordering God. The argument from design, in its modern

---

[7] John Ray, *A Collection of English Words Not Generally Used, with their Significations and Original, in two Alphabetical Catalogues, The One such as are Proper to the Northern, the other to the Southern Countries. With Catalogues of English Birds and Fishes: And an Account of the Preparing and Refining such Metals and Minerals as a Gotten in England* (London: 1674), 129.

form, was mineralogical and crystalline, a beatification of the ultra-complex formations found throughout nature, from the lowest quarry to the highest asteroid.

Into the Newtonian celestial and the Cartesian epistemic vacuums rushed plenty of speculators. Germany was represented by Friedrich Christian Lesser, who produced tract after tract inferring the existence of God from the complex organization of various microscopic and macroscopic things: seashells, insect societies, and, of course, stones.[8] Lesser's sprawling *Lithotheologie* (theology of stones) occupies a rhetorical position somewhere between the genre of the "anatomy"--the collection, like Richard Burton's *Anatomy of Melancholy*, featuring randomly arranged, ever-multitudinous barrages of anecdotes and observations--and the dictionary-encyclopedia, with its commitment to artificial order, alphabetical or otherwise. Arranged like as well as concerned with stones, the *Lithotheologie* balances order and variety in crystaliine equipoise. Another pious mineralogist, Israel Hibner, simultaneously updates alchemy, mineralogy, astronomy, agronomics, and pharmaceutics by establishing an order of correspondences between completely disparate phenomena. Hibner notes, for example, that the lowest brute animals can discover medically miraculous herbs that bear the signatures of assorted (mineral) planets.[9] Minerals, owing to their diversity and their interconnectedness with all aspects of God's highly ordered cosmos, serve as entry portals to more expansive chambers in the mansion of science. A popular literary form in the later eighteenth century was a fictional encounter between the culture of the ladies' drawing room and the rougher culture of men's science. Through dialogue, the barrier between men's cosmological knowledge and women's literary acumen could be penetrated. John Harris offers a dialogue between a young woman and a male virtuoso:

> I thank you, said she, for that explication, Sir, I have often met with the Word, but never knew *fully* what Diameter signified before: But now I know what the ingenious Mr. *Butler* meant when speaking of the Moon, he saith, that *Sydrophil* knew
> > *What her Diameter to an Inch is,*
> > *And prov'd she was not made of green Cheese.*
>
> And now I know what the Plummer meant the other Day, when he talk'd of a Pipe of Lead of such a Diameter; I now know the Meaning of *Diametrically opposite, & c.* But pray, Sir,

---

[8] See Friedrich Christian Lesser, *Testaceo-Theologia, Oder gründiches Beweis des Dasenns und der vollfommenster Eigenschaften eines Göttlichen Wesens, aus natürliches und geistliches Betrachtung der Schnecten und Wuscheln, zur gebührendes Beherrlichung des grossen Gottes und Beförderung des ihm schuldigen Dienstes ausgesertiget* (Leipzig: 1756); Lesser, *Insecto-Theologia, Oder: Bernunft und Schrifftmässiger Versuch Wie ein Mensch durch aufmerchsame Betrachtung derer sonste wenig geachteten Insecten Zu lebendiger Erkanntniss und Bewunderung der Allmacht, Weissheit, der Güte und Gerechtigkeit des grossen Gottes gelangen könne* (Frankfurt and Leipzig: 1738); and Lesser, *Lithotheologie, Das ist: Naturliche Historie und gesitliche Betrachtung derer Stine, Also abgefaßt, daß darauss Die Allmacht, Weißheit, Güte and Gerechtigkeit des grossen Schöpffers* (Hamburg: 1735).

[9] See Israel Hibner, Mysterium Sigillorum, Herbarum & Lapidum. A Compleat Cure of all Sicknesses and Diseases of Mind and Body, by Means of the Influences of the Seven Planets. Adorned with Copper Plates & Figures, Shewing the Foundation of this Astronomical and Coelestial Science (London: 1698).

go on ... O! Sir, said she, this *Astronomy* is mighty instructive; I now understand the just Meaning of usch Expressions, as these,
There vice did in its Zenith reign,
Our bright Meridian Sun decline, & c.[10]

It is in such highly didactical passages, such introductions for beginners or for persons excluded from the mainstream methods of education, that we often find the clearest juxtaposition of insentience and stupidity, whether human or mineral, against wonder, order, and cosmological wit. Here we find avid expressions of the internal dynamism of minerality, of the interplay and the encounter of mind and body, structure and irregularity, that comprises the crystallographic worldview.

Delicate instruction and utter unintelligibility sometimes come together in sensational yet informative periodical essays designed to that explain to lay audiences precisely how the world might come to a disastrous end. Today's tabloid press, full as it is of putatively "scientific" explanations as to how all knowledge and science might be destroyed, resembles the Enlightenment periodical press, in which experts explained in excruciatingly deliberate, ponderously detailed language how cosmological order and apocalyptic destruction encountered one another in cataclysmic events.

> Besides the planets, there are other bodies which may be said to belong to the solar system, and are called comets; but the orbits they move in are so elliptical, that is to say, such a long oval, that they can be seen by us only in their perihelion, or when they come to that end of their orbit, which has the sun for its center. They likewise are opaque spherical bodies, receiving their light and heat from the sun; and some of them go round him at such a small distance, that they must acquire a degree of heat more intense than can possibly be imagined or described. The number of them is not known, nor perhaps ever will; but by late observations the times of some of their revolutions have been calculated; and to what we know, some of them may put an end to the present state of things in this earth; for as they cut or cross the orbit of the earth at least twice, if earth should be in that part of its orbit, or very near it, when the comet crosses, it would occasion a most terrible revolution; and it was computed that the comet which appeared in 1680, came within half the sun's diameter of us, that is to say, within 382,150 miles of us.[11]

Robert Dodsley, the publisher of this chilling vision, includes in the *London Magazine* a diagram [see figure 1] of the interplay of planetary and cometary orbits, showing with precision their regularity and predictability and yet also marking out those comets he considers unusual or prodigious, those that have made some marvellous figure when viewed from earth or whose perfectly orderly orbits might lead to a perfectly calamitous cosmic collision, to a Götterdammerung of culture and intelligence. For the

---

[10] John Harris, *Astronomical Dialogues Between a Gentleman And A Lady: Wherein The Doctrine of the Sphere, Uses of the Globes, And the Elements of Astronomy and Geography are Explain'd, In a Pleasant, Easy and Familiar Way* (London: 1719), pp. 8, 36.

[11] *London Magazine*, December 1752, pp. 564-6.

Enlightenment mind, the consummate expression of divine intelligence turns out to be the regularity and predictability of an "extinction level event," an event carried out by a marauding yet internally organized mineral projectile.

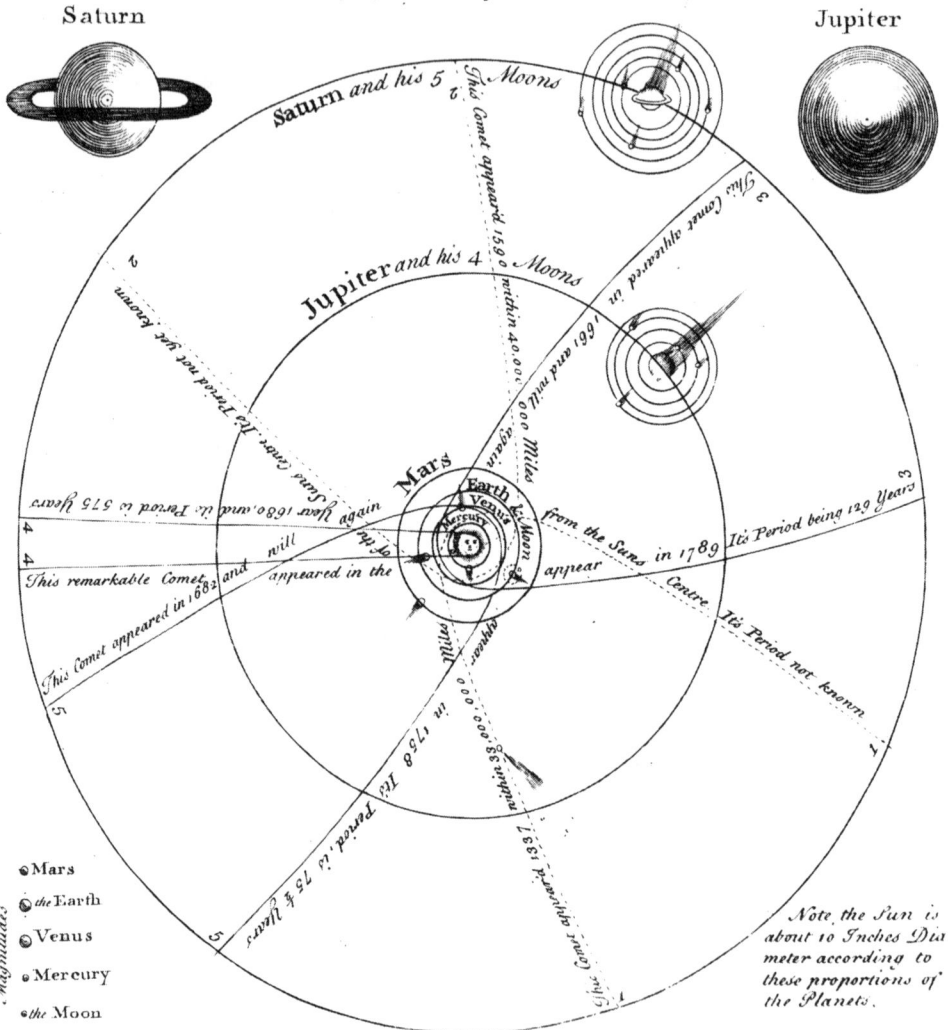

Figure 1: Map of Planetary Orbits, Robert Dodsley's *Preceptor* of 1752. Courtesy McMaster Archives and Research Collections.

II. THE DISPLACEMENT OF THE INVISIBLE IDEAL

The limited technology available to the Royal Society stopped Dodsley from knowing the size of comets and asteroids. Nevertheless, Dodsley and his audience could know from the velocity of these errant bodies that they would be the kernel of a colossal *event*. Through their meditations on cometary destruction, Dodsley and others conducted a mineralogical recodification of colossalism. They redefined immensity as a process. The size of the impinging comet was immaterial; what mattered was that it would stage a really big show. Augustan interest in minerals turned on the *apparent* miraculousness of crystalline structures. The fact that eighteenth-century scientists were unable to see the atomic structures that underlay such wildly diverse yet recurring patterns made those patterns all the more mysterious and enticing. The popular appeal of comets, likewise, turned on the juxtaposition of their invisibility against their destructive potential and calamitous grandeur. Like eighteenth-century "sublimity," the colossal and the mineralogical were no longer intrinsic features of objects, but were becoming psychological and experiential affections. Essayists on the sublime like Immanuel Kant or Edmund Burke were more interested in the affective consequences of a sublime encounter than in the quantity of matter contained in a mountain or seascape; Dodsley and cohort cometeers were more interested in sublime impacts than in measurement. They led the way in the *displacement of the colossal*, from the colossal thing-in-itself to the communication, transmission, movement, rarefaction, and, in general, *dislocation* of colossal*ism*.

The twentieth-century American south is a haven for precisely this kind of displacement. Dynastic families in the American south still enjoy fairly vivid oral-cultural memories of the southern Confederacy and Civil War, that great rupture in the previously crystalline structure of America. An invaded people at once curious and resentful about northern lifestyles, they participate in a collective imagination that they are somewhere other than where they are. This communal commitment to displacement operates at all levels of society: truckdrivers paint large Confederate flags on the grillwork of their engines (thus keeping the ever-displaced south moving down the highway); the English Department at Louisiana State University hires no faculty members who received their degrees from southern universities, thinking that the understanding of southern literary culture is best perfected *somewhere else*. Religiously and philosophically, the south is multiply dislocated. Like Germany, the northern half of the south is Protestant and the southern Catholic; the "high" southern Protestant culture of Mississippi, Alabama, Georgia, South Carolina, and Tennessee is now historically distanced from the dislocated English immigrants who settled it; and the sense of being an occupied, conquered state still persists, long after the Civil War. An excellent new book, *Roadside Revelation*, by Boykin M. Woodruff, has offered pictorial documentation of this political and religious displacement by photographing the billboards that southern Protestant churches set up along roadways, billboards filled with witty aphorisms about God, especially about apocalyptic and eschatological themes. Drivers in the rural south see one such sign after another, all pointing down the highway yet also pointing up toward dislocated visions of the Last Judgment.

"Roadside Revelations" like those described in Woodruff's book are formed by breaking complete heavenly visions into de-contextualized aphorisms, then dispersing them along the highway or other monument to motion. Southern geography cooperates in and mimics this process. Owing to the neo-classical sensibility of the colonial English planters, the entire classical world can be found in the south. Most every southern state has cities like Rome, Athens, Carthage, Troy, Sparta, Memphis, Salem, or Cairo. One extraordinary example of such displacement carried down to the phonetic level is the city of "New Roads," Louisiana, a city that alludes to Hellenic Rhodes but that, owing to a mixture of confusion and ambition, invokes the American sense of manifest destiny and universal mobility by reconfiguring "Rhodes" as "Roads," as novel routes to new destination. New Roads rose to its modest prominence through colossal hydrographical prevarication, by presenting itself as a Utopian recreational community along an ideal body of water called "False River." This immense lagoon resembles an elbow in the Mississippi, but it has no connection to that famous river. Contrary to the destinarianism implied by the city name "New *Roads*," False River is completely landlocked, leading nowhere at all. Places like New Roads and the adjacent False River share with Dodsley's comet-strewn universe the conviction that imposing ancient things or events, whether Rhodes with its colossus or the Mississippi River with all its folklore or the Biblical prophecy of an apocalyptic conclusion to human history, are somewhere other than they ought to be--that the Last Judgment on earthly history is building up in outer space or that the ancient Rhodian colossi have decided to take a stroll in Louisiana's Cajun country.

American geographical onomastics has little to do with geography but a lot to do with mineralogy. The fact that Ontario's "Stratford" has an "Avon" River and an "Old Globe" theater brings it no nearer to the original Stratford in England. Instead, it underscores the often comical differences between a wee town in the English countryside and a "themed" installation way out in the middle of the colossal Canadian prairie. The distance between the two Stratfords is part of the wonder. Those unfamiliar with the Canadian Stratford guffaw that there might be such a thing as a make-believe town in the middle of Ontario, while those of a mineralogical bent see the similarity between crystalline complexity and the complicated relations and divergences between the American and the British Shakespearelands. Creating New World imitations of Old World settlements is less a way of replicating a place than of asserting that this *can* be done, that something comparatively large, like an English settlement, can be made to subsist both in another place and, more importantly, in a concept, in a dimensionless thought or imagination (hence the designation of the numerous Disneylands around the world as "the Magic Kingdom," as a magical means of production and as a "themed" concept rather than as a particular place).

The geographical, the mineral, and the colossal can thus subsist, in the new world, in some very modest manifestations. The catachresis of the mighty mineral and the tiny conceptual is nowhere more fully expressed than in the American obsession with *lifestyle*, with a mode rather than a place for life. One event that has seized the popular imagination in America is the "American Fitness Pageant." The American Fitness Pageant reconciles the most categorical of oppositions. An event for women, it locates the midpoint between the male brute strength displayed in weightlifting or bodybuilding competitions and, contrarily, the celebration of female passivity, subjugation, and observability that characterize old-line beauty pageants such as The Miss America Competition. "Fit" women are not hulking bodybuilders, but perfectly regular and symmetrically chiselled ordinary human beings. They are, by plan, of all races and all cultures. Pretty and strong but not sublime, they are the human equivalent of common crystal [see figure 2]. The American Fitness Pageant has, quite unknowingly, undertaken a critique of structuralism and poststructuralism. Its catachretical mineralism, its continuous reconciliation of seeming opposites, undoes the discourse of binary oppositions that underwrote this critical movement from the time of Northrop Frye and Levi-Strauss to the era of Deconstruction. Indeed, the American Fitness Pageant is physically mineralogical, for it stresses achieving the state of (somatic) *hardness*, yet it also exists in the perfectly soft, pliable spaces of the Internet, where its contestants are perpetually being compared--competing--against one another.[12] Like granite or any other crystal, "Fitness" is a kind of suspended process, a slice of time in the process of freezing and expanding.

Figure 2: Thais Delgado Creegan, Competitor, American Fitness Pageant. Courtesy ESPN Sports Network.

---

[12] Visit www.fitnessamerica.com/index.html

A different example of this assimilation of foreign cultures into familiar lifestyles--of the replacement of geography with gesture--occurs within a curious intercultural encounter now underway in a remote precinct of Texas. There, in the tiny town of Conroe, a group of older men have banded together, joined the "Confederate Air Force," and become Japanese fighter pilots, going so far as to issue colorful calling cards bearing the Japanese war cry, "Tora! Tora! Tora!" [see figure 3]. Such an intercultural recreational lifestyle abounds with more contradictions than its participants realize. There never was a Confederate Air Force, for the Civil War occurred before aviation; Texas was never part of the Confederacy; the aerobatic aircraft used in this club exercise are not Japanese, but Russian YAKs dressed as Japanese planes; the elderly men who indulge in this diversion were enemies, not citizens, of Japan during their service in the Second World War. All of these contradictions become assimilable because, as contradictions go, they are certainly immense, indeed geopolitical ones. They are too vast for placement in time and space; moreover, the Japanese-Confederate Air Force, by its nature, is a moving force. Such vast intercultural encounters thrive in the geography of the imagination, in a crystalline culture that uses disparity as a springboard to complex systematicity. The paradox of the Confederate Japanese Air Corps is represented most efficiently on a tiny business card precisely because its immensity can only be played out in a minimalized, highly plastic space--in the infinitesimal space of consciousness.

Figure 3: Business Card, Confederate Air Force Member. Courtesy General Aviation Services of Conroe, Texas.

Regular crystalline structure emerges within the frozen clash of diverse molecules, in a small space where microscopic and mirror the microscopic. The American search for an invisible and yet amalgamative ideal--for a "more perfect Union"--is most at home in such manageable spaces. America is noted for its "funkiness," for strange mini-monstrosities like a bakery shop in the shape of a giant doughnut, a huge rendering of a tiny pastry that represents an ideal so elusive as to be for all puposes invisible. It is not surprising, therefore, that the search for cosmological ideals should take place in miniature cultural encounters. In the latest book on the Shroud of Turin, *Blood and the Shroud*, forensics expert Ian Wilson ascertains that this relic is the genuine burial shroud of Jesus by subjecting its alleged blood stains to DNA analysis, hoping to prove the stains genuine blood from an ancient middle-eastern ethnic group.[13] Whatever Wilson might prove, his method is literally crystalline, for he catachretically seeks out traces of immense divinity in the tiny molecular salts and oils deposited by bodily fluids. Categorical evil as well as cosmological good can likewise be simultaneously embodied and disembodied. In the World War II epic *Gung Ho!*, the story of a group of Marines who train for a secret mission against the Japanese by pursuing an invisible ideal of unity and cooperation ("gung ho" being the Chinese term for bonding through teamwork), a series of candidates for the secret team are asked why each of them would like to join so dangerous an enterprise. Each of the recruits gives a particular if somewhat idealized answer--desire to defend America, opposition to tyranny, avenging relatives lost in the fighting--save for the last candidate to speak. Portrayed as a usefully psychotic person, this last applicant tells the recruiting sergeant, "Awwww, I just hate Nips" ("Nips" being a contemptuous nickname for Nipponese, or Japanese). This startling expression of pure racial hatred as a consequence of war brings the scene to an abrupt end, to be followed by an innocuous segment on training. It was only in such infinitesimally brief and out-of-the-way moments that American producers, directors, and viewers of the time could confront or articulate the feelings of xenophobia and racism that spurred on the American war effort; it was only such microscopic cameos that could make the big and brutal picture clear. This technique has not run its course with World War II films. Instead, it has come even more into the foreground as a means of voicing background sentiments. In the course of editing my academic journal, I recently received an epistle from a contributor in which assorted frustrations with the contemporary literary-critical scene were expressed in such a tellingly explosive and yet strangely humorous way, all to carry out a cultural encounter from the margins of New Zealand against the central culture of American critical internationalism [see figure 4].

---

[13] See Ian Wilson, *The Blood and the Shroud* (New York: Free Press of Simon and Schuster, 1998).

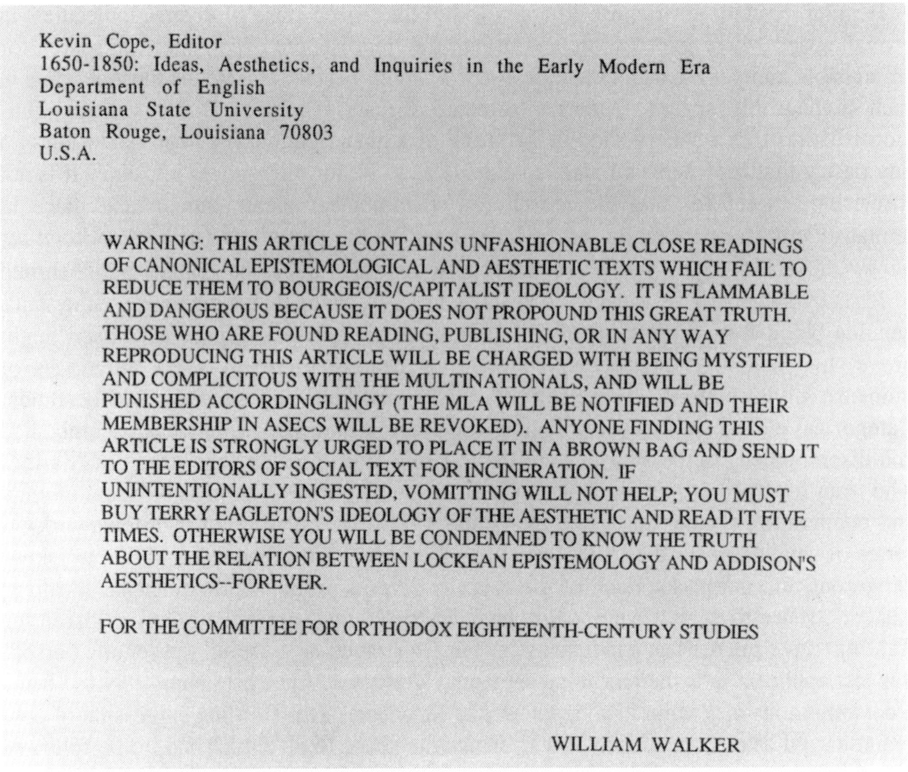

> Kevin Cope, Editor
> 1650-1850: Ideas, Aesthetics, and Inquiries in the Early Modern Era
> Department of English
> Louisiana State University
> Baton Rouge, Louisiana 70803
> U.S.A.
>
>   WARNING: THIS ARTICLE CONTAINS UNFASHIONABLE CLOSE READINGS OF CANONICAL EPISTEMOLOGICAL AND AESTHETIC TEXTS WHICH FAIL TO REDUCE THEM TO BOURGEOIS/CAPITALIST IDEOLOGY. IT IS FLAMMABLE AND DANGEROUS BECAUSE IT DOES NOT PROPOUND THIS GREAT TRUTH. THOSE WHO ARE FOUND READING, PUBLISHING, OR IN ANY WAY REPRODUCING THIS ARTICLE WILL BE CHARGED WITH BEING MYSTIFIED AND COMPLICITOUS WITH THE MULTINATIONALS, AND WILL BE PUNISHED ACCORDINGLINGY (THE MLA WILL BE NOTIFIED AND THEIR MEMBERSHIP IN ASECS WILL BE REVOKED). ANYONE FINDING THIS ARTICLE IS STRONGLY URGED TO PLACE IT IN A BROWN BAG AND SEND IT TO THE EDITORS OF SOCIAL TEXT FOR INCINERATION. IF UNINTENTIONALLY INGESTED, VOMITTING WILL NOT HELP; YOU MUST BUY TERRY EAGLETON'S IDEOLOGY OF THE AESTHETIC AND READ IT FIVE TIMES. OTHERWISE YOU WILL BE CONDEMNED TO KNOW THE TRUTH ABOUT THE RELATION BETWEEN LOCKEAN EPISTEMOLOGY AND ADDISON'S AESTHETICS--FOREVER.
>
> FOR THE COMMITTEE FOR ORTHODOX EIGHTEENTH-CENTURY STUDIES
>
>   WILLIAM WALKER

Figure 4: Provocative-Satirical Letter to the Editor of *1650-1850: Ideas, Aesthetics, and Inquiries in the Early Modern Era*. Photo by the Author.

III. THE IDEAL PERSON

The Iagoesque, metaphysical hatred imprinted in the "Awww, I just hate Nips" remark has a counterpart the American concept of heroism. The two extremes, the sociopathic zealot and the nation-building hero, are inextricably mixed together. It is no accident that one of the most successful American film series of all time was *Rocky*, the story of a violently frenetic, ambitious, and patriotic boxer who, despite some personal difficulties, became the symbolic protector of America. The success of *Rocky* and its sequels was helped by its nominal association with stones, in much the same way that counter-cultural caricature-heroes like Jed Clampett of the smash comedy series *The Beverly Hillbillies* or J. R. Ewing of the perennial serio-soap-opera *Dallas* were easy to love because each had become wealthy through minerals, through oil. The American hero, moreover, is also a crystalline hero because he is always complicated. Seldom a stainless chivalric knight like those of European legend or a superhero like those of classical antiquity, the

American heroe combines opposite elements in a complicated structure and is applauded as much for his resolution of contradictions as for any valorous deeds.

These contradictions often reach the level of genre or even ontology. 1998 is the 200th anniversary of the death of the first American President, George Washington, with many celebratory events planned. In the unending debate over racism in America, George Washington's reputation has been tainted owing to his slaveholding. Event planners have been trying to rehabilitate Washington not by directly confronting Washington's ineptitude in intercultural encounters, but by amplifying the contradictions in his life, by applauding his efforts to resolve them, and finally by merging Washington with the world of fiction. Washington, it is noted, arranged to free his slaves after his death, meaning that his death was a moment of resolution between his status as "Father of a [Free] Country" and his misdeeds as a slaveholder. James Rees, the Director of the Mount Vernon Historical Site, Washington's Plantation home, has declared that Washington's "life was like and eighteenth-century GI Joe," re-hybridizing the historical Washington with a children's toy soldier, a toy soldier presented as a Rambo-like superpatriot--as a socially useful psychopath. A milder version of the same strategy can be found in the trademark icon for Betty Crocker Cake Mix, the most popular baking product in America, in which the image of the imaginary "Betty Crocker" is computer morphed so as to show characteristics of all races, to be no particular person and yet be everyone, all in a domestic crusade for good cakes [see figure 5].

Figure 5: Betty Crocker Cake Mix Logo. Photo by the Author.

A case study of the convergence of Washington-*cum*-GI Joe and Betty-Crocker-*cum*-domestic-multicultural-crusader is Irvin "Magic" Johnson. "Magic" Johnson, whose nickname suggests hybrid or even supernatural origins, compiled a stellar career in the National Basketball Association before testing HIV-positive in 1991, whereupon his career collapsed and his heroical *mana* disappeared. In short order, Johnson's publicity apparatus reconfigured him as a devoted husband in the midst of a trauma, as a well-meaning victim, as a warrior against an epidemic, and as a tormented family man. Within a few years Johnson had once again achieved hero status, this time as a mixture of former warrior and future champion of domestic reform. During this transformation, Johnson began a career as a television commentator on basketball and took up a position on the President's Council on AIDS. He became an ideal warrior against an invisible threat, an atomic, mineralogical expression of an anticipated global disaster--the human equivalent of one of Dodsley's comets. Johnson, who had little education and no philosophical skill, soon distinguished himself by his ability, especially in basketball commentary, to coin strange aphorisms that, despite their redundancy or even internal contradictoriness, had a popular appeal, a natural catchiness. Among his more stunning assertions were phrases like "in all reality that was a good foul" (as if there could be a partial reality), "when you is in the game, you want all the other players in the game" (using redundancy to suggest a lust for team spirit during a rally), and most remarkably of all, "the greatest players of all time are the greatest players in the game at any given time," a marvellous reconciliation of the heroic eternality and the commercial ephemerality of sports, of the mentality that creates a "Football Hall of Fame" drawing many times more tourists than does the Library of Congress. In these cosmological aphorisms, "Magic" Johnson succeeded in speaking about or even being everybody and everyone--all the players and all the greats--while he and his own story became almost invisible. He crystallized the mentality of professional sports like an electric force binding together crystals, by being everywhere and yet having no particular manifestation, by binding together everything and everyone in one strikingly generalized form.

"Magic" Johnson was and is an abstract ideal, an unobtrusive amalgamation of all that there is to amalgamate. In his own quaint way, he is the natural summation of the thought and influence of a whole array of modern thinkers, from mineralogist Friedrich Lesser to social contract theorists like John Locke or Jean-Jacques Rousseau. Johnson was and is good at putting himself at the nexus of disparate forces, forces that he seems to draw together in an unsentient, mineral way. Johnson's rehabilitation is a case study in the dislocationist culture that could create a "New Roads/Rhodes" out of a backwoods town. He directs attention away from objects or persons and toward their affective potential, from measurable phenomena to elastic emotions. Our old friend John Harris, the author of the *Astronomical Dialogues*, tries a similar ploy to explain the incomprehensibilities of long-distance travel by light:

Good God! cry'd she, how immense and wonderful are the Works of thy Hands! Why then, said she, if all the Stars were to be extinct or anihilated this next Night, we should not miss them till about 6 Months after![14]

Harris's point is that the colossal time and space intervals implied by the high velocity of light can be articulated only in the way that "Magic" Johnson dealt with the horror of the AIDS epidemic: by attending to its emotional impact, by treating it as a swoon-inducing hurricane in the heart. The ontological status of the stars wouldn't matter to Harris for half a year, as we would still go on enjoying them even after they had expired. A cosmological catastrophe would have no impact until ages after it had already occurred, in much the same way that fans' adulation for "Magic" Johnson and his persistence in his announcing career keep him alive even despite his terminal illness.

To understand fully the emotional impact of the catachretical-mineralogical mind of American culture, it is necessary to go all the way to the margins of literary expression, to those areas of human expression that are avoided even by those boasting of canon revision. What at one time were called "lonely hearts columns," advertisements by which single persons arranged meetings and liaisons, have lately been, like "Magic" Johnson, re-legitimized by electronic technology. Most newspapers publish lonely-hearts advertisements that are divocal, diachronic, and dyadic, that provide various electronic means, whether secret telephone voice-boxes or Internet encounter points, by which unknown persons may begin and continue conversations. Unfinished and dialogical, these advertisements are initial lines in an open-ended emotional text. Such quasi-dialogical texts provide venues in which the popular *mentalité* may work out, through a code of abbreviations, a picture, like that of Betty Crocker on the cake mix box, of an ideal person, a person with too many diverse qualities to have any instantiation outside the imagination. This recent advertisement from the "Talk to Me" column of the *Baton Rouge Advocate* is a masterpiece in the mixing of cosmology of colloquial, particular ideas of the ideal.

TAKE ME AS I AM
Quiet, romantic, not rich DWM [divorced white male], 49, brown/brown [hair/eyes], enjoys classical literature, easy-listening/big band music, comedy/Sinatra/classic movies, sunsets, rain. Seeking spontaneous S/DWF [single or divorced white female], 5'4" [tall], 40-50 [years old]. All calls answered. Code 3541.

The advertisement is a symphony of harmonized but jumbled ideals. The "quiet romantic" would presumably have no place for the tempestuous Shelley or the ranging Byron; the avoidance of a claim of wealth is presumably a claim of sincerity, as is, covertly, the claim of being divorced, as this guarantees the ensuing romance would not be an "affair"; the hair and eyes approach an extreme ideal of temperate moderation, being a composite of all colors while being nothing threatening or odd; the reference to "classic" literature probably refers to something very recent, say *Gone with the Wind*, rather than Herodotus or Aeschylus; the affirmation of the value of "easy-listening" music insures that no

---

[14] Harris, *Astronomical Dialogues*, 82.

excessive musicological ideals will be pursued, that non-threatening monotony will be celebrated; and the remarkable, truly crystalline-mineralogical composition of "comedy/Sinatra/classic [in its second invocation] movies" compiles everything from the ludic-farcical to the presumed sublimity of America's most renowned pop singer, "Ol' Blue Eyes." The advertiser washes his picture against a J. M. W. Turner wet-and-windy horizon. In a moment of grand contradiction, he asks *methodically* for a *spontaneous* partner of a *specific* age and size. This universe of hope and confusion is drawn into a two-centimeter advertisement buried in a cavalcade of similar notices, all forming a recurring pattern on a highly regular page--a crystal image of hope, despair, pursuit, loss, success, and love.

This incorporation of emotional immensity into a tiny journalistic kaleidoscope is outdone only by a remarkable advertisement, an epitome of thousands that are sent to "target" audiences over the Internet but that are so provocative as to be deleted before being read--that are the *ultimate* marginalized text, because so few people bother to read them. This advertisement offers the ideal person in "virtual" form, without the muss and fuss attendant on dealing with a real partner:

> Date: 18-May-98 09:55 CDT
> From: PREAC14540 > INTERNET:PREAC14540@aol.com
> Subj: Last Chance
>
> The Virtual Girlfriend and Virtual Boyfriend are artificial intelligence programs for your IBM PC or compatible and also for MACINTOSH. You can watch them, talk to them, ask them questions, tell them secrets, and relate with them. Watch them as you ask them to take off different clothes and guide them through many different activities. Watch and participate in the hottest sexual activities available on computer, including: several sexual positions, using many unique toys, even bringing in multiple partners. This is no doubt one of the most realistic, sexually stimulating computer games available. They will remember your name, birthday, your likes and your dislikes. Every time you start the program, they say different things, and act differently. Each time, they have a different personality. With the VGA digital graphics, The Virtual Girlfriend and Virtual Boyfriend software have some of the hottest, sexiest graphics out there. And with a Soundblaster or compatible card, you can actually hear their voice as they talk to you. This is the first adult software title that was designed for both heterosexual and homosexual people. ...
>
> It will run on any 386, 486 or higher, and 100% IBM compatibles. Required is VGA graphics, and a hard drive. The sound card is optional. Macintosh requires at least 4 meg of ram. Virtual Girlfriend and Virtual Boyfriend are artificial intelligence programs, meaning they are completely interactive. It would be just like if you were talking to someone. You can actually have simple conversations. Their attitudes change with the different things you say, so you can say things that will upset them, and then say things that will please them. The more you play/talk with them, the more you learn what they can do, and what they like to do. It really is a blast. With all these movies coming out about virtual reality, it's amazing to actually have a virtual reality program like this for your own computer. It's easy to install, and instructions are easy to follow.[15]

---

[15] Received as an unsolicited advertisement over Compuserve, May 18, 1998.

Of all the perversities embedded in such an advertisement, three are the most striking. First, that the advertisement is authenticated not with reference to experience or reality, but with regard to "all these movies," in the same way that George Washington was re-authenticated by reference not to historical deeds, but with respect to an idealized toy figure, GI Joe. Second, no matter how comprehensive it is touted as being, it is still incomplete; as an artificial intelligence program, it requires complexity--a partner--in order to evolve into new dialogical formations. Third, the program is an intimate version of an intercultural encounter, being aimed at either heterosexuals or homosexuals and presumably designed to compete with the various services offering access to eastern-European or oriental brides or lovers. The advertisement is mineralogical, for it moves away from ordinary, sentient sexual partners and toward an electronic world in which all divergencies and differences can be reconciled, ordered, and arranged by magnetic forces, in which the endless variation of human sexual taste can be set up and regularized in taxons, files, and, as it were, recurring crystalline formations, where the ideal, here the ideal person or partner, is miniaturized down to the size of an electron, to the energetic point at which sublimity meets infinitesimality in the neural activity of digitized passion.

IV. MINERAL DRAMA AND MIRTHFUL MADNESS

Products like the "Virtual Girlfriend and Virtual Boyfriend" fuse the infinity of possibility with the infinitesimality of achievement. On the one hand, the Virtual Girl/Boyfriend can provide any sort of diversion required; it covers the full breadth of all possibility. On the other hand, it delivers nothing at all, being little more than an electronic echo of the user's neurons. In so (not) doing, such products reveal another aspect of "mineral drama": the way in which this genre draws on colossal possibilities but associates those possibilities with events that (almost) never happen. Mineral drama has a natural relationship with stories of miracles or other supernatural doings, with extraordinary events that are not in themselves impossible--there is nothing to say that it is impossible for gothic ghosts to walk the earth or for fakirs to levitate--but that rarely happen. One unanticipated consequence of philosopher David Hume's Enlightenment-era critique of miracles was that it made them all the more believable and secular. When Hume argued that a miracle could never be proved to have happened because there would never be enough credible witnesses to counteract the continued testimony of ordinary experience, he moved the criteria for the recognition of a miracle from ontological to forensic grounds. The question was not really whther miracles happened so much as whether they could be known or reported or affirmed in reliable testimony. As a "modern" mode, mineral drama assimilates Hume's critique, offering events that are nigh on but not utterly impossible, that stagger or bewilder or even annihilate testimony but that *could* happen. It presents colossal doings for which the chances are infinitesimally small.

"Mineral drama," the intercultural and interspecific encounter between sentient and insentient protagonists, has a natural teleology and an inevitable colossism to it. The pursuit of ever more remote possibilities involves the search for ever larger events and phenomena (the current wave of interest in the sunken ocean liner Titanic is a case in point). Apocalyptic themes are natural candidates for treatment in a mineral drama. From the time of St. Stephen onward, stones have been ascribed an aggressive bent. Astronomer J. T. Desaguliers was among the first to pick up on the theme of interplanetary encounters:

> If th' Errours of *Copernicus* may be
> Apply'd to ought within this Century,
> When e'er the want of understanding Laws,
> In Government, might some wrong Measures cause,
> His Bodies rightly plac'd still rolling on,
> Will represent our fix'd Succession,
> To which alone th' united *Britons* owe,
> All the sure Happiness they feel below.
> Nor let the Whims of the Cartesian Scheme,
> In Politicks be taken for thy Theme,
> Nor say that any Prince shou'd e'er be meant,
> By *Phoebus*, in his *Vortex*, indolent,
> Suff'ring each globe a *Vortex* of his own,
> Whose jarring Motions shook their Master's Throne,
> Who governing by Fear, instead of Love,
> Comets, from ours, to other Systems drove.[16]

In Desaguliers's political-astronomical parallel, a reverse collision occurs in which politicians committed to a Cartesian mindset trigger a calamity in the solar system, leading aggrieved comets to stage a mass-exodus to some other Sun King. For co-cometeer Dodsley the threat was more centrifugal: that some celestial object might collide with the earth.

I have discussed elsewhere the American preoccupation with unstoppable beings or forces (the cinematic "Terminator," the relentlessly successful machine of the Gulf War forces, the self-made rich man who makes money despite astonishing obstacles),[17] a literary motif of which the marauding meteor, the completely amoral and unthinking chunk of iron on a perfectly regular trajectory toward mass destruction of thinking beings, is the best of all examples. This kind of gloomy astronomical mineral drama also incorporates the cheerful postmodern chaotic-crystalline hypothesis: that battling planets will produce some new order or better world or other good result. One of the first recurrences of the asteroidal mineral drama in the twentieth century is Immanuel Velikovsky's notorious treatise, *Worlds in Collision*, in which this Russian immigrant (himself an intercultural phenomenon) theorizes that mankind shares in the collective

---

[16] Desaguliers, pp. 30-34.

[17] See my "Norman's Conquest: Red Seas, Gulf Shore, Vigorous Jacuzzis, Depth Charges, Professional Shallows, and the Theory of Theorylessness," for Rüdiger Ahrens and L. Volkmann, eds., *Why Literature Matters: Theories and Functions of Literature* (Heidelberg: Universitätsverlag Carl Winter, 1996), 161-181.

memory of a great celestial calamity involving a planetary collision.[18] Among other things, this great collision spawned an allegedly new planet, Venus, and produced salutary environmental changes on earth, making possible the rise of advanced, sentient, and technologically advanced life forms. Paradoxically, Velikovsky's tome thrives on a kind of insentience. Evidentiary arguments against its validity elicit not doubt, but conspiracy theories involving attempted cover-ups of evidence by researchers with a personal stake in other theories. The book is, like straying planets, always engaged in unintelligible collisions.

With the impending arrival of the millenium, a spate of new and highly advertised films concerning planetary disasters and interplanetary collisions are being produced. Not only is Velikovsky enjoying a second wind, not only are Internet areas concerned with hypothetical planetary catastrophes erupting, but the films *Deep Impact* and *Armageddon* have revived the popular fear of imminent planetary disaster. As the religiously evocative name of the latter film suggests, this popular concern with rampaging rocks is, like the city of New Roads or like mineral drama generally, a displacement, a secular rendering of apocalyptic feelings. This displacement is inadvertently addressed in *Armageddon*, where there characters are careful to inform the audience, erroneously, that Armageddon *is* the Last Judgment. As is typical of mineral drama, the fact and concept of the Last Judgment is geographically displaced into the site where the precursory battle will take place. Venue and vision merge.

Armageddon and *Deep Impact* make for an interesting contrast. The first, as its title suggests, attempts a mythic and yet also colloquial rendering of the last days. An authoritarian NASA is told by the only man technically qualified to drill a hole for a nuclear warhead on the impending asteroid that he rejects the formally trained NASA crew and will take with him, on his spaceship, only the gang of roughnecks with whom he has been drilling for oil in third-world, intercultural venues for the past thirty years. Mineral meets mineral as oilmen fly into space to defeat interplanetary iron in a subtly sentimental allegory of the virtue of ordinary people. *Deep Impact*, on the other hand, postulates an ultra-competent American government that has been secretly preparing plans and equipment to deal with the interplanetary calamity, in this case a collision with a comet. Again, the emphasis falls on sentimental responses to mineral sublimity, most of the film being dedicated to an analysis of how people would resolve interpersonal relationship issues at the end of history and, additionally, how those selected to enter a survival shelter would go about reconciling themselves to their happy fate and putting themselves into the mentality needed to revive a new world "after the dust clears."

Within this framework, both movies address a post-modern, post-political-correctness dilemma of the representation of the many cultures within American society. *Deep Impact* takes a simplistic approach by portraying the American President as a black man surrounded by white experts, although the encounter is made problematic by presenting this black President not as a virtuous or oppressed minority, but as as equally cunning and tough as any of his white predecessors. *Armageddon* avoids the cliché exultation of a minority President by keeping the Chief of State white but making his technocratic

---

[18] Immanuel Velikovsky, *Worlds in Collision* (New York: Doubleday, 1950).

entourage a racially mixed group, even allowing the black Chief of Staff for the Armed Forces to make foolish and prejudicial statements about the rowdy and apparently incompetent white men recruited from the oil rig. Both films stand apart from earlier disaster flicks by postulating the possibility of *surviving* minorities. In *Jurassic Park* and other Steven Spielberg catastrophe films, for example, black characters are always quickly killed by whatever monster or force is afoot, even despite Spielberg's reputation as a liberal cinematographer. In both *Armageddon* and *Deep Impact*, the minority attachés to the President survive the film. The totality of the fictional interplanetary calamity seems to make the intercultural calamity of racism smaller and *a fortiori* survivable. Had the danger only been dinosaurs, blacks would have died; surviving the seemingly total desturction of a Velikovskian planetary collision, however, clears away obstacles to minority survival. Russians and women also make it through these post-cold-war, post-racism pageants. Several comic moments, additionally, address the survivability of another marginalized characteristic, stupidity. Under psychiatric examination for his suitability as an astronaut and crew member, one of the oil-rigger characters in *Armageddon* is asked, by a psychologist, what is the one truth he would like to offer to mankind were he to have the platform and the opportunity to do so, to which this candidate rock-blaster replies that he would like to tell his fellow survivors that rock-music-star "Jethro Tull is not just a person, he is a concept and an institution."

The juncture between the personal, eccentric, or sentimental and the insentiently or obtusely objective is an integral element in mineral drama. Whatever may be the population of outer space, the fact remains that most of the universe is either vacuity or hostile environments. Today's avant-garde American rendering of the universe, however, is infused with this a high degree of individuality and sentimentality. A recent academic conference on "Star Wisdom" articulated a vision of space that is somewhat more than space and substance, that is a field against which American inter- and intra-culturalism can be projected. This "Star Wisdom" conference, convened at Harvard University and the Massachusetts Institute of Technology, presented space as the platform for a full bevy of diverse American cultural activitists, "including "John Mack, M.D., Harvard Psychiatrist; Sequoyah Trueblood, Choctaw Native elder; Edgar Mitchell, D.Sc., Apollo astronaut and founder of the Institute for Noetic Sciences; Dhyani Ywahoo, Cherokee chief and Tibetan Buddhist teacher; [and] Rudy Schild, Astrophysicist at the Harvard-Smithsonian Center for Astrophysics" [see figure 6]. The insentience of space and the rubble in it became the contrasting medium for expressing the fulness of culture. Indeed, it provided a vehicle for ascending into a supernatural world presided over by a variety of intercultural gurus, including a mixed Cherokee shaman and Buddhist sage.

This practice was not altogether new. I have noted elsewhere that eighteenth-century journalist Paul Whitehead used the great London earthquake of 1750 as an opportunity to imagine all sorts of conversations underway while heading into oblivion, while being swallowed up by the earth.[19] Whitehead and the Star Wisdom organizers take a mock-

---

[19] See my "A Spot of Tea on Silken Trunks, Or, The Industry of Experience," in Rüdiger Ahrens and Fritz-W. Neumann, eds., *Historical Fact and Fiction in Anglo-American Literature* (Heidelberg: Carl Winter, 1998), 137-59.

Figure 6: Star Wisdom Conference Brochure. Photo by the Author.

heroical approach to ontology, using either natural horror and disaster or cosmological vacuity to counterpoint grandiose or at least humorous speculations. American popular culture abounds with such mineralogical juxtapositions of the comical against the cosmological, or, perhaps more confusingly if not disconcertingly, of the comical against the horrifically evil, against the supernaturally repugnant. Europeans are often baffled by the strange American habit of making jokes about postal workers. In America, several post offices have been the scenes of shooting sprees and psychotic mass murders. Whereas in most European countries, postal workers are reasonably well-paid or at least respected civil servants, the American stereotype presents postal workers as frustrated and angry persons who couldn't get anything better than what we brutally call "a dumb job." Competitive Americans, animated by the old Puritan sense of manifest destiny, are fascinated by someone who either settles for or is trapped in a tedious career like that of sorting letters or reviewing postal codes but who one day goes off the deep end. The phrase „going postal" has now replaced "going ballistic" as an idiom for "losing one's mind in a sociopathic rage." There are, of course, many boring and demaning jobs, but the work of the postal service exerts a special fascination because of the head-on collision of endlessness--how many letters, how many addresses, and how many postal codes and postage rates must there be?--with employee incompetence and simmering frustrated ambition. Although there have been many shooting rampages in America, it is only those that took place in a post office that persist in popular memory, for it is only these that tap into the deepset interest in the battle between regimentation and sociopathology. This interest has advanced so far as to give rise to a computer game called *Postal* that comes in a box resembling a brown shipping container riddled with bullet holes; in the game, scores increase as the marauding gunman gets closer and closer to the administrators, officers, and finally postmaster.

Mayhem-driven postal humor is exceeded only by the comical discourses found in the most remote regions of Contemporary American dialogue. In America, the Internet has emerged as a vehicle not of Enlightenment, but of perversity. It is estimated that 83% of all "hits" emanating from American terminals are aimed at either pornographic or gambling sites on the World Wide Web. The transmission of socially unacceptable or politically dangerous or simply tasteless jokes among groups of friends has become an important means of bonding and group identification in an era profoundly suspicious of any potentially exclusive group identity. One sample of Internet humor is based almost completely on the expression of suppressed seriocomic laughter over the deficits of certain clamorous, self-righteous, or otherwise "challenged" groups:

> > Should crematoriums give discounts for burn victims?
> > If a mute swears does his mother wash his hands with soap?
> > And whose cruel idea was it to put an "S" in the word "Lisp"?
> > If a man stands in the middle of the forest speaking and there is no woman around to hear him ... Is he still wrong?
> > If someone with multiple personalities threatens suicide ... is it considered a hostage situation?
> > Is there another word for synonym?
> > Isn't it scary that doctors call what they do "practice"?
> > Where do forest rangers go to get away from it all?
> > What should you do if you see an endangered animal eating an endangered plant?
> > If a parsley farmer is sued do they garnish his wages?
> > Would a wingless fly be called a walk?
> > Why do they lock gas station bathrooms? Are they worried someone will clean them?
> > Is a shelless turtle homeless or just naked?
> > Can vegetarians eat animal crackers?
> > If a mime is arrested do they tell him he has the right to talk?
> > Why do they put Braille on the drive thru bank machines?
> > Do they use sterilized needles for lethal injections?
> > Why did kamikaze pilots wear helmets?
> > Is it true that cannibals won't eat clowns because they taste funny?[20]

---

[20] Forwarded e-mail communication from Mary Elizabeth Hughes, July 20, 1998.

The use of in-group and scatological humor as a means of social bonding is nothing new either to anthropologists or literary critics. Here, the conventional arrow "forwarding" figures (" > > ") indicate that this item has circulated through many friendly terminals and hands. Many of these jokes move beyond the ordinary scatological and into the supernatural or even gothic, to macabre topics like the technology of sanitary capital punishment (lethal injections) to the economic privileges of bodies in crematoria. This exploration of forbidden or horrific or frightening topics, of the vastness of obscenity, is possible in part owing to the miniaturization, even the invisibility of the Internet; such comic performances are private, ephemeral, restricted to a screen, digitally encoded, and no larger than an electron. These jokes collide with the brutal facts of life, with all the unstoppable horrors of crime, death, disease, and mutilation, in the same way that comets collide with the earth, as invisible, imaginary confrontations with some unstoppable force and as encounters with cultures that few would otherwise visit. Vulnerability and mortality are unstoppable forces, yet few pay regular visits to mausoleums or critical care units; just as the imaginary marauding comet is a useful if paradoxical vehicle for hypersentient wonder and terror, so gothic and scatological jokes provide entertaining but awkward vehicles for an encounter with the inverse sublime, with the hard human misery. Like mineral drama, like all the odd and faintly comic situations that come from trying to repel an asteroid, mineral comedy, comedy mixing triviality, banality, and smallness with the great horrors of the human condition, sits on the boundary between the serious and the savage, the didactic and the amusing. America's cultural radio network, National Public Radio, supplemented journalistic coverage of the recent execution of Carla Fay Tucker, the first woman executed in Texas in decades, with a visit to a roadside restaurant near the Huntsville Prison, a prison described as "the world's busiest death chamber," only to find that the proprietor, a black woman, feared the possibility of legislation against capital punishment because it would reduce the popularity of her restaurant's signature dish, the "Killer Burger." It was not only the surprising fact that a minority should hold such callous sentiments in a nation where an disproportionate number of minority criminals are executed that made these Brechtian comments so shocking to the NPR audience; it was also the fact that jokes like those in the foregoing Internet citation must remain dimensionless. They cannot be performed in public, outside the film of a screen, lest they become too dangerous, lest they become a real comet in a discursive universe occupied by postmodern meteors.

V. MINERALS, DIVERSITY, MISDIRECTED MEANINGS

The rise (and fall) of Deconstruction has demonstrated that not everyone is opposed to the misdirection of meaning, that there is such a thing as a fortunate linguistic fall or a constructive degeneration of communication. Misdirected comets are the perfect climactic metaphor for the age of semiotics. Errant heavenly bodies are at once inscrutable and clear in their meaning, at once an object of conversation and a sign of the termination of semiosis. The mineralogical worldview fits snugly with the cult of "diversity" and multiculturalism in Anglo-American critical thought, for it is of the essense of a wandering comet to diverge.

The chief leading mineralogist of the eighteenth century, Friedrich Christian Lesser, was religiously committed to diversity. His preoccupation with variation arose from his peculiar variation on the "Chain of Being" theme. While most eighteenth-century theologians and poets regarded the Chain of Being as a ladder of *species* in which every *type* of animal, vegetable, and mineral was represented and ranked, Lesser took a more particularized, horizontal view in which not just every species, but every individual organism, filled a specific and different place in creation. So committed to diversity was Lesser that he left little room for general taxons or categories. He was less interested in establishing what distinguished ants from bees or granite from pyrite *generically* than in celebrating the fact that any one chunk of granite or any one ant was different, sometimes dramatically so, from its compeers.

The only nation that was founded during the Enlightenment, America is caught up in Lesser's and others' celebration of diversity. Often this Lesserian preoccupation leads to odd results or an obsession with freakishness or horror. Miniature public hysteria, like the obsessive television viewing of O. J. Simpson murder trial or the fascination with euthanasia advocate Dr. Jack Kervorkian (and the eery white van in which he assists patients wishing to terminate their lives) are partly moral matters but mostly the product of a fascination with radical difference. It is a cliché of both formal and popular cultural studies that America is a land of innovation, but the origins of this innovation are often misunderstood. Although it is true that Puritanical faith in the manifest destiny of the new world and Baconian commitment to technological progress drive the American innovation machine, much of "Yankee ingenuity" accrues from this rather more aesthetical interest in divergence, diversity, and meteoric careening. The fact that Americans enjoy the production of junk, funkiness, and "kitsch" as much as they revel in scientific or cultural advancement suggests that the origins of these innovative ways go beyond the moral, religious, or scientific-methodological and on into the mineralogical and aesthetic.

The difficulty with celebrating Lesserian variety is that it leaves the celebrant with no general idea as to what is being celebrated. Celebrations usually laud classes and plurals of things--advance*s* in technology, achievement*s* in the arts. The radical individualism advocated by Lesser or the American Founders or American culture over the last two centuries makes celebration more challenging. People cannot collectively laud American poetry when every American poet rejects classification or group identity, when the idea of "American poetry" as a collective class is continually subverted. Academic-political discourse about "political correctness" is now grappling with individual members of minority groups who reject "labelling" and ask not to be counted as representatives of a class, lest being so labelled impair the development of their individual identity.

American culture, material and otherwise, abounds in examples of the meteoric misdirection of meaning through particularization. During the 1990s, the cult of UFOlogy--the study of unidentified flying object and of alien visitors--was a matter of very serious business. It generated religions, conspiracy theories, a spate of speculative and philosophical books, and plenty of movies. So high a level of seriousness and sobriety cannot long subsist in a culture committed to what American President Bill Clinton calls "change." Of late, even those seriously committed to the existence of UFOs have clamored for novelty, for humorous products related to their vocation. One result is a line of men's silk underpants ornamented with images of the images of "greys," the renowned extraterrestrial beings with the swelled heads and almond-shaped eyes. A "reader" of these underpants is at a loss to ascertain their exact meaning--whether comic spoof, serious statement of UFOlogical belief, or sheer erotic novelty--because the meaning of these garments *is* the diversification of meaning, *is* the cometary redirection of high-flying seriousness into something else, something the nature of which is unstable, uncertain, and changing. Oftentimes these semiotic diversions arise as a social process, in ways completely outside the influence of artist's or author's intentions. A big attraction now touring America is Kathryn Stuber's wax rendering of Leonardo Da Vinci's *Last Supper*, a diorama with life-size, three-dimensional wax figures set up in the poses shown in Leonardo's painting, with the polite addition of place- and name-cards for the dining apostles. Efforts to assure viewers that this display really *is* the Last Supper have the opposite, diverging effect. Even the most naive visitor knows that the audio track was recorded neither in Biblical times nor in the time of Leonardo and that the "real human hair" used in the display does not count as a relic of the earliest saints. The wax rendering is colossalized in that the figures are life size, and thereby much larger than those in Leonardo's masterpiece. These efforts at verisimilitude leave the viewer certain only that the meaning of this event--a *tour de force*, an eccentricity, a work of piety, an educational diorama--grows increasingly uncertain, that the distance between the meaning and the vehicle is increasing and mutating.

A more casual example is that of the world's most famous sporting event announcer, Michael Buffer. Michael Buffer is the perfect representation of postmodern *textualization* in that his entire career and professional identity rests on a single five-word phrase, "let's get ready to rumble!" that he enthusiastically announces before any and all kinds of sporting or entertainment events around the world. Buffer often precedes his signature ejaculation with comments in the native language of the event venue, but he always proclaims his signature phrase in English. Buffer, whose name suggests lapidary and gemological arts and who is so heavily made-up and so artfully coiffeured as to resemble a wax museum figure, has no other role or duty outside making this announcement, an art that he has parlayed into a lucrative international industry. His presence alone gives meaning to any and all events because his "ready to rumble" phrase is perfectly stable and always unchanging, not matter what or where he is introducing. Yet the meaning of the phrase is perpetually deviating from itself, possibly because it has no meaning. Buffer's Internet site (www.letsrumble.com/gallery.htm) explains that the phrase is intended to convey optimism and commitment to hard work and the success that comes from right living. This latter-day appeal to Puritanism is yet another mineralogical move, a deferment of meaning to an emotional state, a state of hopefulness or even generic "commitment." Buffer is the very image of the affective stabilization of an object, here a phrase, that, in its unchanging insentience, may mean nothing but that invokes, amalgamates, and in sum *does* a lot.

The high level of mineralogical displacement, the intense encounter between the meaningful and meaningless but motile, seen in a character like Michael Buffer is exceeded only by *mineral characters*, material objects that are credited with a degree of sentience or that become personalities or that achieve an iconic status far beyond what would seem appropriate to their nature or composition. A splendid example is the Alamo, an adobe fortress in San Antonio, Texas, where an American militia was slaughtered by a vastly superior force commanded by the Mexican General Santayana. The Alamo has attained tragic, even mythic status in the American consciousness as a symbol of independence and the American "fighting spirit." Additionally, it has become the subject of a number of epic motion pictures, including the renowned *The Alamo*, starring American film icon John Wayne. What is perhaps most remarkable--and most overlooked--about the cult of the Alamo is that, despite its minerality, it is credited with a kind of personality. Most epics record the adventures of a person--Odysseus, Orlando Furioso, Gilgamesh--but the Alamo stands almost alone as a *building*, a mound of adobe, that has itself become an epic hero, a character, the star of *The Alamo*. One thinks of the cinematic World War II epic, *The Sands of Iwo Jima*, also a cultic and iconic epic expression of the American wartime *mentalité*, in which heroism is titularly ascribed to *sands*, to the mineral silicon. A literal as well as semiotic and cognitive displacement, the Alamo that tourists visit today *is* a mineral--an amalgamation of dried mud--but even at that it *is not* what it is advertised to be. Most of the original Alamo was destroyed, and what remains is only an ancillary building, a church, that was moved from its original location and redecorated to look rather more militaristic. Like "Colonial Williamsburg" and other historic recreations, it contains almost no historical components. The Alamo is not even where the Alamo was, having been moved to make way for commercial developments. This veneration of ersatz historicity through dislocated mineral artifacts is at play in the American fashion for "gated communities," suburban housing developments protected by a gate, a guard, and sometimes a wall [see figure 7]. In a "gated community," modern mineral building materials are used to evoke a nostalgic, even spurious "European" atmosphere through a confused allusion to castles and their ramparts, in much the same way that the Disney enterprise has constructed an exaggerated rendering of Neuschwanstein Castle at all its theme parks (in the character of "Cinderella's Castle"). The gate of a gated community is a counter-intercultural emblem, for it is intended to keep poor and presumably minority "troublemakers" and "criminals" away, although, curiously, the architectural idiom has also been embraced by wealthy black celebrities such as the Rap music star Master P, who also resides in a suburban gated community. As Figure 7 makes clear, one important aspect of the gated community is its porosity, passability, and insecurity. It is essential to be able to see and pass through the gate in order to wonder at the prosperity of the inhabitants. A mineral symbol that means the opposite of what it means--that began as a symbol of European aristocracy and now iconizes the American upper-middle class--is doubly negativized, its superficial meaning being "security" but its primary meaning being reconnoiterability, permeability, and old-fashioned American "openness." So strong is this Alamo-style impulse to fictionalize if not falsify history, to displace epic meaning from sentient to insentient creatures, that sometimes a genuinely historical building that had housed historically significant, real-life occupants can be rendered fictitiously sentient and de-historicized. The Laura Plantation near Donaldsonville, Louisiana, hosted many historical

Figure 7: Gated Community near Baton Rouge, Louisiana. Photo by the Author

personages, including the Marquis de Lafayete and members of the George Washington family, yet its managers prefer to bill it as the residence of a fictional character whose tales were told there, as "The American Home of Brer Rabbit" [see figure 8].

Not every mineral is a rock. Far and away one of the most iconic minerals in America is chrome, derived from chromium, as shiny, silver-colored metal commonly used to ornament automobiles. Chrome has served many iconic purposes on many vehicles, from the declaration of prosperity on the flashy sports cars of the 1950s to the expression of toughness among motorcycle gangs. Like all other movements, the cult of the "easy rider" or "hell's angel," the rough-and-tumble gypsy motorcycle enthusiast who travels the country in small packs drinking, fighting, and troublemaking, is slipping into the past as its acolytes age. An unexpected result of this progress toward cultural obsolescence has been the *apotheosis of chrome*, the process by which Hell's Angels metamorphose into heaven's messengers. As former roughnecks become itinerant evangelists, and the meaning of chrome converts from savagery to salvation. Several national associations of Christian motorcyclists have evolved from these formerly boisterous motorcycle gangs, most notably the Tribe of Judah, in which motorcycles replace camels as the means of

Figure 8: Entry to Laura Plantation, Donaldsonville, Ascension Parish, Louisiana. Photo by the Author.

transportation through the desert of impiety. The Christian Motorcyclists Association wanders from church to church in an effort to renew devotion through novelty, by making startling appearances at sluggard congregations. One member of this brotherhood of the chromed cowl has achieved almost complete iconic displacement. Daniel D. "Woody" Woods [see figure 9] retains the "look" of the "bikey" yet lives a saintly and devoted life as an itinerant motorcycle minister, travelling from city to city showing that his chrome-laden bicycles and his eccentric entourage can rival the great historical hermits for their piety. Mr. Woods's dress features a T-shirt blazoned with a ferocious eagle that no longer carries out rape and raven but instead bears a cross. What appears to be a Harley-Davidson logo on his baseball cap reads not "Harley Davidson," but "Heavenly Davidson." His black-and-leather overall appearance presents a stark contrast to the blazing white of the parking lot in which he carries out his missionary work, as a kind of counter-iconic process in which black represents good and the blistering glare of the pavement represents the vulgarity of material culture and shopperly acquisitiveness.

Essential to Mr. Woods's presentation is a vast quantity of chrome-draped motorcycles, a huge load of mineral material to express the anti-materialistic messages that he carries--or drives--around the world.

Figure 9: Motorcycle Missionary. Photo by the Author.

VI. AFTERWORD: THE "X" FACTOR

In the cold-war monster-movie classic, *Godzilla vs. Monster Zero*, the anonymous "Controller of Planet X" [see figure 10] begs Nick Adams, the incongruous American leader of Japan's space force, to let Godzilla battle his planet's number one adversary, "Monster Zero." When asked for his and the monster's identification documents, the grease-painted Controller proclaims that "everything here is numbered—the monster is zero," even despite the monster's having three heads. Planet X, it seems, combines simple determinism with comical complexity, sentience with insentience. meaning with nullity, and mineral with animal. The robotic, antenna-sprouting Controller's scientifically managed planet abounds with numerous, nay, numbered threats; his greatest bibliographical work is a systematic catalogue of system-smashing disasters; worse still, his culture is suffering from a major shortage of air, water, and other elements. The Controller and his Kodel-costumed crew "control" the surface only through screens and

Figure 10: "The Controller of Planet X" in *Godzilla versus Monster Zero*. Courtesy American International Films.

projections deep within their bunker. Foreign--intercultural--from every point of view, Planet X is perpetually in the process of displacement, onomastic or otherwise. Ravaged by alien monsters, lacking a definitive name, it needs help from a temporally dislocated Jurassic and recruits Anglo-Japanese astronaut crews. This unknown, uncharted, and ungovernable planet looks more like a nexus of jostling possibilities than a possible place in any known world. Contemporary audiences probably doubt that anyone ever made a movie about so cliché a place as "Planet X." Yet the idea of a mysteriously unnameable place, a destination full of dark secrets and concealed information, flourishes in such popular productions as *The Twilight Zone Movie* or *The X Files*. Anonymous location X seems cliché because it is virtually synonymous with American cultural topography. More than an unnamed identity, "X" is also an undefined quantity, a ciphered sum of all the unidentified resources in our land of unlimited opportunity. "X marks the spot" at which to tell countless tales about the uncharted spaces of the vast American landscape.

Like the cinematic Planet X, America never "existed" and never will be "discovered." Rather, it was mined. America from the beginning was a complex vein, a crystalline cohesion of highly charged and highly molecular factions, parties, and diversities. Mineralogical to the core, it is not surprising that, in the twentieth-century critical milieu, America should become the core of peripheralism, the center of margin-seeking multiculturalism. The source of cliché academic interculturalism yet intraculturally resistant to uniformity, America is the X that marks the point of productive uncertainty on every literary, fantasy, and sometimes genuine map. It is the spot where unquantified buried treasure, where mineralogical cultural conceptions are crystallized.

Memory and national identity in postcolonial historical fiction

ULRICH BROICH (München)

The Empire has been writing back for some time, and this also applies to the writing about the past of the former colonial countries. An enormous number of fictional and non-fictional texts have been written in former colonies all over the world in order to rewrite the history of their countries, which, in the period of colonization, had been mainly written by the colonizers. In this postcolonial rewriting of history the colonial past was seen as a period of oppression and resistance. But this writing about the past was not necessarily concerned solely with history. Jan Assmann, in his book on cultural memory, has a useful though not very precise distinction between a sense of history proper and a cultural memory, which can be non-historical and even antihistorical.[1] In this sense, quite a number of postcolonial texts attempt to uncover the cultural past of their countries even before the period of colonization. They describe their social and political structures before their deformation through colonial rule as well as their forms of religion and myth before the advent of Christianity. They try to recover from oblivion their indigenous forms of oral and written literature, which were pushed into the background when the curriculum in the schools and universities of the colonial countries was dominated by texts from the western canon. These texts evoke a cultural memory of a time which, at least in the western sense of the word, often lies beyond and before history

It is obvious that such texts could be of particular political importance for the former colonies after they had obtained their independence. In most cases, the colonial states were artificial units with artificial boundaries, and they were often made up of a number of tribal kingdoms with different languages and religions. When such a colony was dismissed into independence, it was, as a rule, within the boundaries created by the colonial powers. India, for example, had never existed before her independence as a state within the boundaries of 1947. Salman Rushdie has therefore been able to write that "a nation which had never previously existed was about to win its freedom", and he calls India "a collective fiction".[2] Thus new states were formed which were not founded on a consciousness of national identity. It is evident that in this situation historical writing could have been useful to help to create such a national identity – just as epics and historical novels helped to do so when new nation states were created in nineteenth-century Europe.[3]

---

[1] Jan Assmann, *Das kulturelle Gedächtnis. Schrift, Erinnerung und politische Identität in frühen Hochkulturen* (München: Beck, 1992).
[2] Salman Rushdie, *Midnight's Children* (1981) (Picador edition; London: Pan Books, 1982), 112.
[3] For discussions of the relationship between nation and literature see Homi K. Bhabha (ed.) *Nation and Narration* (London: Routledge, 1990).

Therefore, the following paper will be devoted to the question of whether the spate of historical literature in postcolonial countries was a response to the need for establishing a new national identity. In particular, it will investigate the forms of historical fiction in these countries and will inquire to what extent western forms of historical fiction were used or transformed in order to serve the interests of countries in a postcolonial situation. The examples will be taken from various postcolonial literatures from all over the world, but exclusively from literatures written in English. How far the results obtained from a limited number of texts are representative must be left open for the time being.

1.

It may be useful to begin with a brief look at the model of historical fiction created by Sir Walter Scott. Scott wrote his novels on the history of Scotland at a time when the political union between England and Scotland was more than a century old and "sixty years since" the last rebellion of the Scots against the English had been crushed in the battle of Culloden, but at a time when a new British national identity had not yet been established. Thus he wrote his novels on the one hand, as he put it in the postscript to *Waverley*, "for the purpose of preserving" the cultural memory of the Scottish past and "of the ancient manners of which I have witnessed the almost total extinction,"[4] and, on the other hand, in order to make the reader "aware of the progress we have made" (*Waverley*, 492): a progress from archaic feudal structures in Scotland to a more modern society and from conflicting English and Scottish identities to a new overall British identity. In *Waverley*, this new identity is embodied in the final marriage between the English protagonist and the Scottish Rose Bradwardine.

A similar concept can be found those of Scott's novels which are set in the Middle Ages. Thus, his novel *Ivanhoe* presents the conflicts between the Anglo-Saxons and Normans more than a century after the Norman Conquest, but also the developments towards a new cultural and national identity which unites Anglo-Saxons as well as Normans.

Behind all these novels we may discover a somewhat Hegelian concept of history, though Scott may not have been acquainted with Hegel.[5] The two nations within one country may be seen as thesis and antithesis, and the positive ending of the novels represents a synthesis in which the culture of both nations is 'aufgehoben' and in which the transformation of two nations into one represents what Scott unhesitatingly calls "progress".

It is obvious how Scott's model of historical fiction could have been instrumentalized in the new postcolonial countries. But in spite of the fact that the form created by

---

[4] Walter Scott, *Waverley* [1814] (London: Penguin, 1985), 493.

[5] According to Georg Lukács, Scott had no knowledge of Hegel's writings though in his novels he put some of Hegel's ideas into practice. (Georg Lukács, "Scott and the Classical Form," in A. Norman Jeffares, ed., *Scott's Mind and Art* [Edinburgh : Oliver & Boyd, 1969], 93-131, here: 130).

Scott is still alive at least on the level of *Trivialliteratur*, postcolonial writers have rarely used this form. In the few novels from postcolonial countries which do follow Scott's model of historical fiction, the ideology on which it is based has been abandoned. As examples I am now going to discuss briefly two postcolonial historical novels which rather obviously follow the model created by Scott and which, not surprisingly, are not among the best historical fiction from postcolonial countries.

A rather early example is Peter Abrahams's novel *Wild Conquest*. This novel by a South African writer (whose parents were an Ethiopian and a 'coloured') was published in 1951, that is at a time which can, strictly speaking, not be called 'postcolonial'.[6]

The scene of this novel is set in the South Africa of about 1835. The action consists, just as in Scott's *Waverley* and *Ivanhoe*, of conflicts between different peoples living in the same region, that is on the one hand of conflicts between the black tribes of the Matabele and the Barolong, and on the other hand between the blacks and the Boers, who undertake their historical Great Trek from the Cape Colony to the north. The main characters – the Barolong Dabula and the Boer Paul – are fictional, and just as in Scott's novels they meet historical characters like the Boer leader Potgieter and are involved in historical events like the battle of Vegkop (1836).

In spite of the growing hatred between the blacks and the Boers, the two protagonists Dabula and Paul come to a closer understanding in the course of the action. But unlike in Scott's novels there is nothing like a vision of progress towards a union of the peoples which are now fighting each other. The novel ends not with a union but a separation: the Boers, after their victory of Vegkop, settle in the country of the Matabele, and the Matabele, driven away from their country, in their turn move toward the north in order to settle in Zimbabwe. Of this final situation the novel says: "an epoch has ended, an epoch has started"[7] – the new epoch is one of white dominance and black expropriation. It is true that at the end of the novel some of the characters have a vision of "a new day", of a time without violence and of peaceful community. But this is not a vision of a national union in South Africa but a utopian vision of a union of all men in the spirit of humanity, and the realization of this vision at the end of the novel seems to be farther away than ever before.

My second example of adaptations of the Scottian model in postcolonial countries is a more recent one and comes from New Zealand. It is the novel *Season of the Jew* of the year 1986, which was written by the white author Maurice Shadbolt. This rather popular novel narrates, or rather rewrites, the story of the last great Maori rebellion against the whites, which took place in 1868 and 1869 and which was led by the Maori Te Kooti.

---

[6] According to the definition in *The Empire Writes Back. Theory and Practice in Postcolonial Literatures* (London: Routledge, 1989) by Bill Ashcroft, Gareth Griffiths and Helen Tiffin even this novel can be called 'postcolonial': "We use the term 'post-colonial', however, to cover all the culture affected by the imperial process from the moment of colonization to the present day."(2).

[7] Peter Abrahams, *Wild Conquest* [1952] (Hong Kong: Nelson, 1982), 379.

Season of the Jew follows the model created by Scott even more closely than Peter Abrahams's *Wild Conquest*. As in many of the novels in the tradition of Scott, the action is centred around a civil war, and many of the characters, like Te Kooti, and many of the events, like the Poverty Bay Massacre, which forms the climax of the novel, are historical. The protagonist, however, like Waverley and Ivanhoe, is fictional and somehow placed between the fighting parties. He is the white Captain Fairweather, who is a harsh critic of colonial rule and who has strong sympathies with the Maoris, but who nevertheless fights against them. Moreover, like Waverley, Fairweather is attached to a woman from the other side – to Meriana Smith, who bears him several children.

And yet, Shadbolt adopts from Scott only structures and motifs rather than the corresponding ideology. At the end of *Waverley*, Scott first narrates the trial and execution of a Jacobite leader, then has only a few sentences for the battle of Culloden and the ensuing Highland Clearances, in which the society and culture of the Scots were almost eradicated, and finally tells at great length the story of the marriage between Waverley and Rose. Understating the political disaster and overstating private happiness seems to have been the only way for Scott to enable him to end his novel with a vision of national union and progress. This is entirely different in *Season of the Jew*. The novel ends with the trial and execution not of the rebel leader Te Kooti, but of a very young boy who happened to be in the rebel army, and this execution is meant to show the injustice and brutality of the colonial power. It is true that the marriage between Fairweather and a Maori woman could have been used to symbolize a better future, but what we read in the epilogue about the future is only that Fairweather's two sons were killed in the First World War and that he, in an English understatement, realizes that the twentieth century was "no improvement on the last."[8]

In any case, the novel ends not with a vision of national unity for Maoris and whites but with the destruction of Maori culture and the expropriation of Maori land, with even Fairweather settling on land which had belonged to the Maoris. Therefore, Shadbolt does not adopt a concept of history which is, like Scott's novels, based on a belief in progress. On the contrary, whenever any of Fairweather's brother officers use the word "progress" to describe the expansion of white settlements in New Zealand, Fairweather has only scorn for this conviction (e.g. *Season*, 47). The concept of history on which this novel is based is completely different, and Herrick, who thinks very much like Fairweather, puts it into the following words:

> [...] a curse. On our kind, and not just in this country. Trample such a curse here, and it takes fire there. I see more like Kooti to come with terror and a text.[9] If not flourishing the words of one testament, then those of another. There will always be a Biggs to kindle the fuel; always a Whitmore to stoke it [...] I think I am talking original sin. (308)

---

[8] Maurice Shadbolt, *Season of the Jew* (Boston: David R. Godine, 1986), 383.
[9] The word 'text' refers to the Old Testament, on which Te Kooti founded his new religion of rebellion and revenge.

History, therefore, is not governed by the law of progress; it is, rather, marked by a cyclical return of meaningless violence.

In spite of its criticism of white colonial rule, *Season of the Jew* in its turn has been severely criticized by postcolonial critics. Nelson Wattie, for instance, calls the novel's view of the Maori rebellion "British, imperialist, and even racist."[10] This criticism is a bit difficult to understand. But then it has to be admitted that Shadbolt, different from Peter Abrahams, describes the action almost exclusively from the point of view of the whites, does nothing to preserve the cultural memory of the Maoris, and adopts a view of history which is just as foreign to a colonized people as that of Scott.

We can therefore conclude that the Scottian model of historical fiction, though adopted every now and then in postcolonial countries, does not seem to have provided an adequate form and even less an adequate ideology for representing postcolonial views of history and cultural memory. Before turning to alternative models for historical fiction, therefore, I shall sketch some theoretical statements on history and literature by authors from different postcolonial countries.

2.

In an article written after the death of Indira Gandhi, Salman Rushdie says: "Those who forget the past are condemned to repeat it."[11] This statement about the necessity of remembering, and learning from, the past sounds rather conventional – and 'western'. But we shall find that postcolonial writers as a whole see the function of historical memory in a way that differs greatly from 'western' views. I shall now discuss three such rather different opinions.

My first author is the Caribbean historian and poet E.K. Brathwaite. In his article on history and the Caribbean writer, he states that the Caribbeans have "no history" and "no memory."[12] The indigenous population of the Caribbean islands was exterminated by the white conquerors, who then brought slaves from Africa to the islands, a new population who on a different continent seem to have lost their roots and forgotten their past. At school they were given British history instead.

Brathwaite calls upon the Caribbeans "not [to] listen to Prospero's commands [any more] but to the memory of the history of [their] own culture" (Brathwaite,

---

[10] Nelson Wattie, "The New Zealand Land Wars in Novels by Shadbolt and Ihimaera," in Geoffrey Davis and Hena Maes-Jelinek, eds., *Crisis and Creativity in the New Literatures in English* (Amsterdam and Atlanta: Rodopi, 1990), 433-48, here: 445. This article compares *Season of the Jew* with Witi Ihimaera's *The Matriarch* (1986), which was written by a Maori and presents the history of New Zealand from a Maori point of view.

[11] Salman Rushdie, "The Assassination of Indira Gandhi," in Salman Rushdie, *Imaginary Homelands: Essays and Criticism 1981-1991* (London: Granta, 1991), 41-6. Here 41.

[12] Edward K. Brathwaite, "History, the Caribbbean Writer and X/Self," in Geoffrey Davis and Hena Maes-Jelinek, eds., *Crisis and Creativity in the New Literatures in English* (Amsterdam and Atlanta: Rodopi, 1990), 23-46, here 25.

"History", 39). If they do, they will recover the forgotten memory, for example that of the 'Middle Passage', on which the slaves were transported from Africa to the Caribbean, or even of the tremendous catastrophe in which the island of Atlantis was destroyed thousands of years ago. From the echo of this catastrophe, which is still part of the memory of the Caribbeans, Brathwaite concludes that this memory is characterized by a sense of fragmentation, which strongly differs from the "very strong sense of wholeness" (26) of the English. This sense of fragmentation is, according to Brathwaite, increased by the fact that on the Caribbean islands four different languages are spoken.

What Brathwaite demands is apparently, in the terms of Jan Assmann, not so much a historical memory proper but a cultural memory. And this cultural memory establishes not a sense of national identity but rather a sense of fragmentation which the cultural memories of all Caribbeans have in common. It is therefore perhaps not surprising that Brathwaite has avoided writing historical fiction; instead, he has written poems about the fragmented present of the Caribbeans, in which fragments of the past turn up again and again in a coded form. Decoding these fragments accordingly means for the reader to recover his forgotten cultural memory.

My second author is the Indian historian Dipesh Chakrabarty. In his article about "Postcoloniality and the Artifice of History" he analyses the particular problem of history for postcolonial countries from a different angle. Brathwaite had stated that the European colonizers had deprived the colonized of their histories and had forced their own history on them. Chakrabarty goes one step further and calls the concept of history itself European. Thus he writes: "'Europe' remains the sovereign theoretical subject of all histories, including the ones we call 'Indian', 'Chinese', 'Kenyan' and so on."[13] In this manner he implies that 'history' is an imperialist concept in which European history is always the master narrative, of which the history of a postcolonial country is only a subordinated, peripheral part.

At the same time, he emphasizes that this concept of history is deeply linked with the concepts of modernity and of the nation state. The tendency of postcolonial countries toward modernization and toward nationalism appears, therefore, as an ultimately 'western' one.

We may object that Chakrabarty's concept of history is too narrow and that it applies rather to nineteenth-century views of history in Europe. At the same time, however, it is obvious that a concept in which history, modernity, progress, and the nation state are inseparably linked is exactly the concept on which Scott's historical novels are based. And it must also be admitted that the concept of a nation-state is very much a European one.

Chakrabarty does not say that this form of fiction is utterly inadequate to the postcolonial situation, but this conclusion can certainly be drawn from his argument. Instead, he demands an approach to history which 'provincializes' Europe, which liber-

---

[13] Dipesh Chakrabarty, "Postcoloniality and the Artifice of History," in Bill Ashcroft, Gareth Griffiths and Helen Tiffin, eds., *The Post-Colonial Studies Reader* (London, New York: Routledge, 1995), 383-8, here 383.

ates "'history' from the meta-narrative of the nation state" (Chakrabarty, "Artifice of History", 384) and which can even be antihistorical. But at the same time he realizes the impossibility of this project and demands that any postcolonial presentation of history must at least problematize the ideology hidden in the concept of history.

The third and last author whose theoretical view on history and the postcolonial situation I would like to discuss is the Caribbean Nobel Prize winner Derek Walcott. Walcott goes even further than Chakrabarty in his condemnation of history from a postcolonial point of view. In his essay "The Muse of History" (1974), he paradoxically indicates this already at the beginning by using a quotation from a 'western' author as his motto: "*History is a nightmare from which I am trying to awake. James Joyce.*"[14] Also in this article, Walcott calls history an "unbearable burden" ("Muse of History", 371) or even a Medusa, which petrifies everyone who looks at it. He gives the following reason for this verdict on history:

> In the New World servitude to the muse of history has produced a literature of recrimination and despair, a literature of revenge written by the descendants of slaves or a literature of remorse written by the descendants of masters. ("Muse of History", 371)

Thus, literature is marred whenever it looks into the Medusa-like face of history, no matter whether this is done from the perspective of the descendants of the former colonizers or from that of the colonized. The only way out for Walcott is to "reject this sense of history" ("Muse of History", 371), to reject the remorse and recrimination inextricably connected with the sense of history in postcolonial countries, and also to oppose the "obsession with progress" ("Muse of History", 373), which also seems to him closely related with this sense of history. Therefore he wants to avoid the "view of Caliban" ("Muse of History", 371) as well as the view of Prospero, and he refuses to see either of them as part of his history:

> I say to the ancestor who sold me, and to the ancestor who bought me, I have no father, I want no such father, although I can understand you, black ghost, white ghost, when you both whisper 'history' [...] ("Muse of History", 373)

Instead, he wants to turn to a view of man which he calls "Adamic" ("Muse of History", 371), a view of man before and beyond history, which he finds realized in writers like Walt Whitman and Pablo Neruda.

And yet, like Chakrabarty, he finds it impossible to maintain this utter rejection of history. All his poetry, and especially his long poem *Omeros* (1990), is steeped in reminiscences of the history of the former slaves as well as of European history. But there is always the attempt to deconstruct these histories and to find a point beyond history in the nature of the Caribbean archipelago and to find a new identity not in history but in nature, and especially in the Caribbean sea.

---

[14] Derek Walcott, "The Muse of History" (1974). Quoted from an abridged version in Bill Ashcroft, Gareth Griffiths and Helen Tiffin, eds., *The Post-Colonial Studies Reader* (London, New York: Routledge, 1995), 370-374, here 370.

If we assume that this distrust or even rejection of history is more or less general in postcolonial countries, this is bound to have consequences, not only for the poetry of Brathwaite and Walcott but also for historical fiction; and it becomes obvious that historical fictions like the novels by Peter Abrahams and Maurice Shadbolt are not representative of this view of history. We shall therefore now turn to examine three novels – one from Nigeria, one from Kenya and one from India – in which this postcolonial distrust of history is more explicit, and we shall see which constructions of a postcolonial identity they offer.

3.

The first of these three novels, Chinua Achebe's *Things Fall Apart* (1958), is not an historical novel in the usual sense of the word. The greater part of the novel is set in the timeless world of an Igbo village in Nigeria, and there are no historical dates, characters and events. It is only towards the end of the novel,[15] when the English begin to establish colonial rule in Nigeria, that the reader learns that England is reigned by a queen. Therefore the reader can conclude that the action takes place in the late period of Queen Victoria's reign.

Two thirds of the novel, however, are localized before this historical event. They describe the community of an Igbo village, the cycle of the seasons, the planting and harvesting of yams, religious rituals, marriage customs, festivals and games, and the ways of administering justice, and the reader is given the impression that these customs and rituals have existed unchanged for many generations. This society seems to be a society before or without history, at least in the western sense of the word.

Most of the characters are typical and serve to represent timeless customs. The protagonist Okonkwo, however, is an exception. He is very much an individual character and consequently stands in the tradition of the western novel. He is characterized by particular abilities and ambitions, but also by a tendency towards sudden anger, which time and again thwarts his ambitious goals and in the end leads to his tragic downfall.

It is into this timeless world that history breaks towards the end of the novel. The first white missionaries arrive, and they prepare the way for British soldiers and administrators, who turn Nigeria into a British colony. After a time of peaceful coexistence between non-Christian and Christian villagers, some Christian fanatics desecrate an Igbo ritual; in retaliation the Christian church is burnt down, and this in turn leads to intervention by the District Commissioner, who, with the aid of his military power, imprisons and humiliates the leaders of the village. In the end Okonkwo commits suicide, and the Igbo community is irrevocably broken. Incidentally, there are also some other literary works from Nigeria which describe exactly this moment of the irruption of history into Nigerian society through the colonial power and the ensuing

---

[15] Chinua Achebe, *Things Fall Apart* [1958], African Writers Series (Oxford: Heinemann, 1986), 127.

break-up of this society, for example Wole Soyinka's historical drama *Death and the King's Horseman* (1975).

At the end of Achebe's novel, the British District Commissioner, who has successfully suppressed all opposition against colonial rule, smugly intends to write a book on these events, and he wants to give it the title "*The Pacification of the Primitive Tribes of the Lower Niger*" (*Things Fall Apart*, 148). This intention, which gives the novel its ironical ending, shows how the history of Nigeria may have been written in the time of colonization and shows also that Achebe's novel is an attempt at rewriting this history. This means at the same time that Achebe does not seem to share Walcott's view that literature ought to escape the burden of history because it can only produce a literature of recrimination or remorse, for at first sight *Things Fall Apart* seems to belong to that literature of recrimination which Walcott wants to avoid. But is this the real function of history in Achebe's novel?

In one of his critical articles, Achebe characterized the purpose of his historical novels as follows:

> Here then is an adequate revolution for me to espouse – to help my society to regain belief in itself and put away the complexes of the years of denigration and self-abasement. [...] For no thinking African can escape the pain of the wound in our soul. [...] I would be quite satisfied if my novels [...] did no more than teach my readers that their past – with all its imperfections – was not one long night of savagery from which the first European acting on God's behalf delivered them.[16]

In this passage, which is taken from an article with the characteristic title "The Novelist as Teacher", Achebe states not only that in his historical novels he wants to rewrite the history of his people, but also his intention of helping his "society to regain belief in itself", that is to regain its identity. The novel, however, realizes these aims only with some qualifications. It certainly shows that the Igbo society before the advent of Christianity was a more or less humane society with remarkable mechanisms for peacefully settling conflicts, and that the Christian missionaries with their message of peace and humanity only paved the way for the political and military power of the colonizers. But the novel also shows that the Christian missionaries were only able to succeed because of the contradictions and elements of inhumanity in the customs of the Igbos. According to their religious belief, all twins are of demonic origin and have to be killed right after their birth. The novel also narrates how a boy, who has been taken as a hostage after a conflict with another village and who has lived for years in his new home, is brutally killed one day at the order of the priests. Customs such as these are felt to be inhumane by some of the Igbos and induce them to embrace the seemingly more humane Christian religion.

This shows that *Things Fall Apart* is not a nostalgic novel, a novel which merely wants to revive the memory of an ideal Igbo culture and to establish a cultural identity in the present which is based on it. Instead, the novel demonstrates that the old Igbo

---

[16] Chinua Achebe, "The Novelist as Teacher," in C.A., *Hopes and Impediments. Selected Essays 1965-1987* (Oxford: Heinemann, 1988), 27-31, here 30.

culture, just as the Christian culture, was characterized by deep contradictions. At the same time, at the end of the novel there is no synthesis in the manner of Scott's historical novels, but as the title indicates, "things fall apart". This is of course a quotation from Yeats's poem "The Second Coming", and in this poem, just as in Achebe's novel, the falling apart of things indicates the beginning of a new era in which a former unity is lost.

Achebe's novel does not contain a vision of a new Nigerian identity in a new nation which has shaken off colonial rule and which has established a new union of the things that have fallen apart. On the one hand, the novel is only concerned with the cultural identity of the Igbos, and other cultures which are also part of the present Nigeria, like those of the Haussa and the Yoruba, are not mentioned. On the other hand, Achebe sees his new Nigerian nation in a deeply critical manner, which becomes obvious in his later novels, which are localized in the period after independence. And it is significant in this context that Achebe, like so many other postcolonial authors, had to leave his country for good – he has been living in the United States since 1985.

The only synthesis possible to Achebe is his work of fiction. It is only here that western and Igbo culture are linked together. The novel is not only steeped in Igbo culture, contains a lot of Igbo words and draws on the native oral tradition, but at the same time it is written in the English language, employs structures of the western novel and is also based on the conviction that by now the Christian tradition has become a part of Nigerian culture which cannot simply be eradicated.

4.

Ngugi wa Thiong'o's novel *A Grain of Wheat* (1967) may serve as a contrast to Achebe's novel and is much more of a historical novel in the western sense of the word. The present action takes place a few days before, on, and a few days after a very important date in the history of Kenya: Uhuru Day, 12 December 1963, the day when Kenya obtained independence from colonial rule. The novel narrates the celebrations of Uhuru Day in a Kenyan village, but also the historical events leading up to it: strikes and other forms of resistance against British colonial rule, the Mau Mau rebellion, the state of emergency and the establishment of detention camps. All this is presented from the perspective of the Kenyan village and of fictional characters; historical characters like Jomo Kenyatta are mentioned again and again, but they do not appear as characters on the scene of the novel.

Ngugi, however, does not use the traditional form of the historical novel, with a central plot and a single protagonist. The focus shifts between various inhabitants of the village, and at the same time it permanently shifts between the present and the past. Thus we learn about the prehistory of Uhuru Day from a narrator who seems to be an inhabitant of the same village,[17] but even more so through the reminiscences of the different characters. Therefore, the structure of *A Grain of Wheat* is similar to that

---

[17] This narrator always uses the collective "we", indicating the people in the village.

of a modernist novel, and it even seems to have been influenced by a particular novel of early modernism: the story of Mugo, who betrays the leader of the resistance movement against the British, seems to be modelled on the story of Razumov in Joseph Conrad's *Under Western Eyes*, who betrays a member of the Russian resistance movement to the Czarist police.

As the action of the novel is steeped in history and leads up to the foundation of the state of Kenya, Ngugi seems to have far fewer problems with history and national identity than Achebe or Derek Walcott. It is true that he, too, presents history as a burden. Mugo has betrayed the freedom fighter Kihika to the British, other inhabitants of the village collaborated with the British and prosecuted their own countrymen, a white woman was raped by some villagers, a Christian missionary was murdered, and a black woman slept with the commander of the British police in the village while her husband was imprisoned in a detention camp. All these events show that the memory of the past is, in the words of Walcott, inseparably burdened with "remorse and recrimination". And yet, Ngugi does not advocate a forgetting or bypassing of history and a return to Adamic man and nature like Walcott. The novel shows that the suppressed or forgotten burden of the past, in which almost everyone became guilty and which some want to forget, has to be remembered and that it is only this memory that will make it possible for the people to communicate and to work together in their new state in order to create "a new earth."[18] Historical memory thus obtains a therapeutic and cathartic function. At the same time, history also contributes to the formation of a new identity after the end of colonial rule. Thus, on Uhuru Day, the history of the country is presented as a show:

> Again they recreated history, giving it life through the words and voices: Land alienation, [...] taxation, conscription of labour into the white man's land, the break with the missions, [...] Jomo [...] (*Grain of Wheat*, 189)

All this is embodied in the title of the novel, which is taken from Saint Paul's first letter to the Corinthians 15:36 and which is so very different from Achebe's title: at the end of Ngugi's novel, things have not irrevocably fallen apart, but the grain of wheat has yielded a good harvest. History therefore seems to appear as progress, a concept with which Ngugi as a student of English may have become acquainted through English historical novels and histories but certainly much more through the works of the Marxist Frantz Fanon, by whom Ngugi was increasingly influenced when he was writing *A Grain of Wheat*.[19]

---

[18] Ngugi wa Thiong'o, *A Grain of Wheat* [1967] (London, Nairobi, Ibadan: Heinemann. 1986), 203.

[19] There is, however, one concept of history as progress which is severely criticized. It is that of the British District Commissioner, who has studied history and believes in a British Empire which will rule the world and in which all men will be equal (*Grain of Wheat*, 47ff.). Ironically, it is this "Prospero in Africa" who becomes one of the worst tormentors of Africans in the novel.

And yet this reading does not do justice to the complexity of the novel. At the end, it becomes evident to the reader that the newly established national union will be burdened by unsolved problems. In the course of the novel, the villagers are shown to be Christians, but also as defenders of indigenous customs such as the circumcision of women against the humanitarian opposition of the colonizers. During the Uhuru celebrations Christian rhetoric and ritual play a great part, and the new state is compared to a "new Jerusalem" (*Grain of Wheat,* 118), but at the same time black rams are sacrificed to the indigenous gods. Moreover, the whole action is narrated from the point of view of the Gikuyu. They, however, are only one tribe in a country with a strongly mixed population, so that Kenya would stand in need of a national identity beyond Gikuyu, Turkana, Suk and Masai.[20]

These problems admittedly are in no way foregrounded in the novel. But there are other aspects whose problematical nature is emphasized indeed. Kenya on the day of independence is shown to be ruled by one party, but the only representative of the party in the novel is presented as deeply corrupt, and this puts the vision of "a new earth" in Kenya in doubt. The novel, moreover, ends with another dissonance. Mugo, who had betrayed the freedom fighter Kihika to the British, later, in a British detention camp, became a kind of national hero. Therefore, he is asked to give the main speech on Uhuru Day. But in his speech, he confesses his guilt, and he is killed on the following day. This execution, with which the action of the novel ends, is not presented directly. Instead, we are given only the reactions of Warui and Wambui, who took part in his trial and execution:

> "'Something went wrong. I was deceived by his eyes, those eyes. Maybe because I am old. I am losing my sight.'
> Wambui sat on and watched the drizzle and grey mist for a few minutes. Darkness was creeping into the hut. Wambui was lost in a solid consciousness of a terrible anti-climax to her activities in the fight for freedom. Perhaps we should not have tried him, she muttered. Then she shook herself, trying to bring her thoughts to the present. I must light the fire. First I must sweep the room. How dirt can so quickly collect in a clean hut! But she did not rise to do anything. (210)

We are never told what actually "went wrong" with Mugo's execution. But what happened seems to have caused a deep dissonance in those who took part and appears as "a terrible anti-climax" in their fight for freedom. Therefore, the fire is not lit, the dirt not swept. We can read this as a statement that the new state will remain burdened with the dirt and the guilt from the past.

Ngugi himself later was made to suffer from this. A year after the publication of *A Grain of Wheat* he gave up his position at the University of Nairobi in order to protest

---

[20] Ngugi himself has regretted the strong tendency in East Africa to see reality in terms of the tribe and not of the nation. (cf. S.A.K. Mlacha, "Crisis and Conflict in East African Literature. Cultural and Ethnic Identity: the Works of Ngugi wa Thoing'o," in Geoffrey Davis and Hena Maes-Jelinek, eds., *Crisis and Creativity in the New Literatures in English* [Amsterdam and Atlanta: Rodopi, 1990] 123-132, here 129).

against the abolition of academic freedom. In 1978, he was arrested and put into a Maximum Security Prison without trial for a year. After that he spent a long time in exile – just like Achebe.

5.

The last author to be discussed will be Salman Rushdie from India. Like Achebe and Ngugi, he has written several novels which deal with the history of his country. I shall select for discussion his best novel, *Midnight's Children* (1981).[21]

This novel is even farther away from the traditional, Scottian model of historical fiction than any other novel discussed in this paper. Nevertheless there is one basic affinity. *Midnight's Children* contains most of the major historical events in the history of India from the year of its independence up to the late seventies – the murder of Gandhi, the war between India and China in 1962, the war between India and Pakistan in 1965, the division of Pakistan into Pakistan and Bangladesh in 1971, the state of emergency under Indira Gandhi in 1975 etc. As in the traditional historical novel all these historical events are linked with a fictional protagonist, with Saleem Sinai, who is a 'mittlerer Held' like Waverley or Ivanhoe. Just like his predecessors he is "handcuffed to history"[22], that is involved in and affected by all these events. Rushdie goes even further in his connection of historical fact and fictional hero. In his novel the history of India and the history of Saleem Sinai are closely synchronized – from the birth of Saleem at the moment of midnight of 15 August 1947, which is also the moment of the birth of the new Indian state, up to the final dissolution of his body, which corresponds to the advancing dissolution of India. Therefore, *Things Fall Apart* would be an appropriate title also for Rushdie's novel.

Nevertheless, *Midnight's Children* is fundamentally different from traditional historical fiction. The latter was based on the belief in the objective character of history and in the possibility of a true description of history. This belief was still shared by the postcolonial novels previously discussed in this paper. In Rushdie's novel, however, history is nothing objective, but something extremely doubtful. Saleem Sinai, who is also the narrator, is always making mistakes in his narration of the past, he lies and forgets, and above all, as Rushdie himself put it, he always distorts "his material [so] that the reader will be forced to concede his central role" in history and thus shows that "we make the past to suit our present purposes, using memory as our

---

[21] For a more detailed interpretation of this novel see my article "'For a nation of forgetters': der Sinn der Erinnerung im Zeitalter der Dekonstruktion – Salman Rushdie's *Midnight's Children*," to be published in 1998 in Wolfgang Frühwald, Dietmar Peil, Michael Schilling, Peter Strohschneider, eds., *Erkennen und Erinnern in Kunst und Literatur* (Tübingen: Niemeyer).

[22] Salman Rushdie, *Midnight's Children* [1981] (London: Picador, 1982), 9.

tool."[23] This view of history as a subjective construct does not stand somewhere in the background of the novel but is foregrounded time and again by the narrator Saleem. Thus he tells Padma, a young woman of the people to whom he reads his autobiography:

> 'I told you the truth', I say yet again, 'Memory's truth, because memory has its own special kind. It selects, eliminates, alters, exaggerates, minimizes, glorifies, and vilifies also; but in the end it creates its own reality, its heterogeneous but usually coherent version of events; and no sane human being ever trusts someone else's version more than his own.'
> (Rushdie, *Midnight's Children*, 211)

This deconstruction of the belief in historical truth and this emphasis on the subjectivity of the historical memory have further consequences which move the novel far away from the European tradition of the historical novel. One of these consequences is that Saleem – and his author Rushdie – feel free to mix history with fantasy, as is the case, for example, when the novel narrates that on 15 August 1947 the state of India was created and that at the same midnight 1001 children with all sorts of miraculous abilities were born. Another consequence of the subjectivity of historical memory is that Saleem does not attempt to follow the linear, temporal, and causal succession of conventional history, but keeps deconstructing the linearity of his story of himself and India by never refusing to be tempted by interesting digressions. Padma, his listener, who represents the conventional reader, always becomes uneasy when Saleem departs from history into fantasy and from linearity into digressions – therefore Saleem keeps making fun of Padma's "what-happened-nextism" (Rushdie, *Midnight's Children*, 39).

There is yet another element of the traditional historical novel which is also deconstructed in *Midnight's Children*: the belief in progress and its connection with the idea of the nation. Indeed Saleem originally believed in progress, and he also believed that there would be an Indian nation, in spite of the differences of languages, religions and cultures within the subcontinent. But the point of the novel is that the historical events in India after her independence teach Saleem that his belief was an illusion, which he calls his "optimism disease" (Rushdie, *Midnight's Children*, 46), and that India will fall apart just like his own body.

It is tempting to read this deconstruction of traditional convictions and structures concerning history and the historical novel as a postcolonial deconstruction of 'western' conventions, as an indication of the Empire's writing back. This view is held, for example, by Bill Ashcroft *et al.* in their book *The Empire Writes Back*, where they state that *Midnight's Children* "deliberately [...] disrupt[s] European notions of 'history' and the ordering of time" (Rushdie, *Midnight's Children*, 34). Similarly Aruna Srivastava interprets Rushdie's novel as a postcolonial attack on 'western' conceptions of history and the writing of history.

---

[23] Salman Rushdie, "'Errata': or, Unreliable Narration in *Midnight's Children*," in Salman Rushdie, *Imaginary Homelands: Essays and Criticism 1981-1991* (London: Granta, 1991), 22-5, here 24.

This is certainly true if we identify 'western' conceptions with those of the nineteenth century. And it is also true that Rushdie in his novel confronts such conceptions of history and history writing with alternative ones which he characterizes as Indian. Thus he speaks of an Indian view of history according to which history moves in cycles of many thousand years (Rushdie, *Midnight's Children*, 194) and which believes in the essential "changelessness" (Rushdie, *Midnight's Children*, 107) of things. He also points out the "Indian disease, this urge to encapsulate the whole of reality" (Rushdie, *Midnight's Children*, 75), which makes a linear historical narration unIndian.[24]

And yet it seems obvious to me that Rushdie's major models for his deconstruction of history and history-writing are 'western'. He himself has admitted that his novel was stimulated by such historical novels as Günther Grass's *Die Blechtrommel* and Gabriel García Márquez' *Cien años de soledad*,[25] and at the same time it is evident that Rushdie, who read history at Oxford, is familiar with postmodern deconstructions of history from Robin Collingwood to Hayden White.[26]

But in spite of all these postmodernist deconstructions, Rushdie upholds the necessity of memory, and he makes his narrator Saleem tell the story of his own and India's past to "a nation of forgetters", to "an amnesiac nation" (Rushdie, *Midnight's Children*, 37, 460). The memory his novel wants to evoke is partly a historical memory, a memory of the past in spite of the falsifications by government propaganda. But it is even more a cultural memory, a memory of the cultural roots of the country. This certainly also applies to Achebe's and Ngugi's novels. When Achebe presents the indigenous culture mainly before colonization and Ngugi the political and cultural opposition against the colonizers they also invoke memory, and they do so in order to strengthen an identity which, as we have seen, is not so much national and Nigerian or Kenyan, but tribal and Igbo or Gikuyu and in which the contribution of the colonizers is played down. The point of Rushdie's novel is quite different, and it becomes particularly evident in Saleem's story of his fathers. In Grass's *Blechtrommel*, one of Rushdie's models, Oskar Matzerath has two different fathers, and he kills them both (or, to be more precise, feels responsible for the death of both). In *Midnight's Children*, however, Saleem has, as he puts it, three fathers, an English colonial officer, a Muslim businessman and a Hindu street musician, and he not only accepts all of them as his fathers but even 'invents' more fathers for himself. In this way he indicates that he has his roots not in one culture or religion only but in many, and, as his story is that of India, that this also applies to the whole subcontinent. This position is diametrically opposed to that of Walcott, who said: "I have no father. I want no such father." (Walcott, "Muse of History", 373).

---

[24] "Raja Rao has made the point that the digressional obsession of the Indian imagination [...] is as much a quality of Indian literature as Indian oral tale" (Timothy Brennan, *Salman Rushdie and the Third World. Myths of the Nation* [Houndsmills: Macmillan, 1989], 83).

[25] Cf. James Harrison, *Salman Rushdie* (New York: Twayne, 1992), 55-57.

[26] Cf. my article "For a nation of forgetters" (cf. n. 20).

Midnight's Children shows that the Partition of 1947 was based on the conviction that a nation and a state ought, as it were, to comprehend only children of one father. In his next novel, *Shame* (1983), Rushdie goes on to demonstrate that in Pakistan the ruling powers increasingly want to base their state on one national and religious identity, that of a militant Islam, and in his latest novel, *The Moor's Last Sigh* (1995), he satirizes attempts to found India entirely on a militant Hinduism. Rushdie's novels stand in opposition to these tendencies. Just as they are hybrid texts with many textual 'fathers', they also advocate a national and cultural Indian identity which is based on the recognition that India has many cultural 'fathers' none of which ought to be forgotten or suppressed. Of course such a political creed is skilfully encoded in Rushdie's novels and lies deeply hidden under a textual surface which is characterized by fragmentation and deconstruction. In his political essays, Rushdie has been able to advocate his creed more openly. Thus, in his essay written after the assassination of Indira Gandhi, he states that India, if she wants to survive as a nation, will have to become a highly decentralized state in which different cultural identities are allowed to exist side by side on an equal footing. Though I have said earlier that it is a far cry from Sir Walter Scott to Salman Rushdie, in this respect there seems to be a surprising affinity between the two authors and the convictions on which their historical novels are based.

6.

Before I can finally attempt some conclusions, I shall first say a few words on the question of whether the works on which these conclusions will be based are representative of postcolonial literatures and their approach to history. Here, two objections could be raised.

1. The historical novel is, in its different forms, a 'western' genre. Can novels like those by Achebe, Ngugi and Rushdie then be regarded as representative of postcolonial literatures? Would it not have been better to discuss the presence of history in postcolonial poetry, for example in the poems of Brathwaite or Walcott? Would it not have been even more preferable to discuss historical epics, such as *Two Thousand Seasons* (1973), a prose epic by Ayi Kwei Armah from Ghana, which is an imaginative narration of one thousand years of West African history, or *Emperor Shaka the Great* (1979), a verse epic by the South African author Mazisi Kunene, who turns the legendary Zulu king Shaka into a hero of epic dimensions?

    Apart from the fact that a comparative approach to texts from various parts of the world is easier if all these texts more or less belong to the same genre, we should not forget that the epic of Kunene or the poetry of Walcott have also partly been formed by 'western' models. The main argument in favour of discussing historical novels, however, is that there has been a spate of historical fiction in most postcolonial countries, and this is why this genre can well be regarded as representative if only on account of its numbers.

2. The second objection is to be taken more seriously. The novels by Achebe, Ngugi and Rushdie have been widely read all over the world and have at the same time been praised as great works of art also by 'western' critics. In order to be accepted by a 'western' readership these novels as a rule had to fulfil some conditions. They must be published in English, they must have a certain artistic complexity and sophistication, and I think they will also have to avoid a shrill nationalistic and anticolonialist tone (except with readers on the extreme left). The three novels which I discussed at length fulfil these conditions. Indeed, it is probable that their authors did not only write for readers in their native countries but also for readers in Europe and America. This was not too difficult for them because they were well acquainted with 'western' literature and spent a long time in 'western' countries, in some cases even settling there permanently. But can works of such writers in exile be characteristic of the literature of their countries?

Therefore, future research will also have to include postcolonial historical novels and other texts concerning history which are not widely read in 'western' countries. These studies will have to include historical novels which are written in the indigenous languages of postcolonial countries which are less critical of the present political situation in these countries, and which unhesitatingly advocate their new nation-state and a corresponding national identity. Moreover, oral literature with historical subjects and historiography from postcolonial countries will have to be studied as well.

With these qualifications in mind, I shall finally try to draw some generalizations from what I have said before. There is a world-wide revival of interest in history in former colonial countries which has also stimulated a revival of historical fiction. This applies to postcolonial literatures not only in English but also in other languages. Consequently, is therefore to be regretted that there was no room in this paper to discuss the historical novels of such authors as Mario Vargas Llosa or Gabriel García Márquez.

There is a wide variety of themes and periods in all these novels, but there seems to be a preference for two points in the history of a postcolonial nation: that of colonization and that of independence. Apart from that, there is a remarkable interest in post-independence history up to the present. Whenever contemporary history is the background of such a novel, its structure does not essentially differ from that of novels set in historical periods farther away from the present.

Most of the texts attempt to rewrite history. The imperialist approach to history is often directly mentioned in the novels – for example right at the end of *Things Fall Apart*, when the English District Commissioner intends to write a history of the *"Pacification of the Primitive Tribes of the Lower Niger"*, or when the District Commissioner in *A Grain of Wheat* voices his imperialist view of history. In the works of Achebe, Ngugi, Rushdie and many others history is rewritten from an anti-imperialist perspective and from the point of view of the former colonies. This could mean that the 'western' concept of the progress of history towards self-determination, which in colonial times had only been accepted for the countries in Europe, has now been transferred to post-colonial countries, too. This is very rarely the case, however. Such an optimistic view of history is utterly foreign to most postcolonial historical fiction available to me. In spite of many differences, in most cases history is seen to be a heavy burden which deeply oppresses the present, though few writers go as far as Walcott and demand a literature beyond history. If in this pessimistic view of history there is a period at all which appears in a more positive light, it is the period before colonization. But though this 'period before history' is sometimes presented in a nostalgic light, even authors like Achebe show the internal contradictions and rifts in the precolonial culture which, at the advent of the colonizers, contribute to its destruction.

This is why the view of the nation and of national identity in these novels is not optimistic either. Timothy Brennan speaks of "The nation-centredness of the post-colonial world" (Brennan, *Rushdie*, 5) and of the enormous importance of 'nation' and 'nationalism' "in Third-World fiction after the Second World War" (Brennan, *Rushdie*, 4). As far as the historical novels discussed in this paper – and quite a number of similar texts – are concerned, this statement cannot be confirmed. As we have seen, Achebe and Ngugi emphasize a tribal rather than a national identity. Similarly, Kunene, in his epic about the emperor Shaka, emphasizes a Zulu and Soyinka, in his historical drama *Death and the King's Horseman*, a Yoruba and not a national identity.

Apparently the concepts of 'nation' and 'national identity' are at least as problematical for these authors as that of 'history'. This can partly be explained by the fact that the typical post-colonial writer had a partly European education, spent a long time in Europe or America or even lives there for good, and is, as Rushdie repeatedly calls it in *Shame*, a "migrant", somebody placed between different cultures, with either two conflicting cultural identities or even a cosmopolitan identity. But what makes so many of these authors live far away from their country is not their lack of patriotism or their cosmopolitanism, but the political situation in their own countries after they became independent. Many postcolonial states are ruled by regimes which curb the activity of writers by censorship, imprisonment or even, as recently in Nigeria, by capital punishment. As these regimes often appeal to the ideas of the nation and of national identity, although nationhood and statehood in many postcolonial countries are undergoing a process of decomposition in our time rather than one of stabilization, these ideas have become deeply suspect to writers who are not willing to make their literary works subservient to the powers that be.

But at the same time we may assume that the view of history and of the nation – ideas so often combined in traditional historical fiction – as highly problematic and questionable is perhaps the deepest reason why so many postcolonial authors have been stimulated to write so much – and so much excellent – historical fiction.

Postmodernist Re-Writings of the Puritan Commonwealth: Winterson, Ackroyd, Mukherjee"[1]

SUSANA ONEGA (Zaragoza)

In a lecture entitled "Backwards to the Future" (Logroño, 1993) the East Anglia University Professor lately turned novelist, Christopher Bigsby, described the "theatre, film, television and the novel" of the nineteen eighties in Britain as "taking us [....] backwards, and backwards in a number of ways" (Bigsby, "Backwards," 32). In the field of drama, he contended, "the dramatist who inspired some of the more thoughtful productions and attracted some of our leading actors and actresses [was] William Shakespeare" (Bigsby, "Backwards," 32), while a similar influence was felt in the rage for adaptations of Shakespearean plays to film.

However, for Bigsby, the greatest influence on the British art of the late twentieth century was provided by the Victorian period and/or the turn of the nineteenth century. The theatre, for example, recurrently expressed a keen interest in the recuperation of spectacle, melodrama and other Victorian theatre effects, so that, "if the principal playwright of the 80s was Shakespeare, the principal form was the musical" (Bigsby, "Backwards," 33). The television, likewise, produced extremely successful historical series set in the nineteenth century, like Evelyn Waugh's *Brideshead Revisited*, or *The Jewel in the Crown*, "Paul Scott's saga set in the days of the Raj" (Bigsby, "Backwards," 33), while some of the most successful film versions were *Little Dorrit* and Merchant Ivory's *Passage to India*, *Gandhi* and *Heat and Dust*.

Bigsby identified a similar concern with the nineteenth century in the novel, which he traced back to the publication of John Fowles' *The French Lieutenant's Woman* and exemplified with Golding's trilogy of the eighties (*Rites of Passage, Close Quarters* and *Fire Down Below*), Melvyn Bragg's *The Maid of Buttermere* and Timothy Mo's *An Insular Possession*. However, he was also aware that Fowles' novel of the eighties, *A Maggot*, and Peter Ackoyd's *Hawksmoor* and *Chatterton*, are not set in the Victorian period but in the eighteenth century, that Rose Tremain's *Restoration* is set in the seventeenth century, and that Kazuo Ishiguro's novels *A Pale View of Hills*, *An Artist of the Floating World* and *The Remains of the Day* are "dominated by the Second World War" (Bigsby, "Backwards," 34).

Christopher Bigby's explanation for the backward looking trend among British writers, artists and entertainers of the eighties was twofold. It expressed, on the one hand, a longing for a past "safely fixed and transformed by nostalgia. The past is turned into icon. It is a past, moreover, in which Britain had seemed secure,

---

[1] The research carried out for the writing of this paper has been financed by the Spanish Ministry of Education (DGICYT, no. PS94-0057).

powerful, confident, the past of empire and war supremacy" (Bigsby, "Backwards," 35). On the other hand,

> there is a counter current in that the past revisited was a past which tended now to be changed with 80s insecurities [...]. Contemporary doubts about gender roles, racial attitudes and national myopia are projected backwards into the past where their roots are presumed to lie [...]. Those who wish to change the future must first change the past or lay claim to it on their own terms (Bigsby, "Backwards," 12-13).

Bigsby's identification of a "current" and a "counter current" echoes Hal Foster's contention that there are different types of postmodernisms[2] and confirms the presence in Britain of a world-wide phenomenon that had been variously described — after Hutcheon,[3] by Bertens,[4] Onega[5] and others — as characteristic of postmodernism: the renewed interest in history and the proliferation of historical novels precisely at a time when historians and philosophers of history are openly questioning the validity of the traditional concept of history understood as a scientific search for knowledge.

The close relationship of history and the novel may be traced back to the very origins of the literary genre. A clear early exponent of this relationship would be the historical romance, which came to a climax during the second and third decades of the nineteenth century in the work of Scottish writers like Sir Walter Scott, James Hogg or John Galt. This narrative trend may be said to run parallel to the development of Hegelian world history.[6] In general terms, world history aimed at the representation of the historical facts from the perspective of the dominant race, class and culture. Similarly, the aim of the nineteenth-century historical romance was to construct a historical narrative of the past which could make the dominant race, class and culture intelligible and graspable. In keeping with this view, a Marxist sociologist of literature like Georg Lukács would present the historical novel, in Diane Elam's words, as "an artistically faithful image of a concrete historical epoch."[7] Therefore, as

---

[2] Hal Foster, "(Post)Modern Polemics," *New German Critique* 33 (1984): 67-79. On the different kinds of postmodernist historical fiction, see also Ansgar Nünning, "Crossing Borders and Blurring Genres: Towards a Typology and Poetics of Postmodernist Historical Fiction in England since the 1960," *European Journal of English Studies* 1:2 (August, 1997): 217-38.

[3] Linda Hutcheon, *A Poetics of Postmodernism: History, Theory, Fiction* (New York and London: Routledge, 1988).

[4] Hans Bertens, "Postmodern Culture(s)," in Edmund J. Smyth, ed., *Postmodernism and Contemporary Fiction.* (London: B. T. Batsford Ltd, 1991), 123-37.

[5] Susana Onega, "British Historiographic Metafiction in the 1980s," in Theo D'Haen and Hans Bertens, eds., *British Postmodern Fiction* (Amsterdam and Atlanta: Rodopi, 1993), 47-61. Reprinted as "British Historiographic Metafiction," in Mark Currie, ed., *Metafiction* (London and New York: Longman, 1995), 92-103.

[6] On this, see Onega, "'A Knack for Yarns:' The Narrativization of History and the End of History," in Susana Onega, ed., *Telling Histories: Narrativizing History: Historicizing Literature* (Amsterdam and Atlanta: Rodopi, 1995), 7-18.

[7] Diane Elam, *Romancing the Postmodern* (London and New York: Routledge, 1992), 96.

Elam explains, in his analysis of Sir Walter Scott's historical romances, Lukács would systematically disregard the unrealistic, romantic element, stressing only the importance of their realistic historical material. However, as the American critic further observes, Scott's historical romances are articulated around a clash of cultures: Saxon and Norman in *Ivanhoe* or Highland tribal organisation and capitalist modernity in the Jacobite romances (Bigsby, "Backwards," 64 ff.). Invariably, the dominant culture is described realistically by recourse to history, but the "other" culture is accounted for by recourse to romance, for it is a culture already "lost" to history and historicism. And, what is more, as an orally-transmitted culture, it can only be imperfectly fathomed by the members of the dominant culture through translation.[8]

Claire Lamont makes a similar point when she notes that in Walter Scott's historical romances "the history of the dominant culture is written on top of the unwritten histories of the smaller cultures it defeated."[9] In other words, in Sir Walter Scott's historical romances, the power/bondage relationship of the dominant and dominated cultures fictionalized is echoed linguistically in terms of dominant discourse/silence.

In Mikhail Bakhtin's *Rabelais and His World* and in his essays on the novel published in *The Dialogic Imagination*, the target of his attack is language that has organized the world into false relations of hierarchy, domination, repression and silencing. In "Forms of Time and of the Chronotope in the Novel: Notes Toward a Historical Poetics," Bakhtin proposes to rewrite the representation of the objects in the world and to change the relations of human beings to them:

> It is necessary to destroy and rebuild the entire false picture of the world, to sunder the false hierarchical links between objects and ideas, to abolish the divisive ideational strata. It is necessary to liberate all these objects and permit them to enter into the free unions that are organic to them, no matter how monstrous these unions might seem from the point of view of ordinary, traditional associations [...]. It is necessary to devise new matrices between objects and ideas that will answer to their real nature, to once again line up and join together those things that had been falsely disunified and distanced from one another —as well as to disunify those things that had been falsely brought into proximity. On the basis of this new matrix of objects, a new picture of the world necessarily opens up — a world permeated with an internal and authentic necessity.[10]

In the same essay Bakhtin presents Rabelais' laughter as an effective tool for resistance and subversion of these received associations. The subversiveness of Rabelais' laughter is purely linguistic: to the dominant discourse of patriarchy Rabelais opposes "the unofficial side of speech," the "rich store of curses both simple and complex, with its various indecencies, the enormous weight carried by words and expressions

---

[8] As Flora explains to Waverley after she has translated for him the bard's song: "O you cannot guess how much you have lost!" (in Elam, *Romancing*, 68).

[9] Claire Lamont, "Waverley and the Battle of Culloden," in Angus Easson, ed. *History and the Novel* (Cambridge: D.S. Brewer, 1991),14-26, here 26.

[10] Mikhail M. Bakhtin, "Forms of Time and of the Chronotope in the Novel: Notes Toward a Historical Poetics," *The Dialogic Imagination: Four Essays* (Austin: University of Texas Press, (1934-35) 1981), 84-258, here 169.

connected with hard drinking" (Bakhtin, "Forms of Time," 238). Therefore, by opposing the eschatological and coarse "unofficial speech" of common people to the abstract and transcendental official discourse of authority, Rabelais opens up the possibility of "link[ing] up and join[ing] together those things that had been falsely disunified and distanced from one another," and so, the possibility of rewriting the world.

Bakhtin's contention that the links between objects and ideas in any hierarchical system constitute a "false picture of the world" and his definition of the novel as polyphonic, that is, as allowing for the utterance of different voices struggling for cultural preeminence, are paralleled by Hayden White's contention that traditional world history leaves out of its account many facts that remain ungraspable.[11] For White, the source of history's incompleteness and unreliability is also linguistic: it has to do with the fact that historians have always refused to deal with history in terms of "what it most manifestly is: a verbal structure in the form of a narrative prose discourse" (ix). In *Metahistory*, White establishes a deliberate parallelism between the metafictional trend in literature and the metahistorical trend in history. His contention is that both are parallel developments, reflecting the impact of Saussure's linguistic theory and the ulterior questioning of the traditional values of sign, word, and writing carried out by poststructuralist and deconstructive theory.

Drawing on the ideas of Hayden White and of other New Historicists Linda Hutcheon concludes in *The Poetics of Postmodernism* that the contradictory ethos of postmodernism is best expressed in that particular kind of self-conscious historical novel she calls "historiographic metafiction." The Canadian scholar situates the origins of this type of novel in the 1960s, a decade commonly acknowledged as a period of crisis, heralding a complex change of world-view. The development of pacifist, anti-militarist and "green" political options during this decade, as well as popular demonstrations such as the Student Revolt of May 1968 in France, and the anti-Vietnam War and Civil Rights protests in The United States, are early exponents of the widespread cultural and social reaction against the "master-narratives" of bourgeois liberalism which, according to Jean-François Lyotard,[12] characterizes our postmodernist era. These popular movements, generated at the "fringes" of patriarchy, characteristically offered the competing and/or complementary world-views of the sexual, political, ethnic and religious margins of patriarchy, thus aiming, to borrow Bakhtin's words, "to destroy and rebuild the entire false picture of the world, to sunder the false hierarchical links between objects and ideas" and substitute them with other "natural" links, "no matter how monstrous these unions might seem from the point of view of ordinary, traditional associations."

In conclusion, if in Sir Walter Scott's historical romances (and in Bigsby's "current") the past is recreated in order to make the dominant (patriarchal and imperi-

---

[11] Hayden White, *Metahistory: The Historical Imagination in Nineteenth-Century Europe* (Baltimore and London: The Johns Hopkins University Press, 1984).

[12] Jean-François Lyotard, *The Postmodern Condition: A Report on Knowledge* (Minneapolis: University of Minnesota Press, 1984).

alist) culture intelligible and graspable, in this subversive and marginal kind of historical novel (as in Bigsby's "counter current") the recreation of the past is aimed, rather, at finding vital answers for the present and the future.

Christopher Bigsby mentioned Rose Tremain's *Restoration* as an example of a historical novel set in the seventeenth century. Although this novel is focused from the "marginal" perspective of Robert Merivel, a young physician turned Royal Veterinary to the King's dogs, Tremain's novel, set in the court of Charles II, with its display of Frenchified tastes and its anti-Puritan zest for pleasure, may be said to respond to Bigsby's first category, the kind of historical novel whose recreation of the past is "safely fixed and transformed by nostalgia," a novel, that is, which, like Sir Walter Scott's historical romances, seeks to reinforce rather than undermine the discourse of the dominant culture and make it intelligible and graspable.[13] By contrast, more experimental and "marginal" historiographic metafictions like Jeanette Winterson's *Sexing the Cherry* (1989), Peter Ackroyd's *Milton in America* (1996), or Bharati Mukherjee's *The Holder of the World* (1993), also set in the seventeenth century, might be said to respond to Bigsby's second category, that is, to the type of contemporary historical novel evincing "doubts about gender roles, racial attitudes and national myopia," (Bigsby, „Backwards," 12-13) novels, that is, which, in line with Bakhtin's proposal, seek to revisit the past in order to subvert the "false notions" inherited from it as a way of changing the present and the future. In keeping with this aim, the false ideology denounced by these novels is either that of the Puritan Commonwealth, the worst period of religious fanaticism and patriarchal totalitarianism in British history, or that of the effects of its burgeoning imperialism in Asia and America.

In the pages that follow an attempt will be made to show how these three totally different writers go back to the period of the Puritan Commonwealth with Bakhtin's proposal in mind "to destroy and rebuild the entire false picture of [that] world," and how, even though they are writing from different "marginal" positions, they will create strikingly similar "free unions" between objects and ideas, in their attempt to find answers to their "troubled" relationship with the world.

***

Since the Students' Revolt of 1969, French feminism steadily developed in different directions. In particular, the work of Antoinette Fouque, Hélène Cixous and other French feminists associated with the group "Psychanalyse et Politique" (*Psych et Po*), has exerted a great influence on women writers attempting to "rewrite the world" from a feminine perspective. Succintly stated, the aim of *Psych et Po* is to develop revolutionary theories of the oppression of women through the systematic re-reading of the outstanding texts of psychoanalysis. Their basic contention is that the way out of patriarchal oppression lies in an alternative, feminine practice of writing. Thus, to the Lacanian phallus, symbol of male hegemony and power, Cixous opposes the female body, which she de-

---

[13] Another case in point would be Christopher Bigsby's own sequel to Nathaniel Hawthorne's *The Scarlet Letter* entitled *Pearl* (1995).

fines as culturally specific, as caught up in representation, in language. Therefore, for Cixous the new *écriture feminine* should aim at discursively creating subjectivities that would be plural and shifting (bisexual), that would break up the set of hierarchical oppositions which, she argues, have structured Western thought and governed its political practice, such as "culture/nature," "head/heart," "form/matter," "speaking/writing," derived from the basic opposition "man/woman." Cixous insists that, if feminine writing is to escape from and displace man's discourse, if should exist outside the traditional (male) narrative structures, for, as she explains in "Sorties:" "woman has always functioned 'within' man's discourse [...] now it is time for her to displace this 'within,' explode it, overturn it, grab it, make it hers."[14]

In order to achieve this aim, Jeanette Winterson, like Angela Carter, Margaret Atwood and many other contemporary women writers, recurrently has recourse to fantasy, a literature whose subversiveness lies in that it works to dissolve structures, moving both towards an ideal of entropic *undifferentiation,* "of transgression of the limits separating self from other, man from woman, human from animal, organic from inorganic objects,"[15] and towards the opposite pole of constant metamorphosis, with its stress upon instability of natural forms, expressive of its rejection of the notion of the self as a coherent, indivisible and continuous whole held by traditional "realist" fiction. As Rosemary Jackson explains, "it is precisely this subversion of unities of "self" which constitutes the most radical transgressive function of the fantastic"(Jackson, *Fantasy*, 83).

In *Sexing the Cherry*, the pull towards undifferentiation and transgression of the traditional (male) narrative structures is carried out at the narrative level by the fact that, instead of just one narrative instance, the narration alternates and doubles two intradiegetic narrative voices separated by a gap of two hundred years. The novel opens with the retrospective account of the Dog-Woman, running from about 1630 — the year of birth of her adopted son, Jordan[16] — until the Great Fire of London of 1666. This narration is made up of the apparently "real" facts of the Dog-Woman's and her son's meagre and marginal lives by the Thames, on the outskirts of London. With it alternates Jordan's recording in a "travel book" of his journeys to remote lands as helpmate to John Tradescant Jr., Charles I's Royal Gardener and an expert in the new technique of grafting. Echoing T. S. Eliot,[17] Jordan warns us at the beginning of the novel that, unlike traditional travel books, his recorded journeys are "Not the

---

[14] Morag Shiach, *Hélène Cixous: A Politics of Writing* (London and New York: Routledge, 1991), 22. On the way in which female writers deconstruct classical male myths, see Susanne Schmid's "Mythomaniacs: Contemporary Women Writers and Their Use of Myth," in Uwe Böker and Hans Sauer, eds., *Anglistentag 1996 Dresden Proceedings* (Trier: Wissenschaftlicher Verlag, 1997), 363-71.

[15] Rosemary Jackson, *Fantasy: The Literature of Subversion* (London and New York: Methuen, 1981), 73.

[16] Jeanette Winterson, *Sexing the Cherry* (London et. al.: Vintage, (1989) 1990), 21.

[17] Jordan's words echo Eliot's fourth category of time in "Burnt Norton": „what might have been" (T. S. Eliot, *The Four Quartets,* in *Collected Poems (1909-1962)* (London: Faber and Faber, (1963) 1974), 189.

ones I made, but the ones I might have made" (*Sexing the Cherry*, 10). The reader's expectations thus raised, are, however, immediately undermined by the discovery that, instead of a recording of the paths imagined or dreamt by Jordan, the travel book contains, rather, overtly derivative versions of earlier literary texts. Thus, for example, although his search for Fortunata is presented as a mythical hero's quest for individuation of the self,[18] it nevertheless takes Jordan to the well-known folk-tale world of the *Twelve Dancing Princesses*, and what is more, as Elizabeth Langland[19] has pointed out, for all the apparent deviation of the Grimm brothers' version of the tale, Jordan's report of the Princesses' stories is not original but intertextually charged with parodic echoes of well-known Romantic poems:

> For example, [...] the second princess begins her narrative with the words, "That's my last husband painted on the wall... looking as though he were alive," explicitly evoking Browning's Duke, the speaker of "My Last Duchess." In Winterson's revisionary narrative the second princess echoes the Duke's repression and stifling of his Duchess in her own macabre murder of her husband [...]. The third princess parodies Byron, beginning, "He walked in beauty." Denied his beauty because "it was a boy he loved," she "pierced them with a single arrow where they lay" (Langland, "'Sexing the Text,'" 50).

In the last section of the novel, the setting unexpectedly switches from the mid-seventeenth century to the present moment. Two new twentieth-century characters, a naval cadet called Nicholas Jordan and an anonymous ecologist, alternate the narration with the Dog-Woman and Jordan. These characters are clearly identified as the contemporary re-incarnations of the seventeenth-century protagonists, for they share the same vital attitudes, thoughts and even words with them. Like the seventeenth-century characters, these solitary hero and heroine are perfectly aware of their "difference" and "marginality" with respect to the predominant social order, and they are attracted to each other by the realization that they must fight such emblems of patriarchal power as "the World Bank" and "the Pentagon" and "the world leaders" (*Sexing the Cherry*, 121), who are contributing to the destruction of the planet with their policy of unmitigated capitalism.

Structurally, the merging of the seventeenth and the twentieth centuries and the blending of the characters' voices and actions disrupt the linear chronology of history in favour of the cyclical temporality of myth, also suggested by the parallel (apocalyptic) fires with which the stories in both historical periods end: the burning of

London in the Great Fire of 1666, and the destruction of the factory that is poisoning a river with mercury by Nicholas Jordan and the ecologist.

---

[18] Jordan himself suggests that his search for Fortunata is a self-quest when he says that he might not be "searching for a dancer whose name I did not know [but] for the dancing part of myself" (*Sexing the Cherry*, 40).

[19] Elizabeth Langland, "'Sexing the Text:' Narrative Drag as Feminist Poetics and Politics in *Sexing the Cherry*," *Narrative* 5.1 (January, 1997): 99-107.

The fact that Jordan's "literary" travel book of "possible" journeys alternates with the Dog-Woman's factual narration of past events, may be said to provide a (historical) narrative and a (literary) counter-narrative that echoes and parodies at the structural level the traditional separation of reality/unreality, history/storytelling, lived/imagined. However, no sooner has the reader established this dichotomy that he or she will be struck by the realization of its inadequacy. For all the fantastic and literary echoes of his travel book, Jordan himself seems to be a perfectly "real" and "normal" young man who, like other men in patriarchal societies, dreams of being a hero: "I want to be brave and admired and have a beautiful wife and a fine house. I want to be a hero and wave goodbye to my wife and children at the dock, and be sorry to see them go but more excited about what is to come. I want to be like other men [...]" (*Sexing the Cherry*, 101). By contrast, although the Dog-Woman, like women in patriarchy, enjoys gentlemanly deference and feminine grace,[20] she has a fantastically huge, grotesque body and an ugly face pitted with smallpox marks as big as caves where fleas live (24-5).[21] However, she cannot find fault with her physical aspect. She thinks nothing of the fact that the local parson has denied her a place in the parish choir on the grounds that she looks like a gargoyle,[22] and when a frustrated lover complained that she was too big for sexual intercourse, she simply retorted — like Gulliver to the King of Brobdingnag[23] — that her bodily parts seemed "all in proportion" to her (*Sexing the Cherry*, 107).

With Cixous's words in mind, it is easy to see that the Dog-Woman's affirmation of her natural grace and feminine delicacy and her insistence on the perfect proportions of her huge body are meant to destabilize and overturn the conventional canon of beauty attributed to women in patriarchy. In *The Madwoman in the Attic*, Sandra M. Gilbert and Susan Gubar show how patriarchal literature and art constantly display a plethora of repressive mechanisms to dissuade women from attempting to step out of their allotted roles within the patriarchal social order and how the transgressive woman is made to feel in constant danger and fear of being labelled as mad and/or monstrous:

> [...] male ambivalence about female "charms" underlies the traditional images of such terrible sorceress-goddesses as the Sphinx, Medusa, Circe, Kali, Delilah, and Salome, all

---

[20] "I am gracious by nature and I allowed myself to be led" (*Sexing the Cherry*, 20).

[21] She has been compared by the critics to Gargantua (Eugene Wildman, "*Sexing the Cherry*, by Jeanette Winterson," *Chicago Tribune* (5 June, 1990): 3; Lewis Buzbee, "Hidden Journeys, Mythical History," *San Francisco Chronicle* (15 April, 1990): 9; and Michael Dirda, "A Cornucopia of Earthly Delights," *The Washington Post* (13 May, 1990): x09), and also to Jaba the Hutt, (the alien monster in *The Return of the Jedi* in the *Star Wars* series), and Fevvers, the bird-woman in Angela Carter's *Nights at the Circus* (Dirda, "Cornucopia," x09).

[22] "Singing is my pleasure, but not in church, for the parson said the gargoyles must remain in the outside, not seek room in the choir stalls. So I sing against the mountain of my flesh" (*Sexing the Cherry*, 14).

[23] Jonathan Swift, *Gulliver's Travels* (Harmondsworth: Penguin Books, (1726) 1989), 143.

of whom possess duplicitous arts that allow them both to seduce and to steal male generative energy.

The sexual nausea associated with all these monster women helps explain why so many real women have for so long expressed loathing of (or at least anxiety about) their own, inexorable female bodies. The "killing" of oneself into an art object — the pruning and preening, the mirror madness, and concern with odors and aging, with hair which is invariably too curly or too lank, with bodies too thin or too thick — all this testifies to the efforts women have expended not just trying to be angels but trying *not* to become female monsters.[24]

In her book *Powers of Horror: An Essay on Abjection*,[25] Julia Kristeva, drawing on Lacanian theory, offers an interesting analysis of the maternal figure as abject. As she explains, abjection, as a source of horror, works within patriarchal societies as a means of separating the human from the non-human and the fully constituted subject from the partially formed subject. For Kristeva, one of the key figures of abjection in patriarchy is that of the mother, who, she contends, becomes a figure of abjection at that moment when the child, struggling to become a separate subject, rejects her for the father who represents the symbolic order. In order to tackle the danger of the child succumbing to the temptation of remaining locked in the blissful relationship with its mother, patriarchal religions have developed complex rituals of defilement. These rituals, whose function is "to ward off the subject's fear of his very own identity sinking irretrievably into the mother" (Kristeva, *Powers*, 64), are of two basic types: excremental (or external) and menstrual (or internal):

> Excrements and its equivalents (decay, infection, disease, corpse, etc) stand for the danger to identity that comes from without: the ego threatened by the non-ego, society threatened by its outside, life by death. Menstrual blood, on the contrary, stands for the danger issuing from within identity (social or sexual); it threatens the relationship between the sexes within a social aggregate and, through internalization, the identity of each seen in the face of sexual difference (Kristeva, *Powers*, 7).

As Barbara Creed, commenting on Kristeva's theory, explains, "Both categories of polluting objects relate to the mother; the relation of menstrual blood is self-evident, the association of excremental objects with the maternal figure is brought about because of the mother's role in sphincteral training."[26] The mother's teaching of the child to control its body and to distinguish the clean and unclean areas of it — what Kristeva calls the semiotic "primal mapping of the body" — represents the child's first experience of "maternal authority," which is prior to and different from the "paternal

---

[24] Sandra M. Gilbert and Susan Gubar, *The Madwoman in the Attic: The Woman Writer and the Nineteenth-century Literary Imagination* (New Haven and London: Yale University Press, (1979) 1984), 34.

[25] Julia Kristeva, *Powers of Horror: An Essay on Abjection* (New York: Columbia University Press, 1982).

[26] Barbara Creed, "Horror and the Monstrous-Feminine: *An Imaginary Abjection,*" *Screen* 27.1 (1986): 69.

law" which, according to Lacan, will be acquired by the child during the phallic phase through the acquisition of language (Kristeva, *Powers*, 72).

As Creed notes, while the acquisition of "paternal law" involves immersion in a "'totally different universe of socially signifying performances where embarrassment, shame, guilt, desire, etc. come into play,'" the earlier phase of "maternal authority" is characterised by the "exercise of 'authority' without guilt, at a time when there is a 'fusion between mother and nature'" (Creed, "Monstrous-Feminine," 69). Therefore, images of blood, vomit, pus, faeces, etc, which are central to our culturally/socially constructed notions of the horrific, provoke a double reaction that echoes the split between the two orders: the maternal authority and the law of the father:

> On the one hand, these images of bodily wastes threaten a subject that is already constituted, in relation to the symbolic, as "whole and proper." Consequently, they fill the subject —both the protagonist in the text and the spectator in the cinema— with disgust and loathing. On the other hand, they also point back to a time when a "fusion between mother and nature" existed; when bodily wastes, while set apart from the body, were not seen as objects of embarrassment and shame (Creed, "Monstrous-Feminine," 70).

In other words, the contemplation of the abject produces contrary reactions according to whether the beholder is an "already constituted subject" who feels the phallogocentric symbolic system threatened, or whether he (or she) still is in a position to recuperate his (or her) first experience of "maternal authority," and "go back to a time when bodily wastes [...] were not seen as objects of embarrassment and shame." With this distinction in mind, it is easy to see why the Dog-Woman's loving mother, her son Jordan, his friend Tradescant and the Dog-Woman's female friends, the nuns and whores, are not at all revolted or frightened by the Dog-Woman and even yearn to be like her, as happens to Jordan, who, conscious of his bodily limitations, imagines the possibility of using the technique of grafting for himself in order to "become someone else in time, grafted on to something better and stronger" (*Sexing the Cherry*, 87). Indeed, it is only the "already constituted (male) subjects," those who feel their phallogocentric symbolic system threatened, who find the Dog-Woman's body "monstrous:" the parson mentioned above who compared her to a gargoyle, the Dog-Woman's own father, who wanted to sell her as a freak in a travelling fair (*Sexing the Cherry*, 107), and Puritans like Preacher Scroggs and Neighbour Firebrace (*Sexing the Cherry*, 63), who are seized not only by disgust and loathing but sheer terror at the sight of her.

According to Kristeva, the external manifestations of the abject that the subject finds most loathsome are bodily wastes such as blood, faeces or pus, rotting flesh and ultimately the corpse. Consequently, these are the elements the Dog-Woman is constantly associated with. She considers "rotting a common experience" (*Sexing the Cherry*, 105), thinks nothing of helping to collect hundreds of rotting corpses during the Plague of 1665, and when she finds that one of the deceased is a friend of hers, she heroically carries her body on her shoulder to the bottom of the infernal pit where the corpses are being burned, on the simple reflexion that it is an "indignity to be tossed aside" (*Sexing the Cherry*, 140). When, in order to gain admittance to the

King's trial, she has to think of a disguise, she sits on a wheelbarrow "like a heap of manure" (*Sexing the Cherry*, 68), and gains immediate access telling the horrified soldier at the door that she cannot stand, "for I have the Clap and my flesh is rotting beneath me. If I were to stand up, sir, you would see a river of pus run across these flags." (*Sexing the Cherry*, 69).

On this occasion, "the soldier's lip twitch[ed]" (*Sexing the Cherry*, 69) with nausea just *imagining* what her clothes hid. On another, the Dog-Woman provoked "a great swooning amongst the crowd" (*Sexing the Cherry*, 25), simply raising her skirts and showing the naked lower half of her huge body. The reaction of the crowd is as misogynistic as the nausea Gulliver felt when, reduced to one twelfth of his normal size, he was allowed to contemplate the Brobdingnagian Maids of Honour in their nakedness (Swift, *Gullivers' Travels*, 158). As I pointed out elsewhere,[27] the monstrosity of the Dog-Woman's lower half is comparable to that of such mythical half-woman/half-beast monsters as the sirens and harpies, and their English counterparts, like Errour in the *Faerie Queene*, who is half-woman, half-serpent, herself the prototype of a long list of female monsters created by man's fear of female power (according to Gilbert and Gunbar, *Madwoman*, 3-44). Indeed, the Dog-Woman is literally associated with a specifically Puritan monster, Milton's Sin in *Paradise Lost*:[28] when she arrived in Wimbledon with Jordan and her dogs, "a half wit went foaming and stuttering to Mr Tradescant, crying that the garden had been invaded by an evil spirit and her Hounds of Hell" (*Sexing the Cherry*, 29).

The fact that the Dog-Woman lives on the bank of the Thames, in a watery and earthy world inhabited only by hounds and a haggard and derelict witch under her protection, that is, literally outside the bounds of the city governed by Puritan rule, brings to mind Lacan's distinction between the imaginary and the symbolic order.[29] Now, according to Julia Kristeva's reading of Lacan, the relationship between mother and son in the natural realm of the maternal feminine (Lacan's imaginary) is problematic because, while the child tries to break free from her, the mother feels the contrary urge to retain the child as a way to authenticate her existence. Their separation, therefore,

> is a violent, clumsy breaking away, with the constant risk of falling back under the sway of a power as securing as it is stifling. The difficulty the mother has in acknowledging (or

---

[27] Susana Onega, "Jeanette Winterson's Politics of Uncertainty in *Sexing the Cherry*," in Chantal Cornut-Gentille and José Angel García Landa, eds., *Gender Issues in Literature and Film* (Amsterdam and Atlanta: Rodopi, 1996), 351-69.

[28] Sin is the abject mother condemned to give birth to innumerable Hell Hounds, only to be endlessly devoured by her own children, in a dreadful eternal cycle.

[29] According to Lacan, the phallus is the symbol of power, ruling the symbolic order, that is, the order of signs and social and cultural life brought about by the acquisition of language. Before entering the symbolic order, the male child, during the pre-Oedipal period, is in the imaginary, where he feels at one with the mother and has no sense of his own difference from her. Jacques Lacan, "Le stade du miroir comme formateur de la fonction du je," *Ecrits I* (Paris: Seuil, (1949) 1966), 93-5.

being acknowledged by) the symbolic realm — in other words, the problem she has with the phallus that her father or husband stands for — is not such as to help the future subject leave the natural mansion (Kristeva, *Powers*, 13).

The Dog-Woman's indiscriminate fury against the male Puritans might be read as evidence that she has "a problem" with the phallus. She has blinded — that is, symbolically castrated, according to Freud — or murdered hundreds of men starting with her own father, a rapist and a Dog-Man in the literal and also in the symbolic sense of the term. The only time she found a man brave enough to attempt to have sex with her, she "pulled him in, balls and everything" without being stirred (*Sexing the Cherry*, 106). And when an exhibitionist asked her to put his member in her mouth, he was rewarded with the materialization of the abstract fear of castration which, according to Freud[30] is associated to the sight of the female genitals: she bit it off and spat it out disgustedly (*Sexing the Cherry*, 40). Indeed, this episode and the fact that she sleeps on a bed made of watercress and the teeth she has torn from the skulls of the Puritans she has murdered, present the Dog-Woman from the perspective of patriarchy as the monstrous embodiment of Freud's *vagina dentata*, and her counterpart, Joseph Campbell's "phallic mother,"[31] the castrating mother of primitive men's fears.

However, the reason why the Dog-Woman bit off the exhibitionist's member was simply that she agreed to follow his instructions literally, out of innocent curiosity, and not metaphorically, as he had meant her to do: "I like to broaden my mind when I can and I did as he suggested, swallowing it up entirely and biting it off with a snap, [... then] feeling both astonished by his rapture and disgusted by the leathery thing filling up my mouth, spat out what I had not eaten and gave it to one of my dogs" (*Sexing the Cherry*, 41). Similarly, her decision to pluck out the teeth and eyes of every Puritan she came across was triggered off by her desire to fulfill literally the instructions she had been given in a fiery sermon on "the Law of Moses: 'an eye for an eye and a tooth for a tooth'" (*Sexing the Cherry*, 84). In other words, her motivation is not so much the desire to appropriate the phallus, but rather her inability to take for granted what Bakhtin called above "the false hierarchical links between objects and ideas" that make up "the entire false picture of the [Puritan] world" (Bakhtin, "Forms of Time," 169). It is precisely the Dog-Woman's colossal incapacity to accept the metaphors of patriarchy that makes her so terrifying: her literal reading of the Puritans' instructions allows her to show how deadly their metaphors are and to open up a space for the construction of "new links between objects and ideas" that would respond to a new, more authentic picture of the world.

Once this is understood, it is easy to see that the Dog-Woman does not suffer from what Kristeva describes as "the problem she [the abject mother] has with the phallus that her father or husband stands for." The Dog-Woman does not feel the need to appropriate the phallus simply because she is totally unaware of the patriarchal equations man=self, woman=other. As Jordan explains, "She has never been in love, no,

---

[30] Sigmund Feud, "Fetishism," in *On Sexuality* (Harmondsworth: Pelican Freud Library, VII, (1927) 1981), 354.

[31] Joseph Campbell, *The Masks of God: Primitive Mythology* (New York: Penguin, 1969), 73.

and never wanted to be either. She is self sufficient and without self-doubt" (*Sexing the Cherry*, 101). At the beginning of her narration, the Dog-Woman confessed that she would have liked to have a child of her own, but "you have to have a man for that and there's no man who's a match for me" (*Sexing the Cherry*, 11). Therefore, it was Nature itself which provided her with a child: the river deposited at her door a baby "so caked in mud I could have baked him like a hedgehog" (*Sexing the Cherry*, 14). Since that day, the Dog-Woman's relation to her son is built on freedom and undemanding love, not on possessiveness or restraint: "I wanted to give him [Jordan] a river name, a name not bound to anything. When a woman gives birth her waters break and she pours out the child and the child runs free" (*Sexing the Cherry*, 11).[32] It is this water and earth symbolism, with its connotations of maternity, cyclical renewal and cosmic regeneration, and the association of maternal authority with Nature that best expresses the symbolic identity of the Dog-Woman. Her enormous body perfectly responds to Mikhail Bakhtin's description of the grotesque body characteristic of carnival imagery, as found, for example, in Shakespeare, Cervantes, Diderot, Voltaire, Swift and Rabelais.[33] As Bahktin recalls, grotesque imagery, with its emphasis on "the life of the belly and the reproductive organs"[34] symbolizes "the contact with earth as an element that swallows up and gives birth at the same time" (Bahktin, *Rabelais*, 21). It is within the context of the Dog-Woman's close relationship to Nature that we should interpret the basic metaphor the novel proposes in its title: the "sexing" or grafting of cherries. Elizabeth Langland has pointed out how Winterson takes the phrase "sexing the cherry" from Andrew Marvell's speaker in the poem "The Mower, Against Gardens." As she explains, "That speaker posits pastoral against heroic ideals, domestic against imperial virtues, endorsing an idealized and static view of 'plain and pure' nature against a conception of cultivation and innovation as vice ridden" (Langland, "'Sexing the Text,'" 104).

When Jordan was three years old, he was tremendously impressed by the sight of the first banana brought from the Bermudas to England. Watching it, the Dog-Woman concluded that "'Such a thing never grew in Paradise'" (*Sexing the Cherry*, 12), but she found she was wrong when Jordan shared with her his vision of "deep blue waters against a pale shore and trees whose branches sang with green and birds in fairground colours and an old man in a loin-cloth" (*Sexing the Cherry*, 13). This vision of an exotic, paradisal Golden Country untouched by civilization will trigger off Jordan's

---

[32] Jordan is not only aware of his freedom, he is even hurt by the apparent indifference of his mother: "We never discussed whether or not I would go; she took it for granted, almost as though she had expected it. I wanted her to ask me to stay, just as now I want Fortunata to ask me to stay" (*Sexing the Cherry*, 101).

[33] As the Dog-Woman's twentieth-century *alter ego*, the nameless ecologist, explains: "I wasn't fat because I was greedy; I hardly ate at all. I was fat because I wanted to be bigger than all the things that were bigger than me. All the things that had power over me. It was a battle I intended to win [...]. But there is no Rabelaisian dimension for rage" (*Sexing the Cherry*, 124).

[34] Mikhail Bakhtin, *Rabelais and His World* (Indiana: Indiana University Press, (1966) 1984), 21.

yearning for travel, and he himself will return from the Barbados many years later, after Tradescant and Cromwell are dead (*Sexing the Cherry*, 104), with another unheard-of fruit, the first pineapple. Jordan's journey brings to mind another poem by Andrew Marvell, "Bermudas."[35] In it, a providential God leads "a small boat [...] through the watery maze/ Unto an isle so long unknown,/ And yet far kinder than our own?" (ll. 3, 6-8), where, besides oranges, pomegranates and melons, the seafarers find "apples plants [i. e., pineapples] of such a price,/ No tree could ever bear them twice" (ll. 23-4). Marvell's idea that pineapples can only grow once, interestingly undermines the moral scruple against grafting and the manipulation of nature in general that Marvell himself voiced through the speaker in "The Mower, Against Gardens,"[36] for if the pineapple can only grow once, it exists in nature independently of the laws of reproduction. And this is precisely the overall message the novel conveys: the existence of the Dog-Woman, who is both a virgin and a mother[37] questions the very idea of order on which Marvell's nature/culture opposition rests, since it allows for the existence of "exotic" natural forms: the loving mother/son relationship established between herself and Jordan is separated from the biological reproductive functions, and so is the perfect female friendship existing between the Dog-Woman and the nuns and whores living under Puritan rule, whose roles are presented as interchangeable, in clear reference to the patriarchal definition of woman as virgin/whore (the characteristics of Jung's anima).

***

Andrew Marvell's and Jordan's attribution of paradisal features to the Bermudas and the Barbadoes was a common seventeenth-century metaphor that became a literal belief for the most radical Puritans after the fall of the Commonwealth. Basically, the intention of the Puritans was to "purify" the Church of England by eradicating everything that seemed to have no Biblical justification. They were all religious zealots, with a fierce sense of moral rectitude and self-righteousness. Their religious intransigence came to a climax in the "Covenant of Grace" defended by the more radical faction, the "Separatists," who "taught that only those men and women upon whom God sheds His grace are saved because this allows them to believe in Christ; those excluded from God's grace lack the power to believe in a Saviour, thus are not

---

[35] Andrew Marvell, "Bermudas," in Margaret Ferguson, Mary Jo Salter and Jon Stallworthy, eds., *The Norton Anthology of Poetry* (New York and London: Norton, (1681) 1970), 433-4.

[36] He condemns the gardener's "Forbidden mixtures" (l. 22) because they produce "uncertain and adulterate fruit" (l. 25), and transforms the garden into "His green seraglio [that] has its eunuchs too" (l. 27). Andrew Marvell, "The Mower, Against Gardens," in Margaret Ferguson, Mary Jo Salter and Jon Stallworthy, eds., *The Norton Anthology of Poetry* (New York and London: Norton (1681) 1970), 440-41.

[37] The joke is double when we realise that her "unnatural" condition is precisely that of the Virgin Mary.

only not saved but damned."[38] James Hogg's gothic tale, *The Private Memoirs and Confessions of a Justified Sinner* (1824), constitutes a darkly ludicrous, telling parody of the atrocious consequences of believing that the "Elect" can do no wrong, that even their most loathsome and unnatural crimes will eventually be "justified" by God.

Before the Civil Wars, many "Separatists," incapable of accepting Charles I's pro-Catholic policy, went into exile in America, thus becoming the "Pilgrims" who settled in Plymouth, Massachusetts, in the 1620s. Many others joined them after the collapse of the Commonwealth. Looking at the Bible for a justification of their defeat and the restoration of the monarchy, these Puritans convinced themselves that their expulsion from England was a re-enactment of the expulsion from Eden, and that the defeat of the Commonwealth signified the loss of the Covenant between Adam and God. Now, as Emily Miller Budick explains, "In the Old Testament, the story of the sacrifice of Isaac stands between the fall and the promised land. It establishes the covenant with Israel that, in the New Testament, became the type of the new covenant secured by the sacrifice of the divine son, Christ."[39] Therefore, for the Puritans, America became Israel, the promised land of the new covenant and the Pilgrims themselves, "uniquely, American Israelites, the sole reliable exegetes of a new, last book of scripture" (Bercovitch, in Budick, 38). As Budick notes, this biblical interpretation of their recent past, involved the erasure of history:

> The American Puritans claimed to be historical typologists. But identifying themselves so thoroughly and literally with the ancient Israelites as to become "American Israelites," the nation of Israel incarnate, they essentially erased the historical dimension of the text. They allowed for no difference between Old Testament and new America [...]. Rendering the biblical text in their own image, they converted the history of scripture into the history of self (Budick, *Fiction*, 38).

Peter Ackroyd's latest novel, *Milton in America* [40] takes the figure of John Milton as the symbol of the Separatist mentality that materialised in the construction of the first Puritan settlements in New England. He imagines the blind poet travelling to America with the self-imposed task of creating the perfect Commonwealth, instead of staying in England to write *Paradise Lost* and *Paradise Regained*. Milton is accompanied in this journey by a "London poor boy" (*Milton*, 22) he had encountered on the road, nicknamed "Goosequill," who is to act as his scrivener and guide. Their ship, fittingly called *Gabriel*, like the archangel in charge of the gates of Eden, is shipwrecked near the bay of Massachusetts. However, like the sailors led to the Bermudas by God's providential hand in Marvell's above-quoted poem, Goosequill and Milton survive the shipwreck (*Milton*, 59), and manage to preserve their lives in the wilderness until they encounter Eleazar Lusher, the beaver hunter who leads them to New

---

[38] Joyce Carol Oates, "The King of the Weird," *The New York Review* (October, 1996): 46.
[39] Emily Miller Budick, *Fiction and Historical Consciousness: The American Romance Tradition* (New Haven and London: Yale University Press, 1989), 37.
[40] Peter Ackroyd, *Milton in America* (London: Sinclair-Stevenson, 1996).

Tiverton, the Separatist settlement (*Milton*, 81) that will immediately be renamed New Milton in the poet's honour on condition that he becomes their spiritual leader.

Before accepting their offer, the poet submits his leadership to a general vote (*Milton*, 110) and insists that "Where men are equal they ought to have an equal interest in government" (*Milton*, 111). However, Milton will in fact never listen to any of his followers or to Goosequill's frequent criticisms, and he promulgates strictly repressive laws for his own brethren which contemplate all kinds of physical and psychological tortures and even death. What is more, for all the proofs of friendship and good will of their Catholic neighbours, the nearby settlers of Mary Mount, Milton's policy will be invariably aimed at the eradication of the Catholic and Indians from New England for, although he is ready to concede that the Indians were originally "very like the ancient Britons" (*Milton*, 133), that is, innocent and pure "natural men," he believes that they have degenerated and become like "those heathen Irish who used to feed upon the buttocks of boys and the paps of women" (*Milton*, 133). For Milton, the basic difference between the Indians (or any other kind of "heathen," including the Catholics) and the Puritan settlers is precisely that while the former still live according to the "law of nature," the latter live according to the "moral law," a law that "is grounded on the principles of nature and right reason" (*Milton*, 129), but enlightened by ("true") religion.

The narrow-mindedness of Milton and his "Particular Separatist Elect" contrasts with the liberality of the Catholic settlers of Mary Mount, who, like the inhabitants of Thomas More's *Utopia*, have built their settlements on the principles of religious toleration and racial and sexual equality. Like the Utopians, who belonged to "different sects," yet were ready to agree that there is one "Supreme Being [...] identical with Nature"[41], the Catholics of Mary Mount are ready to admit that "Kiwasa [...] is much like our Holy Spirit" (*Milton*, 178) and do not see any harm in allowing the Indians to burn tobacco instead of incense in honour of the Virgin (*Milton*, 178). Where the Utopians had "nothing to be seen or heard in their churches which can't equally well be applied to all religions" (*Milton*, 125), in Mary Mount there are two adjacent tents, one with an image of the Virgin and another with the Indian wooden idol of "a man or god squatting upon the ground" (*Milton*, 178). And both shrines were situated where the Pequots, who had sold the land to Ralph Kempis, the Catholic leader of Mary Mount, had said that there was "a spring of sacred water which cured agues and fever" (*Milton*, 185).

The most characteristic trait of the Mary Mount settlers is their preternatural merriment, which (besides the phonetic similarity of the names of both settlements) aligns them to the carnivalesque world of Nathaniel Hawthorne's sketch "The Maypole of Merry Mount."[42] In this sketch, a "New England annalist" records the history of the "gay colony" of Mount Wollaston or Merry Mount, the site of an early trading com-

---

[41] Thomas More, *Utopia* (Penguin: Harmondsworth, (1516) 1971), 117, 118.
[42] Nathaniel Hawthorne, "The Maypole of Merry Mount," in Thomas E. Connolly, ed., *Nathaniel Hawthorne: The Scarlet Letter and Selected Tales* (Harmondsworth: Penguin, (1837) 1978), 287-98.

pany near Plymouth, Massachusetts, presided over by that ancestral emblem of seasonal renewal, the maypole. The narrator-annalist explains how, in those days "Jollity and gloom were contending for an empire" and how, "should their banner be triumphant, [the settlers of Merry Mount] were to pour sunshine over New England's rugged hills, and scatter flower seeds throughout the soil" ("The Maypole," 287).

It is easy to see the parallelism between "the grim Puritans" ("The Maypole," 293) in Hawthorne's tale and the "Particular Separatist Elect" in New Milton, and between the "mirthful spirit dwell[ing] all the year round at Merry Mount" ("The Maypole," 287) and the jollity of Indians and Catholics at Mary Mount. The narrator in Hawthorne's tale is fascinated by the lively rituals of a community he associates with those of classical paganism: he calls them "people of the Golden Age" and compares them to "Fauns and Nymphs", but also to "Gothic monsters, though perhaps of Grecian ancestry" ("The Maypole," 288). As in Mary Mount, the maypole is at the centre of Merry Mount, and, to the scandal of their grim Puritan neighbours, its "votaries danced round it, once, at least, in every month," and "sang ballads and told tales" ("The Maypole," 293). Indeed, "the Puritans affirmed, that, when a psalm was pealing from their place of worship, the echo, which the forest sent them back, seemed often like the chorus of a jolly catch, closing with a roar of laughter" ("The Maypole," 294). Interestingly, the narrator connects the "merry" settlers to Milton when he calls them "the crew of Comus," in direct reference to a masque written by Milton in 1634. As Thomas E. Connolly explains, Comus is "a pagan god invented by Milton, the son of Bacchus and Circe [who] represents temptation against purity" (*Nathaniel Hawthorne*, 375, note 6). As the narrator-annalist points out, "the future complexion of New England" wholly depended on which of the two models of society would eventually prevail:

> Should the grisly saints establish their jurisdiction over the gay sinners, then would their spirits darken all the clime, and make it a land of clouded visages, of hard toil, of sermon and psalm, for ever. But should the banner-staff of Merry Mount be fortunate, sunshine would break upon the hills, and flowers would beautify the forest, and late posterity do homage to the Maypole! ("The Maypole," 294).

Like the Puritans in Hawthorne's tale, the Milton in Ackroyd's novel is perfectly aware of the subversive potential of the carnivalesque spirit reigning in the neighbouring settlement. He abhors the laughter of children — "there is no whispering and laughter in paradise [...] so wherefore should we suffer them [children] here?" (*Milton*, 163) — and is utterly discomfited by the Rabelaisian merriment, gluttony and incontinence of the Mary Mount settlers: their "wanton and untimely singing" (*Milton*, 192) and the fact that "the papists are daily, gluttonous and incontinent drunkards" (*Milton*, 192). His reaction is to oppose their "evil" example with ever more repressive rules for, as he tells Goosequill: "I must guard and preserve you all. I cannot slacken the reins [of Plato's black horses of passion]" (*Milton*, 194).

On 20th December 1661 Milton, who had gone out for a walk into the forest, fell into an Indian deer trap and found himself "hanging from a pole [suspended] between earth and heaven [...]. His dark world turned upside down" (*Milton*, 158). He, then, discovered in amazement that he could see (*Milton*, 159). That is, Milton found himself in the position of the Hanged Man, the Tarot card symbolizing the quester's opportunity to destroy "the whole 'higher' structure of outlook, attitudes, tastes, acquired mental and emotional habits, which cages the inner man."[43] Rescued by the friendly Powpows, Milton experiences the healing power of the *sachem*'s sympathetic magic (*Milton*, 216-17) and is given the opportunity to correct his opinion about the Indians' beliefs. However, he stubbornly refuses to accept their white magic as good and concludes that these "rare cures in the wilderness must surely be the work of the devil" (*Milton*, 217).

Milton's incapacity to correct what Bakhtin called above his "false picture of the world" reaches its climax during the Indian "feast of dreams," when, incapable of shaking off the Puritan association of love and sin, he mistakes the pure prelapsarian "mix[ture of] soul with soul, or flesh with flesh" offered him by the Indian virgin, for guilty sex, "the cause of all his woe" (*Milton*, 275). The rejection of this opportunity to grow spiritually brings about the return of his physical blindness and confirms his spiritual self-fragmentation, expressed in Milton's narrative voice split into the first and the third person. In terms of Tarot symbolism, it might be said that, at this stage, the Puritan poet has reached the point of no return when the quester, incapable of being reborn into a new spiritual life, becomes a "Black Brother isolated from the rest of the universe in the hard and evil shell of his own egotism." Deprived of spiritual nourishment, "'Such a being is gradually disintegrated [...]. He may indeed prosper for a while, but in the end he must perish...'" (Cavendish, *Magical Arts* 111).

It is then that, panic-striken by the feeling that his whole phallogocentric symbolic system is threatened, Milton undertakes a tour of the main Puritan towns in New England in order to "raise an army of the Lord utterly to destroy [the] papists" of Mary Mount (*Milton*, 242). In Hawthorne's tale, the Puritan leader, John Endicott eventually leads an army against the Merry Mount settlement: he interrupts the wedding of the Lord and Lady of the May ("The Maypole," 296) and cuts down the maypole, thus confirming their "rigorous destiny, in the shape of the Puritan leader, their only guide" ("The Maypole," 297). However, the future predicted by the narrator-annalist is not so gloomy, since, "at the fair spectacle of early love [...] the iron man was softened [...]. And Endicott, the severest Puritan of all who laid the rock-foundation of New England, lifted the wreath of roses from the ruin of the Maypole, and threw it, with his own gauntleted hand, over the heads of the Lord and Lady of the May" ("The Maypole," 298). The sketch ends with the newly married Lord and Lady of the May in a scene that recalls Adam and Eve's expulsion from Paradise at the end of *Paradise Lost*: "their home of wild mirth made desolate," they are condemned to return "to it no more." However, their expulsion from Paradise was assuaged by the knowledge that they still held in their intertwined hands "all the purest and best of their early joys. They went heavenwards, supporting each other along the difficult path which it was their lot to tread" ("The Maypole," 298).

---

[43] Richard Cavendish, *The Magical Arts: Western Occultism and Occultists* (London: Arkana, (1967) 1984), 108-9.

In the novel, Milton and his Puritan army also attack and destroy the Catholic settlement, but unlike "the iron man" John Endicott, Milton allows for no mercy: Ralph Kempis and Goosequill are killed, together with most of the Catholics, and the Indians are unmercifully massacred. Thus, the novel, unlike the tale, seems to end with the imposition of Milton's unmitigated Separatist rule. However, it would be wrong to consider this battle a lasting victory. At the end of the novel, in a scene that also recalls the ending of *Paradise Lost*, Milton's fragmented Self is left sadly narrating how his own sleep-walking Shadow, condemned like Adam/the Lord of the May, (but without the consoling company of Eve/the Lady of the May), "wandered ahead and, weeping, through the dark wood took his solitary way" (*Milton*, 277).

Milton's self-fragmentation brings to mind yet another important intertext of *Milton in America*: William Blake's *Milton, A Poem*.[44] As Essick and Viscomi have pointed out, Blake wrote this poem in order to give the author of *Paradise Lost* the possibility of returning from heaven to the earth to mend the errors committed in his earlier life. As they go on to explain, "In Blake's view, Milton's errors infected his life and writings with classical paganism, moral self-righteousness, and rational materialism."[45] For Blake, the "single vision" of rational materialism was utterly reductionist and evil. He condemned Moses' tablets of the law as a "code of 'thou shalt nots' [...] a negative crime-and-punishment legalism [...] the antithesis of Christ's way of overcoming enemies by forgiving them" (Essick/Viscomi, "Introduction," 13). And he thought that "the Jewish occupation of Canaan exemplified [...] the degeneration of a spiritual ideal into materialist conquest —a conversion of the Holy Land into the Bloody Land" (Essick/Viscomi, "Introduction," 14). Translating Canaan for America, and with Blake's poem in mind, it might be concluded that, by imagining Milton's transatlantic journey, Ackroyd is giving the Puritan poet yet another opportunity to correct the errors that infected his life and writings, allowing him, in Bakhtinian terms, "to destroy and rebuild the entire false picture of [his Puritan] world," with the good example and help of the Catholics and Indians.

We have seen how Milton missed this second opportunity, mistaking the spiritual ideal in the Bible for materialist conquest, thus cutting off for ever the possibility of his spiritual growth. But it would be wrong to assume that the evil he planted in New England would never come to an end, for punishment is always followed by redemption and it should not be forgotten that the author of *Paradise Lost* also wrote *Paradise Regained*.

This is surely the message behind the casual meeting of Milton and a young man called Thornton in Harvard Library near the end of the novel. Thornton was introduced to Milton as a writer working on an epic poem entitled *Paradise Regained*, "celebrat[ing] his country [on] the model of *The Faerie Queen*" (*Milton*, 252). Thus, although the novel ends with the prospect of universal darkness spreading over New

---

[44] For a more detailed analysis of the novel's intertexts, see Susana Onega, *Metafiction and Myth in the Novels of Peter Ackroyd* (Columbia: Camden House, 1998), Ch. IV.

[45] Robert N. Essick and Joseph Viscomi, "Introduction" to *William Blake: Milton, A Poem* (London: The William Blake Trust/ The Tate Gallery, 1993), 16.

England after the destruction of that Rabelaisian paradise of interracial harmony, ancestral wisdom, utopian socio-politics and religious liberty and mirth that was Mary Mount, the subject matter of Thornton's poem can only be the story of the eventual restoration of Edenic happiness and pleasure in New England, a prospect, which, unlike the softened Puritanism prophesied by Hawthorne, signifies the eventual recuperation of Paradise itself.

***

In Ackroyd's novel, the intertextual influence of Hawthorne's writings is pervasive but, like that of Thomas More, Plato, Aristotle, Defoe, Blake or Milton himself, it is never openly acknowledged. By contrast, in Bharati Mukherjee's *The Holder of the World*,[46] the narrator-historian informs the reader at the end of the novel that her account is the true version of the "story of the brave Salem mother and her illegitimate daughter" (*The Holder*, 282) which Hawthorne fictionalised in *The Scarlet Letter*, though "shying away from the real story" (*The Holder*, 282). Therefore, unlike Winterson's and Ackroyd's re-writings of the Puritan Commonwealth, Mukherjee's is presented as the "true" version of concrete historical facts, painfully gathered by an "assets hunter" called Beigh Masters with "a hunger for connectedness" (*The Holder*, 11), who wishes to track down the "secret life of a Puritan woman whom an emperor honoured as Precious-as-Pearl, the Healer of the World" (*The Holder*, 20). Interestingly, the narrator's obsession with this seventeenth-century woman called Hannah Easton, is inseparable from her attempts to trace back her own Puritan origins to the Musters/Masters of Massachusetts (*The Holder*, 11), who are also Hannah's ancestors, while her apparently objective interest in sorting out "the tangled lines of India and New England" through the unravelling of Hannah's life on either continent is also given a subjective colouring by the fact that her boyfriend, Venn Iyer is an Indian working for the MIT who, like the author herself, "grew up in a world so secure I [Beigh] can't imagine it" (*The Holder*, 31).[47] This subjective element was given a further turn of the screw by Bharati Mukherjee in a recent interview[48] when she pointed out that Beigh Masters "has my initials" (Collado Rodríguez, "Multiplicity," 300), thus establishing a parallelism between the fictional American woman with an Indian boyfriend and herself, an Indian woman with an American husband.[49] Although Bharati Mukherjee has a PhD in English, history was her second subject at university and she acknowledges having done extensive historical research in order to

---

[46] Bharati Mukherjee, *The Holder of the World* (New York: Fawcett Columbine, (1993) 1994).

[47] For an interesting summary of Bharati Mukherjee's family background and early life, see Michael Connell, Jessie Grearson, and Tom Grimes, "An Interview with Bharati Mukherjee," *The Iowa Review* 20:3 (Fall, 1990): 7-32.

[48] Francisco Collado Rodríguez, "Naming Female Multiplicity: An Interview with Bharati Mukherjee," *Atlantis* 17:1-2 (May-November, 1995): 293-306.

[49] Bharati Mukherjee was born in Calcutta in a well-to-do Brahmin family, but acquired American citizenship in 1988. Her husband is the American writer of Canadian origin Clark Blaise.

write *The Holder of the World*. However, like her fictional *alter ego*, Mukherjee is most interested in "the story part of History" (Collado Rodríguez, "Multiplicity," 299) and, as she explained, "I don't really see the point in writing a historical novel that is simply a passive retrieval of past data. I need to experience history and have my readers experience history rather than be told historical information"(Collado Rodríguez, "Multiplicity," 300-301). In fact, she added, "each novel [of mine] is, in a sense, covert autobiography" (Collado Rodríguez, "Multiplicity," 302).[50] In the same interview, Mukherjee defined herself as "a woman writing in the 1990s and as a feminist born in India" (Collado Rodríguez, "Multiplicity," 301) and she noted that her approach to history is based on her continuous need to rebel "against a culture that has encouraged women — and everybody else, but particularly women — to be very pliant to gurus, to mentor/disciple relationships" (Collado Rodríguez, "Multiplicity," 296). Mukherjee's words clearly ally her with the writers in Christopher Bigsby's "counter-current," who believe that, in order to change the future, they "must first change the past or lay claim to it on their own terms" (see above).

The author's theoretical position adds meaning to the narrator's decision to analyse the life of a single woman she is personally involved with, instead of devoting her research, as Hegel or Nietzsche would have recommended, to the analysis of the troubled socio-political and religious relationships between England, America and the East Indies in the seventeenth century with a view to developing an overall historical synthesis. Indeed, her approach to history echoes the New Historicist contention that "critics [...] should be less concerned to construct a holistic master story of large-scale structural elements directing a whole society than to perform a differential analysis of the local conflicts engendered in individual authors and local discourses."[51] Similarly, the fact that the narrator-historian gives the same historical value to all kinds of records, from logbooks, annals, travel books, diaries and memoirs to paintings, poems, "captivity narratives," embroidered samplers and orally transmitted tales or myths is in keeping with the New Historicist tenet that literary and non-literary texts circulate inseparably and share a similar narrative nature, an idea further enhanced by the fact that the end-product of her historical research is not a history book, but the very novel that we have in our hands.

Venn Iyer is also a researcher intent on recovering the past, but while Beigh Masters' aim is to fill in one of the many gaps left by traditional totalitarian history recreating the life of a single woman across her life span, he aims at "re-creating the universe, one nanosecond, one minute at a time" (*The Holder*, 5) by means of virtual reality. His method is "the mass ingestion of all the world's newspapers, weather patterns, telephone directories, satellite passes, every arrest, every television show,

---

[50] Peter Ackroyd holds a similar position. As he recently noted, "I do not see any great disjunction, or any great hiatus between the poetry and the fiction. For me they are part of the same process. Similarly the biographies. I don't think of biographies and fictions as being separate activities" in Susana Onega, "An Interview with Peter Ackroyd," *Twentieth-Century Literature* 42:2 (Summer, 1996): 208-20, here 212.

[51] H. Aram Veeser, ed., *The New Historicism* (New York and London: Routledge, 1989), xii.

political debate, airline schedule" (*The Holder*, 5-6) into his macro-computer. His research project shows the impact of relativity theory, in particular, the New Physicists' tenet that reality cannot be known essentially, since human knowledge is inevitably mediated by the senses and the measuring instruments.[52] As a relativist, Venn is ready to admit that every virtual re-creation of the past will vary according to the time-traveller, since each "will create a different reality" (*The Holder*, 6). Thus, when Venn fed into his computer all the data his girl friend had been gathering about the life and times of Hannah Easton, and then tried to interact with it, "all he got was a postcard view of modern Madras" (*The Holder*, 281). By contrast, when Beigh herself attempts the same experiment, she achieves astonishing results, for, as Venn explains, human reality does not exist as an overall abstraction separated from the perceiver but is, on the contrary, wholly interactive: "The program will give you what you most care about; your mind is searching through the program though you don't realize it — it is interacting with my thousand-answer questionnaire — until it finds a place it wants to jump in" (*The Holder*, 281). However, for all the subjectivity and variability of the results, Iyer, paradoxically, also defends the view that all the virtual versions of the past will be real, that they will be re-creations, not re-productions.

Confronted with Beigh's account of Hannah's life, the reader is soon puzzled by the fact that every crucial event in Hannah's biography runs parallel to a decisive event in world history. Thus, for example, the day Hannah turned a year old (the 29th September 1671), is also the day that the colonial government in distant Plymouth humiliated the Wampanoag chief, Metacomet (renamed King Philip by the colonists), an event that would lead to the Indian Wars of 1675 (*The Holder*, 27), and it is also the day that Hannah's father "while in his outdoor privy savouring the poetic paradox in an imported, treasured copy of *Paradise Lost* and the physical paradox of constipation's painful pleasures, died of a bee sting" (*The Holder*, 27).

The improbability of such biographical and historical coincidences produces a realism-undermining effects further enhanced by the constant teasing suggestion that the historical and biographical data might in fact have a fictional origin. Thus, for example, the ludicrous description of Edward Easton's death while in his outdoor privy, reading *Paradise Lost*, has a strong parodic ring of the famous episode in *Ulysses* in which Leopold Bloom peruses "an old number of *Titbits*," while sitting at stool.[53] Likewise, the joyful elopement of Hannah's mother, Rebecca, with a war-painted Wampanoag Hannah acknowledges as "her inadmissible father" (*The Holder*, 28) parodies Hester Prynne's guilt-ridden seduction by the Reverend Mr. Dimmesdale in *The Scarlet Letter*.

---

[52] On the influence of relativity and quantum theories on American historiographic metafiction, see, Francisco Collado Rodríguez, "Uncertain Knowledge, Ideological Discourse: Locating American Historiographic Metafiction," *Foreign Language Teaching* 5:5-6 (Sofia, 1994): 58-66 and 6:1 (Sofia, 1995): 35-46.

[53] James Joyce, *Ulysses* (Harmondsworth: Penguin, (1922) 1960), 70.

Hester Prynne and her little daughter, Pearl, were stigmatised and cast out of the Puritan community. By contrast, Hannah, after her mother's elopement, was deposited by an Indian woman at the door of Robert and Susannah Fitch, who adopted her into their Puritan family. Hannah's ability with the needle is also inherited from Hester Prynne: while Hawthorne's heroine uses her art to embroider her scarlet letter of "Adulteress" and to attire her child as the living emblem of her shame, Hannah's "embroidery is the embodiment of desire" (*The Holder*, 45). Glowing like a rainbow banner on the wall behind her bed, her full-coloured little sampler, framed by her foster brother Thomas "in the finest cherrywood left over from a chest he had made for the fearsome old magistrate, the twisted John Hawthorne (whose excesses in the witch trials would so torment his descendant, Nathaniel Hawthorne) [... cast] a pagan iridiscence [...] when she knelt by it to pray" (*The Holder*, 45).

More than three hundred years before Venn Iyer realized that in interactive virtual reality each human mind creates what it most cares about, the twelve-year-old Hannah (like Jordan with his travel book of "possible journeys" in Winterson's novel) was giving empiric evidence of the same as she embroidered in her sampler "an 'uttermost shore'" (*The Holder*, 44) she had never seen, an imagined coast with colonial gentlemen and colourfully garbed black-skinned men living in harmony under the shadow of a building that "could even be the Taj Mahal" (*The Holder*, 45). In clear allegory, Hannah's pagan art soon developed into a healing art. She learned from a veterinary surgeon how to stitch up wounds in animals and gave a tremendous imaginative leap when she decided to try the same technique on human beings who had been scalped. She then broke an even stricter Puritan taboo when she combined her new scalp-healing technique with the herbal remedies her mother had secretly learned from the Indians (*The Holder*, 49).

Hannah's opportunity to escape from Salem's Puritan grimness has all the ingredients of romance: she marries Gabriel Legge, the fiancé of her best friend, Hester Manning after she jumps off a precipice into the sea and drowns in a bout of romantic dejection (*The Holder*, 67), caused by his having withdrawn his marriage proposal. Hannah's unexpected husband is a one-eyed "treacherous alien" (*The Holder*, 69), openly associated with Robin Hood (*The Holder*, 167), a seafaring adventurer who made a reputation for his "rampant embroidery" (*The Holder*, 68) of fabulous stories about exotic and remote lands, soon after his arrival in Salem in search of "an Empress of his own, fit for the Emperor's Dreams" (*The Holder*, 68).[54]

In the above-mentioned interview Bharati Mukherjee explained that she did not believe in unchangeable fate, but rather in what she called *dynamic destiny*: "You are given choices but you have to cope with the choice" (in Rodríguez, "Multiplicity," 305). It is clear that Hannah's basic choice is between the strict Puritan morality she inherited from her father and her foster parents and the passionate desire her mother yielded to when she eloped with the Indian brave. Therefore, Hannah's decision to marry the one-eyed pirate Gabriel Legge may be read as her first step away from

---

[54] Besides their romantic overtone, Legge's words, as well as the fact that he is a "one-eyed merchant" also connote the devalued Tarot symbolism of T. S. Eliot's *The Waste Land*.

Puritan repression and towards the acknowledgement of desire already unconsciously expressed in her embroidery. Each time Hannah's life comes to a decisive stage, her name changes accordingly. Thus, after her marriage she becomes "Hannah Easton Fitch Legge" (*The Holder*, 61), for, as Mukherjee has noted, she likes "using names as reincarnations; to name yourself is to say, 'I'm going to be this person for the time being'" (in Collado Rodríguez, "Multiplicity," 306).

After the arrival of Hannah and Gabriel Legge at Fort St. Sebastian, the East India Company enclave in the Coromandel where Gabriel had got a job, Hannah is exposed to a further choice. She can behave like the other married women in the White Town of the Fort, or she can follow the dangerous path opened up by Henry Hedges, the former owner of Hannah and Gabriel's residence, a beautiful and haunting "white miniature palace" (*The Holder*, 117).

The first option means conforming to the rules dictated by the Chief Factor of Fort St. Sebastian, Cephus Prynne, whose surname already betrays his Puritanism. Just as his Salem ancestor in Hawthorne's novel had no doubts about the racial inferiority of the Indians, so Prynne is convinced of the "natural" superiority of the Whites over the Muslims and Indians, and of the need to have "An iron will and a heart of flint" (*The Holder*, 119). He also believes that the duty of white women is "to devote themselves to the well-being of their husbands, the keeping of their tables and the education of their children in the Protestant religion" (*The Holder*, 112). However, the male factors knew that "their lives in India were extraordinary and, by most standards of the day, debauched [...] their personal code was Excess in All Things" (*The Holder*, 128). Consequently, the social structure of Fort St. Sebastian is based on sexual discrimination, racial *apartheid* and social hypocrisy: the White Town is strictly forbidden to the inhabitants of the Black Town; the white women, locked inside its walls, are expected to entertain themselves, as Hannah does during Gabriel's long absences, like Penelope, "Only with [her] sewing," (*The Holder*, 153), while at the same time every factor has a numerous progeny of half-caste children with their Hindu or Muslim *bibis* (*The Holder*, 131).

The other option, to break the separatist taboo, is represented by Henry Hedges, the eccentric English humanist working as a translator for the Company whose "interest in India was too acquisitive" (*The Holder*, 127). Unlike the other whites, Hedges "found himself dissatisfied with both sides" (*The Holder*, 127), and was therefore condemned by his colleagues as a "voluptuary:" "a man distracted from the Company's business by the lure of personal pleasure" (*The Holder*, 135). After his untimely death Henry Hedges' beautiful Indian *bibi*, whom he had re-named Bhagmati, i.e. "Gift of God" (*The Holder*, 121), remained in the house where he had dared to bring her. Her name, which not only begins with a B but is also phonetically very close to "Bharati" ("Goddess of Learning"), as well as the fact that she was born into a high-caste Brahmin family, openly links Bhagmati with Bharati Mukherjee. But Bhagmati is also associated with Hester Prynne: like her, she lost honour, caste and family when she was kidnapped and raped at the age of nine and decided to swim instead of drown.⁵⁵ In case the parallelisms are not clear enough for the reader, Mukherjee, with characteristic didacticism, makes Hannah give her new friend the name "Hester" in memory of her drowned friend Hester Manning. With this, the round of associations — or one might say, the re-incarnations — between author, narrator and white and black female protagonists comes full circle.

Through Bhagmati, Hannah will become, like Hedges, a "voluptuary," a white woman "too interested" in Indian culture. Both women develop "a common language" (*The Holder*, 171) in which Bharati tells Hannah endless stories — like that of Sita, "the self-sacrificing ideal Hindu wife" (*The Holder*, 173) — which carry Hannah "into brilliantly hued subterranean worlds" (*The Holder*, 171).

After breaking the separatist taboo, Hannah's next choice seems unavoidable. After Gabriel is taken for dead (*The Holder*, 203), the socially acceptable option would be to return to England as a false widow. Instead, she decides to stay in India, and this decision leads Hannah to a new life as Raja Jadav Singh's lover, the "Salem bibi" of Beigh Masters' historical records.

In an article synthesising the conclusions of a seminar on contemporary minority women's writing in America, Gail Ching-Liang Low noted first that there was general agreement among the participants that "the task of reconstructing cultural lines in the face of racism and denigration was absolutely vital." ⁵⁶ She then went on to make the following observation:

> However, when we turned to the Indian Canadian/American writer Bharati Mukherjee, we found that we could not fit her writing into the model of post-colonial and diasporic texts that we had collectively mapped out as important [...]. Instead of consolidating cultural specificities against a dominant white urban America, she positively rejects it (Low, "In a Free State," 8).

Although the seminar was held before the publication of *The Holder of the World*, it is easy to see that, in this as in her earlier novels and short stories, Mukherjee is not interested in consolidating the "cultural specificities" of Indian culture against white Imperialism, simply because, like Hedges, she finds herself "dissatisfied with both sides." The Indian and Muslim cultures Hannah confronts on the other side of the world are as defective as the Puritan culture she left behind in Salem. It is true that Bhagmati, as an Indian servant, "was invisible to the women of White Town" (*The Holder*, 133),⁵⁷ but it is also true that she was equally invisible for her own Indian

---

⁵⁵ In a sense, Bharati Mukherjee may be said to share even this trait with Bhagmati, for she also lost caste and honour when she married Clark Blaise.

⁵⁶ Gail Ching-Liang Low, "In a Free State: Post-Colonialism and Postmodernism in Bharati Mukherjee's Fiction," *Women: A Cultural Review* 4.1 (1993): 8-17, here 8.

⁵⁷ Angeles de la Concha makes an interesting point when she notes that the white women's incapacity to see Bhagmati reproduces the patriarchal pattern of female objectivization: the white women treat their female servants as objects in order to shake off their own feeling of inferiority with respect to the white men in the Company. "Otras voces, otra Historia," in José Romera Castillo, ed., *La novela histórica a finales del siglo XX* (Madrid: Visor, 1996),

relatives after her loss of caste. Again, the deep hatred leading to constant bloody confrontations between the Hindu Raja Jadav Singh and the Great Mughal, Aurangzeb, like the hatred that caused the King Philip Wars in New England, stems from a similar kind of patriarchal fundamentalism, imperialist zest for power, racism and religious fanaticism.

When Hannah, like Sita in the Indian myth, crosses the white chalk circle that separates her from her demon lover (*The Holder*, 175), she cuts herself off from her earlier life as a white married woman, as her mother had done when she eloped with her Indian lover, sacrificing, like her, social status, family and reputation, in order to "understand the aggressive satiety of total fulfilment" (*The Holder*, 237). However, just as Rebecca's affair with the Wampanoag brave was disrupted by the Indian Wars, so Hannah's passionate relationship with Jadav Singh is soon disrupted by history. The rising animosity between Jadav Singh and the Great Mughal leads to a series of skirmishes that climax in the massacre of the Hindu troops and the fatal wounding of Jadav Singh. It is then that Hannah rejects the possibility of behaving like the perfect Hindu woman, refusing to kill herself or to allow Bhagmati to do so (*The Holder*, 244). Instead, breaking several Indian taboos, Hannah kills the Muslim General Morad Farah, rescues her dying lover and even dares to change his fate, healing him with her pariah hands: "Her white casteless hands had touched him, touched his blood, her hands that had touched beef; even if she brought him back from Yama's grip, what sort of half-human monster would he be?" (*The Holder*, 252). These outraged words are uttered by Jadav Singh's mother, the old fanatic and vengeful Queen, for whom the value of human life wholly depends on one's capacity to fulfill the abstract duty imposed by Hindu ideology: "A mother's duty is to place the needs of her son above her fears. A wife's duty is to walk through fire to please her husband. A king's duty is to sacrifice himself for his subjects" (*The Holder*, 254).

Bhagmati, commenting on the effect Henry Hedges' love had had on her, told Hannah that "when a man craves you like that, you feel very powerful" (*The Holder*, 224). Likewise, the force that triggers off Hannah's actions is the sexual power she acquired with her Hindu lover. As she explained to the furious Queen Mother, when she restored her son's health, "She did not save him to send him back to battle [...]. She saved him in order to have him to herself" (*The Holder*, 253). Later on, when she visits the eighty-year-old Great Mughal, Aurangzeb, in order to see if she "could free

the two warrior-kings from their self-destructive obsession" (261), she again defends religious toleration, inter-racial equality and indiscriminate love:

> Love for a man, love for a place, love for a people. They are not Devgal people or Roopconda people, not Hindu people or Muslim people, not Sunni or Shia, priests or untouchables, servants or kings. If all is equal in the eye of Brahma as the Hindus say, if Allah is all-seeing and all-merciful as you say, then who has committed atrocities on the children, the women, the old people? Who has poisoned the hearts of men? (*The Holder*, 268).

183-88, here 183.

Predictably, her anti-patriarchal, anti-imperialist and anti-racist speech is lost on the ascetic and fanatic Holder of the World, as it was lost on the Queen Mother, for the patriarch of patriarchs can only understand the speech of duty to a god as pitiless and repressive as that of the Puritans: "The duty of the Emperor is to bring the infidel before the throne of judgment. There is no escaping the judgment of Allah" (*The Holder*, 269).

In *The Scarlet Letter*, Dimmesdale's incapacity to confess his sin eventually materialised in a mysterious illness located in his heart. Ironically, the doctor provided by the Puritan community to heal their preacher is Hester's vengeful husband, the old alchemist turned physician Roger Chillingworth. As the narrator explains,

> as he proceeded, a terrible fascination, a kind of fierce, though still calm, necessity seized the old man within its gripe [...]. He [Chillingworth] now dug into the poor clergyman's heart, like a miner searching for gold; or, rather, like a sexton delving into a grave, possibly in quest of a jewel that had been buried on the dead man's bosom, but likely to find nothing save mortality and corruption (*Scarlet Letter*, 150).

The jewel in Dimmesdale's bosom is both his unacknowledged scarlet letter of "Adulterer" and his unacknowledged daughter, Pearl. In Mukherjee's novel, the jewel is the largest and most beautiful diamond in the world, called The Emperor's Tear for "The tear I [Aurangzeb] shed as I discharge my duty" (*The Holder*, 269).

When Beigh Masters virtually/metaleptically enters the picture reproducing the final battle between the Hindus and Muslims, she re-incarnates herself in Bhagmati, just as she is "plung[ing] the knife deep into [her] belly [... and] with [her] dying breath, [she] plung[es] the diamond into the deepest part of [her]" (*The Holder*, 283). Thus, in clear allegory, Bhagmati/Hester/Beigh/Bharati achieves a symbolic victory against patriarchal fundamentalism where Hannah had failed to achieve it by means of argument. Bharati dies and is buried by Hannah in the Christian cemetery as "Hester Hedges." That is, like Sita in the Hindu myth (*The Holder*, 177), she returns to Mother Earth, but taking with her The Emperor's Tear, The Great Mughal's "one stark symbol of power" (*The Holder*, 263).

After this symbolic burial of patriarchy, Hannah, with neat symbolic symmetry, gives birth to a half-Hindu daughter and retuns to Salem in order to find her mother. Thus, the novel ends with the family reunion of the three transgressive women: old Rebecca, "with the shameful *I* boldly sewn in red to her sleeve [...] White Pearl and Black Pearl" (*The Holder*, 284), who, sure enough, will contribute their own female experiences of religious toleration, equality and passionate love to the healing of Salem's aching heart and the construction of the true multi-racial American identity.

***

Thematically, structurally, stylistically and ideologically *Sexing the Cherry*, *Milton in America* and *The Holder of the World* are three very different novels which, however, share one thing in common: the need to go back to the Puritan Commonwealth, that period in Anglo-American history where the roots of contemporary patriarchal capitalism are presumed to lie. As we have seen, where the traditional historical romance would attempt to achieve a faithful representation of the period from its dominant Puritan perspective, these three novels set themselves the opposite task of deconstructing the metaphors of patriarchy on which the Puritan ideology is built, and of rewriting it from alternative marginal perspectives. In each novel the perspective is different, because the marginal positions from which Winterson, Ackroyd and Mukherjee write are also different. However, the three novels convey a similar message: the need to recuperate the human capacity for laughter, passionate desire and love. That is, the need to erase the grim sexual, racial and religious repression prescribed by patriarchal duty, by means of the carnivalesque spirit that Bakhtin considered to be the most effective tool for resistance and subversion of the patriarchal false picture of the world.

The Moor's Last Sigh: Rushdie's Intercultural Family Saga

FRITZ-WILHELM NEUMANN (Erfurt)

The true satirist's outlook is exceedingly bleak. In the exordium of his epic narrative *The Moor's Last Sigh*, Rushdie defines the subject matter of the family saga which he is going to convey to the gentle reader: "the root of the whole matter of family rifts and premature deaths and thwarted loves and mad passions and weak chests and power and money and the even more mortally dubious seductions and mysteries of art" contributing to "the family's long slide" towards the end of what used to be "the age-old da Gama art of turning spice and nuts into gold."[1] The family's decline relates to postcolonial India entering the world of global capitalism under increasing pressure from the American life style. The state of contemporary Mother India is rotten indeed: Bombay's apocalypse, which leads to the collapse of the family empire, is the apogee of a crisis caused by the rush of modernization and, in its extreme form of violence, the image of a nightmare combination of corruption and fundamentalist Hindu fanaticism.

From the individual's point of view, this is a tale of a futile quest for meaning, identity and belonging in an era of change, which crystallizes around traditional forms of the epic: its Homeric conventions and its recent revival under the guise of the family saga. The purpose of this paper is, however, to discontinue the post-structuralist readings of Rushdie in order to underline how deeply Rushdie's thought is rooted in early twentieth-century vitalism when he resorts to biting satire. Therefore, I would first like to have a brief look at the paradigm of the family saga in Anglo-Indian as well as in English literature. Secondly, I would like to discuss the particular status Rushdie's version of the family chronicle has achieved in the tradition of satire rather than in the broad current of postmodern literature. To conclude, we shall thus be in a position to assess properly the nature and meaning of apocalypse which was created by a very blunt and dismal satirist.

The Family Saga

Rushdie's *The Moor's Last Sigh* has its roots in Anglo-Indian as well as in traditional English literature. The Indian novel was created during the latter half of the nineteenth century. Writers were either inspired by the Western model or re-wrote European literature for the evolution of the Anglo-Indian novel. Similiarly to the European tradition, the family served as the stage where social history was enacted, even as early as in mid-nineteenth-century novels. The literary historian Srinivasa Iyengar quotes *Alaler Gharer Dulal* (1858) ('Spoilt Son of a Rich Family'), which was written in

---

[1] Salman Rushdie, *The Moor's Last Sigh* (London et al.: BCA, 1995), 14-17.

Bengali on the lines of the *Jack-Wilton* story, as the initial example of the new genre.² Srinivasa Iyengar further describes Venu Chitale's *In Transit* (1950) as a "history of our own times" with the underlying structure of the family chronicle: "But as a study of Hindu joint family life in Maharashtra, set in the background of the Ghandian Age, *In Transit* merits praise. A joint-family is an intricate microcosm." Likewise, K. N!garajan's *Chronicles of Kedaram* (1961) - just to mention a second forerunner - gives a picture of life in a South Indian district town during the thirties (Srinivasa, *Indian Writing*, 286).

In his earlier novel, *Athawar House*, Nagarajan had drawn more closely on Galsworthy's *Forsyte Saga*, (Srinivasa, *Indian Writing*, 286-7) which we also have to take into account as a possible source for Rushdie's family saga. In Galsworthy's *roman fleuve* that spawned all the best-selling family sagas, a sense of history as an age of former grandeur and decline prevails, as the author states in the preface to the 1922 edition:

> Looking back on the Victorian era, whose ripeness, decline, and 'fall-off' is in some sort pictured in The Forsyte Saga, we see now that we have but jumped out of a frying-pan into a fire. It would be difficult to substantiate a claim that the state of England was better in 1913 than it was in 1886, when the Forsytes assembled at Old Jolyon's to celebrate the engagement of June to Philip Bosinney. And in 1920, when again the clan gathered to bless the marriage of Fleur with Michael Mont, the state of England is as surely too molten and bankrupt as in the eighties it was too congealed and low-percented.³

Most probably, Rushdie was not familiar with Hugh Walpole's *Herries Chronicle* (1930-33), which is even more the prototype of what one might call not the stream-of-consciousness, but the stream-of-life novel. At a more sophisticated level, Virginia Woolf also drew upon this model in *The Years* and, finally more distantly, in *Between the Acts*. When the Whig interpretation of history as progress lost its popularity, English literature as part of the Victorian heritage produced the new biography as a means of escape from harsh reality. This was initiated by Lytton Strachey and it represented life as a mysterious growth of the human personality, and, likewise, by recurrence, the family chronicle which made the substance of life in the continuity of success and decline even more visible. The glorified vitalism or biologism of the life force which lurks behind everyday life gave shape and meaning in an age when, after the catastrophe of the Grand War, the purpose of history had become a doubtful issue.⁴

As a tale of achievement written on the brink of decline, the family chronicle enacts ideological wishful thinking. Its underlying vitalism transcends the incomprehensibility

---

[2] K.R. Srinivasa Iyengar, *Indian Writing in English* (New Dehli: Sterling Publishers, (1962) 1996), 315.

[3] John Galsworthy, *The Forsyte Saga* (London: Heinemann, 1922).

[4] Cf. Fritz-Wilhelm Neumann, *Der englische historische Roman im 20. Jahrhundert: Gattungsgeschichte als Diskurskritik* (Heidelberg: Winter, 1993), 102 ff., 142-53; see, for a good survey, John A. Lester, Jr., *Journey Through Despair 1880-1914: Transformations in British Literary Culture* (Princeton: Princeton University Press, 1968).

of history, which was a common escape from crisis in the early twentieth century. The wide-spread metaphor of the mysterious directedness and force of the river, which stands for the inscrutability of life, reflects the intellectual climate of the twenties. The central myth, which is ultimately rooted in Heraclitus, was a projection of romantic longings in an age of doubt and relativism, when the rational design of history was no longer feasible, but when, equally, the forces of change threatened the groundwork of society. The irrational aura of vitalism - the Wordsworthian growth of the self might be taken as its romantic counterpart - emerges in a situation in which one prefers to believe blindly in history, because the need for direction is being felt most urgently.

But in the India of Rushdie's mind, wishful thinking is no longer possible. In the rush of modernization, his key image of the dynasty primarily serves as an epistemological parable in the same way as the hole in the sheet in *Midnight's Children* where knowledge was represented as being phallic. Ambeen Hai has recently argued that Rushdie's discourse is shaped by bodily functions, which means that archaic emotions experienced in childhood are inextricably linked to the perception of reality in adult life. As an epistemological device, biologism is even more pervasive in *The Moor's Last Sigh*. Emotions take priority over profound rational analysis. The family, with its suffocatingly intimate pattern of human relations including incestuous behaviour, is used to bring to the fore the dilemma of the post-colonial mind in the self-reflection practiced by Rushdie's narrator.

On the level of narrative structure at least, a new post-colonial self is created with the increased awareness of repetition, recurrence, and inheritance, which is, by definition, the family embedded in history, as well as in the act of writing itself[5] by the reciprocity of text and world, which is part of the epistemological myth.[6] Contrary to the current view in literary criticism and cultural studies, the well-known strategies of hybrid formation fail to work in *The Moor's Last Sigh*.[7] Under Rushdie's pen postcolonial hybridity turns into a merely 'garbological' experience of civilisations on the wane. Historical categories of literary criticism might prove more helpful to throw some light on how Rushdie's mind and emotions work in the present situation. Let's argue that in the crisis, the emotional residues, which are shaped by the family structure, come up as soon as the more recent or 'advanced' layers of conditioning crumble, namely the thin crust of civilisation. Furthermore, as another underlying assumption that life is a process of change, the life force which determines growth and

---

[5] Cf. Maria Degabriele, "Trafficking Culture in Postcolonial Literature: Postcolonial Fiction and Salman Rushdie's Imaginary Homelands (1991)," *SPAN. Journal of the South Pacific Association for Commonwealth Literature and Language Studies* 34/35 (1992/93): 69, who refers to Rushdie's Herbert Read Memorial lecture of 1990.

[6] Ambeen Hai discusses current theory; see his *Fathered by History: Figurations of Family and the Writing of Empire* (Ph. Diss. Yale University 1994), *passim*.

[7] Sabine Schülting deconstructs the "nostalgia of myth," which is prevalent in Rushdie's novel, as "explicitly masculine;" her conclusion that "hybridity is little more than a soothing illusion (not only) in twentieth-century India" is inescapbale; see "Peeling off History in Salman Rushdie's *The Moor's Last Sigh*," in Monika Fludernik, ed., *Hybridity and Postcolonialism: Twentieth-Century Indian Literature* (Tübingen: Stauffenburg, 1998), 241, 260.

decay re-enacts the fate of discontinuity inherent in the dynasty's Portuguese/Jewish roots as India's manifest destiny. In Toynbee's terms, post-colonial India will be unable to face the challenge of globalisation. Similarly, the build-up of frustration can only be endured by the use of satire.

The model of *The Moor's Last Sigh* is not the epic, but the mock heroic. In English literature, the late 17th and early 18th-century mock heroic arose when the epic, which was the most prestigious genre because it provided a plan for the world, was no longer possible. During the first half of the century, the novel proved to be the more appropriate medium to depict the rise of the middle classes with their moral values and their sense of empiricism.[8] Rushdie's late 20th-century mock heroic, which makes use of the epic and the novel alike, combines the foundation of the dynasty with the middle class quest for identity in the modern world. In applying the mock heroic (Hammer Moraes in the underworld), the discrepancies between the mind's tools and the object they are applied to lead to black satire *ad hominem* (against Indira Ghandi and Hindu fundamentalists), against present times, and against the tools man uses to build his civilisation. Finding the task impossible, the writer turns the epic into nostalgia as well as into the mock heroic, which needs intertextuality to thrive on, and he turns writing into garbage, as its only purpose can be to prove how futile human civilisation has become. It is no mere coincidence that the narrative process is shaped by the underlying biologism, which is the only law of existence, as the increasing awareness of the narrator shows that he is not only a witness of events affecting the family, but that his own consciousness is determined by the ebb and flow of vital forces and that meaning is possible only in the light of self-reflection, and even then it is limited to the artfully isolated process of narration. Art heightens awareness, which, according to deconstructionists, is linked to a quest for patrilinear genealogy. But the fact that there are archetypal patterns of consciousness at work does not come as a surprise. Archetypal responses are evoked by the use of satire, which in itself results from failure. The longing for continuity and unity, which is set between Walt Disney's universe and the tradition of occidental literature, is frustrated by political upheavals and cultural multiplicity so that any idea of constructing a meaningful form of post-colonial hybridity appears preposterous.

The members of the family act in accordance with the forces which drive post-colonial India, without really being able to master them. They experience history as achievement and failure, while the small world collapses, where they had prospered and fought their feuds. Whenever you are on the losing side, the question of guilt comes up quite naturally, which is a natural human reflex. The apocalyptic crisis of change, which terminates the corruption of the governing Zogoiby dynasty only to unleash the forces of Hindu fundamentalism, ironically reveals the human bias of interpreting history in moral terms. "The family's long slide" (15) is brought about by

---

[8] See Ulrich Broich's comprehensive study, *The Eighteenth-Century Mock-Heroic Poem* (Cambridge: Cambridge University Press, 1990); Werner v. Koppenfels, "Heroic Versus Mock-Heroic: Epos und Epenparodie von Milton bis Pope," in Heinz-Joachim Müllenbrock, ed., *Europäische Aufklärung II*, Neues Handbuch der Literaturwissenschaft (Wiesbaden: Athenaion, 1984), 91-122.

human weakness and failure not as a moral category but as an ebbing away of life's substance. Future historians of the postcolonial era might read it differently, but the novelist is prone to produce archetypal reductions, which is part of his epistemology.

The epistemological process, which is in itself a longing back to the womb, involves the two powerful female characters (Belle and Aurora) incorporating the source of the family's life force (as in Walpole's *Herries Chronicles*), while most of the males are drawn to the water, dabble in politics and practice homosexuality. Abraham Zogoiby, the Jewish progenitor of the narrator, however, pulls the strings in the Bombay export business as well as in the shadow economy of mafia gangs. According to the pattern of the family saga the drama is staged as an effusion of the life force. Moraes, the Moor and last descendant of the family, ages at double speed. As with Virginia Woolf's Orlando, who travelled as a meta-character through the centuries of English culture, or with Grass's tin-drummer, who refused to grow up under the Nazis, Moraes' spell is rapidly consumed, in spite of his prodigious sexual experiences while still surprisingly young. "Premature-ageing disorder" (219) is a symbol of the exhaustion of the family's substance as well as of the acceleration of change in contemporary India. Accordingly, *The Moor's Last Sigh* describes the fruitless quest of an "outcast" (98) picaro who is traumatised by the loss of his original paradise. Being neither English nor Indian, the Jewish-Portuguese family will have no place in modern India.

If the disastrous currents in Indian history can only be grasped and re-enacted in terms of archetypal patterns, Rushdie's postcolonial mind seems to be at the end of its tether indeed. Mother India's "inexhaustible motion" (60) "destroyed and again loved her children" (61). At a deeper level, the self-annihilation of the Zogoiby dynasty stands for the last phase of post-colonial secularization, Rushdie's narrator is overawed by the incomprehensible in the evolution of modern India, which he helplessly reduces to categories of everyday life. Facing the incomprehensible in the same way, Kipling and Forster had resorted to the epistemological myths of secret-service investigation and law-court procedure.

Satire

The comedy of satire disguises the strong feelings of discontent. The intellectual device for reducing *ad absurdum* the contradictions of one's environment expresses a powerful sense of frustration. Accordingly, Rushdie's satire verbalizes the loss of the homeland (cf. Degabriele, "Trafficking Culture," 68). This is the archetypal drama of betrayal which produces an emotional setting that will reject any idea of attributing significance to the linguistic surface beyond the purposes of satire in spite of Rushdie's playing the metafictional game. Rushdie's narration is enhanced by a number of obvious analogies, of which the most prominent is Aurora's sequence of paintings on the evolution of modern India. The so-called Moor painting, 'The Moor's Last Sigh,' which is the copestone of Moraes's quest, converges on a face evoking the "existential torment" displayed by Edvard Munch. On a deeper level, the painting reveals the face of his mother's assassin, namely his father. Rushdie's sense of the human condition is founded on the classical tenets of existentialism: "There is no world but the world" (84); "power, money, kinship and desire: [...] the driving forces behind" (238). So, the dance of life easily turns into the "dance of death" (203), which confirms mutability as the only law in history. "We have chopped away our own legs, we engineered our own fall" (372) - Moraes moralizes about man's actions in history, but there is no poetic justice or divine retribution, even if moments of change assume a truly apocalyptic dimension from the point of view of those falling from fortune's wheel. In the end, Rushdie's picaro realizes that he "was fortune's, and my parents,' fool." Life is "our tragedy enacted by clowns" (412), which echoes similar moments in world literature. The Moor's quest for his mother's love will never be accomplished in this world. His father is disclosed as the instigator of Aurora's death, which robs him of any possibility of finding a guide through the real world. The notorious Hindu fanatic, Mainduck or Raman Fielding, cannot serve as Moraes' instructor, if he is introducing him to street fighting and similar rackets. When Moraes finally kills him, he erroneously believes he has dispatched the chief villain of Bombay, but Mainduck was just one of the many puppets whose strings were pulled by Abraham Zogoiby. In this way, Rushdie repeatedly uses the family pattern to intensify the tragedy of existence. If change means "the destruction of the old shapes by the hated advent of the new" (46), history terminates in an entropy of evil taking the forms of both the new and the old. The meaning of the fiction which was created by analogy with the evolution of modern India, produces a sense of irredeemable tragedy. For this purpose, the Moor reworks a tragicomic version of the *Mahabharata,* "with burlesque and buffoonery replacing the portentous actions of gods and men which comprise the founding myth of the nation" (352),[9] but the tragedy which lurks behind satire can only be endured by comic relief.

Obviously, Rushdie's cherished British ambition to take the torch of civilisation to India has failed. The futility of trying to implant Western or - nowadays - global civilisation onto India has been one of the major concerns in Anglo-Indian literature. When Moraes leaves India, the typically British feeling of melancholy wells up, which Walsh had already perceived in writers such as Paul Scott (*The Raj Quartet,* 1966-75) and J.G. Farrell, whom he aptly quotes.[10] In *The Siege of Krishnapur,* Farrell's Collector realizes

> that there was a whole way of life of the people in India which we would never get to know and which was wholly indifferent to him and his concerns. The Company could pack up here tomorrow and this fellow would never notice [...]. And not only him [...]. The British could leave and half India wouldn't notice us leaving just as they didn't notice

---

[9] Cf. Catherine Cundy, *Salman Rushdie* (Manchester: Manchester University Press, 1997).

[10] William Walsh, *Indian Literature in English* (London: Longman, 1990), 185-6; cf. Allan J. Greenberger, *The British Image of India* (Ph. Diss. Ann Arbor, University of Michigan, 1966).

us arriving. All our reforms of administration might be reforms on the moon for all it has to do with them.[11]

Satire redefines and shortens the boundaries of deconstruction because Rushdie's language is overburdened with infantile feeling and will not leave much for deconstructionists to do. Words may fail or deceive or mislead human consciousness, but our linguistic feelings of loss and emptiness will hardly be untrue. In this way, we can readily accept Ambeen Hai's suggestion that Rushdie's language is particularly material itself, "emanating from the body, a somatic production almost like a purge that reacts violently to self-silencing, or self-censorship, but also uncannily powerful, beyond human or rational control" (Hai, *Fathered by History*, 270). There is a rising tide of archaic emotions which had raged in the small world of the nursery when entering real life or history - behind the intellectual game of writing deconstructable logocentric pieces.

Let us face the so-called Rushdie paradox discussed by Foucauldians - why does Rushdie paradoxically re-write another myth - that of patrilinear genealogy? (Schülting, "Peeling off History," 260). In his 'India of the mind,'[12] men "struggle for their relative authority of interpretation and thus possession of the representation of women." Women are killed by men or by male violence. "Moraes's narrative thus deconstructs the Indian myth of the self-sacrificing woman." - What, then, are "the narrator's childish needs" (Cundy, *Salman Rushdie*, 256, 257-8) - the quest for the mother, namely the disinherited and unloved picaro's quest for the self and a meaningful universe? The image of the self-sacrificing woman - Hammer Moraes and his gang of thugs force unwilling widows to share the funeral pyre with their defunct husbands - is embedded in the overbearing myth of Mother India. Self-sacrifice and absolute power are part of the same cultural fixation on womanhood which verges on the incestuous; this is satirized by Rushdie who refers to the very early practice of sexuality in Moraes' childhood. The father, however, cannot serve as a model for his son's education, nor can the world supply the slightest hope of finding a meaning in life, unless we believe in Mother India as the traditional symbol of fertility, chaos, incomprehensibility, and the continuity of change. *Midnight's Children* (1981) dramatizes the beginnings of independent India, while *The Moor's Last Sigh* stages its apocalypse in corruption and fanaticism under global capitalism. As a metafictional character, the hero of the anti-*Bildungsroman* does not want to accept the world as it is. As the key myth of this novel, the great mother of chaos invites psychoanalytical readings: the pre-oedipal mother is feared and adored at the same time as a world beyond human control - and beyond language - and non-adult.[13] The Rushdie paradox could be recon-

---

[11] J.G. Farrell, *The Siege of Krishnapur* (Harmondsworth: Penguin, 1975), 232.

[12] Cundy, *Salman Rushdie*, 110, who refers to Rushdie's *Imaginary Homelands:* "Effectively exiled not only from the India of his birth but also from the active and engaged life that was such an important source of ideas in his earlier work, Rushdie has been obliged, more than ever, to construct an 'India of the mind.'"

[13] Cf. Gérard Mendel, *La révolte contre le père: Une introduction à la sociopsychoanalyse* (Paris: Payot, 1968).

ciled if we consider how deeply this layer is buried in his thinking and feeling, where the true clash of matriarchal and patriarchal civilisations takes place. Rushdie's archetypal epistemology renders palpable a layer of cultural conditioning which seems to be an additional impediment to a new post-colonial self.

The mock heroic contains a good deal of nostalgia, however masculine the underlying patterns of the heroic appear to be, whereas in Indian mythology matriarchal elements are traditionally prominent. In this way, the epistemological myth of the family proves efficient again. As one critic remarked, Rushdie's satirical pre-oedipalism does not prevent the reader from revelling in the carnival of his prose and in the "bombastic dynamism" of his best work (Cundy, *Salman Rushdie*, 110). The intertext game, which displays a useless amount of erudition, emphasises the character's failing understanding of change. The great epics created a meaningful universe, which, indeed, is the foremost quality of the epic: Homer and Virgil, Dante, Shakespeare, Washington Irving, Kipling, Ramayana form the palimpsestic background of Rushdie's mock-heroic narration.[14] Rushdie uses the palimpsest, which "Homi Bhabba, arch-theorist of hybridity" (329)[15] considers to be a model for the post-colonial era, as a weapon against those who envisage a modern India. If love, however, is the ultimate expression of hybridity - "the blending of the spirits" (289) - , Uma enacts the failure of such an idea which was fostered by Bhabha, with whom Rushdie strongly disagrees. The emotional disorders produced by Uma's different roles will refute any "pluralist philosophy on which we had all been raised" (272).[16] Rushdie's views are very clear indeed, as he disclosed in an interview with Maya Jaggi:

> I was interested to try to suggest there's a flip side to pluralism; the down side can be confusion, formlessness, chaos, a lack of vision or singleness of purpose. There are some very strong, monolithic, brutal views around, and sometimes those who have a clearer view get further.[17]

---

[14] Cf. Theo D'Haen, "Salman Rushdie's *The Moor's Last Sigh*, or, The Emotional Depths of Postmodernism," in Gerhard Hoffmann und Alfred Hornung, eds., *Emotion in Postmodernism*. (Heidelberg: Winter, 1997), 228.

[15] Cf. Homi K. Bhabbha, "DissemiNation," Bhabbha, ed., *Nation and Narration* (London: Routledge, 1990), 291-322.

[16] See, however, Schülting, "Peeling off History," reading Uma in the context of metafiction as a "feminization of writing" (245). "So *Shame* as well as *The Moor's Last Sigh* assume something like an *écriture féminine*, which is employed in the interests of the male narrator's and novelist's project" (246). Discussing "the novel's complex web of gender differences" and "cultural/textual hybridity" Schülting confirms the argument that Rushdie resorts to archetypal patterns: "Surprisingly however, in a novel where there is no fixed identity at all, where hybridity does not only refer to individual biographies and national histories, but also to the dialogic narrative itself, *sexual* difference is never deconstructed, and male and female identities are never questioned. One can thus say that sexual difference serves as the matrix which stabilizes the hybrid or dialogic narrative" (248) - Apart from Foucauldians, to whom does the constructedness of emotions come as a surprise?

[17] Interview with May Jaggi, *New Statesman and Society*, 8 Sept. 1995, 21.

Can any act of writing redeem the reader or his author from the burden of the postmodern loss of the subject and his/her homelands? Can it equally serve as a conscious subversion of the traditional Mother India myth, while the epic annihilates the legendary founding father of the dynasty, of the tribe, of the nation? Hammer the picaro, the heroic outsider or "lachrymose rider" (the lonely cowboy alias John Wayne) is cut off from the nation, the family, from love, from paradise - but not from rendering it as an aesthetic experience. In the deconstruction of the palimpsestic nature of literature and tradition, only emotions are genuine and can be put to the test. Readers familiar with British postmodernism should be aware of the fact that intellectual and intertextual games and sentimentalism can hardly be uncoupled. As with Saleem Sinai (*Midnight's Children*), the Moor is another physically disintegrating narrator, "possessed, from these early moments of self-consciousness, by a terror of running out of time" (152). As any endeavour to define identity through writing beyond one's emotions seems to be thwarted (Interview, 253) Foucauldians tend to expose the veiled links between literature and patriarchy in the Moor's endeavour to transform reality into the art of the narrative process and its sublime or superior state of consciousness, which is "explicitly masculine:" (Interview, 258) "In the end, stories are what's left of us, we are no more than the few tales that persist" (110). *Vita brevis, ars longa*.

Is there a deplorable attitude of male chauvinism involved in the fact that Rushdie's protagonist is unmistakably driven "by homosocial desire by male bonding, which replaces the eroticized mother-son-relationship between Moraes and Aurora?" (Schülting, "Peeling off History," 255). Isn't immaturity of whatever degree - enacted by literature - the price to be paid for true satire and sheer comedy? And, lastly, is it really to the point that there is a reflex leading the writer to aspire to eternity, which is attributed to 'maleness' by C.G. Jung and his school of archetypologists[18] thus being notorious? The rhetorical topos claiming modesty only appears to be a male emotional construct with a long and honourable tradition: To be masculine or not - the final act of the manuscript's launch makes the book a work of art of its own, quite different from the writer's intentions and his fragile subject, transcending the turmoil from which it arose into the work of art which reminds one of Chaucer's concluding "farewell" in *Troilus and Criseyde*:

> Go, litel bok, litel myn tragedye,
> Ther God thi makere yet, er that he dye,
> So sende myght to make in som comedye!
> But litel book, no makyng thow n'envie,
> But subgit be to alle poesye;
> And kis the steppes, where as thow seest pace
> Virgile, Ovide, Omer, Lucan, and stace. (V. 1786.92)

---

[18] See, however, the phenomenology of Gilbert Durand, *Les Structures anthropologiques de l'imaginaire* (Paris: Bordas, 1969).

Apocalypse

Criticism should focus on the essentials of history. As a longing for retribution, the apocalypse is a most irrational vision of history, and it properly concludes Moraes's immature vision of a world of change, which is the emotional backbone of Rushdie's distorted *Bildungsroman*. Historically speaking, on a more rational level, Rushdie's apocalypse reveals the third world's - or modern man's - inability in general to adjust to the speed of twentieth-century progress and globalization. The parable of acceleration and crisis displays change as an apocalyptic experience of loss. There is a contradiction in itself, as secularization, which really takes place in India and elsewhere, normally meant pragmatism and rationalism freed from religion, but nowadays corruption and fundamentalism seem to have taken the largest share of contemporary India, in spite of a powerful software industry emerging in many places and the country's current nuclear armament race with Pakistan. Never in history has the gulf between old and new been so wide. As the ultimate drama of the emotions, Rushdie resorts to a cathartic outlet: he cleanses his imaginary homeland from the madness of modern times. The gain is knowledge, while bathing in nostalgia, but not plunging into bathos. The inhabitants of Rushdie's world are driven by desire, greed and fanaticism, but they are not necessarily dull.[19] Using myth to reject any idea of heroism, Moraes prefers seeing things with the detached eye of the outsider. The anti-hero makes a gesture of desperation, which is a longing for moral reaffirmation to face the modernization of post-colonial India, which, notwithstanding Walt Disney, continues to be incomprehensible as ever. Change causes the loss of paradise and heads towards an apocalypse, although nobody believes in a myth which promises that the old world will be destroyed in order to make way for a better one. As Afzal-Khan rightly stated, "the real pain of history, then, can only be dealt with in mythical, magical fashion - realism must be diluted by myth"[20] - and tuned to the appropriate emotion. Universal disorder leads to entropy, which, according to Grimm, signifies the end of all systems of government and order. However, the myth of the apocalypse suggests meaning and divine-like retribution in the face of the urgent problems of contemporary society and the fears and doubts of the future on a global scale.[21] Rushdie's vision of apocalypse becomes the more forceful the less the reader believes in the progress of post-colonial Indian civilization. Apocalypse builds up the mythical scenario for modern man who is unable to adapt to the speed of change and technology, self-annihilation appears to be the ultimate step of secularization (Grimm et al., *Apokalypse*, 8-9).

---

[19] See v. Koppenfels's references to Alexander Pope's *Peri Bathous* (1727) and contemporary satire, "Heroic versus Mock-Heroic," 111.

[20] Fawzia Afzal-Khan, *Cultural Imperialism and the Indo-English Novel: Genre and Ideology in R.K. Narayan, Anita Desai, Kamala Markandaya, and Salman Rushdie* (University Park, PA.: Pennsylvania State University Press, 1993), 157.

[21] See Gunter E. Grimm, Werner Faulstich und Peter Kuon, eds., *Apokalypse: Weltuntergangsvisionen in der Literatur des 20. Jahrhunderts* (Frankfurt am Main: Suhrkamp 1986), 9-10; K. Ludwig Pfeiffer, "It's Now or Never - Wie und zu welchem Ende geht die Welt so oft unter?" *Sprache im technischen Zeitalter* 81-84 (1982): 181-96.

True satire has to make sure that it hurts, apocalyptic satire can do so more easily. There are quite a number of verifiable attacks on Bombay politicians, whereas the family saga is a construct set up in order to provide a stage for witnessing and furnishing the historical events with the coherence of the artist's work. In following the steps of Moraes through Bombay, the reader picks his way over the debris of the great occidental and oriental cultures. This is where satire and apocalypse join. Rushdie uses the mock-heroic mode in a similar way as the satirists did in early eighteenth-century England. The mock heroic presented the dull world of middle-class England in patterns that referred to a past of epic grandeur. However much satire hurts, the dignity of the epic will never be damaged. Even when the protagonist is taken into custody and detained in the Hades-like prison of Bombay, the presence of epic elements will always sharpen the reader's awareness that present times can never match a past where order and purpose reigned.[22] If the post-colonial discourse cannot persist, because there is no world for a truly post-colonial mind, Rushdie's "striving for new human values under the auspices of eternal change," however, will survive.[23]

Conclusion

The lonely rider through post-colonial Indian history indulges in nostalgia and melancholy. Any reading of *The Moor's Last Sigh,* which is to go beyond deconstruction and the strongholds of postmodernism, will have to recognize the shortcomings of the language game and its concomitant 'garbology,' which is the principal weapon of satire, in order to take the brunt of Rushdie's attack. The garbological nature of hybridity results from the fact that cultural knowledge taken from different areas of civilization and used for creating new forms of expression in literature fails to outline systematically what may be an ordered universe in transition. Rushdie does not build his hopes on the new discourse. In the age in which global lifestyle has been imposed on the turmoil of modern India, literature will never come to terms with reality unless it assumes the voice of mordant satire. Thus the treasure-houses of western and eastern history alike crumble into a heap of debris. This is the problem with a past which is no longer applicable to the present and which rules out any fusion of the worlds we have repeatedly been told to consider as hybrid. Even if scholars of postmodernism such as D'Haen consider *The Moor's Last Sigh* "as a very complex" work,[24] I take its

---

[22] Apart from the description of the tiles, the underworld episode is one of the highlights of Rushdie's novel.

[23] Rüdiger Ahrens, "Shifts of Aesthetic Discourses: National, Post-colonial and Post-structuralist Discourses," in Rüdiger Ahrens and Laurenz Volkmann, eds., *Why Literature Matters: Theories and Functions of Literature* (Heidelberg: Winter, 1996), 60.

[24] "Rushdie's The Moor's Last Sigh," 228. This reminds one of the interview Rushdie granted the German weekly *Die Zeit 15* (5.4.90), where he describes how he pieced together the most discrepant material: "'Des Mauren letzter Seufzer' ist mir schwergefallen. Einige Jahre lang konnte ich nur einzelne Episoden schreiben. Jede für sich. Ohne jeden Bezug aufeinander. Am Ende hatte ich sehr viel Material, aber wieder keinen Roman. Zwei Jahre dauerte

strategy of intertextual and intercultural references to be the messy surface of a carnevalesque code which seeks to prove the entropical nature of a global culture, in which the abundance of information blurs the identity we cannot do without. In a novel presented in the picaresque tradition, this makes more sense than duly acknowledging the ritual of the postmodern intellectual game - are we really proof against anything that postmodernism can throw at us? Myth and emotion, however, persist, as does the quest for one's own roots in the pre-linguistic depths of the soul.

---

es, bis ich aus den vielen Geschichten eine große Erzählung gemacht hatte. Ich habe dabei sehr viel verwenden können von dem, was ich vorher geschrieben hatte. Offenbar war mein Unterbewußtes klüger gewesen als ich und hatte fast alles schon ganz richtig gemacht" (48).

Passing in South African Literature

PAUL GOETSCH (Freiburg)

Definition of Passing

Passing refers to the transgression of lines drawn on the basis of social class, gender, and race. Frequently, the term is used to indicate the crossing of the color line — from the black to the white side in the United States or from the 'colored' to the white group in apartheid South Africa.[1]

The wish to pass for white or play-white emerges in situations of economic, social, cultural, political, and racial inequality. In the United States its origins go back to the sexual exploitation of black slave women and the low social status mulatto children inherited from their mothers. Although "whiteness was reproduced from 'black' female bodies" in successive generations, this whiteness was deemed inauthentic in the light of the one-drop-of-blood theory.[2] As the Supreme Court of the United States ruled in the 1896 case of Plessy v. Ferguson, a person with one-eighth Negro ancestry, even if he appeared to be white, could be defined as Negro under Louisiana law (see Ginsberg, "Introduction," 7).

In South Africa passing has its origins in colonial miscegenation. Intermixing took place between Europeans, indigenous people, slaves and immigrants from other countries. The 'colored' offspring of the Afrikaners (Boers) were sometimes treated better than blacks and occasionally enjoyed "a relationship of ambiguity, and a feeling of almost near-kinship;"[3] nevertheless they were discriminated against. In the course of the hardening of white racist attitudes, various attempts were made to classify people in terms of skin pigmentation. The Population Registration Act of 1950 classified all South Africans as follows:

A Whites (non-Black)	B Non-whites (blacks)
Whites are subdivided into	Non-whites are subdivided into
1 Afrikaans-speaking	1 Coloureds
2 English-speaking	2 Asiatics
3 immigrants, e.g., Italians, Greeks etc.	3 Bantu

(February, *Mind Your Colour*, 3)

---

[1] See Werner Sollors, *Neither Black Nor White Yet Both: Thematic Explorations of Interracial Literature* (Oxford: Oxford University Press, 1997), 247-84.

[2] Elaine K. Ginsberg, "Introduction," in the same, ed., *Passing and the Fictions of Identity* (Durham: Duke University Press, 1996), 5.

[3] Vernie A. February, *Mind Your Colour: The 'Coloured' Stereotype in South African Literature* (London: Kegan Paul, 1981), 2.

The non-white groups were further subdivided, 'Bantu' into eight units, 'Coloreds' into" (1) 'Cape coloured,' (2) Malay, (3) Griqua, (4) Chinese, (5) Indian, (6) 'other' Asiatic, (7), 'other' coloured" (February, *Mind Your Colour*, 4). Individuals were classified and reclassified. As Alan Paton relates in his novel *Ah, But Your Land Is Beautiful* (1981), the state bureaucracy regularly compared racial classifications on birth and marriage certificates in order to find out who was passing as white, with disastrous consequences for the families concerned.[4] The 1950 system of classification, one in a series of similar attempts, was based on such vague or arbitrary criteria as appearance, descent, and general acceptance. And yet it served as a groundplan for creating barriers between the main population groups and regulating their relations with a number of laws forbidding, among other things, sexual intimacies between whites, 'coloreds' or blacks. As Breyten Breytenbach has stated:

> Apartheid is the state and the condition of being apart. It is the no man's land between peoples. But this gap is not a neutral space. It is the artificially created distance necessary to attenuate, for the practitioners, the very raw reality of racial, economic, social and cultural discrimination and exploitation. It is the space of the white man's being. It is the distance needed to convince himself of his denial of the other's humanity. It ends up denying all humanity of any kind to the other and to himself (quoted from February, *Mind Your Colour*, 118).

In such a situation, then, passing for white is a strategy for assimilating to the dominant white group or, to use Erving Goffman's term,[5] it is a type of stigma management, that is, an attempt to conceal and forget the discreditable sign. In real life the term stigma management may express a number of individual motives, which have been listed conveniently by Werner Sollors:

> [...] the possibility of economic advancement and benefits (opportunism); interracial courtship and marriage (love); escape from slavery, proscription, discrimination, and the restrictions that segregation imposed on black life (political reasons); the desire to get away from the hypocrisy, narrowness, and double standard of black life; and [...] many other motives such as curiosity, desire for kicks (an "occasional thrill"), love of deception, preparation for political acts of subversion or revenge, and investigation of white criminal misconduct (Sollors, *Neither Black*, 250).

In literary works on passing all these motives may appear; apart from voluntary passing, acts of involuntary or inadvertent passing may be narrated. In the following survey of South African passing narratives, I will concentrate on how the authors evaluate the passing phenomenon. My brief references to U.S. American works are not meant to give the impression that South African writers are indebted to their American colleagues; rather, they are intended to indicate how passing narratives tend to follow the same conventions, some of which were first developed in American fiction.

---

[4] See Alan Paton, *Ah, But Your Land Is Beautiful* (Harmondsworth: Penguin, 1983), 243-7.
[5] Erving Goffman, *Stigma: Notes on the Management of Spoiled Identity* (Harmondsworth: Penguin, 1968).

Passing-White and the Sin of Miscegenation

Some works dealing with the theme of passing preach racial purity and reflect "the fear-psychosis which infects white South Africa at the mere suggestion of colour in the family" (February, *Mind Your Colour*, 67). While they may concede that play-whites are tragic characters, they leave no doubt that they deserve their fate and have to expiate the sin of their parents or, in some cases, the sin of a white ancestor who, as a pioneer, succumbed to the wilderness and went native. Alex La Guma has an Afrikaner parson say in *Time of the Butcherbird* (1979):

> [...] are the sins of the fathers not visited upon the children? The decline of civilisations, the disappearance of a way of life, does not only come through defeat in war or superiority in victory. The heathens around us have blighted us since the times of our forefathers who delivered this country into our hands. The victors sinned against keeping the blood pure. Sin came with the mixing of blood as sure as Adam ate of the forbidden apple. Blood pollution and the lowering of the racial level which goes with it, are the only cause why old civilisations disappear.[6]

While La Guma satirizes the parson and his doctrines, other writers affirm the purity-of-blood ideology and treat the passing mulatto from a white, racist perspective, reminiscent of such American works as Thomas Dixon's *The Clansman* (1905) and *The Leopard's Spot* (1903) and Robert Lee Durham's *The Call of the South* (1908).[7]

The best-known fictional plea for maintaining racial purity in South Africa is Sarah Gertrude Millin's novel, *God's Stepchildren* (1924). Convinced that there will be "no brotherhood between black and white" in South Africa, at best, "perhaps, a stepbrotherhood,"[8] she regards the sexual transgression of the borderline between the races as socially foolish, morally reprehensible, and racially evil (see Voss in Millin, *Stepchildren*, 9). Time and again, she associates miscegenation with mental and physical degeneration.[9]

She illustrates the consequences of miscegenation in a chronicle novel that focuses on the descendants of Reverend Andrew Flood. A missionary to the Hottentots in the Transvaal in the 1820s, Andrew Flood cannot keep up his civilized front for long. After living with the natives for eighteen months, he adopts their way of life: "He had become used to them. He was himself hardly delicate in his person any more. He had given up shaving and wore a beard — it was less trouble" (Millin, *Stepchildren*, 55).

---

[6] Alex La Guma, *Time of the Butcherbird* (Oxford: Heinemann, 1987), 106.

[7] See Judith R. Berzon, *Neither White Nor Black. The Mulatto Character in American Fiction* (New York: New York University Press, 1978), 25, 32-3.

[8] Sarah Gertrude Millin, *The South Africans* (1926), quoted by Tony Voss, "Preface," in Millin, ed., *God's Stepchildren* (Johannesburg: AD. Donker, 1986), 9.

[9] See Horst Zander, "Millin's Step-Children and Her Grand-Children: 'Miscegenation' in Some Southern African Novels," in Elmar Lehmann and Erhard Reckwitz, eds., *Current Themes in Contemporary South African Literature* (Essen: Die Blaue Eule, 1989), 84-125, 91.

His downfall is completed when, out of loneliness and despair about the usefulness of his missionary work, he gets married to a black woman. His hope that his marriage will help to wipe out the difference in color that stands between him and the natives is soon frustrated.

According to Sarah Gertrude Millin, Andrew Flood's original sin haunts and punishes the succeeding generations. His descendants, whatever their pigmentation, prove equally foolish and weak and illustrate Millin's prejudice that "mixing or contamination of bloods is indulged in by inferior individuals, and the strain of dark (weak, evil) blood never disappears from the 'stock'" (Voss in Millin, *Stepchildren*, 8). Despite her open racism and adoption of degeneration theories, Millin has some understanding and sympathy for her characters. As long as they do not deny their mixed inheritance, they are allowed to lead a more or less 'normal' life among the 'Coloreds.' Whenever they try to suppress their descent from black or 'colored' mothers or fathers, they join the group of tragic mulattos familiar from earlier American literature. For instance, Kleinhans, Andrew Flood's grandson, is told by his mother that he looks like a Boer. He behaves accordingly, only to be rejected as a bastard by the whites. Forced to settle down as a tenant farmer, he marries a light-colored Cape Town girl. His daughter Elmira succeeds in playing-white at a convent school, but after some time her parents are identified and she is forced to leave school as a consequence. Elmira's son Barry is the first member of the family to pass as white for many years. Inwardly, however, he is not happy: "[...] there was not a day but he remembered the secret degradation under his skin (Millin, *Stepchildren*, 246).

From his youth on, he is obsessed with "an instinctive sense of his inferiority" and shudders at the idea of being incapable of maintaining "accepted white standards" (Millin, *Stepchildren*, 246, 251). He develops the habit of passionately attacking "black and brown and yellow" (Millin, *Stepchildren*, 247), thus turning bitterly against part of himself. Thanks to his half-sister, he attends white schools and Oxford University. After World War I he returns to South Africa with a white bride. Driven by jealousy, his half-sister reveals his background. When his pregnant wife suggests that they should return to England, he shows "strength in his face" for the first time in her experience: he decides to leave and spend the rest of his life as a missionary among his "brown people" (Millin, *Stepchildren*, 326). Trying to expiate the sin of miscegenation, he intends to settle in the very same place where his ancestor Andrew Flood had his mission and where the tragedy of blood began. J.M. Coetzee, who studied Millin's racial obsessions and traced them back to various contemporary race theories, says in summary:

> No matter how white the guilty one's line may grow, his ancestral secret will not be safe: the 'vagaries of heredity' [...] may at any time proclaim his shame to the world.
> The flaw in the blood of the half-caste is thus an instinct for death and chaos. He destroys the peace of the community by revisiting its repressed sins upon it, it drives the half-caste himself to a withdrawal from life. Mixed blood is a harbinger of doom.[10]

---

[10] J.M. Coetzee, "Blood, Taint, Flaw, Degeneration: The Novels of Sarah Gertrude Millin," *White Writing* (New Haven: Yale University Press, 1988), 136-62, 152.

When Dr Dönges proposed a law against sexual relations between white and black in 1948, he mentioned Millin's work, Regina Neser's novel *Kinders van Ishmael*, and an essay by Olive Schreiner in support of his bill (February, *Mind Your Colour*, vii). Other works that directly or indirectly warn against racial mixing and deal with the theme of passing include Millin's *The Herr Witch-doctor* (a sequel to *God's Stepchildren*), Abel Coetzee's Afrikaans novel *Warheen vader?* (1940) and Daphne Rooke's *Mittee* (1952). Abel Coetzee demonstrates how the social ambitions of an ostensibly white family are destroyed by the birth of a dark-skinned child (February, *Mind Your Colour*, 67). Daphne Rooke is sensitive to the issue of racism and criticizes some white prejudices. At the same time, she hesitates to endorse the 'colored's' longing for equality.

The action of her novel takes place on an isolated Transvaal farm at the end of the nineteenth century. Mittee, the farmer's daughter, and Selina, a colored servant, have grown up together, almost like sisters. Selina, from whose perspective the story is chiefly narrated, is often made to feel Mittee's whims and prejudices, but she idealizes her nevertheless and envies her white skin. Aspiring to become like her, she distances herself from the 'kaffirs' and also from the 'coloreds:' "I hesitated, thinking I might join in the fun but a feeling of not belonging to my own race was strong upon me [...]."[11] When Selina wishes to see a lantern slide show for whites in Pretoria, Mittee suggests that she should dress up and play-white. Selina does so successfully, but only on this occasion.

Her friendship with Mittee develops into a love-hate relationship when the two women fall in love with the same man, the Boer Paul Du Plessis. While the man officially courts Mittee, he secretly takes Selina as his mistress. J.M. Coetzee describes Selina's situation as follows:

> Selina desires Mittee's beau [...], because Mittee (in her milk-and-water way) desires him, because Mittee is the object of Selina's obsessive imitation in all affairs, because to Selina her own desires are by definition inauthentic, the desires of 'a coloured girl.' The stratifications that set white and black in worlds apart, and leave 'a coloured girl' wandering in a no-girl's land between them, define the consciousness of Mittee and Selina and of everyone in their society [...].[12]

Selina's hopes are rudely shattered by her lover's remark that she will never appear as white in his eyes. From that moment on, the action erupts into rural Gothic. Paul Du Plessis, the racist, marries Mittee, kills their invalid child, rapes his ex-mistress, victimizes other people, and is finally killed by Selina. As in other versions of the tragic mulatto theme, the sympathies of the author seem to be with Selina's psychological problems rather than with her social aspiration to become white. Though Selina is not publicly accused of murder and is granted a modest degree of happiness

---

[11] Daphne Rooke, *Mittee* (Harmondsworth: Penguin, 1991), 31.
[12] J.M. Coetzee, "Afterword," in Daphne Rooke, *Mittee* (Harmondsworth: Penguin, 1991), 206.

with a 'colored' man, she is a variation of the tragic mulatto as an overreacher who must learn to content herself with being a member of the group of 'coloreds.'

Passing as a Betrayal of One's Origins

As the previous examples have shown, crossing the racial barrier is attented by fear of detection and may have tragic consequences for the person concerned. Playing-white can also induce feelings of guilt and a sense of having been unfaithful to one's group. Correspondingly, those who are left behind by the play-whites may feel betrayed and react to the passer's opportunism and hypocrisy with aggressiveness. In any case, passers have to pay a price for abandoning their affiliation with their original community, and that community has to come to terms with being despised and stigmatized by former members. Like some American writers, several authors of South African passing narratives also seem to assume that passing for white conceals or violates the true 'colored' identity.

In Richard Rive's story "Dagga-smoker's Dream,"[13] Karel, a drunkard and drug addict, wants to forget his miserable situation by entertaining the crowd in a train carriage. When a man, who looks white but is probably a middle-class 'colored' passing for a white, ignores his antics, Karel tries to provoke him into a fight and thus regain his self-respect in the eyes of the 'colored' crowd. The stranger continues to ignore him and leaves at the next station. Karel immediately opens all the windows amid raucous laughter. The applause helps him to get over his sense of self-pity and the feeling of inferiority caused by his skin-color.

In Rive's short story "Resurrection" (Rive, *Advance*, 29-37), a 'colored' woman dies and leaves behind three children who pass for white and the 'colored' girl Mavis. During the funeral, segregation is practiced: the white fathers, white friends and relatives and the three light-skinned children occupy the dining-room, where the coffin is placed, and expect Mavis and her 'colored' friends to use the kitchen. This spatial arrangement is the result of the long-standing division within the family. As Mavis remembers, her sisters often attacked her mother for her color, whereas she herself, driven by jealousy and envy, blamed her for having given birth to white children. Realizing that her hatred of her mother is actually self-hatred, she identifies with her dead parent and attacks the white mourners, who ignored their white friend's black wife as long as she lived:

> The room was filled with her mother's presence, her mother's eyes, body, and soul. Flowing into her, filling every pore, becoming one with her, becoming a living condemnation.
> "Misbelievers!" she screeched hoarsely, "Liars! You killed me! You murdered me! Hypocrites! Don't you know your God!!" (Rive, *Advance*, 37).

---

[13] Richard Rive, *Advance, Retreat: Selected Short Stories* (New York: St. Martin's Press, 1983), 5-9.

This "resurrection" marks the first time that the "mother" of the white-looking children is allowed to give voice to her suffering and her sense of having been betrayed by her children.

Like Mavis, Ou Kakkelak in Alex La Guma's story "Out of Darkness" (1957)[14] is made to suffer, because other persons pass. His girlfriend Cora is suddenly attracted by the secondary gains playing-white seem to promise her and goes to places where he cannot accompany her. In the end, she turns on him, slaps his face, calls him a black nigger, and tells him to go to hell. Hell for him means prison, because the story hints that after her outburst he kills her. Kakkelak's tragedy is "the tragedy of internalized values of ethnicity."[15] As Chandramohan argues, La Guma's "denunciation of such values is even more elaborate" in "The Gladiators" (1967) (Chandramohan, *Trans-Ethnicity*, 62). The story's protagonist Kenny, who just misses passing for white, dreams of becoming the star of the white boxing world. He feels so superior racially to his black opponent that he fails to take him seriously and is easily knocked out. In vain does his coach remind him of the fact that slight differences in skin-color do not matter to audiences who "pay cash to see two other black boys knock themselves to hell."[16]

Another theme that sometimes goes along with the passer's self-criticism is the desire to return home again — not necessarily to a physical home and to family obligations, but chiefly to the group one has abandoned for the attractions of the white world. This magnetic pull of home may, or may not, be identified as a "vague and mysterious calling of race."[17] To illustrate this point, Juda Bennett cites a short passage on passers from the American novel *Passing* (1929) by Nella Larsen:

> "They always come back. I've seen it happen time and time again."
> "But why?" Irene wanted to know. "Why?"
> "If I knew that, I'd know what race is" (Bennett, *Passing Figure*, 51).

An impressive American example of such a homecoming[18] is Sinclair Lewis's *Kingsblood Royal* (1947): on discovering that he has black ancestors the novel's protagonist goes through an identity crisis; he ends it by accepting his black origins, risking his position in white society, and fighting for his own people. The theme of homecoming plays an important role in *God's Stepchildren* and in a number of works

---

[14] Alex La Guma, "Out of Darkness," in Richard Rive, ed., *Quartet: New Voices from South Africa* (London: Heinemann, 1974), 33-8.

[15] Balasubramanyam Chandramohan, *A Study in Trans-Ethnicity in Modern South Africa: The Writings of Alex La Guma 1925-1985* (Lewiston: Mellen Research University Press, 1992), 62.

[16] Alex La Guma, "The Gladiators," *A Walk in the Night and Other Stories* (Evanston: Northwestern University Press, 1990), 108-14, 111.

[17] Juda Bennett, *The Passing Figure: Racial Confusion in Modern American Literature* (New York: Peter Lang, 1996), 51.

[18] See Berzon, *Neither White*, 159, for other American returns to one's roots.

still to be discussed. Here it may suffice to mention Ahmed Essop's "The Hajji" (1978), which relates the homecoming from the perspective of a person who did not leave the family fold.

In Essop's short story, Karim uses his fair complexion and grey eyes as passports to cross the color border and live with a white woman. His family is shocked and humiliated. His brother Hajji feels: "By going over to the white Herrenvolk, his brother had trampled on something that was vitally part of him, his dignity and self-respect."[19] His brother's betrayal still rankles with Hajji ten years later. When Karim lies dying and wishes to be given a Muslim burial, Hajji obstinately refuses to have anything to do with the funeral. In the end, however, his fear of how other Muslims might judge his behavior, his regret of the morbid joy he felt at Karim's death, and some childhood memories of his brother make him change his mind. He joins the funeral procession belatedly, but is not recognized by anyone.

Passing as a Political Weapon

As a questionable assimilation to white standards, passing is usually connoted negatively: as opportunism, betrayal, and the cause of suffering. Sometimes it is appreciated as a playful means of temporarily setting aside bothersome restrictions and apartheid rules. Occasionally, it is fully accepted as a political weapon to camouflage underground activities, escape from the police, and help those whose skin-color gives them away as non-whites.

In the American context, for instance, passing helped light-skinned blacks to escape into freedom. In his biographical account *Running a Thousand Miles for Freedom*, or *The Escape*, William Craft tells how his wife, passing as a white lady, and he, impersonating her black servant, escaped to the North. Though Craft's book was first published in 1860, his story, which had already received much publicity, stimulated Harriet Beecher Stowe in *Uncle Tom's Cabin* (1852) to make passing the means by which Eliza gets away from the slave catcher Tom Loker. Later American writers followed suit (see Berzon, *Neither White*).

In the South African situation, passing could be employed to circumvent discriminatory laws, to escape to other counties, cope with police control, and move more freely from one area to another and thus keep in touch with other members of the opposition.

In the short story cycle *You Can't Get Lost in Cape Town* (1987),[20] Zoe Wicomb deals with a 'colored' family that aspires to leave its provincial Afrikaans background behind and rise socially in modern urban society. As Frieda, the narrator, shows, her parents have adopted the English language and English values and prevented her from socializing with Afrikaans-speaking 'coloreds' of the neighbourhood. This strategy of

---

[19] Ahmed Essop, "The Hajji," in Denis Hirson and Martin Trump, eds., *The Heinemann Book of South African Short Stories* (Oxford: Heinemann, 1994), 189-201, 190.

[20] Zoe Wicomb, *You Can't Get Lost in Cape Town* (New York: Pantheon, 1987).

stigma management ignores not only the British legacy of colonialism in South Africa, but also the rigid apartheid laws and norms. In the title story, Frieda, who has a white lover of English descent, wishes to get an illegal abortion, knowing only too well that interracial marriage is forbidden. The white abortionist, who asserts that she would not act on behalf of 'colored' girls, is misled by Frieda's educated language and performs the operation. She is assisted by a 'colored' girl who is aware of Frieda's racial identity. Ironically, it is a white racist who helps someone whose dilemma was caused by racist laws. Embryos may be aborted in apartheid Cape Town, but that is the only way to get lost, because children and adults cannot really escape from a society that enforces racial division and stigmatization.

Richard Rive's novel *Emergency* (1964) concentrates on the lives of a few Cape Town 'colored' activists in the days after the Sharpeville massacre (1960) and outlines the political options the men will have if the State of Emergency is proclaimed: strikes, underground activities or the flight to Basutoland. The novel leaves it open whether the characters can really carry out their various plans. But it takes a clear, if complex stand on passing. The politically committed 'coloreds' usually despise play-whites such as James Dyer who uses his light skin to get around the Immorality Act and enjoy flings with white women. Abe Hanslo, a man who could easily have crossed the line, criticizes too facile condemnations, however. He argues that those who try to pass remain victims of the apartheid system:

> I think we should try and understand people like him. It's easy for Herby to cross the colour-line. He's fair and his hair is O.K. It means advantages. No abuses. Better facilities. All that goes with the divine rights of a white skin.[21]

He himself plays white only for the political purpose of getting away from the police and protecting Andrew Dyer and his white girlfriend from being arrested. In one of the novel's most effective scenes, he joins a queue for non-Europeans at the railway ticket office. When the clerk mistakes him for a white and tells him to go to the office for Europeans, he makes a point of staying and insisting on being served, thus demonstrating to the bystanders how arbitrary racial definitions are (Rive, *Emergency*, 123ff). His stand is in keeping with his opinion that the opposition to the apartheid system should eschew an Africanist or racialist orientation:

> The people must at the very start be made to recognize the indivisibility of oppression. They must look upon themselves not as Africans, Coloureds, Indians or whites, but as a people seeking to abolish national oppression. Racialism cannot be fought with racialism [...] (Rive, *Emergency*, 163).

Richard Rive appoints the 'colored' intellectual as the spokesman for the emancipation of all South Africans and the fight against racialism. At the same time he makes it clear that, given the imminent State of Emergency, Abe Hanslo must be regarded as a political idealist and dreamer by his friends. Rive thus tries to maintain some distance

---

[21] Richard Rive, *Emergency* (London: Collier, 1970), 72.

from the old stereotype that the light-skinned 'coloreds' are predestined to lead their darker brothers.[22] The same stereotype recurs in Rose Moss's *The Schoolmaster* (1979).

Moss's novel is loosely based on a terrorist incident in 1964. David Miller, a teacher, and some of his friends from school days are prepared to blow up installations. The majority have agreed to plan such acts of sabotage carefully in order not to endanger human lives. Convinced that there is no more time for patience and political stalling, David Miller does not abide by the majority decision and plants a bomb in a public place, hoping to signal "the end" of the apartheid regime symbolically.[23] He is caught by the police and condemned to death. In the prison cell he reviews his life and tries to come to terms with the fact that he has killed innocent poeple and endangered the lives of the other conspirators. In particular, he has to cope with the totally unexpected reactions of his old friend and role model Philip Boet: when he comes to his home on his flight from the police, Philip sends him away like "a mad dog," blames him for having betrayed the group's trust, and even threatens to call the police (Moss, *Schoolmaster*, 7). Philip, a 'colored' who can and does pass as white when he wishes to circumvent the apartheid rules, has been an opponent of the regime since their school days and suffered for his views in prison. In the course of the novel, David has to learn to respect differences in opinion on the use of violence against the state and take responsibility for his own actions. He is also forced to appreciate the courage Philip displays when summoned as a court witness: though obviously having undergone torture, Philip does his best not to incriminate his friend. It is David, not Philip, who has betrayed his group's trust. Perhaps, however, such betrayals are inevitable, given the historical situation. In the night before the execution, David, who is white, is cheered up by the songs of the black prisoners:

> They welcomed him. The power was his also. Their power was his power. They would take his power and save it. He had poured out his life. He had not reversed history. He had not broken the dam. But he was not lost (Moss, *Schoolmaster*, 237).

Passing and the Indictment of Racism

Of course the works that employ passing as a weapon and those that explore the suffering and even tragic fates of the play-whites and their relatives are severe indictments of the apartheid regime. This, however, does not automatically mean that they can also be read as attacks on racism in general. As long as they insist that the passers deserve a tragic fate, that they betray their ethnic group, or should pass only to promote the political ends of the oppressed, they remain implicated in racialist constructions of black, 'colored' and white identities. What Horst Zander said about the theme of miscegenation seems to apply to that of passing too: it "usually fails to provide the

---

[22] For the American mulatto as race leader, see Berzon, *Neither White*, ch. 8.
[23] Rose Moss, *The Schoolmaster* (Randburg: Ravon Press, 1995) (first as Terrorist, 1979), 4.

tool for efficient social criticism of a racialist society" (Zander, "Millin's Stepchildren," 125).

A more effective or radical criticism would have to acknowledge the reality of racism and yet demonstrate the arbitrariness of racial classifications and their concomitant legal, economic, political, and cultural fictions. It would emphasize that "all race identity is [...] the product of passing"[24] or that race, in Henry Louis Gates's term, is "the ultimate trope of difference" (Ginsberg, "Introduction," 8), that is, merely a metaphor, not an authentic expression of being.

In the historical situation in South Africa before the dismantling of apartheid, the differences and divisions between the various ethnic groups were stressed by the whites in power and, often for reasons of self-defence and survival, by the oppressed. Visions of equality for all and of a truly multicultural society evolved in the course of time, but did not necessarily unite oppositional groups. Hence, it is little wonder that most South African passing narratives are about the representation of the differences between blacks, 'coloreds,' and whites. A few works are, however, concerned with the failure of color to provide "the grounds for a stable, coherent identity" and raise the question of what is white, if a 'colored' can be white (Kawash, "Autobiography," 63). As such works suggest, passing can insist "on the fallacy of identity as a content of social, psychological, national, or cultural attributes, whether bestowed by nature or produced by society; it forces us to pay attention to the form of difference itself" (Kawash, "Autobiography," 63).

For H.J.E. Dhlomo difference of color, a biological fact, does not justify cultural constructions of racial difference and discriminatory practices. In his story "An Experiment in Colour" (1935), he employs themes from Robert Louis Stevenson's *Dr Jekyll and Mr Hyde* and H.G. Wells's *The Invisible Man* to show that the social information skin-color conveys to prejudiced observers misrepresents that person's character.[25] Frank Mabaso, a highly intelligent black headmaster at an African school, reacts bitterly to daily discrimination and takes refuge in scientific experiments to solve the maddening problem of color. After discovering the secret of how the chameleon changes its color, he is ready to experiment upon himself. With the help of injections, he can turn himself into "a perfect white man" and back into a black man.[26] He tries out his discovery in public and enjoys passing as white. Having gained the love of a white woman, he neglects his black wife and child and soon exhausts his financial resources. Realizing that he cannot keep up his expensive double life, he decides to publicize his discovery and present it as a solution to the race problem. His

---

[24] Samira Kawash, "*The Autobiography of an Ex-Coloured Man*: (Passing for) Black Passing for White," in Ginsberg, *Passing*, 59-74, 70.

[25] Another predecessor, if not model, is George Schuyler, *Black No More* (Boston: Northeastern University Press, 1989). This satire from the 1920s deals with the invention of a whitening process by Doctor Crookman of Black-No-More, Inc. Thanks to the invention, Max Disher is whitened, assumes the name Matthew Fisher, and leaves Harlem for the South; there he marries into a white family and soon begins to defend white supremacy.

[26] Herbert I.E. Dhlomo, *Collected Works*, Nick Visser and Tim Couzens, eds., (Johannesburg: Ravan Press, 1985), 489-99, 494.

demonstration of the experiment is successful, but his message that color is an arbitrary sign, not a stigma, is not appreciated: a white man kills him on the spot, because white kaffirs are not wanted in the Afrikaner country (Dhlomo, *Collected Works*, 499).

In the novel *Let the Day Perish* (1952), Gerald Gordon tells the story of two brothers.[27] Stephen feels stigmatized by his dark skin, broods on racial and social inequality, and later commits himself to the cause of freedom for his people. Light-skinned Anthony passes, attends a white school, and climbs the social ladder. Ironically, he seems to personify "all the myths of white ethno-aestheticians:" "He is blond and handsome, virile and popular, a sportsman of no mean ability — a veritable Apollo" (February, *Mind Your Colour*, 68). When brought to trial for violating the Immorality Act, he publicly admits that he is 'colored' and uses the opportunity to attack the regime as one still persecuting the 'coloreds' for the acts of their ancestors. His later suicide is in keeping with his closing statement to the court:

> "We were tried for the acts of our ancestors, were convicted and sentenced to live in a world of prejudice. Even if you acquit me now, that sentence still stands. It stands until my earthly existence comes to a close. With Job I can truly say: 'Let the day perish wherein I was born and the night in which it was said, there is a man child conceived'" (February, *Mind Your Colour*, 68).

Anthony's suicide, as V.A. February points out, appears less melodramatic in the light of newspaper reports of "well-known farmers (Afrikaners at that), who after being 'caught in the act,'" chose "a shameful death in preference to a lifetime of racial prejudice and ostracism" (February, *Mind Your Colour*, 69). All in all, Anthony is an interesting variation on the tragic mulatto: he suffers in the racist reality of South Africa, but refuses to accept the doctrines that racists invoke to justify their stand.

The theme of the two brothers is taken up again in Athol Fugard's *The Blood Knot* (1961). The play focuses on the relationship between Morris and Zacharias, two 'colored' brothers in a Port Elizabeth township. Light-skinned Morris apparently passed for some time as white, but decided to return home to his brother one year before the play's action begins. As in other works, his homecoming is motivated by Morris's sense of having betrayed his brother, whose eyes, he believes, pursue him into his dreams. As Brian Crow oberves, "[...] Fugard seems to be saying that individuals can never escape the 'eyes' of others, whether one's actions are in the form of role-play or out in the 'real world.'"[28] Another reason for Morris's homecoming is only hinted at in some of his remarks about the past: he may have had frustrating experiences in the world of the whites, including that of being found out as a play-white.

---

[27] Since the text was not available, I follow February, *Mind Your Colour*, 67-9. The theme of the two half-brothers who develop differently is found in a number of American novels, for instance, in Harriet Beecher Stowe's anti-slavery novel *Dred: A Tale of the Dismal Swamp*. See Berzon, *Neither White*, passim.

[28] Brian Crow, "Athol Fugard," in Bruce King, ed., *Post-colonial English Drama. Commonwealth Drama since 1960* (New York: Macmillan, 1992), 150-64, here 155.

In spite of his wish to be with Zach and support him, Morris identifies his brother as a black man and projects everything he dislikes about himself onto him. Zach, for his part, envies Morris's skin-color. The color difference, of which both brothers are painfully aware, is accompanied by other differences. Fugard attributes behavioral traits to the two men that are usually employed in the racist discourse as stereotypes to construct differences between the races. Probably because of his previous life among whites, Morris, the son of an Afrikaner, has internalized 'white values' like self-discipline, thrift, rationality, and Calvinist ascetism. His dark-skinned brother, who takes after his black mother, is, unlike Morris, illiterate. Zach is not really interested in Christian religion, lives from day to day, and fantasizes about having sexual adventures. Whereas Zach works as a watchman in a park for whites, Morris has the say in their shack and feels responsible for its order. Because of this division of spheres and the other differences mentioned, the tense relationship between the brothers mirrors the conflict-ridden co-existence of whites and non-whites under apartheid.

The mirror is, however, a distorting one. As 'coloreds,' both brothers are victims of racial segregation. The fact that Morris and Zach are highly sensitive to the differences between them does not change their fate, for their differences are negated by the classifications the apartheid regime enforces. Hence, the differences acquire meaning only in the psychological and social games the two brothers play with one another. Through these games Morris and Zach learn to question their dreams and illusions and acknowledge their actual social situation.

Morris, for example, dreams of buying a farm and saves their money for this purpose. When his brother wishes to spend his wages on women, Morris suggests instead that he should find a female pen-pal. Zach likes the idea and enters into correspondence with an unknown woman enthusiastically. Morris, who writes the letters for him, is shocked when the woman's 'white identity' is revealed by a photo. He advises his brother to end the correspondence, because, as he probably knows from previous experience, "They don't like these games with their whiteness."[29] Zach, however, insists on continuining the correspondence. Though he realizes that he will not be accepted as a partner by the white woman, his imagination has been so stimulated that he wishes to prolong the game and enjoy a vicarious experience with his brother's help. Expecting Morris to stand in for him during the white woman's visit, he spends all their savings on dressing Morris up as a white gentleman and then rehearses the rendezvous with him. Morris finds the game appealing to his secret wishes and loses himself in the role of the white gentleman to the extent of treating his brother, who mimicks a peanut-seller, brutally as a black "boy." This eruption of the game into a racist conflict shocks both brothers. Zach becomes newly aware of his low status in South African society, feels that his personal identity has been threatened, and asks his dead mother in an imaginary dialogue whether blackness really means ugliness. Morris feels guilty, fears that he has once again played Judas to his bother, and plans to leave again.

---

[29] Athol Fugard, *Selected Plays* (Oxford: Oxford University Press, 1987), 92.

When the woman ends the correspondence for reasons of her own, Zach asks Morris to put on the suit in which he looked like a gentleman. In this new game, Zach plays his real-life role as a watchman in a park, whereas Morris assumes the role of a white racist. In the game, Zach demonstrates how white men usually treat him and then makes it clear to his brother that he does not like 'coloreds' who play-white in order to enter the park reserved for whites. Since each character's self-hatred is vented in anger at the other, the game, like the ones preceding it, threatens to climax in violence.

In the end, however, the two brothers return from the world of make-believe to the reality of their shabby shack. Morris buries his dream of becoming a farmer, affirms the "bond between brothers," and hopes that in the future Zach and he will play harmless games which while away the time, but do not make them forget reality. The brothers' resignation and hopelessness resemble those of Vladimir and Estragon in Beckett's *Waiting for Godot*. Although the 1985 version of the play is even more bleak,[30] the original has been rightly characterized as follows:

> [...] Morris and Zach are in a state of siege: the harsh, outer world is pressing in upon them; they cannot escape their beleaguered castle and they must perforce construct a modus vivendi within their single room upon the meagre rations of human tolerance and understanding. *The Blood Knot* is South Africa's *La Peste*: the "absurdity" of the French novelist, Albert Camus, is here represented by the apartheid world which drives two imprisoned men into each other's arms. At the end of *La Peste*, Dr. Rieux, the doctor in the city attacked by plague, has come to terms with life; similarly *The Blood Knot* explores the methods by which Morris and Zach adjust - both to themselves and to each other.[31]

The Blood Knot is certainly the best treatment of the passing theme to come out of South Africa. It alludes to a number of the clichés associated with the theme, but it presents them, via plays within the play, in a distanced manner. It thus effectively illustrates the suffering caused by differences in skin-color that reflect on the arbitrary distinctions imposed upon society by the racist discourse.

Bessie Head's *Maru* (1971) also sheds light on the racial pecking order. The whites look down upon the coloreds, the coloreds on the blacks, the blacks on specific black tribes and peoples:

> And if the white man thought Africans were a low, filthy nation, Africans in Southern Africa could still smile — at least they were not Bushmen. They all have their monsters. You just have to look different from them, the way the facial features of a Sudra or Tamil do not resemble the facial features of a high caste Hindu, then seemingly anything can be said and done to you as your outer appearance reduces you to the status of a non-human being.[32]

---

[30] See Kim McKay, "The Blood Knot Reborn in the Eighties: A Reflection of the Artist and His Times," *Modern Drama* 30 (1987): 496-504.

[31] R.J. Green, "South Africa's Plague: One View of The Blood Knot," *Modern Drama*, 12 (1970): 331-45, here 333.

[32] Bessie Head, *Maru* (London: Heinemann, 1987), 11.

In the novel, an orphaned Bushman girl is raised by the missionary's wife and given her name, Margaret Cadmore. When the child becomes conscious of herself as a person, she has difficulties defining herself in terms of her family background and the responses of other people. On the one hand, everyone tells her that she is "a Bushman, mixed, half breed, low breed or bastard;" on the other hand, everyone is thrown into confusion when she opens her mouth to speak:

> Her mind and heart were composed of a little bit of everything she had absorbed from Margaret Cadmore. It was hardly African or anything but something new and universal, a type of personality that would be unable to fit into definition of something as narrow as tribe or race or nation (Head, *Maru*, 16).

After leaving school, Margaret becomes a teacher in a small Botswana village, where her people, the Marsawas, are treated as outcasts. Since she freely admits that she is a Marsawa herself and does not try to pass as a 'colored,' she makes the villagers realize how deceptive appearances are: "'The eye is a deceitful thing,' they said. 'If a Marsawa combs his hair and wears modern dress, she looks just like a coloured'" (Head, *Maru*, 52-3). Whereas the more progressive villagers accept her as a teacher, the conservatives turn against her. The gap between these two camps is widened when Maru, one of the local leaders, falls in love with Margaret. The couple wisely leaves the village. Yet as Bessie Head suggests, their marriage instils the discriminated Marsawas with hope and Maru's ideal of mutual tolerance marks a new beginning (see Head, *Maru*, 126).

Carolyn Slaughter's *The Innocents* (1986) uses a number of themes from Daphne Rooke's *Mittee* and can be seen as an updated version of the same in that it anticipates the end of apartheid. Like other South African novels, *The Innocents* associates the possibility of interracial friendship with childhood and adolescence and demonstrates how the apartheid system affects the characters as they move into adulthood. The novel's first generation grows up on an isolated farm. Zelda and her brother Dawie strike up a close friendship with the 'colored' girl Hannah, allow her to play indoors and sleep in their room. This friendship survives their separation when Zelda and Dawie are sent away to a school for whites. Dawie later defines the age of innocence as "all those free, easy years before adolescence:"

> After that, in an unspoken way, it should have stopped, as she [Hannah] should have begun to call him baasie. It was not that they refused those traditions, purposefully broke the rituals and the taboos of centuries, it was just that it never occurred to any of them that they were anything but equals.[33]

The novel's second generation also does not respect racial barriers. Young Ruth, who lives with Zelda and Hannah, plays with the Afrikaner Andries and the black boy Willie, who works on the farm. Only during occasional quarrels does Ruth resort to using racist epithets to humiliate Willie.

---

[33] Carolyn Slaughter, *The Innocents* (New York: Simon & Schuster, 1988), 67.

The rather idyllic time of friendship and mutual respect, which all the characters like to remember, is destroyed by love and sexuality. These themes, but especially that of miscegenation, turn the novel into a rural Gothic reminiscent of Rooke's *Mittee* and American Southern fiction. Zelda kills the man who jilts her shortly before their wedding. Her brother and Hannah fall in love with one another, but have to separate when she gives birth to a daughter. Zelda saves the baby from being drowned by her mother. Sixteen years later, Ruth, who expects a child from Andries, runs away from home to seek Willie's help. After Willie has driven her back to the farm, she gives birth to a 'colored' boy. At first she is shocked and revolted at the sight of the child, but when she is informed that Hannah and Dawie are her parents, she becomes reconciled to her personal history. Dawie and Hannah plan to marry and acknowledge Ruth as their child. The need to keep an interracial affair secret and hide one's child or hope that it will pass in public no longer exists (Slaughter, *The Innocents*, 226), because in real life the Mixed Marriages Act was abolished on June 19, 1985. Another sign that the days of the apartheid regime are numbered is the violence spilling over from the cities into the countryside. The historical context, then, allows Carolyn Slaughter to provide a happy ending both for the tragic mulatto theme (Hannah) and that of passing (Ruth) and demonstrate the viability of interracial friendship.

In Rayda Jacob's novel *The Middle Children* (1994), light-skinned Sabah, who comes from an Indian-Muslim background, plays-white occasionally, for instance, to use the less-crowded European section of the train. At the age of 16 she decides to try to pass in order to be accepted into a restricted business school. Five years later, in 1968, she is arrested for bearing a white pass and forced to emigrate, since she had applied to Canada for a visa already. The novel recalls Sabah's childhood and adolescence under apartheid, her experiences in Canada, and her visits to South Africa. It introduces a great number of characters and intercultural encounters and focuses on survival under apartheid and change in Canada and South Africa, rather than the suffering and identity crises of its protagonist. In one episode Sabah successfully manages to escape the trap three male office-workers have set up to catch her both as a woman and a play-white; in another scene she is amused by a police-officer's insistence that she should go to the section for whites and report a theft there. Sabah refuses to consider her fate as a singular one and is tired of "this singsong over who's more oppressed:"

> The middle people have had it better than the black people, yes but the middle people have suffered too. ... At least, if you have a black skin, you know you're black. The devil isn't at your elbow telling you to just get into the white section of the train 'cause there you'll have a seat, or leave out your race on the job up because you're damn qualified and want the job. Whiteskins are tempted everyday into falseness and deceit.[34]

She welcomes the dismantling of apartheid, admires the lack of bitterness in Mandela, and is herself willling to forgive. She does not return to South Africa, but prefers to become a naturalized citizen of Canada, a country that has "warmed up with the dif-

---

[34] Rayda Jacobs, *The Middle Children* (Toronto: Second Story Press, 1994), 143.

ferent colours of the world" (Jacobs, *Middle Children*, 162) since she first came and thus can serve as a model for the new South Africa to be created after 1990.

Summary

Passing has fascinated many South African writers. As a transgression of the economic, social, cultural and legal boundaries within South African society before and under apartheid, it has caused white writers to rally to the defence of white hegemony. Even if the white authors did not advocate racist policies, they found passing an unsettling theme and preferred to focus on the problems and tragic failures of the play-whites, rather than their successes. 'Colored' and black writers also often critized passing as the assumption of a fraudulent white identity. They recommended that those who were able to pass should not seek success and salvation with the whites, but rather with the oppressed in general, or with the group they came from in particular. They usually tolerated brief, intermittent passing as a political weapon to outwit the police and circumvent apartheid regulations. Like some white writers, they took up the passing theme in order to attack the apartheid regime.

Authors from all groups were interested in reducing the potential threat contained in the act of passing: its threat to the racial categories and hierarchies established by social custom and the law. Given the racist reality under the apartheid regime, most writers found it difficult to conceive of passing as a masquerade demonstrating how arbitrary "the epidermal schema of racial difference" (Frantz Fanon) is (quoted from Ginsberg, "Introduction," 4). They thought rather in terms of opposing racial groups and wished to strengthen the walls around their camps. Now that apartheid has officially been abandoned and replaced by the doctine of multiculturalism, perhaps a less rigidly ethical and partisan, a more relaxed and playful approach to passing will become possible. However, as American literature shows, the stereotypical evaluations of passing and the mulatto seem to stay alive long after the abandonment of restrictive racist laws.

Migrations: Reading Louise Ho and Interleaving the Chinese Diaspora

ANDREW PARKIN (Hong Kong)

We have family trees and we figure the history of our texts by means of the *stemma*. We talk of our roots in a certain culture, geographical region, or mother tongue. We are talking tree dwellers — and once were that. On the other hand, human migration has been a condition of our being and our survival for many thousands of years. It is clear that we are no longer as rooted as we imagine we once were. Human beings are not trees. Nor do we have roots. We have feet. We move about carrying our memories with us.

Human geographers would largely agree that over the last two hundred years there has been more human migration than at any other period since the last ice age. The human story has been one of diaspora. The Chinese diaspora is an astonishing phenomenon and a large chapter in that narrative. An ancient civilization that had progressed in many ways further than the remainder of humanity had its merchants who spread into the neighbouring Asian communities, but China reached its crisis in the late eighteenth century and found itself during the nineteenth century to be weak and humiliated by the foreigners aggressively using the new technologies and sciences developing so rapidly in Europe. As the power of the Chinese Empire declined and the golden mountains of the West beckoned, Hong Kong became a staging post for the Chinese footing it from their towns and villages to escape poverty, seeking another chance at life, another chance at wealth, another modernity. In the twentieth century, revolutions, civil war, and world wars created historical conditions for the Chinese that can only be termed nightmarish tragedy. This again resulted in diaspora. People had to find their feet in other cultures.

Our concern here is one example of the literary consequence of all this. In our contemporary world, where English is no longer the mere imposition of a colonial power, world trading patterns, scientific publications, and the global information network, together with the migration of people in their millions, have resulted in the use of English as a tool for practical affairs and as a literary language for writers of the new literatures in English. An abiding fascination of these new 'English' literatures is that the readers of English around the world may discover a vast array of literary talent with different ethnicities, different sensibilities. Insofar as the Chinese diaspora has created a growing number of ethnic Chinese writers in English, we should not forget the strength of Chinese cultures, the binding significance of Chinese as a written language, and that other phenomenon of new Chinese literature by overseas Chinese written in Chinese. This is different from the new literatures in English, of course, in that it is written by Chinese in 'exile' (voluntary and involuntary) and is therefore akin to other emigré literature (e.g. Polish and Russian). We are not talking of a literature in Chinese written by people who are not ethnically Chinese.

How does the poetry of Louise Ho fit in — if it does? In my view, Louise Ho is rather different from the Chinese writers who have gone into other cultures as children, or been born into immigrant families and have stayed as native speakers of English within the 'new' culture. Louise Ho is a native speaker of Cantonese who has grown up and studied in a number of different places but has worked for most of her adult life in Hong Kong. Because of her early education, she has never really learned to write Chinese characters with any facility for literary purposes. She speaks, writes, and teaches English with native-speaker aplomb. A poet-critic, she publishes in English. She operates on a social level and at work (like many of the Hong Kong elite) as a bilingual 'professional.' Like many of them, too, she has foreign nationality, in her case Australian citizenship. She articulates a distinct kind of *Hong Kong modernity*.

Born in Hong Kong in 1943, when it was under the control of the Japanese forces, Louise Ho was educated in Mauritius, Hong Kong, and England. From her early years in Mauritius, or l'Isle Maurice as it is known to the French — and of course to Baudelaire, who stayed there briefly — she retains an interest in the French language and French literature. Her poetry contains traces of Baudelaire's ironies. Her educated English accent confirms the English part of her education and her frequent visits to a country where she has good friends[1] and a sense of 'home' that comes from its being her 'other world' as she refers to it in 'Migratory,' despite Hong Kong's importance for her as - perhaps - her real home, and despite her recently acquired Australian nationality.

What kind of a home can Hong Kong be? It is a crossroads home. It is a hybrid culture. It is a city culture, a fishing culture, as old as the first fisher folk, it is rural too, in what is left of the New Territories. Her house was on the edge of the Mai Po marshes, very near the Chinese border, on the staging-perch of migratory birds, within the staging-post territory. Hong Kong as a city is full of ancient superstition and modernity, village-like in its networks of old friends, a megalopolis in its wired architecture dominated by the banks. It is a latter-day Byzantium of master jewellers and East/West traders. In "Home to Hong Kong" a few terse lines capture the sense of a hybrid home of migrants:

> A Chinese
> Invited an Irishman
> To a Japanese meal
> By the Spanish steps
> In the middle of Rome
> Having come from Boston
> On the way home
>
> (*New Ends, Old Beginnings*: 77)

The Chinese on the way home will carry in her mental baggage a sense of both America and Europe. And what Chinese could forget the Japanese? The free verse is

---

[1] This information as with subsequent undocumented personal knowledge comes from many conversations between the present writer and Louise Ho from January 1991 onwards.

not entirely North American; the capitals at the beginning of each line belong to the greater formality of English and, indeed, European versification. This third and latest book of verse, *New Ends, Old Beginnings,* reaches back, through its themes of home, self, and migration to her previous book of poems, *Local Habitation.*

The links between the two books are the result of naturally continuing concerns of the writer and are conscious, deliberate. Ho includes in her latest book for example the poem "Remembering June 4, 1989" which was part of her previous collection. The reason is that many migrations from Hong Kong were prompted by the Tiananmen Square events of June 1989.[2] The events provoked thousands of poems around the world in different languages. Louise Ho's poem begins by invoking writers from the English literary tradition: Marvell, Dryden, Yeats, "[...] men who had taken up the pen/While others the sword.[...]" Her next two stanzas plunge from this general context into reportage, recalling the bloodshed, and the "stunned world" that "Pointing an accusing finger, felt cheated." The poem then delivers its 'turn' or 'volta' in thought, for the next stanza asserts that Hong Kong's hopes were dashed by a power that never promised more than "The rock bottom of a totalitarian state." Drawing on Yeats's "Easter 1916" in her next stanza, she celebrates the change in Hong Kong people that the events caused: a new solidarity in which people "rose up as one" thinking and speaking as one so that "We too have changed [...]/And something beautiful was born." It was a bloody birth.

The newborn Hong Kong spirit might nevertheless have its moments of gladness at the prospect of return to the mother, China. For many, however, resistance was stiffened and produced the desire to leave home, to find an 'adolescent' independence, a new sense of Chinese identity separate from that of continental China or that of Taiwan. Another feature of this was the very practical need for an insurance against totalitarianism through emigration and foreign passports. Louise Ho did not leave immediately after June 1989 but some years later. Her emigration spurred the reflections on migration, 'home' and identity. She is now a 'returnee,' poised astride the Pacific, one foot in Hong Kong, one in Australia. This is different from the precarious balancing act at the end of her Tiananmen poem:

> Ours is a unique genius,
> Learning how to side-step all odds
> Or to survive them.
> We have lived
> By understanding
> Each in his own way
> The tautness of the rope
> Underfoot.
> *(New Ends, Old Beginnings*: 23-25)

---

[2] In a note to the present writer about a projected collaboration, Louise Ho noted that the poem "Remembering June 4, 1989" was from *Local Habitation* but also "[...] as it happens, it begins the theme of emigration, so v.[ery] suitable for our new volume" [March 1996].

The genius for side-stepping the odds in order to survive is not unique to the people of Hong Kong, or even of China itself. It is, of course, shared by all the hardy peoples who have survived our blood-soaked century. We are all tight-rope walkers. This is not to denigrate the ability of Hong Kong in itself to survive. It is merely to see our century's battles and migrations as global phenomena.

Another point worth noting about how Louise Ho's work fits the migration theme of our last two centuries is this: *New Ends, Old Beginnings* actually grew from an earlier group of poems that she was collecting to put in a book she would call either *Migrations* or *Migratory* (a title she has used for one poem in the latest book just referred to) or *Tertium Quid* or *Monkey Business*. The last of these working titles illustrates Louise Ho's humorous, bantering mood. The present writer was also going to collect poems he had written about journeying and Australia. If the collection seemed to hold together, it would be a collaborative volume in search of a publisher.

This was an idea we had in March 1996. The collaboration did not get very far; the two poets, though, have not ruled out some future collaboration. They bounce ideas off one another in a jocular way. This is one way in which they combat the pressures of the academy and keep a creative space amid the academic work.

In contrast to flight there is standing one's ground. Many Hong Kong people lacking the education or the resources to emigrate and unable to obtain British passports, because of the British refusal to grant them to all Hong Kong residents as a 'safety net,' have simply stood their ground, proving that wherever they may have come from originally, they are now Hong Kongers. Others have actively welcomed the 'handover,' seeing June 4 as an anomaly. China is now almost free of foreign colonial interference. This is a matter of national pride. It is also a matter of national pride that China's form of communism is pragmatic enough to make needed reforms and steer the economy successfully through special economic zones, one country two systems, significant privatization, infrastructure projects, and joint ventures. Mistakes of the past are being admitted and astute policies have enabled the leadership in Beijing to avoid the sudden collapse of the system that the Soviet bloc suffered. If end-of-the-century China is not a totally post-communist society, it is being described as one that runs a kind of 'socialist capitalism.' This kind of paradox is perfectly possible in the thinking of pragmatic Chinese officials.

If standing one's ground is now feasible as an anti-colonial stance and also an anti-emigration stance, it is worth remembering also that, for many Hong Kong people during the Communist and Red Guard riots of 1967, the standing one's ground of the British forces and local colonial police was in some ways desirable and even admirable. Louise Ho reminds us in the year of the handover, 1997, that thirty years before there had been the riots commemorated in her "Hong Kong riots, 1967 II:"

> Stand your ground
> even if for only
> two foot square.
> The sentry's box
> the railings
> the imposing gate posts

> were plastered
> with posters.
> [...]
> The anti-riot police
> grouped
> like so many Roman turtles
> stood their ground.
> Rain or shine
> surrounded by crowds
> outside
> the Governor's house
> the sentry stood
> khaki shorts
> rifle in hand
> still as a statue
> and held his ground
> of two foot square.
> This too is pomp and circumstance
> without fanfare.
>
> (*New Ends, Old Beginnings*: 15-16)

The lack of fanfare is also part of the poem's versification with its short three or four beat lines with casual variants of more syllables here and there and the off-hand rhyme to give a finish that is almost an afterthought: "foot square" with "fanfare!"

This poem, together with "Hong Kong riots 1967 I" – a short lyric of eight lines dealing with the lifting of the curfew – derives from the earlier volume, *Local Habitation* (1994) were it was printed as two poems, with what has now become the second one following without the interruption of another title. The arrangement with titling I and II is clearer, because we know that both poems are about the same riots, and to my mind it is a better presentation. The first starts with the end of the rioting, the second with the riots themselves. The reverse order fits the title of the new book.

In the late sixties it was known to many in Hong Kong that China could take back the colony in a few hours merely by cutting off the water supply, among other things. There were people ready to flee at the switch of a tap. The horrors of the 'Cultural Revolution' were becoming known. People with families across the border were very worried. Corpses that had been thrown into the Pearl River were sighted off the shore at Shek O, a popular Hong Kong Island beach.[3] 'Home' as a concept was very problematic. The traditional Chinese idea of a family was changed by a hundred years of massive migrations and the horrors of twentieth century Chinese history. This kind of upsetting redefinition of family is known to all migrants and, of course, the displaced peoples of Europe and Africa. Louise Ho takes stock of it in "Hong Kong at the Crossroads:"

---

[3] Imagine the present writer's astonishment, returning to Britain in late 1967, to find naive university students waving little red books of Mao's thoughts and disrupting their own studies for the sake of a 'revolution' they knew very little about.

> The city has become
> adjunct to its airport.
> The airport has become
> a mere coach station
> for families strung out
> across oceans and continents.
> 'The family at home'
> used to refer to one place at a time.
> It will now be redefined.
> (*Local Habitation*: 2)

The fears and uncertainties of the years between 1989 and the handover have subsided because of the determination of Hong Kong people, the business as usual attitude, the careful handling of the People's Liberation Army's presence here, and the concern of Beijing that Hong Kong remain successful. The recent summit with the European powers and now the promised visit to Beijing by the President of the USA with an entourage of 1200, serve also to remind us that the western democracies are not only interested in the survival of Hong Kong but have realized that partnership with China is an economic necessity for them as well as for China. If the next decades are ones in which China, Asia, and western powers realize they have much to learn from and teach one another in mutuality, it is in Hong Kong that one can see this happening as in a laboratory crucible. The acceptance of 1997 and some of the current attitudes are netted by Ho's poem on 1997 entitled "A Good Year:"

> The air is lambent with
> A collective will to succeed
> Almost as if to say
> With feet firmly planted on the ground
> What matters what flag flies above
> We are ourselves to a day
> 1997 is a good year
> As good as any year
> It is here
> (*New Ends, Old Beginnings*: 66)

The Hong Kong success story delivers not only new millionaires but a large measure of pain. There are the illegal migrants and those who start a family and give birth in Hong Kong so that the child will be a Hong Kong Chinese. This can lead to the splitting of families. In addition, for many the hope of success fades fast. Hard work does not always bring riches. For a few there is either the life in the minimal shelter of the infamous cage dormitories or street sleeping. In the nineteen sixties there were street sleepers all over the place, even on traffic roundabouts. Now you have to look hard to find them. "City" gives Louise Ho's description of the merciless side to Hong

Kong. She published the poem in the anthology *VS: 12 Hong Kong Poets*[4] and later included it in *Local Habitation*, from which I quote:

> Between many lanes
> Of traffic, the street-sleeper
> Carves out his island home.
> Or under the thundering fly-over
> Another makes his own peace of mind.
> 					(*Local Habitation*: 24)

The poem mentions three 'derelicts' men whose stubbornly pain-bearing flesh persists amid the concrete and cars. "Home" here is some neglected corner irrelevant to the traffic flow. The fact that it is an "island home" throws up its ironies contrasting with Churchill's proud use of the phrase to describe Britain. But the street sleepers, though anonymous, unknown, are given a touch of individuality by the slight revision of the poem. The version printed in *VS* finished the quoted stanza with the last line lacking the word "own." All three are beggars but they differ from one another. They make their *own* kind of "peace." This revision breaks the regular iambic beat and adds a little more depth to the poem. The tone is restrained, perhaps clinical, seemingly detached. In this poem Ho avoids overt political, sociological, or moral comment. This is a great relief in an age that in the last forty years has become neo-Victorian in its dogma–every action and statement is supposedly political and, despite professions of pluralism and relativism, we all know which politics are supposed to be intellectually acceptable and which not. And yet we know that her poem has compassion for the three anonymous street sleepers. How? Feeling is conveyed at the end through a Biblical or perhaps Lawrentian usage, followed by close observation of a gesture and its image:

> A man entirely unto himself
> Lifts his hand
> And opens his palm.
> His digits
> Do not rend the air,
> They merely touch
> As pain does, effortlessly.
> 					(*Local Habitation*: 24)

---

[4] See *VS: 12 Hong Kong Poets* (Hong Kong: big weather press, 1993). This volume contains poems by Brent Ambacher, Simon Beck, Liam Fitzpatrick, Ulrikka S. Gernes, Jeremy Hardingham, Louise Ho, Richard Lawrence, Gordon T. Osing, Andrew Parkin, Gerard Tannam, Deirdre Tatlow, and Yuen Che Hung. The idea was to collect poems by people writing in English resident in Hong Kong. Most of the poets gave readings at the bar-restaurant, Post 97, in Lan Kwai Fong in 1993-94 and also at Tolo Lights, the Chinese-English poetry readings at Shaw College of the Chinese University organized by Andrew Parkin and K.F. Chor. *VS* was published with help from and dedicated to Nichole Garnaut, owner of Post 97. It was launched at the China Club, then newly opened by the entrepreneur David Tang.

The mention of pain is delivered obliquely. The gesture suggests not some desperate clawing at insubstantial air by someone in agony but some private, inconsolable sorrow. We realize that human beings are fragile; they can be left in ruins by forces so great that the process is accomplished "effortlessly" and this insight is offered by the poet and the poem in a simile, an analogy. An 'as if' renders subtly the inconsolable spectacle of suffering. This symbolic gesture of the street sleeper reminds us of mass suffering we encountered in her "Remembering 4th June, 1989" in the lines

> The shadows of June the fourth
> Are the shadows of a gesture
> *(Local Habitation*: 12)

In "Wood-block Cutting" Ho imagines the inanimate wood's "...response/To the cutter's edge" as

> [...] a willing surrender
> To the unrelenting,
> To the cold of steel
> In a rhythm of movement.
> (*Local* Habitation: 89)

Here is the human gesture that delivers pain. But this 'human touch' renders the wood-block an object that can create an image on paper that is beyond pain, though derived from it. It is the artistic image. The visual artist and the poet are alike in this. It is also worth adding that Louise Ho sketches rather well, is interested in the connexions between literature and visual arts, and illustrates *New Ends, Old Beginnings* with her own art work.

In his brief Introduction to this volume, Michael Hollington also notes the strongly visual element in the poetry:

> She finds a powerful image for the complex process of metamorphosis
> that July 1997 means to her in Mak Hin Yeung's sculptured "Bronze
> Horse," where a horse's torso and a human torso coalesce – both of
> them headless.
> (*New Ends, Old Beginnings*: 11)

In his longer – and wordier – Introduction to her previous volume, the critic Ackbar Abbas also comments on the same poem (Ho likes it enough to include it in both books) as follows:

> [...] the poem that captures best the political tensions and ambiguities of the city is perhaps "Bronze Horse," which restricts itself to a careful description of an art object, a very striking piece of sculpture by Mak Hin Yeung. The sculpture depicts a horse's legs 'flaying the air' and the human legs dangling from the pedestal. This is not a centaur, image of wisdom [...], but a mindless image of violence and obscenity in which no terrible beauty

is born. [...] It is not necessary to translate the image into a political allegory critical of the slogan 'one country, two systems.' The form can speak for itself.

(*Local Habitation*: iv)

Actually the form does speak for itself, as does Ho's poem "Bronze Horse" and it is much more than the rather crude political allegory Abbas translates it into, despite the rhetorical device of denying the very thought he voices. The actual sculpture, shown to me by Louise Ho when I visited her home, delivers the immediate shock of the unexpected and strange. The grotesque six-legged amalgam is weirdly, solidly, yet springingly beautiful. It is some ritual object from a lost religion, as much reminiscent of the depths of the religious mind explored by Peter Shaffer in his play *Equus*, as it is of the famous remark about the future of Hong Kong. Ho's poem does not find the image 'obscene.' The upturned fallen horse is instead presented as an image of vulnerability and pain, as if the creature had just fallen on its back, breaking it on the iron pedestal, rather than landing on the soft, receiving earth. This is the important general point made in the first two sentences of the poem that form its first section. The second and last section begins with another two sentences that describe the sculpture itself – essentially in accord with the photograph of it in *Local Habitation* or Louise Ho's sketch of it in *New Ends, Old Beginnings*. The third and last sentence of this section describes the feeling of movement in the sculpture, movement that is a clash of two kinds of movement flung out of control. The poem itself is firmly in control, on the *qui vive* despite the 'free verse' technique.

What is home, then, for the migrant twentieth century writer? Assuredly it is where the sensibility says it is; it is where one *feels* at home. Just as the personality can change and we can become a succession of selves, historic and simultaneous, so we can have several different 'homes.' At the deepest level, the writer, as opposed to people who lead unexamined lives, is home alone, alone in the artistic imagination. Such a home is not necessarily comfortable. Its inconveniences, its problems, its uncomfortable familiarity may at times bespeak a residue of fear and trembling and pain. These things are always there in the artist's home, waiting in the darkest corners to leap out like a beast, perhaps only partly human, and taking its form either in verse or prose.

A reader of Baudelaire and Rimbaud, like them Louise Ho has published a number of prose poems. One of them connects again with the horse imagery. In "Clip Clop" an unexpected incident during a drive to Kai Tak airport, presents an image of wonderful beauty and unfathomably ordered vitality in the figure of the horse:

One solitary horse, rich chestnut brown, muscles gleaming, was coming towards us in a mechanically steady trot, meticulously following the white line in the middle of the road, oblivious of us, or of anything [...]. The intricate sound pattern began to fade in stages into the distance and then was heard no more. Unharnessed. Cameoed.

(*Local Habitation*: 34)

What is unharnessed in the artist can, through her craft, become a cameo.

Home is also where mother is or was. This is not mere geography. It is where mother is in the imagination. Mother and daughter is a particularly powerful and fascinating subject for the artist. In another prose poem "Mother has just turned seventy [...]" and, on cue, here she is, celebrated as a sort of angel, with a glory of white hair. A moment of recognition and of longed-for meeting occurs:

> Her black eyes penetrated or so I felt. I breathed a sigh of relief. My body sagged, almost sobbing, into a state of complete and utter abandon. It *felt like coming home* [my italics].
> Ten minutes ago, still crouching in the grass, I felt a sharp piercing bite. I started in pain. I then saw a bright green bamboo snake winding its way in big loops over the grass, its scales shimmering in the sun [...] Help is out of the question. This is the wilderness and there is no one within reach.
> <div align="right">(<i>Local Habitation</i>: 42-43)</div>

The womb itself and the maternal home cannot endure for very long as a lost and regained paradise, even in the artistic imagination. In every Eden there is a serpent. Home turns out not to be a safe retreat; it is where we are essentially alone, beyond help, and the last home is where we die.

The bleakness of Ho's imagination seems to me to be shaped by a condition that she describes in another prose poem which begins, "There is a black hole at the back of my head that stretches to infinity. It is always there, blatantly or latently." She feels it as a physical sensation. It seems akin to the black bouts of deepest melancholy that we find in a number of writers. It saps energy. It can "grow, slowly, bigger and bigger, until it gets so big, I find myself in it [...].It enfolds you and you become nothing. All my life, in varying degrees, I've had to fight off that force." It provokes fear and an animal-like apprehension so that she is "on the qui vive all the time." The result is that she lives in her waking moments always "[...] fearing for my life." (*Local Habitation*: 44).

Fortunately for her readers, Louise Ho's bleakness is accompanied by humour and a measure of satire. In *New Ends, Old Beginnings* there is humour in "The Australian O," "Odd Couple," "Party," "On Seeing Promite on the Shelves" and "Did You Know." The sudden appearance of the hawk at the end of the latter poem brings the predatory imagination swooping back.

We make the journey to the last home through the abundant tangle of our languages. The artist in words blazes the trail through the medium itself; it is for the poet or novelist a lonelier trail usually than for the dramatist. Louise Ho has left some of her words to remain in her first published collection, *Sheung-Shui Pastoral and Other Poems*, but others she has carried with her from that book to republish them in the two later books. To give a few examples, "Hong Kong 1967" became "Hong Kong Riots 1967" and "Summer at Warwick 1973" became simply "Summer at Warwick," while "Boston, First Impressions (and therefore a bit raw)" was revised and pruned to become the terser "Jet-lagged In Boston." Another revision to similar ends turned "All in a Row at Tai Po Train Station" into "Babies and Mothers (at Tai-Po train station)." The revision shortens the lines and cuts reflections on the subject. Revision concentrates vision. Words *present the subject* with minimal, if any, discussion. This tendency to reprint work from previous volumes keeps a continuity and an economic reference back and forth in the works for those who want to follow Ho's career as a poet. The revisions also show some development in technique. But they are not such drastic revisions as to suggest dramatic growth or change in her style. She has shorter and terser lines. The keen and clinical observation and the deliberately understated language are there in the early work. So is the preoccupation with the mother-daughter relationship, as well as Hong Kong as physical and psychic home. The cultural home throughout her work is at once local and international. The dedication of *Sheung-Shui Pastoral* is a thank you for Mary Visick and Ian McLachlan "My teachers and friends." It suggests the university world and the international community of scholars. For me, personally, Mary Visick will always represent voracious reading, keen critical insight, and a special kind of political intelligence that never blinds one to humane values and the authentic humanist learning. It is, in my view, homage to these things that is embedded in the dedication to Mary Visick.

Along Louise Ho's tortuous trail through the thickets of language, we find instead of dedications epigrammatic quotations from other writers in the two latest books: Shakespeare and Théophile Gautier for *Local Habitation* and Eric Satie and Tadeusz Rozewicz for *New Ends, Old Beginnings*. Rosewicz's epigram that "[...] a poet's lie/is multilingual" uses the notion that literature uses fictions and therefore lies in the effort to tell the truth about life. The notion is complicated, though, by the idea of the "multilingual." For a monolingual writer this may seem odd. For the 'sledded Polack' whose country, sandwiched between Western and Eastern Europe, has been over the centuries an unwilling host to many conquerors and their languages, it seems almost a condition of writing. Among Hong Kong intellectuals, there are some who in their own way feel similar tensions, because in Hong Kong's Cantonese linguistic seas there float the flotsam and jetsom of many other Chinese dialects, Mandarin Chinese, English from all over the world, other European languages, and, naturally, other Asian languages.

Satie's quoted epigram is "I was born very young into times that were very old." The joke at the beginning of the sentence stiffens into the awareness of the world weariness of the European decadence followed by the catastrophic first world war after which nothing was ever the same. The writer, moreover, always arrives at the *end* of his or her tradition. The pressure to write contains also the pressure to find something to express in oneself that is not mere repetition. But it is easy to feel callow. Louise Ho is acutely aware of this problem. Not long after we met in early 1991, she told me that she was finding it difficult to write, because she was aware of so much excellence in the past. I, too, was very much aware of the problem. Paradoxically, knowledge that supposedly empowers may in effect sap one's confidence. Shakespeare and all the other great writers of the past in their various languages and traditions conspire to keep our own pages blank. The conversation sparked two of my own poems.[5] My

---

[5] "Mountain and Harbour" (I and II) in Andrew Parkin and Laurence Wong, *Hong Kong Poems* (Vancouver: Ronsdale Press, 1997).

reply was my own common-sense credo: "Louise, Shakespeare is dead. You're alive. You have to write the world as you find it." Since then, Louise Ho has told me that the remark spurred her on to keep writing. I did not realize at the time that she had taken so much notice of what we had said.

    I am very pleased that she did.

David Malouf's *Johnno* (1975):
A Study of Post-Colonial Self-Constitution in Modern Australia

HEINZ ANTOR (Düsseldorf)

In a survey article on children's literature in the former British colonies, Mary Rubio points out that "one of the observations of post-colonial theory is that the imperialistic cognitive process has often constructed the 'mother-country/colony' relationship in the 'parent/child' paradigm in children's literature."[1] If the imperial phase of a nation's development is associated with children's literature and with the patriarchal relationship between the young and the old in a family here, the process of becoming an independent country and of entering a post-colonial era must then logically be linked on the symbolic level with the period when adolescents become young adults and begin to lead their own lives away from the parental home and influence. This is indeed what the reader finds quite frequently in the New Literatures in English, in which the process of growing up is often used not only to show how the young protagonists try to find a place in life and to form a personality of their own, but also, by metaphorical extension, to reflect upon the respective ex-colonies' attempts at self-definition and identity constitution. Post-colonial writers thus ironically often take up an imperialistic cognitive paradigm, but only in order to demonstrate through its use the problems both the newly independent countries and their inhabitants have to face as a result of the period of colonialism. In what is to follow, we will analyze such a narrative in order to discuss some of the aspects of the problem mentioned here in an Australian context. The paradigmatic text we have chosen as an example is *Johnno* (1975), the first novel published by the Australian writer David Malouf and by now "one of the most widely read Australian novels,"[2] as Philip Neilsen has pointed out.[3]

Johnno is a hybrid novel which includes elements of the *Bildungsroman*, of the coming-of-age novel, and of autobiographical writing. It is a book about the life of Edward Athol Johnson, called Johnno, the eponymous hero of the text. Moreover, the

---

[1] Mary Rubio, „Children's Literature (Overview)," in Eugene Benson and L.W. Conolly, eds., *Encyclopaedia of Post-Colonial Literatures in English* (London and New York: Routledge, 1994), 228-30, here 229-30.

[2] Philip Neilsen, "Malouf, David," in Benson/Conolly, *Encyclopaedia of Post-Colonial Literatures in English*, 965-66, here 965.

[3] Malouf's relevance in our context is already indicated by such critical remarks as the following by Karin Hansson: "David Malouf [...] indicates in his writing some important prerequisites for [...] a harmonious and sound development towards individual as well as national identity among second-generation immigrants." (Karin Hansson, "The Untold Story: David Malouf and the Issue of Identity," in Mirko Jurak, ed., *Literature, Culture, and Ethnicity: Studies on Medieval, Renaissance and Modern Literatures. A Festschrift for Janez Stanonik* (Ljubljana: Filozofska fakulteta, Znanstveni institut, 1992), 119-125, here 119).

novel is a book about the early life of the first person narrator, but also about Australia, particulary Brisbane,[4] in the forties and fifties.

The short prologue and the brief epilogue form a frame for the story of Johnno, and the book starts off as a personal reminiscence[5] rather than as a novel about Australia. In the prologue, the as yet unnnamed I-narrator is called home to Brisbane from a study leave in Europe because his father is suddenly taken seriously ill after a stroke. By the time he arrives home, his father has already died. The deceased was an Australian self-educated man, a sporting type, healthy and self-reliant, but not very much interested in books. Having left school at eleven, he became a post-boy on the Nanango mails (5).[6] In 1947, he moved with his family from "a suburban farmlet" (4), a wilderness in Edmondstone Street (22)[7] in South Brisbane cultivated by the narrator's grandfather, a man who still "spoke no English" (36), to the "new house at Hamilton" (4), which he built himself, but which his son, the narrator, regards as "stuffily and pretentiously overfurnished and depressingly modern" (4). The house is the symbol of the father's ambitions, "some vision of worldly success and splendour" (4).[8] Although he was a very practical and pragmatic man, the narrator's father's affairs are "in a good deal of disorder" (4) after his death so that the narrator, at the beginning of the book, finds himself in a position "to sort through his 'effects'" (5). This does not only confront the narrator with "evidence of a life [he] had failed to take account of" (6), i.e. with mementoes documenting his parents' past, but he also comes across his own past in the form of what used to be his own desk when he was a pupil. There, he finds a photo in an old back number of the Brisbane Grammar School

---

[4] The role of Australia in general and of Brisbane in particular is so important in this novel that Hadgraft writes: "[...] a third contestant [i.e. in addition to Johnno and the narrator] has slipped in and occupies at frequent intervals those parts of the stage where the spotlight rests. This intruder is Brisbane. It turns out to be the books real concern, a background against which people move and things happen." (Cecil Hadgraft, "Indulgence: David Martin's *The Hero of Too*," Frank Dalby Davidson's *The White Thorntree*, Dal Stivens's *A Horse of Air*, David Malouf's *Johnno*, and Frank Hardy's *But the Dead are Many*," in K.G. Hamilton, ed., *Studies in the Recent Australian Novel* (St. Lucia: University of Queensland Press, 1978), 194-224, here 215-16).

[5] This is why Daniel speaks of the novel's "framework of remembered and reconsidered experience" (Helen Daniel, "Narrator and Outsider in *Trap* and *Johnno*," *Southerly: A Review of Australian Literature* 37 (1977), 184-195, here 184).

[6] All quotations from the novel are taken from the following edition: David Malouf, *Johnno* (Ringwood and Harmondsworth: Penguin, 1976 [11975]).

[7] We have here a clearly autobiographical element of the novel. Malouf himself lived in 12 Edmondstone Sreet in Brisbane as a child, and his collection of essays entitled *12 Edmondstone Street* is even named after his first childhood home. Cf. Hansson, "The Untold Story," 121.

[8] The house is the physical expression of the narrator's father's Australian Dream. Cf. Norbert Schaffeld, *A Future with a Past: Historische und ideengeschichtliche Grundlagen des Australian Dream und seine Spiegelung in der Literatur* (Trier: WVT, 1997) and Horst Prießnitz, "Dreams of Austerica: A Preliminary Comparison of the Australian and the American Dream," *Anglia* 113:1 (1995): 41-70.

Magazine for 1949 (9), which shows the school's Stillwater Lifesaving Team. He is struck by the fact that his one-time schoolmate Johnno is also in the picture wearing gold-rimmed spectacles and "staring diagonally out of the frame" (10) although he was neither a member of the team nor in need of glasses. This irregularity or anomaly immediately causes the narrator to get hooked by his memories of Johnno, and we learn that the latter always had a very special influence on the narrator, who almost thinks that Johnno only sneaked into the picture in order to tease him in a kind of "joke with a time fuse" (11). Now, twenty years after he first had the idea, the narrator writes the book about Johnno he always wanted to write, maybe in order to come to terms with the extraordinary and unusual character his friend presented to him and to the world at large. The act of writing, then, here is both an act of reminiscence and also a taming of the unruly experience of knowing Johnno.

The story of Johnno and his acquaintance with the narrator forms the main part of this novel and is told in fourteen chapters. At school, Johnno "was the class madcap" (13). He puts on an air of innocence, but he drives his teachers mad with his practical jokes and with his refusal to conform. He is often punished for his bad behaviour, but all to no avail. His schoolmates, including the narrator, are impressed by his recklessness and his ability to do anything he sets his mind to, be it ever so outrageous, but the adults look down on him as an anti-social being. This is how the narrator comments on this judgment:

> And it was true he had no sense of responsibility, no school spirit, no loyalty to his country or to his House, no respect for anything as far as we could see. It meant nothing to him that minor servants of the British Raj had sent their sons to be educated here in the years before the Great War, or that a tree had been planted in the grounds by a Royal Duke, the son of Queen Victoria, or that the honour-boards in the Great Hall carried the names of seven generals, nine judges of the Supreme Court and a governor of Queensland, not to mention the war dead, whose names were recited, alphabetically, to the assembled school on Anzac Day. Johnno cared for nothing and nobody. He was a born liar and an elegant shoplifter [...]. It was generally agreed he would have slept with his sister if he'd had one. We were appalled and delighted by him He gave our class, which was otherwise noted only for its high standards of scholarship, a dash of criminal distinction. (16)

This passage defines the two main themes of the book. Johnno here is shown as the rebellious adolescent, who rejects the norms the world of adults confronts him with,[9] something that is typical of young people of his age. But at the same time, it is stressed here that it is through his misdemeanour that he defines himself and even his class. It is not the high standards of scholarship, i.e. an act of conforming to conventional expectations, that confer a special quality upon the class, but the fact that it is Johnno's class, i.e. a group harbouring somebody who defines himself and creates a distinct identity of his own by putting himself beyond the pale of orderliness and ordi-

---

[9] Helen Daniel refers to Johnno as „an errant and subversive outsider" (Daniel, "Narrator and Outsider," 184).

nariness. We are confronted here, then, with a novel about the process of identity constitution in a young man, a book which describes Johnno's and the narrator's efforts to define themselves by placing themselves on the map of life in an individual way, which includes the possibility of unconventional behaviour and rebellion against traditional value systems.

This, however, is also done in a specifically post-colonial and Australian context. Just as Australia as an ex-colony had to grow up from the status of a dominion to that of an independent country, so Johnno, too, tries to free himself from old fetters in order to find his own personal way. When, in the passage quoted above, the narrator notes Johnno's lack of responsibility, this is a reference to Johnno's refusal to let himself be bound up in social structures that would bind him to others, but which at the same time would thereby also restrict his freedom to behave in an unfettered way and thus to define and express his own personality. These social fetters, significantly enough, are associated with the experience of colonialism and post-colonial patriotism, as the references to the Raj, to the British Monarchy, and to the First World War as well as to such authorities as the Supreme Court and a governor of Queensland or to Anzac Day show.[10] Johnno refuses to be colonized by the rules of the adult world,[11] which itself is a world characterized by the power mechanisms of colonialism. His adolescent rebelliousness, then, is closely linked with a rejection of the signifiers of colonial power in an Australian context.[12]

Johnno's refusal to conform and the distinction he thereby gains fascinates some of his classmates, who form a gang around him, although Johnno himself only reacts with the same "unconcealed contempt" (16) he displays towards everything else.[13] The narrator, on the other hand, still finds himself on the side of conventionality and considers Johnno nothing but "a shameless waster of his own and other people's time and

---

[10] This is also why Huang Yuanshen, referring to "Johnno's Hooligan-like traits" (Huang Yuanshen, "Johnno and Some Other Social Misfits in Australian Literature," *Waiguoyu* 5:69 (October 1990): 68-76, here 73), can see these as a sign of his being "a real Australian hero" (Yuanshen, "Johnno," 73).

[11] Hadgraft is therefore wrong when, in a very conservative judgment, he calls Johnno "a rebel without a cause – except himself." (Hadgraft, "Indulgence," 216).

[12] In the passage quoted above, lying is one of the strategies Johnno uses against the colonial gestures of the adult world. The rejection of colonial power in general is often expressed in Australian literature by protagonists who indulge in lying. The eponymous hero of Peter Carey's novel *Illywhacker* (1985) is a good example. Cf. Heinz Antor, "Australian Lies and the Mapping of a New World: Peter Carey's *Illywhacker* (1985) as a Postmodern Postcolonial Novel," *Anglistik: Mitteilungen des Verbandes Deutscher Anglisten* 9:1 (1998): 155-178, esp. 160-61.

[13] The fascination Johnno has for others and the strong independence he displays justifies Daniel's characterization of him as a "protean figure" (Daniel, "Narrator and Outsider," 184).

a thoroughly bad influence" (17), somebody who is dangerous and from whom it is best to keep away.[14]

In chapter two of the novel, we learn that Johnno and the narrator knew each other well before they met again at grammar school in Brisbane. They "had been kids together at the beach at Scarborough" (18), a fishing village in the back of beyond, which in the summer months was transformed into a vast encampment of vacationers. Johnno was "a tearaway even then" (p.19), and the narrator's father, the Australian self-educated practical man trying to live up to the ideal of the Australian Dream, would have liked his son to be like Johnno,[15] while his more finicky mother would have preferred him not to spend so much time in such bad company. The narrator, however, is so unsure of himself that he does not really think of Johnny as 'his company'. He is far too shy and does not really know what he is (19).

Johnno's and the narrator's childhood are characterized by boredom and by the eventlessness of an utterly familiar world. The only events worth following are those of the Second World War. There is a vague fear of invasion by the Japanese (21), and in early 1942, American soldiers are stationed in Australia (20), but the really exciting events take place in Europe:

> Australia was familiar and boring. Now was just days, and events in *The Courier Mail* - even when those events were the Second World War. History was The Past. I had just missed out on it. There was nothing in our own little lives that was worth recording, nothing to distinguish one day of splashing about in the heavy, warm water inside the reef from the next. (21)

Australia here is depicted as a country on the outer edge of the world, far away from the centre of events and of history, a backwater[16] of boring homogeneity where

---

[14] Huang Yuanshen comments on the complementarity of the two by pointing out that "Dante and Johnno in the years of childhood are depicted in contrast to each other, forming, in Malouf's own words, 'a whole set of oppositions that is right at the centre of almost everything'" (Yuanshen, "Johnno," 71).

[15] This may be an act of wish fulfilment via the son on the part of the narrator's father, who himself, as a young man, was "too dutiful, too deeply imbued [...] with Old Country notions of filial piety, to be critical of his father [...]." (Samar Attar, quoted by Hansson, "The Untold Story," 121). Johnno's unruliness, then, to the narrator's father, signifies the overcoming of Old Country notions and thus makes the eponymous hero of the novel an embodiment of the Australian Dream on one level, although on another, as we shall see, he does not come to grips with his home country.

[16] Malouf's choice of Brisbane as the Australian setting of *Johnno* is not only due to the fact that this is the place where he himself grew up. It also allows him to stress the feeling of decenteredness referred to here because „[i]n contrast to Sydney and Melbourne, Brisbane has for a great many years been seen as 'a big country town'; certainly not a 'real city.'" (Garry Winter, "Quensland Literature: Is It Different?, " *LiNQ* 15:3 (1987), 45-51, here 46.

nothing interesting ever happens.[17] This creates a Eurocentric attitude in the narrator, which makes him a decentered being, an ec-centric young boy on the margin of the world, who can melodramatically turn up at school one morning sobbing bitterly because "BELGIUM'S FALLEN" (24).

Johnno comes closer to the events of the war than the narrator,[18] because his father fights in the army, is first sent to Greece and then to Malaya, where he goes missing (21). When he does not come back after the war, Johnno's wildness is generally attributed in a patriarchal argument to this absence of a father figure, i.e. to the lack of a male impersonation of the law (22).

Conversely, the narrator's father is too old to go to the war so that all the boy sees of the great catastrophe is the distribution of air-raid kits against Japanese attacks after Pearl Harbour (26), the establishment of General MacArthur's headquarters for the pacific campaign in Brisbane, which "was suddenly at the centre of things" (27),[19] troop transports in the streets, and the fortification of his family's house with sandbags and trenches (27). Apart from these developments, however, life in Brisbane follows its usual course and nothing changes much really (29-30) so that once again, Australia, despite the presence of the American general, appears to be on the margin from the narrator's point of view. Australia therefore is described as a place of stagnation rather than development, a static region of this world without any dynamics of its own. The only factor that can slightly ruffle the smooth surface of the routine of everyday rituals in Brisbane, next to the war and to the unruliness of Johnno, is the narrator's Uncle Nick, who has criminal tendencies and even had to spend some time in prison "for stabbing an Albanian" (30). But Johnno's mother, who herself can look back on her own well-ordered childhood as the youngest child of a big family in pre-war (i.e. pre-1914) London (32), sees to it that the narrator is properly brought up in orderly circumstances. There is an almost puritanical quality to the way the narrator spends his childhood, as the following remark shows:

> It was a world so settled, so rich in routine and ritual, that it seemed impossible then that it should ever suffer disruption. Life was a serious affair. For that reason we had to be strict with ourselves; the rules and regulations were necessary, we needed them - how else could we discover order and discipline? (35-6.)

The narrator thus grows up in a world governed by fixed rules imported from the imperial centre of London, rules the validity of which is uncritically accepted as simply given and not to be questioned, as the narrator tells us:

---

[17] This is why Neilsen characterizes the novel as one which "deals [...] with the post-colonial problem of establishing a sense of place and belonging that will overcome the residual perception of exile from the centre." (Neilsen, „Malouf, David;" 965).

[18] Huang Yuanshen refers to him as a "war child" (Yuanshen, "Johnno," 69).

[19] General MacArthur's choice of Brisbane as the American Allied headquarters of the Southwest Pacific Theatre in World War II is also referred to in Carey's *Illywhacker*, but it is used there to stress the marginality of Australia in the minds of US neocolonialists. Cf. Antor, "Australian Lies," 163-64.

> The rituals by which my own life was regulated it never occurred to me to doubt. They were so utterly reasonable. [...] All these rules and regulations, I was convinced, not only trained you in the best behaviour, they also taught you discipline, and discipline was character-building. [...] Doing what you didn't like doing gave you moral backbone [...]. (37-8)

The narrator thus is brought up according to the principles of a liberal education tinged with Puritanism. But at the age of thirteen, he starts "sneaking over, as it were, to Johnno's side" (39).[20] This is due to the fact that the adolescent narrator finally does begin to doubt some of the rules he has accepted so far. He speaks of his "defection from the dogma" (38) in this respect and describes the process in the following way:

> I had too many secrets. One of them was a sense of humour (though I had found as yet no good use for it) and the other was the shrewd suspicion, based on irrefutable personal evidence, that there was more going on under people's clean, well-brushed clothes than the building of muscle by silverbeet. I had begun, secretly, to believe some things and disbelieve others, and I was overwhelmed by the discovery that I had a choice. (39).

Johnno now looks behind the façade people present to the world and therefore no longer unquestioningly accepts traditional codes. It is through his fascination with his discovery of individual choice that he tries to define his personal identity. For example, he becomes "shaky about the Catholic Church" (39), and he rejects his mother's stories about the negative impact of masturbation as absurd. Gradually, he even develops "some notion of being a rebel" (39) and glides from his mother's side of order and discipline to Johnno's side of chaos and freedom.[21]

When the narrator is invited to spend a day with Johnno, he first commits an act of theft in order to impress Johnno with his booty. The latter, however, is embarrassed by this indirect expression of the narrator's low opinion of him. This, in turn, puts the narrator to shame, and the two become close friends.

---

[20] Huang Yuanshen comments on this by stating that "as they [i.e. Dante and Johnno] grow up the moral distance diminishes between them [...]" (Yuanshen, "Johnno," 72).

[21] We are of course confronted here with a phenomenon well known to developmental psychologists dealing with puberty and adolescence. The rebelliousness that is so characteristic of this age is often expressed by a transgression of the rules of order in a deliberate embrace of the rulelessness of chaos. This constitutes a step in the development of young people that is not only felt to be problematic by the adults they have to deal with, but also by the young people themselves. Many novelists have dealt with this theme. Ian McEwan, for example, has analyzed the phenomenon extensively in his first novel *The Cement Garden*, albeit in a non-colonial environment. McEwan wonderfully works out there the tension between the lure of chaotic transgression and the need for order of some sort. Johnno feels primarily the need to transgress. On McEwan's novel cf. Heinz Antor, "Sozialisation zwischen Norm und Tabubruch: Ian McEwans Roman *The Cement Garden* als Lektüre im Leistungskurs Englisch," *Literatur in Wissenschaft und Unterricht* 30:4 (1997): 267-286.

When Johnno unexpectedly does very well at school, everybody is quite astonished, and some even refuse to believe it. They want Johnno to conform to their expectations and to confirm the picture they have formed of him. The change is due to the fact that 'The Boys', i.e. the group of followers that had gathered around him without his encouragement, had to leave school and, "[f]ree at last of their expectations, Johnno had simply settled and become himself." (47). Previously, then, Johnno was partly defined from outside by what the others wanted him to be. This is linked with the problem of identity creation because it turns out that the narrator also feels disoriented by Johnno's new self and that the change in his friend leaves the narrator at a loss:

> Ever since those days, long ago at Scarborough, when Johnno had been identified for me as "bad company", I had used him as a marker. His wildness had been a powerful warning to me [...] Now all that was changed. I didn't know where I was. What made me most resentful, I think, was his refusal to stay still. I had found for Johnno a place in what I thought of as *my* world and he refused to stay there or to play the minor role I had assigned him. He had suddenly developed qualities of his own, complexities I hadn't allowed for. [...] Everything I had ever seen of him in these last years began to shift and change its ground. Maybe, after all, it was Johnno who was the deep one. (48)

The narrator here provides us with a typical example of the process of self-constitution through the attempt to place himself on the map of a fixed framework where everything and everybody has a static[22] and reliable character or meaning.[23] Since Johnno does not conform to such a concept through his elusive change of character, the narrator himself experiences a kind of identity crisis and is at a loss how to define his own position. This is even reinforced by Johnno's use of a new nickname for the narrator, whom he used to call "The Prof" so far, but refers to as "Dante" now because the narrator published a poem entitled "To Beatrice" in the school magazine (49):

> I hated it but the name stuck. At the very moment when I was most in doubt about who I was, or where I stood, I had developed a new identity and now not even the name sewn into my gym things was true [...] (49)

The identity crisis the narrator finds himself in due to Johnno's change of character also makes him wonder about his surroundings and about his relationship to the world he lives in. Once again this is expressed in terms of the search for a topographical

---

[22] This is why Daniel can refer to the narrator as "the static figure of Dante" (Daniel, "Narrator and Outsider," 191).

[23] On the epistemological and psychological importance of frameworks cf. Charles Taylor, *Sources of the Self. The Making of the Modern Identity* (Cambridge: Cambridge University Press, 1989) and Heinz Antor, "The Ethics of Criticism in the Age After Value," in Rüdiger Ahrens and Laurenz Volkmann, eds., *Why Literature Matters: Theories and Functions of Literature* (Heidelberg: Winter, 1996), 65-85, esp. 67-69.

position, which is nothing but a metaphor for the value system the adolescent narrator is looking for:[24]

> *Arran Avenue, Hamilton, Brisbane, Queensland, Australia, the World.* That is the address that appears in my schoolbooks. But what does it mean? Where do I really stand? (49)

As he tries to answer these questions and goes through the various locations mentioned in his extended address, from the microcosmic view of the street he lives in to the macroscopic view of the whole world, Dante comes to an overwhelmingly negative conclusion. It turns out that he has never overcome the shock he had when his father left the old but warm and mysterious house at Edmondstone Street in order to move to the "glossy and modern" (50) house in "one of the best suburbs of Brisbane" (49). The narrator feels alienated where he has to live now.[25] He fails to link up with the new house and with his parents:

> What do I have to do with all this, I wonder? I feel odd and independent. There is nothing in what I think or feel these days that relates to my parents, to what they know or might have taught me, nothing at all. Or so I believe. I have left their influence far behind me: having learnt at last to drink beer (though my father is a fanatical teetotaller), and to have left-wing opinions and despise the world of business. We have nothing in common now. (50)

The narrator experiences the same process most adolescents go through, namely that of breaking loose from his parents, although the insistence with which he emphasizes that he has nothing whatsoever to do with them any longer only shows how much his thoughts still centre around them and how uncertain he really is. The narrator finds himself caught up between the contradictory expectations his two parents have for his future, wedged in between his father's wish for him "to get out into the world and start on my own account, as he did, instead of experiencing everything second hand, through books," (51)[26] and his mother's idea of her son becoming a doctor or a lawyer (51):

> How little they understand me! What I am, what I will be, can have nothing to do with them. I feel like a stranger in the house. And what irritates me most of all, is that there is absolutely no hostility between us - they are ideal parents, I have nothing to complain of, they leave me no room to rebel. (51)

---

[24] Mapping is an important theme in post-colonial literature. Peter Carey's *Illywhacker* yet again is another good Australian example. Cf. Antor, "Australian Lies,"167-171.

[25] Hansson also stresses the importance of "the themes of alienation" as well as of "the search for identity" in Malouf's work (Hansson, "The Untold Story," 121).

[26] In view of such quotations as this one, Hansson takes too conservative a view of Dante's father when she writes: "Like Dante, the narrator in *Johnno*, Malouf has expressed his feeling that his father would have preferred him to grow up to become, like himself, a more conventional type." (Hansson, "The Untold Story," 123).

Significantly enough, Dante here knows exactly whom he wants to rebel against and what he rejects without, however, being able to state what it is he wants, what he will be and who he wants to be.

Unlike Dante, the narrator cannot love his home town. Brisbane is rejected by him as a place "so sleepy, so slatternly, so sprawlingly unlovely" (51), "simply the most ordinary place in the world" (52). The prospect of possibly having been shaped by Brisbane is a fearful one to him (51).[27]

Queensland does not fare any better than its capital. The narrator considers it "a joke", calls it the "Moonshine State" and comes to the conclusion that there is "[n]othing to be said about Queensland. Half of it is still wild [...], the rest detained in a sort of perpetual nineteenth century. [...] Aborigenes are herded on to reservations. Kids, even in this well-to-do suburb, go to school all the year round with bare feet."[28] (52). Significantly, Dante's association of Queensland with backwardness is linked with an accusing reference to colonialism and to the inhuman way in which the colonizers treated the aborigenes so that it is its very state as an ex-colony that renders progress improbable there.[29]

The fact that he has grown up in what he considers to be nothing but a colonial backwater in Dante's mind confers upon his existence a quality of arbitrariness and makes it appear to be the result of a random quirk of fate, a totally contingent affair, when he says:

> What an extraordinary thing it is, that I should be here rather than somewhere else. If my fathjer's father hadn't packed up one dayto escape military service under the Turks; if my mother's people, for God knows what reason, hadn't decided to leave their comfortable middle class house at New Cross for the goldfields of Mount Morgan, I wouldn't be an Australian at all. It is practically an accident, an entirely unnecessary fate. (52)[30]

This leads on to the following questions:

> Why Australia? What *is* Australia anyway? (52)

---

[27] Daniel also points out that Johnno rejects and tries to transcend his surroundings "because reality palls." (Daniel, "Narrator and Outsider," 184).

[28] Malouf himself has pointed out that "Queensland still has a Victorian society" (Yuanshen, "Johnno," 70).

[29] According to Stephen Kirby, Johnno's attitude towards Brisbane and Queensland is typical of "Malouf men [who are] desperate to escape stultifyingly closed, conservative milieux." (Stephen Kirby, "Homosocial desire and homosexual panic in the fiction of David Malouf and Frank Moorhouse," *Meanjin* 46:3 (September 1987): 385-393, here390).

[30] Hansson similarly points out that Malouf "is constantly intrigued by the gratuitous and accidental quality of national identity and ethnic belonging, the fatality and coincidence of the place where one happens to be born. Thus his awareness of 'other kinds of possible experience, of alternatives that got shut out', [...] relate to the theme of identity, from a cultural, national, linguistic, individual and religious point of view." (Hansson, "The Untold Story," 120).

When Dante tries to answer this, it soon turns out that although he may know a lot about his home country, a positivistic approach to the fifth continent does not render any useful results, nor does any other way of thinking about it. Australia eventually turns out to be a mysterious unknown, impossible to grasp with our intellect because of its sheer size and of its inhuman dimensions:

> The continent itself is clear enough, burnt into my mind on long hot afternoons in Third Grade, when I learned to sketch in its irregular coastline [...]. I know the outline; I know the names (learned painfully for homework) of several dozen capes, bays, promontories; and can trace in with a dotted line the hopeless journeys across it of all the great explorers, Sturt, Leichhardt, Burke and Wills. But what it is beyond that is a mystery. It is what begins with the darkness at our back door. Too big to hold in the mind! I think my way out a few steps into it and give up on the slopes of a Mount Hopeless that is just over the fence in the vacant allotment next door. Australia is impossible! Hardly worth thinking about. (52-3)

The narrator does not only recoil from the elusiveness of the vast continent that is his home country - a home country he does not feel at home in -, but also from the resulting hopelessness that results from the lack of perspective such an impenetrable enormity as Australia creates. Since he cannot place himself on the unknown map of this ultimately unknowable non-place and isn't able to chart his future and emplot his life in such a gigantic riddle, he feels at a loss and cannot say who he is in an Australian context. His identity crisis, then, is not only the result of puberty and adolescence, but also of the particular problems of growing up in such a country as Australia. As has already been pointed out, we are confronted here with a problem that is dealt with extensively in many of the New English Literatures.

The world as a whole appears to Dante as a battlefield full of temptations and problems, something one is tested by, as the headmaster of the school has warned his boys (53). With such a general feeling, he does not find it easy to cope with his adolescent identity crisis.

At university, Johnno recommends Nietzsche to the narrator, who is enormously excited by the existentialist philosopher without finding satisfactory answers to his questions about life and the world there. In the university library, he is struck by the fact that many vagrant people spend the day there because it provides convenient shelter, but when he and his fellow students go home in the evening, these vagrant people vanish to nowhere, which makes Dante wonder yet again about the meaning of life, something that appears to him to be just as unknowable as Australia itself:

> How, I wondered, had they fallen out of that safe and regular world that the rest of us took for granted as if it was the only world there could be? [...] Life suddenly seemed utterly mysterious to me. What were the mechanics of survival? What did you have to do to stay afloat? (62)

For the time being, there are no answers yet, but Dante spends a lot of time with Johnno, who still pursues a course of recalcitrance and rebellion, drinks a lot, gets excited about Voltaire and Mozart, and likes to provoke the prostitutes in Brisbane.

Sometimes, the two go to watch a boxing match, which reminds Dante of the insistence with which his father stressed the importance of sports as a good training for the battle of life. When Dante finally refused to have anything to do with sports, this was "a terrible disappointment" (71) to his father, who always used to analyze the loser in a fight and who, in his active time, only lost a single fight himself. This is a result of the father's hard childhood during which he had to learn "to scrap in the 'pushes' that terrorized the Southside before the Great War" (73). From the point of view of the self-reliant man of action, life is a battle for survival, which explains the single paternal bit of advice Dante gets from his father:

> "Look after yourself, son" was all my father would offer in the way of advice. (72)

Johnno, who is just as much in search of a way in the world as Dante, tries to find an answer by coming up with fantasies such as that of an anonymous secret Organization guiding the world (75). This product of his imagination[31] allows Johnno to recentre the world and make its confusing heterogeneity and contingency seemingly intelligible as the result of the ineffable considerations of the Organization, as he himself indirectly admits when he comments on his fantasy:

> "It's perfect, don't you see? It's - " he searches for a word, "it's Copernican! Once you've been made to realize it everything suddenly makes sense." (77)

Johnno, just as much as Dante, suffers from life in Brisbane, which he calls "the bloody arsehole of the universe!" (83).[32] The narrator particularly suffers from the lack of permanence he feels there, as if Brisbane was a ghost town - there one day, gone the next (83). Johnno tries to deal with this situation by trying to "emplot" the nothingness of life in Brisbane through his fantasies and thus render it meaningful,[33] which prompts the following remark from Dante:

> [...] what Johnno called life bore an uncanny resemblance, it seemed to me, to what the rest of us called "literature". (84)

---

[31] Daniel also stresses the importance of the imagination in this context when she points out that Johnno "toys with fantasy and delights in the bizarre" (Daniel, "Narrator and Outsider," 184) in order to be able to deal with the supposedly boring world he finds himself surrounded by.

[32] Winter points out that the two protagonists' "perception of home-town Brisbane [...] becomes a limitation of self-discovery" (Winter, "Queensland Literature," 50) and thereby establishes the connection between the post-colonial and the psychological aspects we are discussing here.

[33] On the role of emplotment as a strategy of creating meaning cf. Hayden White, *Metahistory: The Historical Imagination in Nineteenth Century Europe* (Baltimore and London: Johns Hopkins University Press, 1973). That Malouf himself is aware of the importance of emplotment is documented by the following remark he made in an interview he gave Samar Attar: "History is not what happened but what is told." (Quoted in Hansson, "The Untold Story," 125.

Together with the medical student Bill Mahoney,[34] Johnno plans to bring down society and to initiate a general "disintegration of consciousness" so as to destroy all the myths that provide the dominant framework of meaning in Australia. For Dante, such a destructive mood, however, cannot be enough, which is why he asks:

> And the end?
> That, of course, was just the sort of question I *would* ask. Who would know what the end would be, when all the myths had dissolved like so many ghostly chains and we were free to be ourselves? (87)

The narrator here does not only ask the questions a young adolescent in search of an orientation in life is liable to ask, but he also poses the modernist question of what may replace the lost centre in a modern age in which the old myths do not hold any longer.[35] Significantly enough - and this is also typical of the attitude of many moderns - he is not able here to provide an answer himself.

Both Johnno and Dante have their adolescent love affairs, of course, but these don't help them either to come to terms with their situation. Both affairs do not last very long, and the narrator's romance with a girl named Rhoda is abruptly broken off because Rhoda's father does not approve of Dante's Catholicism (93). Personal relationships with girls, then, cannot solve the two protagonists' problems either.

In the end, Johnno, having finished his geological studies at university, decides to leave Australia, because a complete break with this unknowable monster of a country seems to him to be the only way of freeing himself from the problems life in such a vast mystery creates for a young man in search of his own identity. He accepts a mining job in the Congo and thus hopes to liberate himself from all the fetters and problems he has been hampered by so far:

> This, for Johnno, was to be the great escape. His break at last into perfect freedom.
> "I'm going to shit this bitch of a country right out of my system," he told me fiercely. "Twenty fucking years! How long will it take me, do you think, to shit out every last trace of it? At the end of every seven years you're completely new - did you know that? New fingernails, new hair, new cells. There'll be nothing left in me of bloody Australia. I'll be transmuted. I'll say to myself every morning as I squat on the dunny, there goes another bit of Australia. That was Wilson's Promontory. That was Toowong.

---

[34] To the reader of Australian literature, this name is a telling one in so far as it brings to mind that other famous Australian misfit, Richard Mahony, the eponymous hero of Henry Handel Richardson's well-known novel trilogy *The Fortunes of Richard Mahony* (1917-1929). Links to great works of Australian literature such as this one confirm the importance of Johnno in the context chosen here. On similarities between Malouf's Johnno and Richardson's Mahony cf. Yuanshen, "Johnno," 72. For further connections between *Johnno* and other Australian literary texts cf. Kirby, "Homosocial desire," 390.

[35] It is interesting to observe in this context that Huang Yuanshen refers to Johnno as "a misfit of modern version." (Yuanshen, "Johnno," 68).

> Whoosh, down the plughole! And at the end of seven years I'll have squeezed the whole fucking continent out through my arsehole. I'll have got rid of it for ever. All *this*." (98)

Shortly before his departure for the Congo, Johnno braves the forces of Australian nature in an almost existentialist act of defiant self-assertion when he plunges into the torrential floods of a river (102-103). He thus accepts the challenge posed by the unknowable power of the forces of the fifth continent, and when he doesn't come to any harm, this might be interpreted as the beginning of his freeing himself from Australia. On the other hand, however, Johnno has himself photographed with a koala, that most Australian of animals, one week before he leaves, which indicates that there still is an intimate link between him and the country he pretends to despise so much. This supposition is also strengthened by the ostentatious vehemence with which he denounces Australia and everything Australian, as if he still had to persuade himself that his plan to leave is a good one. The narrator, however, is the only person Johnno will obviously miss, which is expressed by his sobs in the farewell scene (105).

Johnno leaves Australia with a Eurocentric outlook, because it turns out that he only uses the three years of his stay in the Congo to read up on all the classics of the Western literary canon,[36] thus supposedly acquiring "civilization" and transforming himself from a "barbarian" into somebody fit to go to Europe (107).[37] Johnno thus displays an Australian's cultural inferiority complex, a result of the colonial heritage of the country.

The narrator, conversely, tries to resist this post-colonial attraction of Europe and doggedly stays in Brisbane while most of his friends go abroad or at least to the capital Canberra and make their careers there:

> And still I hung on. I was determined for some reason, to make life reveal whatever it had to reveal *here*, on home ground, where I would recognize the terms. In Europe, I thought, some false glamour might dazzle me out of any recognition of what was common and ordinary. (109).

However, Brisbane is true to itself, and nothing extraordinary reveals itself to Dante there. His expectations are disappointed, and his prospects shrivel into nothing, while those who went to Europe, such as those among his former classmates who

---

[36] This may be an interesting autobiographical reference to the importance of classical Western literature in Malouf's own life, as the following statement by Hansson shows: "[...] young David, named after David Copperfield, came to know many English classics at an early age thanks to his mother's and the housekeeper's taking turns reading aloud while they were working. He and his sisters were not allowed to use local slang, to »speak or act ‚Australian', which made them think they grew up »as in a foreign land« in which everything outside their own house »had about it the glow of the exotic«." (Hansson, "The Untold Story," 123). Malouf's mother is also described as a "first generation immigrant, who constantly idealized the English heritage [...]" (Hansson, "The Untold Story," 123-24).

[37] Huang Yuanshen rather uncritically sees this in a positive light and states that "Johnno develops a complexity from reading literary works and extending his personal experience to the areas he has not known before" (Yuanshen, "Johnno," 69).

received a Rhodes scholarship and went to study at Oxford, are successful and enjoy a good reputation (110). The narrator, however, does not even envy them, but, to his own astonishment, finds himself "entirely without ambition" (110):

> I was simply immobilized from within (110).

Finally, Dante goes to visit Johnno in Paris. He sets out for Europe with certain misgivings and the vague fear that the old world might prove indeed to be preferable to Australia and do something for him his home country could not provide him with:

> I felt vaguely disturbed that Europe might after all be about to do what Brisbane had refused to do, break the spell that had been over me. (111)

The narrator ultimately is afraid of finding a justification of and new fuel for his so far successfully suppressed Eurocentrism. The result of such a development could be an even further alienation from Australia and an aggravation of his identity problem, because it would make him spiritually homeless and condemn him to live in a mental culture not his own, a foreign culture with a colonial taste to it. He finds Johnno living in Paris where he earns a little money by teaching English as a foreign language. In order to find clients, however, he has to deny his Australian identity and pass himself off as a Scot, because Australian English, in a gesture of belated supercilious linguistic colonialism, is associated with bad English by the Europeans (112, 114).

Johnno is just as dissatisfied in Paris as he was in Brisbane. He is still in search of an absolute meaning to life and to the universe, an orientation in life[38] and he tries to find it by avoiding everything conventional.[39] For example, he advises Dante not to see the Sainte Chapelle, one of the principal sights of Paris, but instead takes him to the murkier quarters of Paris in order to see the prostitutes there (116-17). He is always in search of something "mystical" (117), even in the shabbiest things. Johnno and Dante find themselves caught up in the social violence of France under President de Gaulle immediately before the events of 1968, which, strangely enough, has a positive effect on Johnno, as Dante remarks:

> I also saw now what it was that had happened to Johnno, what it was that was so different about him. His violence was no longer a private disorder. It was part of a whole society's public nightmare. He was free of himself. Cured. (120-21)

Johnno finally has found some kind of integration within society while at the same time not having to surrender the principle of destroying the old patterns of order. He has thus ceased to be an outsider without automatically becoming an insider within a

---

[38] Daniel also points out that "in the section of the novel set in Europe [...] Malouf does suggest the expatriate search for meaning against what Johnno and dante both conceive as a stifling and narrow Brisbane" (Daniel, "Narrator and Outsider," 193).

[39] Kirby is therefore right when he talks about "Johnno's refusal to accept, not just provincial Australian society, but any society." (Kirby, "Homosocial desire," 391).

repressive order he can only reject.⁴⁰ In Paris, therefore, he lives on the precarious borderline between rebellion and conformity, between rejection and acceptance, between disorientation and orientation. This is also expressed by his seemingly paradoxical conversion to Catholicism, which has to be seen not as a conservative move towards social adaptation - after all he still does not want Dante to visit the Sainte Chapelle-, but as an attempt at coming closer to the mystery of existence (118). Johnno's tenuous way of defining his position is also expressed by his constantly making plans to leave Paris and go elsewhere. Sweden, the Massif Central, Nepal, Spain, Greece, Britanny - they all become places where Johnno would like to go with Dante:

> But when Johnno saw that I meant it and would set off the moment he gave the word, his enthusiasm cooled and he began to find difficulties. [...] We didn't go to Greece. Or even top Britanny. Johnno, I soon realized, was mesmerized by Paris, his dreams of leaving it for one corner of Europe or another were simply alternatives that he allowed to exist for a moment because they made Paris itself, and his presence in it, so much more solid and absolute. Paris was the city for which Greece, Spain, Sweden, and other places too numerous to mention, had been rejected. (123-24)

Johnno's way of placing himself on the map and of defining Paris as his point of sojourn is a post-structuralist one in as far as he does not define Paris from within itself without any reference to things outside it, but only by placing it within a whole range of other possibilities from which it differs. Just as the linguistic sign is defined by its difference from other signs and is what the other signs are not, Paris is preferable because the other places are not. In a way, it is defined from outside rather than constituted from within and could always be compared to yet another place, which is why Johnno's travel plans are endless.⁴¹ Since the relationship between the definition and evaluation of Paris and the constitution of Johnno's identity is a metonymic one, the constitution of the subject as well as the process of creating an individual value system for Johnno is one of infinite deferral, similar to the very similar infinite deferral of meaning in Derridean deconstructive readings of texts. Johnno's personality is defined through his rejection of closure of any kind. He cannot accept a final destination, which, in practice, however, means that he stays in Paris for the time being.

The narrator finds himself in a similar plight of finding it difficult to place and thereby define himself. Unlike Johnno, however, he is looking for a destination and thinks more in terms of a finite teleology in this respect. When he goes to London to teach there, he talks about the British capital as a place "which I had always known

---

⁴⁰ Cf. Daniel, "Narrator and Outsider," 191: "Johnno [...] reacts against a categorizing society and finds ist conventions oppressive and constricting but he is not only a subversive and mocking rebel but also a restless and protean figure seeking always to 'bend' reality into more promising shapes and to extract from it some of the infinite possibilities it holds."

⁴¹ Daniel calls him "an errant and ebullient outsider." (Daniel, "Narrator and Outsider," 191) and Huang Yuanshen refers to him as "a typical wanderer" (Yuanshen, "Johnno," 71).

was *my* destination" (127). At the back of his mind, however, again unlike Johnno, he cannot cut himself off completely from the Brisbane of his youth:

> It was the town I would always walk in, in my memory at least, with an assurance I could find nowhere else [...] (127-28)

To Dante, Brisbane, despite all its negative aspects, its stagnation and boredom, still has to offer something, a comfortable security of orientation which he can find in no other place. He differs from Johnno in as far as in London, he finds out that Australia, gigantic and unknowable as it may be, does have to offer something of infinite value to him. In London, then, in the old centre of the Empire, he still feels decentred because he finds himself far away from Australia and because he finds that many of his Australian acquaintances begin to consider him an expatriate who has taken on British habits.[42] This reinforces his feeling of leading an existence in which he is arbitrarily placed and which makes it ever more difficult to define oneself:

> I had once found it odd, gratuitous even, that I should be an Australian. I found it even odder, more accidental, that I should be anything else. Friends who came to visit on working holidays were resentful of my being so settled. Their resentment found its object in certain habits that they thought of as non-Australian and therefore a betrayal. [...] It wasn't something I had chosen. I was here, that's all. I had never left *anywhere* ... (128-29)

Meanwhile, Johnno has left Paris after all, not being able to accept even the French capital as a final destination. After stays in Germany and in Switzerland, he works for the Berlitz School in Athens, thus drifting slowly towards the edge of Europe with the intention of ultimately leaving it again:

> It was to be, for Johnno, the last of Europe. He pointed beyond the harbour wall to where the islands beat east towards Asia: Andros, Naxos, Rodos, Kos - the route Dionysos had come on, stepping from island to island with his message from the heart of the world. "I'll be there in about two years," Johnno said dreamily [...] (132)

Johnno here is put into a Dionysian tradition, and indeed, it is Dante with his stronger yearning for a framework of orientation within his native Australia and with his reflex of looking for a final destination who is the more Apollonian of the two. It is also significant that Johnno, although metaphorically he does walk in the footsteps of Dionysos, does so in reverse direction so that he aims to arrive at where the Greek God started off, i.e. at the heart of the world, a clear indication that Johnno also tries

---

[42] That this is a typical experience in a post-colonial context is illustrated by V.S. Naipaul's novel *The Mimic Men* (1967), the Caribbean protagonist of which goes to London in the hope of recentering himself, only to have feelings very similar to those Johnno has in Malouf's novel. Cf. Heinz Antor, "Aporien postkolonialer Existenz und moderner Persönlichkeitskonstitution in V.S. Naipauls Roman *The Mimic Men*," in Uwe Baumann, ed., *Literaturimport transatlantisch* (Tübingen: Narr, 1997), 211-252, esp. 226-28.

to recentre himself and find an identity of his own as well as to invest the world with meaning, just as much as Dante does. When Dante visits Johnno in Greece, the question of orientation and of what to do with life surfaces again:

> For the first time since I had known him I wondered where he was going, what he was doing with himself. What did he want out of life? What ordinary fate was he in flight from? What would he do next?
> "Well," he enquired of me one day, as if to counter a question I had never put, "what will *you* do next?"
> I answered without thinking: "I'll go home."
> He regarded me scornfully, then nodded. "I always knew you would."
> He looked hurt, as if I had betrayed him, then shrugged his shoulders and went back to his drink. He found my decision incomprehensible; but didn't bother to ask why.
> I'm not sure I could have told him if I had. (135-36)

To Johnno, Dante's decision to go home to Australia amounts to the kind of closure and to the capitulation in front of the forces of traditional order which Johnno has always rejected, a relapse into Apollonian structuralism incompatible with the more Dionysian principles of post-structuralism. For the narrator, Australia does have the potential to turn out to be his centre, while Johnno still refuses to think of it in such terms. While Dante decides to come to terms with the reality of his Australian background, this to Johnno is inacceptable, and he prefers the utopian vision of a constant breaking through of borders and limits in an ever-progressing movement forward without any clearly discernible destination.

Shortly before Dante's departure for Australia, Johnno confesses that he is the firebug who set fire to several churches of various denominations that summer in Greece. The narrator does not know whether to believe Johnno or not, which makes the latter react in a very moody way:

> He looked sulky. Somehow the excitement of it had made him blaze up for a moment like the old Johnno, something impish leaping clear of the heavy body that I had finished off with my failure to respond. I felt mean. As if I had cheated him of some larger dimension of his own improbable existence. Johnno's story was less a confession, I thought, than a rehearsal. I had just rejected one of his finest scenarios. (137)

Johnno tells Dante the story of an *acte gratuit* directed against the institution of the church and thus puts himself in the role of the existentialist protester against the inacceptable closure of traditional world pictures. At the same time, he constructs his own personality by acting the part of the nihilist destroyer of the symbols of meaningfulness. Johnno stages himself in the drama of his life,[43] which he has emplotted in an existentialist context.

---

[43] Daniel also uses the stage metaphor to describe Johnno and stresses that he casts himself in various "dramatic roles." She also emphasizes his "delight in the theatrical and the melodramatic" (Daniel, "Narrator and Outsider," 193).

After his return to Australia, Dante suffers from a feeling of lost opportunity, of possibilities now having been closed off, of a lack of freedom due to finding himself once again caught up in a life of decisions and in "a whole set of little locks I had never cared for, and doubted, even now, if I could accept" (143). In a way, he suffers from what Johnno constantly tries to avoid. Dante has an unhappy love affair with a girl, but it does not last very long. He is considered a failure by his parents and by his former schoolmates so that he grows "increasingly restless and ill at ease" (145) when he runs across Johnno again, who has returned to Australia after all. Together, they find that they have outlived the Brisbane of their youth:

> Brisbane was on the way to becoming a minor metropolis. In ten years it would look impressively like everywhere else. The thought must have depressed Johnno even more than it did me. There wasn't enough of the old Brisbane for him to hate even, let alone destroy. The others had got in before him. (148)

It now turns out that it was Brisbane's and Australia's otherness, their quality as backwaters on the edge of the world, which allowed Dante, but in particular Johnno, to define and centre themselves through their rebellion against the alterity of the supposedly boring margin. Brisbane and Australia thus undergo a paradoxical revaluation, with their very negativity investing them with value for the two protagonists. When Brisbane now becomes more like any other metropolis in the world, its peculiar character and its individuality gets lost in a general urban homogeneity that is the same everywhere, which also deprives Johnno of the opportunity of self-definition through anti-Australian opposition. He still mutters about the need to "destroy the myth" (149), but his position becomes more and more precarious as the necessity for accommodation becomes ever stronger and supercedes the possibility to rebel.

One way out for Johnno may be simply to leave this world. He gets out of a suicide pact with two of his colleagues at the last minute and is the only one of the three to survive (149-50) Shortly afterwards, however, Dante reads in the paper about Johnno's death by drowning, which, the narrator thinks, may well have been suicide. Johnno was pulled out of the water by "the Mango", i.e. one of the Junior Lifesaving Team at school into the photo of which Johnno stole himself in a practical joke at the beginning of the novel (150-51). Dante remembers Johnno at school, with the Mango leaning over his shoulder as he traced the fictitious course of the river he would finally drown in. This, to the narrator, seems to be more than a coincidence, but the working out of a carefully predestined fate:

> The pattern might have been there already if we had had eyes to see it. Now at last it was clear. Or was it? The pattern had been achieved.
> I thought of Johnno's promise, that in seven years every last particle of Australia would be squeezed out of him, he would have freed himself of the whole monstrous continent.
> Well, the seven years were up. Like a bad charm. And it was Johnno who was gone. Australia was still there, more loud-mouthed, prosperous, intractable than ever. Far from

> being destroyed, the Myth was booming. There were suggestions that it would soon be supporting thirty million souls. Australia was the biggest sucess-story of them all. (152-53)[44]

Johnno now has finally lost the race for ascendancy he has had with Australia all his life. Not only did he not succeed in getting rid of Australia and of its myth. As an Australian he was also pulled back by the continent of his birth and ultimately literally swallowed up by it. Australia may be too huge to understand, it may be unintelligible and impossible to grasp, but it canot be denied, nor can it be relegated to the margin and thus deprived of its status of a centre. To Johnno, it *has* proved to be his final centre:

> He too had submitted himself at last to the world of incontrovertible event. Johnno was dead. (153)

And it might be added: dead by the agency of himself and of Australia, one of whose rivers swallowed him.[45] Johnno finally has become part of Australia. At the same time, Johnno symbolizes the identity problems of the post-colonial subject in a vast ex-colony removed from the old metropolitan centre. His existentialist leanings as well as his throwing himself into the vastness of the fifth continent at the end of the book are his way of dealing with the immensity of the ungraspable dimensions of his country. Australia is just as incontrovertible and factual as the event of his death by suicide.[46]

Johnno may have lost his race away from Australia, but he has not lost the whole game in the end. At this funeral, Johnno's one-time girl friend Binkie weeps for the loss of her friend and then says to Dante:

> "But I'm not sad," she insisted when she had recovered a little. "I refuse to be sad. He's happy. I know he is! He's with Nietzsche and Schopenhauer. [...]" (159)

---

[44] This is another of the novel's many references to the Australian Dream. Cf. Schaffeld, *A Future with a Past* and Prießnitz, "Dreams of Austerica."

[45] The fact that Johnno's death cannot with absolute certainty be proved to have been suicide may have contributed to some of the criticisms levelled against the novel: "The book has been described as 'uncertain' and 'elusive', and many critics have been puzzled by it. Laurie Hergenhan complained that 'one looks for a more human and less aesthetic resolution.'" (Kirby, "Homosocial desire," 391). The ending of the book is not uncertain at all, however, with regard to Johnno's having lost his fight against Australia. No matter whether he killed himself and thus willingly and literally became a part of the fifth continent or whether he tried to stick to his otherness from the country where he was born right up to the end and simply died in an accident: in the end, Australia reasserted herself and even physically made him an Australian. Johnno's identity thus may be a precarious and a problematic one, but, ultimately, it is an inescapably Australian one.

[46] Kirby also sees Johnno's death as voluntary suicide: "So incapable is the Maloufian hero of accepting social integration that even death can be seen as preferable." (Kirby, "Homosocial desire," 392).

Johnno's existentialism, in the novel, then, becomes a valid form of coming to terms with the trans-human dimensions of Australia and with the problems of defining oneself as an Australian. At the same time, there is a certain irony in the fact that Johnno can only reach that stage through a reading of some of the major philosophers of central Europe so that in the end there still is some unresolved tension between the colonial centre and what used to be the margin, but what in post-colonial times aspires to a centrality of its own.

Nevertheless, it is only at Johnno's funeral that Dante, the narrator, realizes that he has decided to stay in Australia (160), a decision which implicitly is the result of Johnno's ultimate return to and merger with Australia. Binkie herself is left saying "I wish I understood things" (161) and thus engaged in the same endeavour the narrator and Johnno embarked on throughout the novel.

Dante's final reflection on Johnno in the main part of the novel is a tentative explanation of what the eponymous hero's life and death were all about:

> A suicide with some of the shocking randomness of accident - an accident so aesthetically apt as to have all the elements of a humorous choice. Johnno's death would have to confound us. It would have to be a mystery, and of his own making. It would have also to defy the powers of medicine and the law to establish their narrow certainties. It would need to be explicable, at last, only as some crooked version of art.
>
> For what else was his life aiming at but some dimension in which the hundred possibilities a situation contains may be more significant than the occurrence of any one of them, and metaphor truer in the long run than mere fact. How many alternative fates, I asked myself, lurking there under the surface of things, is a man's life as we know it intended to violate? (164-65)

Johnno defined himself through the avoidance of closure and the preservation of openness, a stance that created a certain mystery and made him ultimately just as ungraspable as the equally mysterious Australia. It is this very element of inexplicability which gave him his unique identity and defined his oneness in the multiplicity of explanations made possible by his existence. In this respect, once again, Johnno becomes the embodiment of the Australian continent with its many faces and its concomitant unintelligibility.

In the epilogue, we find ourselves back with the narrator in his parents' house after his father's death. Dante sifts through his father's belongings, and the way this is described shows that the narrator once again is involved in the process of understanding somebody else, in this case his own father, and this process is yet again intimately connected with the way Australia shapes the lives of those whose home it is. The only two books Dante finds among his father's belongings illustrate this.

> One was a big old-fashioned ledger [...]. It was in fact, as my father had often explained, a graph of the boom years and the years of depression between 1913 when he acquired it and 1994.
>
> My father believed in this sheet of flimsy, yellowing paper as he believed in the Holy Ghost. [...] It was the record, crudely projected, of his life, and at the same time the map

> of an era. [...] Turning back to the old chart now I felt as close as I ever would feel to the forces that had guided my father's life and given it shape. That line on the page was what he had tuned his soul to, taking, as the graph did, the shocks of history." (166-67)

The economic fate of Australia in the twentieth century is so closely interwoven with that of Dante's father that the latter's life is defined by the way his country fares because of his quasi-religious belief in it. This becomes clear when Dante looks at the second of his father's two books:

> It was called *A Young Man with an Oil-Can*, and it celebrated the genius of a young Scot, James MacRobertson, who, beginning with just an oil-can [...] had gone on to found the biggest chocolate factory in the Commonwealth. [...] It was a book, I suppose, that my father turned to as other men in other places have turned to Homer or the *Pilgrim's Progress*, the palpable record of a great national mythology. You began like James MacRobertson with an oil-can and you ended up with a book like this. Or you started like T.C. Beirne and James McWhirter with rival barrows on opposite sides of a street and you ended up with the huge department stores, one firmly Catholic, the other staunchly Protestant, that faced one another across Brunswick Street in the Valley. Success of the golden sort is possible to anyone with the energy and vision to go out for it - that was what the Young Man with the Oil-Can taught; and my father, at least, believed it. (167-68)

Dante's father defined himself by his believe in the Australian dream, which, with its from-rags-to-riches ideology, comes very close to its American counterpart. This Australian myth, just like the pagan classical myths by Homer or the Christian faith embodied in the work of Bunyan, helps the older generation to find its place on the huge map of the new and still partly uncharted fifth continent. Johnno, in a way, also defined himself with implicit reference to this myth, namely by his rebellion against it and by his need to destroy it, to disregard it and to leave Australia behind. The use of the restrictive "at least" in the above quote also indicates that the narrator himself does not fully believe in the promise of the Australian dream. This is also underlined by the way the narrator critically qualifies his father's enthusiasm for the Australian dream:

> But then, any story that matters here is a success story. The others are just literature.
> Still, those troughs at the bottom of the graph are also part of the story. The most impressive fact of my early childhood was the Depression. (169)

We are then also confronted in this novel with the different reactions of two generations towards a national mythology, with the narrator's point of view, i.e. Dante's scepticism both towards his father's uncritical acceptance of the Australian dream[47] and Johnno's wholesale and ultimately unsuccessful rejection of Australia. Dante does not have the heart to burn his father's only two books because he thinks this would be

---

[47] Cf. Kirby, who points out that „[a]t the end of the novel, his [i.e. Dante's] father's belief in a controllable destiny is rejected for the lessons learnt from Johnno [...]" (Kirby, "Homosocial desire," 391).

"like putting a match to the National Gallery" (170). He thereby at least partly revalidates the ideals of his father. This is also due to the fact that he has recognized that our identities and our personalities do not have fixed ontologies of their own and are not something to be found ready-made somewhere out there, but instead consist of the stories we tell about ourselves so that our myths turn out to be our ultimate tools of self-constitution. This comes out in the final passage of the book, in which the narrator Dante reflects on how Johnno would have reacted to his father's belief in Australia and the dream connected with it:

> "It's all lies," Johnno would say. And in the end, perhaps, it is. Johnno's false disguise [in the school photograph] is the one image of him that has lasted, and the only one that could have jumped out from the page and demanded of me these few hours of my attention. Maybe, in the end, even the lies we tell define us. And better, some of them, than our most earnest attempts at the truth. (170)

Cultural Differences and Problems of Understanding in the Short Fiction of Margaret Atwood

HANS-ULRICH SEEBER (Stuttgart)

Introduction

One of the most striking features of Atwood's early short stories is their self-conscious exploration and demonstration of the problem of alterity. Interactions between male and female, young and old, intellectuals and non-intellectuals, foreigners and non-foreigners trigger off endless interpretive activities which are in a sense contrived, because one part of the binary is presented as a more or less impenetrable other. Acts of understanding directed at such alterity break down in a limbo of uncertainties. Hermeneutic understanding fails in the face of actions and words whose code and motivation are beyond the grasp of the fictional interpreter. Thus the stories enact encounters which seem to prove that misunderstandings are the likely results of cultural and gender differences, rather than those utopian areas of in-between, of overlapping and hybrid mixtures envisaged by theorists like Homi Bhaba.[1]

I suggest that many of Atwood's short stories reflect and anticipate a debate concerning cultural tensions and the deficits of hermeneutic understanding. In other words theory and fictional knowledge, or rather knowledge contained in and communicated by fiction, illuminate each other. I hope to shed light on fictional 'intercultural' encounters by viewing them from the vantage point of the theory of hermeneutics. Before proceeding to an analysis of three stories ("The Man from Mars," "Dancing Girls," "Bluebeard's Egg") I shall make an attempt to reconstruct the role of the other in German hermeneutic theory (Dilthey, Gadamer, Figal).

The Other in German Hermeneutics

As one ponders over texts by Hegel, Dilthey and Gadamer one is in for a surprise. 'Difference' and 'the other,' although really the *raison d'être* of a hermeneutic theory of understanding/*Verstehen*, play a strangely marginal role. I attribute this to the persistent influence of a Protestant tradition which stressed the transparent nature of God's word, dismissed allegorical readings and accepted the authority of every believing Christian person as a reader of the holy text.[2] It is no coincidence that Hegel,

---

[1] Homi Bhabha, *The Location of Culture* (London: Routledge, 1994).
[2] Cf. Julian Roberts, "The Politics of Interpretation: Sacred and Secular Hermeneutics in the Work of Luther, J.S. Semler, and H.-G. Gadamer," *Ideas and Production: A Journal in the History of Ideas* 1 (March 1983): 15-32.

Schleiermacher and Dilthey were all Protestants, even theologians, well aware of the hermeneutic tradition since Luther.

In Hegel's aesthetics and in his philosophy of history the interpretive activity of the art critic or the readings of the historian of texts and monuments do not really produce puzzles and unresolved questions, since what is actually going on is an encounter between the "Geist" of the observer and the "Geist" of the observed. The spirit or mind negotiating with itself via the detour of its expressions cannot go astray. What has such groundwork in common cannot fail as a project:

> In dieser ihrer Freiheit nun ist die schöne Kunst erst wahrhafte Kunst und löst dann erst ihre *höchste* Aufgabe, wenn sie sich in den gemeinschaftlichen Kreis mit der Religion und Philosophie gestellt hat und nur eine Art und Weise ist, das *Göttliche*, die tiefsten Interessen des Menschen, die umfassendsten Wahrheiten des Geistes zum Bewußtsein zu bringen und auszusprechen. In Kunstwerken haben die Völker ihre gehaltreichsten inneren Anschauungen und Vorstellungen niedergelegt, und für das Verständnis der Weisheit und Religion macht die schöne Kunst oftmals, und bei manchen Völkern sie allein, den Schlüssel aus. [...] Die Kunst nun und ihre Werke, als aus dem Geiste entsprungen und erzeugt, sind selber geistiger Art, wenn auch ihre Darstellung den Schein der Sinnlichkeit in sich aufnimmt und das Sinnliche mit Geist durchdringt. In dieser Beziehung liegt die Kunst dem Geiste und seinem Denken schon näher als die nur äußere geistlose Natur; er hat es in den Kunstprodukten nur mit dem Seinigen zu tun.[3]

The signs of art, very much like those of the biblical text, express an intellectual substance and truth called "Geist" or even "das Göttliche." By using various forms of sensual representation the spirit harnesses the other ("und der denkende Geist wird sich in dieser Beschäftigung mit dem Anderen seiner selbst nicht etwa ungetreu, so daß er sich darin vergäße und aufgäbe, [...] sondern er begreift sich und sein Gegenteil" [Hegel, *Ästhetik I*, 28]) into its service, but the core and very essence of art is apparently not its form but its intellectual substance, the ideal. This is why philosophy, uncontaminated by "Sinnlichkeit," is ultimately more truthful and more valuable than art. Hegel does not address the hermeneutic problem caused by the cultural differences between the various "Völker" and their art. Since they all, including the observer and the interpreter, evidently partake of the power of the "Geist," their meanings and forms are accessible. Characteristically, for the idealist thinker, Hegel, the other is not to be attributed to gender differences, social differences or ethnic differences, but to the medium of "Sinnlichkeit."

Disposing of metaphysical speculations and placing "Leben" at the very centre of his philosophy, Dilthey wishes to theorize the knowledge gained by the humanities. Hermeneutics, until his time the theory of understanding underpinning theology and philological interpretations of texts, now becomes the very model of philosophy. This happens because Dilthey conceives of life not primarily as a complex set of psycho

---

[3] Georg Wilhelm Friedrich Hegel, *Werke 13: Vorlesungen über die Ästhetik I* (Frankfurt: Suhrkamp, 1970), 27.

logical issues but as an expression, a text, in which the inner self of an individual or a community manifests itself. To gain proper knowledge of life, therefore, human beings and philosophers alike need to interpret the "Lebens-äußerungen," the highest of which and the most truthful are, with reference to the inner life, the languages of art. It is these on which methodical hermeneutic efforts are focused in particular. The expressions or manifestations of life are accessible, since in the process of understanding, with the help of the imagination, it is possible to re-live ("nacherleben") the experience represented in the text or the action.

Despite his antimetaphysical realist turn Dilthey, in a sense, continues the tradition established by Hegel. For him, too, the conditions of understanding are both "Geist" - he uses the terms "Geist" and "Leben" almost interchangeably - and human nature. Since individuation merely emphasizes various components of the "Geist" and of "human nature," imaginative empathy can reconstruct the process of individuation and thereby overcome the strangeness of the historical or ethnic other.

The claims made by Dilthey for this kind of understanding are remarkably high, but also contradictory. According to him, hermeneutics since Luther was concerned with defending the objectivity of understanding ("die Sicherheit des Verstehens gegenüber der historischen Skepsis und der subjektiven Willkür verteidigt").[4] Universal understanding is made possible through the process of "Nacherleben" mediated by the imagination: "Und die Phantasie vermag die Betonung der in unserem eigenen Lebenszusammenhang enthaltenen Verhaltungsweisen, Kräfte, Gefühle, Strebungen, Ideenrichtungen zu verstärken oder zu vermindern und so *jedes fremde Seelenleben nachzubilden*" (Dilthey, *Aufbau*, 215, my italics). Yet the "Sicherheit" of such an understanding is ultimately wholly subjective ("letzte, obwohl ganz subjektive Sicherheit," [Dilthey, *Aufbau*, 218]).

Seeing this contradiction Gadamer quite rightly criticised Dilthey's roots in romantic hermeneutics and universalism. The notion of "Geschichtlichkeit" ("historicity") is not really applied by Dilthey to the observer himself, whose observations are inevitably tinged by his position in the present. Furthermore, understanding always operates in a tradition of preconceptions ("Vorurteile") and interpretations which the interpreter cannot avoid, which in fact are the productive framework of "Verstehen." For us, however, this also means that Gadamer's interpreter is never really confronted with the unmediated other. It is contained and domesticated by a constantly changing tradition of "Horizontverschmelzung" not allowing the other to have a separate existence:

> Wenn sich unser historisches Bewußtsein in historische Horizonte versetzt, so bedeutet das nicht eine Entrückung in fremde Welten, die nichts mit unserer eigenen verbindet, sondern sie insgesamt bilden den einen großen, von innen her beweglichen Horizont, der über die Grenzen des Gegenwärtigen hinaus die Geschichtstiefe unseres Selbstbewußtseins umfaßt. In Wahrheit ist es also ein einziger Horizont, der all das umschließt, was

---

[4] Wilhelm Dilthey, *Der Aufbau der geschichtlichen Welt in den Geisteswissenschaften*, 3. Auflage, Gesammelte Schriften, Bd. VII (Stuttgart: Teubner, 1961), 217-18.

das geschichtliche Bewußtsein in sich enthält. Die eigene und fremde Vergangenheit, der unser historisches Bewußtsein zugewendet ist, bildet mit an diesem beweglichen Horizont, aus dem menschliches Leben immer lebt und der es als Herkunft und Überlieferung bestimmt.[5]

This is precisely the point where Günter Figal and Gadamer part ways. Not only does Figal emphasize "begrenzte Vernunft,"[6] the impossibility of hermeneutic understanding to grasp fully or exhaust the semantic potential of the other, he also modernizes hermeneutics by stressing the relationship between "das Eigene" and "das Fremde." Figal rediscovers the quality of historical and cultural "Fremdheit" (Figal, *Sinn des Verstehens*, 25) lost in classical hermeneutics. Complementing Gadamer's notion of understanding guided by tradition, which, always changing, always synthesizes the horizon of the present and the horizon of the past, he defines his theory of "Hermeneutik der perspektivischen Integration" as "Übersetzen des Fremden ins Eigene" (Figal, *Sinn des Verstehens*, 27), whereby the other - a style, a thought, a mode of belief - can become the true voice of the self and its aspirations. Figal views the relationship between the self (das Eigene) and the other (das Andere, Fremde) as a highly dynamic affair. Distinctions between what belongs to one's own world and what belongs to the other are inevitable. Yet the familiar, as soon as one tries to understand it, loses its familiarity and becomes something strange. Conversely, the other can be metamorphosed or adapted to what is called the familiar:

> Das Eigene kann also zum Fremden umschlagen oder sich bei näherer Betrachtung als ursprünglich fremd erweisen. Fremdheit und Eigenheit stehen zwar als Kategorien fest, doch nichts ist von Natur aus fremd oder gehört ein für allemal zum Eigenen. Deshalb läßt die skizzierte Erfahrung sich umkehren: Wie im Eigenen das Fremde, so kann auch im Fremden das Eigene hervortreten - Aspekte anderen Lebens, die vertraut erscheinen, etwas, das "dort" genauso oder ähnlich ist wie "bei uns," das früher so ähnlich war, wie es heute ist. (102-3)

Other aspects that I believe need stressing concern the notions of *Bildung* and cognition. In the notion of *Bildung* the self does not merely change into the other by a shift of perspective. The personal or collective self expands, grows, acquires its specific contours by the very process of learning and integrating other languages, values, modes of perception, technologies etc. In such a process of accretion and integration the self fashions itself, not necessarily consciously, by growing and changing, yet nevertheless remains recognizable. Furthermore, the self needs the other to define itself. Conversely, the other is not accessible in acts of understanding, unless the self can relate it, to some extent, to its own code and experience. Failure of communication, accompanied by feelings of anxiety and even horror, is therefore a recurring

---

[5] Hans-Georg Gadamer, *Wahrheit und Methode: Grundzüge einer philosophischen Hermeneutik*, 3. Auflage (Tübingen: Mohr, 1972), 288.

[6] Günter Figal, *Der Sinn des Verstehens: Beiträge zur hermeneutischen Philosophie* (Stuttgart: Reclam, 1996), 12.

feature of science-fiction stories. If one adds that the observer's under-standing of the other is not merely determined by his own code and experience, but also by his interests (political, economic, etc.), the whole concept of hermeneutic understanding becomes very doubtful, as critics like Foucault and Said have argued.[7] In colonial literature, for example, the other, regarded as culturally inferior, was given the role of the exploited and the ruled. Even textually, the other was not allowed to retain its otherness, since it was caught and appropriated by a network of analogies and metaphors relating and subjecting it entirely to the knowledge and to the stereotypes of the colonizing subject. After all, this is the main result of Todorov's book *Die Eroberung Amerikas*. For Said, Western orientalism was a mode of forceful appropriation of the East and not the truth.

However, understanding is the condition of any scholarship in the humanities, no matter whether this scholarship turns to ancient cultures or different contemporary cultures. The new hermeneutic modesty of "begrenzte Vernunft," which also, I suggest, implies the notion of varying degrees of understanding depending on the situation and the competence of the observer, seems a realistic response to fundamentalist scepticism. What Figal underestimates, however, is the possibility of radical, unbridgeable difference. Such difference hardens when *Weltanschauungen* take over, when difference becomes the preoccupation of ideological and aesthetic purposes and interpretations. It seems to me that in Atwood's early short fiction, gender differences and cultural differences not only reflect and explore genuine experiences, they are also conscious ploys and strategies of her politically committed art.

"The Man from Mars"[8]

At first sight the point of Atwood's story seems to be to demonstrate the a priori failure of intercultural communication and understanding. Christine, an unattractive, fat student of politics at a Canadian University, meets a similarly unattractive oriental student of (probably) theology, who imposes himself on her as a friend. Her initial polite treatment of him in the park when he asks for the way, which is motivated by her liberal, international outlook, is apparently mistaken by him as an interest in his person. Through the instigation of her mother, who evidently expects the "person from another culture" (10) to be a potential suitor for her daughter, he extracts an invitation to tea, which he exploits by contriving a photo showing himself and Christine standing closely next to each other. From then on the stranger pursues Christine ceaselessly, smiling, wishing to talk to her but actually not doing it, an impossible

---

[7] Cf. Lothar Bredella, "Intercultural Understanding between Relativism, Ethnocentrism and Universalism: Preliminary Considerations for a Theory of Intercultural Understanding," in Günther Blaicher and Brigitte Glaser, eds. *Anglistentag 1993 Eichstätt* (Tübingen: Niemeyer, 1994), 287-306.

[8] Margaret Atwood, "The Man from Mars," in *Dancing Girls and Other Stories* (London: Virago Press, 1984), 9-31.

situation which increasingly awakens fears of rape and murder in Christine. When, by his presence, he frightens the West Indian employee, the police step in and eventually deport him back to his own country. In characteristic fashion the story ends inconclusively with speculations, Christine's in particular, about possible reasons for the strange behaviour of the foreigner. Both Christine, the other characters and the readers are drawn into a debate concerning cultural identity and the nature of understanding. Attempts at understanding or interpreting are inevitable since the characters and the readers need interpretations to guide their actions. But most interpretations, I believe, are not really the result of successful acts of understanding but *attributions* determined by changing points of view, interests and world views.

The foreign student is a puzzle. To function as such the characters and the readers are given precious little information about him. He does not even have a name, we do not know which country he comes from, and we cannot be sure about his chosen area of studies. Neither can we be quite sure whether he is sane or insane. His behaviour is archetypal, he pursues a woman as ancient gods used to pursue nymphs. Since we are never allowed to enter his consciousness we are only left with the two key-words he uses, "friend" and "family," both of which seem to point to an oriental, quasi-feudal notion of culture and social bonding. In some ways his behaviour and outward appearance conform to negative stereotypes of oriental students: he has dark hair, smiles constantly, is intrusive to the point of being rude, uses too much oil for his hair, exploits his host, speaks bad English, pursues women relentlessly. Confronted with a living example of these stereotypes, Christine's liberal, international outlook is sorely tested. Liberalism seems to produce stereotypes not compatible with the realities of human nature and cultural otherness. This at least also seems the point of Christine's dealings with the West Indian girl-servant of their family. Her conscious avoidance of condescending, colonial attitudes towards the girl does not earn her friendship and love, but contempt. Similarly, her liberal notions concerning the foreign student and his culture evidently lead to misunderstandings and unwanted consequences:

> Christine hesitated. If this had been a person from her own culture she would have thought he was trying to pick her up. But then, people from her own culture never tried to pick her up; she was too big. The only one who had made the attempt was the Moroccan waiter at the beer parlour where they sometimes went after meetings, and he had been direct. He had just intercepted her on the way to the Ladies' Room and asked and she said no; that had been that. This man was not a waiter though, but a student; she didn't want to offend him. In his culture, whatever it was, this exchange of names on pieces of paper was probably a formal politeness, like saying thank you. She took the pen from him (11).

The text's mode of presentation evidently emphasizes the non-translatability of foreign cultures. East meeting West in fact makes everyone involved conscious of cultural differences which the title of the story, with its allusion to typical science-fiction patterns ("The Man from Mars"), exaggerates into an intergalactic one. Difference triggers off endless interpretive activities in a double sense. Thus the text explores the conflicting ways in which different members of society explore the other. Generally the perplexing signs of otherness are deprived of their intriguing, unnerving strangeness by acts of reductive attribution. Thus the mechanism of stereotype-formation reduces the understanding and acceptance of contingent individualities to a recognition of self-made formulae and ideologies. Perhaps this is the only way "Fremdverstehen" can operate at all, but it is not the specific achievement understanding aims at which is, after all, a coming to grips with cultural particulars. Political correctness ("a person from another culture," 10) and the match-making instincts of a mother ("he wasn't quite the foreign potentate her optimistic, veil-fragile mind had concocted," 17) explain the image Christine's mother has of the oriental student. The police consider this interpretation to be simply naive, they regard the foreign student, who harasses women, as a potential killer:

> "That kind don't hurt you," one of the policemen said.
> "They just kill you. You're lucky you aren't dead."
> "Nut cases," the other one said.
> Her mother volunteered that the thing about people from another culture was that you could never tell whether they were insane or not because their ways were so different. The policemen agreed with her, deferential but also condescending, as though she was a royal halfwit who had to be humoured. (26)

Yet this professional reading appears ludicrous when it turns out that the police eventually deport the oriental because he is accused of pestering a sixty-year-old Mother Superior. Christine's friends have other explanations to offer. For them he is a sort of lustful Turk who fancies fat women, or a political opportunist who wishes to contrive a marriage in order to gain permanent residence in Canada. If one accepts the reading that the stranger's problem is not a cultural but a psychological one, that his compulsion to chase women is a symptom of a psychological illness, all the other interpretations collapse, unless one assumes that the crisis is induced by his cultural isolation.

These interpretations are surely "perspektivisch" and "begrenzt," but one wonders whether they can be called examples of "perspektivische Integration." Instead of being integrated the other is in a sense displaced and not respected at all. The possible *complexity* of the relationship between "das Eigene" and "das Fremde" is more evi-dent in Christine's case. Her initial responses to the advances of the student fit the options recommended by a liberal form of political correctness. But then, understand-ably, anxieties and suppressed wishes take over which have to do with her unsatisfactory social role as a sexually unattractive woman. As long as she is exposed to the bewildering physical presence and pressure of the ugly foreign man, Christine is obsessed by fears of rape. As soon as this fearful presence is removed, however, the oriental student is transformed into an object of intense romantic interest, no doubt including erotic interest. She keeps thinking of him, examines pictures and television broadcasts about the war in his country, tries to find out whether he has become a victim or not. After all he is the only male ever to show a passionate interest in her.

Christine's view of the other is not stable as it moves from indifference to obsessive preoccupation, and oscillation between revulsion, fear and pity. Even while persecuted she ponders the possibility that he is the victim of his cultural background and her strange, hitherto undiscovered sexual power. She perhaps comes closest to understanding when she surmises that the foreign student must be in desperate search of a home and a family in a frightening cultural environment. Finally the other loses its quality of disturbing otherness when Christine comes to the conclusion that the student is in fact like herself: "He would be something nondescript, something in the background, like herself; perhaps he had become an interpreter" (31).

However inconclusive these perceptions and interpretations must be, they are evidence of Christine's strenuous attempt at understanding. Furthermore, as shown by Figal, the self and the other are not locked in a petrified binary. After studying the foreign country intensely it seems "almost more familiar" (31) to her than her own. As long as the foreigner shows intense interest in her, she herself becomes in a sense a mysterious other for her friends as they reflect upon the reason of her strange power over the man. Under the impact of the stranger's obsession with her person and her friends' recently awakened interest she at least momentarily changes her understanding of her own self, viewing herself, for example, as a "water-nixie" (24) or even as "Marilynn Monroe" (24) while taking a bath. The Christine of the end of the story is a changed woman, haunted by visions and taking refuge in conservative Victorian novels.

Constructing a situation of radical cultural difference, the text explores both the emergence and uses of stereotypes *and* the shifting borders of self and other, sanity and insanity. Attempts at understanding vary according to interest and competence, and they are obviously more successful if motivated by sympathy and intense personal interest. The other of Atwood's stories addressing the theme of multiculturalism is a careful construction, not a given fact. Withholding potentially available information from the reader about African or Asian culture and using a limited point of view, excluding inside views of the other, creates a blank which invites fictional characters and readers alike to project their interpretations on it. The purpose of this strategy is in the first place to increase awareness of cultural difference, suffering, stereotype-formation and the catastrophic breakdown of intercultural communication. Successful understanding would have robbed the story of its tension and its point as an aesthetic construct. However, Atwood's realism also implies the insight that different perspectives on the other result in vastly differing images and constructions which in "Dancing Girls" even include a vision of utopian integration. What is not yet available to her is apparently Homi Bhaba's idea of innovative hybridity, which is celebrated and enacted by Salman Rushdie in the many voices, inversions and complex intercultural relations of his set of short stories *East/West* (1994).

*"Dancing Girls"*⁹

Ann, a Canadian student studying urban design at an American university, lives in a dingy flat rented out by a common, low-class woman called Nolan. Apart from Ann, there are more foreign students in the house, Chinese mathematicians and Leila, a Turkish student of comparative literature, who has moved out because of the noise. Leila's successor is an Arab (African?) student, who pays his rent regularly, borrows the vacuum cleaner equally regularly, but seems to be entirely passive and unhappy in an utterly unfamiliar cultural environment. Ann and her Dutch friend discuss urban design. Ann's vision for the renewed Toronto is a distinctly pastoral one but with no space for people in it. We learn about the Arab only through information provided by Mrs. Nolan and Ann. The simmering crisis comes to a head when the Arab throws a noisy party with two of his friends and three dancing girls, which is abruptly ended by Mrs. Nolan calling the police and chasing them out.

This fictional study of multiculturalism cannot be called pessimistic. The ability to cope with the other varies according to education. People used to learning new ideas and foreign cultures are apparently better equipped to encounter the other than those caught in their narrow horizon of class and nation. This explains the glaring difference between the landlady's and Ann's reactions. Ann, who comes from Toronto, feels like a foreigner in the US, but is not treated as such. She is friendly with the Turkish student Leila, whose "beautiful long auburn hairs" (197) she envies. In fact, the foreigners are in some ways superior to Ann: Leila is perceived by her to be splendidly exotic, the Hong Kong mathematicians are clearly far more intelligent, and her Dutch friend Jetske seems to know more about the world and its ways. In all these cases intercultural communication does not seem to pose a problem. The case of the Arab or African student - his nationality is in fact not clear - is somewhat different since they never engage in conversation, partly because the new tenant is shy, partly because Ann does not wish to become implicated in his situation. Whereas Ann realizes that the foreign student is lonely and cannot cope with his situation, the landlady, after initially praising his quiet ways and regular payments, views his strange passivity with growing suspicion and fear, and is not prepared to excuse the excesses of the party as an inevitable outburst. Drinking excessively, vomiting in the bathtub, leaving heaps of dust in his room and consorting with doubtful women are not acceptable behaviour for her because she makes no attempt whatever to view the situation from the 'Arab's' point of view, in other words, she makes no attempt at understanding. Her interpretation is exclusively determined by her material interest. Nor, of course, is she able to see that her unruly family does not really compare favourably with the foreign students.

Mrs. Nolan has neither the wish nor the will nor the ability to understand the other. This is markedly different with Ann, whose own isolation and ambition, linked to

---

⁹ Margaret Atwood, "Dancing Girls," in *Dancing Girls and Other Stories* (London: Virago Press, 1984), 196-212.

imaginative sympathy, allow her to understand the Arab's plight. Shortly before the party, she sees him watching the traffic and concludes that he is about to "drown" (205). After the uproar she imaginatively reconstructs the Arab's thoughts as he flees, pursued by the frantic landlady:

> She wondered where he had gone, chased down the street by Mrs. Nolan in her scuffies and housecoat shouting and flailing at him with a broom. She must have been at least as terrifying a spectacle to him as he was to her, and just as inexplicable. Why would this woman, this fat crazy woman, wish to burst in upon a scene of harmless hospitality, banging and raving? [...] What unspoken taboo had they violated? What would these cold, mad people do next? (211)

Understanding apparently involves a conscious imaginative effort allowing the understanding person to perceive and to evaluate the world from the other's point of view. While Mrs. Nolan and the foreign student find each other "inexplicable," Ann is able to imagine what the other thinks and feels. His language and his judgements are present in free indirect speech, which does not simply represent Ann's own thoughts but what she thinks the foreigner must think. If Dilthey's "Einfühlung" and "Nacherleben" as the chief instruments of "Verstehen" mean anything, it is in the examples of free indirect speech ("this fat crazy woman," "these cold, mad people") that we see them at work. Understanding means to quote the other correctly or rather to be able to imagine a plausible quotation. Yet this act of quoting and shifting of one's perspective does not mean that one is converted to the other's point of view in the sense that one gives up one's identity.

Even this kind of understanding is not objective, but speculative and subjective. In other words, there is a limitation which, however, cannot be simply accounted for by pointing to the epistemological limitations of understanding itself. After all, a dialogue, the chief mode of encountering the other and the very heart of the hermeneutic project, is not even attempted. Such a dialogue might have clarified the 'Arab's' (or African's?) situation beyond any doubt. Yet if Atwood had attempted that dialogue, the story would have been deprived of its thematic and aesthetic interest, which is to create communicative tension out of cultural difference and to make the reader aware of the ensuing suffering and anxiety. It is precisely such suffering and anxiety which are absent in the pastoral utopia of intercultural peace and understand-ing with which the story ends:

> In the distance, beneath the arches of the aqueduct, a herd of animals, deer or something, was grazing. (She must learn more about animals.) Groups of people walking happily among the trees, holding hands, not just in twos but in threes, fours, fives. The man from next door was there, in his native costume, and the mathematicians, they were all in their native costumes. Beside the stream a man was playing the flute; and around him, in long flowered robes and mauve scuffies, their auburn hair floating around their healthy pink faces, smiling their Dutch smiles, the dancing girls were sedately dancing (212).

All the conflicts tearing cultures and human society apart have become reconciled in this poetic vision of harmony: nature (animals) and technology (aqueduct), various cultures ("native costumes"), stifling, isolating marriages ("not in two, but in threes, fours, fives"), social differences and stigmas ("dancing girls"). The arts of music and dancing ("a man was playing the flute," "sedately dancing") symbolize the new order.

"Bluebeard's Egg"[10]

In "Bluebeard's Egg" problems of understanding do not concern members of different cultures but a married couple. Sally, married to the heart specialist Ed, is obsessively worried about the fascination Ed exercises over women and about his true identity, which seems a "puzzle" (169) to her until she discovers, during a party, that Ed seems to be carrying on an affair with her best friend Marilynn. The story constructs a feminist icon par excellence, i.e. the anxious and betrayed wife. Ever since Elizabeth Hardwick's *Seduction and Betrayal: Women and Literature* (1970) this image has been crucial for Anglo-American feminist theory. In such a scenario the husband is given the role of an indifferent, mysterious womanizer who, without consciously contriving it, exerts power over his wife because of her romantic obsession with him. This seems to represent a recurring situation as the intertextual references testify, namely to the murderous tyrant in Charles Perrault's *Contes du Temps* (1617), as far as the title is concerned ("Bluebeard"), and to "Fitchers Vogel," the Grimm version of the whole text. Since "Bluebeard's Egg" is a rewriting of "Fitchers Vogel," an assignment 'originally' given to Sally in her evening class on "Narrative Forms of Fiction," there are actually two problems of understanding posed by the story, one dramatized in the text, namely Sally's frantic attempts to understand Ed's inner self, and the reader's problem of having to understand the meaning and the function of the difference between Grimm's "Fitchers Vogel" and the Atwood adaptation.

(a) Atwood estranges inter-marital communication by turning the male partner into a mysterious other as if he were a member of an alien culture. This method of marking gender or age differences is quite common in her work. At the end of "Significant Moments in the Life of My Mother," daughter and mother drift apart because of the influence of a 'progressive' university milieu on the daughter:

> At any time I might open my mouth and out would come a language she had never heard before. I had become a visitant from outer space, a time-traveller come back from the future, bearing news of a great disaster (23).
>
> Similarly Ed, while shaving, reminds the wondering Sally of an "Assyrian, sterner than usual" or a "demi-human, a white-bearded forest mutant" (177).

Anxiety concerning his true nature and the spectre of betrayal - she is his third wife after all - are the driving forces behind Sally's ceaseless attempts to interpret Ed's body-language and sentences. Yet the road from the surface of the signs to the depth

---

[10] Margaret Atwood, "Bluebeard's Egg," in *Bluebeard's Egg and Other Stories* (1983, rpt. New York: Ballantine Books, 1990), 144-84.

of their meanings is blocked, Ed's "inner world" (167), the true aim of hermeneutic 'Verstehen' in Dilthey's sense, remains a puzzle to her:

> "Don't be silly," says Ed today, with equanimity. Is he blushing, is he embarrassed? Sally examines his face closely, like a geologist with an aerial photograph, looking for telltale signs of mineral treasure: markings, bumps, hollows. Everything about Ed means something, though it's difficult at times to say what. [...] Is that complacency, in the back turned to her? Maybe there really are these hordes of women, even though she's made them up. Maybe they really do behave that way. His shoulders are slightly drawn up: is he shutting her out? (163)

While Sally's inner world is ruled by Ed, Ed's inner world defies Sally's attempts at understanding. Since the signals coming from him are never evaluated by an omniscient narrator we are left with Sally's uncertainties.

Atwood does not primarily play the postmodern game of stressing the enigmatic character of reality. The darkly powerful and devious male seems, just as in "Betty," to be a strategic device of her feminist art. His power actually stems from the inability of women to see that their romantic devotion to a man, a role for which they are prepared by the popular media, robs them of their independence, their identity, and their professional and creative potential. In other words, their malaise is in other words a self-inflicted one. Romantic love means that Ed controls Sally's heart. When Ed, the "heart man" (152), shows Sally her palpitating heart on the screen with the help of sonography, he also symbolically enacts his power over her. It is only after her discovery of Ed's treachery that she questions his behaviour and his language with critical detachment. His impersonal language ("The woman can do that in the morn-ing," 183) makes her think that he considers women to be "interchangeable" (183) commodities.

(b) Both the title and the end of the text invite the reader in particular to engage in a classical act of understanding. He is expected to compare Atwood's modern version of the fairy tale with the original. Translating the cultural other of Grimm's story into a modern context involves radical adaptations, the purpose of which is to heighten the reader's awareness of the problems of modern gender relations.

"Fitchers Vogel" is the story of a ruthless magician who abducts Fitcher's three daughters one after the other. The first two, not being able to master their curiosity, ignore his strict orders not to enter one of the chambers during his absence. On entering the forbidden chamber with the help of a key entrusted to each of them by the magician, they are so horrified at the sight of chopped limbs and blood that they drop the egg, also given to them by the magician, into the blood. The cunning third daughter, however, manages to outwit, to humiliate and to punish the magician. She also revives her sisters by putting their limbs together. After seemingly passing his test he elects her as his bride and loses all power over her. She makes him suffer on his journey to her parents's home and, with the help of her brothers, arranges his death by fire when she lures him, disguised as a bird ('Fitchers Vogel') into the house on the day of the wedding and then sets fire to it.

Atwood's implicit interpretation of this story is clearly along feminist lines and does not violate the norms of realism. Not only does she dispense with the brutality, supernaturalism and magic of the textual model, she also, significantly, ignores the second of the fairy tales, which demonstrates the power and ruthlessness of the revengeful woman. Such an image would have introduced a jarring note not compatible with the ideas of dependance, suffering and betrayal. Sally, as Ed's third wife, is the equivalent of the clever bride, but all her cleverness does not allow her to see through her husband, nor does her curiosity yield definite insights. It would also seem that the true test of gender relations is no longer the question whether a woman is obedient and a virgin - if one assumes that the bloody egg signifies loss of virginity in the fairy tale - but a marriage, quite contrary to Sally's, in which a woman's identity does *not* "dissolve" (145), because she does not define herself with respect to others, is not exploited by men, and does not indulge in an emotional and erotic dependence depriving her of her self-control.

The magician's realistic version seems to be the devious, indifferent man, whose magic is redefined as erotic fascination. His cruelty seems to reside in a certain indifference and callousness towards the woman, in his inability or unwillingness to send out unequivocal messages of love and reassurance. Finally, the most spectacular rewriting concerns the symbol of the egg. In the fairy tale the white egg's meaning is not expounded, it simply seems to be a mode of discovery in the test and possibly a symbol of virginity and fertility. Since the story is written from Sally's point of view and since her projected version of the tale envisages a text adopting the egg's point of view, it seems logical to identify Sally and the egg. Sally's final vision of a red, growing, palpitating egg might then indicate the emergence and growth of a new life, a new identity for Sally after her shocking discovery. After being Ed's possession ("Bluebeard's Egg") she might be on the threshold of starting a new life.

This is undoubtedly and inevitably a reductive understanding of the story. The openness of the text is such as to allow, even provoke, different readings. Reading the story against the grain one might even claim that Atwood engages in a study of female neuroticism and schizophrenia. Still, the openness, the blanks, create the impression of being contrived. Their primary function does not seem to be to emphasize the notion of undecidability. The other, it seems, also needs to be darkened and mystified for aesthetic and ideological purposes. A transparent Ed would be too banal to cause tension, anxiety, suffering and interpretive efforts. An aesthetic distortion is required to evoke the experience of danger and otherness necessary from a feminist perspective.

The results of the above analyses can be summarized as follows:

Atwood's complex texts seem at first glance to imply that the hopes invested in understanding by hermeneutics are utopian in a negative sense. At best, something like Figal's "begrenzte Vernunft" is possible. Multiculturalism is fraught with potential conflicts which are displaced and overcome in occasional utopian visions.

However true this may be, it is equally true that attempts at understanding and interpretation, although they may be complete or partial failures, cannot be replaced by something else. They are unavoidable, and yield conflicting results according to the perspective and the cultural competence of the observer and interpreter. As soon as petrified binaries are broken up, the borderline between "das Eigene" und "das Fremde" shifts continuously.

Art does not merely represent and interpret the other, it also creates it intentionally for a variety of purposes. This is what the philosophical discourse of (German) hermeneutics seems to overlook when it privileges art as the medium of truth as far as the inner life of human beings is concerned. In Atwood's case the interest and the message of the story demand the construct of a mysterious other to show the ensuing conflicts, anxiety and suffering of the 'real' other, that is the female or the foreign person.

Intercultural Encounters:
Plays by New Zealand, Jamaican and Canadian Authors.

ALBERT-REINER GLAAP (Düsseldorf)

For many years, particularly since the fall of the Berlin wall, Germany has experienced an increasing influx of people from Eastern Europe. Turkish communities have become part of our society. Albanian refugees have sought refuge in Italy and used it as a gateway into countries of Western and Southern Europe. The dismantling of barriers invites the migration of people into Europe. The Euro is expected to bring economic advantages. The world is being confronted with new challenges. More than ever, people from various cultures ask each other how they can live together, further mutual understanding, preserve the traditions and customs of their home country and, at the same time, respect other cultures.

The problems of intercultural encounters hardly crop up on occasional visits, rather when it comes to developing transcultural concepts for a common future, in which each culture has to make sacrifices. This is particularly crucial when one specific culture does not merely bring different traditions and lifestyles and a different language into another country, but is also bigger, relatively more influential, and is considered, or even considers itself, superior. Intercultural, like personal, encounters may result in the domination of one over the other or total "assimilation" of one into the other or mutual recognition. The English word "encounter" implies a "casual or unexpected," a "difficult or dangerous" meeting, or a "particular type of experience" like an encounter "with new ideas."[1] When the word "encounter" was first used in English, in the thirteenth century, its meaning was "meeting in conflict."[2] The twentieth century, which will shortly come to a close, has convincingly proved that only "recognition of each other" is beneficial to intercultural encounters, although, in many cases, it still remains an ideal. Domination often leads to exploitation, subjugation and colonialism. Total assimilation almost always leaves a loss of identity in its wake.

Intercultural encounters which aim at a recognition of each other can be of three different kinds. What has been going on, for instance, between white people or 'Pakeha' and Maori in New Zealand during the past decades could be termed "cohabitation" in the connotative meaning of the word (i.e. "living next to each other"). Maori and Pakeha speak different languages and embrace different cultures, but New Zealand is a country with two official languages. When emigrants from Britain came to New Zealand they started off by grafting their concepts of civilisation, lifestyle and culture onto Maori, who - needless to say - felt fierce antagonism towards them.

---

[1] *Collins Cobuild English Language Dictionary* (London: Collins ELT, 1987), 464.
[2] *The Oxford Dictionary of English Etymology* (Oxford: Clarendon Press, 1966), 312.

Today Maori and Pakeha live next to each other in the same country under legally binding contracts.

The situation in London and other big towns and cities in Britain is different. West Indians, for instance, who have taken refuge in England to find better living conditions and jobs, share a common linguistic ground with the British majority of people. They speak British English, whereas the West Indians speak their particular patois, which is a regional variant of the English language. Most West Indians make an effort to mix and are becoming part of the society in an ongoing process of "integration."

Intercultural encounters have been particularly important to Canadian culture since the nation's foundation. Canada is often referred to as a model of a multicultural society. During this century most racial and ethnic groups have been integrated into society. Since the 1970s Asians have increasingly come to Canada, many of whom however, have the feeling of living inside and outside the Canadian culture, of being Westernised *and* having a foot in the other culture, be it Korean, Chinese or whatever. Their relationship with other Canadians gives an insight into the making of the process of assimilation.

Laws passed, compromises found or agreements made do not as such guarantee that neighbouring or different cultures will get along with each other harmoniously. It is what the different cultures make of their encounters that may in the long run result in intercultural understanding. Encounters with other cultures are always encounters with new ideas and different concepts. It is a continuous process and involves enormous human endeavours.

The fact that intercultural encounters have more and more been thematised in many contemporary stage plays is a highly significant phenomenon. Especially in countries like New Zealand and Britain – also in Canada, where theatre is still very young – playwrights problematise differences and clashes between cultures, and develop concepts and approaches to bring these cultures together. Very often the central characters in their plays are either adolescents or young people between twenty and thirty years of age, who experience a period of transition in their lives. Insights into contemporary plays by New Zealand, Jamaican and Canadian playwrights illuminate some of the facets of intercultural friction and the challenges of multi-ethnic co-existence. They can make theatre-goers realise how important, albeit difficult, it is to fulfil the demands of "intercultural understanding."

Plays on Maori and Pakeha in New Zealand

Plays written both on Maori and by Maori authors, have in the course of the past twenty years, increasingly gained ground in New Zealand. The early eighties were

> a time of great political activity. Those who are coming through *now* don't have that base. There has been a long period of experimentation and building an infrastructure, which comes from a political drive and a creative need,

writes Roma Potiki in a recently published article.³ And Hone Kouka, one of the new generation of Maori dramatists, feels that "Maori, young and old are saying 'Yes, I have my story to tell'" (Huria, "Ma Te Rehia e Kawe, 6). Indeed, there is no need any more for those playwrights to merely represent Maori on stage. Maori theatre "can move away from the directly representational, and become more interpretative" (Huria, "Ma Te Rehia e Kawe, 3 - Briar Grace-Smith). Similar to what happened to Native plays in other so-called post-colonial cultures, Maori plays are no longer primarily being written with the intention to prove that indigenous peoples are there. "So what is Maori theatre? What is Pakeha theatre? We're all different people, we're all individuals," says Hone Kouka (Huria, "Ma Te Rehia e Kawe, 4), and Roma Potiki concurs "Maori are living within a social context that is global. Maori theatre is not a rigid form" (Huria, "Ma Te Rehia e Kawe, 4).

Encounters of Maoris with Pakeha are nevertheless still at the centre of many Maori plays. Two of these are *Te Hokinga Mai (The Return Home)*⁴ by John Broughton and *Mauri Tu*⁵ by Hone Kouka. *Te Hokinga Mai*, written in 1988, is often considered to have been a breakthrough work for Maori theatre. *Mauri Tu*, first staged in 1991, is about "choice," about how to choose one's destiny in New Zealand, the Maori or the Pakeha way. Broughton's play is about the return of a soldier from the Vietnam war. The Te Maori Exhibition which, after a tour through the USA and Europe in 1986/87, came back to New Zealand, was the reason for the title *Te Hokinga Mai* which means "The Return Home." It is an intense 60-minute play. Kouka's *Mauri Tu* was developed from a report in a newspaper about Francis Shaw pleading to have his case heard on the *marae*, the enclosed space in front of a Maori house, as well as in court. This young Maori, alienated from both Maori and Pakeha culture, had exploded into violence. *Mauri Tu* is a typical example of a short play: the performance requires about half an hour. The play was written as a solo piece and was Hone Kouka's first book. *Mauri* can be translated as "life force," and *Mauri Tu* is part of a phrase in a greeting and basically means "it is life." It encompasses the sun, ghost and holy spirit, and is like an awakening; *Mauri Tu* also encompasses the "strength of our life force."

"Te Hokinga Mai"

In *Te Hokinga Mai* Martin Balfour-Davies, a Pakeha, who has just come back from the Vietnam war, is calling on the family of his Maori friend John-Junior Matthews who served with him in the army (Broughton himself was a member of the New

---

[3] John Huria, "Ma Te Rehia e Kawe," *Playmarket News* 16 (1997): 2-7, here 3.
[4] John Broughton, *Te Hokinga Mai (The Return Home)* (Dunedin: Aoraki Productions, 1990). Quotations from the play (numbers in brackets) refer to pages in this edition.
[5] Hone Kouka, *Mauri Tu* (Wellington: Aoraki Press Series, 1992). Quotations from the play (numbers in brackets) refer to pages in this edition.

Zealand Territorial Army and became an officer, some of his comrades were in Vietnam). In the play, Martin arrives outside the Meeting House, the *marae*, to bring the news of his friend's death in the war. On a second level *Te Hokinga Mai* deals with mutual understanding, sympathy and tolerance. Towards the end Martin points out what John-Junior, who was quite alien to him when they first met, eventually meant to him:

> J-J was my friend. I just wanted you to know that my friend taught me a hell of a lot. But for me, the most incredible thing of all, what really gets me, was that I had to leave New Zealand, my home, to go overseas, to a bloody war, to find the treasures on my doorstep (52).

Broughton's play reveals where these "treasures" can be found: in the rituals, symbols and essentials of the Maori culture - a third level of the play. The *karanga*, for example, is the formal call or summon, i.e. the words of welcome, which are characterised as "loud, shrill piercing and emotional" (22). The *hakari* is the traditional meal which is an integral part of every big get-together (called *tui*) of Maori in the *marae*, and *tika* means "in accordance with divine commandments." These and other Maori words are interspersed in the text and are, as a rule, followed by English translations (e.g. "Just to get the soft drink for the *hakari*, the dinner"). They have a double function: they underline the authenticity of the text and introduce the reader or theatre-goer to Maori as both part of a cultural heritage and a living language in New Zealand.

When arriving at the *marae* Martin Balfour-Davies was given a formal friendly welcome (*Te Whaikorero*) which he returns. His first sentence is in the Maori language, then he goes on in English and reports on his friendship with John-Junior, which had started off with prejudices mirrored in racial jokes which the two young men told each other about their respective cultures. It took them a fairly long time before they became real friends. Flashbacks are integral parts of the play illustrating the stages in the development of their relationship. John-Junior appears on stage only four times, talks to Martin and disappears. Martin slips into the role of a commentator, who addresses those present, comments on the respective previous dialogue between John-Junior and himself thereby providing both Martin's family and the audience with insights into how mutual understanding and respect between the representatives of two different cultures are being developed.

But, eventually, when all those present start singing *E Pari Ra*, the song composed on the occasion of the return of the New Zealand soldiers after World War II, Martin "does not know the action, but it doesn't matter, he does his best to follow" (54). In other words: The process of developing intercultural understanding is not completed. It may take a lifetime.

"Mauri Tu"

Tero is the central character in Hone Kouka's *Mauri Tu*. He is Jerry Tahihi's eldest son and has a brother, Waru, aged ten. Jerry, who is in his early forties, is a businessman; his father, Matiu, is in his mid-sixties. The roles of these four characters are played by the same actor, because, as Kouka says, "they are of the one *whanau* - originally of one Woman. Therefore they each have traits of the others, inseparable" (X). The identities of the characters are shown by minimal costume changes: Waru wears a baseball cap and an oversize jacket, Tero black jeans and a black T-shirt, Father a cardigan (to suggest affluence) and Grandfather an aged suit jacket.

Tero has assaulted a stranger in a bar and, when his case is being investigated, pleads for trial on a *marae*. His plea triggers off diverse reactions on the part of the other characters and gives the audience insights into various facets of the co-habitation of Maori and Pakeha. Tero's wish to be tried on a *marae* is all the more astonishing because he does neither speak the Maori language, nor knows anything about Maori rituals. But as he is also an outsider in the Pakeha world, he does not know where he belongs. He must ask his younger brother to tell him how to conduct himself on the *marae*, which - as he admits towards the end of the play - made him "feel small" (29). Their father rejects all things Maori. In his eyes, his son Tero has developed into a criminal - despite his good education - and must suffer the consequences. Jerry is totally absorbed into the Pakeha business world, whereas Matiu, the grandfather, remains the only person with a comprehensive knowledge of Maoritanga, the Maori culture.

At the beginning of the play, after the audience has been called into the theatre, Waru appears, introduces himself and prays to his dead mother to help Tero on the *marae* when his case comes before the court. Then he asks her something that seems to be very important to him:

> What are we? [...] Dad says Grandpa's a Maori. So's Dad ... don't he like being one? I don't sometimes. Tero says he doesn't know what he is. I said you're black man, you must be a Maori. Ha! (7)

What are we? This question, the attempt to define one's Maori identity and to choose one's own destiny, be it Maori or Pakeha, turns out to be the pivotal point of the play. Later in the play, in the first of three scenes on the *marae*, Matiu makes a long speech in untranslated Maori with the lights slowly fading to blackout. Then he addresses the Pakeha in the audience saying:

> So this is what it's like when a Maori speaks in his own tongue ... or, is it that *you* just switch off? No matter, at least we are equal, eh. Me and you. [...] Listen here, listen well. This is what it is like for many of us in this world (21).

Matiu's words, at this point, are used to block communication. He does not try to explain to non-Maori speakers what he was saying in Maori. Matiu wants the Pakeha to understand to what extent intercultural understanding is being impeded when people are literally kept in the dark about the meaning of words spoken in a language they do not understand. And - "as Matiu implies" (in the words of Gilbert and Tomkins):

> [...] the linguistic authority arrogated by English for centuries no longer prevails automatically: English speakers/audiences will also be forced to endure misunderstandings which disrupt their linguistic (and naturalistic) expectations.[6]

Jerry, in the following scene (also on the *marae*) is a typical example of the many people, who all too carelessly drop their mother-tongue and switch over to the prevailing language of the country they live in:

> Jerry: My name is Jerry Tahihi [...]. I'm not going to speak Maori because the majority of the people here today can't understand it and for that matter neither can my son. In the court of law the boy was found guilty, so I can't understand why we're here (24-5).

Jerry does not even question any more if and in what way cultural relations between Maori and Pakeha can be established. He does not say that he is "embarrassed at being a Maori," but "we are culturally inept" (26). And he affirms that Tero "had no contact with anything Maori as long as he was under my control" (25). Tero, however, has not only become alienated from Maori culture but also an outsider in the Pakeha world. In his speech on the *marae*, where he had never been before, he says why he wanted to be tried here: "I wanted to know what I was missing out on. I wanted in" (30). In his life so far he has found out that at school nobody wanted to know him because of his dark skin, and when he came back to the *marae* nobody wanted him because he was considered white (31). In the end we do not know what becomes of Tero. Waru and his grandfather visit him in prison - as Waru points out in his final talk with his dead mother. And it is he who holds hope for a bright future (34).

The four characters in this play are representatives of different generations. What binds them together is that they are all Maori whose reactions and attitudes to the Pakeha, who came into their country as colonisers, are different. Grandfather is rooted in his Mariotanga. He married a white woman; their son (Jerry) grew up in Pakeha surroundings and could not care less about all things Maori. Tero, his son, a representative of his generation, does not know where he belongs and becomes a criminal. Waru, however, is eager to learn all he can about Maori culture and will have the chance to decide of his own free will to live as a Maori in co-habitation with the Pakeha in New Zealand. The search for identity of a Maori family over three generations (from Grandfather's pain of being Maori to Jerry's indifference, to Tero's feeling of being alienated, and finally Waru's having a chance to choose Maori *and* Pakeha, Maori *or* Pakeha) is what Kouka's play is about. It needs a Maori to tell us what the deeper meaning of this search in *Mauri Tu* really is; Rena Owen, for instance, actress and writer, who put it in a nutshell when she said:

> What underlies this play and what we see through the representation of three generations, are the consequences of colonisation. It is a story familiar to many of us Maori (XX-XXI).

---

[6] Helen Gilbert and Joanne Tompkins, *Post-Colonial Drama: Theory, Practice, Politics* (London and New York: Routledge, 1996), 172.

Jamaicans in Britain

There were several incentives for the post-war immigration of Jamaicans to Britain from 1951 onwards: one was the British government's desperate need for cheap labour. Jamaicans thought they would be welcomed as British; after all they had been a trusted part of the war effort. Also, as there was no established University of Jamaica, students, who could afford it, went to Britain and often stayed on. The migrant workers were referred to as the "SS Windrush," which was the name of one of the ships that brought them to Britain.[7] Once they were there, however, many of them did not get the work they expected. What is more, they were treated as inferiors.

In the 1960s, colonial labour force was not in demand any more, independence was granted to Jamaica (1962) and the Commonwealth Immigrants Act (also 1962), which was to control immigration from the Commonwealth to Britain, led to a process of adaptation on the part of Jamaicans in Britain and a search for a new (a black) identity. The second (1970s) and third generations started to consider Britain their home. They were vacillating between adherence to their real mother country and assimilation to Britain, their "new" mother country. They were becoming part of the British mainstream. This development was and still is being mirrored and thematised in plays by writers of West Indian descent, who came to Britain as children or were born there.

Winsome Pinnock is one of these playwrights. She was born in England in 1961, three years after her parents had come over from Jamaica. She attended university in England achieving first a B.A., then her Masters degree. Pinnock encapsulates a blend of different cultures, a mixture of different voices and (what she herself calls) "the new identity" of the Jamaicans, who have left one set of values and try conform to another, trying to combine an English upbringing with their "Caribbean souls." In the seventies when she was growing up, black people in England were angry about being torn between two cultures. Considering the experiences, however, that she and her generation were going through, she was unable to identify with the anger of those people, who were expected to assume roles that were not theirs. She decided to write about identity and the way intercultural encounters and conflicts manifest themselves in different generations. Her play *Leave Taking* (first performed in 1987)[8] is about conflicts in a West Indian immigrant family in England. *Talking in Tongues* (first performed in 1991),[9] which is about how language encapsulates the problems and joys of integration, is set in England and Jamaica.

---

[7] Royal National Theatre, ed., *Leave Taking by Winsome Pinnock: Education Pack* (London: Royal National Theatre, 1995), 10.

[8] Winsome Pinnock, "Leave Taking," in Kate Harwood, ed., *First Run: New Plays by New Writers* (London: Nick Hern Books, 1989), 139-89. Quotations from the play (numbers in brackets) refer to pages in this edition.

[9] Winsome Pinnock, "Talking in Tongues," in Yvonne Brewster, ed., *Black Plays Three* (London: Methuen New Theatre Scripts, 1995), 171-227. Quotations from the play (numbers in brackets) refer to pages in this edition.

"Leave Taking"

None of the characters in this play is truly British or truly Jamaican - apart from the grandmother who is still in Jamaica. Her daughter Enid, being a mother herself, lives in England and tries to bring her two daughters up as respectable British subjects. Viv and Del, however, experience their situation in different ways ending up with different resolutions. Viv appears to tie in with her mother's plans for her British-born daughters' future life. She is an ambitious and successful student and tries to do what is expected of her, but she is troubled because she feels that the role she is playing is an unreal role. Del, on the other hand, does not want to do what other people want her to; she enjoys life and loathes bowing to England. She stays out all night, gets herself pregnant and becomes the apprentice of an Obeah woman, Mai, an arthritic and grumpy sixty-year-old practising the rituals of healing and witchcraft, a catalytic figure, the meeting point of two generations and also the most amusing character in the play. Enid Matthews, the mother, is the epitome of a first generation immigrant who comes to England hoping that she, or at least the children, will be accepted by the English and be given the chance of leading a better life. Enid has given up everything for her daughters. As Charles Spencer, in his review of the play, says: "She feels almost pathetically grateful to England for accepting her and is determined to try and fit in [...] Enid is living vicariously through her daughters."[10]
But these daughters have to break free and want to find out themselves who they really are, Enid must realise that for that reason the family is disintegrating.

Leave Taking mirrors stages, chances and drawbacks in the process of integrating West Indian immigrants into British society, which is "a process of being exiled and exiling oneself."[11] It encompasses cross-generational conflicts, cultural differences, which are liable to rip families apart, and universal themes. A significant feature of this play is the absence of fathers. Apart from Uncle Broderick, the characters are all women. Enid, in John Peter's words, "is one of the walking wounded, carrying the marks of a harsh unloving mother and a dreadful marriage back home."[12] She is contemptuous of her Jamaican roots, but takes her problems to the Obeah woman. She makes the effort to educate her daughters as assimilated English women. But – "at the news of her mother's death, we have seen her English facade demolished by her long pent-up desire for home - whatever that may be: reunion with her birthplace or with her estranged daughter."[13]

---

[10] Charles Spencer in his review of the National Theatre production of *Leave Taking* in *Daily Telegraph*, 9th January 1995.

[11] Albert-Reiner Glaap, "Interview with Winsome Pinnock" (London, 11th March 1995) (typescript).

[12] John Peter in his review of the National Theatre production in *Sunday Times*, 8th January 1995.

[13] Irving Wardle in his review of the National Theatre production in *Independent* on Sunday, 8th January 1995.

The complex experiences of the characters in *Leave Taking* have produced a "new identity;" a mixture, not just a juxtaposition, of two cultures, who speak with different voices. Jamaica is an offstage character; what happens, happens in England:

> I had always wanted to write about more complex characters. People who were more truthful in their relationship both to this country (i.e. Britain) and to ideas about identity [...] I really don't feel immersed in the sense that I'm part of a Caribbean London, although I feel Caribbean. London has influenced me, and it's a very rich culture to have been brought up in (Glaap, "Interview with Pinnock").

These are the words of the author of *Leave Taking* whose main concern, as a Jamaican in Britain, is the integration of one (living) context in a new one. The differences between the three first-generation immigrants in this play (Mai, Enid and Broderick) and those who were born in England (Viv and Del) are clearly marked by the language they speak. The elderly people speak patois (e.g. "In me haht, I wanted to wipe de smile off her fyehce"), the daughters speak straight English, which, in Alistair Macaulay's words, makes us "aware on the one hand that they are talking as their mother hoped they would when she came to England and on the other that they have lost something vivid, for the sake of conformism"[14].

Language being a culture marker in *Leave Taking*, the title of another of Winsome Pinnock's plays, *Talking in Tongues*, points to the building of Babel as reported in *Genesis*, Chapter XI, 1-11: "The whole earth was of one language, but the people decided to build a city and a tower, whose top was to reach unto heaven. Thereupon God confounded their language so that they could not understand one another's speech." And, in the words of Verse 8 of *Genesis* XI: "The Lord scattered them abroad from thence upon the face of all the earth; and they left off to build the city" (i.e. Babel, meaning "confusion").

Talking in Tongues is concerned with different languages, or rather, different levels of language which separate the people in this play: Jamaican patois, black south-London idiom and the English spoken by the white middle class. With language being the overall metaphor, *Talking in Tongues* is about the problems of integration which are illustrated with reference to cross-racial relationships. Leela and Bentley, a black couple, are invited to a party given by Jeff and Fran, a white couple. Curly and Claudette, two other black girls, have also been invited. None of them are married. When Bentley has sex with Fran in an upstairs room, Leela witnesses this. She tries to vent her rage, but realises that she lacks the words needed to articulate this "rage against the continued repression of the voice of one culture by another" (226). Having put an end to her affair with Bentley she goes on vacation to Jamaica together with her black girlfriend Claudette. Leela does not want to meet anyone, just enjoy life on the beach. Claudette, on the other hand, to whom interracial relationships are a betrayal of the community and, more seriously, a betrayal of the black woman, is extremely keen on a muscular black beach boy and is confronted with the fact that he prefers a

---

[14] Alistair Macaulay in his review of the National Theatre production in *Financial Times*, 6th January 1995.

night with a blonde. *Talking in Tongues* is about West Indians who have lost their own language which in turn reflects the loss of their identity. They cannot help but accept their identity as British. The play also illustrates to what extent colour exerts its influence on sexual relationships. After their experiences in London, the two young women go to Jamaica. But they don't find there what they were hoping for. They return to London knowing that they must develop a transcultural identity. With reference to the story about Babel in *Genesis* XI, Winsome Pinnock states in the interview:

> This story suggests that we are potentially more alike than we know and that, while we will never again speak the same language, one of our quests is to find our way back to each other.

Plays on Asians in Canada

Noran Bang: The Yellow Room[15] was the first Korean-Canadian play staged professionally in Canada. It was premiered at Theatre Passe Muraille, Toronto, in 1993. Myung - Jim Kang, usually referred to as M. J. Kang, is its author. This very young playwright-actress who was born in Korea, came to Canada when she was two years old, to a Korean community in which it was impossible to ensconce oneself, because it had lost its very Korean identity. Her play centres around a Korean-Canadian family trying to come to grips with the realities of the new country while at the same time being unable to forget the culture they left behind. The action is set in the late 1970s.

In those days Korean families in Toronto "were affected not only by the immigration experience in Canada but by present and past political events in Korea," writes director Marion de Vries.[16] President Park Chung Hee (1963-79), the leading politician in South Korea after the Korean War (1950-53), had tailored the Constitution to his own liking, in 1972, so that he could stay in office for life. There is no denying the fact that Korea developed from an agrarian society to a modern industrialised nation at that time. However, any opposition to Park Chung Hee's government was suppressed until his assassination in 1979.

M.J. Kang's play is a collage of memories, aspirations, hopes and images. The production shifts between time and place with slide projections illustrating different images of Korea and Canada. The schism in the family encapsulates the clash between the adherence of some of the characters to their former cultural habits and lifestyles and the attempt of others to assimilate the new culture. Thus it mirrors the author's search for identity: Who am I? What makes me up? What made my parents bring me to where I am now? "With any sort of art you draw from what you know," says M. J.

---

[15] Myung Jim Kang, *Noran Bang: The Yellow Room* (Toronto: Playwrights Union of Canada, 1993, updated as of 12th July 1996). Quotations from the play (numbers in brackets) refer to pages in this edition.

[16] Marion de Vries in a Programme Note for Cahoots Theatre Projects 3D (Toronto: Theatre Passe Muraille, December 1993).

Kang, "and that's what I know. I know what it is to be Korean and what it is to try to come to terms with your identity."[17]

Former Korean life, in *Noran Bang: The Yellow Room*, is represented by Umma, the mother. Apba's, the father's, primary target is to better the family's material existence in Canada. He and nine-year-old daughter Mee-Gyung, too young to remember life in Korea, try to assimilate into the new culture, whereas the elder daughter, Gyung-June oscillates between her strong wish to be accepted by her peers and the desire to bring back to mind her early life in Korea. After three years in Canada disillusionment starts spreading in the family which is intensified by the death of the grandmother in Korea. The colour yellow denotes childhood memories, the 'Yellow Room' of the title being the English rendering of the Chinese 'Noran Bang.' M. J. Kang accounts for the title in a programme note:

> On a psychological level the colour yellow signifies childhood memories. *Noran Bang: The Yellow Room* was inspired by the memory of my mother sitting at our kitchen table, holding a picture of her mother. My grandmother had just died.[18]

The members of this family are trying hard to build a life for themselves in Canada. So far they have not yet been wholly successful in joining in the new society. They are still in a process of assimilation, some of them pondering about where they belong. Umma, finally, goes back to Korea, asking Gyung-June to take care of her sister and Apba. "The fridge is stocked with all the Canadian food everyone loves," she says, "no more Korean crap for the family." And she continues: "I am doing what I have to do" (67). Towards the end of the play, when Mee-Gyung asks her sister: "Cah, do you think Umma is coming back?" Gyung-June has this answer:

> I don't know. Halmonee [i.e. Umma's mother] told me that people know in their own hearts where they belong. Maybe Umma belongs in Korea. Maybe she belongs in Canada. Only she knows. But we belong here (74).

M. J. Kang's play is most strongly rooted in a culture that is not mainstream Canadian culture. It is not visibly about race differences, rather about the history of the community from which the author speaks, which is an extraordinarily young community. It exists in the realm of the private, which is the family. It is essentially a view inside a Korean-Canadian family, which carries with it much of the expectations and dreams of immigrants that literally arrived twenty years ago and have set up roots and abandoned others. It is about a un-assimilated family that makes a contrast in values.

When *Noran Bang: The Yellow Room* was first staged, it sold out almost every night, the Korean community came to see it in droves. The combination of Korean dance and percussion traditions and Western performance techniques is certainly a

---

[17] M. J. Kang in Shaun Ray Boyd, ed., *The Metro Word* (Toronto: Theatre Passe Muraille, 1996).

[18] M. J. Kang in Programme Note for Cahoots Theatre Projects 3D (Toronto: Theatre Passe Muraille, December 1993).

fascinating experiment. In the very first scene of the play no word is spoken. The stage directions for this scene read as follows:

> A collage of slides of the family together in Korea and Canada fill the stage as Gyung-June, Mee-Gyung, and Umma dance Korean folk dancing on stage. Apba is playing the Korean hour glass drum. Another drummer is offstage, playing as well. As the dance reaches its climax, a slide of Halmonee comes on stage (1).

Scene Five is a very revealing example of the functions of the flashbacks in the play. It fills the audience in on what was going on in Korea, politically and privately, when Apba and Umma were still living there: Apba works as bank manager, Umma is an assistant calculus professor, as part of her doctorate. They are planning to get married. After Scene Ten, which reflects Apba's disillusionment about his life in Canada and about Umma whose determination had once enchanted him, Scene Eleven - another flashback - mirrors the situation the family found themselves in when they were still in Korea, which made Apba decide to leave their home country, against Umma's will.

The relatively long final scene of the first act illustrates in what way and to what extent stereotyping and clichés can impede intercultural encounters. Gyung-June calls her sister a "chink," which is a very offensive word for a Chinese; Chinks are ugly, have bug eyes, flat noses and coarse bone straight hair (31). When Mee-Gyung walks from the store, a man comes up to her saying: "How come your feet aren't bound?" and: "Go back to where you came from" (33). Mee-Gyung punches and kicks him. When Apba returns, he brings her a doll, which she does not like at all because it is "a doll with blond hair and blue eyes" (39) and "can't be part of our family" (40). Gyung-June gets "a book about Canada," *Anne of Green Gables*, the famous children's classic by Lucy Maud Montgomery, written in 1908, which all Canadian children read. Gyung-June, however, does not consider herself Canadian, and consequently asks for a book about Korea (40).

Flashbacks and cliché-ridden statements underline the contrast between the two cultures which the play is about, while a handful of Korean words which are sprinkled over the otherwise English text of the script show similarities between them. When the two young girls, Mee-Gyung and Gyung-June, are playing the traditional game 'scissors, paper, stone' they talk to each other in English but use the Korean name for the game: "kii, bii, beau" (28-9). Similarly many things that the characters say to each other in Korean correspond closely to frequently used expressions in English: "Moo-sum mah ri-ah!" (1) ("What's that supposed to mean?" or "What are you on about?") and "Shi-ku-wo! (3) ("Shut up").

M. J. Kang's play indeed shows how important intercultural encounters are to Canadian culture. Most encounters, so far, have been encounters between European and Native peoples with continuing political and historical ramifications. In our days the Asian-Caucasian assimilation is increasingly raised as an important issue. M. J. Kang's *Noran Bang: The Yellow Room* is certainly a visceral approach of a very young dramatist to this very issue. The fact that the play deals with the situation at the end of the seventies and the juxtaposition of the two cultures may not mean a lot to those Korean-Canadians whose experience is that they are of both cultures and who believe that no culture is static, that identity is in constant flux. Nevertheless, the interesting thing about Kang's play is the author's thought-provoking attempt to find out where her roots are and how her identity is constructed.

"Mom, Dad, I'm Living With A White Girl"

Marty Chan, born in 1965, is another representative of the up-and-coming young Asian playwrights in Canada. He is a graduate of the University of Alberta. His full-length stage play *Mom, Dad, I'm Living With A White Girl*[19] is very much Western in form. What is not Western is its context. The play is based on Chan's own experiences when he ended up living with a white girl. The inspiration was a specific event, as the author pointed out in an interview:

> I recall, when I was a teenager, my mother told me to never date white girls. I questioned her on this narrow-minded statement. At the time, our family was the only Chinese family in a small town. I wondered who my mother expected me to date if I was not allowed to see Caucasians. This prompted me to examine my mother's motivations, her fears, her racist attitudes, her rural sensibilities. From this point I came up with the play.[20]

The focus of this play is an assimilated Asian-Canadian family. A Chinese son, the auto-mechanic Mark Gee, must tell his parents that he has moved in with his white girlfriend, Sally Davis, the girl of the play's title. She is a script reader for a film production company. Mark's father wants his son to take over from him as an acupuncturist, his mother thinks the same way and - apart from this - wants him to marry a Chinese woman and forget about his white girl. The cultural encounter here is not so much between the white girl and Mark's family, but within his family. Kim's, his father's, profession is one that has been handed down from generation to generation. That is why he wants his son to follow in the family business. Mark's "desire to work on machines rather than people," says the author, "represents his desire to get away from his father's clinic, which stands for family duty, heritage, culture, etc." (Glaap, "Interview with Chan"). Li Fen, the mother, like most wives in traditional Chinese marriages, is a housewife.

There is a counter-narrative to the action of the play. The characters, every now and then, step out of reality and into a hilarious film parody about the Yellow Claw, a vintage Dragon Lady. Yellow Claw, in her brocaded robes and with long fingernails is scheming the downfall of the Western world. She is assisted by Kim and opposed by Sally as the Snow Princess, an RCMP (Royal Canadian Mounted Police) undercover operative, and Mark as Agent Banana. The repeated switch of the actors from do-

---

[19] Marty Chan, *Mom, Dad, I'm Living With A White Girl* (Toronto: Playwrights Union of Canada, 1995, revised draft. 20th February 1995). Quotations from the play (numbers in brackets) refer to pages in this edition.

[20] Albert-Reiner Glaap, "Interview with Marty Chan" (Edmonton, 12th June 1998) (typescript).

mestic drama to B-movie spoof, the replacement of the father's acupuncture table by a torture chamber, and the substitution of the lethal skewers in the satire for what are tiny needles in reality amount to an approach, which, as theatre critic Barbara Crook in her review of the 1996 production of the play at the Firchall Arts Centre, Vancouver, writes, "is an intriguing way to highlight the unspoken hostility behind these 'civilised' family conflicts, and to emphasise the way in which fears and stereotypes on both sides prevent true communication."[21] In addition to this, Marty Chan himself considers the "Yellow Claw" as an extension of the characters' feelings, "their subtext, played out on a grand melodramatic scale" (Glaap, "Interview with Chan"). But he did not want to limit the Yellow Claw scenes to this theatrical device:

> I also wanted to attack Hollywood/North American pop culture for propagating these stereotypes. It is my opinion that pop culture is responsible for generating a lot of the Asian stereotypes that exist today. Often, I think it's a case of people taking one aspect of a culture and making it represent the entire culture. That's the problem with stereotypes. If you look hard enough, you can find some grain of truth under it all. However, one facet of a person does not represent the whole. But in Hollywood that seems to be the norm. Actors get typecast all the time. Big burly men always get cast as thugs. Nebbish women get cast as wallflowers. Asians get cast as martial artists, villains or buffoons. The Yellow Claw scenes in my play are an endeavour to cast these stereotypes out and debunk them. My intention was to make audiences laugh at them at first, then turn the tables and make them feel like accomplices to propagating the stereotypes (Glaap, "Interview with Chan").

Thus Marty Chan brought in some constructs, under the guise of flippant humour, which turn out to be funny stereotypes. What makes *Mom, Dad, I'm Living With A White Girl* so popular, is that part of the material is based on popular culture. Another reason for its popularity is that this play produces a reversal, in the sense that the Chinese family is the family with power, and is the central power. Therefore the disempowered character is the white woman. This reversal is certainly provocative and causes a lot of discussion amongst Canadian audiences, all the more when considering how many people enter into different kinds of ethnic/racial marriages.

Chan's play mirrors the different attempts of Chinese-Canadians to define their identity. There is still the clash between the older generation and their children. Traditional parents still want their sons and daughters to marry other Chinese. The younger generation, however, are increasingly inclined to embrace two cultures rather than advocate cultural purity. Younger immigrant groups do not just abandon the Chinese culture and adopt the Canadian one. "Now many Chinese-Canadians have grown comfortable with their own identities and are less adamant about defining themselves as being anti-Chinese," Marty Chan asserts, and "I think this is a positive trend that will allow the children of inter-cultural relationships to understand both sides of the heritage" (Glaap, "Interview with Chan"). The character of Mark in Chan's play is a

---

[21] Barbara Crook in her review of the Firehall Arts Centre production *Mom, Dad, I'm Living With a White Girl* in *The Vancouver Sun*, 6th February 1996.

representative of those who will take something from China and something from Canada. Whether this will end up as an equal balance of cultures is a moot point. Mark is still in a process of assimilation.

Mom, Dad, I'm Living With A White Girl was workshopped in Cahoots Theatre Projects and then produced in association with Theatre Passe Muraille, Toronto (first performance in March 1995). The Firchall Arts Centre in Vancouver ran a second production in February 1996. Both productions were well received by theatre critics, who, however, unanimously, criticise its ending as "problematic" (Crook, "Review") or "abrupt and not very satisfying."[22]

In the meantime Marty Chan has made revisions to the play[23] and has given its ending more satisfying substance "to keep the sensibilities of these characters, but show enough of their worlds so that non-Asians can understand why the characters make the decisions they do" (Glaap, "Interview with Chan"). The author himself realises that "the critics (all non-Asian) don't buy into a character like Mark or Li Fen:"

> They say these characters can't exist. In contrast I have had many Asians come up and tell me that I've gotten those two characters bang on. I think this is a perfect example of cultural rift (Glaap, "Interview with Chan").

Intercultural Encounters: Co-habitation, Integration, Assimilation

In the past decades the theatre has become a meeting point of, if not mediator between, different cultures in many English-speaking countries. In particular, contemporary Maori playwrights in New Zealand, West Indian dramatists in Britain and Asian-Canadian authors have written thought-provoking plays about the various facets of the complexities of intercultural encounters.

John Broughton, in *Te Hokinga Mai* portrays the lifestyle, customs and rituals of a Maori family in New Zealand, which an *outsider*, a young Pakeha, through his friendship with the son of the family, is eager to learn about and understand. In Hone Kouka's *Mauri Tu*, Tero, also a young man, approaches the problems of intercultural encounters from *within*, i.e. as one of the members of a Maori family who are divided over the issue of cultural co-habitation. Tero is alienated from both Pakeha and Maori culture. He does not know where he belongs and wants to find out what he is missing out on. The characters in these two plays experience both linguistic and cultural barriers and ways of mutual understanding in a country in which co-habitation has been practised over a fairly long period of time.

In Britain, especially in some of the big towns and cities, West Indian immigrants increasingly make an effort to mix. The second generation, i.e. those who came to

---

[22] Renee Doruyter in her review of the Firehall Arts Centre production of *Mom, Dad, I'm Living With a White Girl* in *Province Showcase*, 6th February 1996.

[23] Cp. Marty Chan, "Mom, Dad, I'm Living With A White Girl," in Aviva Ravel, ed., *Canadian Mosaic II: 6 Plays* (Toronto: Simon & Pierre, 1996), 99-163.

Britain when they were still young or were born there, consider this country their home. As opposed to Maori and Pakeha in New Zealand, these immigrants and the British share a common linguistic ground. Winsome Pinnock's *Leave Taking* reveals how differently the two daughters tackle the enforced process of integrating one living context into a new one - in a fatherless family. *Talking in Tongues*, in which language is the umbrella metaphor, illustrates how a sheer juxtaposition of two cultures, or nostalgic images of the home country which are not true to reality any more, impede the ongoing process of speaking with different voices and developing a "new identity" in a process of integration.

In Canada, most ethnic and racial groups have been integrated. But immigrant groups, who have come to this country more recently, especially those from Asian countries, still find themselves in a process of assimilation. Some up-and-coming Asian-Canadian playwrights have thematised aspects of this process in their stage-plays, M. J. Kang, for instance, and Marty Chan. Kang in *Noran Bang* deals with the aspirations and hopes of Korean immigrants who arrived twenty years ago. Descriptions of present situations alternate with flashbacks thereby giving insights into the Asian-Canadian assimilation and the construction of identities. Significantly, as in Pinnock's *Leave Taking*, the grandmother is still in the home country, an offstage character with a catalytic function.

In Marty Chan's *Mom, Dad, I'm Living With A White Girl*, the conflict is not so much a conflict between the white girl and the young Chinese man, but a conflict within the Chinese-Canadian family. Whereas the parents want their son to preserve his Chinese identity, he - a representative of the young generation - does not define himself as Chinese or anti-Chinese. He does not just abandon one culture and adopt a new one, he endeavours to embrace both cultures.

Katherine Mansfield and Witi Ihimaera: A Typology of Reception

UWE BAUMANN (Düsseldorf)

In 1989 the distinguished Maori writer, Witi Ihimaera,[1] published a collection of short stories entitled *Dear Miss Mansfield*.[2] The title calls to mind the opening line of a formal letter, and indeed the book begins with a letter of dedication addressed by the author to Kathleen Mansfield Beauchamp. In the missive Ihimaera recounts his motives for rendering homage to Katherine Mansfield on the centenary of her birthday (WI, 9-10):

> [...] Miss Mansfield, we in New Zealand have laid proud claim to you because you were born and brought up a New Zealander. Although you spent most of your adult years in England and the Continent, you always looked back to these southern antipodean islands as the main source for your stories. [...] They are stories spun sometimes from gossamer, at other times from strong sinew, sometimes kept afloat by a strength of voice, at other times by a mere thread of breath. Near the end, they were stories grabbed from out of the air at great cost. They have kept you in our memory over all the years since you have gone.
>
> It is the modern way, Miss Mansfield, for us to have become as much fascinated with your life as with your stories. I myself have always wished to write about your Maori friend Maata and why, if she had indeed possessed a novel you had written, she may have chosen not to part with it. The novella 'Maata' is my attempt to provide a Maori response to this question. But the main part of this collection, Miss Mansfield, comprises an equally Maori response, not to the life but to the stories.
>
> Like most New Zealanders, Miss Mansfield, I came to know the stories during my school years. My first acquaintance was as a young Maori student, struggling with English, at Te Karaka District High School. This was in 1957 and the story was 'The Fly.' At the time I resisted anything compulsory and I did not really grow to love and appreciate your art until I had left school behind. I can remember, one sunlit afternoon in Wellington, reading 'At the Bay' again, surely, for the fourteenth time. What had simply been words suddenly sprang to life and *there* it all was, happening before me – the sleepy sea sounding Ah-Aah!, the flock of sheep rounding the corner of Coronet Bay, and then Stanley Burnell racing for dear life over the big porous stones, over the cold, wet pebbles,

---

[1] Cf. Richard Corballis & Simon Garrett, *Introducing Witi Ihimaera* (Auckland: Longman, 1984); Cathe Giffuni, "Witi Ihimaera: A Bibliography," *New Literatures Review* 20 (1990), 53-63 and Umelo Ojinmah, *Witi Ihimaera: A Changing Vision* (Dunedin/NZ: University of Otago Press, 1993). Cf. also Elizabeth Alley & Mark Williams, eds., *In the Same Room. Conversations with New Zealand Writers* (Auckland: Auckland UP, 1992), esp. 219-236 and Paul Sharrad, "A Rhetoric of Sentiment: Thoughts on Maori Writing with Reference to the Short-Stories of Witi Ihimaera," in Rajinder Kumar Dhawan; Walter Tonetto, eds., *New Zealand Literature Today* (New Delhi, 1993), 60-72.

[2] Witi Ihimaera, *Dear Miss Mansfield. A Tribute to Kathleen Mansfield Beauchamp* (Auckland: Viking, 1989) [cited as 'WI'].

on to the hard sand to go Splish-Splosh! Splish-Splosh! into the sea. It was all such a revelation to me and I leapt up and down as if I had suddenly discovered a pearl of inestimable value. Does it happen like this for others?

Dear Miss Mansfield, my overwhelming inspiration and purpose comes from my Maori forebears – they are my source as surely as New Zealand was yours. The art of the short story, however, has taken its bearings from your voice also. I do hope that the variations on your stories find some favour with you. They are stories in themselves, some Maori and some with European themes, recognising the common experiences of mankind. But they found their inner compulsion in my wish to respond to your work.

Ah, New Zealand, New Zealand. One hundred years on, Miss Mansfield, and it has changed beyond your recognition. Life, Art, Society – all can be had here now. There is not as much need to make those forays, as you did, to seek it elsewhere. And when we do, it is merely to satisfy our island urgings to go plundering and raiding the world's riches and retreating with them to our island fortress. In the process of exploration within and without, the literary legacy of the New Zealand short story has been greatly enriched. These are the years of fulfilment – of Janet Frame, Patricia Grace, and Keri Hulme among others.

Please accept, Miss Mansfield, my highest regard and gratitude for having been among us and above us all.

Regardless of the slight undertone of irony contained in the closing paragraph ("above us all"), the letter of dedication clearly indicates that Witi Ihimaera considers his own stories a response to the short stories of Katherine Mansfield,[3] the individual reply of a Maori writer to the famous narratives of an author of canonical rank and a New Zealander. New Zealand constituted the main source of inspiration for many of Katherine Mansfield's short stories, and in the same manner Witi Ihimaera consciously draws upon and reflects on his own cultural tradition: "Dear Miss Mansfield, my overwhelming inspiration and purpose comes from my Maori forebears – they are my source as surely as New Zealand was yours." Thus candidly stating his own understanding of his work – a Maori response fed by the Maori traditions of his forefathers, Ihimaera's collection of short stories is clearly a classical work of postcolonial English literature (at least judging by the author's intent). It is conceived as a "counter-discourse" or as "writing back".[4] Significant textual strategies which assist in the recognition of postcolonial literature as part of a conscious "counter-discourse" are the use of untranslated words, glosses, code-switching and interlanguage or syntactic fusion.[5]

---

[3] Katherine Mansfield, *Collected Stories* (London: Constable, 1972) [cited as 'KM'].

[4] Cf. in general Bill Ashcroft, Gareth Griffith & Helen Tiffin, *The Empire Writes Back: Theory and Practice in Post-Colonial Literatures* (London: Routledge, 1989); Patrick Williams & Laura Christman, eds., *Colonial Discourse and Postcolonial Theory: A Reader* (Hemel Hempstead: Harvester Wheatsheaf, 1993); Eberhard Kreutzer, "Theoretische Grundlagen postkolonialer Literaturkritik," in Ansgar Nünning, ed., *Literaturwissenschaftliche Theorien, Modelle und Methoden. Eine Einführung* (Trier: Wissenschaftlicher Verlag Trier, 1995), 199-213.

[5] Cf. Ashcroft, Griffith & Tiffin, *The Empire Writes Back*, 38 ff.

Literary criticism has hitherto failed to accord Witi Ihimaera's collection of short stories the attention it merits. As Helge Nowak's accurate study[6] on continuations of novels provides a descriptive model which is readily applicable to short stories, I will attempt to typologically differentiate Ihimaera's 13 narratives as responses to Katherine Mansfield's individual short stories.

This essay will utilise the terminology coined by Genette and Nowak[7] and will begin by providing, in tabular form, a preliminary account of the transtextual signals. I will then progress from evident, unambiguous interrelations to more complex structures. The diversity of the transtextual references requires detailed analysis for adequate classification and necessitates limitation to a small number of representative examples.[8]

Ihimaera's stories are to provide the focus of our study. However the description and classification of the respective transtextual associations necessitate Katherine Mansfield's pretexts also being accorded due consideration.

Ihimaera's 13 short stories are preceded by the letter of dedication to Katherine Mansfield. Thus the sensitised reader is confronted with the task of identifying the pretextual narrative corresponding to the story at hand, or as a reviewer playfully termed it: "Find the Mansfield Story".[9]

Although Witi Ihimaera, in his dedicatory epistle, explicitly identified his short stories as variations on Katherine Mansfield's fiction he did not expound further. Thus the para-textual signals (title, letter of dedication) are only distinct for the collection as a whole and remain ambiguous for the individual short stories. For example the titles frequently do not suffice to identify the pretext, as the following diagram clearly indicates:[10]

---

[6] Helge Nowak, *'Completeness is all': Fortsetzungen und andere Weiterführungen britischer Romane als Beispiel zeitübergreifender und interkultureller Rezeption* (Frankfurt/M.; Berlin; Bern; New York; Paris; Vienna: Peter Lang, 1994), esp. 21 ff.

[7] Cf. Gérard Genette, *Palimpseste. Die Literatur auf zweiter Stufe*, 2nd ed., (Frankfurt/M.: Suhrkamp, 1993) and Nowak, *Completeness*.

[8] I will focus my analysis on five stories: "The Washerwoman's Children" (WI, 181-191), "The Affectionate Kidnappers" (WI, 110-114), "His First Ball" (WI, 126-135), "The Halcyon Summer" (WI, 156-180) and "A Contemporary Kezia" (WI, 79-88).

[9] Elizabeth Caffin, "KM curious," *NZ Listener* (Auckland: 26.08.1989), 66.

[10] I am much indebted to my students, whose discussions provided me with valuable inspiration for the following diagram and numerous detailed considerations, esp. Nicole Möller (*Die Kurzgeschichten Witi Ihimaeras als Fortsetzung und Weiterführung der Kurzgeschichten Katherine Mansfields*, unpubl. Staatsexamensarbeit Düsseldorf, 1996). Last but not least, I should like to thank Mrs Louise Nieroba and Mrs Mojgan Behmand for their linguistic advice; they helped me to reduce the number of solecisms of style to an acceptable minimum.

Ihimaera (WI)	Mansfield (KM)	Transtextual markers in WI
"The Cicada"	"The Fly"	– title – the insect as central symbol
"Cat and Mouse"	*In A German Pension*	– stylistic borrowing from Mansfield's satires
"The Boy with the Camera"	"The Woman at the Store"	– theme
"A Contemporary Kezia"	—	– title – reference to/incorporation of pretextual character
"Country Life"	"Prelude"	– reference to/incorporation of various pretextual characters
"The Affectionate Kidnappers"	"How Pearl Button was Kidnapped"	– title – continuation of pretextual plot
"This Life is Weary"	"The Garden Party"	– quotation in title
"His First Ball"	"Her First Ball"	– title – plot structure: initiation story
"Summons to Alexandra"	—	– theme (female sexuality, birth and pregnancy)
"On a Train"	—	– Stanley Burnell character
"Royal Hunt Before the Storm"	"Something Childish but very Natural"	– quotation in text – motif (childish love)
"The Halcyon Summer"	"At the Bay"	– elements of the plot
"The Washerwoman's Children"	"The Doll's House"	– title – the names of the characters – quotations and allusions

This sketch lists only the most evident transtextual signals but it suffices to show that the interrelations between Witi Ihimaera's short stories and Katherine Mansfield's narratives are manifold and diverse in nature.[11] Some of Ihimaera's stories cannot be linked indisputably to individual pretexts: Ihimaera's "A Contemporary Kezia" (WI, 79-88) and "On a Train" (WI, 143-147) incorporate two of Katherine Mansfield's central figures (Kezia and Stanley Burnell), who appear in a number of her stories. A transtextual association is achieved here primarily through the characterisation of the figure and not through the plot. Moreover, the proximity to the pretext can differ: in "A Contemporary Kezia" the reader recognises the title's direct reference to Mansfield's presumably most famous child-figure, whereas the transtextual signals required for the identification of Frank Saunders (in "On a Train") as a variation on another prominent Mansfield character, Stanley Burnell, are less distinct. We will begin our study with less elaborate transtextual associations:

1. "The Washerwoman's Children": Continuation by Sequel

Katherine Mansfield's "The Doll's House" (KM, 393-401) is a tale of social exclusion. The Burnell children, Kezia, Lottie and Isabel have been given a present of a doll's house and the gift soon causes a sensation in their social sphere. For the attention-seeking Isabel this constitutes a welcome opportunity to raise her own social consequence (KM, 395): "The girls of her class nearly fought to put their arms round her, to walk away with her, to beam flatteringly, to be her special friend." In the following days, all of the girls' school friends invariably stop by to inspect the celebrated doll's house, but two children, the Kelveys, are excluded. Their mother has to make a living by working as a washerwoman for the wealthy families – such as the Burnells – and numerous rumours circulate about the father: "But everybody said he was in prison" (KM, 396). The adults instil their own attitudes about social separation from the lower classes in their children: many of the children in the Burnells' social circle are not even allowed to speak to the Kelveys. Thus an inspection of the doll's house is rendered impossible for the Kelveys. Kezia defies this social constraint by offering to let Lil and "Our Else" come and see the doll's house in secret. The children are discovered by Kezia's aunt, Beryl, who quickly drives them away, but what the Kelvey children have experienced cannot be undone: "'I seen the little lamp', she [sc. Else] said softly" (KM, 401).

Ihimaera's short story constitutes a continuation of the plot at a much later time: "Our Else" and Lil are respectively Elspeth Fairfax-Lawson and Lilian Bates, widowed or married, have grandchildren (Lilian) or are retired after a successful career.

---

[11] Cf. WI, 58: "Most of the variations have been directly based on short stories as diverse as 'The Woman At The Store,' 'Her First Ball,' 'The Garden Party' and 'The Doll's House.' Some have been less directly based on Katherine Mansfield themes – like the *New Age* 'Pension Sketches' – or the themes of 'Prelude' or 'At The Bay.' Then there are those which have taken their course from characters portrayed in such stories as 'Bliss' or the great New Zealand stories."

(Elspeth).[12] Mrs Justice Fairfax-Lawson, a retired judge, lives in England. One day she receives an invitation to a class reunion from her school in Wellington, and pointedly ignoring her involuntary annoyance, she accepts the invitation in her desire to visit her sister Lilian, who still resides in Wellington. A few weeks later, Lilian proudly presents her sister to her friends and acquaintances in New Zealand. Elspeth's social elevation has been remarkable, prompted by her career and her advantageous marriage to the "Hon. Rupert Fairfax-Lawson." A newspaper article announces that Elspeth Fairfax-Lawson will give the opening address at the forthcoming school reunion and leads to discord between the sisters. Elspeth refuses to speak at the reunion and proceeds to remind Lilian that the time spent at the school was by no means happy: "The way the parents treated Mother and vilified Father was so unspeakable. Just because she had to take in washing and because father was a bankrupt" (WI, 186). Lilian's own consternation serves to reconcile Elspeth. The latter relents and gives the speech. She uses this opportunity to expose the groundless social segregation that she and her sister were subject to and in doing so recounts the key experience which determined the course of her life (WI, 190-191):

> '[...] There was once a little girl and her sisters who came to school one day and told us all about a wonderful gift – a doll's house. [...] Inside was a little lamp. [...] I think that girl died some years ago but what she did stands as a shining symbol to all of us. Certainly it became a symbol for me. [...] Although my sister and I were the children of a washerwoman [...] that girl showed us the little lamp. I have never forgotten that lamp, ever. Its flame has been a constant inspiration to me to always reach out – like that girl did – to others. To extend myself, become a better person and perhaps make the world a better place to live in. Were it not for that kindness, or similar kindnesses which I'm sure you all remember being done to you at this school, none of us would have become the people we are today. I would not have become the person I have.'

The speech is an overwhelming success, but the story ends on a pensive, ambivalent note with the brief, uncommented portrayal of Elspeth's thoughts (WI, 191): "Mrs Justice Fairfax-Lawson smiled a rare smile and thought to herself that what she had said was just the silly common-place sort of thing that Lilian would have liked."

For the readers, who are at least familiar with Katherine Mansfield's most famous story, the title "The Washerwoman's Children" in itself constitutes a transtextual signal, which clearly indicates "The Doll's House" as the pretext. At the outset of the story the transtextual references are few in number but as the tale unravels they become more frequent and increasingly obvious. "Our Else" from "The Doll's House" is introduced in the opening scenes in England as Mrs Fairfax-Lawson and neither the opening address of the letter "Dear *Elspeth*" (WI, 181) nor the name of the sender Lena Holmes (she was Lena Logan in Mansfield's story) necessarily suggest a Mansfield character. A further subtle signal is the name of the sister Lilian ("Lil") and her emphatic warning to her husband to never call her sister "Else." Only as the impend-

---

[12] Cf. In general Wolfgang G. Müller, "Interfigurality. A Study on the Interdependence of Literary Figures", in Heinrich F. Plett, ed., *Intertextuality* (Berlin; New York: Walter de Gruyter, 1991), 101-121.

ing speech awakens memories of a shared traumatic childhood, do the transtextual references increase and the allusions to the pretext become more direct (WI, 186):

> [...] 'You're quite right, Elspeth,' she said, her heart aching from the pain of the reprimand. *And a vivid picture flashed into her mind of Lena Logan sliding, gliding, dragging one foot, giggling behind her hand, shrilling, 'Is it true you're going to be a servant when you grow up, Lil Kelvey?' And taunting her again with 'Yah, yer father's in prison!' before running away giggling with the other girls.* 'We were *always* on the outside,' Elspeth said. 'They never invited us to play in any of their games, because we weren't good enough for them. [...]

The italics are a further transtextual signal and denote passages in Ihimaera's story that are more or less quotations from Mansfield's work.

The above quotation is from a scene in "The Doll's House" in which the two Kelveys are publicly humiliated and branded as social outcasts (KM, 398). The humiliation inflicted upon Else and Lilian becomes a key scene in Ihimaera's continuation and is repeatedly faded in. Thus Lena Logan, now married Mrs Holmes, is the first person Elspeth meets at the reunion (WI, 188):

> No sooner had Mrs Justice Fairfax-Lawson walked through the door of the crowded Assembly Hall than she saw a woman gasp and whisper behind her hand to her companion, and then *sliding, gliding, dragging one foot and shrilling* she came, calling, 'Elspeth! Yoo hoo, Elspeth!'

Here the pretextual description of Lena Logan is made formally conspicuous through italicization and rendered readily recognisable as a quotation (KM, 398). However, it is embedded within the continuation in a manner which is syntactically inconspicuous. Elspeth's flashes of memory, which strongly refer to the pretext without being direct quotations, are increasingly presented in italics. Thus they assume the character of free direct discourse, as the following representative example will show (WI, 189): "Oh, you *must* remember Miss Leckey and that terrible hat she used to wear. *Oh yes. I remember. When Miss Leckey had no further use for it, she gave it to Mother. Lilian used to wear it.*"

Ihimaera utilises the information provided in the pretext for the characterisation of his figures but also emphasises certain features: thus he stresses Lena Logan's merciless malicious glee. The reader learns about the two central characters and the story of the lives that lie between the pretext and the sequel in numerous flashbacks. Between the passages of scenic representation (Elspeth breakfasting in England, the flight to New Zealand, the dialogues of the sisters and the reunion) an omniscient narrator (an external focalizer) recounts the lives of the sisters. From his perspective, that of a discerning judge of New Zealand mentality, he also comments on the sensation created by Elspeth's visit to Wellington with visible ironic detachment (WI, 184-185):

> These ladies knew that New Zealand hospitality was the best in the world, and they weren't going to let the side down – especially with such a famous person in their midst.

And so polite conversation would begin, with everybody minding their p's and q's and trying not to be too colonial.

The postcolonial perspective of New Zealand society is easily discernible here; solely a critical and historical distance to New Zealand's past would permit an assessment of the behaviour of the women as colonial. Ihimaera uses the few suggestions of the pretext for the characterisation of his two central figures, but elaborates on the pretext by elevating the almost mute Else to the position of protagonist (*transvalorisation secondaire*). Furthermore, the individualised Lilian and Elspeth become the literary representation of the society in which they live (WI, 183):

> [...] but no one would ever have taken Lilian for anything but a New Zealander – at a pinch, an Australian perhaps – and that was where the likeness ended. [...] Lilian's spontaneity expressed itself in its overeagerness and anxiousness, whereas Elspeth's was under control, *quite*.

Ihimaera's aged Elspeth Fairfax-Lawson is no longer the childish victim of social ostracism who is incapable of expressing herself; rather she is a universally respected judge, whose address at the class reunion proves worthy of her telling name. In her speech, which constitutes the climax of the story, she passes judgement over all those who participated in the social segregation but proves lenient in her verdict, since she is able to indicate Kezia's conduct as a model to be emulated: "I think that girl died some years ago but what she did stands as a shining symbol to all of us" (WI, 191). Naturally this constitutes another obvious intertextual allusion to the central symbol in Mansfield's narrative: the light in the doll's house which represents an unforgettable encounter for "Our Else." The lamp as a symbol has been interpreted in Mansfield criticism in numerous ways,[13] but is specifically defined in Ihimaera's sequel; the lamp symbolises hope for a humane society and triumph over class-consciousness.

Although several elements (characters, setting) correlate directly to the pretext and serve to clarify ambiguities of the source (e.g. Karori, a suburb of Wellington, as the setting), Ihimaera's story is remarkable due to its autonomy of form and content. The most prominent shift in the perspective of the narrative is caused by the use of the point of view of marginal characters of the pretext. It is above all Elspeth, who advances from a pretextual minor character to the protagonist of the sequel. A re-valuation in the sense of transvalorisation does not occur: in both texts Lil(ian) and Els(peth) are liable to engage the sympathy of the reader as victims of society. However, in "The Washerwoman's Children" the characters have long since cast off their role as victims and have become valued members of a society which has in turn freed itself from colonial class-consciousness. In spite of the progress made by the pretextual minor characters in the sequel, the central figures of the pretext have not been

---

[13] Cf. e.g. C.A. Hankin, *Katherine Mansfield and her Confessional Stories* (New York: St. Martin's Press, 1983), 221: "The lamp, with its ability to irradiate and transform the darkness, represents the imagination of the artist who has the power to transform reality, to create an ideal world subject to his laws – his 'vision'."

devalued: although Kezia only appears in the memories of the protagonist, Elspeth, she advances to a symbol of humanity and tolerance in Ihimaera's story.

By rendering Elspeth an expatriate, Ihimaera supplements the class conflict of the pretext and superimposes a conflict of societies. The former schoolmates seek Elspeth's attention, as they formerly sought Isabel's favour and thus demonstrate the same opportunism and sensationalism. Elspeth is rendered fit for good society not only because she has come up in the world but also because of her immigration to England.

She becomes the sensational object of colonial admiration for all that is English. On the one hand the narrator comments on Elspeth's English reserve with ironic detachment, on the other hand his depiction of the imitative impulse of New Zealand society is almost a caricature. In Mansfield's story the children blindly embrace their parents' class-consciousness, in Ihimaera's story the adults are equally blind in their late-colonial devotion to the English homeland and the emulation of English manners. The narrator (narrator-focalizer) stands outside the plot and also outside English and New Zealand society, thus affording the reader a postcolonial perspective of the pretext. Obviously, within the colonial system suffering was not limited to the ethnic minority – to which Ihimaera belongs –, but also extended to the outcasts produced by the system itself.

As is the case with the pretext "The Doll's House," one may read Ihimaera's narrative from a primarily biographical point of view, a perspective which seems to be prompted by Ihimaera's letter of dedication to Katherine Mansfield. Thus obvious parallels would be discovered between the lives of the protagonist and of Katherine Mansfield. Elspeth Kelvey left the provincialism of New Zealand in order to make a career for herself in England, and her conduct itself testifies to her English identity. Nevertheless, the ties with her native country are still important to her: "She was as much a New Zealander as her family made her one" (WI, 183). The same sentence applies to Katherine Mansfield, who felt bound to flee the colonial narrowness of New Zealand in order to advance her career as a writer in England. However, New Zealand remained an important source of inspiration for a number of her stories, such as "The Doll's House" or "The Garden Party." Significantly, like Ihimaera's heroine, she only received recognition in her native country after she had proved successful in Europe.

2. "The Affectionate Kidnappers": Continuation by Sequel Presenting the Maori Point of View

In choosing "How Pearl Button Was Kidnapped" (KM, 530-534) as a pretext for his narrative "The Affectionate Kidnappers" (WI, 110-114), Ihimaera seemingly chose a simple children's story as inspiration. The plot of Mansfield's story may be summed up very briefly. The little girl Pearl Button is sitting in front of her parents' house and is bored. Two Maori women happen to pass by and are immediately enchanted by the pretty little girl. They take her to their "whare" and on an outing to the seaside. The idyllic journey comes to an abrupt end as "little blue men" (KM, 534) – obviously policemen – charge onto the beach in order to carry Pearl home again.

The plot of the continuation may be summed up just as briefly. It is set in a prison and the narrated time immediately follows that of the pretext. The two Maori women Kuini and Puti have been arrested on charges of kidnapping. The story describes the visit by their tribal chief, Hasbrick, to the prison. Having secured the hesitant permission of the prison guard, Kuini and Puti speak to Hasbrick alone and recount the events of the day from their own point of view. They maintain their good intentions and Hasbrick, who has spoken to Pearl's mother before the visit, realises that an amicable understanding between the two parties may not be reached. The two Maori women know Mrs. Button and believed themselves to be acting with her consent, an assumption which proves to be a momentous misunderstanding. Pearl's mother does not even remember the two women who once worked for her. Hasbrick is forced to leave the two desperate women, stunned by their arrest, in prison.

The support of the members of the tribe, who are keeping vigil outside the prison, fails to console the isolated and uprooted Kuini and Puti, who have never been separated from their tribe before.

The most conspicuous feature of the pretext is the narrative point of view, which is strongly limited to the perceptions of Pearl (character-focalizer). The first sentence immediately confronts the reader with the perspective of the child-narrator: "Pearl Button swung on the little gate in front of the House of Boxes" (KM, 530). The interpretation of signals in the text becomes increasingly difficult as Pearl moves away from her familiar surroundings. At that time the two Maori women are introduced into the story. The most vivid example of this gradual recession behind Pearl's point of view is her first glimpse of the sea: "And down the bottom of the hill was something perfectly different – a great big piece of blue water was creeping over the land" (KM, 533). Thus it becomes clear that everything Pearl experiences on this day is completely new for her, broadening the scope of her knowledge in a most fascinating way. However, her experiences do not only consist of confrontation with the fascinating New Zealand scenery, but especially with the Maoris themselves and their culture (KM, 531-532):

> They set Pearl Button down in a log room full of other people the same colour as they were – and all these people came close to her and looked at her, nodding and laughing and throwing up their eyes. The woman who had carried Pearl took off her hair ribbon and shook her curls loose. There was a cry from the other women, and they crowded close and some of them ran a finger through Pearl's yellow curls, very gently, and one of them, a young one, lifted all Pearl's hair and kissed the back of her little white neck. Pearl felt shy but happy at the same time.

Through focussing on Pearl the narrator recedes strongly into the background,[14] but the impressions of the child are directed by the narrative authority through selection

---

[14] Cf. in general Jochen Ganzmann, *Vorbereitung der Moderne. Aspekte erzählerischer Gestaltung in den Kurzgeschichten von James Joyce und Katherine Mansfield* (Frankfurt/M.; Bern;

and evaluation. Seen through Pearl's eyes, the Maoris are very warm-hearted, hospitable and artless. Scenes of physical contact and tenderness increase in intensity in the course of the narrative. At the beginning of the story, Pearl lets the two women carry her. Later on she snuggles in their lap. Then she is kissed and towards the end of the story is stripped down to her underwear at the beach, so she can play more freely and uninhibitedly. The sensuality and emotional warmth of the Maoris, as well as their direct contact with nature, are in marked contrast to the specifically anti-physical and anti-sensual English Victorian culture that Pearl stems from. Her shy timidity, combined with a deep feeling of natural happiness, serve to engage the reader's sympathy for the uncomplicated naturalness of the Maoris. The entrance of the representatives of white culture into this natural and idyllic setting is hostile and disturbing, frightening even Pearl, who is the object of this rescue attempt (KM, 534):

> Suddenly the girl gave a frightful scream. The woman raised herself and Pearl slipped down on the sand and looked towards the land. Little men in blue coats – little blue men came running, running towards her with shouts and whistlings – a crowd of little blue men to carry her back to the House of Boxes.

The "House of Boxes," referred to in the first and also in the last sentence of the pretext, constitutes the chief metaphor for Victorian class consciousness, which essentially prohibits an intercultural meeting of the kind described.

The point of view of the child-narrator enables Katherine Mansfield to distance herself from traditional patterns of perception and from conventional values. In this story the perspective of the child expediently permits a relatively uninhibited coming together of the English and the indigenous cultures. Such a meeting between adults would have been marred or even made impossible by their colonial dependence on one another. However, Mansfield's picture of Maoris is not devoid of the prejudices of her time; the story conveys a strongly romantic view of the life of New Zealand's ethnic minority: carefree and light-hearted, they seem to live for the day, a shortened version of the late-colonial notion of the Maoris as "noble savages."

The most conspicuous structural feature of the continuation is the absence of an unfolding plot in the sense of a progressive development. The text is an analeptical reassessment of the events of the pretext by the two Maori women. It is mostly organised in the form of a dialogue, a structure which is solely interrupted by portrayals of the consciousness of single characters. The opening of the story "in medias res" at first leaves the reader in the dark as to the reason for the desperation of the two old women (WI, 110): "The two kuia began to weep when their rangatira came in. They wept not because they were frightened but because they were ashamed that their big chief should see them like *this*, in the whareherehere."

New York: Peter Lang, 1986), esp. 202 ff.; Helmut Viebrock, "'The Defeat of the Personal': Katherine Mansfields Theorie und Praxis der Unpersönlichkeit in der Erzählkunst," in Winfried Herget; Klaus-Peter Jochum; Ingeborg Weber; Thomas Finkenstaedt, eds., *Theorie und Praxis im Erzählen des 19. und 20. Jahrhunderts. Studien zur englischen und amerikanischen Literatur zu Ehren von Willi Erzgräber* (Tübingen: Narr, 1986), 127-139.

The reader's disorientation only subsides after the Sergeant, the representative of European culture and its absolute power, has permitted the chief of the tribe to speak privately with the two women. The long passages of dialogue between Hasbrick and the two women not only provide information, but also the shared Maori language emphasises the solidarity of Hasbrick and the two women.[15]

Although the title "The Affectionate Kidnappers" is an aid to the reader in his search for the pretext, the hypertextual context becomes obvious as Kuini speaks of the little girl, whom she refers to as Pearl Button, thus identifying her as the central figure of the pretext (WI, 110-111):

> 'She was such a pretty little blondie girl,' Kuini said. 'She was swinging on a gate, all by herself, you know, down there by the hotera. As soon as I saw her I knew she was the Buttons' little girl. You know, they come every summer to the Sounds and me and Puti, we did some work for Mrs Button last summer, cleaning and that. Ay, Puti?'

The plot elements of the pretext are modified within the succeeding dialogue, in the sense of Genette's terminology of motivation. That is to say the pretext is extended by motives provided for certain actions. In the pretext the perilous behaviour of the women remains unexplained. Ihimaera's story provides reasons that are plausible in retrospect. In contrast to Mansfield's representation of the events, in the modern story the women assume that they have the consent of Pearl's mother for their outing (WI, 111): "And when she saw us she waved back. So we made signs that we would take Pearl with us for our mate. We pointed to the marae. And Mrs Button waved her apron at us as if to say, 'Go right ahead!'" The failure of Mrs Button and the two Maori women to achieve a mutual understanding – then it is solely a simple misunderstanding which precipitates the events – seems to be symbolic of the lack of mutual understanding between two cultures.

While the women recount the events of the pretext in their conversation, Hasbrick is chiefly restricted to the role of listener. He is in an unusual position: he is convinced that the women are innocent, but also acknowledges the arguments of the prosecutor. Repeatedly he interrupts the narration of the women, pointing out to them that another view of the events is possible, that a divergent interpretation of the episode has culminated in the charges against them. In reply to Hasbrick's repeated questions (e.g. "'Didn't you stop to think that this was a Pakeha little girl?'" [WI, 111], 'Didn't it ever pass through your minds [...] how her mother would feel about her daughter eating the Maori kai?'" [WI, 112]) the women react with an appreciable lack of insight. Hasbrick's objections represent a dominant culture's claim of superiority, which in turn culminates in a devaluation of the indigenous culture. The character of Hasbrick becomes a mediator between the two worlds. As he conveys to the reader in long reflective passages, the natural and easy comportment of the two Maori women

---

[15] Cf. in general Susan Beckmann, "Language as Cultural Identity in Achebe, Ihimaera, Laurence and Atwood", *World Literature Written in English* 20 (1981), 117-134.

towards children stands in stark contrast to the white man's distrust of the minority.[16] Thus Hasbrick becomes the most significant figure for the reader, since in his consciousness he scrutinises the events and extends them by another point of view. His mind pictures the reaction of Pearl's mother, which is an elaboration on the pretext (WI, 112):

> *Oh, Pearl, did you eat something from the floor? John, darling, did you hear what the Maoris did? They forced food on her. There's no telling what sorts of diseases she got down there. All those dogs they have. And no hygiene. The place should be burned down. Harbouring diseases and diseased people. Oh darling, she drank some water too. Some filthy Maori water. Oh. Oh.*

The two Maori women utterly fail to comprehend the hysterical reaction of Pearl's mother. However, this reaction not only indicates a complete misinterpretation of the occurrence – Pearl is never coerced into anything in the pretext or in the continuation – but is also clearly founded on common prejudices such as an assumption of a lack of hygiene.

The cultural differences, which render an understanding difficult, are also made formally visible in Ihimaera's tale. A conspicuous linguistic feature of the narrative is the employment of a large number of Maori words in the dialogues.[17] Indeed the first two sentences incorporate three Maori words (WI, 110: "kuia", "rangatira", "whareherehere"). Frequently single words or even whole Maori phrases are integrated into direct speech. Despite this code-switching the story remains comprehensible for the reader who solely speaks English. This is partially achieved through "glossing", although there are passages in the text where there is no such help, especially towards the close of the story (WI, 114): "'Anei, te roimata toroa.' The soft sounds of waiata swelled in the darkness like currents of the wind holding up Kuini's words. 'E noho ra, Pearl Button,' Kuini said, 'taku moko Pakeha'." Kuini and Puti now solely speak Maori and even the narrative voice uses a Maori word ("waiata"), which remains as untranslated and "unglossed" as the dialogue. This seemingly open ending covertly appeals to the reader to seriously examine the marginalised culture of the Maoris. The sounds of waiata, the traditional funeral song of the Maoris, represent the last sensations of the two Maori women, before they enter the night of death (WI, 114): "Then the light went, everything went, life went."

According to Helge Nowak's classification, Ihimaera's "The Affectionate Kidnappers" is an elaboration with an alteration in the point of view. The pretextual portion

---

[16] Cf. WI, 111: "Not only was this a white girl but this was also a pretty as a picture blondie girl. Pakehas didn't like their girls being messed around by Maoris. The idea of a pretty curly-headed white girl being taken away by Maoris brought all sorts of pictures to their minds – of sacrifices to idols, cannibalism, of white girls being captured and scalped by Red Indians – and *he* knew because these were the sorts of questions tourists asked him."

[17] The utilisation of postcolonial linguistic strategies is also evident in the English language historical writing, which labels the English of the Maoris as "vernacular speech" both in dialogue and in delineations of consciousness. Thus its deviation from the standard/norm and the subsequent characterisation as cultural otherness are clearly marked.

of the plot is elaborated, while the point of view is altered. The events immediately follow those of the pretext. The new perspective transforms the minor characters, the two Maori women, into central figures of the continuation. Their delineation of Pearl's supposed kidnapping in no way forms a contrast to Mansfield's version. Instead, the women partly retell the pretext.

The outsider's point of view is integrated into the story through the new figure, Hasbrick. His experience in dealing with the white culture of New Zealand serves as a net of mental concepts (or notions of otherness) through which the events are filtered. In Mansfield's narrative the Maoris, in their inception as "noble savages," constitute a foil against the deficiencies of her own Victorian and colonial society, but her point of view remains – in the terminology of postcolonial literary theory – that of a coloniser. In contrast, Ihimaera endows the Maori with their own voice – partially through the integration of their language – in order to convey a sense of their otherness to the reader. In addition, the plot of the continuation embodies an advance towards an authentic depiction of social reality in New Zealand: the arrest of the two women is a consequence of the existent power structure between the whites and the Maoris. In its position as the dominating culture, white law passes sentence over the two women, who according to the notions of their own culture have committed no wrong. Ihimaera draws a depressing and pessimistic picture of the prospect of understanding and communication between the two cultures of New Zealand. Mrs. Button's unwillingness to acknowledge the good intents of the Maori women is mirrored by the latter's inability to comprehend the white woman's reactions due to their unfamiliarity with her foreign culture. It is solely Hasbrick, propelled into his role of mediator by his position as chief of the tribe, that has an understanding of both cultures and is able to judge them correctly in their otherness. However, he is unable to offer the women more than the full moral support of the tribal community.

Pearl, the child-narrator and character-focalizer of the pretext, has become a secondary matter and a minor character in the continuation. She is only present as an object of conversation, since it is no longer the figure but the cultural conflict expressed through her experience with the Maoris which provides the central link with Ihimaera's story.

3. "His First Ball": "Writing Back" as a Variation on Theme and Structure

The title of Witi Ihimaera's short story "His First Ball" (WI, 126-135) already points to Katherine Mansfield's "Her First Ball" (KM, 336-343) as the pretext, but deviating from the two short stories previously examined, it is not a continuation of a plot and does not incorporate figures from the pretext. Essentially Ihimaera presents an initiation story in the same manner as Mansfield and, as in the earlier narrative, a ball plays the key role. However, Ihimaera's variations on the themes central to Mansfield's pretext, i.e. the ball and the concept of initiation, give the reader a highly interesting postcolonial perspective.

Leila, the daughter of a colonial lord, has been replaced by the Maori Tuta Wharepapa with a typical working-class background. He packs batteries in a factory and lives with his mother Coral, also a factory worker. His free time is spent with his friends, who bear such illustrious names as Crazy-Joe or Desirée Dawn and cover the whole range of social fringe groups from transvestites to car thieves. Unlike Mansfield's upper class daughter Leila, Tuta already lives an independent life and is fully integrated into his social environment. Thus the invitation to the prestigious Governor's ball does not signify an opportunity for integration into the adult world for him as it does for Leila. Indeed it is an obligation utterly devoid of personal interest for him and rather encumbers him in his self-determined life (cf. WI, 128).

For Tuta the ball is an initiation that he does not wish to experience, since it does not signify an initiation into a new period of his life as an individual. He has only been invited as the representative of a group, the workers.[18] Tuta's disinclination not only contrasts sharply with the feelings of the pretextual figure Leila, but also with the enthusiasm of his surroundings. Mother Coral is enjoying the admiration of the neighbours. Tuta's dubious friend, Blackjack, considers it a great opportunity to procure a diplomatic license plate. Mrs. Simmons, on the other hand, believes it her duty to acquaint Tuta with rules of etiquette. Her acceptance of Tuta's participation in the festivities is as unquestioning as her recognition of the need to conform to the norms of the set attending the ball: "One does not say 'No' to the Crown" (WI, 128).

A number of readers may recognise references to the glorious colonial past – as portrayed in the pretext – in the English hierarchy and rules of behaviour portrayed here. Yet, more significantly, Gloria Simmon's English or rather colonial snobbist education and wholehearted admiration for everything English is satirised. Thus, Tuta is advised to always act proud and indifferent and when in doubt to only speak about the weather: "If you're talking you ask about the weather. This is called polite conversation. You say 'Isn't it lovely?' to everything, even if it isn't" (WI, 131).[19]

Of course these phrases provide constant references to the pretext in that they echo precisely the superficiality of the conversation that Leila had at the ball. The ironically parodied and exaggerated worry about "What To Do and How To Do It At A Ball" (WI, 128) becomes social reality at the governor's ball.

All Tuta's efforts to conform to the rules of this society fail to protect him from being branded as an outsider. His uncertainty and lack of grace in the art of dancing

---

[18] Cf. WI, 128: "And he [sc. Tuta] listened as Mrs Simmons explained that Mrs Governor-General had been very impressed by the workers at the factory and that Tuta was being invited to represent them."

[19] Cf. also WI, 131: "Then, suddenly it was time for Tuta to go to the ball. 'Yes, Mum,' he said to Coral as she fussed around him with a clothes brush, 'I've got a hanky, I've brushed my teeth three times already, the invite is in my pocket – 'And when Tuta stepped out the door the whole world was there – the boss, Mrs Simmons, Crazy-Joe, Blackjack, Bigfoot and others from the factory, Desirée Dawn and the neighbours. 'Don't let us down,' the boss said. 'Not too much food on the fork,' Mrs Simmons instructed. [...] The car drew away and as it did so, Mrs Simmons gave a small scream. 'Oh my goodness, I forgot to tell Tuta that if Nature calls he should not use the bushes,' she said."

or conversation are immediately recognised by the closed set of New Zealand's "High Society" and become a source of general amusement: "Everybody seemed to laugh at his every word, even when it wasn't funny, or to accept his way of dancing because it was so *daring*" (WI, 133). Easy prey for their ridicule, the young Maori comes up against a wall of complete disregard for his individuality. None of the other guests deigns to learn his name, which in a subtle comedy sequence goes through numerous variations in the course of the evening (WI, 132):

> 'Your Excellencies, Mr Tutae Tockypocka.' [...] In trembling anticipation Tuta approached the Governor-General. 'Mr Horrynotta?' the Governor-General smiled. 'Splendid that you were able to come along. Dear? Here's Mr Tutae.' And in front of him was Mrs Governor-General. 'Mr Forrimoppa, how kind of you to come. May I call you Tutae? Please let me introduce you to Lord Wells.' And Lord Wells, too. 'Mr Mopperuppa, quite a mouthful, what. Not so with Tutae, what?' *You don't know the half of it*, Tuta thought gloomily.

Thus the ball becomes a caricatured reflection of a society that appears to be a relic of colonial decadence and ignorance. Tuta's invitation is supposed to signify accessibility for all social groups but in a parodic exaggeration it becomes a manifestation of narrow-minded belief in imperial superiority.

Owing to his social status as a worker and also because of his ethnic background as a Maori, Tuta becomes an outsider. The game the other guests play by changing Tuta's first name to Tutae not only indicates their insulting demeanour but also their ignorance, since Tutae is Maori for 'dirt', 'shit.'

Throughout the entire story the concept of imitation and the search for authenticity shape the conduct of both groups. Upper class New Zealand society imitates imperial magnificence in an out-of-date manner, but the English pattern has also impressed itself upon the consciousness of the underprivileged classes. Thus the secretary tries to adopt a presumably Oxford accent when she rings the Governor's mansion: "Ooo, Gahverment Howse? May ay speak to the Aide-de-Camp? Ooo, har do yoo do" (WI, 127). On the other hand, the unwilling Tuta exemplifies the colonial impulse to imitate. His true identity represents the authentic modern New Zealand society but is hidden behind hastily adopted modes of behaviour and non-committal meaningless phrases. Consequently, Tuta feels displaced at the ball and for the hour that he is in the limelight, his main worry is that he will be unmasked and his true personality revealed: "*Oh boy*, he thought. *Look at this red carpet*. He felt quite sure that the paint was running off his shoes and that there were great big black footmarks all the way to where he was now standing" (WI, 132).

Significantly, a new awareness of his true identity comes about through his rapport with the second outsider figure of the story, Joyce. She is the only person at the ball who uses his first name and thus acknowledges his individuality. With her Tuta has his first real conversation of the evening, though she is also forced to hide her true identity. At their first meeting she is sitting behind a large plant and thus beyond the circle of events (WI, 133): "'It always happens this way,' a voice said behind Tuta. 'I wouldn't worry about it.' Startled, Tuta turned around and saw a huge fern. 'Before you,' the fern continued, 'it was me'."

Joyce is a student of sociology and, as signalised by her first appearance, is accorded the role of observer rather than participator in the story. She gives the reader another view of the occurrences: sensible and culturally critical. Unlike Tuta, Joyce observes society from a distance. This is not a consequence of social and ethnic otherness, but rather of her analytical-scientific way of thinking: "This could be India under the Raj. All this British Imperial graciousness and yet the carpet is being pulled from right beneath their feet" (WI, 134). One would not be wrong in discerning an affinity to the author's own position in this penetrating recognition, whose universal validity goes beyond the compass of the observed events.[20]

The sterility and narrow-mindedness of colonial society are only seen by Joyce and Tuta, who are the only true representatives of a postcolonial society – in a historical sense– and who also personify the hopes of that society. Tuta finally grasps the deeper meaning of Joyce's exhortation to beat the other guests at their own game (WI, 135):

> And it came to him that, bloody hell, if you could not join them – as if he would really want to do *that* – then, yes, he could beat them if he wanted to. Not by giving in to them, but by being strong enough to stand up to them. Dance, perhaps, but using his own steps. Listen, also, not to the music of the band but to the music in his head. He owed it, after all, to generous but silly wonderful mixed-up Mum, Mrs Simmons, Desirée Dawn, and the boys – Crazy-Joe, Blackjack and Bigfoot – who were out *there* but wanting to know enough to get *in*. But they needed to come in on their own terms – that's what they would have to learn – as the real people they were and not as carbon copies of the people already on the inside. Once they learnt that, *oh, world, watch out, for your walls will come down in a flash, like Jericho.*

As in Mansfield's pretext, the dance floor becomes a metaphor for society; dancing in their own new way, Joyce and Tuta defy the rigidities of that society. Carried by the knowledge that Tuta and his friends are the true, authentic society of New Zealand, the recognition emerges that they have to avoid the fundamental mistake of imitating the dominant culture and its forms. The narrative closes on a note of hopefulness and with the affirmation of that new-found confidence (WI, 135): "And Tuta smiled and 'It's *my* first ball too,' he said. 'From now on, balls like these will never be the same again.' He took her hand and the band began to wail a sweet but *oh-so-mean* saxophone solo as he led her on to the floor."

The strong didactic intentions of the story, whose turning point is provided by the appearance of Joyce, are obvious. The focal point of the narrative is provided by Tuta, however the narrator furnishes us with insights into his consciousness which go beyond that of the individual. Tuta's initiation is not solely a personal experience but, instructed by Joyce and the 'voice of the author,' he recognises complex social inter-

---

[20] Cf. Jane Wilkinson, "Witi Ihimaera: Interview," *Kunapipi* 7 (1985), 98-110; Paul Sharrad, "Listening to One's Ancestors: An Interview with Witi Ihimaera", *Australian and New Zealand Studies in Canada* 8 (1992), 97-105; and in Alley & Williams, eds., *In the Same Room*, 219-236.

dependencies. The story can be read as an appeal to all marginalised groups to acknowledge their specific cultural traditions and thus find their own positive identity in an effort to finally overcome the imperialist and colonial structures. In the terminology of Genette the relationship between the pretext and the continuation may be described as *transposition heterodiégétique*, as a comprehensive alteration of the pretext in setting and characters. Thus Ihimaera changes the gender of the pretextual central figure from female (Leila) to male (Tuta) and alters their social background. Even the narrated time is changed as Ihimaera's continuation moves closer to the social reality of the time of publication.

The most obvious connection between the two stories lies in their shared plot element of the ball and in their structure as initiation stories. However, the initiation delineated in the continuation is induced by a different impetus. For Leila the initiation signifies an opportunity and is prerequisite for a successful integration into the adult world (cf. KM, 336-337). For the outsider, Tuta, his rejection by high society is mirrored by his own lack of affinity with that society. The element of displacement, central to postcolonial literature,[21] is used here to expose the stiff and narrow-minded postcolonial society, a society which is an imperial relic nursing its old ties with the form and values of the British Empire.

Even though Tuta does not participate in a formal initiation, he does live through an inner process of recognition in the same manner as Leila. Unlike in the pretext, his experience is not an individualistic one providing him with an insight into his own mortality, but rather a recognition of his own social identity within the postcolonial counter-discourse.

4. "The Halcyon Summer": Variation of a Central Theme

The narrative "The Halcyon Summer" (WI, 156-180) recounts the occurrences of a summer in the life of the eleven-year-old Tama. He and his two younger sisters Kara and Pari are to spend a few weeks on the north coast with relatives. At first the children anticipate their vacation with more fear than joyous expectancy: their relatives, their great aunt Nani Puti, her husband Karani Pani and their numerous children live in a remote coastal region north of Gisborne and still keep up many Maori traditions. Tama and his sisters are city children and fear the unknown customs and the strange language (WI, 157): "But Tama still didn't like the idea of going – it was all Maoris up the Coast, no Pakehas [...]. Furthermore, Maoris wore only grass skirts and probably never even wore pyjamas to bed, and he knew that was rude."

Regardless of all their fears, the children live through exciting weeks in which they participate in the daily life of a large family. They learn to milk the cow, to ride and fish, they share in the provincial joy of going to the movie theatre in the neighbouring town of Ruatoria and they learn about the history of their family, which is inseparably linked with the land. However, the almost idyllic life at the coast also has a downside,

---

[21] Cf. Ashcroft; Griffith & Tiffin, *The Empire Writes Back*, 9.

which in those few weeks gradually moves to the foreground of the narrative: the family is involved in law proceedings regarding their rights of possession over the land and they lose the lawsuit. In the following weeks the great aunt and uncle mobilise their relatives living scattered in various regions to assist them in their resistance. As Tama's parents return from Auckland to fetch their children the confrontation with the police is imminent. Tama's parents also wish to aid their clan in their battle over the land and promise to return as soon as they have returned the children to safety in Gisborne.

"The Halcyon Summer" thematically refers to Mansfield's "At the Bay" (KM, 205-245): both stories delineate a vacation spent on the New Zealand coast. Ihimaera's story parallels the earlier narrative in its usage of the beach as the stage on which a large portion of the family life takes place. However, unlike "At the Bay," the structure of "The Halcyon Summer" is best described as an initiation story. Tama is the central figure and everything that he experiences during his stay is, in a way, new to him and widens the horizon of his knowledge. This disparity between the new and the familiar is due to Tama's city origins which contrast sharply with the traditional life on the coast.

The embarkation on this new life is minutely described, from the announcement by the parents to the end of the long car journey. The intention of the mother to familiarise her children with Maori life in the "whanau" is explicitly stated: "You kids are growing up proper little Pakehas" (WI, 157). Indeed the children's notions of their relatives are tinged with fears, that are reminiscent of white man's prejudices and devoid of any identification with the Maori community: "This Nani sounded alarming – she was very old for one thing, being sixty, and had white hair and tattoos on her chin" (WI, 157; cf. also 158).

Tama's initiation progresses slowly and in stages: at first his numerous cousins only see the kid from the city in him, the "townie," and meet him armed with their prejudices – which incidentally mirror his own: "Think you're better than us, ay? Just because you live in the town. Just because you speak all la-di-da – " (WI, 162). His final acceptance by the community occurs after a brawl: nobody wins the fight but Tama is afforded an opportunity to prove his loyalty as he conceals the incident from grown-ups.

After that Tama is acquainted with a life which is governed by such ancient traditions as fishing and searching for clams. From stories he learns much about the spiritual life of the Maoris, such as making an offering of a portion of his day's catch to the Sea God Tangaroa (cf. WI, 169) and also about the inseparable ties binding the family to the land they live on (WI, 164):

> ' [...] In the old days there was a Maori pa, right where our house is. It used to guard the whole Coast. It's famous,' and Kopua puffed the words up with pride. 'And all the land – ' Kopua described a large generous circle' – that you can see once belonged to us. Now, only this – ' Kopua pointed down the beach – 'is left. The pa is gone, the land is gone, but our house and we are still here. And Mum's the big chief here. She'll never leave. Even if people are trying to get us out.'

Compared to the Burnell family of the pretext,[22] the Maoris live a life in harmony with the rhythm of nature. It is nature which does not need to be displaced, as Stanley Burnell does every morning during his swimming practice, but rather revered as a life-giving force. In a reversal of the power structure of the pretext in which Stanley Burnell is obviously the patriarchal head of the family, the modern narrative depicts the wife and mother as the ruler of the clan. Even her husband, Koro, acknowledges her influence and recognises her significance for the community without reservation: "She's the one who keeps us all together" (WI, 168).

Tama's initiation does not only consist of his introduction to the traditional Maori lifestyle, but also includes his developing a political consciousness. Thus the political background of this idyllic life becomes more clear for the reader: the events take place in 1950 ("It was the year Sir Apirana Ngata died" [WI, 156]), a year of intense legal and political conflict pertaining to the land-owning rights of the Maoris.

Tama's initiation reaches its climax as he realises (as Tuta did) that for a Maori a complete assimilation of the life of New Zealand's Pakeha is the wrong path to discovering one's identity (WI, 179):

> Tama watched his parents with growing discomfort because they seemed unaware of what was happening, really *happening*. His parents had brought gifts for Nani and Karani, who accepted them politely, and for the cousins – Grace gave a scream of delight at the new H-line dress that their mother had brought back from Auckland. And the thought came to Tama that his parents and his family were foolish people because they were so privileged that they could never see beyond themselves.

Not only has the range of Tama's experience been widened but also his conception of himself has changed at the end of the story: "Something was happening at the edge of childhood. It was just around the corner and, whatever it was, it would forever change all their lives" (WI, 179). The alteration which the narrative alludes to here manifests itself as a new awareness of his ethnicity and pride in his own indigenous descent. Tama's parents live the town life of the Pakehas and have significantly taken a trip to Auckland to see the "Empire Games," a manifestation of the colonial past, but even they recall their close ties with their tribe: "We – I – my children – have as much say as you about this place" (WI, 179). Thus, once more, the postcolonial point of view is moved to the foreground of the story. This perspective allows a critical view of the past and simultaneously embodies the implicit appeal not to accept the dominance of a Euro-centric culture as irrevocable.

Despite the political earnestness of Ihimaera's story and the central thematic parallels to the pretext(s) in their concentration on the difficulties of establishing one's identity within the family (cf. KM, 11-60 and 205-245), a number of humorous allusions to the pretexts may be discovered. Thus, Tama's cousin Grace is a modern version of the narcissistic Beryl presented from a new perspective (cf. esp. KM, 22). The

---

[22] Compare also Ihimaera's "Country Life" (WI, 89-109) with Mansfield's "Prelude" (KM, 11-60) as another modern – interfigural – version of the Burnells.

disparity between the fantasy of a perfect seductress and the reality of the destitute farm life almost seems a parody (WI, 172): "[...] there was a big difference between brothers and MEN. And was it all worth it? Oh yes, for to see Grace all transfigured by soap and water, gilded by the moon, queening it across the paddock and around the cowpats was to witness – a vision."

Ihimaera's story is framed by a stanza at the beginning and at the conclusion; the stanza is conspicuous in form due to italicization and its distinct "lyrical" language. The central theme of the narrative is re-stated in the figurative and expressive language of poetry (WI, 156): "*Once there was a nest, floating on the sea at summer solstice, and happy voices to charm the wind. The nest is gone now, drifting away on the tides. But somewhere, somewhere must surely float scattered straws, even just a single straw, which I may light upon.*"

The nest is a symbol of safety and may be assumed to denote the original Maori community prior to the social upheavals which commenced with the process of colonisation. This state of being is recalled as happy and idyllic ("[...] *happy voices to charm the wind*"), but this community has been washed away by the tides of time. The last sentence announces the indestructible hope of the lyrical I: the scattered straws of the nest must still exist, the community can be reassembled. If the lyrical I and the author are presumed to be one, then the stanza may be interpreted as an indication of his intention: so long as stories about the solidarity of the Maori tribal community and family exist, then there is hope. Such stories signify hope for a people that have become a minority in their own homeland (about 10% of the population) and that have to keep reassuring themselves of their existence and their cultural heritage.[23]

This frame structure is reminiscent of Mansfield's narrative frame in "At the Bay": The story begins with a description of the sea, the central symbol of the story, and ends also with one. But Ihimaera's "The Halcyon Summer" is surely a borderline case for hypertextuality.

If one utilises Genette's classification of formal and thematic transpositions, significant alterations may be discovered in each area. In regard to form and style it must be said that completely divergent narrative concepts are involved: in the continuation there is only one focalizer – not several as in Mansfield's pretext – and a very clear narrative voice.

Thematically, the changes are at least as extensive. Of significant importance is the fact that none of the characters has a pretextual source. However, an assessment of the story as a variation on the point of view is admissible and thus the short story would constitute a continuation of the pretext – despite minute transtextual signals.[24]

---

[23] Cf. WI, 180: "Once there was a nest, floating on the sea, at the edge of childhood. Then it was gone, its straws scattered across the waves. And I have been a kingfisher searching, always searching."

[24] Cf. also Nan Bowman Albinski, "Witi Ihimaera," in Robert L. Ross, ed., *International Literature in English. Essays on the Major Writers* (New York: Garland, 1991), 39-51, esp. 45-47.

Katherine Mansfield portrays a colonial family with no material cares, whereas Ihimaera's family is drawn to indicate the threatened livelihood of the Maoris who lose their land. The second, and central aspect of the story is portrayed in the contrast between the city-bred child Tama and his relatives, who are familiar with cultural traditions, and indicates the dangers of a loss of identity in this ethnic minority.

5. "A Contemporary Kezia": Interfigurality and the Limits of Transtextuality

The title of the story "A Contemporary Kezia" (WI, 79-88) already indicates a marked transtextual association with the central child figure in Katherine Mansfield's New Zealand Stories. Thus the title itself directs the reader's interpretation: evidently the narrative is conceived as a new perspective on, or a topical rendering of, a pretextual figure. However, it should be stated right away that there is no connection to the plot of a Mansfield story other than this solitary interfigural relationship.

The character of the little girl, Kezia, is present in four of Katherine Mansfield's stories: "Prelude" (KM, 11-60), "At the Bay" (KM, 205-245), "The Doll's House" (KM, 393-401) and "The Little Girl" (KM, 577-582). "The Little Girl" is the earliest Kezia-story (1912): the feelings of a little girl towards her father are tinged with fear but that changes as she feels physically protected by him. In "Prelude" and "At the Bay" Kezia is still tormented by fear of abandonment, but now the women of the family are the individuals she focuses on: a mother who keeps her at a distance and a grandmother who has assumed the role of a substitute mother. In "The Doll's House" she is sensitive but self-willed and defies the injunctions of the grown-ups. Although the character of Kezia is accentuated differently in these stories – a gap of ten years lies between some of these narratives – there are still sufficient shared aspects to render her a central figure. No other child's psyche is drawn so painstakingly and she is a significant focalizer in the stories she appears in: the activities and dialogues of the grownu-ps are filtered through her perception of them. It is partially due to this detailed portrayal and her naturally emotional responses that she engages the reader's affections. Ihimaera's "A Contemporary Kezia" presents the story of a New Zealand family – with a mixture of European and Maori blood - in three episodes. The setting of the first episode is provided by Auckland's airport. The twelve-year-old Kataraina and her father are waiting to board an airplane which will take them to Tauranga. Kataraina's father is fondly reminiscing about his oldest daughter's childhood. The girl is angered by her father's faulty memory and keeps pointing out patiently – but doggedly – that a different version of every anecdote is remembered by her. This results in a sort of dialogue in which each tries to convince the other of his or her own view of the events: the discussion over the colour of Kataraina's stuffed animal almost ends in a dispute. Kataraina is happy when they are requested to board the airplane.

In the second episode Kataraina and her father are waiting for the arrival of her younger sister in the Tauranga airport. In a second conversation he continues with his anecdotes from the girls' childhood and once again Kataraina tries to break the sentimental mood by correcting him; the episode ends with Kataraina's good-natured acquiescence (WI, 84): "And Kataraina smiled at her father, 'We love the way you tell that story Daddy.' Ah yes, their father thought ruefully, he had certainly remembered it well."

In the third episode the father recounts the story of his mother's rough childhood. She grew up in a large Maori family on the east coast. Nani was separated from her family when she was six years old and sent to keep house for two old women, highly respected weavers. With only a dog as a constant companion, the little girl spends the next three years of her life in a remote valley, burdened with the responsibility for the old and the sick. When the dog dies, Nani leaves the old women, who die shortly afterwards.

The father ends the anecdote with an instruction to his two daughters: the grandmother learned to assume responsibility early in her life, and the two granddaughters should do the same.

"A Contemporary Kezia" adheres to the principle of the linearity of time but does not contain a classical plot with cause and effect relationships. In the first two episodes the rapid dialogue of father and daughter dominates, in the third part the embedded narrative of the father makes up the episode. A comic undercurrent is discernible in the first two episodes due to the nostalgic reminiscing of the father and Kataraina's earnestness; the narrator, however, maintains an ironic aloofness towards both focalizers. Thus he (and the reader) is a better judge of Kataraina's behaviour than the father (WI, 83):

> 'There it is, Daddy!' Kataraina cried. The plane touched down and before her father could stop her Kataraina had run out to the gate. The plane was still far away, but Kataraina began to wave and wave – and her father felt his heart lift as he observed this evidence of closeness between his two daughters.

The reader, who is also familiar with Kataraina's thoughts, knows that this is only the father's wishful thinking. To Kataraina the arrival of the plane is only a welcome interruption of her parent's garrulousness ("From out of the sky the plane appeared. Please hurry, Kataraina prayed" [WI, 83]).

Kataraina and her sister Amiria are portrayed as modern, self-confident girls, who will occasionally challenge their father's parental authority. It is especially Kataraina, "poised on the edge of womanhood" (WI, 79), that is about to relinquish her status as a child. Her childhood, adorned with such characteristic accessories as Coca-Cola and worn out jeans, seems to run along the familiar west-European lines. In many respects the third episode presents an unexpected break within the story: it recounts the tale of a number of characters but permits the father to become the narrator.

The cheerfully ironic tone of the narrator provides a distinct contrast to the solemnity and persistence of the father at the outset of his narrative: "Kataraina sweet, I need to tell you about Nani, my mother" (WI, 84). The purpose of the embedded narrative cannot be determined with certainty, since there is no direct association with any of the two earlier episodes. However, if the cultural context, the individual narrator and the indigenous oral narrative tradition of the Maoris are taken into account,[25] the aim of the story becomes clear.

In various interviews Ihimaera has repeatedly stressed the significance of Maori traditions for his own conception of his creative work. He has also drawn attention to their transposition into the literature of the Maoris. The concept of "rope of man", a significant element in the cultural identity of the Maoris, is defined by the author in the following way:[26]

> All Maori people believe in what we call te taura tangata, which translates as being the rope of man. In that particular rope are woven all the generations of man from creation to the present day. It's that rope which forms the basis of the search for whakapapa, the union with the universe that we talk about. It becomes difficult when a population like ours has moved from its rural hearths to an urban area because then there is a discontinuity, a dislocation, in the transmission of the whakapapa and so journeys like 'In Search of the Whakapapa' have become extremely vital for the older generation to take the younger generation on, and it's a way also of ridding ourselves of Western, urbanized traits and concentrating on oral techniques. We believe that the word is a very sacred thing. Most genealogies are only learnt orally and they are the means of cultural continuation for Maori people: we never ever consider ourselves to be just ourselves at this moment; we believe ourselves to be the inheritors and possessors of thousands and thousands of years of a wonderful cultural legacy.

The third part of "A Contemporary Kezia" depicts precisely this moment of oral transmission of familial or tribal genealogy: a father, the representative of the older generation, transmits his knowledge of the family's genealogy to the new generation. Thus the daughters become the upholders of their joint cultural heritage. The father's exhortation to the girls to regard the experiences of the grandmother as consequential for their own lives is a direct testimonial to the crucial importance of oral transmission. Thus the transmission of memory unites three generations: grandmother, child and grandchildren: "She has taught her own children and I, in turn, try to teach you and Amiria, Nani's grandchildren" (WI, 88). The grandmother's task of providing the old people with fire acquires a symbolic meaning: "It's strange, really, but all her life your Nani has been the one who always looks after the fire and blows on the embers and brings us life every day" (WI, 88). Thus Nani becomes the personification of the life-giving force that guarantees the survival of the tribal genealogy and the "Maori-Ancestry" for the ensuing generation. The simulated oral quality of the embedded narrative is discernible in its rhetorical features and in its content. The history is recited with a thoroughly didactic approach and numerous emphatic repetitions. Furthermore the story tells of a cultural achievement, which is transmitted orally. On the whole this indigenous tradition is joined with the rather conventional narrative tech-

---

[25] Cf. in general Peter H. Marsden, "'But Maoris Don't Read Books': Mündliche Überlieferung und Rhetorik der Maori-Dichtung," in Werner Kreisel; Peter H. Marsden, eds., *'First Peoples, First Voices.' Indigene Völker zwischen Fremdbestimmung und Selbstbehauptung* (Aachen: Verlag der Augustinus Buchhandlung, 1995), 23-48.

[26] Wilkinson, "Witi Ihimaera: Interview," 100.

nique which dominates in the first two episodes. The successful synthesis of the two forms can be interpreted on a metaphorical level as a description of modern literature in New Zealand. A literature which, according to Ihimaera, enjoys the privilege of drawing upon two cultural sources for inspiration:[27] "[...] but obviously, when you talk about 'New Zealand literature,' you talk about literatures that are sourced from two different cultures: one that goes back to Anglo-Saxon and one that goes back to Maori oral traditions."

Through the synthesis of the two forms a new, intercultural form is produced, which has little in common with the classical short story.[28]

Nevertheless, the three episodes do produce an integral whole. The father's admonition to the daughters to always remember their grandmother constitutes an appeal to retain their identity as Maoris. The younger generation, especially Kataraina, lives a life formed by the values of the Pakeha culture. Thus Kataraina's Maori descent is barely perceived by the reader in the first two episodes. However, the traditional transmission of cultural knowledge and reverence for that tradition brings the story to an optimistic end: it signifies hope for the survival of indigenous values in a New Zealand society which seems to be guided by western values.

"A Contemporary Kezia" does not constitute a continuation in Nowak's sense, since there is no connection between the pretext and the continuation within the plot. On the other hand the title is a clear transtextual signal, sending the reader in search of the hypertextual transformation of Kezia's character. Terming this phenomenon an "internymic device"[29] in agreement with Wolfgang G. Müller, one may meditate on the connection between the contemporary Kezia and her diffident, fearful counterpart in the pretexts, but the prevalent problem of interfigurality cannot be avoided. However, the title of the continuation is ambivalent, since the narrative presents the reader with two girls belonging to two different generations. Kataraina may be viewed as a contemporary Kezia, being a contemporary at the time of the book's publication. But Nani, the grandmother, would be a contemporary of the pretextual Kezia. In both cases Nani/Kataraina would be Maori versions of Kezia, but they have little in common with the colonial daughter of Mansfield's pretexts. Thus on the formal level of characterisation there is a conspicuous absence of transtextual references or remarks on the pretext.

Nani is the human attestation of an arduous past; Kataraina, however, is a personification of the modern, rising New Zealand. She is heir to both cultural origins, Pakeha and Maori.

In the entire volume of *Dear Miss Mansfield*, "A Contemporary Kezia" is the only narrative whose transtextual identification of its pretext occurs solely through its title.

---

[27] Sharrad, "Listening to One's Ancestors," 98.
[28] Cf. in general on the mediating between two cultures Dieter Riemenschneider, "Intercultural Exchange between Ethnic Minority and English Language Majority: The Writing of Jack Davis and Witi Ihimaera," in M. T. Bindella; G. V. Davis, eds., *Imagination and the Creative Impulse in the New Literatures in English* (Amsterdam; Atlanta, 1993), 271-280.
[29] Cf. Müller, "Interfigurality," 106.

At the same time it is the story which most obviously reverts to the indigenous tradition of oral narrative. Thus it renders a complex transtextual system of reference unfeasible from the outset, since this would be founded on the written word.

* * * * *

In the first two of the stories analysed ("The Washerwoman's Children," "The Affectionate Kidnappers") Witi Ihimaera presents his own individual answer, his Maori response, to Mansfield's pretexts by effecting an alteration in the point of view within the stories. In each case he chooses the point of view unheeded during the course of the narrative. Furthermore both stories are individual continuations of the respective pretextual plot. In "His First Ball" Witi Ihimaera reproduces the pretextual plot in his own new way; the characters and the setting of the pretext are not appropriated, but the main element of the plot, the ball, and the structure of an initiation story are distinct references to the pretext.

Beyond these explicit hypertextual relationships, the transtextual associations between Ihimaera's stories "The Halcyon Summer" and "A Contemporary Kezia" and the respective pretexts are of a much more complex nature. A consequence of this complexity is the inadequacy of Nowak's models and proposals for the classification of these narratives.

As regards the art of narration, Ihimaera's stories are distinguished by their great independence. The author dissociates himself from Mansfield's modern narrative technique which seems to recede into the background behind her characters. Unlike in Katherine Mansfield's fiction, Ihimaera's narrator is noticeably involved in the narrative and is conspicuous as a result of his ironic detachment from the characters. In addition, judging by the author's intent and linguistic execution, Ihimaera's stories are explicit works of postcolonial literature intended to make the voice of the marginalised Maoris heard.

A continuation naturally implies a renewal of discussion and a new assessment of the pretexts, as exemplified particularly by "The Affectionate Kidnappers." Occasionally this aspect recedes into the background in Witi Ihimaera's collection of stories, for example in "The Halcyon Summer" and "A Contemporary Kezia," but at the same time the reader is given a fascinating glimpse of an elegant, humorous and many-faceted literary representation of "Intercultural Encounters."

Appendix

List of Publications by Rüdiger Ahrens

I. Books

1966   *Die moralistische Funktion der Essays von Francis Bacon*, PhD dissertation, University of Erlangen.

1972   *Englische Parodien – von W. Shakespeare bis T. S. Eliot*, with an introduction and annotations, UTB 179 (Heidelberg: Quelle & Meyer).

1974   *Die Essays von Francis Bacon. Literarische Form und Moralistische Aussage*, Anglistische Forschungen 105 (Heidelberg: Winter).

1975   *Englische literaturtheoretische Essays; Volume 1: 17. und 18. Jahrhundert; Volume 2: 19. und 20. Jahrhundert*, with an introduction and annotations, UTB 389/390 (Heidelberg: Quelle & Meyer).

1977   *Shakespeare im Unterricht*, anglistik & englischunterricht 3 (Trier: WVG, 1977), 2nd ed. (Trier, 1978), 3rd rev. ed. (Trier, 1980).
Own contribution: "Die Tradition der Shakespeare-Behandlung im Englischunterricht," 12-38.

1978/79 with Erwin Wolff, *Englische und amerikanische Literaturtheorie – Studien zu ihrer historischen Entwicklung; Volume 1: Renaissance, Klassizismus und Romantik; Volume 2: Viktorianische Zeit und 20. Jahrhundert*. Anglistische Forschungen 126/127 (Heidelberg: Winter).
Own contribution: "Literatur und das System der Wissenschaften in der Literaturtheorie der Renaissance," 121-148.

1979   with Horst W. Drescher and Karl-Heinz Stoll, *Lexikon der englischen Literatur* (Stuttgart: Kröner): 143 own contributions.

1981   *Amerikanische Bildungswirklichkeit heute*, Hildesheimer Beiträge zu den Erziehungs- und Sozialwissenschaften (Hildesheim: Olms).
Own contributions: "Grundzüge des amerikanischen Universitätssystems," 3-24, and "Die Funktion von Tests im amerikanischen Hochschulwesen," 57-86.

1982   *William Shakespeare: Didaktisches Handbuch*, 3 Vols., UTB 1111/1112/1113 (München: Fink).
Own contributions: Volume 1: "Shakespeare-Rezeption in der Literaturdidaktik des 20. Jahrhunderts," 43-68. Volume 2: "Das Thema des Wuchers in Shakespeares The Merchant of Venice und F. Bacons 'Of Usury'," 829-850. Volume 3: "Jan Kotts Analyse von *Macbeth*. Drama und kritischer Text," 885-912.

1992   with Heinz Antor, *Text – Culture – Reception. Cross-Cultural Aspects of English Studies* (Heidelberg: Winter).
Own contribution: "The International Development of English and Cross-Cultural Competence," 3-23.

1995 with Wolf-Dietrich Bald and Werner Hüllen, *Handbuch Englisch als Fremdsprache* (Berlin: Schmidt).
Own contribution: "Literaturwissenschaftliche Modelle," 301-309.

1996 with Laurenz Volkmann, *Why Literature Matters: Theories and Functions of Literature*, Anglistische Forschungen, 241 (Heidelberg: Winter).
Own contribution: "Shifts of Aesthetic Discourses: National, Post-Colonial and Post-Structuralist Discourses," 49-63.

1998 with Fritz-Wilhelm Neumann, *Fiktion und Geschichte in der anglo-amerikanischen Literatur: Festschrift für Hans-Joachim Müllenbrock zum 60. Geburtstag* (Heidelberg: Winter).
Own contribution: "Das Konzept der Natur in *Lear* und *King Lear*: Edward Bond vs. William Shakespeare," 357-376.

II. Editorships

1971-91 Member of the editorial board of *German Studies: Literature, Music, Fine Arts, German-Language Research Contributions. A Current Survey in the English Language*, Tübingen.

1978-92 with Erwin Wolff, *Forum Anglistik, Realien und Probleme der Literaturwissenschaft: Eine Buchreihe zur englischen und amerikanischen Literatur* (Heidelberg: Winter).

1992 - with Erwin Wolff, *Anglistische Forschungen* (Heidelberg: Winter).

1978-80 with Jörg Hasler et al., *Trierer Studien zur Literatur* (Frankfurt/M.: Lang).

1984 - with Franz Link et al., *Beiträge zur englischen und amerikanischen Literatur, im Auftrag der Görres-Gesellschaft* (Paderborn: Schöningh).

1985 - *Anglo-Amerikanische Studien – Anglo-American Studies* (Bern/New York: Lang), since 1995 with Kevin L. Cope, Baton Rouge.

1990 *Anglistentag 1989 Würzburg: Proceedings* (Tübingen: Niemeyer).

1990 - *Anglistik – Mitteilungen des Verbandes deutscher Anglisten* (Heidelberg: Winter).

1996 - with Wolf-Dietrich Bald, *Grundlagen der Anglistik und Amerikanistik* (Berlin: Schmidt).

1998 - with A. Fischer, Ernst Leisi, and Ulrich Suerbaum, *Englisch-deutsche Studienausgabe der Dramen Shakespeares* (Tübingen: Stauffenburg).

1998 - *Symbolism. An International Journal of Critical Aesthetics.* (New York: AMS).

III. Articles

1968 "Limerick-Dichtung im Englischunterricht," *Der Fremdsprachliche Unterricht*, 61-70.

1969 "Sonderthemen im englischen Oberstufenunterricht," *Die Neueren Sprachen* 5, 209-221.

1970 "Das moderne englische Drama. Möglichkeiten der Behandlung im Unterricht der gymnasialen Oberstufe," *Der Fremdsprachliche Unterricht* 1, 15-29.

1971 "Der moderne anglo-amerikanische Essay. Methodisch-didaktische Überlegungen zu seiner Verwendbarkeit in der gymnasialen Oberstufe," *Der Fremdsprachliche Unterricht* 3, 14-30.

1973 "Möglichkeiten der Literaturdidaktik im Englischunterricht der Studienstufe," *Die Neueren Sprachen* 1, 1-8.

1973 "Gedichtinterpretation und Gesellschaftskritik im Englischunterricht der Studienstufe – Literaturdidaktische Analyse einer Parodie zu W. Wordsworths 'The Daffodils'," *Der Fremdsprachliche Unterricht* 1, 50-61.

1973 "Kompositionsprinzipien in S. Becketts *Waiting for Godot* und *Endgame*," *Archiv für das Studium der Neueren Sprachen und Literaturen* 209:124, 363-368; reprinted in K. A. Blüher, ed., *Modernes Französisches Theater: Adamov– Beckett–Ionesco*, Wege der Forschung 532 (Darmstadt: WBG, 1982), 204-211.

1973 "Jeremy Colliers moralistische Intention," in G. Droege, W. Frühwald and F. Pauly, eds., *Verführung zur Geschichte: Festschrift zum 500. Jahrestag der Eröffnung einer Universität in Trier, 1473-1973*, Trier, 220-230.

1973 "Literaturwissenschaft in den lehrerbildenden Curricula," in Konrad Schröder and Gertrud Walter, eds., *Fremdsprachendidaktisches Studium in der Universität* (München), 82-96.

1974 "Antithetische Literaturbetrachtung im Englischunterricht – Das Gedicht und seine Parodie, dargestellt an W. B. Yeats 'The Lake Isle of Innisfree'," *Neusprachliche Mitteilungen* 1, 42-49.

1976 "N. F. Simpson – One Way Pendulum," in Horst Oppel, ed., *Das englische Drama der Gegenwart* (Berlin: Schmidt), 49-64.

1976 "Literatur und Imagination in der Poetik der englischen Renaissance," *Trierer Beiträge* 2, 21-26.

1977 with Werner Hüllen, "Bemerkungen über die 'Einheitlichen Prüfungsanforderungen in der Abiturprüfung: Englisch'," *Neusprachliche Mitteilungen* 1, 25-29.

1977 "Literaturdidaktik," in Konrad Schröder and Thomas Finkenstaedt, eds., *Reallexikon der englischen Fachdidaktik* (Darmstadt: WBG), 147-152.

1979 "Shakespeare und die reformierte Oberstufe: Bericht über ein Informationsseminar bei den Shakespeare-Tagen 1977 in Lahn-Gießen," *Die Neueren Sprachen* 1, 64-67.

1979 "Die bisherige Rolle der Short Story im Englischunterricht der Sekundarstufe II," in Peter Freese, Horst Groene and Liesel Hermes, eds., *Die Short Story im Englischunterricht der Sekundarstufe II* (Paderborn: Schöningh), 11-37.

1979 "Amerikanische Universitäten heute. Ein Blick in die hochschulpolitische Zukunft?," *Mitteilungen des Hochschulverbandes* 27:2, 64-71.

1980 "Grundzüge des Mäzenatentums in der Tudorzeit. Ein Beitrag zum Verhältnis von Literatur und Aristokratie im England des 16. Jahrhunderts," *Trierer Beiträge aus Forschung und Lehre an der Universität Trier* 7, 1-5.

1980 "Visuelle Medien und Unterrichtsphasen im fremdsprachlichen Anfangsunterricht," *Die Neueren Sprachen* 4, 361-377.

1981 "Literaturtheorie und Aristokratie in der Tudorzeit. Ein Beitrag zur Funktion des Mäzens im England des 16. Jahrhunderts," *Anglia* 99:3-4, 279-311.

1981 "Literaturtheorie in ihrem Verhältnis zum Mäzenatentum der Tudorzeit," in A. Buck, G. Kauffmann, B. L. Spahr and C. Wiedemann, eds., *Europäische Hofkultur im 16. und 17. Jahrhundert* (Hamburg: Hauswedell), vol. 2, 171-178.

1982 "Das amerikanische Universitätssystem und die 'Harvard Reform'," in H. A. Glaser, ed., *Hochschulreform – und was nun?* (Frankfurt/M.: Ullstein), 397-423.

1982 "Die Relation von Text und Kontext als perspektivisches Lesen," in Hans Hunfeld, ed., *Literaturwissenschaft – Literaturdidaktik – Literaturunterricht: Englisch, II. Eichstätter Kolloquium zum Fremdsprachenunterricht 1981* (Königstein/Ts.: Scriptor), 75-93.

1982 "Transzendenz und lyrisches Ich in Ted Hughes' 'Gnat Psalm' und Geoffrey Hills *Mercian Hymns*," in H. Kunisch, Th. Berchem and F. Link, eds., *Literaturwissenschaftliches Jahrbuch, im Auftrag der Görres-Gesellschaft*, Neue Folge 23 (Berlin: Duncker & Humblot), 265-296.

1983 "History and the Dramatic Context: John Osborne's Historical Plays," *Fu Jen Studies* 16, 49-75.

1984 "The Poetics of the Renaissance and the System of Literary Genres," in Ulrich Broich, Theodor Stemmler and Gerd Stratmann, eds., *Functions of Literature: Essays Presented to Erwin Wolff on his 60th Birthday* (Tübingen: Niemeyer), 101-117.

1984 "Die 'Harvard Reform' und das kulturelle Selbstverständnis der USA," in Lothar Bredella, ed., *Die USA in Unterricht und Forschung* (Bochum: Kamp), 259-273.

1985 "Die Fiktionalisierung der Historie in den Dramen John Osbornes," in Manfred Pfister, ed., *Anglistentag 1984: Vorträge* (Gießen: Hoffmann), 351-367.

1985 "Grenzen der Richtlinien und Chancen der Fachdidaktik," in Karl-Richard Bausch, Herbert Christ, Werner Hüllen and Hans-Jürgen Krumm, eds., *Forschungsgegenstand Richtlinien. Arbeitspapiere der 5. Frühjahrskonferenz zur Erforschung des Fremdsprachenunterrichts* (Tübingen: Narr), 11-16.

1986	"Ted Hughes' 'Gnat Psalm': The Poet in Search of a New Transcendence," *Fu Jen Studies* 19, 15-36; reprinted in *Gaéliana* 8 (1986), 239-255.
1987	"Fremdsprachenunterricht zwischen Kontextualismus und absoluter Sprache," in Karl-Richard Bausch, Herbert Christ, Werner Hüllen and Hans-Jürgen Krumm, eds., *Sprachbegriffe im Fremdsprachenunterricht, Arbeitspapiere der 7. Frühjahrskonferenz zur Erforschung des Fremdsprachenunterrichts* (Tübingen: Narr), 9-18.
1987	"Die Aktualität des Malthusianismus," in M. Lindauer and A. Schöpf, eds., *Die Erde unser Lebensraum* (Stuttgart: Klett), 17-58.
1987	"The Educative Paradigm of the Modern Novel of Initiation," in W. Lörscher and R. Schulze, eds., *Perspectives on Language in Performance: Studies in Linguistics, Literary Criticism, and Language Teaching and Learning, To Honour Werner Hüllen on the Occasion of his 60th Birthday* (Tübingen: Narr), vol. 1, 611-641.
1988	"The Modern Poet in View of Nature: Ted Hughes' 'Gnat Psalm'," *Poetica* (Tokyo) 28, 60-74.
1988	"National Myths and Stereotypes in Modern Irish Drama: Sean O'Casey, Brendan Behan, Brian Friel," *Fu Jen Studies* 21, 89-110.
1988	"Sprachkompetenz als Bestandteil der Bildung," in W. Böhm and M. Lindauer, eds., *"Nicht Vielwissen sättigt die Seele." Wissen, Erkennen, Bildung, Ausbildung heute* (Stuttgart: Klett), 147-182.
1988	"Sprache und Bildung. Sprachenpolitik in Europa," in Thomas Goppel, ed., *Aktionskreis Wirtschaft Politik Wissenschaft e.V.*, October 1988, 1-33.
1989	"Das Universitätssystem in Großbritannien," *Forum (Deutscher Hochschulverband)* 47, May 1989, 43-66.
1989	"The Critical Reception of Shakespeare's Tragedies in Twentieth-Century Germany," in R. Dotterer, ed., *Shakespeare. Text, Subtext, and Context, Susquehanna University Studies* (London/Toronto: Associated University Presses), 97-106.
1989	"Political History and Satire in William Shakespeare's *Macbeth* and Barbara Garson's *MacBird!*," in J. E. Peters and Th. M. Stein, eds., *Scholastic Midwifery: Studien zum Satirischen in der englischen Literatur 1600-1800. Festschrift für Dietrich Rolle zum 60. Geburtstag* (Tübingen: Narr), 7-25.
1989	"The Impact of the Collage Technique on Charles Marowitz's *A Macbeth*," in Ulrich Horstmann and Wolfgang Zach, eds., *Kunstgriffe – Auskünfte über die Reichweite von Literaturtheorie und Literaturkritik: Festschrift für Herbert Mainusch* (Frankfurt/M.: Lang), 11-26.
1990	"Motivgeschichtliche Aspekte der New Woman im englischen Drama der Jahrhundertwende," in A. Klein and H.-J. Müllenbrock, eds., *Motive und Themen in englischsprachiger Literatur als Indikatoren literaturgeschichtlicher Prozesse: Festschrift zum 65. Geburtstag von Theodor Wolpers* (Tübingen: Niemeyer), 293-320.
1990	"Sprache und Bildung – Sprachenpolitik in Europa," *Almanach des Deutschen Hochschulverbands* III, 9-30.

1991	"The Political Pamphlet (1660-1714): Pre-Revolutionary and Post-Revolutionary Aspects," *Anglia* 109, 1-2, 21-43.
1992	"Satirical Norm and Narrative Technique in the Modern University Novel: David Lodge's Changing Places and Small World," in J. Schwend, S. Hagemann and H. Völkel, eds., *Literatur im Kontext – Literature in Context: Festschrift für Horst W. Drescher* (Frankfurt/M.: Lang) 277-295.
1992	"Rhetorical Means and Comic Effects in William Shakespeare's *Twelfth Night*," in Toshiyuki Takamiya and Richard Beadle, eds., *Chaucer to Shakespeare: Essays in Honour of Shinsuke Ando* (Cambridge: Brewer), 195-209.
1993	"Rhetorik und Komik in William Shakespeare's Twelfth Night," *Anglia*, 111:1-2, 19-38.
1994	"Zwischen Tradition und Erneuerung: Bildungssystem und berufliche Ausbildung," in Hans Kastendiek, Karl Rohe and Angelika Volle, eds., *Länderbericht Großbritannien* 327 (Frankfurt/M.: Campus), 438-455; reprinted in 1999, 523-543.
1995	"The Art of Poetry" and "The Defence of Poesie," in Rolf Günter Renner and Engelbert Habekost, eds., *Lexikon literaturtheoretischer Werke* (Stuttgart: Kröner), 43-44 and 79-80.
1995	"Invertierte Welten bei William Shakespeare und Tom Stoppard: Das Beispiel Hamlet" in Bernd Engler and Klaus Müller, eds., *Exempla. Studien zur Bedeutung und Funktion exemplarischen Erzählens*. Schriften zur Literaturwissenschaft 10, (Berlin: Duncker & Humblot), 425-448.
1995	"Curricular Goals of Reading Modern Drama: Textual Strategies of Samuel Beckett and Harold Pinter," in Wolfgang Riehle and Hugo Keiper, eds., *Anglistentag 1994 Graz: Proceedings* (Tübingen: Niemeyer), 421-438.
1995	with Shen Yuanping, "Vom kommunikativen zum interkulturellen Lernen," in Chinese in *Dang Dai Cai Jing* 2, 68-71.
1995	"Typen des ästhetischen Diskurses: Nationaler, post-kolonialer und post-strukturalistischer Diskurs im Englischen," *Anglia* 113:4, 464-487.
1995	"Zwischen Tradition und Erneuerung: Bildungssystem und berufliche Ausbildung," in Hans Kastendiek, Karl Rohe and Angelika Volle, eds., *Großbritannien: Geschichte – Politik – Wirtschaft – Gesellschaft* (Frankfurt/M.: Campus), pp.438-455 (2nd edition 1999, 523-543).
1996	---- with A. Tschida, "Neusprachlicher Philologe/Neusprachliche Philologin (Anglistik, Romanistik)," in Bundesanstalt für Arbeit, ed., *Blätter zur Berufskunde* (Nürnberg: Bundesanstalt für Arbeit), p. 59.
1996	" 'Gentleman' and 'scholar athlete': Der Universitätssport in Großbritannien und den USA," *Forschung & Lehre, Mitteilungen des Deutschen Hochschulverbandes* 7, 348-352.
1996	"Weimar and the German Romantics," in Malcolm Bradbury, ed., *The Atlas of Literature* (London: De Agostini Editions), 74-77.
1996	"Die Herausforderung des Fremden im post-kolonialen Roman: Yasmine Gooneratne, *A Change of Skies* (1991)," in Herbert Christ and Michael K.

Legutke, eds., *Fremde Texte verstehen: Festschrift für Lothar Bredella zum 60. Geburtstag* (Tübingen: Narr), 246-259.

1996   "Theo Stemmler zum Sechzigsten," in S. Horlacher and M. Islinger, eds., *Expedition nach der Wahrheit. Poems, Essays and Papers in Honour of Theo Stemmler: Festschrift zum 60. Geburtstag von Theo Stemmler* (Heidelberg: Winter), XXIII-XXXII.

1996   "Shakespeares Musicals: *Kiss Me Kate, West Side Story* und *Your Own Thing,*" in S. Horlacher and M. Islinger, eds., *Expedition nach der Wahrheit. Poems, Essays, and Papers in Honour of Theo Stemmler: Festschrift zum 60. Geburtstag von Theo Stemmler* (Heidelberg: Winter), 471-487.

1997   "Die interkulturelle Dimension der englischen Fachdidaktik," in Hans Hunfeld and Konrad Schröder, eds., *Was ist und was tut eigentlich Fremdsprachendidaktik?* Augsburger I.-&I.-Schriften 75 (Augsburg: Wißner), 71-77.

1997   "Universitäre Fachdidaktik Englisch – der Stand der Dinge: Universität Würzburg," in Hans Hunfeld and Konrad Schröder, eds., *Was ist und was tut eigentlich Fremdsprachendidaktik?* Augsburger I.&I.-Schriften, 75 (Augsburg: Wißner), 166-188.

1998   "Hermeneutik," in A. Nünning, ed., *Metzler Lexikon Literatur- und Kulturtheorie* (Stuttgart: Metzler), 207-210.

1998   "Krieger, Murray," in A. Nünning, ed., *Metzler Lexikon Literatur- und Kulturtheorie* (Stuttgart: Metzler), 285-6.

IV. Reviews

1971   Slettengren and Widén, *Moderne englische Kurzgrammatik*, in *Die Neueren Sprachen* 9, 500-501.

1971   F. Bürmann and J. Moreau, eds., *Nouvelles Poésies Françaises*, in *Die Neueren Sprachen* 12, 676-7.

1971   U. Dreysse, *Realität als Aufgabe*, in *German Studies: Literature, Music, Fine Arts*, IV:1, 15-18.

1972   Dieter Mehl, ed., *Das englische Drama*, in *German Studies: Literature, Music, Fine Arts*, V:2, 178-181.

1973   Dietrich Schwanitz, *G.B. Shaw – Künstlerische Konstruktion und unordentliche Welt*, in *German Studies: Literature, Music, Fine Arts*, VI:2, 176-7.

1973   K. H. Köhring and J. T. Morris, *Instant English I*, in *Die Neueren Sprachen* 3, 180-181.

1973   Lothar Hönnighausen, *Präraphaeliten und Fin de Siècle*, in *German Studies: Literature, Music, Fine Arts*, VI:2, 158-160.

1974 Rudolf Sühnel and Dieter Riesner, eds., *Englische Dichter der Moderne. Ihr Leben und Werk*, in *German Studies: Literature, Music, Fine Arts* VII:2, 226-28.

1974 G. Leeming and S. Trussler, *The Plays of Arnold Wesker*, in *Archiv* 211, 166-168.

1974 S. Wells, *Literature and Drama*, in *Archiv* 211, 116-117.

1974 R. Hindmarsh and J. T. Morris, *On Education*, in *Die Neueren Sprachen* 1, 86-7.

1974 Rudolf Sühnel and Dieter Riesner, eds., *Grundlagen der Anglistik und Amerikanistik*, 4 vols., in *German Studies: Literature, Music, Fine Arts* VII:1, 59-63.

1975 H. Itschert, ed., *Das amerikanische Drama von den Anfängen bis zur Gegenwart*, in *German Studies: Literature, Music, Fine Arts* VIII:174-176.

1975 J. Nünning, ed., *Das englische Drama*, in *German Studies: Literature, Music, Fine Arts* VIII:2, 199-201.

1975 Wolfgang Karrer and Eberhard Kreutzer, *Daten der englischen und amerikanischen Literatur*, in *Neusprachliche Mitteilungen* 1, 46-7.

1976 Horst W. Drescher, *Themen und Formen des periodischen Essays im späten 18. Jahrhundert: Untersuchungen zu den schottischen Wochenschriften The Mirror und The Lounger*, in *Archiv* 213, 190-192.

1976 Klaus Lubbers, ed., *Die amerikanische Lyrik: Von der Kolonialzeit bis zur Gegenwart*, in *German Studies: Literature, Music, Fine Arts*, IX:2, 151-153.

1976 Robert Fricker, *Das moderne englische Drama*, in *Neusprachliche Mitteilungen* 2, 90-92.

1976 Paul Goetsch, *Das amerikanische Drama*, in *German Studies: Literature, Music, Fine Arts* IX:1, 20-22.

1978 Kurt Tetzeli von Rosador, *Das englische Geschichtsdrama seit Shaw*, in *German Studies: Literature, Music, Fine Arts*, XI:2, 204-207.

1978 Norbert H. Platz, *Ethik und Rhetorik in Ben Jonsons Dramen*, in *German Studies: Literature, Music, Fine Arts*, XI:2, 195-6.

1978 Heinz Kosok, ed., *Das englische Drama im 18. und 19. Jahrhundert: Interpretationen*, in *German Studies: Literature, Music, Fine Arts*, XI:2, 174-176.

1978 B. Haferkamp, *Das literaturwissenschaftliche Proseminar heute*, in *Neusprachliche Mitteilungen* 3, 185-6.

1978 Hans Weber, ed., *Der englische Essay: Analysen*, in *Neusprachliche Mitteilungen* 1, 53-55.

1979 Paul Goetsch, *Bauformen des modernen englischen und amerikanischen Dramas*, in *German Studies: Literature, Music, Fine Arts* XII:2, 173-4.

1980 Rolf Breuer, *Die Kunst der Paradoxie, Sinnsuche und Scheitern bei Samuel Beckett*, in *German Studies: Literature, Music, Fine Arts* XIII: 2, 138-9.

1980 K. Kloth, James Beatties ästhetische Theorien. Ihre Zusammenhänge mit der Aberdeener Schulphilosophie, in *Anglia*, 1/2, 245-247.

1980 Heinz Reinhold, *Der englische Roman im 18. Jahrhundert*, in *German Studies: Literature, Music, Fine Arts* XIII:1, 32-3.

1980 Heinz Kosok and Horst Prießnitz, eds., *Literaturen in englischer Sprache: Ein Überblick über englischsprachige Nationalliteraturen außerhalb Englands*, in *German Studies: Literature, Music, Fine Arts* XIII:1, 20-22.

1980 Gerhard Hoffmann, *Raum, Zeit, erzählte Wirklichkeit: Poetologische und historische Studien zum englischen und amerikanischen Roman*, in *German Studies: Literature, Music, Fine Arts* XIII:1, 14-16.

1981 Horst Priessnitz, ed., *Anglo-amerikanische Shakespeare-Bearbeitungen des 20. Jahrhunderts*, in *German Studies: Literature, Music, Fine Arts* XIV:2, 155-7.

1981 J. Hermand, ed., *Literatur nach 1945*, in *German Studies: Literature, Music, Fine Arts* XIV:1, 15-17.

1983 E. Austermühl, *Poetic Language and Lyrical Understanding*, in *German Studies: Literature, Music, Fine Arts*, XVI:1, 5-6.

1983 W. J. Kennedy, *Rhetorical Norms in Renaissance Literature*, in *Anglia* 101:1-2, 243-5.

1983 Dieter Buttjes, ed., *Landeskundliches Lernen im Englischunterricht: Zur Theorie und Praxis des inhaltsorientierten Fremdsprachenunterrichts*, in *American Studies* 28, 130-34.

1983 Ina Schabert, *The Historical Novel in England and America*, in *German Studies: Literature, Music, Fine Arts* XVI:2, 131-32.

1984 D. Schulz, *Search and Adventure. The "Quest" in English and American Fiction*, in *German Studies: Literature, Music, Fine Arts* XVII:1, 43-44.

1984 J. Martini, ed., *The Problem of Alienation in Samuel Beckett's Plays*, in *German Studies: Literature, Music, Fine Arts* XVII:2, 140-141.

1984 Lothar Hönnighausen, *Grundprobleme der englischen Literaturtheorie des neunzehnten Jahrhunderts*, in *Anglia* 102:3-4, 543-6.

1984 Dieter Mehl, ed., *Die Tragödien Shakespeares: Eine Einführung*, in *German Studies: Literature, Music, Fine Arts* XVII:2, 141-42.

1985 Paul Goetsch, ed., *Englische Literatur zwischen Viktorianismus und Moderne*, in *German Studies: Literature, Music, Fine Arts* XVIII:1, 25f.

1985 H. Blinn, ed., *Shakespeare-Rezeption: Die Diskussion um Shakespeare in Deutschland I: Ausgewählte Texte von 1741-1788*, in *German Studies: Literature, Music, Fine Arts* XVIII:1, 10-11.

1985 Klaus Peter Steiger, ed., *Das englische Drama nach 1945*, in *German Studies: Literature, Music, Fine Arts* XVIII:2, 162-3.

1985 W. F. Schirmer, ed., *Geschichte der englischen und amerikanischen Literatur*, in *German Studies: Literature, Music, Fine Arts* XVIII:2, 156-7.

1985 Thomas Finkenstaedt, ed., *Kleine Geschichte der Anglistik in Deutschland: Eine Einführung*, in *German Studies: Literature, Music, Fine Arts* XVIII:2, 135-36.

1986 W. Kluge, ed., *Der Stil der dramatischen Sprache in den Stücken George Bernard Shaws*, in *German Studies: Literature, Music, Fine Arts* XIX:2, 113-114.

1988 H. Wurmbach, *Christopher Marlowes Tamburlaine-Dramen: Struktur, Rezeptionslenkung und historische Bedeutung: Ein Beitrag zur Dramenanalyse*, in *German Studies: Literature, Music, Fine Arts* XXI:1, 68.

1988 Therese Fischer-Seidel, *Mythenparodie im modernen englischen und amerikanischen Drama: Tradition und Kommunikation bei Tennessee Williams, Edward Albee, Samuel Beckett und Harold Pinter*, in *German Studies: Literature, Music, Fine Arts* XXI:2, 170-71.

1988 J. N. Schmidt, *Ästhetik des Melodrams: Studien zu einem Genre des populären Theaters im England des 19. Jahrhunderts*, in *German Studies: Literature, Music, Fine Arts* XXI:2, 194.

1988 Artemis Einführungen in die anglo-amerikanische LiteratuR
Vol. 3: Willi Erzgräber, *Virginia Woolf* (München: Artemis, 1982).
Vol. 7: Ingeborg Weber, *Der englische Schauerroman* (München: Artemis, 1983).
Vol. 9: Hans-Joachim Lang, *George Orwell* (München: Artemis, 1983).
Vol. 15: Franz Link, *Ezra Pound* (München: Artemis, 1984).
Vol. 21: Helmbrecht Breinig, *Mark Twain* (München: Artemis, 1985).
Vol. 28: Paul Goetsch, *Dickens* (München: Artemis, 1986).
Vol. 32: Andreas Barth, *Moderne englische Gesellschaftskomödie: Von Oscar Wilde zu Tom Stoppard* (München: Artemis, 1987):
In H. Kunisch, Th. Berchem, E. Heftrich, F. Link and A. Wolf, eds., *Literaturwissenschaftliches Jahrbuch im Auftrag der Görres-Gesellschaft*, Neue Folge 29, 326-332.

1989 Rüdiger Imhof, *Contemporary Metafiction: A Poetological Study of Metafiction in English since 1939*, in *German Studies: Literature, Music, Fine Arts* XXII:1, 24.

1989 Manfred Pfister, *Oscar Wilde: The Picture of Dorian Gray*, in *German Studies: Literature, Music, Fine Arts* XXII:1, 36.

1989 Klaus Peter Steiger, *Die Geschichte der Shakespeare-Rezeption*, in *German Studies: Literature, Music, Fine Arts* XXII:2, 162-63.

1990 M. Raab, *"The music hall is dying": Die Thematisierung der Unterhaltungsindustrie im englischen Gegenwartsdrama*, in *German Studies: Literature, Music, Fine Arts* XXIII:2, 153-4.

1990 Jürgen Klein, *Francis Bacon oder die Modernisierung Englands*, in *German Studies: Literature, Music, Fine Arts* XXIII:1, 27-8.

1990 Jürgen Wolter, *Die Suche nach nationaler Identität: Entwicklungstendenzen des amerikanischen Dramas vor dem Bürgerkrieg*, in *German Studies: Literature, Music, Fine Arts* XXIII:1, 28-9.

1990 Hubert Zapf, *Das Drama in der abstrakten Gesellschaft: Zur Theorie und Struktur des modernen englischen Dramas*, in *German Studies: Literature, Music, Fine Arts* XXIII:1, 29-30.

1990 Meinhard Winkgens, *Die kulturkritische Verankerung der Literaturkritik bei F. R. Leavis*, in *Literaturwissenschaftliches Jahrbuch* im Auftrag der Görres-Gesellschaft 31, 430-36.

1991 René Wellek, *Geschichte der Literaturkritik: 1750-1950*, 4 vols., in *Anglia* 110:3-4, 551-3.

1991 M. Frank and A. Haverkamp, eds., *Individualität*, in *Anglia* 110:3-4, 555-7.

1991 Herbert Grabes, *Das englische Pamphlet I: Politische und religiöse Polemik am Beginn der Neuzeit (1521-1640)*, in *Anglia* 111:1-2, 220-22.

1991 Gerhard Hoffmann, ed., *Der zeitgenössische amerikanische Roman: Von der Moderne zur Postmoderne*, 3 vols., in *German Studies: Literature, Music, Fine Arts* XXIV:1-2, 20-22.

1991 Thomas Kullmann, *Abschied, Reise und Wiedersehen bei Shakespeare: Zu Gestaltung und Funktion epischer und romanhafter Motive im Drama*, in *German Studies: Literature, Music, Fine Arts* XXIV:1-2, 25.

1992 H. Blinn *Shakespeare-Rezeption: Die Diskussion um Shakespeare in Deutschland II: Ausgewählte Texte von 1793-1827*, in *Anglia* 110:3-4, 518-19.

1992 R. Herzog and R. Kosellek, eds., *Epochenschwelle und Epochenbewußtsein*, in *Anglia* 110:3-4, 553-55.

1992 M. Frank and A. Haverkamp, eds., *Individualität*, in *Anglia* 110:3-4, 555-57.

1993 Franz Link, ed., *Paradeigmata: Literarische Typologie des Alten Testaments*, 2 vols., in *Anglia* 111:3-4, 550-56.

1995 Hans Braun and Wolfgang Klooß, eds., *Kanada: Eine interdisziplinäre Einführung*, in *Zeitschrift für Anglistik und Amerikanistik* 4, 373-76.

V. *Essays and Shorter Articles*

1979 "Amerikanische Universitäten heute – Ein Blick in die hochschulpolitische Zukunft?," *Mitteilungen des Hochschulverbandes* 2, 64-71.

1981 "Moderne Shakespeare-Übersetzungen in Prosa," *Der fremdsprachliche Unterricht* 60, 298-301.

1982 "Die 'Harvard Reform' und der neue Trend zur Allgemeinbildung," *Mitteilungen des Hochschulverbandes* 6, 311-16.

1984 "Das Studium an angelsächsischen Universitäten. 'Public and Private Education'," *Mitteilungen des Hochschulverbandes* 4, 199-205.

1985 "Der Test als wissenschaftliche Prüfungsform," *Mitteilungen des Hochschulverbandes* 5, 255-61.

1986 "Die Gefahren einer globalen Bevölkerungsexplosion. Die heutige Bedeutung des Malthusianismus," *Informationen* 5:20 (31.7.1986), 5-10.

1986 "Die Allgemeinbildung an der Harvard Universität – ein Vorbild für Würzburg?," *Informationen* 8:20 (22.12.1986), 10-13.

1987 "Geistige Selbständigkeit als Bildungsziel," *Innovatio* (1.2.1987), 21-22.

1987 "New Developments in English and American Higher Education," *Dynamena Monthly* 12, 15-19.

1988 "Das deutsche und das japanische Universitätssystem. Gemeinsamkeiten und Unterschiede," *Mitteilungen des Hochschulverbandes* 5, 267-73.

1989 "Europäische Sprachenpolitik. Ein bisher noch wenig beachteter Aspekt des europäischen Binnenmarktes." *Mitteilungen des Hochschulverbandes* 3, 163-66.

1989 "Die Novellierung der Bayerischen Hochschulgesetze," *Mitteilungen des Hochschulverbandes* 4, 183-88.

1989 "ERASMUS in Würzburg: Europäische Literaturkritik im Vergleich," *Informationen der Bayerischen Julius-Maximilians-Universität Würzburg* 3:23, 38.

1989 with E. M. White, "European vs. American Higher Education. Two Issues and a Clear Winner," *Change* 21:5, 52-55. Reprinted as "European and American Higher Education: Some Comparisons," *American Studies Newsletter* 24, May 1991, 31-3.

1989 "Würzburg und die englische Literatur," *Anglistentag. Verband deutscher Anglisten e. V., Jahrestagung 1989 in Würzburg vom 24.-27. September,* 16-17.

1989 "Deutscher Anglistenverband tagte in Würzburg," *Informationen der Bayerischen Julius-Maximilians-Universität Würzburg* 4:23, 30-31.

1991 "Im Vergleich: Weiterführende Schulen in Europa und Amerika," *Amerika Dienst* 22 (June 1991), 1-3.

1991 "Würzburger Anglisten, Romanisten und Germanisten beim ERASMUS-Seminar in Caen," *Informationen der Bayerischen Julius-Maximilians-Universität Würzburg* 1-2:25, 28-29.

1991 "National Traditions of Literary Criticism: An Intensive Programme of the Universities of Würzburg, London (Royal Holloway and Bedford New College) and Caen." *Messenger* 1:1 (Autumn 1991), 35-36.

1992 "Der Frühbeginn des Fremdsprachenunterrichts," *Die Bayerische Schule* 4, 25-26.

1992 "Eine Europäische Kulturakademie (EKA)," *Mitteilungen des Hochschulverbandes* 1, 8-10.

1992 "Die 'Preis-Politik' des Deutschen Anglistenverbandes," *Mitteilungen des Deutschen Anglistenverbandes* 1, 68-70.

1993 "Die zukünftige Struktur des Universitätsstudiums," *Mitteilungen des Hochschulverbandes* 1, 21-24.

1993 "English and American Studies in Reunified Germany," *I.A.U.P.E.-Bulletin,* Summer 1993, 1-5.

1993 "I.A.U.P.E. 15th Triennial Conference," in *Mitteilungen des Deutschen Anglistenverbandes* 1, 75-79.

1994 "Die Bedeutung der kulturellen Renaissance für das heutige Europa," *Philia* I, 34-37.

1996 "16th Triennial Conference of the International Association of University Professors of English (I.A.U.P.E.)," in *Anglistik: Mitteilungen des Verbandes Deutscher Anglisten* 1, 146-151.

1998 "Journalistenpreis 1997: Laudatio auf Patrick Bahners," in *Anglistik: Mitteilungen des Verbandes Deutscher Anglisten* 1, 19-26.

1998 "PMLA Abroad," in *Publications of the Modern Language Association of America* 113:4, 1124-1126.

Tabula Gratulatoria

JOCHEN ACHILLES
Mainz

GÜNTER AHRENDS
Bochum

SHINSUKE ANDO
Tokyo

ANDREA ANTOR
Würzburg

HEINZ ANTOR
Düsseldorf

ULRICH BACH
Kürnach

WOLF-DIETRICH BALD
Köln

UWE BAUMANN
Düsseldorf

TODD BENDER
Madison

THEODOR BERCHEM
Würzburg

CHRISTOPH BODE
Bamberg

UWE BÖKER
Dresden

MALCOLM BRADBURY
Norwich

LOTHAR BREDELLA
Giessen

ULRICH BROICH
München

URSULA BRUMM
Berlin

HORST BRUNNER
Würzburg

ERNST BURGSCHMIDT
Würzburg

KEVIN L. COPE
Baton Rouge

KATHLEEN CURRY
Rostherne

BERND DIETZ
Cordoba

PAUL EGGERT
Canberra

RUDOLF EMONS
Passau

EILERT ERFLING
Heidelberg

ANDREAS FISCHER
Zürich

LOTHAR FIETZ
Tübingen

MONIKA FLUDERNIK
Freiburg

NORBERT GREINER
Heidelberg

HERBERT FOLTINEK
Wien

RENATE HAAS
Kiel

BRUNO FORSTER
Würzburg

INGRID HAMPEL
Würzburg

NEIL FORSYTH
Lausanne

MONIKA HOFFARTH-ZELLOE
Alexandria

PETER FREESE
Paderborn

STEFAN HORLACHER
Mannheim

CHRISTIAN J. GANTER
Würzburg

GABRIEL HORNSTEIN
New York

WOLFGANG GEHRING
Würzburg

WERNER HÜLLEN
Essen

JACQUELINE GENET
Caen

KARIN IKAS
Würzburg

ALBERT-REINER GLAAP
Düsseldorf

WILLIAM J. JONES
London

WALTER GÖBEL
Saarbrücken

JOHN E. JOSEPH
Edinburgh

KARL HEINZ GÖLLER
Kelheim

GERTRUD KALB-KRAUSE
München

PAUL GOETSCH
Freiburg

MICHAEL KEEFER
Guelph

YASMINE GOONERATNE
Sydney

GEORGE KNOX
Riverside

KENNETH GRAHAM
Guelph

ROLAND KOFER
Würzburg

VERNON GRAS
Fairfax, Va./Washington, DC

STEPHAN KOHL
Würzburg

EVANGELOS KONSTANTINOU
Würzburg

MURRAY KRIEGER
Irvine

THOMAS KULLMANN
Göttingen

LUCIEN LEBOUILLE
Caen

RUTH FREIFRAU VON LEDEBUR
Bonn

ERNST LEISI
Zürich

JOSETTE LERAY
Fontenay-sous-Bois

LEUNG PING-KWAN
Hong Kong

LEONHARD LIPKA
München

PIERRE LURBE
Caen

HENA MAES-JELINEK
Liège

CHRISTINE MERTEL
Würzburg

PETER MÜHLHÄUSLER
Adelaide

HEINZ-JOACHIM MÜLLENBROCK
Göttingen

WOLFGANG G. MÜLLER
Jena

MAX NÄNNY
Zürich

FRITZ-WILHELM NEUMANN
Erfurt

ERICH OETHEIMER
Caen

SUSANA ONEGA
Zaragoza

ARUNA PANDEY
Jaipur

ANDREW PARKIN
Hong Kong

HELMUT PFOTENHAUER
Würzburg

ALBERT FRANÇOIS POYET
Toulouse

MARY REID
München

RUDOLF RIEKS
Bamberg

ANGUS ROSS
Brighton

IAN ROSS
Vancouver

GEORGE S. ROUSSEAU
Aberdeen

HANS SAUER
München

HARTMUT SCHIEDERMAIR
Köln

RAINER SCHÖWERLING
Paderborn

JOACHIM SCHWEND
Leipzig

HANS-ULRICH SEEBER
Stuttgart

SHEN YUANPING
Guangzhou

FRANZ K. STANZEL
Graz

THEO STEMMLER
Mannheim

KLAUS STIERSTORFER
Würzburg

BRIAN TAYLOR
Sydney

EDWIN THUMBOO
Singapore

JOHN W. VELZ
Austin, TX

WOLFGANG VIERECK
Bamberg

LAURENZ VOLKMANN
Würzburg

HORST WEINSTOCK
Aachen

MEINHARD WINKGENS
Mannheim

ERWIN WOLFF
Erlangen

MICHAEL WOLLENSCHLÄGER
Würzburg

SIBYLLE WOLLENSCHLÄGER
Würzburg

HUBERT ZAPF
Augsburg